PRINCIPLES OF ARBITRATION LAW

Second Edition

Stephen J. Ware
Frank Edwards Tyler Distinguished Professor of Law
University of Kansas

Ariana R. Levinson
Professor of Law
Brandeis School of Law
University of Louisville

CONCISE HORNBOOK SERIES™

WEST
ACADEMIC
PUBLISHING

860 Blue Gentian Road, Suite 350
Eagan, MN 55121
1-877-888-1330

Printed in the United States of America

ISBN: 978-1-63659-355-5

For

Adam and Spencer Ware

&

Kathy and Stanley Levinson

Preface

Arbitration law has a long history. Even "modern" arbitration statutes like the Federal Arbitration Act are now about a century old. And the last few decades have witnessed the growth of a large body of legal doctrine—from statutes, judicial decisions, and other sources—focused on arbitration. This book is written with the goal of providing a clear and reliable summary of that body of law, so this book should be useful to lawyers and scholars researching arbitration law and to students learning about arbitration.

We thank the student research assistants who helped with various portions of this second edition, Howard Mahan, Steven Hendler, Alex Telesca, Claudia Armstrong, Kyler Womack, Brittany Ussery, Nick Heintz, Aimee Wuthrich, Anshul Banga, Emma Bishop, Evan Mitchell, David DeKold, Jessie Hagan, and Shane Creason. And, we are grateful for the support we have received from the University of Kansas and the University of Louisville.

As we expect to write future editions of this book, we welcome comments and suggestions.

STEPHEN J. WARE
Frank Edwards Tyler
Distinguished Professor of
Law
University of Kansas
ware@ku.edu
(785) 864-9209

ARIANA R. LEVINSON
Professor of Law
University of Louisville
Brandeis School of Law
a.levinson@louisville.edu
(502) 852-0794

October 31, 2022

Note to Teachers

This Hornbook is designed to be used as the primary or secondary text in a law school course. In the United States, casebooks, rather than Hornbooks or other treatises, are the primary texts in most law school courses, and casebooks work well at the center of law school courses that emphasize Socratic dialog and "thinking like a lawyer." By contrast, many teachers of dispute-resolution, including arbitration, design their courses to develop a wider array of practice skills, generally through the use of role-playing exercises. We believe this Hornbook is especially well-suited to be the primary text for such courses. Because this book is clear and concise, students reading it can quickly gain a solid understanding of arbitration's central concepts and legal doctrines. This efficient use of time enables the teacher to devote many class sessions to role-playing exercises, and discussion of them. Excellent role-playing exercises are available from several sources, including:

- Harvard Program on Negotiation http://www.pon.harvard.edu/store/
- University of Missouri Center for the Study of Dispute Resolution https://law.missouri.edu/csdr/drle/teaching/
- Employment Law Arbitration Exercises, developed by Gary Spitko, Santa Clara University School of Law, gspitko@gmail.com
- Securities Dispute Resolution Triathlon, St. John's University School of Law Hugh L. Carey Center for Dispute Resolution & FINRA, https://www.stjohns.edu/law/about/places/hugh-l-carey-center-dispute-resolution (click on Carey Center/FINRA Securities Dispute Resolution Triathlon)
- American Bar Association Law Student Competitions http://abaforlawstudents.com/events/law-student-competitions/practical-skills-competitions/competition-videos/
- American Bar Association's Dispute Resolution Resource Database, (scroll to Legal Education) https://www.americanbar.org/groups/dispute_resolution/resources/ which links to several resources, including https://www.adrvideo.org/

Of course, individual instructors can also create their own role-playing exercises.

Also helpful in teaching practice skills is viewing others engage in arbitration hearings and processes. As with role-playing exercises, excellent videos are available from several sources, including:

- The Pennsylvania State University School of Labor and Employment Relations Labor Arbitration Case Study: The Suspension of Nurse Kevin https://ler.la.psu.edu/product/arbitration-dvd/
- YouTube, Labor Management Arbitration Excerpts, Part I & II, https://www.youtube.com/watch?v=ZkaLoZOKf4I
- American Bar Association, Advanced Arbitration Insight: 20/20, https://www.americanbar.org/products/ecd/ebk/217823/
- American Bar Association Law Student Competitions http://abaforlawstudents.com/events/law-student-competitions/practical-skills-competitions/competition-videos/
- The Center for American and International Law, Arbitral Advocacy, Mock Arbitration Proceedings and Commentary, http://www.cailaw.org/Institute-for-Transnational-Arbitration/onlineeducation/video-library/arbitral-advocacy.html

In addition to serving as the primary text for arbitration courses that emphasize role-playing exercises, this Hornbook can also serve as the primary text for arbitration seminars. In a seminar course, students generally read scholarly articles and write their own substantial papers. Before venturing into a field of scholarship, students generally need a solid foundation in the field's central concepts and legal doctrines. This book provides that foundation with only a limited amount of reading, thus enabling students to devote substantial time to the seminar's more-advanced work of reading scholarly articles and writing original papers.

Summary of Contents

Table of Contents

PRINCIPLES OF ARBITRATION LAW

Second Edition

Chapter 1

WHAT IS ARBITRATION

Table of Sections

---

§ 1 Arbitration Defined

Arbitration is private (non-government) adjudication.[1]

---

[1] Adjudication is the process by which somebody (the adjudicator) decides the result of a dispute. Rather than the disputing parties agreeing on the result of the dispute, as in negotiation, adjudication is the adjudicator telling the parties the result. See, e.g., Alan Scott Rau, Edward F. Sherman & Scott R. Peppet, Processes of Dispute Resolution 21 (4th ed. 2006) (" 'Adjudication' refers to the process by which final, authoritative decisions are rendered by a neutral third party who enters the controversy without previous knowledge of the dispute."); Lon Fuller, The Forms and Limits of Adjudication, 92 Harv. L. Rev. 353, 364 (1978) ("the distinguishing characteristic of adjudication lies in the fact that it confers on the affected [disputing] party a peculiar form of participation in decision, that of presenting proofs and reasoned arguments for a decision in his favor."); id. at 365 (from this participation by the parties, "the office of judge or arbitrator and the requirement of impartiality follow as necessary implications.")

Arbitration is private adjudication. See Ian R. Macneil, Richard E. Speidel & Thomas J. Stipanowich, Federal Arbitration Law § 2.6.1, at 2:37 n.1 (1994) ("Arbitration is a form of adjudication because the parties participate in the decisional process by presenting evidence and reasoned arguments to an arbitrator whose final decision should be responsive to the dispute as presented."); Restatement (Third) U.S. Law of Int'l Comm. Arb. § 1.1 (2019) (" 'Arbitration' is a dispute resolution method in which the disputing parties empower an arbitral tribunal to adjudicate a dispute in a final and binding manner."); Gary B. Born, International Commercial Arbitration 2124 (2d ed. 2014) (describing "the adjudicative character of international arbitration, in which the arbitrators are obligated to decide the parties' dispute impartially and objectively, based upon the law and evidence the parties present."); Pamela K. Bookman, Arbitral Courts, 61 Va. J. Int'l L. 161, 171 (2021) ("At their core, the difference is that courts are public and arbitration is private. Courts' public nature means that courts should be open to the public—available to all comers to use them, to read their decisions, to observe their proceedings. They employ judges paid by the

Arbitrators, selected by the disputing parties (directly or indirectly),[2] are the adjudicators in arbitration. In contrast, judges and jurors are the adjudicators in *litigation*, which is adjudication in a government forum, a court.

In addition to being "private" in the non-governmental sense, arbitration is also often "private" in the confidential sense, but it does not have to be.[3] Arbitration could occur on a busy city sidewalk in full view of the public, and it would still be *private* adjudication. In short, the essence of arbitration is that it is a private-sector alternative to government courts. It is to the court system what private schools are to public schools, or what private housing is to public housing. One might think of different arbitration organizations—such as the American Arbitration Association or its main competitor, JAMS—offering their adjudication services as like FedEx and UPS offering their delivery services. Continuing this analogy, the government court system is like the U.S. (Government's) Postal Service. Much as law confers on the Postal Service a monopoly in the delivery of first-class mail, law confers on the government court system a monopoly in the adjudication of criminal cases. And much as FedEx and UPS may say they deliver packages faster or more reliably than the Government's Post Office, arbitration organizations may say they adjudicate some civil cases faster or more reliably than the government courts.

§ 2 Contractual Arbitration and Non-Contractual Arbitration; Constitutional Right to Jury Trial

Arbitration can be divided into two types, contractual and non-contractual.[4] The duty to arbitrate a dispute can be created by contract or by other law. If the duty to arbitrate is created by contract, then enforcement of that duty is unlikely to violate the constitutional right to a jury trial. Courts overwhelmingly hold that, by forming a contract to arbitrate—even an adhesive arbitration agreement, as is common in consumer and employment transactions—a party waives its right to a trial by jury.[5] In contrast,

state whose role is to be public servants—adjudicating not just for the parties but with the public good in mind.")

[2] See § 33(a).

[3] See § 32.

[4] See § 66(a).

[5] See, e.g., Hicks v. Cadle, 436 F. App'x 874, 879 (10th Cir. 2011) ("Because arbitration 'necessarily waives jury trial,' our conclusion that this case was properly referred to arbitration undercuts Mr. Cadle's objection that he was wrongly denied a jury trial"); Harrington v. Atl. Sounding Co., 602 F.3d 113, 126 (2d Cir. 2010) ("courts may not rely on the uniqueness of an agreement to arbitrate, which necessarily waives jury trial, as a basis for a state-law holding that enforcement would be unconscionable. It is well-settled that waivers of jury trial are fully enforceable under the FAA.") (internal quotations omitted); Caley v. Gulfstream Aerospace Corp., 428 F.3d 1359,

the parties to non-contractual arbitration have rarely waived the right to a jury trial, so non-contractual arbitration generally must be non-binding to avoid violating this right.[6]

Non-contractual, yet binding, arbitration is discussed at the end of this book, under the heading "Processes Similar to Arbitration."[7] Otherwise, the term "arbitration" is used throughout this book to mean "contractual arbitration."

§ 3 Arbitration Law Summarized

(a) Post-Dispute and Pre-Dispute Agreements to Arbitrate

A dispute goes to arbitration only when the parties have contracted to send it there.[8] Sometimes parties with an existing

1371 (11th Cir. 2005) (the "agreement to arbitrate and waiver of jury trial rights are governed by contract principles and are not subject to the heightened knowing and voluntary standard argued by plaintiffs"); Antonucci v. Curvature Newco, Inc., 270 A.3d 1088, 1096 (N.J. App. Div. 2022) ("The waiver of the right to go to court and receive a jury trial is one of the primary objectives or 'defining features' of an arbitration agreement."); American Heritage Life Ins. Co. v. Orr, 294 F.3d 702, 711 (5th Cir. 2002) (" '[t]he Seventh Amendment does not confer the right to a trial, but only the right to have a jury hear the case once it is determined that the litigation should proceed before a court. If the claims are properly before an arbitral forum pursuant to an arbitration agreement, the jury trial right vanishes.' ") (*quoting* Cremin v. Merrill Lynch, Pierce, Fenner & Smith, Inc., 957 F. Supp. 1460, 1471 (N.D.Ill.1997)); Sydnor v. Conseco Fin. Servicing Corp., 252 F.3d 302, 307 (4th Cir. 2001) ("the right to a jury trial attaches in the context of judicial proceedings after it is determined that litigation should proceed before a court."); Geldermann, Inc. v. Commodity Futures Trading Comm'n, 836 F.2d 310, 323–24 (7th Cir. 1987) ("In a non-Article III forum [arbitration] the Seventh Amendment simply does not apply. Because we hold that Geldermann is not entitled to an Article III forum, the Seventh Amendment is not implicated.") (citations omitted); Hays Grp., Inc. v. Biege, 193 P.3d 1028, 1030 (Or.App.2008) (parties waived jury right by agreeing to arbitrate); Turner v. Vulcan, Inc., 190 Wash. App. 1048 (2015) ("there is no dispute that Turner signed the agreement at issue. Once that has been established 'a party implicitly waives his [or her] right to a jury trial by agreeing to an alternative forum, arbitration.' ") (quoting Adler v. Fred Lind Manor, 153 Wash. 2d 331, 360–61, 103 P.3d 773, 789 (2004) ("by knowingly and voluntarily agreeing to arbitration, a party implicitly waives his right to a jury trial by agreeing to an alternate forum, arbitration").

The Seventh Amendment, preserving the right to jury trial, is one of the few provisions of the Bill of Rights that constrains only federal, not state, government. See Curtis v. Loether, 415 U.S. 189, 192 n.6 (1974). The Seventh Amendment applies in federal, not state, court. Gasperini v. Ctr. for Humanities, Inc., 518 U.S. 415, 418 (1996); GTFM, LLC v. TKN Sales, Inc., 257 F.3d 235, 245 (2d Cir. 2001). While many state constitutions contain a provision that similarly protects the right to trial by jury, the Federal Arbitration Act prevails in a conflict between it and a state constitutional provision. See U.S. Const. art. VI, § 2 (the Supremacy Clause). Thus, an arbitration agreement's effectiveness as a waiver of the right to jury trial is determined solely by federal, rather than state, law unless the arbitration agreement is one of the few not governed by the FAA. See § 5.

[6] See § 66.

[7] See id.

[8] See, e.g., Howsam v. Dean Witter Reynolds, Inc., 537 U.S. 79, 83 (2002) (" 'arbitration is a matter of contract and a party cannot be required to submit to

dispute contract to send that dispute to arbitration, but such *post-dispute* arbitration agreements (or "submission agreements") are relatively rare and non-controversial.[9] More common, and more controversial, are *pre-dispute* arbitration agreements. These are contracts containing a clause providing that, if a dispute arises, the parties will resolve that dispute in arbitration rather than in court. Pre-dispute arbitration agreements typically are written broadly to cover any dispute the parties' transaction might produce, but can be written more narrowly to cover just some of those potential disputes.[10] Arbitration clauses appear in a wide variety of contracts including those relating to employment, credit, goods, services, land, intellectual property, and other intangibles.

(b) Enforcement of Arbitration Agreements

In the case of most contracts containing pre-dispute arbitration clauses, like most contracts generally, the parties never have any dispute. But if the parties do have a dispute, the arbitration clause often will be enforceable, so a party who would rather litigate than arbitrate will nevertheless have to perform its agreement to arbitrate. If, for example, Seller sues Buyer despite an arbitration agreement between them, Buyer can get a court to stay or dismiss Seller's lawsuit.[11] As a result of the court's order, Seller's only forum to pursue its claim is arbitration.[12] Another possibility is that Seller asserts a claim against Buyer in arbitration, but Buyer simply refuses to participate in arbitration. Seller can get a court order

---

arbitration any dispute which he has not agreed so to submit.' " (quoting United Steelworkers v. Warrior & Gulf Naval Co., 363 US 574, 582 (1960)); First Options of Chicago, Inc. v. Kaplan, 514 U.S. 938, 943 (1995) ("arbitration is simply a matter of contract between the parties"); Granite Rock Co. v. Int'l Bhd. of Teamsters, 561 U.S. 287, 297 (2010) ("a court may order arbitration of a particular dispute only where the court is satisfied that the parties agreed to arbitrate *that dispute*.") (emphasis in original).

[9] See Christopher R. Drahozal & Samantha Zyontz, Private Regulation of Consumer Arbitration, 79 Tenn. L. Rev. 289, 346 (2012) (noting 96.3% of cases arose out of pre-dispute agreements, while only 3.7% arose out of post-dispute agreements to arbitrate); Lewis L. Maltby, Out of the Frying Pan, into the Fire: The Feasibility of Post-Dispute Employment Arbitration Agreements, 30 Wm. Mitchell L.Rev. 313, 319 (2003) (analyzing the American Arbitration Association data on the infrequency of post-dispute arbitration clauses in employment cases).

Post-dispute arbitration agreements resemble settlement agreements.

[10] See § 26.

[11] See § 5(b).

[12] With respect to this dispute, arbitration has replaced litigation as the default process of dispute resolution. Disputing parties who have previously agreed to arbitrate can contract into some other process of dispute resolution, but if they do not do so then each party has the right to have the dispute resolved in arbitration. See Stephen J. Ware, Principles of Alternative Dispute Resolution § 1.7(b) (4th ed. 2022) (distinguishing arbitration from other alternative processes of dispute resolution in this regard).

compelling Buyer to participate.[13] In this manner, the court enforces Buyer's agreement to arbitrate.

Parties seeking to litigate rather than arbitrate a claim generally make three types of arguments:

1. I never formed an arbitration agreement;
2. The arbitration agreement I formed is not enforceable; and
3. The enforceable arbitration agreement I formed does not cover this claim.

Formation is discussed in Sections 17–19, enforceability is discussed in Sections 20–25, and the scope of arbitration agreements is discussed in Sections 26–29. These sections are preceded by discussions of which law—federal or state—governs (Sections 4–16).

(c) The Arbitration Process

Not only does the parties' contract usually determine *whether* a dispute goes to arbitration, the contract also largely determines *what occurs* during arbitration.[14] Like any *adjudication*,[15] arbitration involves the presentation of evidence and argument to the adjudicator. The presentation of evidence and argument in *litigation* is governed by rules of procedure and evidence enacted by government. In contrast, the rules of procedure and evidence in arbitration are, with few exceptions, whatever the contract says they are. Rather than detailing such rules in a contract, pre-dispute arbitration agreements usually incorporate the rules of an arbitration organization, such as the American Arbitration Association or its competitor, JAMS. Arbitration organization rules commonly provide for less discovery and motion practice than is typical of litigation and commonly provide for fewer rules of evidence than are typical in litigation.[16] But parties are free to draft their arbitration agreement almost any way they like. So, arbitration privatizes procedural law by largely allowing parties to create their own customized rules of procedure and evidence.

(d) Enforcement of Arbitrator's Decision or "Award"

Arbitration agreements typically provide that the arbitrator's decision (or "award") will be final and binding. Once an arbitrator renders an award, either party may obtain court enforcement of that award. Judicial enforcement may not be needed because losing

---

13 See § 5(b).

14 See §§ 31–35.

15 See § 1.

16 See §§ 31–34.

parties often comply with arbitration awards. Nevertheless, the winning party can get a court order *confirming* the arbitration award; confirmation converts the award into a judgment of the court.[17] A confirmed arbitration award in favor of the plaintiff (or "claimant") can be enforced in the same manner as other court judgments. Arbitration awards also are enforced through the preclusion of court actions. An arbitration award in favor of the defendant (or "respondent") precludes the plaintiff from litigating the claim that was already resolved in arbitration.[18] This prevents the plaintiff from having more than one "bite at the apple," as lawyers say.

Judicial enforcement of arbitration awards is an example of courts enforcing contracts. Refusing to comply with the arbitrator's award breaches the arbitration agreement, which includes a promise to comply with the arbitrator's award.[19]

---

17 See § 36.

18 See § 37.

19 See § 39(c).

Chapter 2

SOURCES OF CONTEMPORARY AMERICAN ARBITRATION LAW

Table of Sections

§ 4 State Law

State arbitration law is, as discussed below, largely preempted by federal law.[1] Nevertheless, state arbitration law continues to govern those arbitration agreements not governed by federal law.[2]

State arbitration law in nearly every state—Alabama is the exception[3]—is similar to federal arbitration law in generally

---

1 See §§ 6–16.

2 See § 5(c)–(e).

3 See Ala. Code § 8–1–41(3) (1975)("The following obligations cannot be specifically enforced: * * * An agreement to submit a controversy to arbitration"). See

enforcing arbitration agreements and arbitration awards.[4] In addition, federal arbitration law incorporates much of state contract law,[5] and perhaps much of other bodies of state law, such as agency.[6]

§ 5 Federal Law

(a) Sources of Federal Arbitration Law

The Federal Arbitration Act ("FAA")[7] is by far the most important source of arbitration law in the United States. Other sources of federal arbitration law exist, but they govern only specific types of arbitration, such as labor arbitration, which typically arises out of a collective bargaining agreement between a labor union and an employer.[8]

The FAA was originally drafted by counsel to the New York Chamber of Commerce and was enacted by a Republican-majority congress in 1925—same year Republican President Calvin Coolidge captured the spirit of the times in saying "[t]he business of America is business." Befitting that origin, the FAA is pro-contract. Its main rule instructs courts to enforce arbitration agreements "save upon such grounds as exist at law or in equity for the revocation of any contract."[9] This language reflects an intent to reverse judicial hostility to the enforcement of arbitration agreements and to place

---

also Stephen J. Ware, The Alabama Story: Arbitration shows law's connection to politics, culture, Disp. Resol. Mag. 24 (Summer 2001).

4 Many states have adopted the Uniform Arbitration Act ("UAA"), drafted in 1955, or the Revised Uniform Arbitration Act ("RUAA"), drafted in 2000. The UAA, drafted by the National Conference of Commissioners on Uniform State Laws, is currently enacted in 27 states. See Unif. Arbitration Act (1956), 7 U.L.A. 99 (2009). The RUAA, also drafted by the National Conference of Commissioners on Uniform State Laws, has been enacted by 12 states, plus the District of Columbia. See Unif. Arbitration Act (2000), 7 U.L.A. 1 (2009).

5 See §§ 17–20, 26(d).

6 Ian R. Macneil, Richard E. Speidel & Thomas J. Stipanowich, Federal Arbitration Law § 5.4.2; id. § 10.6.2.1 (Supp. 1999) ("contract law alone is an insufficient foundation for the FAA. The FAA also presupposes the existence of a whole corpus of general law: property, torts, agency, corporations, criminal, and regulation, to mention a few of countless possible examples.").

7 9 U.S.C. §§ 1–16, 201–08, 301–07, 401–02.

8 See § 44.

9 The full text of § 2 is as follows:

> A written provision in any maritime transaction or a contract evidencing a transaction involving commerce to settle by arbitration a controversy thereafter arising out of such contract or transaction, or the refusal to perform the whole or any part thereof, or an agreement in writing to submit to arbitration an existing controversy arising out of such a contract, transaction, or refusal, shall be valid, irrevocable, and enforceable, save upon such grounds as exist at law or in equity for the revocation of any contract.

9 U.S.C. § 2.

arbitration agreements "upon the same footing as other contracts."[10] The FAA's enactment was "motivated, first and foremost, by a congressional desire to enforce agreements."[11]

(b) The FAA's Specific Enforcement of Arbitration Agreements

Before the FAA, courts generally enforced arbitration awards, but not executory agreements to arbitrate. This distinction, like so many legal rules in the United States, traces back to England. This history is perhaps most influentially explained by Judge Frank's opinion for the Second Circuit in *Kulukundis Shipping Co. S/A v. Amtorg Trading Corp.* It said that "English courts, while giving full effect to agreements to submit controversies to arbitration after they had ripened into arbitrators' awards, would—over a long period beginning at the end of the 17th century—do little or nothing to prevent or make irksome the breach of such agreements when they were still executory."[12] Judge Frank further explained that "courts of this country were [similarly] unfriendly to executory arbitration agreements."[13] In other words, if the disputing parties went to arbitration—presenting their evidence and arguments to the arbitrator—and the arbitrator ruled, then courts would enforce that arbitration award. But if one of the parties to an arbitration agreement simply refused to arbitrate a dispute covered by that agreement, courts would not compel arbitration.

For example, suppose Seller sued Buyer despite an arbitration agreement between them. Before the FAA, nearly all courts in the U.S. would allow Seller's litigation to proceed, as they would deny Buyer's motion to stay or dismiss Seller's case.[14]

In some courts, Buyer could seek money damages for Seller's breach of the arbitration agreement, but how would the amount of those damages be calculated? To put the non-breaching party in the

---

10 H.R. Rep. No. 68-96, at 2 (1924).

11 Volt Info. Sciences, Inc. v. Board of Trustees, 489 U.S. 468, 478 (1989). See also Buckeye Check Cashing, Inc. v. Cardegna, 546 U.S. 440, 443 (2006) ("To overcome judicial resistance to arbitration, Congress enacted the Federal Arbitration Act * * *. Section 2 embodies the national policy favoring arbitration and places arbitration agreements on equal footing with all other contracts.")

12 126 F.2d 978, 982 (2d Cir. 1942).

13 Id. at 984.

14 See Ian R. Macneil, Richard E. Speidel & Thomas J. Stipanowich, Federal Arbitration Law § 4.3.2.2 (1994) (explaining that in the period 1800–1920, agreements to arbitrate future disputes were not enforced with remedy of specific performance); Wesley A. Sturges, Commercial Arbitration and Awards § 87 (1930). New York and New Jersey enacted statutes providing specific enforcement for arbitration agreements a few years before the FAA's 1925 enactment. See Ian R. Macneil, American Arbitration Law: Reformation, Nationalization, Internationalization 34–47 (1992).

position it would have been in had the contract been performed,[15] the court would have to predict the results of both arbitration and litigation, then award as damages the difference (in terms of value to the non-breaching party) between the two. The speculative-ness of such an approach is daunting and courts did not use it. Instead, a court might award Buyer nominal damages of one dollar or so,[16] but Buyer would receive no other remedy for Seller's breach. In short, the law basically allowed Seller to breach its arbitration agreement.

Alternatively, suppose that Seller performed its agreement to arbitrate by asserting its claim against Buyer in arbitration, but Buyer breached its promise to arbitrate by simply refusing to participate in arbitration of the claim against it. Prior to the FAA, Seller could not get a court order compelling Buyer to participate in arbitration. So, if Seller wanted to pursue its claim against Buyer, Seller would have to do so in litigation. Seller would have no meaningful remedy for Buyer's breach of the arbitration agreement, so Buyer could breach its arbitration agreement with impunity.

The FAA changed the result in both of these Seller/Buyer scenarios. Under the FAA, the remedy for breach of an arbitration agreement is specific performance, that is, an order to arbitrate.

Consider, first, Seller's suit against Buyer. A plaintiff who sues, despite an arbitration agreement with the defendant, is in breach of that agreement. By staying the lawsuit, a court effectively orders the plaintiff to perform its agreement to arbitrate as the only path for the plaintiff to receive a remedy.[17] This stay follows from FAA § 3, which says:

> If any suit or proceeding be brought in any of the courts of the United States upon any issue referable to arbitration under an agreement in writing for such arbitration, the court in which such suit is pending, upon being satisfied

---

[15] This is the way to calculate the "expectation damages" normally awarded for breach of contract. See Restatement (Second) of Contracts §§ 344 & 347 (1981).

[16] See Munson v. Straits of Dover S. S. Co., 102 F. 926 (2d Cir. 1900) (ship owner sued charterer despite arbitration agreement between them and charterer's offer to arbitrate; court ruled against owner; charterer sought damages in the form of lawyer's fees and costs incurred in defending the lawsuit; court held "only nominal damages are recoverable.")

[17] Restatement (Third) U.S. Law of Int'l Comm. Arb. § 2.1 Note a(i) (2019) ("A stay is a form of indirect enforcement; it eliminates access to the court granting the stay, and to that extent curtails the plaintiff's options."); id. ("Unless the defendant has claims of its own to press, the defendant may seek only a stay in hopes that the plaintiff, limited to the arbitral forum, will decide not to pursue its claims."); LaPrade, 146 F.3d at 903 (a district court stay instructs plaintiff, in effect, that it may not litigate claims directly in court, but could only arbitrate them or abandon them); Cabinetree of Wisc., Inc. v. Kraftmaid Cabinetry, Inc., 50 F.3d 388, 389 (7th Cir. 1995) ("[A] defendant who wants arbitration is often content with a stay, since that will stymie the plaintiff's effort to obtain relief unless he agrees to arbitrate.").

> that the issue involved in such suit or proceeding is referable to arbitration under such an agreement, shall on application of one of the parties stay the trial of the action until such arbitration has been had in accordance with the terms of the agreement, providing the applicant for the stay is not in default in proceeding with such arbitration.[18]

Although FAA § 3 only mentions stays, not dismissals,[19] most circuits permit dismissal of the suit when the arbitration agreement covers all of the claims before the court.[20] The distinction between a stay and a dismissal matters because dismissals are immediately appealable under FAA § 16, but stays are not.[21]

Now consider the second scenario, Buyer's refusal to arbitrate Seller's claim against it. A defendant who refuses to participate in arbitration will be ordered by a court to do so. This order follows from FAA § 4, which says, in part:

---

18 9 U.S.C. § 3.

19 Lloyd v. Hovensa, LLC., 369 F.3d 263, 269 (3d Cir. 2004) ("the plain language of § 3 affords a district court no discretion to dismiss a case where one of the parties applies for a stay pending arbitration."); Adair Bus Sales, Inc. v. Blue Bird Corp., 25 F.3d 953, 955 (10th Cir. 1994) ("where a defendant moved for a stay pending arbitration under 9 U.S.C. § 3, the District court erred in instead entering a dismissal and the proper course would have been to enter the stay"); Bender v. A.G. Edwards & Sons, Inc., 971 F.2d 698, 699 (11th Cir. 1992) ("We find that the state law claims are subject to arbitration, but that it was error to dismiss these claims rather than staying them pending arbitration."); Hewitt v. St. Louis Rams P'ship, 409 S.W.3d 572, 574 (Mo. Ct. App. 2013) ("Rather than dismissal, the proper course of action for the trial court, upon finding an agreement to arbitrate, is to stay the action pending arbitration.");.

20 Next Step Med. Co., Inc. v. Johnson & Johnson Int'l, 619 F.3d 67, 71 (1st Cir. 2010) (a district court has discretion to dismiss "if all claims asserted in the case are found arbitrable."); Soucy v. Capital Mgmt. Servs., L.P., No. 14 C 5935, 2015 WL 404632, at *6 (N.D. Ill. Jan. 29, 2015) ("The Seventh Circuit . . . has repeatedly affirmed district courts' decisions dismissing suits where all of the claims must be arbitrated according to the agreement."); Knall Bev., Inc. v. Teamsters Local Union No. 293 Pension Plan, 744 F.3d 419, 421 (6th Cir. 2014) ("[T]he district court correctly ruled that the Act requires that this claim be arbitrated, and properly dismissed the case without prejudice."); Ozormoor v. T-Mobile USA, Inc., 354 Fed. Appx. 972 (6th Cir. 2009) (rejecting argument "that 9 U.S.C. § 3 requires district courts to stay suits pending arbitration rather than dismiss them."); Alford v. Dean Witter Reynolds, Inc., 975 F.2d 1161, 1164 (5th Cir. 1992) ("[t]he weight of authority clearly supports dismissal of the case when all of the issues raised in the district court must be submitted to arbitration"); Green v. Ameritech Corp., 200 F.3d 967, 973 (6th Cir. 2000) (same); Sparling v. Hoffman Const. Co., Inc., 864 F.2d 635, 638 (9th Cir. 1988); Choice Hotels Intern., Inc. v. BSR Tropicana Resort, Inc., 252 F.3d 707, 709–10 (4th Cir. 2001) ("Notwithstanding the terms of § 3, however, dismissal is a proper remedy when all of the issues presented in a lawsuit are arbitrable."); Bercovitch v. Baldwin School, Inc., 133 F.3d 141, 156 & n.21 (1st Cir. 1998) (remanding to dismiss or stay).

21 FAA § 16(a)(3), (b)(1). See Lloyd v. Hovensa, LLC., 369 F.3d 263, 270–271 (3d Cir. 2004) ("[G]iving the District Court discretion to dismiss the action rather than enter a stay [would deprive] a party who has been held entitled to arbitration . . . of an important benefit which the FAA intended him to have—the right to proceed with arbitration without the substantial delay arising from an appeal.").

> A party aggrieved by the alleged failure, neglect, or refusal of another to arbitrate under a written agreement for arbitration may petition any United States district court * * * for an order directing that such arbitration proceed in the manner provided for in such agreement * * *. The court shall hear the parties, and upon being satisfied that the making of the agreement for arbitration or the failure to comply therewith is not in issue, the court shall make an order directing the parties to proceed to arbitration in accordance with the terms of the agreement * * *.[22]

To summarize, FAA §§ 3 and 4 require courts to enforce arbitration agreements with orders of specific performance. Rather than ordering the payment of money, courts order parties in breach of arbitration agreements to perform their agreements, that is, to arbitrate.

(c) The FAA's Broad Applicability: Interstate Commerce, Including Consumer Transactions

The FAA applies to a written[23] arbitration agreement "in any maritime transaction or a contract evidencing a transaction involving commerce."[24] FAA § 1 defines "commerce" to mean interstate or international commerce,[25] and the Supreme Court

> interpret[s] the term 'involving commerce' in the FAA as the functional equivalent of the more familiar term 'affecting commerce'—words of art that ordinarily signal the broadest permissible exercise of Congress' Commerce Clause power. * * * [The FAA] provides for the enforcement of arbitration agreements within the full reach of the Commerce Clause.[26]

---

[22] 9 U.S.C. § 4.

[23] See § 17.

[24] 9 U.S.C. § 2.

[25] "Commerce" is defined as:

> commerce among the several States or with foreign nations, or in any Territory of the United States or in the District of Columbia, or between any such Territory and another, or between any such Territory and any State or foreign nation, or between the District of Columbia and any State or Territory or foreign nation, but nothing herein contained shall apply to contracts of employment of seamen, railroad employees, or any other class of workers engaged in foreign or interstate commerce.

9 U.S.C. § 1.

[26] Citizens Bank v. Alafabco, Inc., 539 U.S. 52, 56–57 (2003) (citing U.S. Const. art. I, § 8, cl. 3 (granting Congress the power "To regulate Commerce with foreign Nations, and among the several States, and with the Indian Tribes.")) See also Allied-Bruce Terminix Co. Inc. v. Dobson, 513 U.S. 265, 281–82 (1995).

So interpreted, FAA § 1's definition of commerce is extremely broad, bringing the vast majority of arbitration agreements within the coverage of the FAA.[27]

This broad reach of the FAA results in it routinely enforcing most consumer arbitration agreements today, even though when the FAA was enacted in 1925 "very few" consumer transactions "would have involved interstate commerce and thus fallen under the jurisdiction of the FAA."[28] Back then—before most consumers had landline telephones, let alone cellphones, computers, and internet service—consumer transactions tended to be with local merchants. In contrast, a century of advances in communications technology have greatly spurred the growth of consumer transactions across state and national lines.

In addition, the Supreme Court expanded its interpretation of federal legislative power under the Commerce Clause in the 1930s to permit the New Deal proposed by President Franklin Delano Roosevelt. In 1935 and 1936, the Supreme Court struck down several key pieces of New Deal legislation.[29] President Roosevelt "chastise[d] the Justices for their 'horse and buggy interpretation' of the Commerce Clause."[30] After his landslide 1936 reelection, Roosevelt announced a plan to enlarge the Court's membership from nine to fifteen, which would have allowed him to appoint enough justices to reverse the Court's recent decisions, and thus uphold the New Deal. But "before the bill came to a vote in Congress, two Supreme Court justices came over to the liberal side and by a narrow majority upheld as constitutional the National Labor Relations Act and the Social Security Act."[31] This "switch in time that saved nine," greatly

---

[27] For exceptions, see Garrison v. Palmas Del Mar Homeowners Ass'n, Inc., 538 F. Supp.2d 468, 475 (D.P.R. 2008) ("these deeds are inherently intrastate and do not constitute 'transactions involving commerce' within the meaning of the FAA"); Arkansas Diagnostic Center, P.A. v. Tahiri, 257 S.W.3d 884, 891–92 (Ark. 2007) (employment agreement); Brown v. Hyatt Corp., 128 F. Supp.2d 697, 699–700 (D. Haw. 2000); Baronoff v. Kean Development Co., Inc., 818 N.Y.S.2d 421, 424–25 (Sup. Ct. 2006); Ex parte Webb, 855 So.2d 1031 (Ala. 2003); City of Cut Bank v. Tom Patrick Construction, Inc., 963 P.2d 1283 (Mont. 1998).

[28] Jean R. Sternlight, Panacea or Corporate Tool? Debunking the Supreme Court's Preference for Binding Arbitration, 74 Wash. U. L. Rev. 637, 647 (1996).

[29] Barry Cushman, The Court-Packing Plan as Symptom, Casualty, and Cause of Gridlock, 88 Notre Dame L. Rev. 2089, 2090 (2013).

[30] Id.

[31] Roosevelt announces "court-packing" plan, HISTORY (2010), http://www.history.com/this-day-in-history/roosevelt-announces-court-packing-plan (last visited Dec. 22, 2922). See also Daniel E. Ho & Kevin M. Quinn, Did a Switch in Time Save Nine?, 2 J. of Leg. Analysis 69, 70 (2010) ("The prevailing popular . . . account of the 'switch in time that saved nine' begins with a Court of four stalwart conservatives who battled with three liberal 'musketeers' for the survival of the New Deal. Holding the balance were the swing votes of Chief Justice Hughes and Justice Roberts, who in the 1934–1935 terms sided with the four conservatives to successively demolish New Deal infrastructure. When Roosevelt unveiled the court-packing plan, the story has it, the

expanded federal power, including—although this would not be fully evident until the 1980s[32]—the FAA. In sum, "[b]ecause the FAA predates the massive expansion of the federal Commerce power, matters that Congress did not intend to regulate in 1925 now fall squarely within the statute's text."[33]

(d) The FAA's Exclusions for Employment and Labor Arbitration

An exception to the FAA's extremely broad reach is FAA § 1, which says "nothing herein contained shall apply to contracts of employment of seamen, railroad employees, or any other class of workers engaged in foreign or interstate commerce."[34] This language may have originally excluded all workers' employment agreements from FAA § 2's instruction to enforce arbitration agreements, because in 1925 the Supreme Court narrowly interpreted "commerce" subject to federal legislative power.[35] So quite plausibly, in 1925 all workers either worked directly in interstate commerce—like "seamen" and "railroad employees"—and so were excluded from the FAA by § 1, or did not work directly in interstate commerce, and so were not even presumptively covered by FAA § 2, which governs only "transaction[s] involving commerce." Consequently, it was likely that when the FAA "was passed in 1925, Congress excluded all contracts of employment over which it then had jurisdiction."[36]

However, as discussed above, the Supreme Court expanded its interpretation of federal power under the Commerce Clause in the 1930s.[37] This big constitutional change expanded the types of workers covered by FAA § 2, much as it expanded the types of consumer transactions covered by FAA § 2. Courts could have responded to the expansion of workers covered by FAA § 2 by "interpreting [FAA § 1's] 'workers engaged in . . . commerce' flexibly to broaden along with the Court's broadening of 'commerce.' "[38] Under this interpretation, "as the types of jobs in 'commerce'

Court—or more specifically Justice Roberts—caved * * *. Thus, in a somersault of constitutional history, the switch in time resurrected the New Deal and spared the Court from packing."); id. at 72 ("Roberts shifted sharply (and statistically significantly) to the left in the 1936 term").

[32] See § 7.

[33] David Horton, The Federal Arbitration Act and Testamentary Instruments, 90 N.C. L. Rev. 1027, 1077 (2012).

[34] 9 U.S.C. § 1.

[35] See § 5(c).

[36] Matthew W. Finkin, Employment Contracts Under the FAA—Reconsidered, 48 Labor L.J. 329, 334 (1997).

[37] See § 5(c).

[38] Stephen J. Ware, A Short Defense of Southland, Casarotto, and Other Long-Controversial Arbitration Decisions, 30 Loy. Consumer L. Rev. 303, 333–34 (2018).

expanded to bring employees under FAA section 2, the types of employees excluded from the FAA by section 1 would have similarly expanded, thus leaving most employment arbitration agreements excluded from the FAA."[39]

In contrast, the Supreme Court's 2001 decision in *Circuit City Stores, Inc. v. Adams*,[40] held that FAA § 1 retained its original 1925 scope even as FAA § 2's scope expanded with the Court's expansion of the Commerce Clause. *Circuit City* distinguished FAA § 2's "involving commerce"—which the Court construed as extending to the full reach of Congress's Commerce power—from FAA § 1's "in commerce"—a term of art the Court had, in several contexts, construed more narrowly.[41] *Circuit City* recognized that "the FAA was enacted when congressional authority to regulate under the commerce power was to a large extent confined by our decisions," and "not[ed] that Supreme Court decisions beginning in 1937 ushered in an era of Commerce Clause jurisprudence that greatly expanded the previously defined authority of Congress under that Clause."[42] However, *Circuit City* said this change in constitutional interpretation had not caused the Supreme Court to change its interpretation of other statutes. That is, *Circuit City* cited non-arbitration cases declining to "afford significance, in construing the meaning of the statutory jurisdictional provisions 'in commerce' and 'engaged in commerce,' to the circumstance that the statute predated shifts in the Court's Commerce Clause cases."[43] In short, *Circuit City* rejected giving FAA § 1 "a broader construction than justified by its evident language simply because it was enacted in 1925 rather than 1938."[44]

Consequently, *Circuit City* interpreted FAA § 1 narrowly to exclude from the FAA only transportation workers—"seamen, railroad employees," and the like—while leaving other employment arbitration agreements covered by FAA § 2's rule of enforcing arbitration agreements.[45] This yields the strange result of a federal statute governing employees less closely connected to interstate commerce, while state law governs employees most closely connected to it. For instance, the Supreme Court's 2022 decision in *Southwest Airlines Co. v. Saxon*, held that "[w]orkers * * * who load cargo on and off airplanes belong to a class of workers in foreign or interstate

39 Id.

40 532 U.S. 105 (2001).

41 532 U.S. at 115–19.

42 Cir. City Stores, Inc. v. Adams, 532 U.S. 105, 116, 121 S. Ct. 1302, 1309–10, 149 L. Ed. 2d 234 (2001).

43 532 U.S. at 117.

44 532 U.S. at 118.

45 Id. at 119.

commerce," so the arbitration agreement of such a worker is not governed by the FAA.[46] Such transportation workers' arbitration agreements are instead governed by state law.[47] This distinction between transportation workers and other workers applies as well to independent contractors, the Supreme Court held in 2019's *New Prime Inc. v. Oliveira*.[48]

Distinct from employment arbitration, which arises out of a contract between an employer and an employee, is labor arbitration, which typically arises out of a contract—a collective bargaining agreement—between an employer and a labor union. Labor arbitration is primarily governed not by the FAA but by federal common law developed under the Labor Management Relations Act (Taft-Hartley Act) of 1947.[49] And labor arbitration in the public sector is governed by its own set of laws.[50]

(e) Other Exceptions to the FAA's Enforcement of Arbitration Agreements

(1) Federal Statutory Claims—from Wilko to McMahon and Gilmer

Although most non-labor arbitration agreements are governed by the FAA, several federal statutes and regulations remove particular types of arbitration agreements, or particular claims, from FAA § 2's rule of enforcing executory arbitration agreements. Such statute-by-statute exceptions to the FAA were more readily found by courts before the 1980s. In fact, from the FAA's 1925 enactment into the 1980s, courts found such exceptions so easily that they became the norm; courts generally refused to enforce pre-dispute agreements to arbitrate federal statutory claims.

The leading case in this refusal was *Wilko v. Swan*,[51] a 1953 Supreme Court decision involving an arbitration clause in a securities broker's form customer agreement. Despite this agreement to arbitrate, the customer brought a federal Securities Act claim against the broker in court rather than arbitration. The broker cited the FAA in moving to stay litigation and thus enforce the arbitration

---

[46] Sw. Airlines Co. v. Saxon, 142 S.Ct. 1783, 1970 (U.S. June 6, 2022) ("one who loads cargo on a plane bound for interstate transit is intimately involved with the commerce (e.g., transportation) of that cargo").

[47] The Seventh Circuit judgment affirmed by the Supreme Court in Southwest Airlines Co. v. Saxon noted the worker "could still face arbitration under state law or through an agreement outside of her contract of employment." S.W. Airlines Co. v. Saxon, 142 S. Ct. 1783, 1793 (2022).

[48] New Prime Inc. v. Oliveira, 139 S. Ct. 532 (2019).

[49] See § 44.

[50] See §§ 44(d), 66(b)(2)–(3).

[51] See Wilko v. Swan, 346 U.S. 427 (1953).

agreement. But the Supreme Court refused to enforce it, citing language in Section 14 of the Securities Act voiding any "condition, stipulation, or provision binding any person acquiring any security to waive compliance with any provision" of the Securities Act.[52] *Wilko* found the pre-dispute arbitration agreement to be such a prohibited waiver. "As the protective provisions of the Securities Act require the exercise of judicial direction to fairly assure their effectiveness, it seems to us that Congress must have intended § 14 to apply to waiver of judicial trial and review," that is, to arbitration agreements.[53]

Did *Wilko* prohibit arbitration of Securities Act claims? One might think so from a later Supreme Court case, *Mitsubishi Motors Corp. v. Soler Chrysler-Plymouth, Inc.*, saying *Wilko* "held nonarbitrable claims arising under the Securities Act."[54] But *Wilko* did not prohibit parties from arbitrating their Securities Act claims. And if parties did arbitrate Securities Act claims after *Wilko*, a court would enforce the arbitrator's decision (the arbitration award).[55] So, *Mitsubishi*'s description of claims under a particular statute as "non-arbitrable" does not mean parties cannot arbitrate them, or even that such arbitration awards will be denied enforcement by courts. Saying claims under a particular statute are "non-arbitrable" merely means they are claims with respect to which a court will not enforce a *pre-dispute* agreement to arbitrate. In contrast, an "arbitrable" claim in this context is one with respect to which a pre-dispute arbitration agreement will be enforced by courts.[56]

In holding Securities Act claims non-arbitrable, *Wilko* contrasted claims under this investor "protective" statute with "commercial controversies" where the *Wilko* Court "[r]ecogniz[ed] the advantages that prior agreements for arbitration may provide."[57] In other words, *Wilko* refused to enforce a pre-dispute agreement to arbitrate claims under a protective statute but would have enforced a pre-dispute agreement to arbitrate commercial claims. This distinction between statutory claims and commercial claims largely prevailed until the 1980s, so before then, and leaving aside labor

---

52 Id. at 435.

53 Id. at 437.

54 Mitsubishi Motors Corp. v. Soler Chrysler-Plymouth, Inc., 473 U.S. 614, 621 (1985).

55 See § 5(b) (explaining that pre-FAA courts enforced arbitration awards but not executory arbitration agreements).

56 A separate meaning of "arbitrable" claim is a claim within the scope of an arbitration agreement. See § 26(a).

57 Wilko v. Swan, 346 U.S. 427, 438 (1953) ("Recognizing the advantages that prior agreements for arbitration may provide for the solution of commercial controversies, we decide that the intention of Congress concerning the sale of securities is better carried out by holding invalid such an agreement for arbitration of issues arising under the Act.")

arbitration, which is governed by separate law,[58] "arbitration * * * functioned almost entirely * * * in 'ordinary disputes between merchants as to questions of fact,' "[59] rather than cases involving statutes protecting investors, consumers, employees, or the broader public.

Consider, for example, a contract between Buyer and Seller obligating each party to arbitrate any "controversy or claim arising out of or relating to this contract, or the breach thereof." If a dispute arises and one party seeks to litigate, while the other party seeks to arbitrate, a court will have to decide whether to hear the case on the merits or order arbitration. Assuming there is no generally applicable contract defense,[60] a court will order arbitration if, for example, Seller alleges that Buyer failed to pay, or Buyer alleges that Seller breached a warranty. By sending contract and warranty claims to arbitration over the objection of a party that seeks to litigate, courts hold that such claims are arbitrable.

But what if Buyer alleges that Seller violated the Sherman Antitrust Act? Until the 1980s, courts held that antitrust claims, like securities claims, were not arbitrable.[61] In our example, the court likely would have concluded that Buyer and Seller agreed to arbitrate Buyer's antitrust claim because it, like the contract and warranty claims, "ar[ose] out of" or at least "relate[d] to" the contract.[62] However, the court would have heard the antitrust claim on the merits—allowed Buyer to litigate it—rather than order arbitration of it because antitrust claims were non-arbitrable.

In addition to securities and antitrust, pre-1980s courts held many other federal statutory claims nonarbitrable, including RICO,[63]

---

[58] See § 44.

[59] See Mitsubishi Motors Corp. v. Soler Chrysler-Plymouth, Inc., 473 U.S. 614, 650 (1985) (Stevens, J., dissenting).

[60] See §§ 20–25.

[61] See, e.g., American Safety Equip. Corp. v. J. P. Maguire & Co., 391 F.2d 821, 828 (2d Cir. 1968) (declaring antitrust claims "inappropriate for arbitration"), overruled by Mitsubishi Motors Corp., 473 U.S. 614, 640 (1985) (holding an agreement to arbitrate a claim arising under the Sherman Antitrust Act enforceable).

[62] See § 26.

[63] See Page v. Moseley, Hallgarten, Estabrook & Weeden, Inc., 806 F.2d 291, 298–300 (1st Cir. 1986). "RICO" is an abbreviation for "Racketeer Influenced and Corrupt Organizations." 18 U.S.C. §§ 1961–68.

patent,[64] copyright,[65] "non-core" bankruptcy proceedings,[66] Title VII,[67] ADEA,[68] and ERISA.[69]

Then in the 1980s, the Supreme Court revolutionized arbitration law to require enforcement of agreements to arbitrate federal statutory claims. The Court held that the FAA

> mandates enforcement of agreements to arbitrate statutory claims. Like any statutory directive, the [FAA]'s mandate may be overridden by a contrary congressional command. The burden is on the party opposing arbitration, however, to show that Congress intended to preclude a waiver of judicial remedies for the statutory rights at issue * * *. If Congress did intend to limit or prohibit waiver of a judicial forum for a particular claim, such an intent will be deducible from [the statute's] text or legislative history, * * * or from an inherent conflict between arbitration and the statute's underlying purposes.[70]

The Supreme Court first made a statement to this effect in 1985,[71] and over the next several years the Supreme Court greatly increased the variety of federal statutory claims that are arbitrable.[72] So only

---

64 See Beckman Instruments, Inc. v. Technical Dev. Corp., 433 F.2d 55, 63 (7th Cir. 1970).

65 See Kamakazi Music Corp. v. Robbins Music Corp., 522 F. Supp. 125, 137 (S.D.N.Y. 1981), aff'd, 684 F.2d 228 (2d Cir. 1982).

66 See Zimmerman v. Continental Airlines, 712 F.2d 55, 59 (3rd Cir. 1983). But see Hays and Co. v. Merrill Lynch, Pierce, Fenner & Smith, Inc., 885 F.2d 1149, 1155 (3d Cir. 1989) (overruling Zimmerman and holding that non-core bankruptcy proceedings are arbitrable). Since Hays, courts have generally held that non-core bankruptcy proceedings are arbitrable. See, e.g., In re Gandy, 299 F.3d 489, 495 (5th Cir. 2002) ("it is generally accepted that a bankruptcy court has no discretion to refuse to compel the arbitration of matters not involving 'core' bankruptcy proceedings under 28 U.S.C. § 157(b)"). For the arbitrability of core bankruptcy matters, see § 5(e)(7).

67 See Utley v. Goldman Sachs & Co., 883 F.2d 184, 187 (1st Cir. 1989).

68 See Nicholson v. CPC Int'l Inc., 877 F.2d 221, 231 (3rd Cir. 1989). "ADEA" is an abbreviation for the Age Discrimination in Employment Act. See 29 U.S.C. §§ 621–634.

69 See Barrowclough v. Kidder, Peabody & Co., 752 F.2d 923, 941 (3d Cir. 1985). "ERISA" is an abbreviation for the Employment Retirement Income Security Act. 29 U.S.C. §§ 1001 et seq.

70 Shearson/American Express Inc. v. McMahon, 482 U.S. 220, 226–27 (1987) (citations omitted).

71 Mitsubishi Motors Corp. v. Soler Chrysler-Plymouth, Inc., 473 U.S. 614, 628 (1985) ("Having made the bargain to arbitrate, the party should be held to it unless Congress itself has evinced an intention to preclude a waiver of judicial remedies for the statutory rights at issue.")

72 Mitsubishi Motors Corp. v. Soler Chrysler-Plymouth, Inc., 473 U.S. 614 (1985) (antitrust); Shearson American Express, Inc. v. McMahon, 482 U.S. 220 (1987) (Securities Exchange Act and RICO); Rodriguez de Quijas v. Shearson/American Express, Inc., 490 U.S. 477 (1989) (Securities Act); Gilmer v. Interstate/Johnson Lane Corp., 500 U.S. 20 (1991) (employment discrimination); CompuCredit Corp. v. Greenwood, 132 S. Ct. 665 (2012) (Credit Repair Organization Act).

a few exceptions from before the 1980s remain. However, some newer exceptions have been created by Congress more recently. Both old and new exceptions are surveyed in the following paragraphs.

(2) Sexual Assault and Sexual Harassment

An exception from the FAA's instruction to enforce arbitration agreements is the Ending Forced Arbitration of Sexual Assault and Sexual Harassment Act, added to the FAA as a new Chapter 4 of Title 9 in 2022.[73] Enacted as a result of the #MeToo movement,[74] FAA Chapter 4 permits a person alleging a sexual harassment or sexual assault dispute to avoid enforcement of a pre-dispute arbitration agreement. FAA § 402(a) says:

> Notwithstanding any other provision of this title, at the election of the person alleging conduct constituting a sexual harassment dispute or sexual assault dispute, or the named representative of a class or in a collective action alleging such conduct, no predispute arbitration agreement or predispute joint-action waiver shall be valid or enforceable with respect to a case which is filed under Federal, Tribal, or State law and relates to the sexual assault dispute or the sexual harassment dispute.[75]

Thus, § 402(a) apparently permits a party asserting such claims to effectively remove the entire case—not just the sexual harassment or sexual assault claims—from the FAA's mandate to enforce predispute arbitration agreements. In contrast, if the party asserting such claims wants to enforce a predispute arbitration agreement, § 402(a) does not authorize the opposing party to prevent such enforcement.

---

[73] Ending Forced Arbitration of Sexual Assault and Sexual Harassment Act of 2021, 9 U.S.C. §§ 401–2.

[74] David Horton, The Limits of the Ending Forced Arbitration of Sexual Assault and Sexual Harassment Act, 132 Yale L.J. Forum (2022) ("antiarbitration momentum accelerated in 2016 with the rise of #MeToo. A parade of disturbing allegations against powerful men led to a 'reckoning and an airing of truths about sexual harassment and assault at work.' These stories highlighted that arbitration's privacy and confidentiality permit 'offender[s] to potentially evade accountability and continue the harassment.' For example, Fox News anchor Gretchen Carlson became a vocal opponent of forced arbitration after her boss, Roger Ailes, invoked the process in her sexual harassment cases against him. As Carlson put it, 'Forced arbitration is a sexual harasser's best friend: It keeps proceedings secret, findings sealed, and victims silent.' * * * As public pressure mounted, a variety of white-shoe law firms and tech companies voluntarily exempted claims of sexual misconduct from their forced arbitration clauses.")

[75] 9 U.S.C. § 402(a).

(3) Military Personnel

Statutes remove certain agreements and claims by military personnel from the FAA's rule of enforcing arbitration agreements. The Military Lending Act prohibits enforcement against military personnel of predispute arbitration agreements in credit agreements.[76] And several years' federal appropriations acts prohibit military contractors from requiring, as a condition of employment, employees to arbitrate claims under Title VII of the Civil Rights Act of 1964 or claims for sexual assault and sexual harassment.[77]

(4) Residential Mortgage Loans and Whistleblowers

Another statute removing particular agreements and claims from the FAA's instruction to enforce arbitration agreements is the Dodd Frank Wall Street Reform Act,[78] enacted in 2010 in the wake of a financial crisis and the Great Recession. Dodd-Frank generally bans the use of predispute arbitration agreements in connection with residential mortgages and home-equity loans.[79] For instance, the Fourth Circuit in 2022 applied Dodd Frank to prevent enforcement of an arbitration agreement in a home-equity line of credit.[80] Dodd Frank also prohibits enforcement of predispute arbitration agreements in the context of certain whistleblowers,[81] as does the American Recovery and Reinvestment Act of 2009.[82]

---

[76] 10 U.S.C. § 987(f)(4) ("Notwithstanding section 2 of title 9, or any other Federal or State law, rule, or regulation, no agreement to arbitrate any dispute involving the extension of consumer credit shall be enforceable against any covered member or dependent of such a member, or any person who was a covered member or dependent of that member when the agreement was made.")

For another possible exception, also relating to military personnel, compare Lopez v. Dillard's Inc., 382 F. Supp.2d 1245 (D. Kan. 2005) (claims under Uniformed Services Employment and Reemployment Rights Act of 1994 (USERRA) are nonarbitrable), with Garrett v. Circuit City Stores, Inc., 449 F.3d 672 (5th Cir. 2006) (claims under USERRA are arbitrable), Landis v. Pinnacle Eye Care, LLC, 537 F.3d 559, 563 (6th Cir. 2008) (same); Ernest v. Lockheed Martin Corp., 2008 WL 2958964, at *9 (D. Colo. 2008) (same).

[77] Department of Defense Appropriations Act, Pub. L. No. 111-118, § 8116, 123 Stat. 3409, 3454 (2010) (uncodified); 48 C.F.R. § 222.7402.

[78] Pub.L. 111–203, 124 Stat. 1376 (2010). 12 U.S.C. § 5301 note (detailing the complete classification of the Dodd Frank Wall Street Reform Act to the U.S. Code).

[79] 15 U.S.C. § 1639c(e). The Dodd Frank Act also authorized the Securities and Exchange Commission and the newly created Consumer Financial Protection Bureau to "prohibit or impose conditions or limitations on the use of" pre-dispute arbitration clauses in many consumer financial services contracts. 12 U.S.C. § 5518, 15 U.S.C. § 78o.

[80] Lyons v. PNC Bank, Nat'l Ass'n, 26 F.4th 180, 186 (4th Cir. 2022) ("The plain language of § 1639c(e)(3) is clear and unambiguous: a consumer cannot be prevented from bringing a TILA action in federal district court by a provision in an agreement 'relate[d] to' a residential mortgage loan—like a HELOC.")

[81] 7 U.S.C. § 26(n)(2).

[82] Pub. L. No. 111-5 § 1553, 123 Stat. 115 (2009).

(5) Auto Dealers and Poultry Farmers

Additional statutes add to the mix of groups who have persuaded Congress to remove their contracts from the FAA's rule of enforcing arbitration agreements. The Motor Vehicle Franchise Contract Arbitration Fairness Act prohibits enforcement of predispute arbitration agreements between auto manufacturers and auto dealers.[83] The Food, Conservation, and Energy Act of 2008 allows covered poultry farmers to opt out of arbitration agreements with poultry processors.[84]

(6) Consumer Product Warranties

Courts split over whether the Magnuson-Moss Warranty Act (Mag-Moss) removes any claims from the FAA's rule of enforcing arbitration agreements. Mag-Moss governs consumer product warranties.[85] The Federal Trade Commission construes Mag-Moss as barring predispute agreements for binding arbitration of consumer warranty claims and the FTC issued a rule prohibiting such arbitration agreements.[86] Some courts enforce this rule,[87] but most courts find that Mag-Moss does not except consumer warranties from the FAA's enforcement of binding arbitration agreements.[88]

---

[83] 15 U.S.C. § 1226(a)(2) ("Notwithstanding any other provision of law, whenever a motor vehicle franchise contract provides for the use of arbitration to resolve a controversy arising out of or relating to such contract, arbitration may be used to settle such controversy only if after such controversy arises all parties to such controversy consent in writing to use arbitration to settle such controversy.") Courts have considered whether this statute governs arbitration clauses in documents related to a motor vehicle franchise contract. Arciniaga v. General Motors Corp., 460 F.3d 231 (2d Cir. 2006) (stockholders agreement was not a "motor vehicle franchise contract" within the meaning of the Motor Vehicle Franchise Contract Arbitration Fairness Act (MVFCAFA)); Pride v. Ford Motor Co., 341 F. Supp.2d 617, 619 (N.D. Miss. 2004) (an automobile dealership investment and employment contract was not a "motor vehicle franchise contract").

[84] 7 U.S.C. § 197c ("Any livestock or poultry contract that contains a provision requiring the use of arbitration to resolve any controversy that may arise under the contract shall contain a provision that allows a producer or grower, prior to entering the contract to decline to be bound by the arbitration provision.")

[85] 15 U.S.C. § 2301 et seq.

[86] See 16 C.F.R. § 703.5; 40 Fed.Reg. 60167, 60210 (Dec. 31, 1975).

[87] See Breniser v. Western Recreational Vehicles, Inc., 2008 WL 5234528, at *6 (D. Or. 2008); Rickard v. Teynor's Homes, Inc., 279 F. Supp.2d 910 (N.D. Ohio 2003); Browne v. Kline Tysons Imports, Inc., 190 F. Supp.2d 827 (E.D. Va.2002); Pitchford v. Oakwood Mobile Homes, Inc., 124 F. Supp.2d 958 (W.D. Va. 2000); Koons Ford of Baltimore, Inc. v. Lobach, 919 A.2d 722, 732–35 (Md. 2007); Parkerson v. Smith, 817 So.2d 529 (Miss. 2002).

[88] Davis v. Southern Energy Homes, Inc., 305 F.3d 1268 (11th Cir. 2002); Walton v. Rose Mobile Homes LLC, 298 F.3d 470 (5th Cir. 2002). See also Brown v. BYRV, Inc., 2015 WL 4507159, at *18 (D. Or. 2015) (following "the well-reasoned opinions of the Fifth and Eleventh Circuits"); Krusch v. TAMKO Bldg. Prods., 34 F. Supp. 3d 584, 594 (M.D. N.C. 2014) ("MMWA does not prohibit enforcement of its provision for binding pre-dispute arbitration of Krusch's written warranty claims."); Seney v. Rent-

(7) Bankruptcy

Courts generally hold that the federal bankruptcy code[89] removes certain claims from the FAA's rule of enforcing predispute arbitration agreements. In particular, federal appellate courts generally hold that courts may decline to enforce arbitration agreements with respect to core bankruptcy proceedings[90] if such enforcement would conflict with an important purpose of the bankruptcy code, such as coordinating in a single forum resolution of all of the debtor's disputes with its various creditors.[91]

A-Center, Inc., 909 F. Supp. 2d 444, 452–453 (D. Md. 2012) ("More persuasive are decisions of the Fifth and Eleventh that have analyzed the MMWA and have concluded that predispute agreements to arbitrate claims arising under the statute are valid and enforceable."); McKinney v. Google, Inc., 2010 WL 11489027, at *6 (N.D. Cal. 2010) ("Here, following the reasoning outlined in the Fifth and Eleventh Circuit, the Court finds that there is no indication of Congressional intent that MMWA claims not be made subject to an arbitration agreement. Nothing in the text, history, or purposes of the MMWA suggests Congressional intent to preclude binding arbitration."); Patriot Mfg. v. Jackson, 929 So. 2d 997, 1006 (Ala. 2005) ("The Magnuson-Moss Act requires disclosure in the warranty itself only to the extent required by the rules of the [FTC] and the FTC has seen fit to require disclosure of required resort to an informal dispute-settlement mechanism, not the completely separate process of binding arbitration."); Abela v. GMC, 677 N.W.2d 325, 327–328 (Mich. 2004) ("Persuaded by these analyses [of the federal court of appeals, we conclude that plaintiffs' agreement with defendant to address the warranty claim through defendant's dispute resolution process, including mandatory arbitration, is enforceable."); Jones v. General Motors Corp., 640 F. Supp. 2d 1124, 1138–43 (D.Ariz. 2009); Hemphill v. Ford Motor Co., 206 P.3d 1, 11 (Kan. Ct. App. 2009); Borowiec v. Gateway 2000, Inc., 808 N.E.2d 957 (Ill.2004); Stacy David, Inc. v. Consuegra, 845 So.2d 303 (Fla. Ct. App. 2003); Abela v. General Motors Corp., 669 N.W.2d 271 (Mich. Ct. App.2003); Southern Energy Homes, Inc. v. Ard, 772 So.2d 1131 (Ala. 2000); In re American Homestar of Lancaster, Inc., 50 S.W.3d 480 (Tex. 2001); Results Oriented Inc. v. Crawford, 538 S.E.2d 73 (Ga. Ct. App.2000).

89 11 U.S.C. § 101 et seq.

90 A core proceeding traditionally involves "the administration of the estate; the allowance of claims against the estate; the voidance of preferences or fraudulent transfers; determinations as to dischargeability of debts; priorities of liens; or the confirmation of a plan." Hays and Co. v. Merrill Lynch, Pierce, Fenner & Smith, Inc., 885 F.2d 1149, 1156 n.9 (3d Cir. 1989). However, not all of what the bankruptcy code says is core may constitutionally be core. Stern v. Marshall, 564 U.S. 462 (2011); Ralph Brubaker, A "Summary" Statutory and Constitutional Theory of Bankruptcy Judges' Core Jurisdiction After *Stern v. Marshall*, 86 Am. Bankr. L.J. 121, 133 (2012).

91 Anderson v. Credit One Bank, N.A. (In re Anderson), 884 F.3d 382, 387 (2d Cir. 2018) ("If the proceeding is non-core, bankruptcy courts generally must stay the proceedings in favor of arbitration. If the matter involves a core proceeding, the bankruptcy court is tasked with engaging in a particularized inquiry into the nature of the claim and the facts of the specific bankruptcy."); id. at 392 (affirming order declining to enforce arbitration agreement because "arbitration will seriously jeopardize a particular core bankruptcy proceeding") (internal quotations and citations omitted); In re EPD Inv. Co., LLC, 821 F.3d 1146, 1150 (9th Cir. 2016) (trustee's "fraudulent conveyance, subordination, and disallowance causes of action" were core proceedings, giving the bankruptcy court discretion to weigh the competing bankruptcy and arbitration interests at stake. The court determined the arbitration provisions at issue conflicted with Bankruptcy Code purposes "of having bankruptcy law issues decided by bankruptcy courts; of centralizing resolution of bankruptcy disputes; and of protecting parties from piecemeal litigation"); In re Relativity Fashion, LLC, 696 F. App'x 26, 30 (2d Cir. 2017) ("a bankruptcy court may retain

(8) Regulations of Nursing Homes, Student Loans, Securities

Long-term care facilities ("LTCs" or nursing homes) contract with the federal government through its Center for Medicaid and Medicare Services (CMS), which is part of the U.S. Department of Health and Human Services. In 2016, CMS enacted a rule that "prohibited the use of pre-dispute arbitration agreements by LTC facilities receiving Medicare and Medicaid funding."[92] A court stopped this rule from going into effect because of its conflict with the FAA.[93] So, in 2019 CMS promulgated a rule, not prohibiting pre-dispute arbitration agreements, but withholding federal funding from LTCs who make agreements to arbitrate "a condition of admission to" or "a requirement to continue to receive care at, the facility."[94] This rule was challenged as conflicting with the FAA, but the Eighth Circuit upheld it on the ground that it:

> does not invalidate or render unenforceable any arbitration agreement. Instead, it establishes the conditions for receipt of federal funding through the Medicare and Medicaid programs. So, for example, if an LTC facility entered into an arbitration agreement with a resident without complying with the Revised Rule by requiring the resident

---

jurisdiction over a core proceeding in spite of a mandatory arbitration provision if, in the exercise of its discretion, it concludes that any underlying purpose of the Bankruptcy Code would be adversely affected by enforcing the arbitration clause. Relevant considerations include the goal of centralized resolution of pure bankruptcy issues, the need to protect creditors and reorganizing debtors from piecemeal litigation, and the undisputed power of a bankruptcy court to enforce its own orders. If the bankruptcy court has properly considered the conflicting policies in accordance with law, we acknowledge its exercise of discretion and show due deference to its determination that arbitration will seriously jeopardize a particular core bankruptcy proceeding.") (internal quotations and citations omitted); In re White Mountain Mining Co., L.L.C., 403 F.3d 164, 169–70 (4th Cir. 2005) ("Congress intended to centralize disputes about a debtor's assets and legal obligations in the bankruptcy courts. Arbitration is inconsistent with centralized decision-making because permitting an arbitrator to decide a core issue would make debtor-creditor rights contingent upon an arbitrator's ruling rather than the ruling of the bankruptcy judge assigned to hear the debtor's case.") (internal citations omitted).

[92] Northport Health Servs. of Arkansas, LLC v. United States Dep't of Health & Hum. Servs., 438 F. Supp. 3d 956, 962 (W.D. Ark. 2020), aff'd sub nom. Northport Health Servs. of Arkansas, LLC v. U.S. Dep't of Health & Hum. Servs., 14 F.4th 856 (8th Cir. 2021). "Residents and facilities could still agree to arbitrate once a dispute arose, but the facility could not enter into a general agreement to arbitrate any dispute with a resident or resident's family before the dispute arose." Id. See CMS Long-Term Care Rule. Reform of Requirements for Long-Term Care Facilities, 81 Fed. Reg. 68,688 (Oct. 4, 2016).

[93] American Health Care Association v. Burwell, 217 F. Supp. 3d 921 (N.D. Miss. 2016), held that the plaintiff was likely to prevail in its challenge to the CMS rule based on its conflict with the FAA.

[94] See Revision of Requirements for Long-Term Care Facilities: Arbitration Agreements, 84 Fed. Reg. 34,718, 34,718 (July 18, 2019) (codified at 42 C.F.R. § 483.70(n)).

> to sign as a condition of admission to the facility, the arbitration agreement would nonetheless be enforceable, * * *. CMS would simply enforce the regulation through a combination of administrative remedies, including denial of payment and civil monetary penalties.[95]

On similar reasoning, a federal court rejected a FAA-based challenge to a U.S. Department of Education rule prohibiting schools that participate in the federal direct loan program from using predispute arbitration agreements covering "borrower defense claims."[96] The court said the rule was consistent with the FAA because it did not prevent enforcement of arbitration agreements, but rather imposes a condition on the participation of a school in the direct loan program.

The Securities Exchange Commission largely prevents public offerings of securities by companies whose charters or bylaws require arbitration of shareholder claims against the corporation.[97] While no statute or regulation specifically empowers the SEC to so discriminate against arbitration provisions, "a long-held view of SEC commissioners and staff [is] that these provisions are inconsistent with the securities laws' non-waiver provisions."[98] Courts have yet to rule on arguments that the SEC's practice is precluded by the FAA.

(9) Bills to Reduce FAA's Applicability

Bills introduced in Congress would remove other types of arbitration agreements from the FAA's rule of enforcing arbitration agreements. Particularly sweeping is the Forced Arbitration Injustice Repeal Act, which would prohibit enforcement of a predispute arbitration agreement "with respect to an employment

---

[95] Northport Health Servs. of Arkansas, LLC v. U.S. Dep't of Health & Hum. Servs., 14 F.4th 856, 868 (8th Cir. 2021) (citations omitted).

[96] Cal. Ass'n of Priv. Postsecondary Schs. v. DeVos, 436 F. Supp. 3d 333, 344 (D.D.C. 2020), vacated as moot, No. 20-5080, 2020 WL 9171125 (D.C. Cir. Oct. 14, 2020).

[97] Alison Frankel, Shareholder Alert: SEC Commissioner Floats Class-Action-Killing Proposal, REUTERS (July 18, 2017), https://www.reuters.com/article/us-otc-arbitration-idUSKBN1A326T. More technically, the SEC refuses to grant accelerated registration to such IPOs. Claudia H. Allen, Bylaws Mandating Arbitration of Stockholder Disputes?, 39 Del. J. Corp. L. 751, 778–79 (2015) (if the SEC denied acceleration "the company could presumably seek recourse through the courts. But, to date, no company has pursued such a time-consuming and expensive course of action. Such an approach would also, as a practical matter, attract negative publicity, be problematic for underwriters who want to take an offering to market at the time they believe optimal, and complicate the ability of a company to work with the Staff on a going-forward basis.")

[98] Andrew K. Jennings, Firm Value and Intracorporate Arbitration, 38 Rev. Litig. 1, 3–4 (2018). See also SEC, Div. of Corp. Fin., No-Action Letter, Pfizer, Inc. (Feb. 22, 2012) ("We note that there appears to be some basis for your view that implementation of the [mandatory arbitration bylaws] proposal would cause the company to violate the federal securities laws.").

dispute, consumer dispute, antitrust dispute, or civil rights dispute."[99] This so-called FAIR Act passed the House of Representatives in 2019,[100] and was referred to the Senate Judiciary Committee, but never received a vote in the Senate.[101] The FAIR Act again passed the House in 2022.[102]

Other bills would remove from the FAA's rule of enforcing arbitration agreements nursing home agreements,[103] and agreements between Amtrak and its customers.[104]

---

[99] Forced Arbitration Injustice Repeal Act, S. 505, 117th Cong. (2021) ("Notwithstanding any other provision of this title, no predispute arbitration agreement or predispute joint-action waiver shall be valid or enforceable with respect to an employment dispute, consumer dispute, antitrust dispute, or civil rights dispute.")

[100] H.R. 1423, 116th Cong. (as passed by H.R., Sept. 20, 2019).

[101] Benjamin Goldstein, Congress Considers Ban on Mandatory Predispute Arbitration and Class Action Waivers, Am. Bar Ass'n. (June, 3, 2021), https://www.americanbar.org/groups/labor_law/publications/labor_employment_law_news/winter-spring-2021-issue/congress-considers-ban/.

[102] Forced Arbitration Injustice Repeal Act of 2022, H.R. 963, 117th Cong. (as passed by H.R., March 17, 2022).

[103] Fairness in Nursing Home Arbitration Act, H.R. 2812, 117th Cong. (2021) ("A pre-dispute arbitration agreement shall not be valid or specifically enforceable against a resident or former resident of a skilled nursing facility, without regard to whether the agreement was made prior to or after the effective date of this paragraph."); id. ("For home and community-based services or home health care services provided under a waiver under this section, section 1902(a)(10)(D), or any other provision authorizing the provision of home and community-based services or home health care services under this title, the provider of such services (and any employee, agent, related entity, or affiliate of such provider) may not require, solicit, accept, or move to enforce a pre-dispute arbitration agreement from or on behalf of any individual receiving such services, whether the agreement is made before, during, or after the first date on which services are received. A pre-dispute arbitration agreement between such a provider (or entity or person) and an individual receiving services (or who formerly received services) shall not be valid or enforceable, without regard to whether such agreement was made prior to the effective date of this subsection.")

[104] Ending Passenger Rail Forced Arbitration Act, S. 2342, 117th Cong. (2021) ("All predispute arbitration agreements and predispute joint-action waivers shall be invalid and unenforceable with respect to a consumer or civil rights dispute between Amtrak (in its capacity as a rail passenger carrier) and a customer of Amtrak.")

Chapter 3

FAA PREEMPTION OF STATE LAW

Table of Sections

A. FAA PREEMPTION WITHOUT CREATING FEDERAL JURISDICTION

Table of Sections

Sec.

---

§ 6 FAA as (Non-Preemptive) Procedural Law

Federal preemption of state law importantly shapes arbitration law. The Supremacy Clause of the United States Constitution says that a federal law within the constitutional scope of federal power is supreme over conflicting state law.[1] Consider, for example, a case in which Defendant is liable to Plaintiff under state tort and contract law. If Defendant can show that enforcement of that state law would conflict with a federal statute, such as the Employee Retirement Income Security Act ("ERISA"), then Defendant wins the case.[2] What would have been the result under state law is reversed by federal law.

What has just been said about the preemptive effect of ERISA can also be said about all federal *substantive* law. Federal substantive law preempts state law inconsistent with that federal law, and this is true whether the case is heard in federal or state court.[3] In contrast, federal *procedural* law does not necessarily preempt state law.[4] For instance, the Federal Rules of Civil

---

1 U.S. Const. art. VI, cl. 2 ("This Constitution, and the Laws of the United States which shall be made in Pursuance thereof; and all Treaties made, or which shall be made, under the Authority of the United States, shall be the supreme Law of the Land; and the Judges in every State shall be bound thereby, any Thing in the Constitution or Laws of any State to the Contrary notwithstanding.")

2 See, e.g., Aetna Health Inc. v. Davila, 542 U.S. 200, 210–14 (2004) ("respondents' state causes of action fall within the scope of ERISA * * * and are therefore completely pre-empted by ERISA") (internal quotations omitted); Pilot Life Insurance Co. v. Dedeaux, 481 U.S. 41, 45–47 (1987).

3 Howlett v. Rose, 496 U.S. 356, 367 (1990) ("Federal law is enforceable in state courts * * * because the Constitution and laws passed pursuant to it are as much laws in the States as laws passed by the state legislature. The Supremacy Clause makes those laws 'the supreme Law of the Land,' and charges state courts with a coordinate responsibility to enforce that law according to their regular modes of procedure.")

4 "No one disputes the general and unassailable proposition * * * that States may establish the rules of procedure governing litigation in their own courts." Felder v. Casey, 487 U.S. 131, 138 (1988). However, "Federal law takes state courts as it finds them only insofar as those courts employ rules that do not impose unnecessary burdens upon rights of recovery authorized by federal laws." Id. at 150 (internal quotations omitted).

Procedure do not preempt inconsistent state rules of civil procedure because the Federal Rules of Civil Procedure only apply in federal court and the "inconsistent" state rules of civil procedure only apply in state court. Federal and state law on civil procedure, even though different, do not conflict because each governs in its own forum.

The same was true of federal and state arbitration law prior to the FAA's 1925 enactment. Federal arbitration law governed only in federal court and state arbitration law governed only in state court.[5] Scholars disagree about whether the FAA was designed to preserve or change this state of affairs. While many believe that the FAA was originally understood to be merely a *procedural* law governing only in federal courts,[6] some evidence suggests that those who enacted the FAA understood its key provision enforcing arbitration agreements, § 2, to be *substantive* federal law governing in both federal and state courts.[7] Whatever the original understanding at the time of the FAA's enactment, several decades passed before courts began to hold that any of the FAA applies in state court and thus preempts inconsistent state law.

§ 7 FAA as (Preemptive) Substantive Law

Until the late 1950's, no case held that the FAA applies in state court or preempts inconsistent state law.[8] However, in 1959 the Second Circuit held that FAA § 2 was "federal substantive law * * *

---

5 Ian R. Macneil, American Arbitration Law 21–24 (1992); Ian R. Macneil, Richard E. Speidel & Thomas J. Stipanowich, Federal Arbitration Law § 10.1 (1994 & Supp.1999).

6 See, e.g., David Horton, Federal Arbitration Act Preemption, Purposivism, and State Public Policy, 101 Geo. L.J. 1217, 1219 (2013) ("Most courts and commentators believe that Congress intended the statute to be a mere procedural rule for federal courts. Yet three decades ago, in Southland Corp. v. Keating, the Court held that the FAA applies in state court and eclipses contrary state law"); Id. at 1227–28 ("Few modern opinions have weathered as much criticism as *Southland*. * * * Ironically, FAA preemption, though widely seen as illegitimate, is now well-established.")

7 Compare, e.g., Ian R. Macneil, American Arbitration Law 92–121 (1992) (only federal courts), with Christopher R. Drahozal, In Defense of Southland: Reexamining the Legislative History of the Federal Arbitration Act, 78 Notre Dame L.Rev. 101, 123 (2002) ("The language of [FAA] section 2 broadly makes 'valid, irrevocable, and enforceable' both pre-dispute and post-dispute arbitration agreements. Nothing in the language of the section limits its application to cases in the federal courts"; "By contrast, the remaining sections of the FAA by their terms apply only in federal court"). This topic continues to inspire passionate criticism of the Supreme Court. See Brown ex rel. Brown v. Genesis Healthcare Corp., 724 S.E.2d 250, 278 (W. Va. 2011) ("With tendentious reasoning, the United States Supreme Court has stretched the application of the FAA from being a procedural statutory scheme effective only in the federal courts, to being a substantive law that preempts state law in both the federal and state courts."), vacated by, Marmet Health Care Center, Inc. v. Brown, 565 U.S. 530 (2012).

8 Ian R. Macneil, American Arbitration Law 122–38 (1992).

equally applicable in state or federal court."[9] The Second Circuit explained:

> To be sure much of the Act is purely procedural in character and is intended to be applicable only in the federal courts. But Section 2 declaring that arbitration agreements affecting commerce or maritime affairs are 'valid, irrevocable, and enforceable' goes beyond this point and must mean that arbitration agreements of this character, previously held by state law to be invalid, revocable or unenforceable are now made 'valid, irrevocable, and enforceable.' This is a declaration of national law equally applicable in state or federal courts.[10]

This view of FAA § 2 was adopted by the Supreme Court in the 1984 case of *Southland Corp. v. Keating*.[11] *Southland* applied the FAA to a case arising out of California state courts and held that FAA § 2 preempts inconsistent state law. *Southland* stated that "The Federal Arbitration Act rests on the authority of Congress to enact substantive rules under the Commerce Clause."[12]

This *Southland* holding was reaffirmed in a 1995 Supreme Court case, *Allied-Bruce Terminix Cos. v. Dobson*,[13] and countless state court cases have applied FAA § 2, so Section 2's applicability in state court is well-established. However, the applicability in state courts of other FAA provisions is less clear, as discussed below.[14]

§ 8 FAA Creates No Federal Jurisdiction

While the Supreme Court has established that FAA § 2 is substantive law,[15] it is unusual federal substantive law because it creates no federal jurisdiction.[16] Ordinarily, a party asserting its

---

9 Robert Lawrence Co., Inc. v. Devonshire Fabrics, Inc., 271 F.2d 402, 407 (2d Cir. 1959).

10 Id. at 407.

11 465 U.S. 1, 11 (1984).

12 Id.

13 513 U.S. 265, 281 (1995).

14 Whether FAA §§ 3 and 4 apply in state court is discussed in § 11. Whether FAA § 10 (grounds for vacating arbitration awards) applies in state court and preempts inconsistent state law on grounds for vacatur is discussed in § 42.

15 See § 7.

16 Southland, 465 U.S. 1, 16 n.9 (1984).

> While the Federal Arbitration Act creates federal substantive law requiring the parties to honor arbitration agreements, it does not create any independent federal-question jurisdiction under 28 U.S.C. § 1331 (1976) or otherwise. This seems implicit in the provisions in § 3 for a stay by a "court in which such suit is pending" and in § 4 that enforcement may be ordered by "any United States district court which, save for such agreement, would have jurisdiction under

federal rights is entitled to have a federal court hear its claims. But that is not true of parties asserting FAA rights. Such parties must use state court unless they can point to some other source of federal jurisdiction. As the Supreme Court said in *Vaden v. Discover Bank*,[17] the FAA:

> is something of an anomaly in the realm of federal legislation: It bestows no federal jurisdiction but rather requires for access to a federal forum an independent jurisdictional basis over the parties' dispute. Given the substantive supremacy of the FAA, but the Act's nonjurisdictional cast, state courts have a prominent role to play as enforcers of agreements to arbitrate.[18]

Vaden began with a (state-law) breach-of-contract claim brought in state court, followed by state-law counterclaims, also asserted in state court. The counterclaims, however, were preempted by federal banking law, so the plaintiff (defending against the counterclaims) argued that its federal banking law defense gave a federal court jurisdiction to compel arbitration of the case.[19]

The Supreme Court disagreed because of the "longstanding well-pleaded complaint rule," which is that "a suit arises under federal law only when the plaintiff's statement of his own cause of action shows that it is based upon federal law. Federal jurisdiction cannot be predicated on an actual or anticipated defense. * * * Nor can federal jurisdiction rest upon an actual or anticipated counterclaim."[20] In sum, "a party seeking to compel arbitration may gain a federal court's assistance only if, 'save for' the [arbitration] agreement, the entire, actual 'controversy between the parties,' as they have framed it, could be litigated in federal court."[21] In cases

---

Title 28, in a civil action or in admiralty of the subject matter of a suit arising out of the controversy between the parties." Ibid.

Id. (citations omitted). In contrast, the international sections of the FAA, 9 U.S.C. §§ 201–208 and 301–307, do create federal jurisdiction. See Vaden v. Discover Bank, 556 U.S. 49, 58 (2009) ("Chapter 2 of the FAA, not implicated here, does expressly grant federal courts jurisdiction to hear actions seeking to enforce an agreement or award falling under the Convention on the Recognition and Enforcement of Foreign Arbitral Awards.")

17 556 U.S. 49, 58 (2009).

18 Id. at 1271–72 (internal quotations omitted).

19 Id. at 1268–69. See 28 U.S.C. § 1331 (giving federal courts jurisdiction over "all civil actions arising under the Constitution, laws, or treaties of the United States.").

20 Id. at 1272 (internal quotations omitted). "Under the well-pleaded complaint rule, a completely preempted counterclaim remains a counterclaim and thus does not provide a key capable of opening a federal court's door." Id. at 1276.

21 Id. at 1275 (quoting 9 U.S.C. § 4). "[F]ederal jurisdiction cannot be invoked on the basis of a defense or counterclaim. Parties may not circumvent those rules by asking a federal court to order arbitration of the portion of a controversy that implicates federal law when the court would not have federal-question jurisdiction

lacking federal jurisdiction, such as *Vaden*, the party seeking to compel arbitration can seek such an order from a state court.

While *Vaden* involved an attempt to enforce an executory arbitration agreement, issues of federal jurisdiction can also arise after arbitration when a party asks a federal court to confirm or vacate an arbitration award. There too, the Supreme Court explained in *Badgerow v. Walters*, the FAA confers no federal jurisdiction, so "an applicant seeking, for example, to vacate an arbitral award under [FAA] Section 10 must identify a grant of jurisdiction, apart from Section 10 itself, conferring 'access to a federal forum.' If she cannot, the action belongs in state court."[22] An action to confirm or vacate has a basis for federal diversity jurisdiction "if it shows that the contending parties are citizens of different States (with over $75,000 in dispute)."[23] An action to confirm or vacate an arbitration award has a basis for federal question jurisdiction "if it alleges that federal law (beyond Section 9 or 10 itself) entitles the applicant to relief."[24] But federal question jurisdiction is not alleged by showing the underlying dispute resolved in arbitration included a federal claim. An action to confirm or vacate an award is not re-contesting that dispute, *Badgerow* explains, but merely contesting "the enforceability of an arbitral award. That award is no more than a contractual resolution of the parties' dispute—a way of settling legal claims. And quarrels about legal settlements—even settlements of federal claims—typically involve only state law, like disagreements about other contracts."[25]

Badgerow held that to determine jurisdiction federal courts should not, on applications to confirm or vacate an arbitration award, look through those applications to the underlying claim (such as the unlawful-termination claim in *Badgerow*) brought by the claimant in that case. This holding contrasts with *Vaden* "approv[ing] the look-through approach for a Section 4 petition" to enforce an executory arbitration agreement. *Badgerow* drew that distinction because FAA §§ 9 and 10 (governing confirmation and vacatur) lack the § 4 language (governing enforcement of executory agreements) on which *Vaden* relied. As *Badgerow* explained,

> Under Section 4, a party to an arbitration agreement may petition for an order to compel arbitration in a "United

over the controversy as a whole. It does not suffice to show that a federal question lurks somewhere inside the parties' controversy, or that a defense or counterclaim would arise under federal law." Id. at 1278.

22 Badgerow v. Walters, 142 S. Ct. 1310, 1316 (2022) (quoting Vaden).

23 Id.

24 Id.

25 Id.

> States district court which, save for [the arbitration] agreement, would have jurisdiction" over "the controversy between the parties." That text, we stated, 'drives our conclusion that a federal court should determine its jurisdiction by "looking through" a § 4 petition to the underlying substantive controversy'—to see, for example, if that dispute "arises under federal law."[26]

In contrast, FAA §§ 9 and 10 lack similar language. So, parties seeking federal jurisdiction for confirmation and vacatur must find a source federal jurisdiction other than by pointing to an underlying claim arising under federal law.

B. FAA PREEMPTION OF STATE LAW IMPEDING CONTRACT ENFORCEMENT

Table of Sections

Sec.

---

[26] Id. at 1317.

§ 9 FAA Preemption Generally Enforces Executory Arbitration Agreements

The core of the FAA is § 2, which instructs courts to enforce arbitration agreements "save upon such grounds as exist at law or in equity for the revocation of any contract."[27] This contract-enforcing command largely adopts state contract law, while generally preempting state law that would override contract law. That is, under the FAA "state law, whether of legislative or judicial origin, is applicable if that law arose to govern issues concerning the validity, revocability, and enforceability of contracts generally."[28] But FAA § 2 preempts state law that "imposes prerequisites to enforcement of an arbitration agreement that are not applicable to contracts generally."[29] The Supreme Court holds that FAA § 2 "establish[es] an equal-treatment principle: A court may invalidate an arbitration agreement based on generally applicable contract defenses like fraud or unconscionability, but not on legal rules that apply only to arbitration or that derive their meaning from the fact that an agreement to arbitrate is at issue."[30] As the Restatement[31] explains,

> The FAA makes arbitration clauses subject to the same state law grounds for nonenforcement as other contract provisions and does not permit them to be subject to discriminatory treatment. * * *
>
> If a ground for nonenforcement makes an arbitration clause less enforceable than other provisions in the contract (or a comparable contract without an arbitration clause)—even if the ground applies to some other (but not all) contract provisions in addition to the arbitration clause—it does not apply to contracts generally and thus is preempted.[32]

---

27 The full text of § 2 is as follows:

> A written provision in any maritime transaction or a contract evidencing a transaction involving commerce to settle by arbitration a controversy thereafter arising out of such contract or transaction, or the refusal to perform the whole or any part thereof, or an agreement in writing to submit to arbitration an existing controversy arising out of such a contract, transaction, or refusal, shall be valid, irrevocable, and enforceable, save upon such grounds as exist at law or in equity for the revocation of any contract.

9 U.S.C. § 2.

28 Perry v. Thomas, 482 U.S. 483, 493 n.9 (1987).

29 Preston v. Ferrer, 552 U.S. 346, 356 (2008).

30 Viking River Cruises, Inc. v. Moriana, 142 S. Ct. 1906, 1917 (2022) (internal quotations omitted).

31 The Restatement of U.S. Law of International Commercial and Investor-State Arbitration was approved by the American Law Institute in 2019. It is cited throughout this chapter as simply the Restatement.

32 Restatement (Third) U.S. Law of Int'l Comm. Arb. § 1.6 cmt. b (2019).

This aspect of FAA preemption—the enforceability of executory arbitration agreements—is the most important area of FAA preemption and is discussed in the following several sections.[33] In contrast, other issues relating to FAA preemption of state law are discussed throughout this chapter as they arise amid various topics.

§ 10 FAA Preempts State Law Prohibiting Courts from Enforcing Arbitration Agreements

The clearest case for FAA preemption is state law making arbitration agreements unenforceable. Alabama courts have declared that predispute arbitration agreements are "void."[34] The U.S. Supreme Court held in *Allied-Bruce Terminix Cos., Inc. v. Dobson*,[35] that the FAA preempts this Alabama law.[36]

§ 11 FAA Preempts State Law Denying Specific Performance to Arbitration Agreements

While the previous paragraph discussed Alabama case law declaring that predispute arbitration agreements are void, Alabama also has a statute that goes not quite as far in the anti-arbitration direction. This statute prohibits courts from enforcing arbitration agreements with the remedy of specific performance, that is, orders to arbitrate.[37] While the Supreme Court held in *Allied-Bruce Terminix Cos., Inc. v. Dobson*, that the FAA preempts this statute,[38] Justice Thomas's dissent pointed out that this statute does not, by its terms, make arbitration agreements unenforceable but merely limits the remedies courts can use in enforcing arbitration agreements.[39] For example, the Alabama statute permits courts to award money damages for breach of an arbitration agreement. Therefore, Justice Thomas concluded, the Alabama statute does not conflict with the

---

33 See §§ 10–16.

34 See, e.g., Wells v. Mobile County Bd. of Realtors, 387 So.2d 140, 144 (Ala. 1980). See generally Stephen J. Ware, The Alabama Story: Arbitration shows law's connection to politics, culture, Disp. Resol. Mag. 24 (Summer 2001).

35 513 U.S. 265 (1995).

36 Id. at 281. See also State ex rel. Wells v. Matish, 600 S.E.2d 583, 591 n.7 (W.Va. 2004) ("The Federal Arbitration Act pre-empts state law * * * [so] state courts cannot apply state statutes that invalidate arbitration agreements." (citation omitted)).

37 Ala.Code § 8–1–41(3) (1975) ("The following obligations cannot be specifically enforced: * * * An agreement to submit a controversy to arbitration").

38 513 U.S. 265, 281 (1995).

39 See 513 U.S. at 293 (Thomas, J. dissenting) ("A contract surely can be 'valid, irrevocable, and enforceable' even though it can be enforced only through actions for damages."); id. at 294 ("the [Alabama] statute does not itself make executory arbitration agreements invalid, revocable, or unenforceable").

FAA's requirement that arbitration agreements be "valid, irrevocable and enforceable."[40]

On the other hand, though, the ineffectiveness of money damages as a remedy for breach of executory arbitration agreements is the main problem the FAA was enacted to solve.[41] Central to the FAA is its requirement that courts enforce arbitration agreements with the remedy of specific performance. Accordingly, the FAA directly conflicts with, and therefore preempts, a state law precluding specific performance as a remedy for breach of an arbitration agreement.

Here, however, the text of the FAA cuts against preemption. The portions of the FAA requiring courts to enforce arbitration agreements with the remedy of specific performance are FAA §§ 3 and 4.[42] The text of these provisions indicates that they apply only in federal, not state, court. FAA § 3 covers "any suit or proceeding * * * brought in any of the courts of the United States."[43] FAA § 4 is even clearer, applying to "any United States district court."[44]

The Supreme Court has not directly resolved the question of whether, despite this apparently limiting language, FAA §§ 3 and 4 nevertheless apply in state court. In 1984, the Supreme Court first applied § 2 of the FAA to a state court case, *Southland Corp. v. Keating*.[45] In 1983, the year preceding *Southland*, the Court said in *Moses H. Cone Mem'l Hosp. v. Mercury Constr. Corp.*, that "state courts, as much as federal courts, are obliged to grant stays of litigation under § 3 of the Act."[46] But *Southland* backtracked: "we do not hold that §§ 3 and 4 of the Arbitration Act apply to proceedings in state courts."[47] And in 1989, the Supreme Court stated: "we have never held that §§ 3 and 4, which by their terms appear to apply only to proceedings in federal court, are nonetheless applicable in state court."[48] The 1995 *Allied-Bruce* case reaffirmed *Southland*, but did not discuss whether FAA §§ 3 and 4 apply in state court. However, the effect of *Southland* and *Allied-Bruce* is to require state courts to

---

40 9 U.S.C. § 2.

41 See § 5(b).

42 See id.

43 9 U.S.C. § 3.

44 9 U.S.C. § 4.

45 465 U.S. 1, 11 (1984).

46 Moses H. Cone Mem'l Hosp. v. Mercury Constr. Corp., 460 U.S. 1, 26 n.34 (1983).

47 See Southland, 465 U.S. 1, 16 n.10 (1984).

48 Volt Info. Sciences, Inc. v. Bd. of Trustees of the Leland Stanford Junior Univ., 489 U.S. 468, 477 n.6 (1989). Accord Vaden v. Discover Bank, 556 U.S. 49, 70 (2009) ("This Court has not decided whether §§ 3 and 4 apply to proceedings in state courts, and we do not do so here.") (citing Volt).

enforce arbitration agreements with the remedy of specific performance, that is, orders to arbitrate. In effect, *Southland* and *Allied-Bruce* have made the specific-performance gist of FAA §§ 3 and 4 applicable in state court even while maintaining that it is still an open question whether those provisions technically apply in state court.[49]

§ 12 FAA Preempts State Law Denying Enforcement of Agreements to Arbitrate Certain Claims

FAA § 2 preempts most state law denying enforcement of agreements to arbitrate certain claims. An example is *Southland Corp. v. Keating*,[50] which held preempted California law denying enforcement of an agreement to arbitrate claims under the California Franchise Investment Law ("CFIL"). *Southland* involved an arbitration clause in a franchise agreement for a convenience store. Franchisees sued the franchisor (Southland) in state court, alleging a variety of claims including torts, breach of contract, and breach of the disclosure requirements of CFIL.[51] The trial court granted Southland's motion to compel arbitration of all claims except for the CFIL claim.[52] In other words, the trial court ruled that the dispute should be split, with one claim litigated and other claims arbitrated.[53] The Supreme Court of California agreed, enforcing the arbitration agreement with respect to all claims except for the CFIL claim.[54] In

49 See Southland, 465 U.S. at 24 (O'Connor, J., dissenting) ("the Court reads [FAA] § 2 to require state courts to enforce § 2 rights using procedures that mimic those specified for federal courts by FAA §§ 3 and 4."); Ian R. Macneil, Richard E. Speidel & Thomas J. Stipanowich, Federal Arbitration Law § 10.8.2.4, at 10:91–10:92 (Supp. 1999) ("although the Court holds that FAA §§ 3 and 4 do not govern state courts, it is equally clear that FAA § 2, which does govern them, carries with it duties indistinguishable from those imposed on federal courts by FAA §§ 3 and 4.").

While the Court has made the core of FAA §§ 3 and 4 applicable in state court, some of its details have been held not to apply in state court. See Rosenthal v. Great Western Fin. Sec. Corp., 926 P.2d 1061 (Cal. 1996) (FAA § 4's jury trial right for issues about the making of the arbitration agreement not applicable in state court); St. Fleur v. WPI Cable Systems/Mutron, 879 N.E.2d 27, 33 (Mass. 2008) (same; state court should apply state statute otherwise similar to FAA § 4 rather than FAA § 4).

50 465 U.S. 1 (1984).

51 Id. at 4. See Cal. Corp. Code Ann. §§ 31000 et seq.

52 465 U.S. at 4.

53 This raises questions about whether one action should be stayed while the other proceeds and about possible conflicting rulings in the two actions. See KPMG LLP v. Cocchi, 565 U.S. 18, 22 (2011) ("when a complaint contains both arbitrable and nonarbitrable claims, the [FAA] requires courts to 'compel arbitration of pendent arbitrable claims when one of the parties files a motion to compel, even where the result would be the possibly inefficient maintenance of separate proceedings in different forums.' ") (quoting Dean Witter Reynolds Inc. v. Byrd, 470 U.S. 213 (1985)).

54 465 U.S. at 5.

other words, it held that the franchisees' tort and contract claims were *arbitrable*, but their CFIL claims were not.[55]

The California courts' rationale for treating CFIL claims differently from tort and contract claims is the language of CFIL, which says that "any stipulation purporting to waive compliance with any provision of this law is void."[56] The California Supreme Court interpreted this language to void an agreement to arbitrate CFIL claims.[57] Whether the California court was correct in treating an arbitration clause as a waiver of statutory compliance is an interesting question,[58] but the United States Supreme Court did not address it in *Southland*. The United States Supreme Court deferred to the California Supreme Court as the highest interpreter of California statutes. The United States Supreme Court therefore considered only whether the California statute, as interpreted by California's highest court, was preempted by federal law.

Southland held that the California statute, as interpreted by California's highest court, was preempted by FAA § 2 which says that arbitration agreements "shall be valid, irrevocable, and enforceable, save upon such grounds as exist at law or in equity for the revocation of any contract."[59] *Southland* explained that the CFIL conflicts with, and is therefore preempted by, FAA § 2.

> We agree, of course, that a party may assert general contract defenses such as fraud to avoid enforcement of an arbitration agreement. We conclude, however, that the defense to arbitration found in the California Franchise Investment Law is not a ground that exists at law or in equity "for the revocation of any contract" but merely a ground that exists for the revocation of arbitration provisions in contracts subject to the California Franchise Investment Law.[60]

Justice Stevens' dissent in *Southland* argued that "a state policy of providing special protection for franchisees * * * can be recognized

---

55 See § 5(e)(1) (discussing a common meaning of "arbitrable").

56 Cal. Corp. Code § 31512.

57 465 U.S. at 10.

58 Compare Wilko v. Swan, 346 U.S. 427 (1953) (holding arbitration agreement is a "provision binding [a] person * * * to waive compliance with" the Securities Act), with Shearson American Express, Inc. v. McMahon, 482 U.S. 220, 229 (1987) ("[b]y agreeing to arbitrate a statutory claim, a party does not forgo the substantive rights afforded by the statute.")

59 9 U.S.C. § 2.

60 Southland, 465 U.S. at 16 n.11.

without impairing the basic purposes of the federal statute."[61] The majority rebutted Stevens' analysis.

> If we accepted this analysis, states could wholly eviscerate Congressional intent to place arbitration agreements "upon the same footing as other contracts," simply bypassing statutes such as the Franchise Investment Law. We have rejected this analysis because it is in conflict with the Arbitration Act and would permit states to override the declared policy requiring enforcement of arbitration agreements.[62]

Southland was the first of several Supreme Court cases holding that state courts may decline to enforce arbitration agreements only on "such grounds as exist at law or in equity for the revocation of any contract."[63]

This holding is important, because many states have laws denying enforcement to agreements—at least predispute agreements—to arbitrate certain claims, such tort claims, personal injury claims, or medical malpractice claims.[64] These laws are preempted by FAA § 2 because they create a ground for denying enforcement to arbitration agreements that is not a ground "for the revocation of any contract."[65] For example, the Supreme Court's 2012 decision in *Marmet Health Care Center, Inc. v. Brown*, held that the FAA preempts a rule of West Virginia case law prohibiting enforcement of predispute agreements to arbitrate personal injury negligence claims against nursing homes.[66]

The Court's 2022 decision in *Viking River Cruises, Inc. v. Moriana*, held that the FAA preempts a rule of California case law

[61] Southland, 465 U.S. at 21 (Stevens, J., dissenting).

[62] Southland, 465 U.S. at 16 n.11 (quoting H.R.Rep.No. 68-96 (1924)).

[63] 9 U.S.C. § 2. See § 9.

[64] See, e.g., Ark. Code Ann. 16–108–233(b)(1) (personal injury, tort, employment, insurance); Ga. Code Ann. 9–9–2(c)(10) (personal injury); Iowa Code Ann. 679A.1(2)(c) (tort); Mont. Code Ann. 27–5–114(2)(a) (personal injury); Neb. Rev. Stat. 25–2602.01(e), (f) (workers compensation, personal injury tort, Fair Employment Practices Act); N.C. Gen. Stat. 90–21.60(a) ("all claims for damages for personal injury or wrongful death based on alleged negligence in the provision of health care"); S. C. Code Ann. 15–48–10(b)(3), (4) (medical malpractice, personal injury, insurance).

[65] 9 U.S.C. § 2. See, e.g., Perry v. Thomas, 482 U.S. 483, 490–91 (1987) (FAA preempts state law denying enforcement of agreements to arbitrate California Labor Code claims); Ting v. AT & T, 319 F.3d 1126, 1147 (9th Cir. 2003) (FAA preempts California's Consumer Legal Remedies Act); Shepard v. Edward Mackay Enterprises, Inc., 56 Cal. Rptr.3d 326 (Ct. App. 2007) (FAA preempts California statute denying enforcement of agreements to arbitrate bodily injury or wrongful death claims arising out of real estate transactions); Triad Health Management of Georgia, III, LLC v. Johnson, 679 S.E.2d 785, 789–90 (Ga. App .2009) (FAA preempts Georgia statute denying enforcement of agreements to arbitrate medical malpractice claims).

[66] 565 U.S. 530 (2012).

prohibiting enforcement of predispute agreements to arbitrate claims under California's Labor Code Private Attorneys General Act ("PAGA").[67] In addition to the authority of a state agency to sue employers for violations of the state's labor code, PAGA allows suits against the employer by an employee as a representative of the state, with the recovery divided 75% for the state and 25% for the employee.[68] The California Supreme Court held that its refusal to enforce agreements to arbitrate PAGA claims was not preempted by the FAA.[69] The California Supreme Court reasoned that "a PAGA claim lies outside the FAA's coverage because it is not a dispute between an employer and an employee arising out of their contractual relationship," but rather "a dispute between an employer and the state," which is not party to and thus not bound by an arbitration agreement.[70] The California Supreme Court analogized PAGA claims to a government agency (the Equal Employment Opportunity Commission) suing an employer on behalf of an employee bound by an arbitration agreement, which the U.S. Supreme Court allowed because the EEOC was not a party to the arbitration agreement.[71] In contrast, the U.S. Supreme Court did not find PAGA claims analogous to government enforcement actions because "[t]he contractual relationship between the parties [employer and employee] is a but-for cause of any justiciable legal controversy between the parties under PAGA. And regardless of whether a PAGA action is in some sense also a dispute between an employer and the State, nothing in the FAA categorically exempts claims belonging to sovereigns from the scope of § 2."[72]

---

[67] Viking River Cruises, Inc. v. Moriana, 142 S. Ct. 1906, 1921 (2022).

[68] Id. at 1914.

[69] Iskanian v. CLS Transportation Los Angeles, LLC, 327 P.3d 129, 151 (Cal. 2014). Accord Sakkab v. Luxottica Retail N. Am., Inc., 803 F.3d 425, 432 (9th Cir. 2015). Similarly, California courts also hold that the FAA does not preempt state law prohibiting enforcement of pre-dispute arbitration agreements with respect to claims for injunctive relief under certain state statutes. Cruz v. Pacificare Health Sys., Inc., 66 P.3d 1157 (Cal.2003); Broughton v. Cigna Healthplans, 988 P.2d 67 (Cal. 1999). However, the Ninth Circuit limited these California holdings. Kilgore v. KeyBank, Nat. Ass'n, 718 F.3d 1052 (9th Cir. 2013) (en banc) (FAA preempts Broughton-Cruz rule except in narrow circumstances in which the injunctive relief sought mostly benefits the general public rather than the individual party pursuing the claim).

[70] Iskanian, 327 P.3d at 133.

[71] Id. at 151 ("In *EEOC v. Waffle House, Inc.* (2002) 534 U.S. 279, 122 S. Ct. 754, 151 L.Ed.2d 755, the high court held that an employment arbitration agreement governed by the FAA does not prevent the Equal Employment Opportunity Commission (EEOC) from suing an employer on behalf of an employee bound by that agreement for victim-specific relief, such as reinstatement and back pay. The court based its conclusion primarily on the fact that the EEOC was not a party to the arbitration agreement.")

[72] Viking River Cruises, Inc. v. Moriana, 142 S. Ct. 1906, 1919 n.4 (2022). See also § 29(a)(3) (further discussing *Viking River*).

§ 13 FAA Preempts State Law Denying Enforcement of Arbitration Agreements in Certain Types of Transactions

(a) Generally Preempted

Many states prohibit enforcement of arbitration agreements in certain types of transactions, such as consumer contracts, adhesion contracts, insurance contracts, or employment contracts.[73] These transaction-focused anti-arbitration laws differ from the claim-focused anti-arbitration laws discussed in the previous section. For example, a breach of contract claim might arise out of a consumer transaction and a tort claim might arise out of a transaction between businesses. An anti-arbitration law focused on consumer transactions would apply to the first example but not the second, while an anti-arbitration law focused on tort claims would apply to the second example but not the first. However, like state laws prohibiting enforcement of agreements to arbitrate certain claims, state laws prohibiting enforcement of arbitration agreements in

---

[73] See, e.g., Ark.Code Ann. 16–108–233(b) (2022) ("This subchapter does not apply to: (1) Personal injury or tort matters; (2) Employer-employee disputes; or (3) An insured or beneficiary under any insurance policy or annuity contract."); Iowa Code Ann. 679A.1(2) (2018) ("This subsection shall not apply to any of the following: (a) A contract of adhesion; (b) A contract between employers and employees; (c) Unless otherwise provided in a separate writing executed by all parties to the contract, any claim sounding in tort whether or not involving a breach of contract."); Ky. Rev. Stat. Ann.417.050(2) (2019) ("This chapter does not apply to: (1) Arbitration agreements contained within the collective bargaining agreements entered into by employers and the respective representatives of member employees; (2) Insurance contracts."); Md. Code Ann., Cts. & Jud. Proc. 3–206.1(b) (2020) ("any provision in an insurance contract with a consumer that requires arbitration is void and unenforceable"); Mo.Ann.Stat. 435.350 (2022) ("A written agreement to submit any existing controversy to arbitration or a provision in a written contract, except contracts of insurance and contracts of adhesion, to submit to arbitration any controversy thereafter arising between the parties is valid, enforceable and irrevocable save upon such grounds as exist at law or in equity for the revocation of any contract."); Mont. Code Ann. 27–5–114 ("this subsection does not apply to: (a) claims arising out of personal injury, whether based on contract or tort; (b) any contract by an individual for the acquisition of real or personal property, services, or money or credit when the total consideration to be paid or furnished by the individual is $5,000 or less; (c) any agreement concerning or relating to insurance policies or annuity contracts except for those contracts between insurance companies."); N.Y. Gen. Bus. Law 399–c(2)(a) (2021) ("No written contract for the sale or purchase of consumer goods, entered into on or after the effective date of this section, to which a consumer is a party, shall contain a mandatory arbitration clause."); S.C. Code Ann. 15–48–10(b)(2–4) (2022) ("(3) A pre-agreement entered into when the relationship of the contracting parties is such that of lawyer-client or doctor-patient. . . (4) Any claim arising out of personal injury, based on contract or tort, or to any insured or beneficiary under any insurance policy or annuity contract."); S.D. Codified Laws 21–25A–3 (2022) ("This chapter does not apply to insurance policies and every provision in any such policy requiring arbitration or restricting a party thereto or beneficiary thereof from enforcing any right under it by usual legal proceedings in ordinary tribunals or limiting the time to do so is void and unenforceable.").

certain types of transactions are generally preempted by FAA § 2 because they create a ground for denying enforcement of certain arbitration agreements that is not a ground "for the revocation of any contract."[74] Partial exceptions to FAA preemption relate to insurance[75] and employment.[76]

(b) Possible Exceptions

(1) Child Custody

The FAA may not preempt state law denying enforcement of agreements to arbitrate child custody. State law generally permits a court to void a child-custody agreement that the court finds is not in the best interests of the child.[77] Will courts transfer this child-protective role to an arbitrator who is (directly or indirectly) chosen by the adults disputing custody? Some courts refuse to transfer their child-protective role to the arbitrator, so they deny enforcement to agreements to arbitrate child custody.[78] These denials have not been held preempted by the FAA.

---

[74] 9 U.S.C. § 2. See also Preston v. Ferrer, 552 U.S. 346, 356 (2008) (FAA preempts state statute denying enforcement to arbitration agreements in talent agency contracts); Sutcliffe v. Mercy Clinics, Inc., 856 N.W.2d 382 (Iowa Ct. App. 2014) (FAA preempts Iowa statute denying enforcement to employment arbitration agreements); Am. Fin. Serv. Assn. v. Burke, 169 F. Supp.2d 62, 68 (D. Conn. 2001) (FAA preempts state statute denying enforcement to arbitration clauses in high-cost home loan agreements).

[75] See § 15.

[76] See § 5(d).

[77] See § 3.39(b)(4). See also Restatement (Second) of Contracts § 191 (1981) ("A promise affecting the right of custody of a minor child is unenforceable on grounds of public policy unless the disposition as to custody is consistent with the best interest of the child.")

[78] Compare Cohen v. Cohen, 600 N.Y.S.2d 996, 996–97 (App. Div. 1993) (refusing to enforce an executory agreement to arbitrate a custody dispute before rabbinical tribunal because "[d]isputes over custody and visitation are not subject to arbitration"); Pulfer v. Pulfer, 673 N.E.2d 656, 659 (Ohio Ct. App. 1996) (refusing to enforce an executory agreement between parents to arbitrate child custody disputes, because "matters of child custody may only be decided by the trial court and are not subject to arbitration despite any agreement entered into by the parties"), with Fawzy v. Fawzy, 973 A.2d 347, 360–61 (N.J. 2009) (enforcing an arbitration award, holding that "the constitutionally protected right to parental autonomy includes the right to submit any family controversy, including one regarding child custody and parenting time, to a decision maker chosen by the parents. * * * [T]he review of an arbitration award is to take place within the confines of the Arbitration Act, unless there is a claim of adverse impact or harm to the child. Only in that case will further review be required"); In re Marriage of Popack, 998 P.2d 464, 469 (Colo. Ct. App.2000) (upholding the enforceability of an executory arbitration agreement between parents to arbitrate child custody disputes subject to the court's determination that the agreement is conscionable and subject to the court's de novo review of the award); Wojnar v. Wojnar, 2006 WL 473789, at *1 (Mich. App. 2006) (enforcing an arbitration award pursuant to state statute: "parties in a divorce action may consent to binding arbitration through a signed agreement providing for an award on disputed matters, including property division, child custody, child support, parenting time, and spousal support.").

(2) Probate

The FAA may not preempt state law denying enforcement of arbitration clauses to the extent they cover probate disputes. Many courts have long refused to enforce arbitration clauses in wills and trusts against parties who did not manifest assent to the document containing the arbitration clause.[79] The FAA may not preempt such refusals because the FAA may not apply to arbitration clauses in documents that are not contracts, such as wills and trusts.[80] This interpretation of the FAA was adopted by the Virginia Supreme Court in 2022:

> The FAA by its plain terms applies to contracts. A trust is not a contract. In the absence of contrary binding precedent, and under a straightforward textual interpretation of this statute, we conclude that the FAA does not apply to the arbitration clause at issue here.[81]

In contrast, arbitration scholar David Horton argues the FAA "does not require an arbitration clause to appear in a contract. Instead, the FAA applies if the parties have agreed to arbitrate. When an executor, trustee, or beneficiary accepts fees or property under an estate plan, they fall within the FAA's coverage."[82] So, perhaps the Virginia Supreme Court decision just quoted will not be followed by all future courts.

§ 14 FAA Preempts State Law Raising the Standard of Assent for Forming an Arbitration Agreement

FAA § 2 preempts state law applying a higher standard of assent to make arbitration agreements than to make other contracts. For example, the FAA preempts the following Montana statute: "Notice that a contract is subject to arbitration * * * shall be typed in underlined capital letters on the first page of the contract; and unless such notice is displayed thereon, the contract may not be subject to arbitration."[83] *Doctor's Associates, Inc. v. Casarotto*,[84] involved a franchise agreement that did not comply with this statute because the arbitration clause was on page nine and in ordinary type.[85] The

---

79 See § 18(i).

80 David Horton, The Federal Arbitration Act and Testamentary Instruments, 90 N.C. L. Rev. 1027, 1049 (2012).

81 Boyle v. Anderson, 871 S.E.2d 226, 230 (Va. 2022) (denying enforcement of a trust's arbitration clause).

82 David Horton, The Federal Arbitration Act and Testamentary Instruments, 90 N.C. L. Rev. 1027, 1073 (2012).

83 Mont. Code Ann. § 27–5–114(4) (1995). This language was deleted from the statute in 1997.

84 517 U.S. 681 (1996).

85 Id. at 684–85.

Supreme Court held that the Montana statute is preempted by FAA § 2 because the Montana statute "conditions the enforceability of arbitration agreements on compliance with a special notice requirement not applicable to contracts generally."[86] The FAA "precludes States from singling out arbitration provisions for suspect status, requiring instead that such provisions be placed 'upon the same footing as other contracts.' "[87] Other state laws preempted on the reasoning of *Casarotto* are numerous.[88]

Despite *Casarotto*, the Montana Supreme Court continues to hold arbitration agreements to a higher standard of assent than it holds contracts generally.[89] The Montana Supreme Court's rationale is that arbitration agreements waive a constitutional right (the right to jury trial) and Montana courts require all contracts (not just

---

[86] Id. at 687.

[87] Id.

[88] With the possible exceptions of state statutes relating to insurance, see § 15, and employment, see §§ 5(d), other statutes preempted on the reasoning of *Casarotto* include: Cal. Bus. & Prof. Code § 7191(a) (2019) (arbitration clauses in certain residential contracts shall contain prescribed notice in at least ten-point roman boldface type or if in red print in at least eight-point boldface type and if provision is included in typed contract, it shall be set out in capital letters); Colo. Rev. Stat. Ann. § 13–64–403(4) (2018) (arbitration clauses in agreements for medical services shall contain prescribed notice in at least ten-point boldface type); Ga. Code Ann. 9–9–2(c)(8), (9), (10) (2013) (arbitration clause for residential real estate purchase or financing, employment, personal injury or wrongful death based on tort must be initialed to be valid); N.Y. Pub. Health Law §§ 4406–a(2), (3) (2022) (arbitration provisions of health maintenance organization contracts must contain statutorily prescribed language and be in at least twelve-point boldface type immediately above spaces for the enrollee's signature); S.C. Code Ann. § 15–48–10(a) (2021) (arbitration clause must be underlined and capitalized, or rubber-stamped prominently, and on first page); S.D. Codified Laws § 21–25B–3 (2021) (arbitration clauses relating to medical services must be in twelve-point boldface type immediately above the space for signature); Tenn. Code Ann. § 29–5–302(a) (2021) (arbitration clause in certain contracts must be signed or initialed by the parties); Vt. Stat. Ann. tit. 12, § 5652(b) (2020) (arbitration clause must use prescribed or substantially similar language and be signed by parties and displayed prominently). See also Munoz v. Green Tree Financial Corp., 542 S.E.2d 360, 364 (S.C. 2001) (FAA preempts statute requiring that arbitration notice be "typed in underlined capital letters, or rubber-stamped prominently, on the first page of the contract"); In re Nexion Health at Humble, Inc., 173 S.W.3d 67 (Tex. 2005) (FAA preempts Texas statute requiring the signature of a party's counsel on arbitration agreements in personal injury cases).

[89] Kelker v. Geneva-Roth Ventures, Inc., 303 P.3d 777, 786 (Mont. 2013) ("Outside the arbitration context, our generally applicable principles of contract law presume that '[a]bsent incapacity to contract, ignorance of the contents of a written contract is not a ground for relief from liability' under its provisions. . . . Because an arbitration provision waives fundamental rights, however, we have applied a more stringent standard when faced with a consumer's claim that she has not read or understood the arbitration clause in a contract."); Kortum-Managhan v. Herbergers NBGL, 204 P.3d 693, 699 (Mont. 2009); Kloss v. Edward D. Jones & Co., 54 P.3d 1 (Mont. 2002).

arbitration agreements) that waive constitutional rights, to the higher standard of assent, "knowing and voluntary" assent.[90]

§ 15 Reverse Preemption in Insurance: The FAA and McCarran-Ferguson

FAA preemption of state law has an added complication in the insurance context because of the McCarran-Ferguson Act,[91] which states:

> (a) State regulation
>
> The business of insurance, and every person engaged therein, shall be subject to the laws of the several States which relate to the regulation or taxation of such business.
>
> (b) Federal regulation
>
> No Act of Congress shall be construed to invalidate, impair, or supersede any law enacted by any State for the purposes of regulating the business of insurance, * * * unless such Act specifically relates to the business of insurance. * * *[92]

Some state laws that would otherwise be preempted by federal law are protected from that preemption by McCarran-Ferguson. For example, McCarran-Ferguson precludes application of the FAA to certain insurance cases, leaving those cases to state arbitration law. The challenge then, is to identify which state laws are protected from FAA preemption by McCarran-Ferguson.

The Supreme Court holds that, to be protected from preemption by McCarran-Ferguson, a state "law must not just have an impact on the insurance industry, but be specifically directed toward that industry."[93] For this reason, McCarran-Ferguson does not protect from FAA preemption state laws regulating arbitration generally, even when those laws are applied to insurance arbitration.[94] In

[90] "Montana law generally applicable to the waiver of constitutional rights, requires that the waiver will not be lightly presumed; that it must be proved to have been made voluntarily, knowingly and intelligently—typically by the party seeking the waiver; and that it will be narrowly construed." Kloss, 54 P.3d at 16.

[91] 15 U.S.C. §§ 1011–1015.

[92] 15 U.S.C. § 1012(a)–(b).

[93] Pilot Life Insurance Co. v. Dedeaux, 481 U.S. 41, 50 (1987). See also United States Dep't of Treasury v. Fabe 508 U.S. 491, 500–503 (1993) (" '[s]tatutes aimed at protecting or regulating this relationship [between insurer and insured], directly or indirectly, are laws regulating the "business of insurance.")' "; id. ("[t]he broad category of laws enacted 'for the purpose of regulating the business of insurance' consists of laws that possess the 'end, intention, or aim' of adjusting, managing, or controlling the business of insurance.")

[94] See Miller v. Nat'l Fidel. Life Ins. Co., 588 F.2d 185, 187 (5th Cir. 1979) (where state insurance code contains no provisions relating to arbitration, applying the FAA to an insurance arbitration clause does not—to use McCarran-Ferguson's language—

contrast, McCarran-Ferguson does protect from FAA preemption state statutes providing that arbitration clauses in insurance policies are unenforceable, while arbitration clauses in other contracts are enforceable.[95] McCarran-Ferguson also protects from FAA preemption certain state law regarding insurance company liquidations and receiverships.[96] In the international arbitration context, courts are divided on the extent to which McCarran-Ferguson protects state law from preemption by the most important arbitration treaty, the New York Convention.[97]

"invalidate, impair, or supersede any state law regulating the business of insurance."); Hart v. Orion Ins. Co., 453 F.2d 1358, 1360 (10th Cir. 1971); Hamilton Life Ins. Co. v. Republic Nat'l Life Ins. Co., 408 F.2d 606, 611 (2d Cir. 1969) ("arbitration statutes * * * are not statutes regulating the business of insurance, but statutes regulating the method of handling contract disputes generally."); Ainsworth v. Allstate Ins. Co., 634 F. Supp. 52 (W.D. Mo. 1985).

95 Kremer v. Rural Cmty. Ins. Co., 788 N.W.2d 538, 553 (2010) ("a statute precluding the parties to an insurance contract from including an arbitration agreement for future controversies regulates the insurer-insured contractual relationship. Thus, it regulates the business of insurance. So we agree with federal courts that the FAA does not preempt such statutes"); For other cases finding that McCarran-Ferguson protects a state law from FAA preemption, see Mutual Reinsurance Bureau v. Great Plains Mutual Ins. Co., Inc., 969 F.2d 931 (10th Cir. 1992); American Bankers Ins. Co. of Florida v. Inman, 436 F.3d 490 (5th Cir. 2006); McKnight v. Chicago Title Ins. Co., Inc., 358 F.3d 854, 859 (11th Cir. 2004); Standard Sec. Life Ins. Co. v. West, 267 F.3d 821, 823 (8th Cir. 2001); Nat'l Home Ins. Co. v. King, 291 F. Supp.2d 518, 530 (E.D. Ky. 2003); Imbler v. PacifiCare of Cal., Inc., 126 Cal. Rptr. 2d 715, 723 (Ct. App. 2002); Allen v. Pacheco, 71 P.3d 375, 384 (Colo.2003); United Ins. Co. of America v. Office of Ins. Regulation, 985 So.2d 665 (Fla.App.2008); Love v. Money Tree, Inc. 614 S.E.2d 47, 50 (Ga. 2005); Friday v. Trinity Universal of Kansas, 939 P.2d 869 (Kan. 1997); In re Kepka, 178 S.W.3d 279, 292–93 (Tex. Ct. App. 2005); Kruger Clinic Orthopaedics, LLC v. Regence BlueShield, 138 P.3d 936, 940–41 (Wash. 2006); State, Dept. of Transp. v. James River Ins. Co., 292 P.3d 118 (Wash. 2013). But see Little v. Allstate Ins. Co., 705 A.2d 538, 541 (Vt. 1997).

With respect to federal crop insurance, courts find that the FAA preempts state arbitration law. State of Kansas ex rel. Todd v. United States, 995 F.2d 1505, 1511 (10th Cir. 1993); In re 2000 Sugar Beet Crop Ins. Litigation, 228 F. Supp.2d 992 (D. Minn. 2002); IGF Ins. Co. v. Hat Creek P'ship, 76 S.W.3d 859 (Ark. 2002).

96 See Munich American Reinsurance Co. v. Crawford, 141 F.3d 585 (5th Cir. 1998) (Oklahoma has formulated a "complex and comprehensive scheme of insurance regulation" which vests state courts with "exclusive original jurisdiction" over all delinquency proceedings involving insolvent insurance companies; held, petition to compel arbitration was properly dismissed); Corcoran v. Universal Reinsurance Corp., 713 F. Supp. 77 (S.D.N.Y. 1989).

97 Compare, e.g., Safety Nat. Cas. Corp. v. Certain Underwriters At Lloyd's, London, 587 F.3d 714, 731 (5th Cir. 2009) ("implemented treaty provisions, self-executing or not, are not reverse-preempted by state law pursuant to the McCarran-Ferguson Act"); Goshawk Dedicated v. Portsmouth Settlement Co. I, 466 F. Supp.2d 1293, 1306 (N.D. Ga. 2006) ("the [New York] Convention prevails over the McCarran-Ferguson Act"), with Stephens v. American International Insurance Co., 66 F.3d 41 (2d Cir. 1995) (anti-arbitration provision in the Kentucky Insurers Rehabilitation and Liquidation Law protected by McCarran-Ferguson from preemption by the Federal Arbitration Act provision implementing New York Convention).

§ 16 Contracting out of FAA Preemption

(a) Agreeing to State Arbitration Law, Instead of the FAA

Because of the United States Constitution's Supremacy Clause, when there is a conflict between federal and state law, the federal law prevails.[98] In this regard, federal arbitration law is no different from any other federal law[99] and the FAA preempts many state laws.[100] However, an oddity of FAA preemption is that, with respect to at least some issues, parties have the power to contract out of it. That is, otherwise-preempted state arbitration law may nevertheless govern particular parties if those parties have, by contract, chosen to be governed by that state law.[101] The parties' power to do this is found in the Supreme Court's opinion in *Volt Information Sciences, Inc. v. Board of Trustees of the Leland Stanford Junior University*.[102]

Volt involved an arbitration clause in a construction contract. The California trial court stayed arbitration pending resolution of related litigation,[103] as a California statute permitted.[104] In contrast, the FAA probably does not permit such a stay.[105] The California Court of Appeal held that California arbitration law, rather than the FAA, applied because the construction contract included a choice-of-law clause stating that the contract would be "governed by the law of the place where the project is located."[106] The project at issue was located in California.[107] The California Court of Appeal held that the parties "have agreed, as we interpret their choice of law provision, that the laws of California, of which [the stay provision] is certainly a part, are to govern their contract."[108] It also held "that enforcement of the arbitration agreement in accordance with the chosen California rules of procedure does not create a conflict with the [FAA], since the

---

98 U.S. Const. art. VI, cl. 2 ("This Constitution, and the Laws of the United States which shall be made in Pursuance thereof; and all Treaties made, or which shall be made, under the Authority of the United States, shall be the supreme Law of the Land; and the Judges in every State shall be bound thereby, any Thing in the Constitution or Laws of any State to the Contrary notwithstanding.")

99 See §§ 6–7.

100 See §§ 9–14.

101 See, e.g., Alan Scott Rau, Federal Common Law and Arbitral Power, 8 Nev. L.J. 169, 203 n.108 (2007) ("parties may choose to subject themselves to state rather than federal rules of arbitration—as long as their intention to do so is particularly explicit.")

102 489 U.S. 468 (1989).

103 Board of Trustees of the Leland Stanford Junior Univ. v. Volt Info. Sciences, Inc., 240 Cal.Rptr. 558, 559 (Ct.App.1987), aff'd, 489 U.S. 468 (1989).

104 Cal. Civ. Proc. Code § 1281.2(c)(4).

105 See § 28.

106 Volt, 240 Cal. Rptr. at 559.

107 Id.

108 Id.

purpose of the [FAA] was to ensure that private agreements to arbitrate are enforceable contracts."[109] The United States Supreme Court agreed and affirmed.[110]

While the Supreme Court's opinions in *Volt* included a dissent, the Court was unanimous in ruling that parties can make an enforceable agreement that California arbitration law, rather than the FAA, determines whether to stay arbitration pending resolution of related litigation. The majority in *Volt* affirmed the holding that the parties in *Volt* had made such an agreement. And while the dissenting justices did not believe the parties in *Volt* had made such an agreement, the dissenters agreed that the parties had the power to make such an agreement. The dissent said that parties "are free if they wish to write an agreement to arbitrate outside the coverage of the FAA. Such an agreement would permit a state rule, otherwise preempted by the FAA, to govern their arbitration."[111] So the Court unanimously held that, at least with respect to some topics, parties have the power to form an enforceable arbitration agreement providing that their dispute will be governed by state arbitration law, instead of by the FAA.

What divided the majority and dissent in *Volt* was whether the parties in that case had exercised their power to make an enforceable agreement providing for California arbitration law, rather than the FAA. The *Volt* Court's majority did not review, but accepted as a matter of state law, the California Court of Appeal's interpretation of the choice-of-law clause "to mean that the parties had incorporated the California rules of arbitration into their arbitration agreement."[112] In contrast, the dissent stated "I can accept neither the state court's unusual interpretation of the parties' contract, nor this Court's unwillingness to review it."[113] The dissent pointed out that "the normal purpose of such choice-of-law clauses is to determine that the law of one State rather than that of another State will be applicable; they simply do not speak to any interaction between state and federal law."[114] Thus, the choice-of-law clause in *Volt* is best interpreted as the parties' choice of California law over other state law, rather than California law over federal law. The California Court of Appeal misinterpreted the contract.

---

109 Id.

110 Volt Info. Sciences, Inc. v. Board of Trustees of the Leland Stanford Junior Univ., 489 U.S. 468, 479 (1989).

111 Id. at 485 (Brennan, J., dissenting).

112 Id. at 474.

113 Id. at 481 (Brennan, J., dissenting).

114 Id. at 488 (Brennan, J., dissenting) (citing authority).

So, the narrow question dividing the Supreme Court in *Volt* was whether to correct the California court's misinterpretation of the contract. The majority chose not to, while dissent would have done so. Ordinarily, the Supreme Court reviews *de novo* state court rulings on federal law but defers to state courts on matters of state law,[115] and contract interpretation is usually a matter of state law.

However, arbitration agreements are also the subject of federal law. The FAA provides that arbitration agreements "shall be valid, irrevocable, and enforceable, save upon such grounds as exist at law or in equity for the revocation of any contract."[116] And states could easily nullify this federal command if the Supreme Court did not police state courts' interpretations of arbitration agreements. For example, the Supreme Court's 2015 decision in *DirecTV, Inc. v. Imburgia* held preempted a state court interpretation of an arbitration agreement.[117] As the Restatement summarizes, *Imburgia*

> Held preempted a state court's interpretation of the phrase "law of your state" in an arbitration agreement to include "invalid California law." The court determined "that California courts would not interpret contracts other than arbitration contracts the same way," but "[r]ather . . . that the [California] court's interpretation of this arbitration contract is unique, restricted to that field." As a result, the FAA preempted the state court's interpretation of the arbitration agreement.[118]

Imburgia's holding that the FAA preempts some state court contract interpretation shows a limit to *Volt's* deference to state court interpretation of arbitration agreements.

(b) Rare to Contract out of FAA Preemption

Since *Volt*, the Supreme Court has twice considered whether parties contracted out of FAA preemption of state law by including a general choice-of-law clause in their arbitration agreement. In both cases, *Mastrobuono v. Shearson Lehman Hutton, Inc.*,[119] and *Preston v. Ferrer*,[120] the Court held that the parties did not contract out of FAA preemption.

---

[115] Erwin Chemerinsky, Federal Jurisdiction § 10.1 (4th ed. 2003) ("The Court may decide only questions of federal law. The Court has no authority to decide matters of state law in reviewing the decisions of state courts.")

[116] 9 U.S.C. § 2.

[117] 136 S.Ct. 463 (2015)

[118] Restatement (Third) U.S. Law of Int'l Comm. Arb. § 1.6 (2019).

[119] 514 U.S. 52 (1995).

[120] 552 U.S. 346, 356 (2008) (FAA preempts state statutory provision denying enforcement to arbitration agreements in talent agency contracts).

Mastrobuono involved a contract between investors and their securities broker. The contract contained both an arbitration clause and a choice-of-law clause stating that the contract "shall be governed by the laws of the State of New York."[121] New York law at the time prohibited arbitrators from awarding punitive damages.[122] When the arbitrator awarded punitive damages to the investor, the broker (citing *Volt*) asked the court to vacate that portion of the arbitrator's award on the ground that New York law governed.[123] The Supreme Court rejected the broker's argument and confirmed the award of punitive damages.[124]

Unlike *Volt*, which began in state court, the *Mastrobuono* case began in federal court. So, in *Mastrobuono* the Supreme Court could interpret the contract as it wished, without considering whether to defer (as it did in *Volt*) to a state court's interpretation of the contract.[125] The *Mastrobuono* Court interpreted the contract as not requiring application of New York's law prohibiting arbitrators from awarding punitive damages. Among other things, the Court suggested that the choice-of-law clause was simply a choice of New York law over the law of other states, rather than a choice to avoid FAA preemption of New York law. The Court did this by pointing out that the broker wrongly interpreted the contract's choice of "the laws of the State of New York" to "include[ ] the caveat, 'detached from otherwise-applicable federal law.' "[126] In other words, *Mastrobuono* held that the choice-of-law clause chose New York law over the law of other states, not over federal law, such as the FAA.

The 2008 *Preston* case involved a contract with an arbitration clause and a choice-of-law clause providing that the "agreement shall be governed by the laws of the state of California."[127] Preston sought to arbitrate his claim for payment for services he rendered to Ferrer.[128] Preston's demand for arbitration was countered by Ferrer's petition to the California Labor Commissioner charging that the contract was unenforceable under the California Talent Agencies Act (TAA),[129] which vests the Labor Commissioner with exclusive original jurisdiction to determine whether a particular agreement is subject to a California statute that requires parties to exhaust

121 514 U.S. at 52, 58–59.

122 Id. at 55.

123 Id. at 54–55.

124 Id. at 64.

125 Whether to so defer is the issue that split the majority and dissent in *Volt*. See § 16(a).

126 Mastrobuono, 514 U.S. at 55.

127 552 U.S. at 361.

128 Id. at 350.

129 Cal. Lab. Code Ann. § 1700 et seq.

administrative remedies before resorting to arbitration.[130] In other words, Preston wanted the case decided in arbitration and Ferrer wanted at least some preliminary portion of the case decided by the Labor Commissioner.

Had there been no choice-of-law clause, the case would have been sent to arbitration simply because that is what the agreement provided and the agreement is enforceable under the FAA.[131] While the TAA purports to make portions of that arbitration agreement unenforceable, the FAA preempts such conflicting state law.[132] So, one issue in *Preston* was whether the parties contracted out of this preemption by including in their contract a California choice-of-law clause. In holding they did not, the *Preston* Court distinguished *Volt* and was "guided by [its] more recent decision" in *Mastrobuono*.[133] The *Preston* Court concluded that the California choice-of law clause should be read to incorporate "prescriptions governing the substantive rights and obligations of the parties, but not the State's 'special rules limiting the authority of arbitrators.' "[134]

In sum, *Mastrobuono* and *Preston* reinforce *Volt*'s main holding—that parties can contract out of at least some aspects of FAA preemption—but indicate that it typically takes more than a general choice-of-law clause to do so. Similarly, most lower court cases treat a general choice-of-law clause as a choice among states, rather than a choice of the chosen state over the FAA.[135] For parties to contract

---

130 Preston, 552 U.S. at 356 (citing Cal. Lab. Code Ann. § 1700.44(a)).

131 See § 12. See also AT & T Mobility LLC v. Concepcion, 563 U.S. 333, 342 (2011) (citing *Preston* for the proposition that "When state law prohibits outright the arbitration of a particular type of claim, the analysis is straightforward: The conflicting rule is displaced by the FAA.")

132 Preston, 552 U.S. at 356 ("Procedural prescriptions of the TAA thus conflict with the FAA's dispute resolution regime in two basic respects: First, the TAA grants the Labor Commissioner exclusive jurisdiction to decide an issue that the parties agreed to arbitrate, * * * ; second, the TAA imposes prerequisites to enforcement of an arbitration agreement that are not applicable to contracts generally * * * .")

133 Id. at 361.

134 Id. at 363 (quoting Mastrobuono, 514 U.S. at 63–64). See Supreme Court Addresses Volt's Choice-of-Law Trap: Is the End of the Problem in Sight?, 64 J. Disp. Resol. 22 (May–July 2009) (noting that what is significant about Preston "but largely overlooked" is that it "departs from the approach in Volt, which left the interpretation of choice-of-law cases to the state courts.")

135 Gulfstream Aero. Corp. v. Oceltip Aviation, 31 F.4th 1323, 1328–31 (11th Cir. 2022) (applying Mastrobuono to conclude "the Agreement does not evidence a clear intent by the parties that the Georgia Arbitration Code—as opposed to federal arbitral-award vacatur standards—control", because although agreement said 'This contract shall be governed by the laws of the State of Georgia," "the Georgia Arbitration Code is not mentioned once in the Agreement. Given that the parties specified arbitration rules—it makes little sense that the parties would have intended and expected that the Georgia Arbitration Code nonetheless would govern review of any award resulting from arbitration."); Dialysis Access Ctr., LLC v. RMS Lifeline, Inc., 932 F.3d 1, 8 (1st Cir. 2019) (quoting P.R. Tel. Co. v. U.S. Phone Mfg. Corp., 427 F.3d 21, 29 (1st Cir. 2005)) ("The mere inclusion of a generic choice-of-law clause within the arbitration

out of FAA preemption, they need more specific language stating not only which state's law they choose to govern the merits of any dispute, but also that they want this state's arbitration law.[136]

agreement is not sufficient to require the application of state law concerning the scope of review, since there is a strong federal policy requiring limited review. A generic choice-of-law clause, standing alone, is insufficient to support a finding that contracting parties intended to opt out of the FAA's default regime for vacatur of arbitral awards."); Cooper v. WestEnd Capital Mgmt., LLC, 832 F.3d 534, 544 (5th Cir. 2016) ("A choice of law provision is insufficient, by itself, to demonstrate the parties' clear intent to depart form the FAA's default rules. The Operating Agreement here does not expressly reference California arbitration law but instead contains only a choice-of-law provision. This is insufficient to compel the application of California's arbitration standards."); BNSF R. Co. v. Alstom Transp., Inc., 777 F.3d 785, 790 (5th Cir. 2015) ("arbitration under non-FAA [state] rules [only] if a contract expressly references state arbitration law"); Jung v. Ass'n of Am. Med. Colleges, 300 F. Supp.2d 119, 153 (D.D.C. 2004) ("Numerous courts of appeals have concluded that Mastrobuono requires that the intent of the contracting parties to apply state arbitration rules or law to arbitration proceedings must be explicitly stated in the contract and that under Mastrobuono, a general choice of law provision does not evidence such intent.")

The exceptions include Ekstrom v. Value Health, Inc., 68 F.3d 1391, 1393 (D.C. Cir. 1995); Restaurant Consulting Servs., Inc. v. Mountzuris, 253 F. Supp.2d 45, 51 (D. Mass. 2003) ("Because the agreement calls for the use of Massachusetts law in determining the rights and obligation of the parties, the Massachusetts Uniform Arbitration Act, rather than the Federal Arbitration Act, applies.").

[136] Star Dev. Grp., LLC v. Darwin Nat'l Assur. Co., 813 Fed. Appx. 76, 81–82 (4th Cir. 2020) ("We presume that an agreement involving interstate commerce, like the Contract, will be arbitrated under the FAA absent clear indication by the parties to the contract. And a generic choice-of-law provision stating generally that a contract is subject to state law is typically insufficient to invoke state arbitration law." However, "the Contract explicitly invoked the Maryland Uniform Arbitration Act as the governing law for arbitration." This "is not the type of generic choice-of-law provision generally found insufficient to invoke state arbitration law. Rather, as its plain language shows, it is an 'unequivocal expression of the parties' intent to invoke Maryland, rather than federal, arbitration law."); Foulger-Pratt Residential Contracting, LLC v. Madrigal Condominiums, LLC, 779 F. Supp. 2d 100, 110 (D.D.C. 2011) (while "a generic choice of law clause is insufficient to displace the FAA, * * * In this case * * * the parties included a specific clause stating that '[t]his [a]greement to arbitrate shall be specifically enforceable pursuant to and interpreted under the laws of the District of Columbia.' [and thus] specifically and unambiguously evidences their clear choice of D.C. law rather than the FAA to govern their agreement to arbitrate.")

Chapter 4

FORMATION OF ENFORCEABLE ARBITRATION AGREEMENTS

Table of Sections

A. FORMATION OF ARBITRATION AGREEMENTS

Table of Sections

§ 17 The FAA and State Law in Contract Formation

(a) Written and Electronic Agreements

The FAA makes enforceable only a "*written* provision in any maritime transaction or a contract * * * or an agreement in *writing* to submit to arbitration an existing controversy."[1] Most state arbitration statutes similarly require enforcement only of "written" arbitration agreements.[2] So, an oral arbitration agreement may well be unenforceable. However, while "the FAA requires arbitration agreements to be written, it does not require them to be signed."[3] In addition, the E-Sign Act has been interpreted as amending the FAA to require enforcement of electronic, as well as paper written, agreements.[4]

---

1 9 U.S.C. § 2 (emphasis added).

2 See Unif. Arbitration Act §§ 1, 2, 7 U.L.A. 102, 240 (2005).

3 Tinder v. Pinkerton Sec., 305 F.3d 728, 736 (7th Cir. 2002); Valero Ref., Inc. v. M/T Lauberhorn, 813 F.2d 60, 64 (5th Cir. 1987) ("It is established that a party may be bound by an agreement to arbitrate even in the absence of his signature.").

4 See Campbell v. General Dynamics Gov't Systems Corp., 407 F.3d 546, 556 (1st Cir. 2005). And the Revised Uniform Arbitration Act uses the word "record" instead of "writing" and defines "record" to mean "information that is inscribed on a tangible medium or that is stored in an electronic or other medium and is retrievable

(b) The FAA Incorporates State Law of Contract Formation

The FAA does not create law governing the formation of arbitration agreements. So the Supreme Court has said that "[w]hen deciding whether the parties agreed to arbitrate a certain matter * * *, courts generally * * * should apply ordinary state-law principles that govern the formation of contracts."[5] The general state-law requirements to form a contract are: (1) mutual manifestations of assent, and (2) consideration.[6] These contract-formation requirements apply to arbitration agreements, as discussed in the following sections.

§ 18 Mutual Manifestations of Assent

(a) Manifesting Assent, Generally

Formation of a contract requires a manifestation of assent by each party.[7] The process by which parties manifest assent is frequently called "offer and acceptance."[8] This process often still culminates, as it has for centuries, in a paper document signed in ink. However, "[c]ontracts are increasingly signed electronically," the Texas Supreme Court observed in enforcing an arbitration agreement in an employer's online hiring ("onboarding") process over the employees' objections that there could have been a "glitch" in the system.[9]

"Parties traditionally manifest assent by written or spoken word, but they can also do so through conduct."[10] For example, a homeowner making a mortgage payment through Speedpay's automated phone payment service was informed by that automated system that " 'the terms and conditions applicable to this payment are located at Speedpay.com/terms,' " and the homeowner was directed by that automated system "to press 1 'to complete your transaction and accept these terms.' "[11] Pressing 1, the Eleventh

---

in perceivable form." Unif. Arbitration Act (2000) §§ 1, 6(a) & cmt. 1, 7 U.L.A. 10, 22–23 (2005).

5 First Options of Chicago, Inc. v. Kaplan, 514 U.S. 938, 944 (1995).

6 Restatement (Second) of Contracts § 17 (1981) ("the formation of a contract requires a bargain in which there is a manifestation of mutual assent to the exchange and a consideration.")

7 Restatement (Second) of Contracts § 17 (1981) ("the formation of a contract requires a bargain in which there is a manifestation of mutual assent to the exchange and a consideration.")

8 See generally Joseph M. Perillo, Calamari & Perillo on Contracts ch.2 (6th ed.2009).

9 Aerotek, Inc. v. Boyd, 624 S.W.3d 199, 207 (Tex. 2021).

10 Berman v. Freedom Fin. Network, LLC, 30 F.4th 849, 855 (9th Cir. 2022).

11 Attix v. Carrington Mortg. Servs., LLC, 35 F.4th 1284 (11th Cir. 2022).

Circuit held, manifested assent to the arbitration agreement at Speedpay.com/terms.[12]

As this example suggests, manifestation of assent often includes assent to form contract terms the non-drafting party may not have read, let alone understood, so long as the court finds the drafting party provided an opportunity to read the terms.[13] In other words, the "blanket" assent non-drafting parties routinely give to form contracts[14] often includes assent to the arbitration clauses within those contracts. These "adhesive" arbitration agreements, which many people call "mandatory" or even "forced arbitration," arise from routine contractual consent.

(b) Apps and Websites

Courts often enforce the arbitration agreements in the Terms of Service (ToS) of the apps and websites that consumers and gig economy workers access on their phones and other electronic devices. It is especially routine for courts to find assent to the contract terms on apps and sites that require a user to scroll through those terms before clicking a button that says "I Agree" or the like ("scrollwrap").[15] For example, a federal court enforced an arbitration agreement in Lyft's ToS:

> The screen explicitly stated: "Before you can proceed you must read & accept the latest Terms of Service." The Terms of Service were set out on the screen to be scrolled through.

---

[12] Attix v. Carrington Mortg. Servs., LLC, 35 F.4th 1284 (11th Cir. 2022) ("before making his mortgage payment, Attix agreed to be bound by Speedpay's terms and conditions.")

[13] Restatement of Consumer Contracts § 2 (2022) ("A standard contract term is adopted as part of a consumer contract if the business demonstrates that the consumer manifested assent to the transaction after receiving: (1) a reasonable notice of the term and of the intent to include the term in the consumer contract, and (2) a reasonable opportunity to review the term."); Russell Korobkin, Bounded Rationality, Standard Form Contracts, and Unconscionability, 70 U. Chi. L. Rev. 1203, 1204 (2003) ("If the non-drafting party indicates his general assent to the form, courts will enforce the terms contained therein whether or not that party approves of the terms provided, understands those terms, has read them, or even has the vaguest idea what the terms might be about. Limited exceptions are made to this rule, most notably if the terms are found to be 'unconscionable.' The prevailing rule of form-term enforcement upsets many scholars").

[14] The Uniform Commercial Code's lead drafter, Karl Llewellyn described the typical buyer's assent to the typical seller's form document as "specific" assent to the "few dickered terms" buyer and seller discuss, and "blanket" assent "to any not unreasonable or indecent term the seller may have on his form, which do not alter or eviscerate the reasonable meaning of the dickered terms." Karl Llewellyn, The Common Law Tradition: Deciding Appeals 370 (1960).

[15] Sellers v. JustAnswer LLC, 289 Cal. Rptr. 3d 1, 21 (Ct.App.2021) ("there should be little doubt scrollwrap agreements are enforceable under California law because the consumer is given the contract, a sufficient circumstance to place the consumer on inquiry notice of the contractual terms.")

> No subtle hyperlink was needed. The Terms of Service begin with the warning: "These Terms of Service constitute a legally binding agreement . . . between you and Lyft, Inc." Before proceeding, the user was required to click on a conspicuous bar that said: "I accept."[16]

An alternative to scrollwrap is hyperlinked terms near the button users click to indicate agreement. Courts generally find assent to such "clickwrap" agreements. For example, the Tenth Circuit enforced AT & T's U-verse arbitration agreement because "U-verse customers are given notice of the U-verse terms and must affirmatively manifest assent to the terms by clicking 'I Acknowledge' and 'I Agree' buttons."[17]

However, assent to clickwrap can be more doubtful when none of the buttons on which users click say "Agree" or the like, and where the hyperlink is hard to see. For instance, slightly different versions of Uber's arbitration agreement were held enforceable by the Second Circuit and unenforceable by the First Circuit. In the Second Circuit case, the user clicked a "REGISTER" button near the words "By creating an Uber account, you agree to the Terms of Service & Privacy Policy." And the app's hyperlink to its "Terms of Service & Privacy Policy" (including an arbitration clause) was blue and underlined, which made it conspicuous enough, the court held, to put the user on notice of the terms.[18] By contrast, in the First Circuit case the Uber app's link to the arbitration clause "was presented in a gray rectangular box in white bold text", which the court held did not have the appearance of a hyperlink, and thus did not adequately notify a user as to the existence of the terms and conditions.[19]

Compared to scrollwrap and clickwrap, courts are less likely to find assent to arbitration agreements where the app or website says that merely using it constitutes assent to terms it somewhere contains. For instance, the Ninth Circuit refused to enforce an arbitration provision where "the design and content of the webpages

---

16 Applebaum v. Lyft, Inc., 263 F. Supp. 3d 454, 469 (S.D.N.Y. 2017).

17 Hancock v. Am. Tel. & Tel. Co., 701 F.3d 1248, 1257 (10th Cir. 2012). Meyer v. Uber Techs., Inc., 868 F.3d 66, 75 (2d Cir. 2017) ("Courts routinely uphold clickwrap agreements for the principal reason that the user has affirmatively assented to the terms of agreement by clicking 'I agree.' ")

18 Meyer v. Uber Techs., Inc., 868 F.3d 66, 79–80 (2d Cir. 2017).

19 Cullinane v. Uber Technologies, Inc., 893 F.3d 53, 62–64 (1st Cir. 2018). See also Kauders v. Uber Techs., Inc., 159 N.E.3d 1033, 1052 (Mass. 2021) (no assent where "The user could fully register for the service and click 'done' without ever clicking the link to the terms and conditions. The connection between the creation of the account and the terms and conditions was also somewhat oddly displayed in the two-part format, with the significant information (i.e., that by creating the account, the user expresses his or her agreement) being displayed less prominently than other information.")

[plaintiffs] visited did not adequately call to their attention either the existence of the terms and conditions or the fact that, by clicking on the 'continue' button, they were agreeing to be bound by those terms."[20] Similarly, the Second Circuit held that "a consumer's clicking on a download button does not communicate assent to contractual terms if the offer did not make clear to the consumer that clicking on the download button would signify assent to those terms."[21]

(c) Assent by Performance

Even without clicking, let alone signing, one may manifest assent to a contract by performing it. For instance, an insurance policy is a contract the policyholder performs by paying a premium. As the Alabama Supreme Court reasoned,

> although the policyholders did not execute stand-alone arbitration agreements or necessarily even read or receive the insurance policies containing the arbitration provisions, they have nevertheless manifested their assent to those policies and, necessarily, the arbitration provisions in them, by accepting and acting upon the policies, inasmuch as they all affirmatively renewed their policies and paid their premiums, thus ratifying the policies.[22]

Assent-by-performance is also an argument made by banks because many bank account and credit card contracts say that the bank may send revised terms to its customer and then the customer's continued use of the account or card constitutes assent to the revised terms, including their arbitration provisions.[23] And assent-by-performance

---

[20] Berman v. Freedom Fin. Network, LLC, 30 F.4th 849, 858 (9th Cir. 2022). See also Schnabel v. Trilegiant Corp., 697 F.3d 110, 127 (2d Cir. 2012) (no assent to arbitration because website "effectively obscured the details of the terms and conditions and the passive manner in which they could be accepted").

[21] Specht v. Netscape Commc'ns Corp., 306 F.3d 17, 29–30 (2d Cir. 2002); id. at 20 ("a reasonably prudent Internet user in circumstances such as these would not have known or learned of the existence of the license terms before responding to defendants' invitation to download the free software, * * * defendants therefore did not provide reasonable notice of the license terms. In consequence, plaintiffs' bare act of downloading the software did not unambiguously manifest assent to the arbitration provision contained in the license terms.")

[22] Am. Bankers Ins. Co. of Fla. v. Tellis, 192 So. 3d 386, 391 (Ala. 2015).

[23] Compare, e.g., Nev. Rev. Stat. Ann. § 97A.140 ("A cardholder shall be deemed to have accepted the written terms and conditions provided by the issuer upon subsequent actual use of the credit card."); Hartranft v. Encore Capital Grp., Inc., 543 F. Supp. 3d 893, 919 (S.D. Cal. 2021) (acceptance of card agreement and arbitration provision therein by use of the credit card; "South Dakota Codified Laws contain a specific provision governing acceptance of credit card agreements, which provides: 'The use of an accepted credit card or the issuance of a credit card agreement and the expiration of thirty days from the date of issuance without written notice from a card holder to cancel the account creates a binding contract between the card holder and the card issuer with reference to any accepted credit card.' " (quoting S.D. Codified

arguments are made by employers who present employees with an employee handbook containing an arbitration clause and then argue that the employee's continued performance of the job manifested assent to the arbitration clause.[24]

At least one consumer successfully turned the tables by sending payment with notice that the seller's acceptance of the payment manifested assent to eliminating the arbitration agreement in the seller's form contract.[25]

(d) Is the Document a Contract?

An arbitration clause may appear on a document that says it is not a contract, which might initially seem to negate the possibility that parties have manifested assent to an arbitration agreement. For instance, many employee handbooks say they are not contracts. Employers typically add this contract-disclaiming language to keep

---

Laws § 54-11-9)); Mounts v. Midland Funding LLC, 257 F. Supp. 3d 930 (E.D. Tenn. 2017) (assent to arbitration through continued use of credit card); Ineman v. Kohl's Corp., No. 14-CV-398, 2015 WL 1399052 (W.D. Wis. Mar. 26, 2015) (under the laws of Delaware, Ohio or Wisconsin "a credit card agreement becomes enforceable once a cardholder uses the card"); Krutchik v. Chase Bank USA, N.A., 531 F. Supp.2d 1359, 1364–65 (S.D.Fla.2008) (assent); Hutcherson v. Sears Roebuck & Co., 793 N.E.2d 886 (Ill. Ct. App. 2003) (assent); MBNA America Bank, N.A. v. Bibb, 2009 WL 1750220 (N.J. Super. App. Div.,2009) ("the cardholder's decision to use the card provides the requisite assent to the terms of the offer extended by the card's issuance, such that a contract is formed."), with Sevier Cnty. Sch. Fed. Credit Union v. Branch Banking & Tr. Co., 990 F.3d 470, 476 (6th Cir. 2021), cert. denied sub nom. Branch Banking & Tr. Co. v. Sevier Cty. Sch. Union, No. 21-365, 142 S. Ct. 2770 (U.S. May 31, 2022) ("What is lacking in this case is the Plaintiffs' consent to the arbitration provision"); Stone v. Golden Wexler & Sarnese, P.C., 341 F. Supp. 2d 189, 198 (E.D.N.Y. 2004) ("the change-in-terms provision does not authorize the Bank to unilaterally add an arbitration clause. Thus, the arbitration clause does not bind plaintiff"); Badie v. Bank of Am., 79 Cal. Rptr. 2d 273 (Ct. App. 1998)(no assent); Union Planters Bank, Nat'l Ass'n v. Rogers, 912 So.2d 116 (Miss. 2005)(no assent); Kortum-Managhan v. Herbergers NBGL, 204 P.3d 693, 699 (Mont. 2009)(no assent).

[24] Compare, e.g., Tillman v. Macy's, Inc., 735 F.3d 453, 455 (6th Cir. 2013) ("Macy's provided sufficient notice of its offer to enter into an arbitration agreement, and Tillman accepted by continuing her employment with Macy's"); Hardin v. First Cash Fin. Services, Inc., 465 F.3d 470 (10th Cir. 2006) (assent); Berkley v. Dillard's Inc., 450 F.3d 775, 777 (8th Cir. 2006) (assent), with Shockley v. PrimeLending, 929 F.3d 1012, 1019 (8th Cir. 2019) ("continued employment may constitute acceptance where the employer's document clearly states that continued employment constitutes acceptance, and the employer informs all employees that continued employment constitutes acceptance.") See Berkley v. Dillard's Inc., 450 F.3d 775, 777 (8th Cir. 2006). This is not, however, what happened here."); Hergenreder v. Bickford Senior Living Group, LLC, 656 F.3d 411, 419 (6th Cir. 2011) ("Hergenreder had no reason to believe that electing to work for Bickford would constitute her acceptance of *anything*. She therefore did not voluntarily undertake some unequivocal act sufficient for the purpose of accepting the arbitration terms contained in the DRP.")

[25] Cook's Pest Control, Inc. v. Rebar, 852 So.2d 730, 737 (Ala.2002) (service-provider assented to terms—eliminating arbitration clause—customer enclosed with payment).

employment at will,[26] so the employer can end employment at any time without liability for breach of contract. But this not-a-contract language can come back to haunt employers when courts rely on it in refusing to enforce the handbook's arbitration clause.[27] On the other hand, some courts have found assent to, and thus enforced, employee handbooks' arbitration agreements, notwithstanding the handbook's contract-disclaiming language,[28] including at least one case in which the former employee sought to compel arbitration of the employer's suit.[29]

(e) Incorporation by Reference

While the previous paragraph discusses documents that might or might not be contracts, other cases involve two documents, one of which received the parties' assent and the other of which contains an arbitration clause. So, the legal issue is whether the former document incorporates the latter document into the contract. For example, the Supreme Court's 2012 decision in *CompuCredit Corp. v. Greenwood*, enforced an arbitration agreement incorporated by reference in a

---

26 In re 24R, Inc., 324 S.W.3d 564, 567 (Tex. 2010) ("The employee policy manual is not a contract. In fact, it contains an express disclaimer that '[t]he policies and procedures in this manual are not intended to be contractual commitments by The Boot Jack. . . .' Express disclaimers in employee handbooks 'negate[ ] any implication that a personnel procedures manual places a restriction on the employment at will relationship.' ")

27 Etienne v. Hang Tough, Inc., No. 08-CV-61682, 2009 WL 1140040, at *3 (S.D.Fla.2009) (arbitration clause not binding); Mankin Media Systems, Inc. v. Corder, No. 19CV-48300W, 2022 WL 2359275 at *3 (Tenn. Ct. App. June 30, 2022) (arbitration clause in employee handbook not binding because "the Handbook clearly states that it is not intended to be a contract, and further states that the provisions therein are subject to unilateral change without the employee's consent."); Ex Parte Beasley, 712 So.2d 338 (Ala. 1998) (same); Hubner v. Cutthroat Commc'n, Inc., 80 P.3d 1256 (Mont. 2003) (same).

28 Patterson v. Tenet Healthcare, Inc., 113 F.3d 832, 834–35 (8th Cir. 1997) (although handbook did not create a binding contract, "the arbitration clause is separate from the other provisions of the handbook and * * * constitutes an enforceable contract."); Curry v. MidAmerica Care Found., No. TH 02-0053-C T/H, 2002 WL 1821808, at *4 (S.D. Ind. June 4, 2002) (following *Patterson* because "[l]ike the arbitration agreement in *Patterson*, the arbitration agreement in the employee handbook is a separate and distinct section of the handbook").

29 See Vero Water, Inc. v. Shymanski, No. 17-23320-CIV, 2018 WL 5098980, at *4 (S.D. Fla. Aug. 30, 2018), report and recommendation adopted, No. 17-23320-CIV, 2018 WL 5098878 (S.D. Fla. Sept. 20, 2018) ("Vero Water contends that, because the Handbook specifically disclaimed the creation of any contractual relationship," "the Arbitration Policy was not an enforceable agreement to arbitrate," but the court said, "the Handbook stated that Shymanski's compliance with the policies contained therein was a condition of his employment. Moreover, the Arbitration Policy in the Handbook stated that Shymanski's agreement to arbitrate was in consideration of his employment, his compensation and benefits, and Vero Water's own promise to arbitrate all employment-related disputes. Thus, the plain language of the Arbitration Policy indicates that Vero Water intended for itself and Shymanski to be bound to an agreement to arbitrate. Consequently, the undersigned finds that the Arbitration Policy was an enforceable agreement.")

consumer's application for a credit card.[30] As the dissent pointed out, "The contract signed by cardholders did not itself require arbitration. Rather, it incorporated by reference an 'enclosed insert' providing that all disputes would be resolved by arbitration."[31]

The document incorporated by reference can be surprising. For example, in *Metro East Center for Conditioning & Health v. Qwest Communications*,[32] a phone company placed an arbitration clause in its tariff with the Federal Communications Commission. The phone company sought to compel arbitration of a dispute with its customer. The district court denied the motion, reasoning that tariffs—regulatory filings to which customers never affirmatively agree—are not contracts. However, the Seventh Circuit reversed, reasoning that the "The tariff is an offer that the customer accepts by using the product."[33]

Other courts require more to incorporate an arbitration provision. For example, the West Virginia Supreme Court held that U-Haul's rental contract did not incorporate an addendum's arbitration agreement because the rental agreement's mention of the addendum was "brief" and "general" and "U-Haul's practice was to provide customers a copy of the Addendum only after the Rental Agreement had been executed."[34]

(f) Organization's Charter or Bylaws

An arbitration clause in an organization's charter or bylaws may be a particularized example of incorporation by reference. Courts have enforced arbitration clauses in bylaws when the party seeking to avoid arbitration had by contract agreed to comply with the

---

30 CompuCredit Corp. v. Greenwood, 565 U.S. 95, 103 (2012). See also Jureczki v. Banc One Texas, N.A., 252 F. Supp.2d 368 (S.D. Tex. 2003) (Texas law required bank account depositors to arbitrate a dispute since they executed a signature card which contained a provision acknowledging receipt of and agreement to be bound by bank's account rules and regulations, which included arbitration provision, despite depositors' claim they never received terms and conditions); Harby ex rel. Brooks v. Wachovia Bank, N.A., 915 A.2d 462 (Md. 2007) (bank customer consented to arbitration by signing an initial terms and conditions agreement that incorporated by reference the arbitration agreement); Robert J. Denley Co., Inc. v. Neal Smith Const. Co., Inc., 2007 WL 1153121, at *2–4 (Tenn. Ct. App. 2007) (mutual assent when a signed contract referenced a separate arbitration document).

31 CompuCredit Corp. v. Greenwood, 565 U.S. 95, 132 n.1 (2012) (Sotomayor, J. dissenting).

32 294 F.3d 924 (7th Cir. 2002).

33 Id. at 926.

34 State ex rel. U-Haul Co. of W. Virginia v. Zakaib, 752 S.E.2d 586, 598 (2013), cert. denied sub nom. W. Virginia ex rel. U-Haul Co. of W. Virginia v. Zakaib, 574 U.S. 816 (2014). See also Etienne v. Hang Tough, Inc., 2009 WL 1140040 (S.D. Fla. 2009) (no assent to arbitrate because acknowledgment form did not incorporate by reference the arbitration provision of the Handbook).

bylaws, thus incorporating them by reference into the contract.[35] Conversely, courts generally refuse to enforce such arbitration clauses without evidence of agreement to abide by the organization's bylaws. For example, the Third Circuit refused to enforce an arbitration clause in by-laws the plaintiff shareholder averred she never received and thus did not incorporate by reference.[36]

---

[35] Meshel v. Ohev Sholom Talmud Torah, 869 A.2d 343, 361 (D.C. 2015) (enforcing arbitration agreement in religious organization bylaws against congregation members, stating "[i]t is well established that the formal bylaws of an organization are to be construed as a contractual agreement between the organization and its members, . . . since the continuing relationship between the organization and its members manifests an implicit agreement by all parties concerned to abide by the bylaws.") (internal citations omitted); Maine Cent. R. Co. v. Bangor & Aroostook R. Co., 395 A.2d 1107, 1119 (Me. 1978) ("It is well established law that the constitution and bylaws of a voluntary unincorporated association . . . constitute a valid enforceable contract between the members and the association. The obligation also runs between each member and the others.") (internal quotations omitted); id. ("Agreements to arbitrate are within the ambit of such rules and regulations."); Rushing v. Gold Kist, Inc., 567 S.E.2d 384, 387–88 (Ga. Ct. App. 2002) ("the arbitration clause is contained in the By-Laws, and Rushing expressly consented to be bound by the By-Laws. It is inconsequential that the By-Laws did not contain the arbitration clause when Rushing signed his membership agreement—he agreed to be subject not only to existing By-Laws, but also to By-Laws 'hereafter in effect.' Such is consistent with a provision in the By Laws that specifically authorized the membership to amend provisions and adopt new ones."); Elbadramany v. Stanley, 490 So.2d 964, 964–65 (Fla. Dist. Ct. App. 1986)(where application for membership promises "to abide by" organization's "Constitution, Bylaws, and Rules and Regulations," "a provision in the constitution, charter or by-laws of a voluntary association which requires that disputes between members be submitted to arbitration constitutes a binding agreement between such members"); Ann M. Lipton, Manufactured Consent: The Problem of Arbitration Clauses in Corporate Charters and Bylaws, 104 Geo. L.J. 583, 590 (2016) ("There are many examples of states enforcing predispute arbitration agreements in close corporations and membership associations (sometimes, though not always, on the basis of arbitration clauses contained in the charter or bylaws). In these disputes, however, there has always been privity of contract between the member and the corporation. The member may have personally signed an agreement promising to abide by the bylaws, or may have entered into a stock purchase agreement containing the relevant provisions, or at least has entered into some kind of direct agreement to be associated with the firm.") See also Elf Atochem N. Am., Inc. v. Jaffari, 727 A.2d 286, 295 (Del. 1999) (enforcing agreement among members of limited liability company—LLC—requiring arbitration of disputes, including claims for breach of fiduciary duty).

[36] Kirleis v. Dickie, McCamey & Chilcote, P.C., 560 F.3d 156, 162 (3d Cir. 2009) ("Kirleis averred that she 'was never provided with a copy of the By-Laws of defendant Firm' "). Id. at 164–65 ("The Firm claims that employee handbooks are different from corporate bylaws because members of a corporation are presumed to understand bylaws in a way that employees are not presumed to understand handbooks. We find this argument persuasive to a point. A shareholder/director of a professional corporation who has had the benefit of advanced education and training and who has been involved in law firm management typically would be more knowledgeable regarding corporate bylaws than an entry-level worker would be likely to know about an employee handbook. But this factual distinction, as cogent as it may be, is immaterial to the fact that Pennsylvania law requires arbitration agreements to be explicit. To the extent the Firm argues that this rule of law does not apply to a corporate shareholder/director, we have rejected that argument.")

However, a couple of courts have gone beyond express incorporation by reference to find that investing in a Maryland real estate investment trust (REIT) constitutes assent to the REIT's bylaws.[37] Whether corporate bylaws similarly bind shareholders who have not otherwise assented to arbitration remains an important open issue.[38] As noted above, the Securities Exchange Commission largely prevents public offerings of securities by companies whose charters or bylaws require arbitration of shareholder claims against the corporation.[39]

(g) Assent by Agent

Another assent issue is whether a party (the principal) who did not assent to an arbitration agreement is nevertheless bound by it because someone else (the agent) assented to it on behalf of the principal. Basic agency law allows one party to act through another,[40]

---

37 Del. County Emps. Ret. Fund v. Portnoy, 2014 WL 1271528 (D. Mass. 2014) (real estate investment trust (REIT) trustees amended bylaws to require arbitration of claims by trust's shareholders against trust or its officers); id. at *5 (applying Maryland court's ruling that "because the ordinary shareholders had constructive knowledge of the arbitration bylaw, the provision was also enforceable against them"); id. at *11 ("each of the Company's share certificates included a provision stating that shareholders were "to be bound by all of the provisions of the Declaration of Trust and Bylaws of the Trust and any amendments thereto."); Corvex Mgmt. LP v. Commonwealth Reit, No. 24-C-13-001111, 2013 WL 1915769 at *8–9 (Md. Cir. Ct. Balt. City, May 8, 2013) (denying plaintiff-shareholder's petition to stay arbitration where plaintiffs were found to mutually assent to arbitration agreement in corporation's bylaws. "Maryland courts as well as other courts from other jurisdictions have frequently ruled that constructive knowledge, constructive notice, and knowledge/notice through incorporation-by-reference are adequate to inform and bind a party to a contract, thereby satisfying mutuality." Because each share certificate included language that "every transferee or assignee hereof by accepting or holding the same agrees to be bound by all of the provisions of the Declaration of Trust and Bylaws of the Trust, as amended from time to time." The court determined that "[p]laintiffs purchased shares with at least constructive knowledge that the Arbitration Bylaws were in effect and that their shares were subject to them. This Court finds that this is enough to constitute mutual assent of the parties to the Arbitration Bylaws at issue.").

38 Ann M. Lipton, Manufactured Consent: The Problem of Arbitration Clauses in Corporate Charters and Bylaws, 104 Geo. L.J. 583, 586 (2016) (The Commonwealth cases cited in the previous footnote "represent the first time a publicly traded company actually both included an arbitration provision in its governing documents, and persuaded a court to enforce it. The cases therefore raise important questions about whether the FAA should be applied to corporate governance documents in the same way that it applies to 'ordinary' contracts, and the suitability of arbitration as a forum for resolving shareholder disputes.")

39 See § 5(e)(8).

40 See Restatement (Third) of Agency § 1.01 (2006).

> Agency is the fiduciary relationship that arises when one person (a "principal") manifests assent to another person (an "agent") that the agent shall act on the principal's behalf and subject to the principal's control, and the agent manifests assent or otherwise consents so to act.
>
> Id.

including to form a contract.[41] In fact, for some parties the only way to form a contract is through an agent. For example, a corporation can form a contract only through the actions of its agents,[42] who often, but not always, are employees of the corporation.[43] Some cases involve the issue whether a corporation or other organization is bound by an arbitration agreement because of assent manifested on its behalf by its agent.[44]

Agency issues can arise in other contexts as well.[45] For example, does a lawyer have authority to bind her client to an arbitration

---

[41] "Perhaps the really distinguishing characteristic of the agent is that he represents his principal contractually, which means that, given proper authorization, the agent makes contracts or conducts negotiations of a business nature on behalf of his principal and by which his principal is bound." William A. Gregory, The Law of Agency and Partnership 113 (3d ed.2001).

[42] "That a corporation can act only through agents is too elementary a proposition to require the citation of authority." William Meade Fletcher, 2 Fletcher Cyclopedia of the Law of Private Corporations § 434 (2005). Corporations are not the only parties that must act through their agents to form contracts. That is also true of other business organizations and other non-human parties such as governments.

[43] "The servant, qua servant, has no power to bind his master in contract. It is apparent, however, that one can be and often will be employed in a capacity where he is alternatively or simultaneously a servant and an agent. So an express company's truck driver may be a servant in driving the truck and an agent when receiving a package and signing a bill of lading binding his company to deliver it." William A. Gregory, The Law of Agency and Partnership 114 (3d ed. 2001).

[44] Trina Solar US, Inc. v. Jasmin Solar Pty Ltd, 954 F.3d 567, 569–72 (2d Cir. 2020) ("Jasmin authorized JRC * * * to act as Jasmin's agent for all business dealings between Jasmin and Trina, although it also recognized that Trina might contract with JRC as a principal in its own right rather than as an agent"; arbitrator and district court held that JRC as agent bound Jasmin as principal to JRC's agreement with Trina, so Jasmin was bound by its arbitration clause, but Second Circuit held that the contract " 'explicitly excludes' Jasmin as a party," so "the District Court erred when it determined that Jasmin was bound as a principal to the Contract under an agency theory."); Merrill Lynch Inv. Managers v. Optibase, Ltd., 337 F.3d 125, 130 (2d Cir. 2003) ("mutual benefits derived from affiliation * * * insufficient to bind a non-signatory on agency principles to an arbitration agreement signed by an affiliate"); Thomson-CSF, S.A. v. Am. Arbitration Ass'n, 64 F.3d 773, 777 (2d Cir. 1995) (agency principles do not bind parent corporation to arbitration agreement signed by subsidiary before parent bought subsidiary); Three Valleys Mun. Water Dist. v. E.F. Hutton & Co., Inc., 925 F.2d 1136 (9th Cir. 1991) ("On remand, the district court must first determine whether the signatory had authority to bind the other plaintiffs to the agreements containing the arbitration clauses.").

[45] Valentine v. Plum Healthcare Grp., LLC, 37 Cal. App. 5th 1076, 1086 (2019) ("a person who is authorized to act as the patient's agent can bind the patient to an arbitration agreement"); Dye v. Tamko Bldg. Prod., Inc., 908 F.3d 675, 686 (11th Cir. 2018) (The homeowners, through their roofer agents, validly accepted those terms—Tamko's binding arbitration provision included."); Scone Investments, L.P. v. American Third Market Corp., 992 F. Supp. 378, 381 (S.D.N.Y.,1998) (broker signed arbitration agreement on customer's behalf); In re Labatt Food Service, L.P., 279 S.W.3d 640 (Tex. 2009) (employee's arbitration agreement requires employee's wrongful death beneficiaries to arbitrate their wrongful death claims against employer even though those beneficiaries did not sign the agreement).

agreement?[46] Some agency cases involve family members. Courts have found that a parent had authority to bind her child to an arbitration agreement,[47] and an adult child had authority to bind her elderly parent to an arbitration agreement.[48] This latter scenario resulted in a Kentucky Supreme Court case holding that an agent could deprive her principal of an "adjudication by judge or jury" only if the power of attorney granting authority to the agent "expressly so provide[d]." But the U.S. Supreme Court reversed because Kentucky's "clear-statement rule" "fails to put arbitration agreements on an equal plane with other contracts."[49] In short, the FAA preempts state efforts to make it harder for agents to bind principals to arbitration agreements than to other agreements.

(h) UCC Article 2 on the Sale of Goods

Distinct assent issues arise in transactions governed by Uniform Commercial Code Article 2 on the sale of goods. For example, merchants may engage in the "battle of the forms" in which one party's form (either the buyer's purchase order or the seller's acknowledgment of an order) contains an arbitration clause, while the other party's form does not. These cases, decided under Uniform Commercial Code § 2–207, sometimes find assent to arbitration and sometimes do not.[50]

Related but different issues arise when a seller provides goods in a box that also contains documents that purport to be a contract, including an arbitration clause. Courts split over whether the buyer's

---

46 Compare Brooks v. BDO Seidman, LLP, 883 N.Y.S.2d 450 (N.Y. Sup. Ct. 2009) (authority), with Louis Michel, Inc. v. Whitecourt Constr. Co., 189 N.E. 767 (N.Y. Ct. App. 1934) (no authority).

47 Global Travel Mktg., Inc. v. Shea, 908 So.2d 392 (Fla. 2005) (parent had authority to bind minor to arbitration clause); Hojnowski v. Vans Skate Park, 901 A.2d 381 (N.J. 2006)(same).

48 Covenant Health Rehab. of Picayune, L.P. v. Brown, 949 So.2d 732 (Miss. 2007) (adult daughter of the patient, acting as a healthcare surrogate, had the authority to contractually bind her mother in healthcare matters), overruled on other grounds, Covenant Health & Rehabilitation of Picayune, LP v. Estate of Moulds ex rel., 14 So.3d 695 (Miss. 2009).

49 Kindred Nursing Centers Ltd. P'ship v. Clark, 137 S. Ct. 1421, 1426–27, 197 L. Ed. 2d 806 (2017).

50 Aceros Prefabricados, S.A. v. TradeArbed, Inc., 282 F.3d 92, 100 (2d Cir. 2002) ("arbitration agreements do not, as a matter of law, constitute material alterations to a contract; rather, the question of their inclusion in a contract under section 2–207(2)(b) is answered by examining, on a case-by-case basis, their materiality under a preponderance of the evidence standard as we would examine any other agreement."); ICC Chem. Corp. v. Vitol, Inc., 425 F. App'x 57, 59 (2d Cir. 2011) (arbitration agreement became part of contract under UCC 2–702(2)(b) because not a "material alteration")); PCS Nitrogen Fertilizer, L.P. v. Christy Refractories, L.L.C., 225 F.3d 974 (8th Cir. 2000); Dorton v. Collins & Aikman Corp. 453 F.2d 1161 (6th Cir. 1972); Dumont Telephone Co. v. Power & Telephone Supply Co., 962 F. Supp.2d 1064, 1079–80 (N.D. Iowa 2013) (arbitration clause became part of contract).

failure to return the goods within the time period specified on the document constitutes assent to the terms on the document.[51]

(i) Wills and Trusts

Although George Washington's will had an arbitration clause,[52] the enforceability of such clauses remains "unresolved in almost every jurisdiction."[53] Many courts have long refused to enforce arbitration clauses in wills and trusts against parties who did not manifest assent to the document containing the arbitration clause.[54] For example, in 2022 the Virginia Supreme Court denied enforcement of a trust's arbitration clause against a beneficiary because "the beneficiary of a trust is not a party to a 'written agreement to submit any existing controversy to arbitration agreement.' "[55] Similarly, in 2021 a New Jersey court refused to enforce a will's arbitration clause against a beneficiary who had not agreed to it. The court said, "a will is not a contract;" it is "not an

---

[51] Compare, e.g., Hill v. Gateway 2000, Inc., 105 F.3d 1147 (7th Cir. 1997) (assent); Brower v. Gateway 2000, Inc., 676 N.Y.S.2d 569, 572 (N.Y. App. Div. 1998) (arbitration clause of standard terms and conditions agreement valid where consumer informed that by keeping product beyond thirty days after delivery he was accepting terms) (assent); Kahan Jewelry Corp. v. Venus Casting, Inc., 847 N.Y.S.2d 366, 372 (Sup. Ct. 2007) ("As UCC § 2–201(2) would make other terms of the Delivery Receipt binding, if not objected to within ten days of receipt, the FAA requires the arbitration clause in the Delivery Ticket also to be enforced if it was not objected to within such ten day period."), with Klocek v. Gateway, Inc., 104 F. Supp.2d 1332 (D. Kan. 2000) (no assent), dismissed for lack of subject matter jurisdiction, 2000 WL 1372886 (D. Kan. Sept.6, 2000); Reedy v. Cincinnati Bengals, Inc., 758 N.E.2d 678 (Ohio Ct. App. 2001) (no assent); DeFontes v. Dell, Inc., 984 A.2d 1061 (R.I.2009)(no assent).

[52] Founders online: George Washington's Last will and testament, 9 July 1799, National Archives and Records Administration, https://founders.archives.gov/documents/Washington/06-04-02-0404-0001 ("My Will and direction expressly is, that all disputes (if unhappily any should arise) shall be decided by three impartial and intelligent men, known for their probity and good understanding; two to be chosen by the disputants--each having the choice of one--and the third by those two. Which three men thus chosen, shall, unfettered by Law, or legal constructions, declare their sense of the Testators intention; and such decision is, to all intents and purposes to be as binding on the Parties as if it had been given in the Supreme Court of the United States.").

[53] Erin Katzen, Arbitration Clauses in Wills and Trusts: Defining the Parameters for Mandatory Arbitration of Wills and Trusts, 24 Quinnipiac Prob. L.J. 118, 119 (2011). See also David Horton, The Federal Arbitration Act and Testamentary Instruments, 90 N.C. L. Rev. 1027, 1036 (2012).

[54] Carpenter v. Bailey, 60 P. 162, 163 (Cal. 1900) (declining to enforce agreement by a group of beneficiaries to arbitrate a will contest that would bind others because "[a] few individuals, claiming to be the heirs, cannot by stipulation, determine such controversy.") See also In re Calomiris, 894 A.2d 408 (D.C. 2006) (declining to enforce provision in will, which created a trust, requiring arbitration of disputes among trustees; "a will is not a contract").

[55] Boyle v. Anderson, 871 S.E.2d 226, 230 (Va. 2022).

instrument that reflects a consensual understanding between parties."[56]

On the other hand, a transferor of property generally has the power to place conditions on such transfer, and several courts have enforced wills' and trusts' arbitration clauses, conceptualizing them as such conditions. On this property-oriented reasoning, a testator's power to mandate arbitration follows from the testator's power to "annex conditions * * * to his bequests."[57] If a beneficiary wants property from the testator, then the beneficiary must comply with the strings the testator has attached to such property. For instance, the Supreme Court of Texas in 2013 enforced a trust's arbitration provision against a beneficiary because "the settlor determines the conditions attached to her gifts."[58]

However, this property-oriented reasoning perhaps only applies if the assent of the testator or settlor is conceded by all parties to make the will or trust or valid. So, some states have enacted statutes making enforceable "[a] provision of a will or trust requiring the arbitration of disputes, other than disputes of the validity of all or part of a will or trust."[59] And parties who dispute validity of the instrument containing the arbitration—alleging for example the trustee's undue influence on a trustor "who had taken heavy narcotics"—have been permitted to litigate the question of validity.[60]

§ 19 Consideration

Consideration is required to form a contract.[61] "To constitute consideration" for a promise, "a performance or a return promise

---

56 In re Hekemian, No. P-47921, 2021 WL 6884165, at *6 (N.J. Super. Ch. Dec. 03, 2021).

57 David Horton, The Federal Arbitration Act and Testamentary Instruments, 90 N.C. L. Rev. 1027, 1037–38 (2012) (quoting Wait v. Huntington, 40 Conn. 9, 11 (1873)). See also Moore v. Harper, 27 W. Va. 362, 374 (1886) (enforcing arbitration clause in will because "[t]he testator has full dominion over his property with the absolute right . . . to do with and dispose of it in any manner or to whomever his will or caprice may suggest").

58 Rachal v. Reitz, 403 S.W.3d 840, 842 (Tex. 2013).

59 Fla. Stat. Ann. § 731.401(1). Ariz. Rev. Stat. Ann. § 14–10205; Ohio Rev. Code Ann. § 5802.05. Mo. Rev. Stat. § 456.2–205.

60 Gibbons v. Anderson, 575 S.W.3d 144, 150 (Ark. 2019) (denying co-trustee's motion to compel arbitration of beneficiaries' breach of trust claim when a beneficiary challenged the validity of the trust because "an arbitration provision within a trust agreement cannot compel arbitration to determine the validity of the trust.") See also McArthur v. McArthur, 168 Cal. Rptr. 3d 785, 787 (Ct. App. 2014) (refusing to compel arbitration of claim seeking declaration that trust was void because of undue influence on testator).

61 Restatement (Second) of Contracts § 17 (1981) ("the formation of a contract requires a bargain in which there is a manifestation of mutual assent to the exchange and a consideration.")

must be bargained for."[62] Common consideration for one party's promise to arbitrate rather than litigate some set of possible disputes is the other party's reciprocal promise to arbitrate rather than litigate those same disputes. Most arbitration agreements describe possible disputes—such as all disputes arising out of the parties' transaction—and obligate each party to arbitrate those disputes, so each party's promise to arbitrate serves as consideration for the other party's promise.[63]

However, some courts have refused to enforce agreements in which the set of disputes each party promises to arbitrate consists entirely or largely of claims by one party, while neither party promises to arbitrate claims by the other party.[64] These cases tend to involve consumers' or employees' adhesive arbitration agreements where the court sees the business drafter of the form contract trying to "use[ ] an arbitration agreement to shield itself from litigation, while reserving to itself the ability to pursue relief through the court system."[65] Although such agreements might be unconscionable,[66] characterizing them as lacking consideration (or "mutuality") conflicts with the usual understanding of consideration as merely requiring a bargain, not necessarily an even or fair bargain.[67] So more standard are courts that find consideration for one party's promise to pursue its claims in arbitration in the other party's

---

[62] Restatement (Second) of Contracts § 71(1) (1981).

[63] See Lombardi v. DirecTV, Inc., 549 Fed.Appx. 617, 619 (9th Cir. 2013) (holding that reciprocal promises between satellite television service provider and customers to arbitrate all claims with the exception of theft of service provided sufficient consideration for arbitration agreement under Arizona and Illinois law).

[64] Hull v. Norcom, Inc., 750 F.2d 1547, 1550 (11th Cir. 1985) (refusing to enforce employment arbitration agreement that permitted employer "to institute and prosecute proceedings in any court of competent jurisdiction, either at law or in equity, to obtain damages for any breach of this Agreement, or to enforce the specific performance thereof by [employee] Hull, or to enjoin Hull from performing services for any such other person, firm, or corporation, during the period herein agreed"); id. "the consideration exchanged for one party's promise to arbitrate must be the other party's promise to arbitrate at least some specified class of claims."); id. at 1549 ("an arbitration agreement will not be enforced unless it is "mutually binding," and an agreement is not mutually binding where one party reserves the option to raise and resolve any and all disputes that it may have against the other party in a court of law rather than through arbitration").

[65] E-Z Cash Advance, Inc. v. Harris, 139, 60 S.W.3d 436, 441 (Ark. 2001) ("There is no mutuality of obligation where one party uses an arbitration agreement to shield itself from litigation, while reserving to itself the ability to pursue relief through the court system.")

[66] See § 24(a).

[67] Restatement (Second) of Contracts § 79 (1981) ("If the requirement of consideration is met, there is no additional requirement of * * * equivalence in the values exchanged; or 'mutuality of obligation.' ")

promise to be bound by the arbitrator's decision of claims brought by the first party.[68]

Suppose though that a contract's arbitration clause obligates only one party to arbitrate some set of disputes, thus giving the other party the post-dispute choice of arbitrating or litigating those disputes.[69] The one party's promise to arbitrate has no consideration within the arbitration clause and thus is unenforceable unless the court finds consideration for this promise somewhere else in the contract. However, some courts refuse to look elsewhere, either because of the separability of arbitration agreements from the contracts containing them[70] or because giving "the holder of the option absolute discretion to select the means of dispute resolution" is "inequitable."[71]

---

[68] Cir. City Stores, Inc. v. Najd, 294 F.3d 1104, 1108 (9th Cir. 2002) ("Najd argues that the [arbitration agreement] is not supported by adequate consideration because Circuit City is not required to submit any of its claims against employees to arbitration. However, Circuit City's promise to be bound by the arbitration process itself serves as adequate consideration. In other words, Circuit City's promise to submit to arbitration and to forego the option of a judicial forum for a specified class of claims constitutes sufficient consideration."); Michalski v. Cir. City Stores, Inc., 177 F.3d 634, 636 (7th Cir. 1999) ("Circuit City's promise to be bound by the arbitration process itself serves as mutual consideration here"); Johnson v. Cir. City Stores, 148 F.3d 373, 378 (4th Cir. 1998) (enforcing agreement while "recogniz[ing that it] apparently requires the arbitration only of Johnson's claims against Circuit City and does not appear to require the arbitration of any claims Circuit City might have against Johnson"). See also Sevier Cnty. Sch. Fed. Credit Union v. Branch Banking & Tr. Co., 990 F.3d 470, 476 (6th Cir. 2021), cert. denied sub nom. Branch Banking & Tr. Co. v. Sevier Cty. Sch. Union, No. 21-365, 142 S. Ct. 2770 (U.S. May 31, 2022) ("Both state and federal courts have consistently found that consideration exists so long as the arbitration agreement binds both parties.")

[69] U.S. ex rel. TBI Invs., Inc. v. BrooAlexa, LLC, 119 F. Supp. 3d 512, 535 (S.D.W. Va. 2015) (agreement said "Should [Plaintiff] and [Defendant BrooAlexa] be unable to resolve said dispute(s) through mediation, any and all dispute(s), at the sole discretion of [Defendant BrooAlexa], shall be settled by the [AAA] in accordance with it [sic] Construction Industry Arbitration Rules"). Courts are not always clear on whether they interpret an arbitration agreement to obligate both parties to arbitrate only claims by one party or obligate only one party to arbitrate some set of claims while giving the other party the post-dispute choice of arbitrating or litigating those disputes. See, e.g., Noohi v. Toll Bros., 708 F.3d 599 (4th Cir. 2013).

[70] See § 21. Stevens/Leinweber/Sullens, Inc. v. Holm Development and Management, Inc., 795 P.2d 1308, 1313 (Ariz. App. 1990) ("Because under the separability doctrine the arbitration provision is an independent and separate agreement, Holm Development cannot 'borrow' consideration from the principal contract to support the arbitration provision. As a result, we conclude that the arbitration provision, which clearly lacks mutuality, is void for lack of consideration.")

[71] Stevens/Leinweber/Sullens, Inc. v. Holm Development and Management, Inc., 795 P.2d 1308, 1313 (Ariz. App. 1990) ("A unilateral arbitration option clearly does not promote the public policy favoring arbitration. This court cannot close its eyes to the reality of the facts before us. The arbitration provision at issue here grants the holder of the option absolute discretion to select the means of dispute resolution and to change its mind at any time prior to final judgment. This is so grossly inequitable that it runs counter to the philosophy of encouraging arbitration. By its terms, this arbitration provision undermines the purpose and intent of arbitration.")

Even if a court may look at other contract terms outside the arbitration clause to find consideration for a clause giving one party a post-dispute choice of arbitration or litigation, such consideration may still be lacking in contracts terminable at will because "promises" in such contracts are not really promises at all—they are "illusory."[72] For example, employment is commonly terminable at-will,[73] so an employee's promise to arbitrate, without a reciprocal promise to arbitrate by the employer, may lack consideration even where the employer has paid the employee for almost 29 years. This was the case for an employee of the Kansas City Chiefs who, upon starting her job, signed a document providing that

> In consideration of my employment by Kansas City Chiefs Football Club, Inc., (hereinafter "the Club"); I hereby agree * * * that all matters in dispute between me and the Club shall be referred to the Commissioner, and that his decision shall be accepted as final, binding and conclusive on me and on the Club.[74]

When the Chiefs terminated the employee, she sued, and the Chiefs moved to compel arbitration before the Commissioner. The Missouri Court of Appeals denied that motion, finding the employee's promise to arbitrate unsupported by consideration. "The Chiefs could have fired her fifteen minutes after she signed the Agreement without suffering any legal consequences because her employment was at-will," so employment "was not sufficient consideration to support her promise to arbitrate,"[75] even though it lasted 29 years.

Other employers avoid this consideration ground for non-enforcement by making reciprocal promises to arbitrate with their at-will employees. So long as each party's duty to arbitrate employment disputes survives termination of employment, then the fact that employment is terminable at will only makes illusory the promises to work and to pay for work, not the promises to arbitrate disputes.[76]

---

[72] Restatement (Second) of Contracts § 77 ("Illusory and Alternative Promises"). Id. cmt. a ("Words of promise which by their terms make performance entirely optional with the 'promisor' do not constitute a promise.")

[73] For a brief discussion of employment-at-will, see §§ 45(a)(1)(C) & 48(b)(1).

[74] Sniezek v. Kansas City Chiefs Football Club, 402 S.W.3d 580, 582 (Mo. Ct. App. 2013).

[75] Id. at 585–86. See also Gibson v. Neighborhood Health Clinics, Inc., 121 F.3d 1126 (7th Cir. 1997) ("when an employer has made no specific promise, the mere fact of continued employment does not constitute consideration for the employee's promise").

[76] Koveleskie v. SBC Capital Markets, Inc., 167 F.3d 361, 368 (7th Cir. 1999) (at-will employee's "contract with [her employer] was supported by adequate consideration" because it "bound both parties" "and allowed arbitration at the insistence of either party"); In re 24R, Inc., 324 S.W.3d 564, 566–67 (Tex. 2010)

In contrast, even with reciprocal promises to arbitrate, one party's promise to arbitrate may lack consideration and thus be unenforceable if found in a document providing that the other party may unilaterally amend it. For example, Maryland's highest court held that an "arbitration agreement in which employer reserved the right to, within its sole discretion, alter, amend, modify, or revoke the arbitration agreement at any time and without notice, was unenforceable for lack of consideration."[77] The Maryland Court of Appeals refused to look outside the arbitration agreement to the broader employment contract to find consideration for the employee's promise to arbitrate.[78]

B. DEFENSES TO ENFORCEMENT OF ARBITRATION AGREEMENTS

Table of Sections

Sec.

("Mutual agreement to arbitrate claims provides sufficient consideration to support an arbitration agreement. At-will employment does not preclude employers and employees from forming subsequent contracts, so long as neither party relies on continued employment as consideration for the contract."); In re Halliburton Co., 80 S.W.3d 566, 569 (Tex. 2002) ("When Myers reported for work," "both Myers and Halliburton became bound to arbitrate any disputes between them. Even if Myers' employment had ended shortly thereafter, the promise to arbitrate would have been binding and enforceable on both parties").

[77] Cheek v. United Healthcare of the Mid-Atlantic, Inc., 835 A.2d 656 (Md. 2003)(arbitration agreement in which employer reserved the right to alter, amend, modify, or revoke the arbitration agreement at any time and without notice, was unenforceable for lack of consideration, even though employer had not exercised that option against employee; employer's promise to arbitrate was illusory, and the employment could not serve as consideration for the arbitration agreement). See also Coady v. Nationwide Motor Sales Corp., 32 F.4th 288, 293 (4th Cir. 2022) ("Because the Modification Clause gives Nationwide the right to change or abolish those policies, procedures, and benefits without notice, the Arbitration Agreement is illusory under Maryland law."); Thompson v. Bar-S Foods Co., 174 P.3d 567, 577 (Okla. 2007)(no consideration because document signed by employee allowed employer to modify arbitration clause at any time without notice),

[78] Cheek, 835 A.2d at 152 (rejecting employer's position that its employment or continued employment of Cheek constituted independent consideration for the Arbitration Policy, reasoning that, "To agree with United would place this Court in the untenable position of having to go beyond the confines of the arbitration agreement itself and into an analysis of the validity of the larger contract, an inquiry which we cannot make" under the separability doctrine discussed in Section 21).

---

§ 20 Defenses Only from Contract Law

FAA § 2 says that arbitration agreements "shall be valid, irrevocable, and enforceable, save upon such grounds as exist at law or in equity for the revocation of any contract."[79] So, the Supreme Court holds that under the FAA, "state law, whether of legislative or judicial origin, is applicable if that law arose to govern issues concerning the validity, revocability, and enforceability of contracts generally."[80] But FAA § 2 preempts state law that "imposes prerequisites to enforcement of an arbitration agreement that are not applicable to contracts generally."[81] The Supreme Court says that FAA § 2 "establish[es] an equal-treatment principle: A court may invalidate an arbitration agreement based on generally applicable contract defenses like fraud or unconscionability, but not on legal rules that 'apply only to arbitration or that derive their meaning from the fact that an agreement to arbitrate is at issue."[82] As the Restatement explains,

> The FAA makes arbitration clauses subject to the same state law grounds for nonenforcement as other contract provisions and does not permit them to be subject to discriminatory treatment. * * *
>
> If a ground for nonenforcement makes an arbitration clause less enforceable than other provisions in the contract (or a comparable contract without an arbitration clause)—even if the ground applies to some other (but not all) contract provisions in addition to the arbitration clause—it does not apply to contracts generally and thus is preempted.[83]

---

79 9 U.S.C. § 2.

80 Perry v. Thomas, 482 U.S. 483, 493 n.9 (1987).

81 Preston v. Ferrer, 552 U.S. 346, 356 (2008).

82 Viking River Cruises, Inc. v. Moriana, 142 S. Ct. 1906, 1917 (2022) (internal quotations omitted).

83 Restatement (Third) U.S. Law of Int'l Comm. Arb. § 1.6 cmt. b (2019).

Consequently, parties seeking to avoid enforcement of their arbitration agreements must rely on "generally applicable contract defenses, such as fraud, duress, or unconscionability."[84] Other permitted defenses—because they are in general contract law—include misrepresentation, mistake, undue influence, impracticability, frustration of purpose, the statute of frauds, and illegality. However, parties seeking to use these defenses often must raise them in arbitration, rather than in court to prevent arbitration, because of the separability doctrine, which is discussed next.

§ 21 The Separability Doctrine

(a) The Separability Doctrine Adopted in Prima Paint

The separability doctrine is complex and, for many people, counter-intuitive. So, it can perhaps best be understood by starting with the facts of the Supreme Court case that adopted it, *Prima Paint Corp. v. Flood & Conklin Manufacturing Co.*[85] F & C sold Prima Paint a list of F & C's customers and promised not to sell paint to those customers for six years.[86] F & C also promised to act as a consultant to Prima Paint during these six years.[87] This consulting agreement included an arbitration clause.[88] Prima Paint did not make the payments provided for in the consulting agreement.[89] Prima Paint contended that F & C had fraudulently represented that it was solvent and able to perform its contract, but was in fact insolvent and intended to file for bankruptcy shortly after executing its consulting agreement with Prima Paint.[90]

F & C served on Prima Paint a "notice of intention to arbitrate."[91] Prima Paint then sued in federal court for rescission of the consulting agreement because of the alleged misrepresentation, and Prima Paint sought a court order enjoining F & C from proceeding with arbitration.[92] F & C cross-moved to stay Prima Paint's suit pending arbitration.[93] The trial court granted F & C's motion to stay litigation, and the Second Circuit dismissed Prima Paint's appeal.[94] The Supreme Court affirmed.

---

84 Doctor's Assocs., Inc. v. Casarotto, 517 U.S. 681, 687 (1996).

85 388 U.S. 395 (1967).

86 Id. at 397.

87 Id.

88 Id. at 398.

89 Id.

90 Id.

91 Id.

92 Id. at 398–99.

93 Id. at 399.

94 Id.

Although the Court ruled against Prima Paint, the Court did not address Prima Paint's argument that F & C fraudulently induced Prima Paint to sign the consulting agreement. In fact, the Court held that no court should address this argument because it should instead be addressed by the arbitrator.

The Court said that its result is compelled by FAA § 4, which provides that if

> [a] party [claims to be] aggrieved by the alleged failure * * * of another to arbitrate * * * [t]he court shall hear the parties, and upon being satisfied that the making of the agreement for arbitration or the failure to comply therewith is not in issue, the court shall make an order directing the parties to proceed to arbitration * * *. If the making of the arbitration agreement or the failure, neglect, or refusal to perform the same be in issue, the court shall proceed summarily to the trial thereof.[95]

More simply, § 4 says that the court shall not order the parties to arbitration if "the making *of the arbitration agreement*" is in issue.[96] If the making of the arbitration agreement *is* in issue, then the court shall proceed to trial on that issue. If the trial determines that the parties made an arbitration agreement, then the court shall order the parties to arbitration. Conversely, if the trial determines that the parties did not make an arbitration agreement then the court shall not order the parties to arbitration. In short, FAA § 4 rests on the basic premise that the parties should be ordered to arbitration if, but only if, they have contracted to be there.

Prima Paint held that there would be no trial to determine whether the parties made an arbitration agreement because Prima Paint alleged fraud in the inducement *of the consulting contract*, not in the inducement *of the arbitration agreement*.[97] The term "arbitration agreement," as used in FAA § 4, refers specifically to the arbitration clause itself, not more broadly to the consulting contract of which the arbitration clause was a part. So, if Prima Paint had argued that there was fraud "directed to the arbitration clause itself,"[98] then the making of the arbitration agreement would have been at issue and Prima Paint would have been entitled to a trial on that issue.[99] But the Supreme Court held that FAA § 4 "does not

---

[95] 9 U.S.C. § 4.

[96] Id. (emphasis added).

[97] Prima Paint, 388 U.S. at 404–06.

[98] 388 U.S. at 402.

[99] See, e.g., Sutton v. David Stanley Chevrolet, Inc., 475 P.3d 847, 852 (Okla. 2020) ("Here, the Suttons specifically challenged the enforceability of the arbitration agreement contained in the purchase agreement's DRC based upon grounds that exist

permit the federal court to consider claims of fraud in the inducement of the contract generally."[100]

This holding is known as the separability doctrine because it treats the arbitration clause as if it is a separate contract from the contract containing the arbitration clause. The *Prima Paint* Court held that:

> arbitration clauses as a matter of federal law are "separable" from the contracts in which they are embedded, and that where no claim is made that fraud was directed to the arbitration clause itself, a broad arbitration clause will be held to encompass arbitration of the claim that the contract itself was induced by fraud.[101]

While the separability doctrine has its critics,[102] its practical benefits can be appreciated by considering what would happen without it. Without the separability doctrine, if Prima Paint alleges fraudulent inducement of the consulting agreement, then a court would "proceed summarily to the trial thereof."[103] A court would decide whether F & C made a fraudulent misrepresentation. If the court found that F & C did not make a fraudulent misrepresentation, then the court would refer F & C's claim for payment to arbitration. But Prima Paint's defense for its non-payment *is* F & C's misrepresentation, so the court would have already decided the issue of the case it was sending to arbitration, thus defeating the usual point of agreeing to arbitrate, which is resolving disputes in arbitration rather than litigation.

As this example suggests, in the absence of the separability doctrine, courts deciding whether to send disputes to arbitration often would, as in this example, become entangled with the merits of the dispute. If the court sent a dispute to arbitration after effectively

---

at law or in equity for the revocation of a contract, i.e., fraudulent inducement. This specific challenge as to the enforceability of the arbitration agreement itself, places the matter correctly in the district court."); id. at 858 ("we hold, under a theory of constructive fraud, the order of the trial court overruling the motion to compel arbitration, which was based upon her oral findings of fraudulent inducement, finds full support in the evidence."); Engalla v. Permanente Medical Group, Inc., 938 P.2d 903 (Cal. 1997).

100 Prima Paint, 388 U.S. at 404.

101 Id.

102 Stephen J. Ware, The Centrist Case Against Current (Conservative) Arbitration Law, 68 Fla. L. Rev. 1227, 1234–48 (2016); id. at 1241 ("the separability doctrine deprives the right to litigate of the protection offered by contract law's defenses and thus enforces agreements (manifestations of assent) to alienate that right under circumstances that deprive the agreements of their normal moral significance and thus should also deprive the agreements of their legal significance. This, at bottom, is why the separability doctrine should be repealed.")

103 9 U.S.C. § 4.

ruling on the merits, the arbitrator would have two choices. The arbitrator could reconsider the merits *de novo*, which would require the parties to adjudicate the merits twice and create the possibility of inconsistent results.[104] Or the arbitrator could rubber-stamp the court's view of the merits, which would make the arbitration agreement effectively unenforceable because the parties would get a court's, rather than an arbitrator's, decision on the merits.

(b) The Separability Doctrine Preempts State Law

Prima Paint's adoption of the separability doctrine occurred in 1967, but for the following four decades some courts did not apply it.[105] To some extent, this was due to belief that *state* courts were free to depart from the separability doctrine.[106] This belief followed from the fact that *Prima Paint*'s reasoning rested on FAA §§ 3 and 4, which by their terms apply only in federal court.[107]

However, the Supreme Court's 2006 decision in *Buckeye Check Cashing, Inc. v. Cardegna*,[108] held that the separability doctrine applies in state court and preempts any inconsistent state law.[109] *Buckeye* said that, "[a]lthough § 4, in particular, had much to do with

---

[104] See Ian R. Macneil, Richard E. Speidel & Thomas J. Stipanowich, Federal Arbitration Law § 15.3.5.1 (1994 & Supp.1999) (discussing Rush v. Oppenheimer & Co., 681 F. Supp.1045 (S.D.N.Y. 1988), in which a broker allegedly told Rush, a customer, that "there was no need to read [the documents], that they were just a formality and that they were just like the documents at Drexel."

> The court treated this allegation as an attack on the arbitration clause in particular, but upheld the clause on its merits. In doing so it made several findings of facts pertaining to Rush's not being misled. Is the arbitrator bound by those findings of fact when Rush attacks the entire agreement for misrepresentation before the arbitrator?
>
> There is much to be said for giving no preclusive effect to the court's determinations when the substantive dispute goes on to arbitration. In other words, the arbitrator should decide de novo whether the defect in the underlying contract exists.

Macneil et al., § 15.3.5.1.

[105] There were "a wide range of cases where *Prima Paint* issues were in fact present, but where the courts * * * refused to apply them or simply ignored their presence." Ian R. Macneil, Richard E. Speidel & Thomas J. Stipanowich, Federal Arbitration Law § 15.3.2, at 15:28 (1994).

[106] See, e.g., Atcas v. Credit Clearing Corp. of Am., 197 N.W.2d 448 (Minn.1972) (recognizing Prima Paint but declining to the adopt the separability doctrine); Marks v. Bean, 57 S.W.3d 303 (Ky. App. 2001) (same); City of Blaine v. John Coleman Hayes & Associates, Inc., 818 S.W.2d 33, 37–38 (Tenn. Ct. App. 1991) (same). None of these cases continues to be good law. The Wyoming Supreme Court thought "the 'separability doctrine' espoused by *Prima Paint* ha[d] been modified by subsequent United States Supreme Court rulings." Fox v. Tanner, 101 P.3d 939, 943 (Wyo. 2004) (citing First Options of Chicago, Inc. v. Kaplan, 514 U.S. 938 (1995), Doctor's Associates, Inc. v. Casarotto, 517 U.S. 681 (1996), Howsam v. Dean Witter Reynolds, Inc., 537 U.S. 79 (2002)).

[107] See § 11.

[108] 546 U.S. 440 (2006).

[109] Id. at 445–47.

Prima Paint's understanding of the rule of severability, this rule ultimately arises out of § 2, the FAA's substantive command that arbitration agreements be treated like all other contracts."[110] As FAA § 2 applies in state court,[111] *Buckeye* held "that, regardless of whether the challenge is brought in federal or state court, a challenge to the validity of the contract as a whole, and not specifically to the arbitration clause, must go to the arbitrator."[112] In short, *Buckeye* holds that state courts must apply the separability doctrine or "*Prima Paint*'s rule of severability" as *Buckeye* called it.[113]

While *Buckeye* held that the separability doctrine "ultimately arises out of [FAA] § 2," *Buckeye* did not explain this as thoroughly as a much earlier Second Circuit opinion, *Robert H. Lawrence Co. v. Devonshire Fabrics, Inc.*:[114]

> That the Arbitration Act envisages a distinction between the entire contract between the parties on the one hand and the arbitration clause of the contract on the other is plain on the face of the statute. Section 2 does not purport to affect the contract as a whole. On the contrary, it makes "valid, irrevocable, and enforceable" only a "written provision in any maritime transaction or a contract evidencing a transaction involving commerce to settle by arbitration a controversy thereafter arising out of such contract or transaction."
>
> * * *
>
> The agreement described in Section 2 is the arbitration "provision" or clause of the principal contract. If this arbitration clause was induced by fraud, there can be no arbitration; and if the party charging this fraud shows there is substance to his charge, there must be a judicial trial of that question before a stay [of litigation] can issue * * *. It is not enough [that] there is substance to the charge that the contract to deliver merchandise of a certain quality was induced by fraud.[115]

The Supreme Court used similar reasoning in a post-*Buckeye* case, *Rent-A-Center, West, Inc. v. Jackson*,[116] which said:

---

110 Id. at 445.

111 See § 7.

112 Id. at 449.

113 Id. at 447.

114 271 F.2d 402 (2d Cir. 1959).

115 Id. at 409–11.

116 561 U.S. 63 (2010).

> [FAA] § 2 states that a "written provision" "to settle by arbitration a controversy" is "valid, irrevocable, and enforceable" *without mention* of the validity of the contract in which it is contained. Thus, a party's challenge to another provision of the contract, or to the contract as a whole, does not prevent a court from enforcing a specific agreement to arbitrate.[117]

In sum, the Supreme Court has reaffirmed the separability doctrine adopted in *Prima Paint* but has shifted the doctrine's foundation from FAA § 4 to FAA § 2.[118] As § 2 applies in state court, the separability doctrine applies in state, as well as federal, court and thus preempts inconsistent state law.[119]

§ 22 Separability Applies to Defenses (Validity), Not Formation

While fraud was the basis of the challenge to the arbitration agreement in the Supreme Court case adopting the separability doctrine, *Prima Paint,* illegality was the basis of the challenge in *Buckeye Check Cashing, Inc. v. Cardegna.*[120] The contract containing the arbitration clause in *Buckeye* was a payday loan's "Deferred Deposit and Disclosure Agreement," pursuant to which Buckeye provided Cardegna with cash in exchange for a personal check in the amount of the cash plus a finance charge.[121] Cardegna sued, "alleging that Buckeye charged usurious interest rates and that the Agreement violated various Florida lending and consumer-protection laws, rendering it criminal on its face."[122] The Florida Supreme Court in *Buckeye* distinguished *Prima Paint* on the ground that

> in *Prima Paint,* the claim of fraud in the inducement, if true, would have rendered the underlying contract merely voidable. In [*Buckeye*], however, the underlying contract at issue would be rendered void from the outset if it were determined that the contract indeed violated Florida's usury laws. Therefore, if the underlying contract is held

---

117 Id. at 2778.

118 Id. at 1209.

119 This preemption applies both to the question of whether an arbitrator or court will resolve an issue and to the question of whether an arbitrator or administrative agency will resolve an issue. Preston v. Ferrer, 552 U.S. 346, 349–50 (2008) ("Does the FAA override not only state statutes that refer certain state-law controversies initially to a judicial forum, but also state statutes that refer certain disputes initially to an administrative agency? We hold today that, when parties agree to arbitrate all questions arising under a contract, state laws lodging primary jurisdiction in another forum, whether judicial or administrative, are superseded by the FAA.")

120 546 U.S. 440 (2006). See § 21.

121 Buckeye, 546 U.S. at 442.

122 Id.

> entirely void as a matter of law, all of its provisions, including the arbitration clause, would be nullified as well.[123]

The Florida Supreme Court was not alone in making this distinction; several other courts had also applied the separability doctrine to voidable-contract arguments but not to void-contract arguments.[124] However, the United States Supreme Court's decision in *Buckeye* ruled that the separability doctrine applies to void-contract arguments as well as to voidable-contract arguments.[125] Either sort of defense to the enforceability (validity) of a contract containing an arbitration clause should be sent to arbitration upon request of a party.

In contrast, *Buckeye* did not hold that courts should send to arbitration parties who argue they did not form a contract containing an arbitration clause. *Buckeye* said:

> The issue of the contract's validity is different from the issue of whether any agreement between the alleged obligor and obligee was ever concluded. Our opinion today addresses only the former, and does not speak to the issue decided in the cases cited by respondents (and by the Florida Supreme Court), which hold that it is for courts to decide whether the alleged obligor ever signed the contract, *Chastain v. Robinson-Humphrey Co.*, 957 F.2d 851 (C.A.11 1992), whether the signor lacked authority to commit the alleged principal, *Sandvik AB v. Advent Int'l Corp.*, 220 F.3d 99 (C.A.3 2000); *Sphere Drake Ins. Ltd. v. All American*

---

123 Cardegna v. Buckeye Check Cashing, Inc., 894 So.2d 860, 863 (Fla.2005).

124 Jolley v. Welch, 904 F.2d 988 (5th Cir. 1990); Three Valleys Mun. Water Dist. v. E.F. Hutton & Co., 925 F.2d 1136, 1140–41 (9th Cir. 1991); Rainbow Investments, Inc. v. Super 8 Motels, Inc., 973 F. Supp. 1387, 1390–91 (M.D. Ala. 1997); Allstar Homes, Inc. v. Waters, 711 So.2d 924, 927 (Ala. 1997).

125 Buckeye Check Cashing, Inc. v. Cardegna, 546 U.S. 440 (2006). Respondents argue,

> the only arbitration agreements to which § 2 applies are those involving a "contract," and since an agreement void ab initio under state law is not a "contract," there is no "written provision" in or "controversy arising out of" a "contract," to which § 2 can apply. * * * We do not read "contract" so narrowly. The word appears four times in § 2. Its last appearance is in the final clause, which allows a challenge to an arbitration provision "upon such grounds as exist at law or in equity for the revocation of any contract." (Emphasis added.) There can be no doubt that "contract" as used this last time must include contracts that later prove to be void. Otherwise, the grounds for revocation would be limited to those that rendered a contract voidable—which would mean (implausibly) that an arbitration agreement could be challenged as voidable but not as void. Because the sentence's final use of "contract" so obviously includes putative contracts, we will not read the same word earlier in the same sentence to have a more narrow meaning.

Id. at 447–48.

Ins. Co., 256 F.3d 587 (C.A.7 2001), and whether the signor lacked the mental capacity to assent, *Spahr v. Secco*, 330 F.3d 1266 (C.A.10 2003).[126]

Thus, *Buckeye* does not preclude courts from hearing arguments about whether any arbitration agreement between the alleged obligor and obligee was ever "concluded," that is, formed.[127] As the Restatement explains, the rationale for the separability doctrine is that "[a] finding that the underlying contract is invalid or subject to some other defense that renders it unenforceable * * * does not ordinarily call into question the validity of the arbitration agreement." In contrast, "[w]hen the existence of the underlying contract is challenged, that challenge implicates both the underlying contract and the arbitration agreement."[128]

Similarly, other Supreme Court cases suggest that courts rather than arbitrators decide whether parties formed a contract containing an arbitration agreement. For instance, in *First Options of Chicago, Inc. v. Kaplan*,[129] Kaplan contended that he never formed an arbitration agreement with First Options, although he conceded that his wholly-owned company, MKI, had done so.[130] The arbitrators decided that they had the power to rule on whether Kaplan had formed an arbitration agreement with First Options and ruled that he had.[131] Kaplan sought to have the arbitration award vacated,[132] and the Supreme Court ruled for Kaplan, affirming the Third Circuit's holding that Kaplan did not form an arbitration agreement with First Options.[133] In so doing, the Court ruled that the Third Circuit correctly reviewed the arbitrators' contrary decision "independently" (de novo), rather than under the deferential standard of review FAA § 10 requires courts to use when reviewing an arbitrator's decisions on matters properly before the arbitrator.[134] Thus, *First Options* supports the proposition that courts, not

---

[126] 546 U.S. at 444 n.1.

[127] See also Rent-A-Ctr. W., Inc. v. Jackson, 561 U.S. 63, 71 n.2 (2010) ("The issue of the agreement's 'validity' is different from the issue whether any agreement between the parties 'was ever concluded,' and, as in [Buckeye], we address only the former.")

[128] Restatement (Third) U.S. Law of Int'l Comm. Arb. § 2.7 cmt. b (2019).

[129] 514 U.S. 938, 944 (1995).

[130] Id. at 941.

[131] Id.

[132] Id.

[133] Id. at 947 ("We conclude that, because the Kaplans did not clearly agree to submit the question of arbitrability to arbitration, the Court of Appeals was correct in finding that the arbitrability of the Kaplan/First Options dispute was subject to independent review by the courts.")

[134] Id. at 943. See §§ 39–41 (discussing FAA § 10).

arbitrators, decide whether a party has formed an arbitration agreement.

Moreover, a 2002 Supreme Court case, *Howsam v. Dean Witter Reynolds, Inc.*,[135] cites *First Options* for the proposition that "a gateway dispute about whether the parties are bound by a given arbitration clause raises a 'question of arbitrability' for a court [rather than an arbitrator] to decide."[136] And in a 2010 labor arbitration case, *Granite Rock Co. v. Int'l Bhd. of Teamsters*, the Supreme Court cited *First Options* and *Buckeye* for the proposition that it is "well settled that where the dispute at issue concerns contract formation, the dispute is generally for courts to decide."[137]

In sum, the separability doctrine does not apply to the question whether a particular party formed an arbitration agreement,[138] but does apply to questions about the validity of that agreement, that is, defenses to the enforcement of that agreement.[139] Following this distinction sends to courts questions about mutual assent,[140] including an agent's authority to assent on behalf of others,[141]

---

135 537 U.S. 79 (2002).

136 Id. at 84.

137 Granite Rock Co. v. Int'l Bhd. Of Teamsters, 561 U.S. 287, 296 (2010). *Granite Rock* involved the question "when (not whether) the [collective bargaining agreement] that contains the parties' arbitration clause was ratified and thereby formed." Id. at 297.

138 Id. at 298–300 ("courts should order arbitration of a dispute only where the court is satisfied that neither the formation of the parties' arbitration agreement nor (absent a valid provision specifically committing such disputes to an arbitrator) its enforceability or applicability to the dispute is in issue.")

139 Clayton v. Davidson Contractors, LLC, No. 071016, 2015 WL 1880973, at *7 (Tenn.Ct.App.2015) ("When read together, Prima Paint, Buckeye, Rent-A-Center, and Granite Rock stand for the proposition that the court resolves two types of issues relating to an agreement to arbitrate: (1) a challenge to the validity of the specific arbitration clause sought to be enforced; and (2) a challenge to the formation of a contract, which may include an agreement to arbitrate.")

140 See the many cases in § 18 in which courts rather than arbitrators resolve issues of assent to arbitration agreements. See also Bowles v. OneMain Fin. Grp., L.L.C., 954 F.3d 722, 726–27 (5th Cir. 2020) (affirming district court order finding mutual assent ("meeting of the minds between Bowles and OneMain necessary for contract formation") and sending to arbitration "procedural unconscionability challenge [that] went to whether the Arbitration Agreement should be enforced rather than to whether an agreement had been formed between the parties.")

141 Sandvik AB v. Advent Int'l Corp., 220 F.3d 99, 107 (3d Cir. 2000) ("the District Court was correct in determining that it must decide whether Huep's signature bound Advent before it could order arbitration."); Sphere Drake Ins. Ltd. v. All American Ins. Co., 256 F.3d 587, 591 (7th Cir. 2001) (court decides whether agent had authority to bind the principal to arbitration agreement unless parties agreed to send that question to arbitration); Midwest Mem'l Grp., LLC v. Singer, No. 301861, 2012 WL 470203, at *5 Mich. Ct. App. Feb. 14, 2012) (trial court had the power to decide * * * Smart signed [arbitration agreements] in an individual capacity and did not have the power to bind plaintiffs to the agreements.); Global Travel Mktg., Inc. v. Shea, 908 So.2d 392 (Fla. 2005) (parent had authority to bind minor to arbitration clause); Hojnowski v. Vans Skate Park, 901 A.2d 381 (N.J. 2006) (same); Cross v. Carnes, 724 N.E.2d 828 (Ohio App. 1998) (court holds that parent had authority to bind minor to arbitration clause,

consideration,[142] and perhaps capacity to contract,[143] while sending to arbitrators questions about misrepresentation (fraud in the inducement),[144] mistake,[145] duress,[146] undue influence,[147]

---

and sends to arbitrators the question of whether parent had authority to bind minor to the rest of the container contract).

142 See the many cases in § 19 in which courts rather than arbitrators resolve issues of consideration for arbitration agreements.

143 Most courts have decided capacity arguments rather than send them to arbitrators. Compare, e.g., Spahr v. Secco, 330 F.3d 1266, 1273 (10th Cir. 2003) (court decides defense of mental incapacity); In re Morgan Stanley & Co., Inc., 293 S.W.3d 182, 190 (Tex. 2009) ("Prima Paint reserves to the court issues like the one here, that the signor lacked the mental capacity to assent. Accordingly, the trial court did not abuse its discretion in declining to yield the question to the arbitrator."); Mayorga v. Ronaldo, 491 F. Supp. 3d 840 (D. Nev. 2020), appeal dismissed, No. 20-17148, 2021 WL 296046 (9th Cir. Jan. 15, 2021) (mental incapacity defense decided by court; finding Spahr "well reasoned and persuasive"); Burgoon v. Narconon of N. California, 125 F. Supp. 3d 974, 983 (N.D. Cal. 2015) ("both mental incapacity and undue influence are issues concerning contract formation. It is thus the Court's duty, and not the arbitrator's, to assess Plaintiffs' assertions of mental incapacity and undue influence."); In re StockX Customer Data Sec. Breach Litig., 19 F.4th 873, 887 (6th Cir. 2021) (Moore, J., dissenting) ("In an unpublished decision, this court has treated a mental-capacity challenge as a challenge based on a contract's formation and, thus, one that should be decided by a court.") (citing Rowan v. Brookdale Senior Living Cmtys., Inc., 647 F. App'x 607, 609–10 (6th Cir. 2016)); Amirmotazedi v. Viacom, Inc., 768 F. Supp. 2d 256 (D.D.C. 2011) (court decides mental capacity defense that went to the formation of the arbitration agreement), with Primerica Life Ins. Co. v. Brown, 304 F.3d 469, 472–73 (5th Cir. 2002) (arbitrator decides defense of mental incapacity).

144 Prima Paint, 388 U.S. 395 (1967).

145 Masco Corp. v. Zurich American Ins. Co., 382 F.3d 624, 629–30 (6th Cir. 2004); Unionmutual Stock Life Ins. Co. of Am. v. Beneficial Life Ins. Co., 774 F.2d 524, 528–29 (1st Cir. 1985).

146 SBRMCOA, LLC v. Bayside Resort, Inc., 707 F.3d 267, 274 (3d Cir. 2013) (under *Buckeye*, "the Condominium Association's coercion claim is arbitrable because it is a challenge to the validity (rather than the formation) of the" contract containing the arbitration clause); Service Corp. Intern. v. Lopez, 162 S.W.3d 801, 810 (Tex. App. 2005) ("duress * * * issue relates to the contract as a whole and not solely the arbitration provision. It is therefore an issue to be decided in arbitration"); In re FirstMerit Bank, N.A., 52 S.W.3d 749, 756 (Tex. 2001) ("The defenses of unconscionability, duress, fraudulent inducement, and revocation * * * must specifically relate to the Arbitration Addendum itself, not the contract as a whole, if they are to defeat arbitration. Defenses that pertain to the entire installment contract can be arbitrated."); Farnsworth v. Towboat Nantucket Sound, Inc., 790 F.3d 90, 98 (1st Cir. 2015) ("Under the Prima Paint line of cases, party must claim that the arbitration clause itself is invalid in order to obtain court resolution of the duress issue.") But see Flannery v. Tri-State Div., 402 F. Supp.2d 819, 825 (E.D. Mich. 2005) ("plaintiff's claim of duress challenges the existence of the contract itself, and therefore relates to all the clauses and provisions in it, including the arbitration clause. The argument that the arbitration clause is invalid and unenforceable, therefore, is not barred by the rule in *Prima Paint*.")

147 Compare Merrill Lynch, Pierce, Fenner & Smith, Inc. v. Haydu, 637 F.2d 391 (5th Cir. 1981) (duress and undue influence); Stone v. Mid Am. Bank & Tr. Co., 2:18-CV-87-RMP, 2018 WL 4701843, at 4 (E.D. Wash. Aug. 31, 2018) ("The undue influence argument references Plaintiff's inability to review the terms of the agreement prior to signing, and the coercive nature of sitting in a doctor's office when she signed the contract. This argument relates not to the arbitration provision specifically, but to the entire contract" and thus should be decided by the arbitrator rather than the court), with Burgoon v. Narconon of N. California, 125 F. Supp. 3d 974, 983 (N.D. Cal. 2015)

unconscionability,[148] impracticability,[149] frustration of purpose,[150] the statute of limitations,[151] and illegality.[152] To reiterate, these latter issues are sent to the arbitrator if they are challenges to the contract as a whole. In contrast, if they are challenges "directed to the arbitration clause itself,"[153] then they are presumptively heard by courts.

§ 23 Delegation Clauses

The previous section explains that the separability doctrine sends to arbitrators defenses to enforcement of the contract

---

(the issue of undue influence concerns contract formation, so it is the court's duty to decide such an issue when considering whether to compel arbitration).

148 Substantive unconscionability of contract terms other than the arbitration clause is an issue for the arbitrator, Bob Schultz Motors, Inc. v. Kawasaki Motors Corp., U.S.A., 334 F.3d 721 (8th Cir. 2003), while substantive unconscionability of the arbitration clause is generally an issue for the court. Biller v. S-H OpCo Greenwich Bay Manor, LLC, 961 F.3d 502, 516 (1st Cir. 2020) (whether "arbitration agreement was unconscionable" is "for the courts to resolve, because under the FAA, an arbitration agreement may still 'be invalidated by 'generally applicable contract defenses, such as fraud, duress, or unconscionability.' Where a party challenges the validity of an arbitration agreement specifically, absent a clear intent to commit the dispute to the arbitrator, the court has to resolve that dispute"); Banc One Acceptance Corp. v. Hill, 367 F.3d 426 (5th Cir. 2004). For a discussion of unconscionability, see § 24.

149 Simplicity Int'l v. Genlabs Corp., No. CV 09-6146 SVW (RCX), 2010 WL 11507526, at *6 n.6 (C.D. Cal. May 6, 2010) ("To the extent that the Plaintiff is arguing instead that a valid contract was formed, but Plaintiff's performance became excused by the denial of credit—i.e., that the acceptance of credit was a basic assumption upon which the contract was made and the non-occurrence of that event excused Plaintiff's performance—the issue is one of enforceability of the contract, which would be decided by the arbitrator. See Buckeye Check Cashing, Inc., 546 U.S. at 446; Restatement (Second) Contracts § 261 (discharge of performance by impracticability). This does not appear to be Plaintiff's argument; however, even if it were, arbitration would be the proper forum to resolve that issue.")

150 Unionmutual Stock Life Ins. Co. of Am. v. Beneficial Life Ins. Co., 774 F.2d 524, 528–29 (1st Cir. 1985) ("[T]he arbitration clause is separable from the contract and is not rescinded by * * * [defendant]'s attempt to rescind the entire contract based on * * * frustration of purpose."); Commonwealth Edison Co. v. Gulf Oil Corp., 541 F.2d 1263, 1271 (7th Cir. 1976).

151 Allianz Glob. Risk U.S. Ins. Co. v. Gen. Elec. Co., 470 F. App'x 652, 654 (9th Cir. 2012) (citing Rent-A-Center, 561 U.S. 63 (2010), for the proposition that "The parties' remaining contentions regarding the statute of limitations, which go to the enforceability of the contract as a whole, are for the arbitrator to decide"). See also O'Keefe Architects, Inc. v. CED Construction Partners, Ltd., No. SC05-1417, 2006 WL 2971783 (Fla. Oct.19, 2006).

152 Buckeye, 546 U.S. 440 (2006). See Nitro-Lift Technologies, L.L.C. v. Howard, 568 U.S. 17, 20 (2012) (whether employee's non-competition agreement is void as against public policy to be determined by arbitrator rather than court; "attacks on the validity of the contract, as distinct from attacks on the validity of the arbitration clause itself, are to be resolved by the arbitrator in the first instance, not by a federal or state court.")

153 Prima Paint, 388 U.S. at 402. Accord Buckeye, 546 U.S. at 449 ("a challenge to the validity of the contract as a whole, and not specifically to the arbitration clause, must go to the arbitrator.")

containing the arbitration clause, but not defenses directed to the arbitration clause itself. However, even defenses directed to the arbitration clause itself are sent to arbitrators if the parties have agreed to that. This was the case in *Rent-A-Center, West, Inc. v. Jackson*,[154] in which the Supreme Court enforced an arbitration agreement clause that said:

> [t]he Arbitrator, and not any federal, state, or local court or agency, shall have exclusive authority to resolve any dispute relating to the interpretation, applicability, enforceability or formation of this Agreement including, but not limited to any claim that all or any part of this Agreement is void or voidable.[155]

In *Rent-A-Center*, Jackson argued that the arbitration agreement was unconscionable, so he should be free to litigate rather than arbitrate his claims against Rent-A-Center.[156] The Supreme Court rejected Jackson's argument on the ground that the just-quoted "delegation" clause constituted his agreement to arbitrate the question of whether his arbitration agreement was unconscionable.[157] By contrast, had Jackson argued that the delegation clause itself was unconscionable then that argument would, the Supreme Court suggested, be heard by a court, rather than sent to arbitration.[158]

In other words, the Court treated the delegation clause as separable from the broader arbitration clause in much the same way the separability doctrine treats an arbitration clause as separable

---

154 561 U.S. 63 (2010). Id. at 65 ("the Mutual Agreement to Arbitrate Claims (Agreement), which Jackson signed on February 24, 2003, as a condition of his employment there").

155 Id. at 2775.

156 Id.

157 Id. at 2777–79.

158 "[U]nless Jackson challenged the delegation provision specifically, we must treat it as valid under § 2, and must enforce it under §§ 3 and 4, leaving any challenge to the validity of the Agreement as a whole for the arbitrator." Id. at 2779. Since *Rent-A-Center*, some parties have successfully challenged delegation clauses. See, e.g., MacDonald v. CashCall, Inc, 883 F.3d 220, 227–28 (3d Cir. 2018) ("Here, unlike in *Rent-A-Center*, MacDonald specifically challenged the delegation clause."); id. ("we conclude that the arbitral forum provided for in the Loan Agreement is nonexistent. As a result, and as explained herein, there is no arbitration forum in which an arbitrator could evaluate whether the arbitration provision is enforceable."); Citizens of Humanity, LLC v. Applied Underwriters Captive Risk Assurance Co., Inc., 909 N.W.2d 614 (2018) (finding that manufacturer specifically challenged validity of delegation clause, rather than entire arbitration clause, of reinsurance participation agreement as contrary to state law; and reinsurance participation agreement was subject to the McCarran-Ferguson Act's "reverse preemption" of FAA so state anti-arbitration statute rendered arbitration provision invalid.)

from the still-broader contract containing it.[159] So, much as the separability doctrine does not prevent courts from hearing contract-defenses to the arbitration clause itself, delegation clauses do not prevent courts from hearing contract-defenses to the delegation clause itself. And occasionally courts find defenses to enforcement of delegation clauses.[160] But perhaps more typical are cases denying challenges to the enforceability of delegation clauses. For example, an Eleventh Circuit decision noted that

> Because the Wells Fargo Agreement delegates issues of interpretation, scope, and enforceability to the arbitrator, we only retain jurisdiction over challenges directed specifically at that delegation. * * * Plaintiffs do not identify any specific defect in the delegation clause and instead argue only that it is unconscionable "for the same reasons" as the contract more generally. Without Plaintiffs pointing to any specific deficiencies in the delegation clause, we find no reason to deem it unconscionable. Plaintiffs may take up their challenges to the contract as a whole with the arbitrator.[161]

---

[159] Jack M. Graves & Yelena Davydan, Competence-Competence and Separability-American Style in International Arbitration and International Commercial Law: Synergy, Convergence and Evolution 165 (2011). See also David Horton, The Federal Arbitration Act and Testamentary Instruments, 90 N.C. L. Rev. 1027, 1058 n.181 (2012). ("[T]he Court conceptualized the delegation clause as an independent arbitration clause ('an agreement to arbitrate threshold issues concerning the arbitration agreement') within a broader contract to arbitrate (the Mutual Agreement to Arbitrate Claims).")

For cases applying *Rent-A-Center*, see, e.g., Momot v. Mastro, 652 F.3d 982, 988 (9th Cir. 2011) (finding that language in arbitration agreement providing that parties agree to arbitrate any dispute that " 'arises out of or relates to . . . the validity or application of any of the provisions of this Section 4' . . . constitutes 'an agreement to arbitrate threshold issues concerning the arbitration agreement' " under *Rent-A-Center*); Hawkins v. Region's, 944 F. Supp. 2d 528, 530 (N.D. Miss. 2013) ("While the holding in *Jackson* leaves a number of unanswered questions, it appears to place a heavy burden on plaintiffs to make challenges which are tailored specifically to arbitration *delegation* clauses within contracts, rather than to the contract as a whole or even to arbitration clauses within those contracts. * * * The court recognizes that the Supreme Court's decision in Jackson might be regarded by some as creating a legal "black hole" which inevitably sucks in disputes and sends them to arbitration (at least in cases involving a delegation clause).")

[160] See Citizens of Humanity, LLC v. Applied Underwriters Captive Risk Assurance Co., Inc., 909 N.W.2d 614 (2018) ((finding that manufacturer specifically challenged validity of delegation clause, rather than entire arbitration clause, of reinsurance participation agreement as contrary to state law; and reinsurance participation agreement was subject to the McCarran-Ferguson Act's "reverse preemption" of FAA so the state anti-arbitration statute rendered the arbitration provision invalid.) See also MacDonald v. CashCall, Inc, 883 F.3d 220, 227–28 (3d Cir. 2018) ("Because the arbitration procedure described in the agreement is fabricated and illusory, any provision requiring that the enforceability of the arbitration procedure must be decided through arbitration is also illusory and unenforceable.").

[161] In re Checking Acct. Overdraft Litig., 856 F. App'x 238, 245 (11th Cir. 2021). See also In re StockX Customer Data Sec. Breach Litig., 19 F.4th 873, 886 (6th Cir.

As this passage suggests, challenging delegation clauses is difficult. However, delegation clauses do not prevent courts from hearing arguments that the alleged contract containing the delegation clause was not formed.[162]

While the delegation clause in *Rent-A-Center* was written into the contract Jackson signed, more common are delegation clauses incorporated by reference into the contract parties sign.[163] That is because many such contracts provide for arbitration under the rules of an arbitration organization whose rules include broad delegations to the arbitrator. For example, American Arbitration Association Commercial Arbitration Rule R-7 says, "The arbitrator shall have the power to rule on his or her own jurisiction including any objections with respect to the existence, scope, or validity of the arbitration agreement or to the arbitrability of any claim or counterclaim." Several courts have held that agreements incorporating such rules

2021) ("An arbitrator must also decide plaintiffs' argument that the arbitration agreement and delegation provision are procedurally and substantively unconscionable. In particular, plaintiffs argue the arbitration agreement is procedurally unconscionable because: the contract is a 'contract of adhesion,' 'comprised of boilerplate language, drafted by StockX'; the arbitration opt-out provision contains an 'exacting set of instructions' and is 'illusory'; and the arbitration clause incorporates the AAA rules 'as modified by [the] Agreement to Arbitrate.' But these arguments do not relate specifically to the delegation provision. As in Rent-A-Center, plaintiffs have not explained how any of those provisions 'causes the arbitration of [their] claim that the [Arbitration] Agreement is unenforceable to be unconscionable.' ")

[162] See, e.g., Theroff v. Dollar Tree Stores, Inc., 591 S.W.3d 432, 440 (Mo. 2020), reh'g denied (Jan. 30, 2020), aff'd (Jan. 14, 2020) ("Theroff's challenge to the existence of the mutual agreement in its entirety because of a lack of assent necessarily challenges the existence of any delegation provision it contains. Theroff denied the existence of the agreement to arbitrate * * *, convincing the circuit court the agreement did not exist. It follows that there is not clear and unmistakable evidence of the existence of assent to a delegation provision. Under these facts, the circuit court cannot delegate the matter to an arbitrator whose very existence depends upon an agreement"); Bowles v. OneMain Fin. Grp., L.L.C., 954 F.3d 722, 726 (5th Cir. 2020) (distinguishing mutual assent ("meeting of the minds") challenge "to the formation of the Arbitration Agreement [which is] therefore to be decided by the courts" from a "procedural unconscionability challenge [which] went to whether the Arbitration Agreement should be enforced rather than to whether an agreement had been formed [and thus should under the delegation clause be referred] to the arbitrator for decision."); Dixon v. Daymar Colleges Grp., LLC, 483 S.W.3d 332, 341 (Ky. 2015) ("Rent-A-Center has a limited application: when the validity of a written agreement to arbitrate is in question, i.e., when a party challenges whether an arbitration agreement is legally binding. When a party challenges whether the arbitration agreement—and, by extension, the delegation provision—was in fact agreed to, Rent-A-Center 's analytical approach does not apply"); Subcontracting Concepts (CT), LLC v. De Melo, 245 Cal. Rptr. 3d 838, 849 (Ct. App. 2019) (holding that the worker did not understand the adhesive agreement because he did not speak English, so although the agreement referenced the AAA rules for arbitration—it did not effectively incorporate them).

[163] See § 18(e) (discussing incorporation by reference more generally).

delegate to arbitrators challenges to the validity (enforceability) of the arbitration agreement, such as its unconscionability.[164]

§ 24 Unconscionability and Similar Regulation of Arbitration

(a) Unconscionability, Generally

As the previous sections explain, courts generally send to arbitration challenges to the enforceability of contracts containing arbitration agreements and, if those agreements delegate this to the arbitrator, challenges to the enforceability of the arbitration agreement itself. But some arbitration agreements do not so delegate, or no party makes a delegation argument, so courts sometimes decide whether particular arbitration agreements are enforceable.

A common challenge to enforceability is unconscionability, which is often thought of as coming in two forms: procedural and substantive. Procedural unconscionability relates to the process of contract formation. It encompasses "not only the employment of sharp bargaining practices and the use of fine print and convoluted language, but a lack of understanding and an inequality of bargaining power."[165] So procedural unconscionability is often found in contracts of adhesion—the form contracts businesses draft and present on a take-it-or-leave-it basis to consumers, employees, and others who do not typically read, let alone understand, all the contract terms.[166]

Substantive unconscionability refers to terms that are "unreasonably favorable" to one side.[167] "Most cases of unconscionability involve a combination of procedural and substantive unconscionability, and it is generally agreed that if more

---

164 See, e.g., Edwards v. Doordash, Inc., 888 F.3d 738, 746 (5th Cir. 2018) ("Here, the [contract] contained an agreement to arbitrate, which, through incorporation of the AAA rules, contained an agreement to delegate issues of arbitrability to the arbitrator. Because DoorDash sought to compel arbitration on the basis of that delegation clause, we must treat it as valid absent any specific challenge to the delegation clause by Edwards. Edwards's unconscionability arguments target the [contract] as a whole and the arbitration agreement, but he fails to challenge the delegation clause. Therefore, we treat the delegation clause as valid. Edwards's remaining arguments regarding the validity of the arbitration agreement or the [contract] as a whole should be addressed by the arbitrator."); In re Checking Acct. Overdraft Litig., 856 F. App'x 238, 244 (11th Cir. 2021) (sending to arbitration unconscionability challenge to contract containing arbitration agreement, "The Wells Fargo Agreement explicitly incorporates commercial AAA Rules * * * This alone is sufficient for us to find the requisite clear and unmistakable intent to arbitrate arbitrability.")

165 E. Allan Farnsworth, Contracts, § 4.28, at 301 (4th ed. 2004).

166 See § 18(a) (discussing adhesion contracts).

167 E. Allan Farnsworth, Contracts, § 4.28, at 301 (4th ed. 2004).

of one is present, then less of the other is required to defeat enforcement."[168]

Courts have held unconscionable arbitration clauses that:

- allow the party drafting the clause to pursue its claims in litigation, while requiring the non-drafting party to pursue its claims in arbitration,[169]
- require the non-drafting party to pay a significant portion of fees charged by the arbitrator or arbitration organization,[170]

---

[168] Id. at 302.

[169] Compare, e.g., Pokorny v. Quixtar, Inc., 601 F.3d 987, 1001 (9th Cir. 2010) ("Requiring one party to arbitrate its claims but not the other is a paradigmatic form of substantive unconscionability under California law."); Iberia Credit Bureau, Inc. v. Cingular Wireless LLC, 379 F.3d 159, 168–69 (5th Cir. 2004) (unconscionable); Peavy by Peavy v. Skilled Healthcare Grp., Inc., 2020-NMSC-010, ¶ 2, 470 P.3d 218, 220 (affirming holding that nursing home facility's "Agreement was substantively unconscionable because it forced residents to arbitrate their most likely and most important claims, but allowed the Facility to litigate its most likely claims"); Armendariz v. Foundation Health Psychcare Services, Inc., 99 Cal. Rptr. 2d 745 (Cal.2000) (unconscionable); Iwen v. U.S. West Direct, 977 P.2d 989 (Mont.1999) (unconscionable); Taylor v. Butler, 142 S.W.3d 277 (Tenn.2004) (unconscionable); Caplin Enterprises, Inc. v. Arrington, 145 So. 3d 608, 616 (Miss. 2014) ("the arbitration clause was oppressive because it forced the plaintiffs to arbitrate their claims, while permitting Zippy Check to pursue remedies for the plaintiffs' breach in court"); Dan Ryan Builders, Inc. v. Nelson, 737 S.E.2d 550, 559 (W.Va. 2012) ("In a majority of jurisdictions, it is well-settled that a contract which requires the weaker party to arbitrate any claims he or she may have, but permits the stronger party to seek redress through the courts, may be found to be substantively unconscionable"), with Caley v. Gulfstream Aerospace Corp., 428 F.3d 1359, 1378 (11th Cir. 2005) ("Under the DRP, some claims, many of which would typically be brought by an employee, are subject to arbitration and others, many of which would be brought by Gulfstream, are not. However, this fact does not render the DRP unconscionable"); Oblix, Inc. v. Winiecki, 374 F.3d 488, 491 (7th Cir. 2004) (not unconscionable); Harris v. Green Tree Fin. Corp., 183 F.3d 173 (3d Cir. 1999).

See also § 19 (discussing consideration).

[170] Compare Cal. Civ. Proc. Code § 1284.3 ("All fees and costs charged to or assessed upon a consumer party by a private arbitration company in a consumer arbitration, exclusive of arbitrator fees, shall be waived for an indigent consumer. For the purposes of this section, 'indigent consumer' means a person having a gross monthly income that is less than 300 percent of the federal poverty guidelines."); Lim v. TForce Logistics, LLC, 8 F.4th 992 (9th Cir. 2021) ("substantive unconscionability exists when a fee-shifting clause creates for employees a "greater financial risk in arbitrating claims than they would face if they were to litigate those same claims in federal court", so affirming holding unconscionable "the requirement that Lim pay half of the arbitration fees," as a "type of expense that [Lim] would not be required to bear if he [ ] were free to bring the action in court."); Chavarria v. Ralphs Grocery Co., 733 F.3d 916, 927 (9th Cir. 2013) (arbitration agreement unconscionable because it would require employee pay half of the arbitrator fees, which would range from $7,000 to $14,000 per day); Capili v. Finish Line, Inc., 699 F. App'x 620, 622 (9th Cir. 2017) ("The district court properly determined that the cost-sharing provision was substantively unconscionable. The provision required Capili, a retail employee making $15 per hour, to pay up to $10,000 at the outset of arbitration, not including the fees and costs for legal representation."); Armendariz v. Foundation Health Psychcare Services, Inc., 99 Cal. Rptr. 2d 745 (Cal. 2000) (fees excessive and unconscionable); Brower v. Gateway

- require the non-drafting party to pay its own attorney's fees even when bringing a claim under which successful plaintiffs are entitled to have such fees paid by the defendant,[171]
- severely limit discovery,[172]

2000 Inc., 676 N.Y.S.2d 569, 574 (App. Div. 1998) (same); D.R. Horton, Inc. v. Green, 96 P.3d 1159 (Nev. 2004) (same), Bekele v. Lyft, Inc., 918 F.3d 181, 188 (1st Cir. 2019) (AAA Rules required Bekele and Lyft to split equally the arbitration's costs. Bekele argues that he and other Lyft drivers cannot afford such high fees and that this arrangement is substantively unconscionable. Under the precedent of this court and the Massachusetts Supreme Judicial Court, Lyft's offer before the district court to pay all fees for an arbitration with Bekele sinks this argument"), with Am. Fam. Life Assurance Co. of New York v. Baker, 778 F. App'x 24, 27 (2d Cir. 2019) ("New York courts have rejected the proposition that cost-splitting provisions are per se unconscionable, instead holding that "the issue of a litigant's financial ability is to be resolved on a case-by-case basis." Brady v. Williams Capital Grp., L.P., 14 N.Y.3d 459, 902 N.Y.S.2d 1, 928 N.E.2d 383, 387–88 (2010). Because Appellants have not put forth any evidence of their financial inability to pursue arbitration under the terms of this Agreement, their unconscionability claim predicated on the cost-splitting provision must accordingly fail"); Carbajal v. H & R Block Tax Services, Inc., 372 F.3d 903, 906 (7th Cir. 2004) (arbitration clause in a loan agreement is not rendered unconscionable by its provision requiring parties to bear their own costs of arbitration); Shadeh v. Circuit City Stores, Inc., 334 F. Supp.2d 938 (W.D. Ky. 2004) (Under Kentucky law, agreement to arbitrate employment disputes was not rendered unenforceable by cost-splitting provision, under which employee's exposure for costs was limited to greater of $500 or three percent of annual income); Norwest Fin. Mississippi, Inc. v. McDonald, 905 So.2d 1187, 1196 (Miss. 2005); Leeman v. Cook's Pest Control, Inc., 2004 WL 2757414 (Ala. 2004); Lovey v. Regence BlueShield of Idaho, 72 P.3d 877 (Idaho 2003); State ex rel. Wells v. Matish, 600 S.E.2d 583 (W.Va. 2004).

See also § 33(c) (discussing arbitration fees).

171 Quilloin v. Tenet HealthSystem Philadelphia, Inc., 673 F.3d 221, 230–31 (3d Cir. 2012) ("Provisions requiring parties to be responsible for their own expenses, including attorneys' fees, are generally unconscionable because restrictions on attorneys' fees conflict with federal statutes providing fee-shifting as a remedy"); Sec. Serv. Fed. Credit Union v. Sanders, 264 S.W.3d 292, 298–301 (Tex. Ct. App. 2008) (arbitration agreements' attorney-fee provisions unenforceable because in conflict with Texas Deceptive Trade Practices-Consumer Protection Act, but severable from arbitration agreement, and arbitration agreement otherwise enforceable).

172 Compare, e.g., Armendariz v. Foundation Health Psychcare Services, Inc., 99 Cal.Rptr.2d 745 (Cal. 2000); De Leon v. Pinnacle Prop. Mgmt. Servs., LLC, 287 Cal. Rptr. 3d 402, 411–13 (Ct. App. 2021) (discovery provision of arbitration agreement substantively unconscionable because 20 interrogatories and three depositions per side were "insufficient for plaintiff to pursue his 13 causes of action concerning wage and hour claims, whistleblower retaliation, wrongful termination, and FEHA issues."); Ramirez v. Charter Commc'ns, Inc., 290 Cal. Rptr. 3d 429, 446 (Ct. App. 2022) ("limitation on depositions is sufficient to show substantive unconscionability" because "[plaintiff] would be deprived of the opportunity to prepare her case because of her inability to depose three of the minimum seven necessary witnesses."); Ostroff v. Alterra Healthcare Corp., 433 F. Supp. 2d 538, 545 (E.D. Pa. 2006) (allowing plaintiff to depose only defendant's expert witnesses unconscionable), with Hopkins v. World Acceptance Corp., 798 F. Supp. 2d 1339, 1350 (N.D. Ga. 2011) ("[D]iscovery limitations [that are] set forth in the Arbitration Rules of the AAA, and [that] allow for a limited number of depositions based upon mutual agreement of the parties or the arbitrator's determination [are not unconscionable]."); Torrecillas v. Fitness Internat., LLC, 266 Cal. Rptr. 3d 181, 189 (Ct. App. 2020) ("the absence of provisions for requesting documents and admissions is not substantively unconscionable."); Gullett v. Kindred

- severely limit remedies, such as punitive damages,[173]
- shorten limitations periods,[174]
- require the parties (not just the arbitrator) to keep the arbitration confidential,[175]

Nursing Ctrs. W., Ltd. Liab. Co., 241 Ariz. 532, 536–37 (Ct. App 2017) (agreement was not unconscionable because "the amount of discovery [was not] so low [,] and the burden to obtain [additional discovery was not] so high" as to deny the plaintiff's right to vindicate his claim); Sanchez v. Carmax Auto Superstores Cal., LLC, 168 Cal. Rptr. 3d 473, 480 (Ct. App. 2014) (discovery provisions not unconscionable because "[they were] considerably more liberal, [ ] the standard for additional discovery was lower ("substantial" rather than "compelling" need) [and the plaintiff did] not make any showing that he could not maintain his claim without more discovery than that provided by the agreement."); Cockerham v. Sound Ford, Inc., No. C06-1172JLR, 2006 WL 2841881, at *3 (W.D. Wash. Sept. 29, 2006) (declining to find discovery clause that allowed each side to take one deposition and granted discretion as to remaining discovery to arbitrator unconscionable under Washington law); Roman v. Superior Court, 92 Cal. Rptr. 3d 153, 164–65 (Ct. App. 2009) (clause allowing arbitrator to deny depositions not unconscionable).

173 Kristian v. Comcast Corp., 446 F.3d 25, 48 (1st Cir. 2006) (in case involving arbitration of antitrust claims, concluding that arbitration agreement's ban on treble damages was unenforceable, because right to recover treble damages is a substantive right); Booker v. Robert Half Int'l, 413 F.3d 77 (D.C. Cir. 2005); Ingle v. Circuit City Stores, Inc. 328 F.3d 1165 (9th Cir. 2003); Armendariz v. Foundation Health Psychcare Services, Inc., 99 Cal. Rptr. 2d 745 (Cal. 2000); Young Seok Suh v. Superior Court, 105 Cal. Rptr. 3d 585, 595–96 (Ct. App. 2010) (American Health Lawyers Association arbitration rules); State ex rel. Dunlap v. Berger, 567 S.E.2d 265 (W.Va. 2002); Penilla v. Westmont Corp., 207 Cal. Rptr. 3d 473, 488 (Ct.App.2016) (limitation on punitive damages [ ] support[ed] a finding of substantive unconscionability); Lange v. Monster Energy Co., 260 Cal. Rptr. 3d 35, 45 (Ct. App. 2020) ("waiver of punitive damages as a remedy for all nonstatutory claims . . . is substantively unconscionable regardless of its mutuality."); Shotts v. OP Winter Haven, Inc., 86 So. 3d 456, 474 (Fla. 2011) ("the limitations of remedies provisions . . . violate public policy [because] they directly undermine[d] specific statutory remedies created by the Legislature."). Contra Torgerson v. One Lincoln Tower, LLC, 166 Wash. 2d 510, 522 (Wash. 2009) (holding that the "remedies limitations" clause in the purchase and sale agreements of a real estate property was not unconscionable because petitioners had expertise in real estate transactions and the opportunity to provide input into the contracts.)

174 Compare Ingle v. Circuit City Stores, Inc. 328 F.3d 1165 (9th Cir. 2003); Parilla v. IAP Worldwide Services, VI, Inc., 368 F.3d 269 (3d Cir. 2004) (agreement unconscionable because it required that "Employee must present Employee's claim in written form to the Company within thirty (30) calendar days of the event which forms the basis of the claim, unless a different time for presentation of the claim is provided for by the [AAA Rules]."); McKee v. AT & T Corp., 191 P.3d 845, 859 (Wash. 2008) ("Washington Consumer Protection Act provides a four year statute of limitations, but AT & T's agreement cuts that period in half." "We hold AT & T's limitation on actions is substantively unconscionable as against public policy as to Consumer Protection Act claims"); In re Juul Labs, Inc., Antitrust Litig., 555 F. Supp. 3d 932, 955 (N.D. Cal. 2021) (arbitration agreement reducing four-year statute of limitations to one year is substantively unconscionable so court "will sever it, leaving the remaining provisions of the arbitration agreements enforceable"), with Bracey v. Lancaster Foods LLC, 838 F. App'x 745, 749 (4th Cir. 2020) (employment arbitration agreement "shortening the statute of limitations period to one year" not unconscionable).

175 Compare Pokorny v. Quixtar, Inc., 601 F.3d 987, 1001 (9th Cir. 2010) ("Another indicator of substantive unconscionability is the confidentiality requirement"); Larsen v. Citibank FSB, 871 F.3d 1295, 1319 (11th Cir. 2017) ("The obvious informational advantage KeyBank holds at the outset of a dispute may therefore have the effect of

- require the arbitrators to be members of occupations similar to that of the drafting party,[176]
- give the drafting party greater control than the non-drafting party in the selection of the arbitrator,[177]
- give the drafting party the power to unilaterally modify the arbitration clause,[178] and

---

discouraging consumers from pursuing valid claims. We thus conclude that under Washington law, the confidentiality clause here is substantively unconscionable."); Bain v. Airoom, LLC, 2022 WL 169933 6 (Ill. App. Ct. 2022) (confidentiality agreement "contributes to the substantive unconscionability of the contract by ensuring that none of the [defendant's] potential opponents will have access to precedent while, at the same time, [the defendant] accumulates a wealth of knowledge. * * * The confidentiality provision in Airoom's arbitration agreement is also substantively unconscionable."); Ramos v. Superior Ct., 239 Cal. Rptr. 3d 679, 701 (Ct. App. 2018), as modified (Nov. 28, 2018) ("requiring discrimination cases be kept secret unreasonably favors the employer to the detriment of employees seeking to vindicate unwaivable statutory rights and may discourage potential plaintiffs from filing discrimination cases. We therefore conclude the provision requiring all aspects of the arbitration be maintained in strict confidence is substantively unconscionable"); McKee v. AT&T Corp., 191 P.3d 845, 858 (Wash. 2008) ("A confidentiality clause in a contract of adhesion is a one-sided provision designed to disadvantage claimants and may even help conceal consumer fraud. Confidentiality unreasonably favors repeat players such as AT & T."), with Biller v. S-H OpCo Greenwich Bay Manor, LLC, 961 F.3d 502, 519 (1st Cir. 2020) (plaintiffs' "attack on the confidentiality provision can't succeed. They don't address any facts (like the number of residents subject to the agreement) that bear on the strength of [defendant's] repeat-player advantage; they don't argue that the confidentiality provision is broad enough to stymie their evidence-gathering efforts"); Iberia Credit Bureau, Inc. v. Cingular Wireless LLC, 379 F.3d 159, 175 (5th Cir. 2004) ("While the confidentiality requirement is probably more favorable to the cellular provider than to its customer, the plaintiffs have not persuaded us that the requirement is so offensive as to be invalid. Confidentiality can be desirable to customers in some circumstances"); Guyden v. Aetna, Inc., 544 F.3d 376, 385 (2d Cir. 2008) (citing *Iberia* and enforcing confidentiality agreement: "Because confidentiality is a paradigmatic aspect of arbitration, our determination that SOX whistleblower claims are arbitrable precludes Guyden's challenge to the privacy of the resulting arbitration."); Parilla v. IAP Worldwide Services, VI, Inc., 368 F.3d 269 (3d Cir. 2004) (not unconscionable); Vasquez-Lopez v. Beneficial Or., Inc., 575, 152 P.3d 940, 953 (Or. Ct. App. 2007) ("nonconfidential information, while not officially reported, is widely available to plaintiffs' lawyers through informal networks and organizations. Thus, any advantage conferred on repeat players and their counsel is marginal and, we conclude, it is roughly offset by the advantage that privacy about their financial affairs confers on plaintiffs.")

[176] See § 33(a)(3) (discussing judicial and regulatory constraints on arbitrator selection).

[177] See id.

[178] Compare, e.g., Al-Safin v. Circuit City Stores, Inc., 394 F.3d 1254, 1259 (9th Cir. 2005); Circuit City Stores, Inc. v. Mantor, 335 F.3d 1101,1107 (9th Cir. 2003); Ingle v. Circuit City Stores, Inc. 328 F.3d 1165, 1179 (9th Cir. 2003), with Ashbey v. Archstone Prop. Mgmt., Inc., 612 F. App'x 430, 432 (9th Cir. 2015) ("unilateral modification provisions, such as the one in the acknowledgment Ashbey signed, are not substantively unconscionable because they are always subject to the limits imposed by the covenant of good faith and fair dealing implied in every contract."); Iberia Credit Bureau, Inc. v. Cingular Wireless LLC, 379 F.3d 159 (5th Cir. 2004) (change-in-terms provision did not render the clause unconscionable); Martin v. Citibank, Inc., 567 F. Supp.2d 36, 45 (D.D.C.2008) (requirement that employer

- place the location of arbitration far from the non-drafting party.[179]

Some cases decline to enforce arbitration agreements on the basis of procedural unconscionability alone.[180]

(b) The FAA's Constraint on the Scope of the Unconscionability Doctrine

The FAA constrains the grounds on which courts may hold arbitration clauses unconscionable. For example, in the 2011 case of *AT & T Mobility LLC v. Concepcion*, the Supreme Court held that a California case law rule on the unconscionability of arbitration agreements prohibiting class actions was preempted by the FAA.[181] The *AT & T* opinion said "The overarching purpose of the FAA, evident in the text of §§ 2, 3, and 4, is to ensure the enforcement of arbitration agreements according to their terms so as to facilitate streamlined proceedings."[182] The Court's reasoning built on this premise that an important purpose of the FAA was to enforce agreements in which parties choose the more streamlined process

---

provides thirty days' notice of prospective modifications to arbitration agreement "affords employees sufficient protection against inequitable assertions of power").

[179] Compare Domingo v. Ameriquest Mortg. Co., 70 Fed.Appx. 919 (9th Cir. 2003); Newton v. Am. Debt. Serv., Inc., 854 F. Supp. 2d 712, 726 (N.D. Cal. 2012) (finding the arbitration clause unconscionable because it "requires that consumers arbitrate their claims in Tulsa Oklahoma, thus giving Defendants GCS and RMBT at [sic] unfair advantage at the consumer's expense by requiring that the consumer come to GCS's home city to arbitrate her claims."; Bolter v. Superior Court, 104 Cal. Rptr. 2d 888, 894 (Ct.App.2001); Swain v. Auto Services, Inc., 128 S.W.3d 103, 108 (Mo. Ct. App. 2003), with Poublon v. C.H. Robinson Co., 846 F.3d 1251, 1265 (9th Cir. 2017) (enforcing California employee's agreement to arbitrate in Minnesota; "Poublon claims that this venue provision is substantively unconscionable because it requires her to litigate her California claims in Minnesota, a thousand miles away from her home in California. We have previously rejected this argument"); Ramos v. Superior Ct., 239 Cal. Rptr. 3d 679, 702 (Ct. App. 2018), as modified (Nov. 28, 2018) ("Ramos's only complaint is that arbitration in Chicago would be inconvenient and expensive for her and more convenient for Winston. She does not argue her claims could not be resolved in that forum or she would not receive substantial justice. Accordingly, we conclude the provision requiring that the arbitration take place in Chicago, Illinois is not substantively unconscionable").

[180] Stancil ex rel. Gentry v. Dominion Crossville, LLC, No. E202101378COAR3CV, 2022 WL 3010499, at *6 (Tenn. Ct. App. July 29, 2022) ("arbitration provision at issue here was buried within the" nursing home admission contract, "appearing on pages eight and nine of the thirteen-page agreement," "the text and heading of the provision are not distinguished in any way relative to the text and headings utilized in other provisions," the same "is also true of the waiver of jury language, which as it turns out, is not even included in the arbitration provision itself but is instead included in a separate provision that does not cross-reference the arbitration provision. Moreover, the arbitration provision does not explain what arbitration is, state how the arbitration procedures would work, or provide any opt-out option or period for revocation. In order to admit Ms. Gentry to Dominion Crossville, agreeing to the arbitration provision was required.")

[181] 563 U.S. 333 (2011). The AT & T case is discussed in greater detail in § 29.

[182] 563 U.S. 333 (2011).

(arbitration) over the more elaborate process (litigation). The Court suggested that the FAA would preempt (hypothetical) state law deeming unconscionable arbitration agreements lacking "judicially monitored discovery,"[183] "adherence to the Federal Rules of Evidence,"[184] or "arbitration-by-jury"[185] because requiring arbitration to include any of these aspects of litigation would effectively convert the more streamlined process into the more elaborate process, so it would no longer be "arbitration," as that process was understood by those who enacted the FAA.[186] Similarly, the Court held that state law "[r]equiring the availability of classwide arbitration interferes with fundamental attributes of arbitration and thus creates a scheme inconsistent with the FAA."[187]

In 2015, the Court supplemented *AT & T* with *DirecTV v. Imburgia*, which policed state court interpretation of arbitration agreements where the state court at least arguably engaged in an unusual interpretation to try to preserve the very state law held preempted by *AT & T*.[188] As the Restatement summarizes, *Imburgia*

> held preempted a state court's interpretation of the phrase "law of your state" in an arbitration agreement to include "invalid California law." The Court determined "that California courts would not interpret contracts other than arbitration contracts the same way," but "[r]ather . . . that the [California] court's interpretation of this arbitration contract is unique, restricted to that field." As a result, the FAA preempted the state court's interpretation of the arbitration agreement.[189]

Imburgia is then a decision preempting state court contract interpretation that would have discriminated against arbitration and led to application of a state unconscionability rule that the Supreme Court had previously held (in *AT&T*) discriminated against arbitration.

---

183 Id. at 361.

184 Id.

185 Id. at 349 n.7.

186 In fact, arbitration is generally less elaborate than litigation; arbitration agreements commonly provide for less discovery and motion practice than is typical of litigation and commonly provide for fewer rules of evidence than are typical of litigation. See §§ 31–34. The *AT & T* Court said that "[p]arties could agree to arbitrate pursuant to the Federal Rules of Civil Procedure, or pursuant to a discovery process rivaling that in litigation. Arbitration is a matter of contract, and the FAA requires courts to honor parties' expectations. * * * But what the parties in the aforementioned examples would have agreed to is not arbitration as envisioned by the FAA, lacks its benefits, and therefore may not be required by state law." 563 U.S. 333 (2011).

187 Id. at 1748.

188 577 U.S. 47 (2015).

189 Restatement (Third) U.S. Law of Int'l Comm. Arb. § 1.6 (2019).

(c) The "Prospective Waiver" Doctrine

While not technically unconscionability, a similar doctrine—the "prospective waiver" doctrine—applies to agreements to arbitrate federal statutory claims. As explained above, courts generally refused to enforce predispute agreements to arbitrate federal statutory claims until the 1980s, when the Supreme Court began enforcing such agreements.[190] The Court did so on the reasoning that "so long as the prospective litigant effectively may vindicate its statutory cause of action in the arbitral forum, the statute will continue to serve both its remedial and deterrent function."[191] The Court reiterated this in *Green Tree Financial Corp.-Alabama v. Randolph*, which considered compelling arbitration of a consumer's Truth in Lending Act claims. The consumer argued "she will be required to bear prohibitive arbitration costs" "and thereby force[d] to forgo any claims she may have," so "she argues, she is unable to vindicate her statutory rights in arbitration."[192] The *Randolph* Court went on to hold that while "the existence of large arbitration costs could preclude a litigant such as Randolph from effectively vindicating her federal statutory rights in the arbitral forum," "the record does not show that Randolph will bear such costs."[193] In contrast, some lower courts have found that consumer or employee claimants showed that arbitration fees "would deter a substantial number of similarly situated persons from attempting to vindicate their statutory rights in the arbitral forum."[194]

Some courts used similar reasoning to render unenforceable arbitration agreement provisions prohibiting class actions,[195] until the Supreme Court rejected this in *American Express Co. v. Italian Colors Restaurant*.[196] Plaintiffs in *American Express* pursued class litigation despite an agreement requiring individual (as opposed to class) arbitration.[197] While the district court dismissed the suits and ordered individual arbitrations, the Second Circuit reversed, based in part on a declaration from an economist who estimated that the cost of an expert analysis necessary to prove the antitrust claims would be "at least several hundred thousand dollars, and might exceed $1 million," while the maximum recovery for an individual

---

190 See § 5(e)(1).

191 Mitsubishi Motors Corp. v. Soler Chrysler-Plymouth, Inc. 473 U.S. 614, 638 (1985).

192 Green Tree Fin. Corp.-Alabama v. Randolph, 531 U.S. 79, 90 (2000).

193 Id.

194 Morrison v. Cir. City Stores, Inc., 317 F.3d 646, 670 (6th Cir. 2003).

195 Kristian v. Comcast Corp., 446 F.3d 25, 45–61 (1st Cir. 2006) (agreement also required each party to pay its own attorney's fees and limited remedies).

196 133 S. Ct. 2304 (2013).

197 Id. at 2308.

plaintiff would be $38,549.[198] The Second Circuit stated that because "the class action waiver in this case precludes plaintiffs from enforcing their statutory rights, we find the arbitration provision unenforceable."[199] The Supreme Court disagreed.

> [T]he fact that it is not worth the expense involved in proving a statutory remedy does not constitute the elimination of the right to pursue that remedy. The class-action waiver merely limits arbitration to the two contracting parties. It no more eliminates those parties' right to pursue their statutory remedy than did federal law before its adoption of the class action for legal relief in 1938. Or, to put it differently, the individual suit that was considered adequate to assure "effective vindication" of a federal right before adoption of class-action procedures did not suddenly become "ineffective vindication" upon their adoption.[200]

Nevertheless, *American Express* reiterated its "desire to prevent prospective waiver of a party's right to pursue statutory remedies," and said "[t]hat would certainly cover a provision in an arbitration agreement forbidding the assertion of certain statutory rights. And it would perhaps cover filing and administrative fees attached to arbitration that are so high as to make access to the forum impracticable."[201]

Since *American Express*, courts have continued to refuse to enforce arbitration agreements that prospectively waive federal statutory claims,[202] or that burden such claimants with excessively high arbitration fees.[203] For example, the Fourth Circuit notes that,

---

198 Id.

199 In re American Express Merchants' Litigation, 634 F.3d 187, 199 (2d Cir. 2011).

200 133 S. Ct. 2304, 2310–11 (2013).

201 Am. Exp. Co. v. Italian Colors Rest. , 570 U.S. 228, 236 (2013).

202 Smith v. Bd. Of Dirs. Of Triad Mfg., 13 F.4th 613, 619–22 (7th Cir. 2021) (affirming denial of motion to compel arbitration of ERISA claim because agreement's class action waiver would preclude a remedy—removal of a fiduciary—and thus "acts as a 'prospective waiver of a party's right to pursue statutory remedies,' so the 'effective vindication' exception applies."); Williams v. Medley Opportunity Fund II, LP, 965 F.3d 229, 238–39 (3d Cir. 2020) (holding arbitration agreement unenforceable because the agreement called for only tribal law to apply to any claim in arbitration, therefore denying plaintiff's effective vindication of their federal and state law claims. "By limiting the claims available to borrowers to tribal-law claims, the arbitration agreement here requires a borrower to prospectively waive claims based on any other law.").

203 Nesbitt v. FCNH, Inc., 811 F.3d 371, 375 (10th Cir. 2016) (affirming denial of motion to compel arbitration; agreement requiring each party to bear its own expenses and split arbitration fees would effectively preclude employee from vindicating her claims under the Fair Labor Standards Act).

"[p]ursuant to the prospective waiver doctrine, courts * * * have refused to enforce arbitration agreements that limit a party's substantive claims to those under tribal law, and hence forbid federal claims from being brought."[204]

(d) Arbitration Organizations' Policing Against Unconscionability

Courts are not the only entities policing the fairness of arbitration agreements. Some of the leading arbitration organizations have enacted policies on the subject.[205] For example, the American Arbitration Association has a "Due Process Protocol" for employment disputes.[206] The AAA has refused to administer arbitration under agreements that do not comply with the protocol.[207] After one such refusal, a court allowed the employee to litigate claims, rejecting the employer's argument that the court should instead appoint an arbitrator outside the AAA.[208] More broadly, the AAA announced in 2002 that it would no longer allow its arbitrators to handle claims brought by patients against managed care providers if they originated from predispute arbitration clauses.[209] In 2003, the AAA announced that it would not administer healthcare arbitrations between individual patients and healthcare service providers that relate to medical services, such as negligence and medical malpractice disputes, unless all parties agreed to submit the matter to arbitration after the dispute arose.[210]

In at least one significant case, an arbitration organization stopped handling a controversial category of claims after it was sued. In 2009, the Minnesota Attorney General sued the National Arbitration Forum (NAF), which at the time was the largest provider of consumer debt collection arbitrations nationwide.[211] This case

---

[204] Id.

[205] See, e.g., Am. Arbitration Ass'n, Consumer Due Process Protocol, https://www.adr.org/sites/default/files/document_repository/Consumer%20Due%20Process%20Protocol%20(1).pdf, (last visited Aug. 5, 2022); JAMS Policy on Consumer Arbitrations Pursuant to Pre-Dispute Clauses Minimum Standards of Procedural Fairness (2009), https://www.jamsadr.com/consumer-minimum-standards/ (last visited Nov. 27, 2022).

[206] Am. Arb. Ass'n, Employment Due Process Protocol, https://www.adr.org/sites/default/files/document_repository/Employment%20Due%20Process%20Protocol_0.pdf (last visited Aug.7, 2022).

[207] Martinez v. Master Protection Corp., 12 Cal. Rptr. 3d 663 (Ct. App. 2004).

[208] Id. at 674–75.

[209] Charles Ornstein, Health Care Disputes at Issue, L.A. Times, at B1 (Mar. 11, 2002).

[210] Ciccio v. SmileDirectClub, LLC, 2 F.4th 577, 581 (6th Cir. 2021) (holding that application of this policy was a question for the arbitrator not the AAA or a court).

[211] Nancy A. Welsh, What Is "(Im)partial Enough" in A World of Embedded Neutrals?, 52 Ariz. L. Rev. 395, 428 (2010) ("by 2006, NAF had become this country's

alleged that NAF committed "consumer fraud, deceptive trade practices, and false advertising," and was hiding extensive ties to a debt collection firm that brought many of NAF's cases. NAF settled the Minnesota AG's case with an agreement to stop arbitrating consumer disputes, although it could continue arbitrating internet domain disputes and other disputes.[212] Also in 2009, the American Arbitration Association announced a moratorium on administering most consumer debt collection arbitrations.[213] And in a third 2009 development, four of the largest issuers of credit cards agreed to remove the arbitration provisions from their credit card agreements for three and a half years as part of the settlement of an antitrust lawsuit.[214]

(e) Quasi-Governmental Policing of Securities Arbitration

Perhaps the arbitration organization that most actively polices against unconscionability is a quasi-governmental entity, the Financial Industry Regulatory Association. FINRA administers securities arbitration and regulates it in conjunction with a federal agency—the Securities and Exchange Commission (SEC). While other domestic commercial and consumer arbitration arises out of private contract and is administered by private-sector organizations like the American Arbitration Association and trade associations, the duty of securities brokerage firms and their registered representatives to participate in securities arbitration is imposed by FINRA, backed by the SEC, as a condition of doing business in this highly-regulated industry.[215] This occupational licensing regime has

---

largest provider of consumer debt arbitration services, handling 214,000 claims in that year alone.").

[212] Consent Judgment, Minnesota v. National Arbitration Forum, Inc., No. 27-CV-09-18550 (Minn. Dist. Ct. July 17, 2009), available at http://pubcit.typepad.com/files/nafconsentdecree.pdf.

[213] See Arbitration or Arbitrary: The Misuse of Mandatory Arbitration to Collect Consumer Debts: Hearing Before the Subcomm. On Domestic Policy of the H. Comm. On Oversight, 111th Cong. 123–32 (2009) (testimony of Richard W. Naimark, American Arbitration Ass'n), available at https://www.govinfo.gov/content/pkg/CHRG-111hhrg64915/pdf/CHRG-111hhrg64915.pdf.

[214] Peter B. Rutledge & Christopher R. Drahozal, Contract and Choice, 2013 B.Y.U. L. Rev. 1, 63 (2013).

[215] Stephen J. Ware, What Makes Securities Arbitration Different from Other Consumer and Employment Arbitration? 76 U. Cin. L. Rev. 447 (2008). See also Jill I. Gross, McMahon Turns Twenty: The Regulation of Fairness in Securities Arbitration, 76 U. Cin. L. Rev. 493, 512 (2008) ("The Securities Exchange Act of 1934 established a complex scheme to regulate and maintain capital markets as well as to protect the investing public, and it created the SEC to administer the Act and oversee these regulations. Under the 1934 Act, a major portion of the day-to-day regulation of broker-dealers and their associated persons was delegated to [FINRA], subject to SEC supervision. Since virtually all broker-dealers are members of FINRA, 'no broker-dealer can escape the self-regulatory system.' ")

been used by "FINRA, with prodding from the Securities and Exchange Commission (SEC) * * * to require broker-dealers to alert customers to the [arbitration] agreement and to provide information about the arbitration process."[216]

> Besides disclosure, FINRA also regulates the arbitration process to a degree that commercial arbitration forums may not and prohibits firms from placing any condition in [an arbitration agreement] that limits or contradicts any FINRA rule. Notably, FINRA does not permit class arbitrations in its forum because it views courts as better equipped to handle complex procedures.[217]

FINRA's ban on arbitral class waivers was upheld by FINRA's Board of Governors in a 2014 ruling that the Securities Exchange Act overcomes the requirement in the FAA (as interpreted by *AT&T Mobility LLC v. Concepcion*,[218]) to enforce such waivers.[219] While a decision by FINRA's board can be appealed to the SEC and then to a federal court,[220] FINRA's ban on arbitral class waivers has not been so appealed.[221] Instead, a securities firm persuaded the Second Circuit to enforce a class waiver by changing the firm's form contract to provide for arbitration before a non-FINRA forum, the Judicial Arbitration and Mediation Service (JAMS).[222] The Second Circuit held that "a pre-dispute private agreement to arbitrate before a non-FINRA arbitral forum is enforceable."[223] FINRA responded to the

---

[216] Barbara Black & Jill I. Gross, Investor Protection Meets the Federal Arbitration Act, 1 Stan. J. Complex Litig. 1, 5–6 (2012).

[217] Id.

[218] 563 U.S. 333, 339 (2011).

[219] Dep't of Enforcement v. Schwab, Disciplinary Proceeding No. 2011029760201 (FINRA Board of Governors Apr. 24, 2014), available at https://www.finra.org/sites/default/files/NACDecision/p496824.pdf. See also Jill Gross, FINRA Reverses Hearing Panel in Schwab Enforcement Case: Class Action Waiver Violates FINRA Rules, Indisputably (Apr. 24, 2014), http://www.indisputably.org/?p=5593.

[220] FINRA, Rule 9370 (2008) ("A Respondent aggrieved by final disciplinary action pursuant to the Rule 9200 Series or the Rule 9300 Series may apply for review by the SEC pursuant to Section 19(d)(2) of the Exchange Act."); 15 U.S.C § 78s(d) ("Any action with respect to which a self-regulatory organization is required by paragraph (1) of this subsection to file notice shall be subject to review by the appropriate regulatory agency for such member, participant, applicant, or other person, on its own motion, or upon application by any person aggrieved thereby . . . ."); FINRA, Adjudication and Decisions, http://www.finra.org/industry/decisions. (last visited July 11, 2018).

[221] See Teresa J. Verges, Evolution of the Arbitration Forum as a Response to Mandatory Arbitration, 18 Nev. L.J. 437, 451 (2018) ("FINRA has effectively used Rule 2268(d) to prohibit member firms from inserting class-action waivers in customer agreements.").

[222] Credit Suisse Sec. (USA) LLC v. Tracy, 812 F.3d 249, 252–54 (2d Cir. 2016).

[223] Id. at 254. See also You've Been Warned: Ignoring FINRA Rules in Favor of Recent Second Circuit Precedent May Invite Disciplinary Action, Herrick Securities Alert (Aug. 2016), http://www.mondaq.com/unitedstates/x/516496/Arbitration+

Second Circuit's decision by issuing Regulatory Notice 16-25,[224] which "reminds member firms that customers have a right to request arbitration at FINRA's arbitration forum at any time and do not forfeit that right under FINRA rules by signing any agreement with a forum selection provision specifying * * * an arbitration venue other than the FINRA arbitration forum." It also says "[a] member firm's failure to comply with FINRA's rules relating to predispute arbitration agreements with customers or predispute agreements with associated persons, or failure to submit a dispute to FINRA arbitration as required by FINRA's rules, would violate FINRA rules, and member firms may be subject to disciplinary action."[225]

§ 25 Waiver of the Right to Arbitrate

Many contract rights can be waived, including the right to arbitrate. So, a defense to enforcement of an arbitration agreement is that the party seeking arbitration has waived its right to enforce the other party's promise to arbitrate.[226] If a court finds that a party has waived the right to compel arbitration then the dispute will be resolved in litigation rather than arbitration.[227] For example, suppose that Buyer and Seller have an arbitration clause in their contract for the sale of goods. If Seller sues Buyer, then Seller is in breach of its promise to arbitrate and Buyer has the right to compel arbitration of Seller's claim.[228] Suppose, however, that Buyer does not promptly ask the court to compel arbitration. Instead, Buyer participates in litigation for a year or two before asking the court to compel arbitration. The court may refuse to compel arbitration on the ground that Buyer waived its right to compel arbitration by participating in litigation.

Most courts hold that the court (rather than arbitrator) should decide whether a party has waived its right to compel arbitration,[229]

Dispute+Resolution/Youve+Been+Warned+Ignoring+FINRA+Rules+In+Favor+Of+Recent+Second+Circuit+Precedent+May+Invite+Disciplinary+Action.

[224] FINRA Rules, Regulatory Notice, 16–25 (2016), https://www.finra.org/rules-guidance/notices/16-25.

[225] Id.

[226] Restatement (Third) U.S. Law of Int'l Comm. Arb. § 2.19 Note a (2019) ("Under U.S. law, the right to arbitrate pursuant to an arbitration agreement may be waived. The effect of waiver is to preclude the waiving litigant from subsequently invoking the arbitration agreement.")

[227] Of course, the parties can form a post-dispute agreement to use some other process, but if they do not then litigation is the default process.

[228] See § 5(b).

[229] JPD, Inc. v. Chronimed Holdings, Inc., 539 F.3d 388, 394 (6th Cir. 2008) ("Howsam [v. Dean Witter Reynolds, Inc., 537 U.S. 79 (2002)] did not disturb the traditional rule that the courts presumptively resolve waiver-through-inconsistent-conduct claims."); Ehleiter v. Grapetree Shores, Inc., 482 F.3d 207, 217–18 (3d Cir. 2007) ("[T]he Supreme Court did not intend its pronouncements * * * to upset the 'traditional rule' that courts, not arbitrators, should decide the question of whether a

but a few cases are to the contrary,[230] sometimes because courts find the arbitration agreement delegates waiver issues to the arbitrator.[231] The Restatement explains that "confusion has been promoted by Supreme Court dictum" stating, "the presumption is that the arbitrator should decide allegation[s] of waiver, delay, or a like defense to arbitrability."[232] "Despite the Court's dictum," the Restatement continues, "lower courts have inferred, rather uniformly, that the Court's observation governs only cases in which waiver is alleged based on acts not occurring in the context of litigation."[233] In contrast, "courts are in the best position to evaluate litigation activities" as waivers of the right to arbitrate.[234] And FAA § 3 gives courts that role by instructing courts to stay litigation "referable to arbitration" "providing the applicant for the stay is not in default in proceeding with such arbitration."[235]

Until 2022, when courts decided whether waiver of the right to compel arbitration had occurred, they often looked to "whether the opposing party would be prejudiced by a subsequent order requiring it to submit to arbitration."[236] This fact-specific inquiry generally

---

party has waived its right to arbitrate by actively litigating the case in court."); Marie v. Allied Home Mortg. Corp., 402 F.3d 1 (1st Cir. 2005) (the issue of waiver by conduct is for the court, and not for the arbitrator, at least in situations where the alleged waiver occurred due to conduct before the court); Tristar Fin. Ins. Agency, Inc. v. Equicredit Corp. of Am., 97 Fed. Appx. 462, 464, 2004 WL 838633 (5th Cir. 2004) (same); Blanco v. Sterling Jewelers Inc., 09-CV-01330, 2010 WL 466760, at *4 (D. Colo. 2010); Scott v. First Union Securities, Inc., 761 N.Y.S.2d 770 (Sup. Ct. 2003) (same),

[230] Nat'l Am.Ins.Co. v. Transamerica Occidental Life Ins. Co., 328 F.3d 462, 466 (8th Cir. 2003); Bellevue Drug Co. v. Advance PCS, 333 F. Supp. 2d 318, 324 (E.D. Pa. 2004) (overturned on other grounds) (relying on Howsam v. Dean Witter Reynolds, Inc., 537 U.S. 79 (2002), for the proposition that "the issue of whether the defendant, by litigating in this Court the present case, has waived the right to demand arbitration should properly be presented in the first instance to the arbitrator").

[231] For instance, the Alabama Supreme Court held that under an agreement to arbitrate "in accordance with the rules of the American Arbitration Association" "whether the arbitration provision in the 2006 contract has been terminated and whether [a party] waived its right to arbitration are issues for the arbitrator, not the circuit court." Managed Health Care Admin., Inc. v. Blue Cross & Blue Shield of Alabama, 249 So. 3d 486, 492 (Ala. 2017). See also Avant Petroleum, Inc. v. Pecten Arabian, Ltd., 696 F. Supp. 42, 45 (S.D.N.Y. 1988) (determination of waiver under a broad arbitration clause for arbitrator).

[232] Restatement (Third) U.S. Law of Int'l Comm. Arb. § 2.19 Note c (2019) (quoting Howsam v. Dean Witter Reynolds, Inc., 537 U.S. 79, 84 (2002)).

[233] Id. (citing Grigsby & Assoc., Inc. v. M Sec. Inv., 664 F.3d 1350, 1352–1354 (11th Cir. 2011); JPD, Inc. v. Chronimed Holdings Inc., 539 F.3d 388, 391–394 (6th Cir. 2008); Ehleiter v. Grapetree Shores, Inc., 482 F.3d 207, 215–221 (3d Cir. 2007); Marie v. Allied Home Mortg. Corp., 402 F.3d 1, 9–15 (1st Cir. 2005); Hong v. CJ CGV Am. Holdings, 222 Cal. App. 4th 240, 243 (2013) ("Based upon the near-unanimous analysis of federal and state courts, we conclude the foregoing language in Howsam does not apply here.")).

[234] Id.

[235] Id.

[236] Mutual Assurance, Inc. v. Wilson, 716 So.2d 1160, 1163 (Ala.1998)(quoting Companion Life Ins. Co. v. Whitesell Manufacturing, Inc., 670 So.2d 897, 899 (Ala.

turned on the costs the opposing party had incurred in litigating,[237] and whether the party seeking arbitration had benefitted from features of litigation, such as extensive discovery, that may not have been available to it in arbitration.[238] Several courts stated that requiring prejudice to show waiver of the right to arbitrate was supported by "the strong federal policy favoring arbitration."[239] However, the Supreme Court's 2022 decision in *Morgan v. Sundance Inc.*,[240] held that prejudice is not required to show waiver of the right to arbitrate. Prejudice is not required to show waiver of other rights, and "the FAA's 'policy favoring arbitration' does not authorize federal courts to invent special, arbitration-preferring procedural rules."[241]

Morgan said, "[o]utside the arbitration context, a federal court assessing waiver does not generally ask about prejudice."[242] The Supreme Court said waiver "focuses on the actions of the person who held the right," not "the effects of those actions on the opposing party."[243] *Morgan* said this general approach to waiver applies to contracts and thus also to arbitration because the FAA's policy "is

---

1995)). See also Patten Grading & Paving, Inc. v. Skanska USA Building, Inc., 380 F.3d 200, 206 (4th Cir. 2004) ("participation in litigation activity alone will not suffice, as the dispositive question 'is whether the party objecting to arbitration has suffered actual prejudice.' ") (citing MicroStrategy, Inc. v. Lauricia, 268 F.3d 244, 249 (4th Cir. 2001)); Perry Homes v. Cull, 258 S.W.3d 580, 594 (Tex. 2008) ("of the twelve regional circuit courts, ten require a showing of prejudice and the other two treat it as a factor to consider"); Steele v. Lundgren, 935 P.2d 671 (Wash. 1997). But see St. Mary's Med. Ctr. of Evansville, Inc. v. Disco Aluminum Prods. Co., 969 F.2d 585, 590–91 (7th Cir. 1992) ("prejudice is but one relevant circumstance to consider in determining whether a party has waived its right to arbitrate"); Raymond James Fin. Services, Inc. v. Saldukas, 896 So.2d 707 (Fla. 2005).

237 Compare, e.g., Gen. Star Nat'l Ins. Co. v. Administratia Asigurarilor de Stat, 289 F.3d 434, 438 (6th Cir. 2002) ("for 17 months, Astra remained idle while General Star incurred the costs associated with this action"), with Rose v. Volvo Const. Equipment North America, Inc., 1:05-CV-168, 2007 WL 846123, at *7 (N.D. Ohio 2007) ("Unlike the party in *Gen. Star Nat'l Ins. Co.* who failed to assert its right to arbitrate until after a default judgment had been entered against it, in the instant case, EHHE requested that this court * * * compel arbitration less than five months after" complaint).

238 Alan Scott Rau, Edward F. Sherman & Scott R. Peppet, Processes of Dispute Resolution: The Role of Lawyers 728 (4th ed. 2006).

239 Joca-Roca Real Est., LLC v. Brennan, 772 F.3d 945, 948 (1st Cir. 2014) ("In considering whether a waiver can be implied, we start with the strong federal policy favoring arbitration agreements. Given the strength of this policy, mere delay in seeking [arbitration] without some resultant prejudice is insufficient to ground a finding of conduct-based waiver. The party advocating waiver has the burden of demonstrating prejudice.")

240 142 S. Ct. 1708 (2022).

241 Id. at 1713.

242 Id.

243 Id.

about treating arbitration contracts like all others, not about fostering arbitration."[244]

Morgan can be expected to increase the frequency with which parties waive the right to arbitrate. But *Morgan* may not end the fact-specific, perhaps sometimes inconsistent, waiver rulings of lower courts. Courts have held that parties waived the right to arbitrate by filing litigation pleadings,[245] engaging in litigation discovery,[246] or removing to federal court.[247] In contrast, other courts have declined to find a waiver by parties who engaged in similar litigation conduct.[248] Courts are more likely to find waiver by plaintiffs who initiate litigation before seeking arbitration than by defendants who respond in litigation before seeking arbitration.[249]

---

[244] Id.

[245] Robinson v. Food Service of Belton, Inc., 415 F. Supp.2d 1221 (D. Kan. 2005) (defendant did not seek to compel arbitration until after filing amended answer listing arbitration as affirmative defense and counterclaims against parties it later sought to compel to arbitrate); Lapidus v. Arlen Beach Condominium Ass'n Inc., 394 So.2d 1102 (Fla. Dist. Ct. App. 1981); Ex Parte Prendergast, 678 So.2d 778 (Ala. 1996).

[246] Rankin v. Allstate Ins. Co., 336 F.3d 8 (1st Cir. 2003)(Defendant insurance company waived its right to arbitrate by waiting until discovery had closed and the long-scheduled trial date had almost arrived before invoking the arbitration clause); In re Citigroup, Inc., 376 F.3d 23 (1st Cir. 2004) (15 depositions); Com-Tech Assoc. v. Computer Assoc. Int'l, Inc., 938 F.2d 1574 (2d Cir. 1991); Ex Parte Smith, 706 So.2d 704, 705 (Ala. 1997); Green Tree Servicing, LLC v. McLeod, 15 So.3d 682, 694 (Fla. Dist. Ct. App. 2009) ("a party's participation in discovery related to the merits of pending litigation is activity that is generally inconsistent with arbitration. Such activity-considered under the totality of the circumstances-will generally be sufficient to support a finding of a waiver of a party's right to arbitration."); MS Credit Center, Inc. v. Horton, 926 So.2d 167, 180 (Miss. 2006).

[247] Ex Parte Hood, 712 So.2d 341, 345 (Ala. 1998).

[248] See, e.g., Hill v. Ricoh Americas Corp., 603 F.3d 766 (10th Cir. 2010) (employer did not waive its right to arbitration by failing to demand arbitration until four months after its answer);

Patten Grading & Paving, Inc. v. Skanska USA Building, Inc., 380 F.3d 200, 206 (4th Cir. 2004) ("party's filing of minimal responsive pleadings, such as an answer or compulsory counter-claim, are not necessarily inconsistent with an intent to pursue arbitration"); Sharif v. Wellness Int'l Network, Ltd., 376 F.3d 720 (7th Cir. 2004)(parties did not waive right to arbitrate under distributorship agreements, even though they waited 18 months after action was filed to seek to compel arbitration and filed four motions to dismiss before filing motion to compel arbitration); Tristar Fin. Ins. Agency, Inc. v. Equicredit Corp. of Am., 97 Fed. Appx. 462, 464, 2004 WL 838633 (5th Cir. 2004) (filing motions, conducting discovery); Coca-Cola Bottling Co. of New York, Inc. v. Soft Drink and Brewery Workers Union Local 812, Int'l Brotherhood of Teamsters, 242 F.3d 52 (2d Cir. 2001)(Union did not waive its right to arbitrate employer's suit by answering complaint, claiming a violation of temporary restraining order, entering into a protective order and stipulation for discovery, and obtaining substantial discovery); Walker v. J.C. Bradford & Co., 938 F.2d 575 (5th Cir. 1991); Stifel, Nicolaus & Co., Inc. v. Freeman, 924 F.2d 157 (8th Cir. 1991).

[249] For plaintiffs' waiver, see, e.g., Grumhaus v. Comerica Securities, Inc., 223 F.3d 648 (7th Cir. 2000) (shareholders litigated their claims for several months and waited several months after dismissal of their complaint and more than one year after filing initial action to demand arbitration formally, and rights and remedies underlying the different claims were the same); Cabinetree of Wis., Inc. v. Kraftmaid

Morgan also leaves open the extent to which courts will enforce anti-waiver agreements. For instance, courts have declined to enforce a contract clause providing that participation in litigation "shall not be deemed a waiver of a party's right to demand arbitration or to continue arbitration."[250] On the other hand, courts have enforced agreements providing that bringing a debt collection claim in court does not waive the right to compel arbitration of a counterclaim by the debtor.[251]

Finally, *Morgan* also leaves open the extent to which courts will characterize waiver of arbitration as a matter of state law. For instance, the Ninth Circuit has held that a federal district court erred in applying federal law to the question of waiver.[252] And the Maryland Court of Appeals held that "[b]ecause waiver is a 'generally applicable contract defense,'" state law on waiver is incorporated into the FAA by the savings clause of FAA § 2.[253] So, "we analyze whether the arbitration clause was waived, and is therefore unenforceable, under state—not federal—law."[254]

Cabinetry, Inc., 50 F.3d 388, 390 (7th Cir. 1995) (finding that a plaintiff, having chosen a judicial forum for the resolution of a dispute is presumed to have waived its right to arbitrate); Aguilar v. Lerner, 12 Cal. Rptr. 3d 287 (Cal. 2004)(client who filed a lawsuit against attorney alleging professional malpractice, thereby waived his rights to arbitrate under the mandatory fee arbitration act, even though lawsuit also sought resolution of attorney fee dispute).

In contrast, the Seventh Circuit rejected the argument that a defendant waived the agreement to arbitrate simply by failing to seize its earliest opportunity to invoke the agreement. See Kawasaki Heavy Indus., Ltd. v. Bombardier Recreational Prod., Inc., 660 F.3d 988 (7th Cir. 2011) (involvement in the judicial process was of a type that was consistent with the intention to arbitrate; waiver not established, reversing Kawasaki Heavy Indus., Ltd. v. Bombardier Recreational Prod., Inc., No. 3:10-cv-00641-DRH-DGW, 2011 WL 1706740 (S.D. Ill. May 5, 2011) (which had found waiver for failure to seek an order to arbitrate or stay "at the first opportunity")).

250 Republic Ins. Co. v. PAICO Receivables, LLC, 383 F.3d 341, 348 (5th Cir. 2004). See also S & R Co. of Kingston v. Latona Trucking, Inc., 159 F.3d 80 (2d Cir. 1998).

251 Reifenberger v. Autovest LLC, 2021 WL 212237, at *5 (D. Utah Jan. 21, 2021) (enforcing "[e]ven if you and we elect to litigate a Claim in court, you or we may elect to arbitrate any other Claim, including a new Claim in that lawsuit or any other lawsuit."); Morrison v. Midland Funding, LLC, 2021 WL 2529618, at *4 (W.D.N.Y.) (enforcing "[w]e will not require you to arbitrate: * * * a case we file to collect money you owe to us. However, if you respond to the collection lawsuit by claiming any wrongdoing, we may require you to arbitrate.")

252 Cox v. Ocean View Hotel Corp., 533 F.3d 1114, 1121, 1124 (9th Cir. 2008).

253 Cain v. Midland Funding, LLC, 156 A.3d 807, 814 (2017).

254 Id.

Chapter 5

TERMS OF ARBITRATION AGREEMENTS

Table of Sections

A. SCOPE OF ARBITRATION AGREEMENTS

Table of Sections

Sec.

§ 26 Scope of Arbitration Agreements

(a) Two Meanings of "Arbitrable"

If a party seeks to litigate rather than arbitrate a claim, the court will send that claim to arbitration only if the parties agreed to arbitrate that claim.[1] That the parties agreed to arbitrate *some* claim is not enough. They must have agreed to arbitrate *that* claim.[2] Whether they did is a question of contract interpretation about the

[1] See § 3(a)–(b).

[2] Granite Rock Co. v. Int'l Bhd. of Teamsters, 561 U.S. 287 (2010) (emphasis in original) ("a court may order arbitration of a particular dispute only where the court is satisfied that the parties agreed to arbitrate *that dispute*."); First Options of Chi., Inc. v. Kaplan, 514 U.S. 938, 945 (1995) ("a party can be forced to arbitrate only those issues it specifically has agreed to submit to arbitration").

scope of the arbitration agreement. The Supreme Court has described this "question [of] whether the parties have submitted a particular dispute to arbitration," as "the 'question of arbitrability.' "[3]

This question of "arbitrability" is, however, very different from another use of the word "arbitrable." An example of this other meaning of arbitrable is the Supreme Court's statement that *Wilko v. Swan*[4] "held nonarbitrable claims arising under the Securities Act."[5] In *Wilko*, the parties' agreement submitted Securities Act claims to arbitration and the issue was whether something in the Securities Act prevents enforcement of agreements to arbitrate claims arising under that Act. *Wilko* refused to enforce a predispute agreement to arbitrate Securities Act claims. So, describing *Wilko* as holding "nonarbitrable claims arising under the Securities Act" uses the word "arbitrable" to describe claims with respect to which a predispute arbitration agreement will be enforced by courts. And that is a very different question from the topic of this section, which is about interpreting contracts to see which claims the parties have agreed to arbitrate. Both contractual arbitrability (this section) and statutory arbitrability (discussed in Section 5) may be involved in the same case because a party may argue both (1) that her arbitration agreement does not cover a particular claim (such as a sexual harassment claim) and (2) even if the court finds that her agreement does cover sexual harassment claims, such agreements are unenforceable because a statute prohibits enforcement of such agreements.[6] In other words, whether parties' arbitration agreement includes—as a matter of interpreting that agreement—a particular claim is different from whether courts will enforce that agreement with respect to that claim.

(b) Scope Is Presumptively Decided by Courts

The threshold issue with respect to interpreting an arbitration agreement is who—court or arbitrator—does it. Who decides whether a particular claim is within the scope of a particular arbitration agreement? Consider, for example, a contract between Buyer and Seller obligating each party to arbitrate any "controversy or claim

---

3 First Options of Chicago, Inc. v. Kaplan, 514 U.S. 938, 944 (1995). See also Howsam v. Dean Witter Reynolds, Inc., 537 U.S. 79, 83 (2002) ("the question whether the parties have submitted a particular dispute to arbitration, i.e., the 'question of arbitrability,' is an issue for judicial determination unless the parties clearly and unmistakably provide otherwise. * * * Similarly, a disagreement about whether an arbitration clause in a concededly binding contract applies to a particular type of controversy is for the court.")

4 See § 5(e)(1).

5 Mitsubishi Motors Corp. v. Soler Chrysler-Plymouth, Inc., 473 U.S. 614, 621 (1985).

6 See § 5(e)(2).

arising out of this contract, or the breach thereof." Suppose that Buyer sues Seller, alleging antitrust violations, and Seller moves to stay the litigation and to compel arbitration. Buyer may concede that the parties agreed to arbitrate breach-of-contract claims but argue that antitrust claims do not "arise out of" the contract so the parties did not agree to arbitrate them. In other words, Buyer may argue that the scope of the agreement is not broad enough to include antitrust claims.

If Buyer sues in some nations outside the United States, the foreign court is likely to grant Seller's motion. Some nations' laws generally prohibit courts from ruling on the agreement's scope until after the arbitrator has so ruled.[7] In contrast, the domestic FAA sends disputes about an arbitration agreement's scope to courts, rather than to arbitrators,[8] unless the agreement delegates scope issues to the arbitrator.[9] If the court interprets the arbitration clause to cover Buyer's antitrust claim, then the court will grant Seller's motion and send the claim to arbitration. In contrast, if the court finds that the arbitration clause does not cover Buyer's antitrust claim, the court will deny Seller's motion. This approach follows from FAA § 3, which provides:

> If any suit or proceeding be brought in any of the courts of the United States upon any issue referable to arbitration under an agreement in writing for such arbitration, the court in which such suit is pending, *upon being satisfied that the issue involved in such suit or proceeding is referable to arbitration under such an agreement*, shall on application of one of the parties stay the trial of the action until such arbitration has been had in accordance with the terms of the agreement, providing the applicant for the stay is not in default in proceeding with such arbitration.[10]

FAA § 3 requires the court to satisfy itself that the issue involved in the suit is covered by the arbitration agreement before compelling arbitration. While the FAA is not the primary law governing labor

---

7 See § 56.

8 First Options of Chicago, Inc. v. Kaplan, 514 U.S. 938, 943 (1995) (arbitration is "a matter of contract between the parties; it is a way to resolve those disputes—but only those disputes—that the parties have agreed to submit to arbitration.") See also Howsam v. Dean Witter Reynolds, Inc., 537 U.S. 79, 83 (2002) ("the question whether the parties have submitted a particular dispute to arbitration, i.e., the 'question of arbitrability,' is an issue for judicial determination unless the parties clearly and unmistakably provide otherwise. * * * Similarly, a disagreement about whether an arbitration clause in a concededly binding contract applies to a particular type of controversy is for the court.")

9 See § 26(c).

10 9 U.S.C. § 3 (emphasis added).

arbitration,[11] the rule that courts, rather than arbitrators, resolve contractual arbitrability disputes applies to labor arbitration, too.[12]

(c) Delegating Scope Issues to Arbitrators

The just-discussed rule that courts, rather than arbitrators, resolve disputes about the scope of arbitration agreements is merely a default rule, because parties can contract around this rule if they do so "clearly and unmistakably."[13] Parties do this routinely by agreeing to arbitrate under arbitration organization rules that delegate scope issues to arbitrators. For example, an agreement can incorporate the American Arbitration Association's Commercial Arbitration Rules, which provide that "[t]he arbitrator shall have the power to rule on his or her own jurisdiction, including any objections with respect to the existence, *scope* or validity of the arbitration agreement or to the arbitrability of any claim or counterclaim."[14] Had Buyer and Seller, in the example above, used such an agreement then the court would likely grant Seller's motion to compel arbitration.[15]

---

11 See § 44(a).

12 AT & T Technologies, Inc. v. Communications Workers of Am., 475 U.S. 643 (1986). Granite Rock Co. v. Int'l Bhd. of Teamsters, 561 U.S. 287, 296 (2010) ("it is well settled in both commercial and labor cases that whether parties have agreed to 'submi[t] a particular dispute to arbitration' is typically an 'issue for judicial determination.' ")

13 Howsam v. Dean Witter Reynolds, Inc., 537 U.S. 79, 83 (2002) ("the question whether the parties have submitted a particular dispute to arbitration, i.e., the 'question of arbitrability,' is an issue for judicial determination unless the parties clearly and unmistakably provide otherwise.") See also First Options of Chicago, Inc. v. Kaplan, 514 U.S. 938, 946–47 (1995); § 22 (discussing facts and reasoning of *First Options*); AT & T Technologies, Inc. v. Communications Workers of Am., 475 U.S. 643 (1986).

14 Am. Arb. Ass'n, Commercial Arbitration Rules, R–7(a) (2022) (emphasis added).

15 See Airbnb, Inc. v. Doe, 336 So. 3d 698, 705 (Fla. 2022) ("The AAA Rules empower the arbitrator 'to rule on his or her jurisdiction,' the 'scope . . . of the arbitration agreement,' and 'the arbitrability of any claim or counterclaim.' Accordingly, this language is clear and unmistakable and expressly delegates arbitrability determinations to the arbitrator."); Ciccio v. SmileDirectClub, LLC, 2 F.4th 577, 583 (6th Cir. 2021) ("incorporation of [AAA] rules provides clear and unmistakable evidence that the parties agreed to arbitrate gateway arbitrability questions"); Terminix Int'l Co., LP v. Palmer Ranch Ltd. P'ship, 432 F.3d 1327, 1332–33 (11th Cir. 2005) (holding that by incorporating AAA Rules into arbitration agreement, parties clearly and unmistakably agreed that arbitrator should decide whether arbitration clause was valid); Contec Corp. v. Remote Solution, Co., 398 F.3d 205, 208 (2d Cir. 2005) ("[W]hen . . . parties explicitly incorporate rules that empower an arbitrator to decide issues of arbitrability, the incorporation serves as clear and unmistakable evidence of the parties' intent to delegate such issues to an arbitrator.")

See also JAMS Comprehensive Arbitration Rules and Procedures, Rule 11(c) ("Jurisdictional and arbitrability disputes, including disputes over the formation, existence, validity, interpretation or scope of the agreement under which Arbitration is sought, and who are proper Parties to the Arbitration, shall be submitted to and ruled on by the Arbitrator. The Arbitrator has the authority to determine jurisdiction and arbitrability issues as a preliminary matter."), available at https://www.jamsadr.com/rules-comprehensive-arbitration/#Rule-11; Monex Deposit Co. v. Gilliam, 616 F.

Buyer would have to go to arbitration to persuade the arbitrator that the arbitration agreement should be interpreted not to cover Buyer's antitrust claim. Only after getting a ruling from the arbitrator to that effect could Buyer litigate the antitrust claim.

The Supreme Court unanimously enforced this AAA rule in *Henry Schein, Inc. v. Archer and White Sales, Inc.*[16] The relevant contract said:

> Any dispute arising under or related to this Agreement (except for actions seeking injunctive relief and disputes related to trademarks, trade secrets, or other intellectual property of [Schein]), shall be resolved by binding arbitration in accordance with the arbitration rules of the American Arbitration Association.[17]

Archer brought suit, seeking both money damages and injunctive relief, and Schein moved to compel arbitration. The Fifth Circuit affirmed a denial of that motion because—although AAA rules delegate to the arbitrator the power to rule on the scope of the arbitration agreement—Schein's argument that Archer's action seeking injunctive relief was covered by an arbitration agreement was "wholly groundless" because the agreement excepted from arbitration "actions seeking injunctive relief."[18] The Supreme Court unanimously reversed. Quoting the principle that "a court may not 'rule on the potential merits of the underlying' claim that is assigned by contract to an arbitrator, 'even if it appears to the court to be frivolous,' "[19] the *Henry Schein* Court said this "principle applies with equal force to the threshold issue of arbitrability."[20]

The Second Circuit held in 2021 "that incorporation of the AAA Rules (or analogous rules) into an arbitration agreement * * * does not, per se, demonstrate clear and unmistakable evidence of the parties' intent to delegate threshold questions of arbitrability to the arbitrator where other aspects of the contract create ambiguity as to

---

Supp.2d 1023, 1025 (C.D. Cal. 2009) (granting motion to compel arbitration and noting that agreement "incorporates JAMS Rules providing that the arbitrator decides scope and validity disputes with respect to particular claims."); Greenspan v. Ladt, LLC, 111 Cal. Rptr. 3d 468, 494–95 (Ct. App. 2010) ("LADT interprets the concluding language of Rule 11(c) to mean the arbitrator makes an initial decision on arbitrability, and, later, the courts independently make the final decision. Not so. For one thing, LADT's interpretation would conflict with JAMS Rule 11(a), which provides that "[t]he resolution of the issue by the Arbitrator shall be final." * * * [T]he arbitrator decides arbitrability issues at the outset, and his decision is final.")

16 139 S. Ct. 524 (2019).

17 Id. at 528.

18 Id.

19 Id. at 529.

20 Id. at 530.

the parties' intent."[21] The Second Circuit said, "where the arbitration agreement is broad and expresses the intent to arbitrate all aspects of all disputes, this—coupled with incorporation of rules that expressly empower an arbitrator to decide issues of arbitrability—constitutes clear and unmistakable evidence of the parties' intent to delegate the question of arbitrability to the arbitrator."[22] On the other hand, "[w]here, by contrast, the arbitration agreement is narrower, vague, or contains exclusionary language suggesting that the parties consented to arbitrate only a limited subset of disputes, incorporation of rules that empower an arbitrator to decide issues of arbitrability, standing alone, does not suffice to establish the requisite clear and unmistakable inference of intent to arbitrate arbitrability."[23]

(d) How Courts Decide the Scope of an Arbitration Agreement

When courts determine the scope of an arbitration agreement, they generally use the same methods of interpretation they use to interpret other contract terms. That is, courts generally try to effectuate the parties' apparent intentions by interpreting the contract's terms as those terms would ordinarily be understood by reasonable people in the positions of the parties.[24] However, to determine the scope of an arbitration agreement, some courts begin by classifying the arbitration clause as "narrow" or "broad." Narrow arbitration clauses are typically written to cover only claims relating to the interpretation and performance of the contract containing the narrow clause. So, narrow clauses may not cover non-contract claims such as "conversion, tortious interference, unfair competition, unjust enrichment, misappropriation of trade secrets, breach of a different contract, and statutory violations," "even if the dispute would not have arisen 'but for' the parties' agreement."[25]

In contrast, as the Second Circuit wrote, "[w]here the arbitration clause is broad, there arises a presumption of arbitrability and arbitration of even a collateral matter will be ordered if the claim alleged implicates issues of contract construction or the parties' rights and obligations under it."[26] Tort claims, for example, are often

---

[21] DDK Hotels, LLC v. Williams-Sonoma, Inc., 6 F.4th 308, 318 (2d Cir. 2021).

[22] Id. at 318–19.

[23] Id.

[24] Restatement (Second) of Contracts § 202(3) (1981).

[25] David Horton, Infinite Arbitration Clauses, 168 U. Pa. L. Rev. 633, 651–52 (2020) (citing cases) (internal quotes omitted).

[26] Louis Dreyfus Negoce S.A. v. Blystad Shipping & Trading Inc., 252 F.3d 218, 224 (2d Cir. 2001) (internal quotation marks and citations omitted).

covered by broad arbitration clauses.[27] Of course, the classifications "broad" and "narrow" are just generalizations and will often be insufficiently precise.[28] Rather than just mechanically placing an arbitration clause in one of two categories, the task of contract interpretation requires a court to be sensitive to the particular language and context of the arbitration agreement in that case.[29]

However, FAA § 2 only requires courts to enforce agreements "to settle by arbitration a controversy thereafter arising out of such contract or transaction,"[30] so the enforceability of an agreement covering claims not "arising out of such contract or transaction" should be determined by state law. Most states have followed New York in enacting statutes enforcing predispute agreements to arbitrate, not just claims arising out of the contract or transaction, but "any controversy * * * between the parties."[31]

---

[27] CD Partners, L.L.C. v. Grizzle, 424 F.3d 795 (8th Cir. 2005) (tort claims covered by broad arbitration clause); Sears Authorized Termite and Pest Control, Inc. v. Sullivan, 816 So.2d 603 (Fla. 2002) (same); Accomazzo v. CEDU Education Services, Inc. 15 P.3d 1153 (Idaho 2000) (intentional tort claims arose out of contract and thus covered by clause). See also Simula, Inc. v. Autoliv, Inc., 175 F.3d 716 (9th Cir. 1999) (agreement to arbitrate "all disputes arising in connection with this agreement" includes antitrust, defamation, and trade secret claims); Hicks v. Cadle Co., 355 Fed.Appx. 186, 189, 193 (10th Cir. 2009) (clause which required arbitration of, among other claims, "any claim based on or arising from an alleged tort," broad enough to require arbitration of defamation and intentional infliction of emotional distress claims). Some broad clauses are even written to expressly cover claims based on "statutory law, common law, equitable claims, or claims for breach of fiduciary duty or other wrongful acts." Herrington v. Union Planters Bank, No. Civ. A 2:98CV231 GR, 2000 WL 424232, *2 (S.D. Miss. Jan.21, 2000).

[28] Ian R. Macneil, Richard E. Speidel & Thomas J. Stipanowich, Federal Arbitration Law § 20.2.1 (1994) ("the form of an arbitration agreement may assume an unfortunate talismanic function, going somewhat beyond simply looking at the language to ascertain party intention."). See, e.g., Local 827, Intern. Broth. of Elec. Workers, AFL-CIO v. Verizon New Jersey, Inc., 458 F.3d 305, 306 (3d Cir. 2006)("In this appeal, we must decide between the conflicting conclusions reached by two district judges in the same court regarding the interpretation of the same collective bargaining contract. One has held that the contract's arbitration clause is narrow, while the other has held that it is broad."); id. at 309 ("The District Court in this case stated that there was some ambiguity in the CBA's arbitration clause, as evidenced by the fact that several arbitrators had held that the clause was broad, while others had found it narrow.")

[29] Neither the FAA nor Supreme Court precedent suggests that courts should classify arbitration clauses as broad or narrow. Ivax Corp. v. B. Braun of Am., 286 F.3d 1309, 1320 n.23 (11th Cir. 2002) ("It appears to us . . . that the [Supreme] Court in Moses Cone made no such distinction" between broad and narrow clauses.); Chelsea Family Pharmacy, PLLC v. Medco Health Solutions, Inc., 567 F.3d 1191 (10th Cir. 2009) (Gorsuch, J., concurring) ("I write separately only to question this business of classifying arbitration clauses as 'broad' or 'narrow.' ")

[30] For an argument that the FAA should be amended to repeal this limitation, see Stephen J. Ware, Interstate Arbitration: Chapter 1 of the Federal Arbitration Act, in Arbitration Law in America: A Critical Assessment 88, 104–05 (2006).

[31] David Horton, Infinite Arbitration Clauses, 168 U. Pa. L. Rev. 633, 678 (2020) (citing statutes).

(e) Resolving Ambiguities in Favor of Arbitration

While courts determining the scope of arbitration agreements often straightforwardly apply standard techniques of contract interpretation, courts sometimes put a finger on the scale in favor of arbitration by interpreting arbitration agreements broadly. The Supreme Court has long said that "in applying general state-law principles of contract interpretation to the interpretation of an arbitration agreement * * * , due regard must be given to the federal policy favoring arbitration, and ambiguities as to the scope of the arbitration clause itself [are] resolved in favor of arbitration."[32] The Court reaffirmed this requirement that interpretation "give due regard" "to the federal policy favoring arbitration " as recently as its 2015 decision in *DIRECTV, Inc. v. Imburgia.*[33]

This interpretive agenda to favor arbitration is especially prominent in labor arbitration cases. Courts have long favored a broad interpretation of collective bargaining agreements' arbitration clauses.[34] In nearly all cases, a broader interpretation benefits the employee and labor union rather than the employer. That is because nearly all labor arbitration cases are grievances (claims) against the employer,[35] and if the arbitration clause is interpreted to cover the dispute, then the employee and union may win in arbitration. In contrast, if the arbitration clause is interpreted not to cover the dispute, then there will probably not be any adjudication of the dispute.[36] So in the labor context, a broad interpretation of the arbitration clause is nearly always favored by the employee and union. That broad interpretation is often provided by courts who make statements like this oft-quoted one by the Supreme Court: "[a]n order to arbitrate the particular grievance should not be denied unless it may be said with positive assurance that the arbitration

---

32 Volt Information Sciences, Inc. v. Board of Trustees of the Leland Stanford Junior University, 489 U.S. 468, 475–76 (1989). See also Safra Sec., LLC v. Gonzalez, 764 F. App'x 125, 126 (2d Cir. 2019) ("Whether parties have agreed to arbitrate a matter is fundamentally a question of contractual interpretation. But the analysis differs from ordinary contract interpretation in that any doubts concerning the scope of arbitrable issues should be resolved in favor of arbitration.* * *. Under these principles, an order to arbitrate "should not be denied unless it may be said with positive assurance that the arbitration clause is not susceptible of an interpretation that covers the asserted dispute.")

33 DIRECTV, Inc. v. Imburgia, 577 U.S. 474 (2015).

34 See, e.g., AT & T Technologies, Inc. v. Communications Workers of America, 475 U.S. 643, 649–51 (1986); United Steelworkers of America v. Warrior & Gulf Navigation Co., 363 U.S. 574, 582–83 (1960).

35 See § 43.

36 Id.

clause is not susceptible of an interpretation that covers the asserted dispute. Doubts should be resolved in favor of coverage."[37]

In other cases, by contrast, the court's agenda is to confine arbitration by interpreting the arbitration clause narrowly. This tends to occur when the court strains its interpretation to favor an employee or consumer plaintiff who seeks to litigate, rather than arbitrate, her claims despite having signed a take-it-or-leave-it arbitration agreement. For example, a New Jersey case interpreted an arbitration clause not to cover statutory employment discrimination claims because it did not, in "clear and unmistakable" language, include them.[38]

While a court's agenda in interpreting arbitration clauses affects the outcome in some cases, most cases are not controversial because the scope of the arbitration agreement is clearly broad enough to cover the claim in question. The typical arbitration clause is written broadly to cover any "controversy or claim arising out of or relating to this contract, or the breach thereof." In the bulk of cases, all claims do plainly arise out of or at least relate to the contract or its breach, so any fair-minded court (or arbitrator) will hold that the parties agreed to arbitrate the claims.

However, a complaint may include multiple claims, some of which are covered by the arbitration agreement and others of which are not. If this occurs and a party moves to compel arbitration, the FAA requires courts to grant the motion with respect to the arbitrable claims "even where the result would be the possibly inefficient maintenance of separate proceedings in different forums."[39]

B. MULTI-PARTY AGREEMENTS AND DISPUTES

Table of Sections

---

[37] United Steelworkers of America v. Warrior & Gulf Navigation Co., 363 U.S. 574, 582–83 (1960).

[38] Alamo Rent a Car, Inc. v. Galarza, 703 A.2d 961, 966 (N.J. 1997).

[39] KPMG LLP v. Cocchi, 565 U.S. 18, 26 (2011) (quoting Dean Witter Reynolds Inc. v. Byrd, 470 U.S. 213 (1985)).

---

§ 27 Claims by or Against Those Not Party to the Arbitration Agreement

The previous section discusses interpreting arbitration agreements to decide if they cover a particular claim.[40] A specific application of that "scope" question is whether a particular arbitration agreement covers particular claims by or against a non-party to the arbitration agreement.[41]

(a) Party Plaintiff vs. Non-Party Defendant

A party to an arbitration agreement may have claims against those who are not party to the agreement, and yet those non-parties may be able to compel arbitration pursuant to the agreement. Consider, for example, an arbitration clause in a contract between Buyer and Seller for the sale of goods. Suppose Buyer sues not just Seller, but also the manufacturer of the goods, the lender who financed Buyer's purchase, an insurance company involved in the transaction, and the individual salesperson who actually made the sale. May any of these defendants other than Seller compel Buyer to arbitrate even though these other defendants are not parties to the arbitration agreement?

This is mainly a question of contract interpretation because contracts often confer rights on those who are not party to it, "intended beneficiaries."[42] To qualify as an intended beneficiary, one must show that "recognition of a right to performance in the beneficiary is appropriate to effectuate the intention of the parties."[43] So, if the arbitration clause in the contract between Buyer and Seller is written broadly to cover "all disputes, claims, or controversies

---

40 See §§ 26.

41 Those not party to the arbitration agreement are often called "non-signatories" but this should not lead us believe the only way to be a party to an arbitration agreement is to sign it. Other methods of manifesting assent are also effective to make one a party to an arbitration agreement. See §§ 17–18.

42 See generally E. Allan Farnsworth, Contracts ch.10 (4th ed. 2004).

43 Restatement (Second) of Contracts § 302(1) (1981).

arising from or relating to this Contract or the relationships which result from this Contract," then Buyer is subject to a motion to compel arbitration of its claims against defendants (such as the manufacturer or salesperson) who are not party to the arbitration agreement.[44] In contrast, if the arbitration clause is expressly limited to disputes between Buyer and Seller then Buyer should defeat a motion to compel by the other defendants.[45] And some arbitration agreements are written to make third-party beneficiaries of some but not all the parties listed above. For instance, the Eleventh Circuit held that an agreement conferred the right to compel arbitration on the buyer, seller, and lender, but not the insurer, so the Eleventh Circuit affirmed denial of the insurer's motion to compel arbitration of the buyer's suit against it.[46]

Not only buyers of goods agree to arbitrate with parties beyond their sellers. For example, consumers buying plane tickets on Hotwire agreed with Hotwire to arbitrate the consumers' claims against "companies offering products or services through us (which are beneficiaries of this arbitration agreement)," such as American Airlines, which compelled arbitration of consumers' claims arising out of pandemic cancellations.[47] In contrast, the Second Circuit held that an employer-employee agreement to arbitrate "all legal claims arising out of or relating to employment" did not cover employee's ERISA claims against the fiduciary managing a profit-sharing fund sponsored by the employer.[48]

Third-party beneficiary law allows hub-and-spoke contracting to obligate each spoke to arbitrate with the other spokes even though

---

44 Sherer v. Green Tree Servicing, LLC, 548 F.3d 379, 383 (5th Cir. 2008) ("the language of the Loan Agreement demonstrates that Sherer has agreed to arbitrate his claims that arise against nonsignatories whose 'relationships . . . result from th[e] [a]greement.' Sherer is bound by the language of the Loan Agreement, and Green Tree, as a nonsignatory whose relationship resulted from the Loan Agreement, may therefore compel Sherer to arbitrate his claims."); Blinco v. Green Tree Servicing LLC, 400 F.3d 1308, 1311 (11th Cir. 2005); Ex Parte Gates, 675 So.2d 371, 374 (Ala. 1996).

The Supreme Court held that "third-party beneficiary theories" could be applied to arbitration because they are "traditional principles' of state law allow[ing] a contract to be enforced by or against nonparties to the contract." Arthur Andersen LLP v. Carlisle, 556 U.S. 624, 630–31 (2009).

45 Monsanto Co. v. Benton Farm, 813 So.2d 867 (Ala.2001); Ex parte Martin, 703 So.2d 883, 888 (Ala. 1996). The same is true of an arbitration clause expressly limited to disputes between general contractor and subcontractor; it does not cover disputes between subcontractor and a third party. In re Application of Diesel Constr. Co., Inc., 234 N.Y.S.2d 349 (Sup. Ct., Special Term 1962).

46 Lawson v. Life of the S. Ins. Co., 648 F.3d 1166, 1172 (11th Cir. 2011) ("The loan agreement does not show, on its face or elsewhere, an intent to allow anyone other than the Lawsons, the car dealership, Chase Manhattan, and the assignees of the dealership or Chase Manhattan to compel arbitration of a dispute, and Life of the South is none of those").

47 Ward v. Am. Airlines, Inc., 498 F. Supp. 3d 909, 915 (N.D. Tex. 2020).

48 Cooper v. Ruane Cunniff & Goldfarb Inc., 990 F.3d 173, 175 (2d Cir. 2021).

they contract only with the hub and not with each other. For instance, a realtor's individual contracts with each of its agents may obligate each of the agents to arbitrate commission disputes with any other agent, even though no agent forms a contract with any other agent.[49]

While intended third-party beneficiaries can compel arbitration, they cannot be compelled to arbitrate.[50] In other words, the beneficiaries have the right, but not the duty, to arbitrate. This follows from the consensual nature of contracts generally and arbitration agreements in particular. Parties to a contract can grant rights to non-parties but cannot impose duties on non-parties. Contractual duties belong only to parties who agree to them and the non-party to an arbitration agreement, by definition, did not agree to arbitrate.[51] So third-party beneficiary law, as a part of contract law, understandably confers on a non-party the right, but not the duty, to arbitrate.

Similarly, although other doctrines beyond third-party beneficiary law, are sometimes discussed as allowing a non-party to bind or be bound to an arbitration agreement, these doctrines in practice usually involve the non-party compelling arbitration of claims against it, rather than being compelled to arbitration when it seeks to litigate.[52] For example, the Supreme Court's 2009 *Arthur Andersen LLP v. Carlisle* opinion said that "assumption, piercing the corporate veil, alter ego, incorporation by reference, third-party beneficiary theories, waiver and estoppel," could be applied to arbitration because they are "traditional principles' of state law allow[ing] a contract to be enforced *by or against* nonparties to the

---

[49] Shapiro v. Sankarsingh, 114 N.Y.S.3d 68, 69 (2019) ("Plaintiff, an independent contractor with nonparty Douglas Elliman (DE), brought this action against defendant, a licensed real estate broker with DE, based on an alleged oral agreement concerning commissions. Plaintiff signed a form acknowledging receipt of the DE policy manual and that she was obligated to follow the corporate policies and rules. The policy manual includes an arbitration clause requiring "any disputes between DE Agents relating to commissions" to be resolved through the company's internal arbitration procedures").

[50] Ian R. Macneil, Richard E. Speidel & Thomas J. Stipanowich, Federal Arbitration Law § 18.3.1.6 (Supp. 1999).

[51] Although one may later become a party to an earlier arbitration agreement by assuming the duties (including the duty to arbitrate) of one of the parties to the earlier agreement. See, e.g., Trippe Mfg. Co. v. Niles Audio Corp., 401 F.3d 529, 531–33 (3d Cir. 2005); Employers Ins. of Wausau v. Bright Metal Specialties, Inc., 251 F.3d 1316 (11th Cir. 2001).

[52] The "theory of estoppel * * * is generally only used by non-signatories to bind signatories to arbitration, not the reverse." B.F. v. Amazon.com Inc, 858 F. App'x 218, 221 (9th Cir. 2021). The Ninth Circuit made this observation in denying Amazon's motion to compel arbitration of statutory claims brought by minor children who allege that Amazon's Alexa service intercepted or recorded their communications without their consent. The Ninth Circuit said, "It is undisputed that, if the parents brought the same claims as Plaintiffs, the terms to which they agreed would bind them to arbitration." Id. at 220.

contract."[53] But when the Supreme Court actually applied one of these doctrines, estoppel, in 2021's *GE Energy Power Conversion France SAS, Corp. v. Outokumpu Stainless USA, LLC*,[54] it did so to permit a defendant that did not sign an arbitration agreement to compel arbitration of claims against it. *GE Energy* said the state-law equitable estoppel doctrine "allows a nonsignatory to a written agreement containing an arbitration clause to compel arbitration [of claims against it] where a signatory to the written agreement must rely on the terms of that agreement in asserting its claims against the non-signatory."[55]

(b) Non-Party Plaintiff vs. Party Defendant

Plaintiffs, like defendants, can be intended third-party beneficiaries of another party's promise to arbitrate.[56] For example, a plaintiff injured while test driving an auto dealer's car "could be considered" a third-party beneficiary of the dealer's insurance policy—the contract between the dealer and its insurer.[57] If that plaintiff brings a breach-of-contract claim against the dealer's insurer then the insurer may rely on the policy's arbitration clause to require the plaintiff to arbitrate, rather than litigate, his claims against the insurer. In other words, if the plaintiff wants to enforce some of the policy's terms (by suing on them) then he "cannot pick and choose the portions of the contract that he wants to apply."[58]

---

[53] Arthur Andersen LLP v. Carlisle, 556 U.S. 624, 630–31 (2009) (emphasis added).

[54] 140 S. Ct. 1637 (2021).

[55] Id. at 1644. See also CD Partners, L.L.C. v. Grizzle, 424 F.3d 795, 798 (8th Cir. 2005) ("[a] nonsignatory can enforce an arbitration clause against a signatory to the agreement * * * [w]hen each of a signatory's claims against a nonsignatory makes reference to or presumes the existence of the written agreement").

[56] Topolski v. Helena Ass'n of Realtors, Inc., 15 P.3d 414 (Mont. 2000) (client sought arbitration against real estate broker and court ordered broker to arbitrate, even though client's contract with broker lacked an arbitration clause, because broker had assented to association rules requiring broker to arbitrate client's claims).

[57] Ex Parte Dyess, 709 So.2d 447, 449–50 (Ala. 1997). "Dyess is suing American Hardware under the uninsured motorist provision in the policy American Hardware issued to Jack Ingram Motors. In effect, Dyess is a third-party beneficiary of the policy between American Hardware and Jack Ingram Motors." Id. at 450.

[58] Id. at 451; Washington Mut. Fin. Group, LLC v. Bailey, 364 F.3d 260 (5th Cir. 2004); Int'l Paper Co. v. Schwabedissen Maschinen & Anlagen GMBH, 206 F.3d 411 (4th Cir. 2000); Friedman v. Yula, 679 F. Supp.2d 617, 628 (E.D. Pa. 2010) ("having embraced the written agreement between Robert and Defendants to prove his claims and his damages, Allan cannot now walk away from the arbitration clauses in the Agreements. * * * Therefore, Plaintiff Allan Friedman must be compelled to arbitration claims under the Joinder Agreement"); Sam Houston Elec. Coop., Inc. v. Berry, 582 S.W.3d 282, 288 (Tex. App. 2017) (holding non-signatories to Texas utility cooperative's bylaws were subject to an enforceable arbitration agreement because of the equitable doctrine of "direct benefits estoppel" . . . "[a] non-signatory that engages the litigation process to bring claims based on certain terms of a contract cannot avoid an arbitration provision within that same contract." ". . . [R]ather, such a non-

However, several courts hold that this reasoning applies only to plaintiffs whose claims rest on the contract containing the arbitration clause. These courts hold that an arbitration clause in a contract to which the plaintiff could be considered a third-party beneficiary is no obstacle to that plaintiff's desire to litigate, rather than arbitrate, non-contract claims, such as tort claims.[59] Nevertheless, such a plaintiff might be required to arbitrate due to non-contractual doctrines such as those noted at the end of the previous subsection: estoppel, agency, and corporate veil-piercing.[60]

(c) Assignee's Right to Compel Arbitration

A non-party to an arbitration agreement can become a party to it through assignment. Most contract rights are assignable,[61] and courts have long held "the arbitration clause is an integral part of the contract and may be availed of, not only by the original parties but also by assignees."[62] For example, if a consumer's credit card issuer assigns its contractual rights to a third party who tries to collect payment from the consumer, and the consumer sues the assignee (debt collector) under, say, the Fair Debt Collections Practices Act or a state consumer statute, the assignee may compel arbitration of the consumer's claim based on the arbitration clause in the consumer's

---

signatory should be compelled to arbitrate if he or she seeks, by his claims, 'to derive a direct benefit from the contract containing the arbitration provision.'") (internal citations omitted). An exception is where the arbitration clause is expressly limited to disputes among the contracting parties, as opposed to disputes involving the third party. Lewis v. CEDU Educational Services, Inc., 15 P.3d 1147, 1150—52 (Idaho 2000).

The principle that one ought not be able to "pick and choose" some portions of a contract, but not others, also applies to a non-party who "steps into the shoes" of a party to the arbitration agreement because the non-party is the executor or receiver of the party's estate. Isp.com LLC. v. Theising, 805 N.E.2d 767 (Ind. 2004); Briarcliff Nursing Home, Inc. v. Turcotte, 894 So.2d 661 (Ala. 2004).

[59] Fleetwood Enters., Inc. v. Gaskamp, 280 F.3d 1069 (5th Cir. 2002); E.I. DuPont de Nemours & Co. v. Rhone Poulenc Fiber & Resin, 269 F.3d 187 (3d Cir. 2001); Infiniti of Mobile, Inc. v. Office, 727 So.2d 42 (Ala. 1999).

[60] See § 37(a).

[61] Restatement (Second) of Contracts § 317(2) ("A contractual right can be assigned unless * * *); 6 Am. Jur. 2d Assignments § 7 ("There is a general right to assign common law and statutory rights unless there is an express prohibition in a statute or a showing that an assignment would clearly offend an identifiable public policy").

[62] Lipman v. Haeuser Shellac Co., Inc., 289 N.Y. 76, 81, 43 N.E.2d 817 (1942). See also I.S. Joseph Co. v. Michigan Sugar Co., 803 F.2d 396, 400 (8th Cir. 1986) (stating that, assuming a valid assignment, the assignee could enforce an arbitration provision entered into by the assignor); Chatham Shipping Co. v. Fertex S.S. Corp., 352 F.2d 291, 294 (2d Cir. 1965) (stating that "absent contrary expression, assignment of a contract carries with it a right to arbitration therein provided"); Ocwen Loan Servicing, LLC v. Washington, 939 So.2d 6, 9–10 (Ala. 2006) ("As a general rule, an assignee stands in the shoes of the assignor and may enforce an arbitration agreement entered into between the assignor of another party").

credit card contract.[63] However, the assignee will lack a right to compel arbitration if the original creditor assigned only "the receivables" (the claim for money) but not the right to compel arbitration.[64] So an assignee must prove not only the breadth of the original arbitration agreement but also the assignment.[65]

§ 28 Consolidation of, and Stays Pending, Related Proceedings

In litigation, rules of civil procedure encourage courts to consolidate related cases and to join multiple parties in a single action if their disputes arise out of the same transaction or occurrence.[66] Consolidation or joinder can avoid multiple litigation over the same facts, thus saving time and money and helping to avoid inconsistent results. These same goals similarly argue for arbitrators to consolidate cases and to join parties. The obstacle to doing so, however, is the contractual basis of arbitration. Parties who have not agreed to arbitrate have a right to litigate rather than arbitrate.[67]

---

[63] Fontaine v. Resurgent Capital Services, L.P., 540 F. Supp.3d 353 (W.D.N.Y. 2021) (assignee adequately proved assignment and broad enough arbitration agreement to cover claims against "affiliate" of original creditor); In re Midland Credit Mgmt., Inc. Tel. Consumer Prot. Litig., No. 11md2286-MMA (MDD), 2019 WL 1676015, at *3 (S.D. Cal.) ("assignees have a right to compel arbitration where there is a valid assignment"); Campbell v. Jacob, No. 4:19-cv-179-JM, 2019 WL 4284106, at *3 (E.D. Ark.) ("Because Citibank sold all of its rights under the agreement to Midland, this caused Midland to substitute for Citibank in the arbitration provision, accordingly, the omission of successors or assigns in the 2016 cardholder agreement is not a legal bar to Midland's enforcement of the arbitration provision.") See also Green Tree-AL LLC v. White, 55 So. 3d 1186, 1191 (Ala. 2010) ("Green Tree Financial was an assignee of a sales contract and installment agreement between the purchasers of the mobile home and Johnson Mobile Homes, the seller of the mobile home. The purchasers later sued Green Tree Financial and Johnson Mobile Homes, both of which moved to compel arbitration. We stated: "As an assignee, Green Tree [Financial] simply steps into the shoes of the assignor, Johnson Mobile Homes, a signatory to the installment agreement, which contained the arbitration clause").

[64] Pounds v. Portfolio Recovery Assocs., LLC, 274 N.C. App. 201, 211, 851 S.E.2d 423, 430 (2020), writ denied, review denied, 379 N.C. 164, 863 S.E.2d 610 (2021), and review dismissed, 863 S.E.2d 613 (N.C. 2021) ("PRA purchased Plaintiffs' debts pursuant to the Bills of Sale, which specifically and solely identify the assignment of Plaintiffs' Accounts and Receivables. The Bills of Sale in this case contrast with the language of other bills of sale or purchase agreements where the documents effectuating the assignments expressly assign all of the rights of the original creditors to the assignee"); Lester v. Portfolio Recovery Assocs., LLC, No. 1:18-CV-0267-VEH, 2018 WL 3374107, at *2 (N.D. Ala. 2018).

[65] Frontline Asset Strategies, LLC v. Rutledge, No. 20-0395, 2021 WL 1972277, at *5 (W. Va. May 17, 2021) ("Frontline has not established that the arbitration rights of the original creditors were effectively assigned to it.")

[66] See, e.g., Fed.R.Civ.P. 14 (third-party practice), 19 (joinder of persons needed for just adjudication), 20 (permissive joinder of parties), 22 (interpleader), 23 (class actions), and 24 (intervention).

[67] See § 3(a).

And parties who have agreed to arbitrate have a right to arbitrate rather than litigate.[68]

Consider a construction project in which the owner of the land has a contract with the general contractor and a separate contract with the architect.[69] Suppose that Owner's contract with Contractor has an arbitration clause but Owner's contract with Architect does not. Owner claims that Contractor breached the construction contract because the construction work had defects. Contractor replies that any defects are due to negligence by Architect in specifying the wrong materials, for example. Assume that either Architect or Contractor must be liable to Owner and the only question is to determine which one is liable.

Owner could pursue separate proceedings, suing Architect and asserting a claim in arbitration against Contractor. But this imposes on Owner the cost of two proceedings and the risk of inconsistent results. A court might rule for Architect on the belief that Contractor (who is not a party to the litigation) is liable, while the arbitrator might rule for Contractor on the belief that Architect (who is not a party to the arbitration) is liable. So, Owner would lose both cases even though, as assumed above, one of the defendants must be liable to Owner.[70]

Under the FAA, Owner is stuck with these problems.[71] Owner may not compel the other two parties into a single proceeding. Owner may not compel Architect to arbitrate because Architect never agreed to arbitrate. And Owner may not compel Contractor to litigate because Contractor has a contractual right to arbitrate its disputes with Owner. The FAA "requires piecemeal resolution when necessary to give effect to an arbitration agreement."[72]

---

68 See § 5(b).

69 These facts are loosely based on Moses H. Cone Memorial Hospital v. Mercury Construction Corp., 460 U.S. 1 (1983).

70 Owner is not saved from this result by ordinary principles of claim preclusion (res judicata) and issue preclusion (collateral estoppel) because preclusion may only be asserted against a party to the prior proceeding. See Jack H. Friedenthal, Mary Kay Kane & Arthur R. Miller, Civil Procedure § 14.14 (4th ed. 2005). Contractor is not bound by the court's ruling because Contractor was not a party to the litigation. Architect is not bound by the arbitrator's ruling because Architect was not a party to the arbitration.

71 Moses H. Cone Memorial Hospital v. Mercury Construction Corp., 460 U.S. 1 (1983).

72 Id. at 20. The Court went on to say:

> Under the Arbitration Act, an arbitration agreement must be enforced notwithstanding the presence of other persons who are parties to the underlying dispute but not to the arbitration agreement. If the dispute between [Contractor] and [Owner] is arbitrable under the Act, then [Owner's] two disputes will be resolved separately—one in arbitration, and the other (if at all) in state-court litigation.

In contrast, Owner's situation is more favorable under the arbitration law of some states, such as California. A California statute allows a court to refuse enforcement of an arbitration agreement if one of the parties to it is also a party to pending litigation with a third party arising out of the same transaction.[73] So under California law, a court could order Contractor to litigate in one proceeding with Owner and Architect to prevent conflicting rulings.

Ordinarily, state law (such as California's) on consolidation is irrelevant because the FAA governs nearly all arbitration and preempts inconsistent state law.[74] But in *Volt Information Sciences, Inc. v. Board of Trustees of the Leland Stanford Junior University*,[75] the Supreme Court held that the parties were governed by California arbitration law, rather than the FAA, because of a provision in their agreement to that effect.[76]

If consolidation of related cases only one of which is subject to arbitration, does not occur, the question arises which proceeding (arbitration or litigation) will reach a decision first. The FAA does not directly address whether: (1) arbitration should be stayed until litigation concludes, (2) litigation should be stayed until arbitration concludes, or (3) neither should be stayed. The Supreme Court has not directly addressed this question, but has held in a two-party dispute that arbitrable claims should not be stayed until litigation of non-arbitrable claims concludes.[77] In a multi-party dispute, a stay of arbitration pending litigation might "violate[ ] the spirit if not the

---

Id. See also Reliance Ins. Co. v. Raybestos Prods. Co., 382 F.3d 676 (7th Cir. 2004) (insured had arbitration clause in contracts with some, but not all, of its insurers); MPACT Constr. Group v. Superior Concrete Constructors, Inc., 802 N.E.2d 901 (Ind. 2004) (enforcing arbitration agreement between owner and contractor but refusing to force sub-contractors to arbitrate when they had not agreed to do so).

[73] Cal. Civ. Proc. Code § 1281.2(c). This provision provides, in pertinent part, that when a court determines that

> a party to the arbitration is also a party to litigation in a pending court action or special proceeding with a third party as set forth under subdivision (c), the court (1) may refuse to enforce the arbitration agreement and may order intervention or joinder of all parties in a single action or special proceeding; (2) may order intervention or joinder as to all or only certain issues; (3) may order arbitration among the parties who have agreed to arbitration and stay the pending court action or special proceeding pending the outcome of the arbitration proceeding; or (4) may stay arbitration pending the outcome of the court action or special proceeding.

Id.

[74] Film Finances, Inc. v. Superior Court, No. B155230, 2002 WL 228205 (Cal. Ct. App. 2002) (unpublished opinion). See generally §§ 6–14 (explaining breadth of FAA preemption of state law).

[75] 489 U.S. 468 (1989).

[76] See § 16.

[77] See KPMG LLP v. Cocchi, 565 U.S. 18, 22 (2011) (per curiam); Dean Witter Reynolds Inc. v. Byrd, 470 U.S. 213 (1985).

letter" of this holding.[78] In contrast, a California statute allows a court to stay arbitration until litigation concludes.[79]

§ 29 Class Actions and Mass Individual Arbitrations

(a) Class Arbitration and Agreements Barring It

(1) Class Arbitration's Brief Growth

The previous section explains that rules of civil procedure encourage courts to join multiple parties in a single action because joinder tends to save time and money and helps to avoid inconsistent results. Taking this reasoning further is the class action, which can effectively join millions of parties in one case. However, preventing class actions has become an important and controversial effect of agreeing to arbitrate.

Before the 21st Century, classwide arbitration was rare.[80] In 2003, though, the Supreme Court seemed to bless class arbitration in *Green Tree Financial Corp. v. Bazzle*.[81] The *Bazzle* case involved an

---

[78] Ian R. Macneil, Richard E. Speidel & Thomas J. Stipanowich, Federal Arbitration Law § 10.9.1, at 10:107 (1994). See AgGrow Oils, Inc. v. Nat. Union Fire Ins. Co., 242 F.3d 777 (8th Cir. 2001) (district court should consider whether to stay litigation until completion of arbitration involving one of the parties to litigation).

> There is now arbitration pending, and it should be given priority to the extent it is likely to resolve issues material to this lawsuit. On the other hand, the lawsuit involves more parties and claims than the arbitration. In a complex, multi-party dispute of this type, issues such as the risk of inconsistent rulings, the extent to which parties will be bound by the arbitrators' decision, and the prejudice that may result from delays must be weighed in determining whether to grant a discretionary stay, and in fashioning the precise contours of any stay.

Id. at 783. Sunopta, Inc. v. Abengoa Bioenergy New Technologies, Inc., No. 4:08CV78 JCH, 2008 WL 782656, at *5–6 (E.D. Mo. 2008) (staying litigation until completion of arbitration involving one of the parties to litigation).

[79] Cal. Civ. Proc. Code § 1281.2(c).

[80] Jean R. Sternlight, As Mandatory Binding Arbitration Meets the Class Action, Will the Class Action Survive?, 42 Wm. & Mary L. Rev. 1, 38 & n.135 (2000).

[81] 539 U.S. 444 (2003). *Bazzle* involved Green Tree's form consumer loan contract, which contained an arbitration clause. Id. at 447. Plaintiffs sued Green Tree in South Carolina state court and asked the court to certify a class action. Id. at 449. Green Tree sought to stay the court proceedings and compel arbitration. Id. The trial court both (1) certified a class action and (2) entered an order compelling arbitration. Id. Green Tree then selected an arbitrator with the plaintiffs' consent and the arbitrator, administering the proceeding as a class arbitration, awarded the class $10,935,000 in statutory damages, along with attorney's fees. Id. The trial court confirmed the award, and Green Tree appealed claiming, among other things, that class arbitration was legally impermissible. Id. On appeal, the South Carolina Supreme Court held that the contracts were silent with respect to class arbitration, that they consequently authorized class arbitration, and that arbitration had properly taken that form. Id. at 450. The Supreme Court granted certiorari to consider whether that holding is consistent with the FAA. Id.

While three dissenting justices thought the arbitration clause prohibited class arbitration, id. at 458–59, the Court agreed with the South Carolina Supreme Court that the clause was silent on whether class arbitration was permitted. Id. at 450–51.

arbitration agreement that neither permitted nor prohibited class arbitration, but rather was silent on that question. *Bazzle* decided that it was for the arbitrator, rather than a court, to interpret this silence,[82] and many arbitrators after *Bazzle* interpreted "silent" contracts to permit class arbitration.[83] Some of the major arbitration organizations developed special rules for handling the growing number of demands for class arbitration.[84]

(2) Enforcing Agreements for Individual Arbitration

The trend toward class arbitration began to reverse with the Supreme Court's 2010 decision in *Stolt-Nielsen S.A. v. AnimalFeeds International Corp.*,[85] which interpreted arbitration agreement silence on class arbitration as a prohibition of it. While the arbitrators in *Stolt-Nielsen* "imposed class arbitration even though the parties concurred that they had reached 'no agreement' on that issue," the Court said "the differences between bilateral and class-action arbitration are too great for arbitrators to presume, consistent with their limited powers under the FAA, that the parties' mere silence on the issue of class-action arbitration constitutes consent to resolve their disputes in class proceedings."[86] *Stolt-Nielsen* held that "a party may not be compelled under the FAA to submit to class arbitration unless there is a contractual basis for concluding that the party agreed to do so."[87] And a 2019 Supreme Court decision, *Lamps Plus, Inc. v. Varela*, held that contractual basis may not be found in an adhesive arbitration agreement's ambiguity about the availability of class arbitration combined with state law resolving adhesion contract ambiguities against the party that drafted the contract.[88] So, the combination of *Stolt-Nielsen* and *Lamps Plus* apparently means

---

Rather than affirming the South Carolina Supreme Court, however, the Court held that the arbitrator, rather than a court, should decide whether this silent contract should be interpreted to permit or prohibit class arbitration. Id. at 451–52. Therefore, the Court remanded for further proceedings. Id. at 454.

[82] See id.

[83] P. Christine Deruelle & Robert Clayton Roesch, Gaming the Rigged Class Arbitration Game: How We Got Here and Where We Go Now—Part I, Metropolitan Corp. Counsel, Aug. 2007, at 9 ("As of June 15, 2007, AAA arbitrators have rendered 51 Clause Construction Awards concerning otherwise silent arbitration agreements, and in all but two of those decisions, the arbitrators have allowed class wide proceedings.")

[84] Am. Arb. Ass'n, AAA Supplementary Rules For Class Arbitrations (2011), available at adr.org/sites/default/files/Supplementary_Rules_for_Class_Arbitrations.pdf (last visited Feb. 6, 2022); JAMS, JAMS Class Action Procedures (2009), http://www.jamsadr.com/rules-class-action-procedures/ (last visited Apr. 20, 2022).

[85] 559 U.S. 662 (2010).

[86] Id. at 684.

[87] Id.

[88] 139 S. Ct. 1407, 1411 (2019).

courts may find the necessary contractual basis for class arbitration only when

- an arbitration agreement expressly provides for it; or
- parties agree that the arbitrator should decide whether their contract authorized class arbitration and the arbitrator decides that it does.[89]

In all other cases an agreement to arbitrate is effectively an agreement to resolve disputes on an individual rather than classwide basis.

Whether to enforce such "class waivers" long divided courts, with some courts enforcing them,[90] and others, often on unconscionability grounds, refusing to, particularly in adhesive arbitration agreements.[91] For instance, in *Discover Bank v. Superior Court*,[92] the California Supreme Court said:

> We do not hold that all class action waivers are necessarily unconscionable. But when the waiver is found in a consumer contract of adhesion in a setting in which disputes between the contracting parties predictably involve small amounts of damages, and when it is alleged that the party with the superior bargaining power has carried out a scheme to deliberately cheat large numbers of consumers out of individually small sums of money, then, at least to the extent the obligation at issue is governed by California law, the waiver becomes in practice the exemption of the party "from responsibility for [its] own fraud, or willful injury to the person or property of another." (Civ. Code, § 1668.) Under these circumstances, such waivers are unconscionable under California law and should not be enforced.[93]

This "*Discover Bank* rule is preempted by the FAA," the U.S. Supreme Court held in *AT & T Mobility LLC v. Concepcion*.[94] The *AT & T* case involved a federal court's application of the *Discover Bank* rule to hold unconscionable an arbitration clause in a cell phone

89 This occurred in Oxford Health Plans LLC v. Sutter, 569 U.S. 564, 566 (2013).

90 See, e.g., Jenkins v. First Am. Cash Advance of Ga., LLC, 400 F.3d 868, 877–78 (11th Cir. 2005); Johnson v. West Suburban Bank, 225 F.3d 366, 373–74 (3rd Cir. 2000); Livingston v. Associates Fin., Inc., 339 F.3d 553, 557 (7th Cir. 2003); Snowden v. Checkpoint Check Cashing, 290 F.3d 631, 638 (4th Cir. 2002).

91 See, e.g., Dale v. Comcast Corp., 498 F.3d 1216 (11th Cir. 2007); Ting v. AT & T, 319 F.3d 1126, 1150 (9th Cir. 2003); Ingle v. Circuit City Stores, Inc., 328 F.3d 1165 (9th Cir. 2003); Omstead v. Dell, Inc., 594 F.3d 1081 (9th Cir. 2010).

92 30 Cal. Rptr. 3d 76 (Cal. 2005).

93 Id. at 87.

94 563 U.S. 333 (2011).

contract. The Ninth Circuit held that the *Discover Bank* rule was not preempted by the FAA because that rule was simply "a refinement of the unconscionability analysis applicable to contracts generally in California,"[95] and thus fell within the savings clause at the end of FAA § 2, which states that arbitration agreements "shall be valid, irrevocable, and enforceable, save upon such grounds as exist at law or in equity for the revocation of any contract."[96]

The Supreme Court's majority[97] disagreed. It said "[t]he overarching purpose of the FAA, evident in the text of §§ 2, 3, and 4, is to ensure the enforcement of arbitration agreements according to their terms so as to facilitate streamlined proceedings."[98] The Court's reasoning built on this premise that an important purpose of the FAA was to enforce agreements in which parties choose the more streamlined process (arbitration) over the more elaborate process (litigation). The Court suggested that the FAA would preempt (hypothetical) state law deeming unconscionable arbitration agreements lacking "judicially monitored discovery,"[99] "adherence to the Federal Rules of Evidence,"[100] or "arbitration-by-jury"[101] because requiring arbitration to include these aspects of litigation would effectively convert the more streamlined process into the more elaborate process so it would no longer be "arbitration" as that process was envisioned by those who enacted the FAA.[102] Similarly, the Court concluded, "Requiring the availability of classwide arbitration interferes with fundamental attributes of arbitration and thus creates a scheme inconsistent with the FAA."[103] Quoting its decision in *Stolt-Nielsen*, the *AT & T* Court said:

---

95 Laster v. AT & T Mobility LLC, 584 F.3d 849, 857 (9th Cir. 2009).

96 9 U.S.C. § 2.

97 Four justices joined the opinion with Justice Thomas concurring in the result. AT & T Mobility LLC v. Concepcion, 563 U.S. 333, 343 (2011). (Thomas, J., concurring). (FAA § 2 "does not include all defenses applicable to any contract but rather some subset of those defenses").

98 Id. at 344.

99 Id.

100 Id.

101 Id. at 349 n.7.

102 In fact, arbitration is generally less elaborate than litigation; arbitration agreements commonly provide for less discovery and motion practice than is typical of litigation and commonly provide for fewer rules of evidence than are typical of litigation. But the parties are free to draft their agreement otherwise. See § 31. The *AT & T* Court said that "Parties could agree to arbitrate pursuant to the Federal Rules of Civil Procedure, or pursuant to a discovery process rivaling that in litigation. Arbitration is a matter of contract, and the FAA requires courts to honor parties' expectations. * * * But what the parties in the aforementioned examples would have agreed to is not arbitration as envisioned by the FAA, lacks its benefits, and therefore may not be required by state law." 563 U.S. 333 (2011).

103 Id. at 344.

> "[C]hanges brought about by the shift from bilateral arbitration to class-action arbitration" are "fundamental." * * * The conclusion follows that class arbitration, to the extent it is manufactured by *Discover Bank* rather than consensual, is inconsistent with the FAA.
>
> First, the switch from bilateral to class arbitration sacrifices the principal advantage of arbitration—its informality—and makes the process slower, more costly, and more likely to generate procedural morass than final judgment. * * *
>
> * * *
>
> Second, class arbitration requires procedural formality. The AAA's rules governing class arbitrations mimic the Federal Rules of Civil Procedure for class litigation. * * *
>
> [I]t is at the very least odd to think that an arbitrator would be entrusted with ensuring that third parties' due process rights are satisfied.
>
> * * *
>
> Third, class arbitration greatly increases risks to defendants. Informal procedures do of course have a cost: The absence of multilayered review makes it more likely that errors will go uncorrected. * * *
>
> * * * We find it hard to believe that defendants would bet the company with no effective means of review, and even harder to believe that Congress would have intended to allow state courts to force such a decision.[104]

In sum, *AT & T* and *Stolt-Nielsen* see "bilateral" arbitration—the simple type of arbitration contemplated by the FAA—as the norm and see class arbitration as a strange process that a few parties might choose, but which should not be imposed on parties who have agreed to arbitrate without specifically approving class arbitration. And *AT & T* strongly suggests that courts may not consider it a strike against the enforceability of an arbitration agreement that the agreement provides only for arbitration, and not for class arbitration. *AT & T* reads the FAA as preempting state law—even state law categorized as "unconscionability" or some other ground for the revocation of any contract—that "[r]equir[es] the availability of classwide arbitration."[105]

---

[104] Id. at 347–51.

[105] Id. at 344. See also American Express Co. v. Italian Colors Restaurant, 570 U.S. 228 (2013).

The Supreme Court majority's resistance to class arbitration continued in *Epic Systems Corp. v. Lewis*,[106] which involved employment agreements requiring disputes be resolved in individualized arbitration, with claims "pertaining to different [e]mployees [to] be heard in separate proceedings."[107] The employee plaintiffs seeking to litigate a class action argued that enforcement of the agreement for individual arbitration violates the National Labor Relations Act, § 7 which says:

> Employees shall have the right to self-organization, to form, join, or assist labor organizations, to bargain collectively through representatives of their own choosing, and to engage in other concerted activities for the purpose of collective bargaining or other mutual aid or protection.[108]

The *Epic Systems* majority saw no conflict between § 7 and the command of the FAA, as interpreted by *AT & T* and *Stolt-Nielsen*, to enforce arbitration agreements requiring individual rather than class proceedings. *Epic Systems* points out that § 7 "does not express approval or disapproval of arbitration. It does not mention class or collective action procedures. It does not even hint at a wish to displace the Arbitration Act—let alone accomplish that much clearly and manifestly, as our precedents demand."[109]

In 2021, the U.S. House of Representatives has passed a bill to overrule *Epic Systems*, but the bill ("the PRO Act") has not, as of this writing, passed the Senate.[110] Moreover, *Epic Systems* does not resolve all tension between the FAA's enforcement of class waivers and other federal statutes or the agency rulemaking they authorize. For instance, the Securities Exchange Commission prohibits class waivers, so they are not enforceable in securities brokers' contracts with their customers and employees.[111] The Consumer Financial Protection Bureau enacted a similar prohibition for agreements within its jurisdiction, but the U.S. Senate overturned it, under the

---

[106] 138 S. Ct. 1612 (2018).

[107] Id. at 1620.

[108] 29 U.S.C. § 157.

[109] Epic Systems Corp. v. Lewis, 138 S. Ct. 1612, 1624 (2018).

[110] H.R. 842, 117th Cong. § 104(5) (2021) ("[I]t shall be an unfair labor practice under subsection (a)(1) for an employer to enter into or attempt to enforce any agreement, express or implied, whereby prior to a dispute to which the agreement applies, an employee undertakes or promises not to pursue, bring, join, litigate, or support any kind of joint, class, or collective claim arising from or relating to the employment of such employee in any forum that, but for such agreement, is of competent jurisdiction.").

[111] See FINRA Rule 13204. The Commodities Futures Trading Commission has a similar rule for the industry it regulates. See CFTC Regulation 7.201.

Congressional Review Act, with Vice President Pence casting the tie-breaking vote.[112]

(3) Private Attorneys General Act ("PAGA")

Although not technically a class action, California's Private Attorneys General Act ("PAGA") also permits many individual "low-value claims [to] be welded together into high-value suits."[113] In addition to the authority of a state agency to sue employers for violations of the state's labor code, PAGA allows suits against the employer by an employee as a representative the state and, in that capacity, on behalf of other employees. In a successful PAGA action, the state receives 75% of the award, while the remaining 25% "is distributed among the employees affected by the violations at issue."[114] The California Supreme Court said that its refusal to enforce agreements requiring individual arbitration of PAGA claims was not preempted by the FAA.[115] The U.S. Supreme Court's 2022 decision in *Viking River Cruises, Inc. v. Moriana*,[116] disagreed.

In *Viking*, an employee brought a PAGA suit against her former employer, both individually and, as a representative of the state, for other employees. The plaintiff's employment agreement required her to arbitrate individual claims and said she could not bring a class, collective, or representative action under PAGA. Plaintiff's employer moved to compel arbitration of her individual PAGA claim and to dismiss her PAGA claims for other employees. The California courts denied those motions, but the Supreme Court reversed.

Citing *Stolt-Nielsen* and *Lamps Plus*, *Viking* emphasized the freedom of parties to determine "the issues subject to arbitration" and

---

112 Arbitration Agreements, 82 Fed. Reg. 33,210 (July 19, 2017), repealed by Pub. L. No. 115-74, 131 Stat. 1243 (2017). Republicans, Wall Street score victory in dismantling class-action rule, Oct. 25, 2017, https://www.cnbc.com/2017/10/24/senate-kills-cfpb-rule-on-arbitration-class-action-lawsuits.html ("Vice President Mike Pence appeared on the Senate floor * * * to cast the tie-breaking vote as the chamber's president and approve the most significant roll-back of Obama-era financial policy since President Donald Trump took office vowing to loosen the leash on Wall Street. The final count was 51 to 50").

113 Viking River Cruises, Inc. v. Moriana, 142 S. Ct. 1906, 1915 (2022).

114 Cal. Lab. Code § 2699(i).

115 Iskanian v. CLS Transportation Los Angeles, LLC, 327 P.3d 129, 151 (Cal. 2014). Accord Sakkab v. Luxottica Retail N. Am., Inc., 803 F.3d 425, 432 (9th Cir. 2015). Similarly, California courts also hold that the FAA does not preempt state law prohibiting enforcement of pre-dispute arbitration agreements with respect to claims for injunctive relief under certain state statutes. Cruz v. Pacificare Health Sys., Inc., 66 P.3d 1157 (Cal. 2003); Broughton v. Cigna Healthplans, 988 P.2d 67 (Cal. 1999). However, the Ninth Circuit limited these California holdings. Kilgore v. KeyBank, Nat. Ass'n, 718 F.3d 1052 (9th Cir. 2013) (en banc) (FAA preempts Broughton-Cruz rule except in narrow circumstances in which the injunctive relief sought mostly benefits the general public rather than the individual party pursuing the claim).

116 142 S. Ct. 1906 (2022).

"the rules by which they will arbitrate."[117] The *Viking* agreement required individual arbitration, but California law would allow the "employee to abrogate that agreement after the fact and demand either judicial proceedings or an arbitral proceeding that exceeds the scope jointly intended by the parties."[118] This, *Viking* held, is preempted by the FAA. "[S]tate law cannot condition the enforceability of an arbitration agreement on the availability of a procedural mechanism that would permit a party [the employee] to expand the scope of the arbitration by introducing claims [on behalf of other employees] that the parties did not jointly agree to arbitrate."[119] *Viking* held "that the FAA preempts [California law] insofar as it precludes division of PAGA actions into individual and non-individual claims through an agreement to arbitrate."[120]

Additionally, the Court said that PAGA provides no mechanism for an individual employee whose claims are in arbitration to litigate her claims as a representative of the state on behalf of other employees. In other words, this employee lost standing under PAGA to litigate representative claims once the Supreme Court sent her individual claims to arbitration.[121] Justice Sotomayor's concurring opinion noted that *Viking* permits California to change PAGA's standing requirements to give an arbitrating employee standing to litigate claims as a representative of the state on behalf of other employees.[122]

(b) Mass Individual Arbitrations

Enterprising plaintiffs' lawyers responded to enforcement of agreements requiring individual arbitration by filing many of them together in what has come to be known as "mass individual arbitration." As arbitration organizations' rules tend to require lower

---

[117] Viking River Cruises, Inc. v. Moriana, 142 S. Ct. 1906, 1918 (2022).

[118] Id. at 1924.

[119] Id. at 1912.

[120] Id. at 1911.

[121] Id. at 1925 ("PAGA provides no mechanism to enable a court to adjudicate non-individual PAGA claims once an individual claim has been committed to a separate proceeding. Under PAGA's standing requirement, a plaintiff can maintain non-individual PAGA claims in an action only by virtue of also maintaining an individual claim in that action. When an employee's own dispute is pared away from a PAGA action, the employee is no different from a member of the general public, and PAGA does not allow such persons to maintain suit.")

[122] Id. at 1926 (Sotomayor, J.) ("if this Court's understanding of state law is wrong, California courts, in an appropriate case, will have the last word. Alternatively, if this Court's understanding is right, the California Legislature is free to modify the scope of statutory standing under PAGA within state and federal constitutional limits.")

filing fees of individual claimants than responding businesses,[123] those businesses have balked at the costs of mass individual arbitration. For example, one law firm "filed over 31,000 substantively identical arbitration demands with AAA on behalf of the Uber Eats customers against Uber."[124] AAA agreed to administer the claims under its Consumer Arbitration Rules, which included a fee schedule under which "Uber would owe AAA a $500 filing fee, a $1,400 standard case management fee, and a $1,500 arbitrator fee, for a total of approximately $107 million if charged the full amount under the fee schedule."[125] AAA also invoked a California statute, which provides that

> In an employment or consumer arbitration that requires, either expressly or through application of state or federal law or the rules of the arbitration provider, the drafting party to pay certain fees and costs before the arbitration can proceed, if the fees or costs to initiate an arbitration proceeding are not paid within 30 days after the due date the drafting party is in material breach of the arbitration agreement, is in default of the arbitration, and waives its right to compel arbitration.[126]

Uber sued AAA alleging that its invoicing was unlawful and seeking a preliminary injunction, which was denied by the trial and appellate courts. The Appellate Division said, "The balance of the equities weighs in favor of AAA. While Uber is trying to avoid paying the arbitration fees associated with 31,000 nearly identical cases, it made the business decision to preclude class, collective, or representative

---

123 See, e.g., Abernathy v. DoorDash, Inc., 438 F. Supp. 3d 1062, 1064 (N.D. Cal. 2020) ("AAA's Commercial Arbitration Rules require each individual to pay a filing fee of $300 and the responding company to pay a filing fee of $1,900.")

124 Uber Techs., Inc. v. Am. Arb. Ass'n, Inc., 167 N.Y.S.3d 66, 68 (App. Div. 2022).

125 Id.

126 Cal. Civ. Proc. Code § 1281.97(a)(1). California statutes further require courts to impose on drafting parties that breach this fee-paying duty a duty "to pay the reasonable expenses, including attorney's fees and costs, incurred by the employee or consumer as a result," and the court may order:

> (1) An evidence sanction by an order prohibiting the drafting party from conducting discovery in the civil action.
>
> (2) A terminating sanction by one of the following orders:
>
> (A) An order striking out the pleadings or parts of the pleadings of the drafting party.
>
> (B) An order rendering a judgment by default against the drafting party.
>
> (3) A contempt sanction by an order treating the drafting party as in contempt of court.

Cal. Civ. Proc. Code § 1281.99.

claims in its arbitration agreement with its consumers, and AAA's fees are directly attributable to that decision."[127]

Similar mass individual arbitrations against DoorDash led the federal district court ordering DoorDash to pay more than $9 million in arbitration filing fees to write:

> For decades, the employer-side bar and their employer clients have forced arbitration clauses upon workers, thus taking away their right to go to court, and forced class-action waivers upon them too, thus taking away their ability to join collectively to vindicate common rights. The employer-side bar has succeeded in the United States Supreme Court to sustain such provisions. The irony, in this case, is that the workers wish to enforce the very provisions forced on them by seeking, even if by the thousands, individual arbitrations, the remnant of procedural rights left to them. The employer here, DoorDash, faced with having to actually honor its side of the bargain, now blanches at the cost of the filing fees it agreed to pay in the arbitration clause. No doubt, DoorDash never expected that so many would actually seek arbitration. Instead, in irony upon irony, DoorDash now wishes to resort to a class-wide lawsuit, the very device it denied to the workers, to avoid its duty to arbitrate. This hypocrisy will not be blessed, at least by this order.[128]

The innovation of mass individual arbitration led the AAA to institute new rules for them, such as "where party submissions are substantially similar across a Multiple Case Filing, the submission may be filed in a single document and need not be filed separately in each individual case."[129] Mass individual arbitration has also led some businesses to remove arbitration clauses from their form contracts. For instance, Amazon removed arbitration from its terms of service in 2021 "after plaintiffs' lawyers flooded Amazon with more than 75,000 individual arbitration demands on behalf of Echo users. That move triggered a bill for tens of millions of dollars in filing fees."[130]

---

127 Uber Techs., Inc. v. Am. Arb. Ass'n, Inc., 167 N.Y.S.3d 66, 70 (App. Div. 2022).

128 Abernathy v. DoorDash, Inc., 438 F. Supp. 3d 1062, 1067–68 (N.D. Cal. 2020).

129 Supplementary Rules for Multiple Case Filings, Am. Arb. Ass'n, https://www.adr.org/sites/default/files/Supplementary_Rules_MultipleCase_Filings.pdf (Jan. 27, 2022).

130 Sara Randazzo, Amazon Faced 75,000 Arbitration Demands. Now It Says: Fine, Sue Us, Wall St. J., June 1, 2021, https://www.wsj.com/articles/amazon-faced-75-000-arbitration-demands-now-it-says-fine-sue-us-11622547000.

C. CONDITIONS TO ARBITRATION

§ 30 Conditions to Arbitration

Sections 2.21–2.23 explain that, in the absence of an enforceable contract clause delegating such issues to an arbitrator, courts may hear contract defenses such as fraud and unconscionability "directed to the arbitration clause itself." In contrast, one might also use a phrase like "defenses to arbitration" to refer to arguments that arbitration should not occur because a contractual condition to arbitration—like trying negotiation or mediation before arbitration[131]—has not been satisfied. Such arguments, the Supreme Court held in *Howsam v. Dean Witter Reynolds, Inc.*, should be heard by the arbitrator even if they are directed to the arbitration clause itself.[132] *Howsam* said "procedural questions which grow out of the dispute and bear on its final disposition are presumptively not for the judge, but for an arbitrator, to decide."[133] As examples, the *Howsam* Court endorsed authorities stating that the "arbitrator should decide whether the first two steps of a grievance procedure were completed, where these steps are prerequisites to arbitration," and "whether prerequisites such as time limits, notice, laches, estoppel, and other conditions precedent to an obligation to arbitrate have been met, are for the arbitrators to decide."[134]

D. ARBITRATION PROCEDURE

Table of Sections

Sec.

---

[131] See, e.g., Molton, Allen & Williams, LLC v. Cont'l Cas. Ins. Co., No. 09-CV-6924, 2010 WL 780353, at *1 (N.D. Ill. Mar. 3, 2010) ("The Agreement contains a mandatory arbitration clause which states: 'In the event of any dispute arising out of or relating to this agreement which cannot be resolved by negotiation, the parties shall endeavor to settle the dispute by non-binding mediation. * * * Any dispute which has not been resolved by mediation within 60 days of the demand for such procedure shall be resolved by final and binding arbitration under the Commercial Arbitration Rules of the American Arbitration Association.")

[132] 537 U.S. 79, 84–85 (2002).

[133] Id.

[134] Id.

---

§ 31 Procedure by Contract

Arbitration, like any *adjudication*,[135] involves the presentation of evidence and argument to the adjudicator. The presentation of evidence and argument in litigation is governed by rules of procedure and evidence enacted by government. In contrast, the rules of procedure and evidence in arbitration are, with few exceptions, whatever the parties' arbitration agreement says they are. The procedures of arbitration are largely determined by contract. According to the Supreme Court,

> The point of affording parties discretion in designing arbitration processes is to allow for efficient, streamlined procedures tailored to the type of dispute. It can be specified, for example, that the decisionmaker be a specialist in the relevant field, or that proceedings be kept confidential to protect trade secrets. And the informality of arbitral proceedings is itself desirable, reducing the cost and increasing the speed of dispute resolution.[136]

As this passage suggests, arbitration tends to be less elaborate than litigation. Compared to litigation, arbitration tends to have less elaborate pleadings, discovery, motion practice, and evidentiary

---

[135] See § 1.

[136] AT & T Mobility LLC v. Concepcion, 563 U.S. 333, 343 (2011).

rules. That is largely because parties typically agree to arbitrate under the rules of arbitration organizations—such as the AAA—that tend to provide more streamlined processes than provided by courts' rules of procedure and evidence. But parties are generally free to draft their arbitration agreement almost any way they like. Arbitration privatizes procedural law by allowing parties to create their own customized rules of procedure and evidence.

However, courts impose some limits on the parties' freedom of contract, particularly in adhesive arbitration agreements. If arbitration occurs and does not meet a court's definition of a "fundamentally fair hearing" then the court will grant a motion to vacate the arbitration award.[137] And courts have refused to compel arbitration of employment and consumer disputes when persuaded that the agreement's procedures for arbitration would have been unfair. These cases rest on contract law's unconscionability doctrine, or special concerns regarding the vindication of federal statutory rights.[138] For example, an oft-cited case, *Cole v. Burns Int'l Security Services,*[139] enforced an employee's agreement to arbitrate statutory employment discrimination claims, but only because:

> the arbitration arrangement (1) provides for neutral arbitrators, (2) provides for more than minimal discovery, (3) requires a written award, (4) provides for all of the types of relief that would otherwise be available in court, and (5) does not require employees to pay either unreasonable costs or any arbitrators' fees or expenses as a condition of access to the arbitration forum.[140]

While other courts use different words, the substance of this list is generally typical. The more of these five factors that are present, the more likely a court is to enforce the arbitration agreement.

§ 32 Privacy, Confidentiality, and #MeToo

Trials are in government buildings open to the public, including news media, and other aspects of litigation—from pleadings and motions through jury verdicts and judicial opinions—are typically public records. In contrast, arbitration filings, hearings, and awards are typically private.[141] But while arbitration organization rules

---

137 See § 40(c).

138 See § 24.

139 105 F.3d 1465 (D.C. Cir. 1997).

140 Id. at 1482 (quoting Gilmer v. Interstate/Johnson Lane Corp., 500 U.S. 20, 28 (1991)).

141 See, e.g., Am. Arb. Ass'n, Commercial Arbitration Rules, R–26 (2022) ("The arbitrator and the AAA shall maintain the privacy of the hearings unless the law provides to the contrary. Any person having a direct interest in the arbitration is entitled to attend hearings. The arbitrator shall otherwise have the power to require

typically require the arbitrator and arbitration organization to maintain confidentiality, arbitration organization rules do not typically impose any duty of confidentiality on the parties or their lawyers.[142] So, parties to arbitration agreements are free to share with the public, including news media, whatever they like about their claims, their arbitration, and their arbitration agreement, unless they have agreed not to.[143] "Indeed, the whole reason contracts with arbitration clauses [sometimes] include separate nondisclosure provisions is that the default view of arbitration in the United States does not extend as far [toward confidentiality] as the nondisclosure agreements would require."[144]

A study published in 2004 found confidentiality agreements (also known as non-disclosure agreements or NDAs) in only 13.5% of arbitration agreements,[145] and the Consumer Financial Protection Bureau reported in 2015 that "most arbitration clauses" in the consumer agreements the CFPB studied "were silent on confidentiality and did not impose any nondisclosure obligation on

---

the exclusion of any witness, other than a party or other essential person, during the testimony of any other witness. It shall be discretionary with the arbitrator to determine the propriety of the attendance of any other person."); id. R–45(a) ("Unless otherwise required by applicable law, court order, or the parties' agreement, the AAA and the arbitrator shall keep confidential all matters relating to the arbitration or the award."); id. R-35(b) ("Upon the agreement of the parties or the request of any party, the arbitrator may make orders concerning the confidentiality of the arbitration proceedings or of any other matters in connection with the arbitration and may take measures for protecting trade secrets and confidential information."). However, "[t]he presumption of privacy and confidentiality in arbitration proceedings shall not apply in class arbitrations. All class arbitration hearings and filings may be made public, subject to the authority of the arbitrator to provide otherwise in special circumstances." Am. Arb. Ass'n, Supplementary Rules for Class Arbitrations, 9(a) (2003).

142 See, e.g., Statement of Ethical Principles, Am. Arb. Ass'n, https://www.adr.org/StatementofEthicalPrinciples ("An arbitration proceeding is a private process. In addition, AAA staff and AAA neutrals have an ethical obligation to keep information confidential. However, the AAA takes no position on whether parties should or should not agree to keep the proceeding and award confidential between themselves. The parties always have a right to disclose details of the proceeding, unless they have a separate confidentiality agreement."); JAMS R. 26(a)–(c) ("JAMS and the Arbitrator shall maintain the confidential nature of the Arbitration proceeding and the Award, including the Hearing, except as necessary in connection with a judicial challenge to or enforcement of an Award or unless otherwise required by law or judicial decision").

143 Christopher R. Drahozal, Confidentiality in Consumer and Employment Arbitration, 7 Y.B. On Arb. & Mediation 28, 37 (2015) ("unless subject to a separate confidentiality agreement, a party is always free to disclose that it has a dispute and the nature of the dispute. Agreeing to arbitrate the dispute does not preclude the party from making such disclosure") (providing examples).

144 Christopher R. Drahozal, FAA Preemption After Concepcion, 35 Berkeley J. Emp. & Lab. L. 153, 167 (2014).

145 Linda J. Demaine & Deborah R. Hensler, "Volunteering" to Arbitrate Through Predispute Arbitration Clauses: The Average Consumer's Experience, 67 Law & Contemp. Probs. 55, 69 (2004).

the parties."[146] However, parties' agreements to keep arbitration confidential, especially in employment, became very controversial around 2018, largely due to the #MeToo movement and its characterization of arbitration agreements required by employers as a condition of employment as "forced." For example, Fox News anchor Gretchen Carlson said "Forced arbitration is a sexual harasser's best friend: It keeps proceedings secret, findings sealed, and victims silent."[147] The settlement agreement between Donald Trump and Stephanie Clifford (a/k/a Stormy Daniels) included both confidentiality and arbitration clauses.[148] When Clifford threatened to publicize her alleged intimate relationship with Trump, an arbitrator prohibited Clifford from doing so, but Clifford nevertheless filed suit and made public the agreement as well as her allegations about the affair.[149] In 2018, attorneys general from all 50 states sent a letter to Congress opposing enforcement of agreements to arbitrate sexual harassment claims, adding that

> concerns arise from the secrecy requirements of arbitration clauses, which disserve the public interest by keeping both the harassment complaints and any settlements confidential. This veil of secrecy may then prevent other persons similarly situated from learning of the harassment claims so that they, too, might pursue relief. Ending mandatory arbitration of sexual harassment claims would help to put a stop to the culture of silence that protects perpetrators at the cost of their victims.[150]

While the 2022 enactment of FAA Chapter 4 presumably ends enforcement of predispute arbitration agreements against parties

---

146 Consumer Financial Protection Bureau, Arbitration Study: Report to Congress Pursuant to Dodd-Frank Wall Street Reform and Consumer Protection Act § 1028(a), § 2, at 52 (2015).

147 Gretchen Carlson, Gretchen Carlson: The Supreme Court Tried to End #MeToo. Here's How We're Fighting Back., FORTUNE (May 31, 2018, 11:06 AM EDT), http://fortune.com/2018/05/31/gretchen-carlson-supreme-court-ruling-arbitration-metoo [https://perma.cc/HV53-WP8H].

148 Brian Farkas, Donald Trump and Stormy Daniels: An Arbitration Case Study, 24 Disp. Resol. Mag. 12, 13 (Summer 2018), https://www.americanbar.org/content/dam/aba/publications/dispute_resolution_magazine/summer-2018/8-an-arbitration-case-study.authcheckdam.pdf.

149 See Jim Rutenberg and Peter Baker, Trump Lawyer Obtained Restraining Order to Silence Stormy Daniels, N.Y. Times, Mar. 7, 2018, at A1, https://www.nytimes.com/2018/03/07/us/politics/stormy-daniels-trump.html ("Ms. Clifford's agreement, though it was made public through her lawsuit, calls for disagreements to be settled through confidential, binding arbitration. It gives Mr. Trump the right to seek financial penalties of more than $1 million in arbitration should Ms. Clifford break or threaten to break her agreement to stay silent. It also gives him the right to obtain an injunction barring her from speaking while disputes are considered in arbitration or open court.")

150 Nat'l Ass'n of Attorneys General, Feb. 12, 2018.

asserting sexual harassment claims,[151] no federal legislation addresses confidentiality in arbitration. However, courts have sometimes pointed to confidentiality provisions in holding arbitration agreements unconscionable.[152]

A few state statutes protect arbitration materials from discovery or admissibility in litigation.[153] Absent such a statute, the evidence and arguments produced in arbitration may discoverable and admissible in litigation,[154] even if the arbitration is subject to a confidentiality agreement.[155] In contrast, other courts have refused discovery of arbitration materials in reliance on the "important public interest in protecting the rights of parties who submit to confidential arbitration."[156]

§ 33 Pre-Hearing

(a) Selection of Arbitrator(s)

(1) Methods of Selection

Arbitration requires at least one arbitrator. Selection of the arbitrator or arbitrators typically occurs through agreement of the

---

151 See § 5(e)(2).

152 See § 24(a).

153 See, e.g., Ark. Code Ann. § 16–7–206 (2022); Cal. Evid. Code § 703.5 (2022); Mo. Ann. Stat. § 435.014 (2022). See also Group Health Plan, Inc. v. BJC Health Sys., Inc., 30 S.W.3d 198 (Mo. Ct. App. 2000); Cox v. Bonni, 241 Cal. Rptr. 3d 359, 379 (Ct. App. 2018) ("Evidence Code section 703.5 broadly prohibits arbitrators from 'testify[ing], in any subsequent civil proceeding, as to any statement, conduct, decision, or ruling, occurring at or in conjunction with' an arbitration over which they presided. There are limited exceptions to this prohibition, one of which permits an arbitrator to provide testimony that 'addresses [a] charge of bias, partiality or improper conduct.' Here, the proceedings in the trial court concerned the neutral arbitrator's purported improper conduct, thus potentially implicating the exception noted above").

154 Sandoz Inc. v. Lannett Co., Inc., 2021 WL 3022431, at *1 (E.D. Pa. July 16, 2021) (ordering the production of arbitration materials in a separate proceeding "[g]iven the close relationship between" the two proceedings. The court observed that the proponent's compelling "interest in discovery . . . outweigh[ed] any institutional concerns about preserving the confidentiality of arbitration proceedings."); Legent Grp., LLC v. Axos Fin., Inc., No. CV 2020-0405-KSJM, 2021 WL 4593775, at *3 (Del. Ch. Oct. 6, 2021) ("the mere fact that the FINRA Arbitration materials are confidential does not immunize them from discovery. Indeed, this court has ordered the production of arbitration materials in the past, and other courts have reached similar conclusions.")

155 Lohnn v. Int'l Bus. Machines Corp., No. 21-CV-6379 (LJL), 2022 WL 36420, at *1 (S.D.N.Y. Jan. 4, 2022) (defendant's motion to seal denied "to the extent that it seeks a blanket order maintaining under seal documents and information in this Court simply because it was conveyed in arbitrations that were subject to a confidentiality agreement.")

156 Pasternak v. Dow Kim, No. 10 CIV. 5045 LTS JLC, 2013 WL 1729564, at *3 (S.D.N.Y. Apr. 22, 2013) (quoting Guyden v. Aetna, Inc., 544 F.3d 376, 385 (2d Cir. 2008)).

parties. If the parties cannot agree on an arbitrator, however, the court will appoint one. FAA § 5 gives courts the authority to do so:

> If in the agreement provision be made for a method of naming or appointing an arbitrator or arbitrators or an umpire, such method shall be followed; but if no method be provided therein, or if a method be provided and any party thereto shall fail to avail himself of such method, or if for any other reason there shall be a lapse in the naming of an arbitrator or arbitrators or umpire, or in filling a vacancy, then upon the application of either party to the controversy the court shall designate and appoint an arbitrator or arbitrators or umpire, as the case may require, who shall act under the said agreement with the same force and effect as if he or they had been specifically named therein; and unless otherwise provided in the agreement the arbitration shall be by a single arbitrator.[157]

Many states have similar provisions.[158] The Seventh and Third Circuits cited FAA § 5 in holding that the district court should appoint an arbitrator where the agreement provided for arbitration by an organization that no longer arbitrated that sort of case.[159] The Second Circuit disagrees.[160]

Court appointment of an arbitrator is rarely necessary because the parties usually agree on an arbitrator. Agreements selecting an arbitrator fall into three categories. First, the parties can name an arbitrator (*e.g.*, "Sylvia Rome") in their arbitration agreement. While this is fairly common in post-dispute arbitration agreements,[161] it is rare in predispute arbitration agreements. At the time a predispute agreement is formed, the parties probably hope and expect that no dispute will ever occur. Why take the time to negotiate agreement on

---

157 9 U.S.C. § 5. See, e.g., Astra Footwear Indus. v. Harwyn Int'l, Inc., 442 F. Supp. 907 (S.D.N.Y. 1978).

158 Unif. Arbitration Act § 11 (2000); NY C.P.L.R. § 7504 (Consol. 2012).

159 Green v. U.S. Cash Advance Illinois, LLC, 724 F.3d 787, 793 (7th Cir. 2013) ("Section 5 allows judges to supply details in order to make arbitration work. The district judge must appoint an arbitrator, who will resolve this dispute using the procedures in the National Arbitration Forum's Code of Procedure."); Khan v. Dell Inc., 669 F.3d 350 (3d Cir. 2012).

160 Moss v. First Premier Bank, 835 F.3d 260, 265–66 (2d Cir. 2016) ("Appellants contend that NAF's inability to accept this case constitutes a 'lapse' within the meaning of Section 5 such that the district court was required to appoint a substitute arbitrator." But there is no lapse where "the parties designated an exclusive arbitral forum, the district court compelled the parties to arbitrate before that forum, and the forum declined to accept the case." "[U]nder such circumstances, a court cannot use Section 5 to circumvent the clear text of the parties' agreement and appoint a substitute arbitrator.")

161 See e.g., Smith v. DHL Express (USA) Inc., 2005 WL 3111013 (N.D. Cal. 2005); DeOliveira v. Liberty Mutual Ins. Co., 2003 WL 21101303 (Conn. 2003).

who the arbitrator should be when arbitration is so unlikely? Even if the parties consider the possibility of a dispute, they do not know what that dispute will involve. Maybe Sylvia Rome would be the best arbitrator for one sort of dispute but not for another. Finally, at the time a predispute agreement is formed, the parties do not know *when* a dispute will occur. Perhaps by then, Sylvia Rome will be unavailable or unwilling to serve as an arbitrator. For all these reasons, predispute agreements rarely name an arbitrator.

What predispute agreements typically do is commit to a procedure for selecting an arbitrator. Many predispute agreements commit the parties to arbitrate according to the rules of an arbitration organization, like the American Arbitration Association. AAA rules, like the rules of other arbitration organizations, contain procedures for selecting an arbitrator. For example, under its Commercial Rules, the AAA sends the parties a list of ten potential arbitrators with some information about each person.[162] Then each party can strike the potential arbitrators to which that party objects, except that the AAA may, at its discretion, limit the number of strikes permitted.[163] Each party also ranks the remaining people in order of that party's preference.[164] The AAA invites those people with the highest combined ranking to serve as arbitrators.[165] If this process does not produce an arbitrator willing to serve, the AAA picks an arbitrator.[166]

Diversifying the rosters of leading arbitration organizations has become an increasingly high-profile issue, thanks in part to Jay-Z. According to critics of "forced arbitration," the plaintiffs' lawyers' American Association for Justice, 88% of arbitrators at AAA and JAMS are white and 77% are male.[167] In 2018, Jay-Z (Shawn Carter) in a dispute stemming from the $200 million sale of his clothing line "challenged an arbitration clause as discriminatory, stating it would force him to select an arbitrator from a list nearly devoid of his ethnic group. Only three of 200 arbitrators on the large and complex case roster provided by the American Arbitration Association identified themselves as African-American, and one of them had a conflict, he argued."[168] "While acknowledging there should be diversity in

---

162 Am. Arb. Ass'n, Commercial Arbitration Rules, R–13(a) (2022).

163 Id., R–13(b).

164 Id.

165 Id.

166 Id.

167 American Association for Justice, Where White Men Rule: How the Secretive System of Forced Arbitration Hurts Women and Minorities (June 2021), https://www.justice.org/resources/research/forced-arbitration-hurts-women-and-minorities.

168 Darlene Ricker, Jay-Z's ADR Problems: Mogul's Case Spotlights Lack of Diverse Arbitrators, ABA J. May 2019, at 9.

arbitration, Justice Saliann Scarpulla stated at a hearing on the Jay-Z matter, * * * 'If people are dissatisfied with the diversity of the AAA, don't put the AAA panel in your agreement. Go somewhere else.' "[169]

An alternative to using the rules of an arbitration organization for selecting arbitrators is to agree to *tripartite* arbitration. The agreement specifies that there will be three arbitrators: each party picks one arbitrator and those two arbitrators agree on the third.[170] Tripartite arbitration, which also occurs under the auspices of arbitration organizations,[171] raises legal and ethical issues, addressed below, about the extent to which the party-appointed arbitrator may be partial, rather than neutral.[172] In some circumstances the party-appointed arbitrators are expected to be neutral; in other, they function as partisans, representing the interests of the party that appointed them. Because additional arbitrators tend to make arbitration more expensive and slower, tripartite arbitration is normally used only in high-value disputes.

Nearly all arbitrations have either one or three arbitrators, but any number is possible.

(2) Arbitrator Fees

Arbitrators are normally paid market rates for their work.[173] Some arbitrators get paid a lot. One or two thousand dollars per day

---

169 Id.

170 See, e.g., Delta Mine Holding Co. v. AFC Coal Properties, Inc., 280 F.3d 815, 817 (8th Cir. 2002) ("Paragraph 8.2 provided that disputes over this provision were subject to arbitration by a panel of three arbitrators, one selected by Delta Mine, one by AFC, 'and a third selected by the other two arbitrators in accordance with the then applicable rules of the American Arbitration Association.' "); U.S. Life Ins. Co. v. Superior Nat. Ins. Co., 591 F.3d 1167, 1170–71 (9th Cir. 2010) (arbitration panel "consisted of an arbitrator appointed by each party and a neutral arbitrator selected by the parties' arbitrators").

171 See, e.g., Am. Arb. Ass'n, Commercial Arbitration Rules, R–14 (2022).

172 See § 40(b)(3). See also David J. McLean & Sean-Patrick Wilson, Is Three a Crowd? Neutrality, Partiality and Partisanship in the Context of Tripartite Arbitrations, 9 Pepp. Disp. Resol. L.J. 167 (2008).

173 In contrast, some arbitrators provide their services for free. These volunteer arbitrators range from merchant members of a trade association (who arbitrate disputes among members of that association) to a local lawyer who arbitrates consumer disputes for the Better Business Bureau. See Sasha A. Carbone & Jeffrey T. Zaino, Increasing Diversity Among Arbitrators, 84 N.Y. St. B.J. 33 (2012) ("Getting the first arbitration case can be difficult for the new practitioner, but there are opportunities to serve on a pro bono basis or on reduced fee cases that may provide future opportunities."); Samuel Estreicher & Matt Ballard, Affordable Justice Through Arbitration, 57 Disp. Resol. J. 8, 11 (2003) ("[T]he AAA has formalized the process for a claimant to receive a waiver or deferral of the AAA administration fee based on financial hardship. And now it has a roster of over 3,000 arbitrators who have volunteered to serve pro bono where an individual would otherwise be financially unable to pursue his or her rights in the arbitral forum.")

is common and some arbitrators earn much more than that.[174] Particularly in high-dollar cases, disputing parties are willing to pay high arbitrator fees to get high-quality arbitrators. But few arbitrators outside the labor context are in such demand that they can make a living arbitrating. Even well-respected arbitrators may be asked to arbitrate only one or two cases a year. Many arbitrators have full-time jobs doing something else and arbitrate only as a side job.

Labor arbitration is a distinct and quite different market for arbitrators. Because almost all collective bargaining agreements include arbitration clauses, the nation's millions of workers represented by unions produce enough grievances to make it possible for experienced labor arbitrators to make a full-time career out of arbitrating.[175]

In many contexts, the parties agree that the arbitrator's fee will be split equally between the parties.[176] In some cases, however, courts refuse to enforce consumer and employment arbitration agreements unless the business or employer relieves the consumer or employee of any obligation to pay significant arbitrator fees.[177]

(3) Judicial and Regulatory Constraints on Party Selection of Arbitrator(s)

Courts limit party-selection of arbitrators in two ways. First, courts have refused to enforce arbitration awards on the ground that the parties selected an arbitrator who had a previous relationship of some sort with one of the parties. This topic, discussed in a later

---

174 See, e.g., Deborah Rothman, Trends in Arbitrator Compensation, 23 Disp. Res. Mag. 8 (Spring 2017). ("At JAMS, which also does not publish its arbitrator rates, there is a great deal of variance, with fees ranging from $400 per hour to $15,000 or more per day")

175 Dennis R. Nolan & Richard A. Bales, Labor and Employment Arbitration in a Nutshell 25–27 (4th ed. 2020) ("Several thousand people hold themselves out as competent labor arbitrators. Only about 600 of these are members of the National Academy of Arbitrators, but that small percentage handles a large majority of labor arbitration cases. * * * On average, members have arbitrated for 26 years and earn three-quarters of their income from their work as a neutral."); Mark D. Gough, Characteristics and Professional Practices of Labor and Employment Neutrals October 2020, 12 Penn. St. Arb. L. Rev. 117, 125 (2020) ("labor and multi-neutrals are nearly twice as likely to describe themselves as full-time relative to employment neutrals").

176 Linda J. Demaine & Deborah R. Hensler, "Volunteering" to Arbitrate Through Predispute Arbitration Clauses: The Average Consumer's Experience, 67 Law & Contemp. Probs. 55, 70 (2004) (of a sample of arbitration clauses in consumer contracts, "[t]he most common overarching rule (found in thirteen of the thirty clauses that mention expenses) is that the parties will divide the expenses of arbitration equally."); Andrew Kramer et al., Mandatory Arbitration as an Alternative Method of Resolving Workplace Disputes, 1999 ALI-ABA Course of Study: Hot Issues in Employment and Litigation 177, 216 (There is a "nearly universal custom" in favor of equal cost-splitting).

177 See § 24(a).

section,[178] is a judicial limit on the arbitrators the parties may select for legally binding arbitration insofar as it denies legal force to their agreement to have their dispute resolved by certain arbitrators.

Second, courts have refused to enforce executory arbitration agreements when dissatisfied with the agreement's method of selecting an arbitrator. This is a distinct possibility when parties to a form contract select an arbitrator closely connected to the party that drafted the form contract. Some drafting parties even write contracts that reserve to themselves complete discretion over the selection of the arbitrator.[179] Only slightly less one-sided are agreements naming a close affiliate of the drafting party to be the arbitrator.[180] More debatable are agreements requiring the arbitrators to share a profession or membership in an organization with the drafting party. As Judge Easterbrook wrote for the Seventh Circuit:

> Industry arbitration, the modern law merchant, often uses panels composed of industry insiders, the better to understand the trade's norms of doing business and the consequences of proposed lines of decision. See Lisa

---

[178] See § 40(b).

[179] Compare Trout v. Organizacion Mundil de Boxeo, Inc., 965 F.3d 71, 81 (1st Cir. 2020) (arbitration agreement between boxer and World Boxing Association unconscionable because it "grants the WBO exclusive control over the appointment of the arbitrators"); Murray v. United Food and Commercial Workers Intern. Union, 289 F.3d 297 (4th Cir. 2002) (employment arbitration agreement unconscionable, where, though the parties ostensibly engaged in an alternate strike method to select the single arbitrator from a list of prospective arbitrators, they were to exercise these alternate strikes from a list of arbitrators provided by the employer); Hooters of America, Inc. v. Phillips, 173 F.3d 933, 938–39 (4th Cir. 1999) (breach of duty of good faith and fair dealing where, although "the employee and Hooters each select an arbitrator, and the two arbitrators in turn select a third. Good enough, except that the employee's arbitrator and the third arbitrator must be selected from a list of arbitrators created exclusively by Hooters. This gives Hooters control over the entire panel and places no limits whatsoever on whom Hooters can put on the list"); Ditto v. Re/Max Preferred Properties, Inc., 861 P.2d 1000, 1004 (Okla. App. 1993) (independent contractor's arbitration agreement was unconscionable because it "would exclude [her] from any voice in selection of the arbitrators."); Rodriguez v. Windermere Real Estate/Wall Street, Inc., 175 P.3d 604, 607 (Wash. App.2008) (same), with Greenwald v. Weisbaum, 785 N.Y.S.2d 664 (Ct. App. 2004) (Arbitration provision of accounting firm's partnership agreement, which required that arbitration panel be comprised exclusively of partners and members of firm's board of directors, did not create situation in which one of parties to dispute adjudicated its own cause, so as to make provision invalid and unenforceable); Hottle v. BDO Seidman LLP, 846 A.2d 862 (Conn. 2004).

[180] See, e.g., Sehulster Tunnels/Pre-Con v. Traylor Brothers, Inc./Obayashi Corp., 4 Cal. Rptr. 3d 655 (Ct. App. 2003); Graham v. Scissor Tail, Inc., 171 Cal. Rptr. 604 (Cal. 1981) (refusing to enforce arbitration agreement between musician and concert promoter where agreement named musician's union as arbitrator). For a more subtle fact pattern in which the party drafting the agreement encouraged the non-drafting party to select among arbitrators who attended an "orientation" conducted by the drafting party, see Pokorny v. Quixtar, Inc., 601 F.3d 987, 1002–03 (9th Cir. 2010).

> Bernstein, Private Commercial Law in the Cotton Industry: Creating Cooperation Through Rules, Norms, and Institutions, 99 Mich. L. Rev. 1724, 1728 (2001). The more experience the [arbitration] panel has, and the smaller the number of repeat players, the more likely it is that the panel will contain some actual or potential friends, counselors, or business rivals of the parties. Yet all participants may think the expertise-impartiality tradeoff worthwhile; the Arbitration Act does not fasten on every industry the model of the disinterested generalist judge.[181]

Other courts may be less deferential to party autonomy in making that "expertise-impartiality tradeoff," especially in contracts of adhesion.[182]

Courts are no longer the only branch of government to regulate arbitrators. A California statute requires extensive disclosures by neutral arbitrators of potential conflicts of interest,[183] and California statutes regulate organizations that administer consumer arbitrations.[184] California even has a statute responding to the

---

[181] Sphere Drake Ins. Ltd. v. All Am. Life Ins. Co., 307 F.3d 617, 620 (7th Cir. 2002).

[182] For example, the drafting party in Broemmer v. Abortion Services of Phoenix, Ltd., 840 P.2d 1013 (Ariz. 1992), was an abortion clinic. The court did not enforce the arbitration clause requiring arbitration before "licensed medical doctors who specialize in obstetrics/gynecology." Id. at 104. *Compare* State ex rel. Vincent v. Schneider, 194 S.W.3d 853, 859 (Mo. 2006) (holding unconscionable provision stating that "the arbitrator shall be selected by the President of the Homebuilders Association of Greater St. Louis"), with Lynes v. Calcagni Associates, 2006 WL 894913 (Conn. Super. 2006) (enforcing clause providing that "If any dispute arises out of or in connection with this Agreement * * * such dispute shall be submitted to arbitration * * * . Only licensed architects, home inspectors, ASHI members, engineers or professional contractors will be eligible to serve as an arbitrator."); Brown v. Wells Fargo Bank, NA, 85 Cal.Rptr.3d 817, 832 (Ct. App. 2008) (rejecting investors' argument that National Association of Securities Dealers "arbitration is substantively unconscionable because under the NASD Code, a minority of arbitrators may be affiliated with the securities industry").

[183] Cal. Civ. Proc. Code §§ 1281.9, 1281.91. At least some of these statutory rules have been interpreted to override contrary language in the arbitration agreement or applicable arbitration organization rules. Azteca Const., Inc. v. ADR Consulting, Inc., 18 Cal. Rptr. 3d 142 (Ct. App. 2004) (statute permitting party uncomfortable with the disclosures of any proposed arbitrator to disqualify him or her within 15 days overrides AAA rule giving AAA sole power to disqualify arbitrator). See also Judicial Council of California, Ethics Standards for Neutral Arbitrators in Contractual Arbitration (Jan. 1, 2016), available at https://www.courts.ca.gov/documents/ethics_standards_neutral_arbitrators.pdf. Courts have held that these state standards, as applied in securities arbitrations, are preempted by the federal securities laws. Credit Suisse First Boston Corp. v. Grunwald, 400 F.3d 1119 (9th Cir. 2005); Jevne v. Superior Court, 111 P.3d 954 (Cal. 2005).

[184] Cal. Civ. Proc. Code § 1281.92 (prohibiting private arbitration companies from administering consumer arbitrations for parties in which they have financial interest); id. § 1281.96 (requiring disclosures by private arbitration companies administering consumer arbitrations); id. § 1284.3 (regulating fees charged in consumer arbitrations).

phenomenon of judges, still on the bench, talking with arbitration organizations about becoming arbitrators after the judge leaves the bench.[185] All of these statutes are, among other things, limits on the arbitrators certain parties may select for legally-binding arbitration insofar as they deny legal force to the parties' predispute agreement to have their dispute resolved by certain arbitrators.

Another source of regulation of arbitrators is Minnesota's Attorney General who effectively ended consumer arbitration agreements providing for arbitrators selected by the National Arbitration Forum (NAF). In 2009, Minnesota's AG sued NAF, which at the time was the largest provider of consumer credit arbitrations nationwide. This case alleged that NAF committed "consumer fraud, deceptive trade practices, and false advertising," and was hiding extensive ties to a debt collection firm that brought many of NAF's cases.[186] NAF settled the Minnesota AG's case with an agreement to stop arbitrating consumer disputes, although it could continue arbitrating internet domain disputes and other disputes.[187]

(b) Pleadings

Litigation generally begins with a complaint filed and served by the plaintiff, followed by an answer filed and served by the defendant. Arbitration is analogous but the terminology may be different. Arbitration typically begins with a *demand* for arbitration filed and served by the *claimant*, followed by an answer filed and served by the *respondent*. However, respondents seem to omit answers more often in arbitration than in litigation. Perhaps that is because in litigation

---

Some of these state statutes may be preempted by the FAA. Compare Arbitration between Lemoine Skinner III v. Donaldson, Lufkin & Jenrette, 2003 WL 23174478, at *8–9 (N.D.Cal.Dec.29, 2003) (FAA preempts Cal. Civ. Proc. Code 1281.92(b) to the extent it creates a ground, not found in the FAA, for vacating an arbitration award), with Ovitz v. Schulman, 35 Cal.Rptr.3d 117, 130–32 (Ct. App. 2005) (rejecting FAA preemption challenge to Cal. Civ. Proc. Code 1286.2(a)(6)(A), which requires vacatur for arbitrator's failure to comply with state disclosure requirements).

185 Cal. Civ. Proc. Code § 170.1(a)(8) (disqualifying judge if "The judge has a current arrangement concerning prospective employment or other compensated service as a dispute resolution neutral or is participating in, or, within the last two years has participated in, discussions regarding prospective employment or service as a dispute resolution neutral, or has been engaged in that employment or service, and * * *").

186 Nancy A. Welsh, What Is "(Im)partial Enough" in A World of Embedded Neutrals?, 52 Ariz. L. Rev. 395, 428 (2010) ("by 2006, NAF had become this country's largest provider of consumer debt arbitration services, handling 214,000 claims in that year alone.").

187 Consent Judgment, Minnesota v. National Arbitration Forum, Inc., No. 27-CV-09-18550 (Minn. Dist. Ct. July 17, 2009), available at http://pubcit.typepad.com/files/nafconsentdecree.pdf.

not answering a claim typically has the effect of admitting it,[188] while under many arbitration rules a claim not answered is denied.[189]

Omitting answers is one way arbitration can be less elaborate than litigation. Another way is that arbitration complaints tend to be more concise and less legalistic than complaints in litigation.[190] An arbitration complaint typically includes only basic factual allegations, the nature or source of the claims and defenses, the remedies sought, and the adjudicator's jurisdiction.[191]

While plaintiffs often show a court's jurisdiction by citing a statute, arbitration claimants often show the arbitrator's jurisdiction by submitting the agreement to arbitrate.[192]

(c) Filing Fees and Un-Administered Arbitration

In litigation, parties generally pay court fees too low to cover the full cost of the judge, jury, court clerk, other administrative personnel, and the courthouse itself—all of which tend to be subsidized by government spending. By contrast, parties to arbitration generally must fully pay the analogous costs: the arbitrator's fee, the arbitration organization's fee, and any cost for a hearing room. Arbitration organizations, such as the AAA, generally charge the parties an arbitrator's fee (which the organization pays to the arbitrator) and a separate administrative fee, which the organization keeps.

Parties can arbitrate without an arbitration organization. This un-administered arbitration saves the parties from paying the fees of an arbitration organization. But it also requires the parties to agree

---

188 Fed.R.Civ.P. 8(b)(6) ("An allegation—other than one relating to the amount of damages—is admitted if a responsive pleading is required and the allegation is not denied."); Fed.R.Civ.P. 12(a)(1)(A)(i) (defendant must serve an answer within 21 days after being served with the summons and complaint).

189 See, e.g., Am. Arb. Ass'n, Commercial Arbitration Rules, R–5(a) (2022) ("If no answering statement is filed within the stated time, respondent will be deemed to deny the claim. Failure to file an answering statement shall not operate to delay the arbitration.")

190 Richard Chernick et al., How to Conduct a Complex Financial Arbitration Part 1: Matters to Consider Prior to the Hearings, 1440 Practicing Law Institute Corporate Law and Practice Course Handbook 453, 456 (2004) ("A statement of Claim or Demand for Arbitration is a far different document than a Complaint in litigation. A claim is much more informal than a pleading and is usually much shorter. There are virtually no 'rules of pleading' in arbitration [and] technical pleading rules need not be followed.")

191 See, e.g., Am. Arb. Ass'n, Commercial Arbitration Rules, R–4(a) (2022) ("a statement setting forth the nature of the claim including the relief sought and the amount involved").

192 See, e.g., id. R–4(a)(i) ("Arbitration under an arbitration provision in a contract shall be initiated by the initiating party ('the claimant') filing with the AAA a Demand for Arbitration, the administrative filing fee, and a copy of the applicable arbitration agreement from the parties' contract which provides for arbitration.")

on their own to an arbitrator and to conduct the arbitration with the help of only the arbitrator. That requires the arbitrator to perform administrative tasks that an organization would otherwise handle. Because the arbitrator's hourly rate may be high,[193] the parties may find it cheaper to pay the fees of an arbitration organization.

Arbitration organization fees, like court filing fees, are generally imposed at the time a case is filed. Arbitration filing fees vary widely and often depend on the size of the case, as measured by the remedy sought by the claimant.[194] Filing fees required of consumers in small arbitrations are generally modest, usually no more than a court fee.[195] In contrast, filing fees for larger commercial cases can run into the thousands of dollars, far exceeding court fees.[196] After the initial filing fee, additional administrative fees (along with an arbitrator's fee) may be required of the parties to hold a hearing or otherwise complete the arbitration.[197] In short, arbitration organizations and arbitrators generally receive higher payments from parties who require more work by the arbitration organization and arbitrator, while courts generally charge parties who consume a lot of the court system's resources about the same as parties who consume little of those resources.

(d) Discovery

"Traditionally, arbitration included minimal pre-hearing discovery."[198] And the Supreme Court recognizes that often "[a] prime objective of an agreement to arbitrate is to achieve 'streamlined proceedings and expeditious results.' "[199] Moreover, the

---

[193] See § 33(a)(2).

[194] See, e.g., Am. Arb. Ass'n, Commercial Arbitration Rules, Administrative Fee Schedules (2018), available at http://www.adr.org/feeschedule.

[195] See also Am. Arb. Ass'n, Consumer Arbitration Rules, Costs of Arbitration, Effective November 1, 2020, https://www.adr.org/sites/default/files/Consumer_Fee_Schedule_2.pdf.

[196] See, e.g., Am. Arb. Ass'n, Commercial Arbitration Rules, Administrative Fee Schedules (2018), available at https://go.adr.org/feeschedule.

[197] Id.

[198] Neal M. Eiseman, et. al., A Tale of Two Lawyers: How Arbitrators and Advocates Can Avoid the Dangerous Convergence of Arbitration and Litigation, 14 Cardozo J. Conflict Resol. 683, 686 (2013). See also Jay Folberg, Dwight Golann, Thomas J. Stipanowich, Jennifer Reynolds, Amy J. Schmitz, Resolving Disputes: Theory, Practice, and Law 486 (4th ed. 2021) ("Pre-hearing practice in arbitration—motion practice and discovery—tends to be more abbreviated and attenuated—perhaps much more so—than in litigation."); Bruce A. McAllister & Amy Bloom, Evidence in Arbitration, 34 J. Mar. L. & Com. 35, 42 (2003) ("It is axiomatic that discovery is not as available in arbitration as it may be in court litigation.")

[199] Preston v. Ferrer, 552 U.S. 346, 357 (2008). See also Hyatt Franchising, L.L.C. v. Shen Zhen New World I, LLC, 876 F.3d 900, 901–02 (7th Cir. 2017) ("nothing in the Federal Arbitration Act requires an arbitrator to allow any discovery. Avoiding the expense of discovery under the Federal Rules of Civil Procedure and their state-law equivalents is among the principal reasons why people agree to arbitrate.")

Court has suggested that while "[p]arties *could* agree to arbitrate * * * pursuant to a discovery process rivaling that in litigation," the FAA would preempt (hypothetical) state law deeming unconscionable arbitration agreements lacking "judicially monitored discovery."[200] On the other hand, courts have held particular arbitration agreements unconscionable because of their insufficient discovery.[201]

Discovery, like other aspects of arbitration, is primarily determined by the arbitration agreement. And as most arbitration agreements incorporate the rules of an arbitration organization, such rules can influence the amount of discovery. For instance, several practicing lawyers suggest that American Arbitration Association rules "support the proposition that discovery is disfavored in arbitration," while "other rule-making organizations," such as JAMS, "have increasingly made way for litigation-style discovery—including depositions—in their rules."[202] Other arbitration agreements customize discovery, either in the direction of constraining it,[203] or expanding it to the levels of discovery under the rules of civil procedure in federal,[204] or state court.[205]

---

[200] AT&T Mobility LLC v. Concepcion, 563 U.S. 333, 341–42, 351 (2011).

[201] See § 24(a).

[202] Neal M. Eiseman, et. al., A Tale of Two Lawyers: How Arbitrators and Advocates Can Avoid the Dangerous Convergence of Arbitration and Litigation, 14 Cardozo J. Conflict Resol. 683, 686 (2013).

[203] See, e.g., Robert A. Weiner & B. Ted Howes, Arbitration Discovery: When should discovery provisions be included in an arbitration agreement?, Disp.Resol.Mag., Summer 1999, at 30, 30–32; John Wilkinson, Arbitration Contract Clauses: A Potential Key to a Cost-Effective Process, Disp. Resol. Mag. Fall 2009, at 9 (many parties are expanding their arbitration clauses to "place meaningful limits on discovery").

[204] See, e.g., Medicine Shoppe International, Inc. License Agreement, in Christopher R. Drahozal, "Unfair" Arbitration Clauses, 2001 U. Ill. L. Rev. 695, 776, App. II; Scott Atlas & Nancy Atlas, Potential ADR Backlash, Disp. Resol. Mag., Summer 2004, 14, 16 ("parties increasingly have attempted to build into their contracts procedural safeguards akin to rules of civil procedure. Arbitrators are now charged with judge-like ethical and procedural duties. They must * * * allow more discovery * * * and increasingly conduct hearings under rules of procedure * * * . [T]hese protections have made the arbitration process more like, and sometimes as expensive as, court proceedings.")

[205] Cox v. Bonni, 241 Cal. Rptr. 3d 359, 371 (Ct. App. 2018) ("the arbitration agreements at issue here expressly granted the parties the same ability to obtain discovery that they would have in the trial court. The arbitration agreements provided that discovery would be conducted pursuant to section 1283.05, under which parties to an arbitration have the same right to obtain discovery 'as if the subject matter of the arbitration were pending before a superior court of this state in a civil action other than a limited civil case.' "); id. ("The arbitration agreements * * * stated that 'depositions may be taken without prior approval of the neutral arbitrator,' thus eliminating the only difference between judicial discovery and discovery under section 1283.05.")

Arbitrators seem to be authorizing more discovery in recent decades.[206] Perhaps this is a result of the increasing variety of parties and claims going to arbitration,[207] as arbitration has broadened beyond disputes over commercial and labor agreements to statutory claims brought by consumers, employees, and other parties.[208]

FAA § 7 authorizes the arbitrators to "summon in writing any person to attend before them or any of them as a witness and in a proper case to bring with him or them any book, record, document, or paper which may be deemed material as evidence in the case."[209] Courts are split on whether this provision authorizes subpoenas of non-parties for pre-hearing discovery or, as most circuits have held, only for the hearing itself.[210] Therefore, some parties seeking to enforce arbitral subpoenas of non-parties for pre-hearing discovery do so in state courts.[211] The Revised Uniform Arbitration Act (RUAA) authorizes subpoenas of non-parties for pre-hearing discovery for testimony and specifically authorizes depositions, which

---

206 Deborah R. Hensler & Damira Khatam, Re-Inventing Arbitration: How Expanding the Scope of Arbitration Is Re-Shaping Its Form and Blurring the Line Between Private and Public Adjudication, 18 Nev. L.J. 381, 399 (2018) ("Extensive discovery [in commercial arbitration], including substantial document production and witness depositions, leading to longer proceedings and higher costs is said to have become the norm, replacing the streamlined and less expensive approach of the past."); Thomas J. Stipanowich, Arbitration: The "New Litigation", 2010 U. Ill. L. Rev. 1, 12.

207 See Edward Brunet, Replacing Folklore Arbitration with a Contract Model of Arbitration, 74 Tul. L. Rev. 39 (1999)(connecting increased discovery with broader changes in arbitration law and practice).

208 See § 5(e)(1).

209 9 U.S.C. § 7.

210 Compare In re Security Life Insurance Co. of America, 228 F.3d 865, 870–71 (8th Cir. 2000) ("We thus hold that implicit in an arbitration panel's power to subpoena relevant documents for production at a hearing is the power to order the production of relevant documents for review by a party prior to the hearing."); American Federation of Television and Radio Artists, AFL-CIO v. WJBK-TV, 164 F.3d 1004, 1009 (6th Cir. 1999) (under LMRA, "a labor arbitrator is authorized to issue a subpoena duces tecum to compel a third party to produce records he deems material to the case either before or at an arbitration hearing."); with Life Receivables Trust v. Syndicate 102 at Lloyd's of London 549 F.3d 210, 216–17 (2d Cir. 2008) ("we join the Third Circuit in holding that section 7 of the FAA does not authorize arbitrators to compel pre-hearing document discovery from entities not party to the arbitration proceedings."); Hay Group, Inc. v. E.B.S. Acquisition Corp., 360 F.3d 404 (3d Cir. 2004) (no authority for pre-hearing discovery subpoena); COMSAT Corp. v. National Science Foundation, 190 F.3d 269, 275 (4th Cir. 1999)("Nowhere does the FAA grant an arbitrator the authority to order non-parties to appear at depositions, or the authority to demand that non-parties provide the litigating parties with documents during prehearing discovery."); CVS Health Corp. v. Vividus, LLC, 878 F.3d 703, 708 (9th Cir. 2017); Managed Care Advisory Grp., LLC v. CIGNA Healthcare, Inc., 939 F.3d 1145, 1160 (11th Cir. 2019) ("because the plain meaning of the statute does not permit pre-hearing discovery from non-parties, the policy argument does not supersede the text of the statute.")

211 Charles E. Harris II, Enforcing Arbitral Subpoenas: Reconsidering Federal Question Jurisdiction Under FAA Section 7, 66 Disp. Resol. J. 24, 25 (2011).

traditionally are rare in arbitration.[212] However, these provisions of RUAA "can be waived or varied by agreement of the parties,"[213] so presumably have no effect on arbitration arising out of an arbitration agreement that, expressly or by incorporating arbitration organization rules, limits discovery.

If the arbitration agreement or the applicable arbitration organization rules authorize it, arbitrators may impose sanctions on parties (or lawyers) who fail to comply with the arbitrators' discovery orders. Courts enforce those sanctions like any other arbitration award.[214]

§ 34 Hearing

(a) General Comparison with Trial

A hearing is to arbitration what a trial is to litigation. Hearings look like trials in some respects: adversaries trying to persuade a neutral adjudicator with evidence and argument. Like trials, arbitrations typically proceed with opening statements, presentation of witnesses by the claimant for examination and cross-examination under oath, followed by similar presentation of the respondent's witnesses, and concluding with closing statements by lawyers for each side. But arbitration hearings differ from trials in other respects. While juries may consist of twelve people, an arbitration panel rarely consists of more than three. While judges sit up high, wear black robes, and expect to be called "Your Honor," arbitrators generally do not, although some arbitrators are former judges. While litigation typically has a transcript or other record of the hearing, arbitration traditionally often did not,[215] although that may have

---

212 "If an arbitrator permits discovery under subsection (c), the arbitrator may order a party to the arbitration proceeding to comply with the arbitrator's discovery-related orders, issue subpoenas for the attendance of a witness and for the production of records and other evidence at a discovery proceeding, and take action against a noncomplying party to the extent a court could if the controversy were the subject of a civil action in this State." Unif. Arbitration Act § 17(d) (2000).

213 Id. cmt.1.

214 McDaniel v. Bear Stearns & Co., 196 F. Supp. 2d 343, 364 (S.D.N.Y. 2002); Superadio Ltd. Partnership v. Winstar Radio Productions, LLC, 844 N.E.2d 246, 252–54 (Mass. 2006).

215 Records and information on hearings, 2 Domke on Com. Arb. § 29:18 ("The value of transcripts has long been a debatable issue in arbitration. Generally, the parties find the delay in delivery of the award, which transcripts necessitate, more justified in technical or complex cases. A study of the subject showed that stenographic records of hearings in institutional arbitration were taken in a little more than 10% of the cases"); Ronald M. Sandgrund, Jennifer A. Seidman, Leslie A. Tuft, Claim and Issue Preclusion Arising from Residential Construction and Other Arbitrations-Part 2, Colo. Law., March 2022, at 18, 22 ("in many cases no record exists of the arbitration proceedings other than the written award"); Am. Arb. Ass'n, Commercial Arbitration Rules, Rule R–29 (2022) ("Any party desiring a transcribed record of a hearing shall make arrangements directly with a transcriber or transcription service and shall

changed particularly with the prevalence of online arbitration during the Covid-19 pandemic.[216]

(b) Role of Lawyers

Lawyers in many arbitration hearings do what they do at trial: make opening statements, call and examine witnesses, cross-examine opposing witnesses, submit briefs, and make closing arguments.[217] But not all hearings look like this. In some arbitration contexts, such as trade association arbitration, lawyers often are not present.[218] In labor arbitration, employees are often represented by a union representative, rather than a lawyer,[219] although the Rhode Island Supreme Court questioned whether some of these nonlawyer representatives might be engaged in the unlicensed practice of law.[220] Going further, the Florida Supreme Court prohibited nonlawyer

---

notify the arbitrator and the other parties of these arrangements at least seven calendar days in advance of the hearing. The requesting party or parties shall pay the cost of the record.")

216 Kristen M. Blankley, Finra's Dispute Resolution Pandemic Response, 13 Penn. St. Arb. L. Rev. 27, 37 (2021) ("FINRA staff can "host" the zoom meeting if the Chair does not feel comfortable running the meeting. The arbitration full video and audio of the hearing will be recorded on Zoom, which is arguably a better recording option compared to the default of audio-only recording at live hearings. Video recording is a standard Zoom feature and does not require any additional equipment as it would for in-person hearings."); Nortek Home Control Holdings, LLC v. Baalbergen, No. 3:20-CV-09319-WHA, 2021 WL 706461, at *1 (N.D. Cal. Feb. 23, 2021) ("The arbitration was held over four days in July 2020, via Zoom, due to the pandemic. The transcript of the arbitration runs some 350 pages.")

217 See Jay E. Grenig & R. Wayne Estes, Arbitration Advocacy, §§ 2.4, 4.18–4.19, & 4.21 (2000).

218 See Ian R. Macneil, Richard E. Speidel & Thomas J. Stipanowich, Federal Arbitration Law § 32.5.5, at 32:49–32:50 (1994) ("[S]ome trade groups have long followed the practice of requiring that parties appear without counsel.") For an arbitration hearing in which both corporate parties were represented by their presidents rather than lawyers, see Arvys Protein, Inc. v. A/F Protein, Inc., No. 206100683S, 2021 WL 2593894, at *9–10 (Conn. Super. Ct., June 7, 2021). The law of many states provides that a pre-hearing waiver of the right to an attorney is void. See Unif. Arbitration Act § 6 (1956), 7 U.L.A. 383 (2009); Unif. Arbitration Act § 4(b)(4) (2000), 7 U.L.A. 19 (2009). For an employment arbitration agreement providing that employer will not hire a lawyer if employee does not hire one, see Johnson v. Long John Silver's Restaurants, Inc., 320 F. Supp.2d 656 (M.D.Tenn.2004).

219 Laura J. Cooper et al., ADR in the Workplace 23 & n.17 (2nd ed. 2005); Judith A. McMorrow, The Advocate as Witness: Understanding Context, Culture and Client, 70 Fordham L. Rev. 945, 973 (2001) ("The formal structure of labor arbitration involves a union representative and management representative making presentations to the neutral person. The representatives need not be lawyers. Figures vary, but somewhere between twenty-five and thirty-five percent of the union advocates are lawyers.") .

220 In re Town of Little Compton, 37 A.3d 85, 95 (R.I. 2012) ("although the conduct involved in this case may be the practice of law pursuant to the language of § 11–27–2, because of the long-standing involvement of nonlawyer union employees at public grievance arbitrations, we will not limit this involvement at this time. We may in the future, however".) See also Alabama Ethics Opinions, https://www.alabar.org/assets/2019/02/2014-01-1.pdf (non-lawyer may not represent party in court-ordered arbitration).

representatives in securities arbitration as the unlicensed practice of law.[221] The same argument has been used to challenge the representation of parties in arbitration by out-of-state lawyers.[222] ABA Model Rule of Professional Conduct 5.5(c) provides that

> A lawyer admitted in another United States jurisdiction, and not disbarred or suspended from practice in any jurisdiction, may provide legal services on a temporary basis in this jurisdiction that:
>
> * * *
>
> (3) are in or reasonably related to a pending or potential arbitration, mediation, or other alternative dispute resolution proceeding in this or another jurisdiction, if the services arise out of or are reasonably related to the lawyer's practice in a jurisdiction in which the lawyer is admitted to practice and are not services for which the forum requires pro hac vice admission.[223]

If lawyers are present at the arbitration hearing, they may behave somewhat differently than they do at trial. Depending on

---

[221] The Florida Bar Re: Advisory Opinion on Nonlawyer Representation in Securities Arbitration, 696 So.2d 1178 (Fla.1997).

[222] Compare Birbrower, Montalbano, Condon & Frank v. Superior Court, 949 P.2d 1 (Cal. 1998) (New York lawyers barred from recovering fees for work performed in California in connection with an impending California arbitration, because they had done so in violation of the California Business and Professions Code § 6125 which states "No person shall practice law in California unless the person is an active member of the State Bar."), with Williamson v. John D. Quinn Constr. Corp., 537 F. Supp. 613, 616 (S.D.N.Y. 1982) (rejecting claim that out-of-State attorney and firm were foreclosed from recovery obtained in connection with services rendered in arbitration proceeding because not authorized to practice law in that State); Siegel v. Bridas Sociedad Anonima Petrolera Industrial Y Comercial, 1991 WL 167979, at *5 (S.D.N.Y. 1991) (quoting and following Williamson "representation of a party in an arbitration proceeding by a non-lawyer or a lawyer from another jurisdiction is not the unauthorized practice of law."); Prudential Equity Group, LLC v. Ajamie, 538 F. Supp.2d 605, 607–08 (S.D.N.Y. 2008) (following *Williamson*); Colmar, Ltd. v. Fremantlemedia North America, Inc., 801 N.E.2d 1017, 1026 (Ill. App. 2003) (relying on Model Rule of Professional Responsibility 5.5(c) as persuasive authority that "an out-of-state attorney's representation of a client during arbitration does not violate the rules prohibiting the unlicensed practice of law"). See also Cal.Civ.P. Code § 1282.4 (West 2007) (allows non-resident lawyers to participate in California arbitrations, creating limited exception to *Birbrower*); Fla.Bar Rule 1–3.11 (permitting out-of-state attorneys to participate in arbitrations taking place in Florida under limited circumstances); Doctor's Associates, Inc. v. Jamieson, 2006 WL 2348849 (Ct. App. Conn .2006) (holding that the absence of a specific statute or rule concerning an out-of-state attorney's participation in private arbitration proceeding is not a bar to the authority of the court to allow such an out-of-state attorney to represent client in Connecticut, as long as attorney otherwise complies with Connecticut requirements); Disciplinary Counsel v. Alexicole, Inc., 822 N.E.2d 348 (Ohio 2004) (A non-attorney who was not licensed to practice law in Ohio cannot represent his or her client in an arbitration taking place in Ohio); In re Creasy, 12 P.3d 214, 217 (Ariz. 2000) (examining witness in arbitration constitutes practice of law).

[223] Model Rules of Professional Conduct R.5.5(c) (2013).

context, the rules of evidence in arbitration can be minimal.[224] So, lawyers may find that raising objections to hearsay and the like accomplishes nothing other than irritating the arbitrator. If the arbitrator has some expertise on the subject matter of the dispute,[225] the lawyer may not need to lay the sort of factual and evidentiary foundations required for a generalist judge or lay jury.[226] Also, lawyers may find that certain personal styles successful in front of a jury are less successful in front of an arbitrator. Many lawyers who succeed in arbitration remain seated and businesslike throughout the hearing, without the sort of movement or drama that might effectively capture a jury's attention.[227]

(c) Rules of Evidence

Evidentiary rules, like other aspects of arbitration, are primarily determined by the arbitration agreement. Many agreements incorporate the rules of an arbitration organization such as the American Arbitration Association. The AAA's Commercial Arbitration Rules allow the parties to offer into evidence whatever is relevant and material.[228] These rules also say that the parties *shall* produce evidence the arbitrator deems necessary.[229] This suggests a more active role for the arbitrator than is typical of judges and juries. In the United States, judges and juries are typically passive triers-of-fact, receiving only the evidence presented by the parties. In contrast, some arbitrators are more inquisitorial—sometimes

---

224 See § 34(c).

225 See, e.g., Star Ins. Co. v. Nat'l Union Fire Ins. Co. of Pittsburgh, PA, 656 F. App'x 240, 243 (6th Cir. 2016) (agreement between two insurance companies provided "any dispute arising out of this Agreement . . . shall be submitted to the decision of a board of arbitration composed of two arbitrators and an umpire. * * * The members of the board of arbitration shall be active or retired disinterested officials of the insurance or reinsurance companies . . . not under the control of either party to this Agreement. * * * The board shall make its decision with regard to the custom and usage of the insurance and reinsurance business.")

226 Jay Folberg, Dwight Golann, Thomas J. Stipanowich, Jennifer Reynolds, Amy J. Schmitz, Resolving Disputes: Theory, Practice, and Law 486 (4th ed. 2021) ("attorneys should remember that because their panel of adjudicators may bring significant expertise to the table, the latter may find extensive explication or foundation-laying unnecessary or even offensive.")

227 Id. ("Experienced lawyers and arbitrators warn that arbitration is not a forum for the strutting and posturing employed by some lawyers in civil trials.")

228 Am. Arb. Ass'n, Commercial Arbitration Rules, R–35(a) (2022) ("The parties may offer such evidence as is relevant and material to the dispute and shall produce such evidence as the arbitrator may deem necessary to an understanding and determination of the dispute. Conformity to legal rules of evidence shall not be necessary. All evidence shall be taken in the presence of all of the arbitrators and all of the parties, except where any of the parties is absent, in default or has waived the right to be present.").

229 See id.

questioning witnesses,[230] or making other investigations into evidence.[231]

Courts' rules of evidence are historically intertwined with the jury,[232] so unsurprisingly arbitration (without a jury) nearly always has less elaborate rules of evidence than those used in jury trials. Some arbitrations have few rules of evidence, so parties can present most any evidence they want, and arbitrators can give it whatever weight they choose.[233] For example, a party seeking to vacate an arbitration award "argue[d] that the arbitrator wrongly relied on hearsay evidence," but the West Virginia Supreme Court rejected this argument, "recogniz[ing] that under the rules applicable to the arbitration proceeding, the rules of evidence were not required to be followed."[234] Arbitrators' general openness to admitting evidence is due in part to the fact that "refusing to hear evidence pertinent and material to the controversy" is one of the few grounds for vacating the arbitration award,[235] while hearing evidence that would not be admissible in court is not a ground for vacatur.[236]

---

[230] Jay Folberg, Dwight Golann, Thomas J. Stipanowich, Jennifer Reynolds, Amy J. Schmitz, Resolving Disputes: Theory, Practice, and Law 486 (4th ed. 2021) ("Perhaps most importantly, rather than act as passive recipients of the evidence adduced by counsel, arbitrators may join in the questioning of witnesses."); Carpenter v. Brooks, 139 N.C. App. 745, 753, 534 S.E.2d 641, 646 (2000) ("an arbitrator is permitted to ask questions of witnesses, as is a judge at trial. Such questioning, which seeks to clarify testimony, is proper even if the questions are perceived as hostile so long as the examination does not prejudice either party").

[231] See, e.g., Am. Arb. Ass'n, Commercial Arbitration Rules, R–37 (2022) ("An arbitrator finding it necessary to make an inspection or investigation in connection with the arbitration shall direct the AAA to so advise the parties. The arbitrator shall set the date and time and the AAA shall notify the parties. Any party who so desires may be present at such an inspection or investigation. In the event that one or all parties are not present at the inspection or investigation, the arbitrator shall make an oral or written report to the parties and afford them an opportunity to comment.")

[232] Ellen E. Sward, The Decline of the Civil Jury 82–84, 243–60 (2001).

[233] Cunningham v. LeGrand, 237 W. Va. 68, 71, 785 S.E.2d 265, 268 (2016) ("The arbitrator advised the parties that he would take all evidence 'for what it's worth and discard it if it's not relevant.' ")

[234] Cunningham v. LeGrand, 237 W. Va. 68, 75, 785 S.E.2d 265, 272 (2016)(quoting rules of the International Institute for Conflict Prevention & Resolution (CPR)). See also ARMA, S.R.O. v. BAE Sys. Overseas, Inc., 961 F. Supp. 2d 245, 263 (D.D.C. 2013) ("An arbitrator has substantial leeway to admit any evidence that it finds useful—even hearsay evidence.")

[235] See § 40(c). 9 U.S.C. § 10(a)(3). "To too many arbitrators, [this provision] has meant one thing: let everything remotely relevant in, no matter how prejudicial, cumulative, incredible, suspect or otherwise useless, for fear that ruling out anything may lead to vacatur." Bruce A. McAllister & Amy Bloom, Evidence in Arbitration, 34 J. Mar. L. & Com. 35, 36 (2003).

[236] Bowles Fin. Group, Inc. v. Stifel, Nicolaus & Co., 22 F.3d 1010, 1013 (10th Cir. 1994) (refusing to vacate award won by lawyer who introduced evidence that would not have been admissible in litigation; "This court has no power to judicially impose our rules of evidence on an arbitration proceeding."); U.S. ex rel. Nat'l Roofing Services, Inc. v. Lovering-Johnson, Inc., 53 F. Supp. 2d 1142, 1145–47 (D. Kan. 1999)(extending *Bowles* rule to case where arbitrator may well have relied on

Evidence in arbitration is often introduced by affidavit or declaration, rather than orally at hearing.[237] In this manner, direct examinations of witnesses can be submitted to the arbitrator before the hearing, with the hearing "then limited to cross-examination, and any redirect examination. Doing so offers the benefit of reducing hearing/trial time."[238]

If evidence is required from someone other than the parties, the arbitrator may obtain it through subpoena. Those who fail to comply with an arbitrator's subpoena may be compelled to do so by a court.[239]

(d) Substitutes for In-Person Hearing

(1) Online Arbitration Hearings

Arbitration hearings, perhaps even more than trials in courts, moved online in and after 2020 due to the Covid-19 pandemic. In Canada, for example, "Arbitration Place, a Toronto-based hearing venue and service provider, reports that the hearings it hosts went from over ninety-five percent in-person before the pandemic to over ninety-five per cent semi- or fully remote by early 2021."[240] As a 2021 article by several practicing lawyers in the U.S. put it,

> With courthouses shuttered across the county, litigants and courts have turned to remote ADR procedures as a way to continue to resolve disputes. Consistent with the inherent flexibility that underlies alternative dispute resolution, mediators and arbitrators alike adapted to the realities of the world-wide pandemic. Third party neutrals have embraced technology and have continued to conduct

---

evidence—of settlement offer—that would not have been admissible in litigation); A.G. Edwards & Sons, Inc. v. McCullough, 764 F. Supp. 1365, 1368 (D. Ariz. 1991) ("evidence of settlement offer, while inadmissible in court, was admissible in arbitration where rules of evidence are inapplicable"); WHD, LP. v. Mayflower Capital, LLC, 673 S.E.2d 168, 2009 WL 368335 at *5 (N.C. App. 2009) (refusing to vacate arbitration award where arbitrator may have relied on evidence that would not have been admissible in litigation).

[237] Weizmann Institute of Science v. Neschis, 421 F. Supp.2d 654, 681 (S.D.N.Y.2005) ("the Tribunal's decision to forego live testimony in favor of affidavits from some witnesses is common practice").

[238] See Gale R. Peterson, Trade Secret Law Update 2008: Including Restrictive Post-Employment Covenants, in Patents, Copyrights, Trademarks, and Literary Property, at 799, 944 (Practicing Law Inst. ed., 2008).

[239] 9 U.S.C. § 7. See, e.g., Washington Nat'l Ins. Co. v. OBEX Grp. LLC, 958 F.3d 126, 136 (2d Cir. 2020) ("The summonses here accorded with section 7. They required the respondents to appear at a hearing at the New York City offices of Proskauer Rose LLP, and to bring with them the documents identified in instructions annexed to the summonses").

In contrast, the law on subpoenas for pre-hearing discovery is more complicated. See § 33(d).

[240] Joshua Karton, The (Astonishingly) Rapid Turn to Remote Hearings in Commercial Arbitration, 46 Queen's L.J. 299 (2021).

> mediations and arbitrations remotely. Initial concerns about presentation of documents and the ability to effectively create "break out rooms" have been resolved.[241]

Online arbitration hearings save the time, money, and stress of traveling to in-person hearings, which is especially important in a pandemic, and likely to continue long-term. Participants generally have become comfortable with the technology,[242] and leading arbitration organizations have provided additional comfort by publishing online hearing guides, so parties and arbitrators are not adapting on the fly as they did early in the pandemic.

However, online hearings raise legal issues. While most federal circuit courts hold that FAA § 7 authorizes arbitrators to subpoena non-parties not for pre-hearing discovery, but only for the hearing itself,[243] even compelling testimony for the hearing itself is doubtful if the hearing is online. A few months before the pandemic, the Eleventh Circuit held that FAA § 7 does not empower arbitrators to summon non-parties to testify outside the physical presence of the arbitrator.[244]

(2) Arbitration on the Documents (Desk Arbitration) and Dispositive Motions

While online hearings are still hearings, arbitration sometimes lacks any hearing, as the arbitrator instead resolves the case (issues an arbitration award) based solely on the documentary evidence submitted. For example, the AAA Commercial Arbitration rules for cases under $25,000 say "the dispute shall be resolved by submission of documents, unless any party requests an oral hearing, or the

---

[241] Deborah Greenspan, Fredric Brooks, Jonathan Walton, Grace Chamoun, Recent Developments in Alternative Dispute Resolution, 56 Tort Trial & Ins. Prac. L.J. 231, 248–50 (2021).

[242] Amy J. Schmitz, Arbitration in the Age of Covid: Examining Arbitration's Move Online, 22 Cardozo J. Conflict Resol. 245, 248, 264 (2021).

[243] See § 33(d).

[244] Managed Care Advisory Grp., LLC v. CIGNA Healthcare, Inc., 939 F.3d 1145, 1160 (11th Cir. 2019) ("Section 7 does not authorize district courts to compel witnesses to appear in locations outside the physical presence of the arbitrator, so the court may not enforce an arbitral summons for a witness to appear via video conference"). See also Dodson Int'l Parts, Inc. v. Williams Int'l Co., No. 19-MC-50489, 2019 WL 5680811, at *2 (E.D. Mich. June 26, 2019) ("According to the plain language of Section 7, an arbitrator can direct a third-party to testify and/or produce documents only at a hearing 'before the arbitrator,' " but testifying remotely is not "before the arbitrator," so the Court should dismiss petition to enforce the subpoena). But see Latoya C. Brown, Bad Law or Just Bad Timing?: Post-Pandemic Implications of Managed Care Advisory Group, LLC v. Cigna Healthcare, Inc.'s Ban on the Use of Virtual Technology for Taking Non-Party Evidence Under Section 7 of the Federal Arbitration Act, 75 U. Miami L. Rev. 1037, 1038 (2021) ("in light of the pandemic and its related health risks, the Eleventh Circuit's opinion raises concerns about the conduct of arbitration proceedings, particularly when disclosure of information by non-parties is needed for a full and fair hearing").

arbitrator determines that an oral hearing is necessary."[245] Such arbitration on the documents is traditionally called "desk arbitration,"[246] perhaps because the arbitrator can issue an award without having to leave her desk to go to an arbitration hearing. And as a result of technological change and the Covid-19 pandemic, "there are now many OArb [online arbitration] providers who provide text-only arbitration with no in-person hearings."[247]

Similar to arbitration on the documents is arbitration resolved by summary judgment. While much litigation ends on a grant of a motion to dismiss or for summary judgment, such dispositive motions are generally thought less likely to succeed in arbitration than in litigation.[248] Perhaps this is because the lesser pleadings and discovery traditionally typical of arbitration make it less likely that all factual issues can be resolved without a hearing of some sort. However, widely used arbitration organization rules allow dispositive motions,[249] and the Sixth Circuit relied on those rules in

---

[245] Am. Arb. Ass'n, Commercial Arbitration Rules, E–6 (2022) ("Where no party's claim exceeds $25,000, exclusive of interest, attorneys' fees and arbitration costs, and other cases in which the parties agree, the dispute shall be resolved by submission of documents, unless any party requests an oral hearing, or the arbitrator determines that an oral hearing is necessary. Where cases are resolved by submission of documents, the following procedures may be utilized at the agreement of the parties or the discretion of the arbitrator. (a) Within 14 calendar days of confirmation of the arbitrator's appointment, the arbitrator may convene a preliminary management hearing, via conference call, video conference, or internet, to establish a fair and equitable procedure for the submission of documents * * * .")

[246] "In a 'Desk' Arbitration, the parties submit their arguments and evidence to the arbitrator in writing. The arbitrator then makes an award based only on the documents. No hearing is held." Am. Arbitration Ass'n, Supplementary Procedures for Consumer-Related Disputes, Glossary of Terms, eff. July 1, 2003, quoted in Ragan v. AT & T Corp., 1160, 824 N.E.2d 1183, 1196 (Ill. App. 2005).

[247] Amy J. Schmitz, Arbitration in the Age of Covid: Examining Arbitration's Move Online, 22 Cardozo J. Conflict Resol. 245, 264 (2021).

[248] See, e.g., Zev J. Eigen & David Sherwyn, Deferring for Justice: How Administrative Agencies Can Solve the Employment Dispute Quagmire by Endorsing an Improved Arbitration System, 26 Cornell J.L. & Pub. Pol'y 217, 262 (2016) ("Most arbitration policies do not allow for motions to dismiss or summary judgment motions."); Eastern Air Lines, Inc., 79 Lab. Arb. Rep. 61, 64, n.3 (BNA 1982) ("a summary judgment is extraordinary (although not unheard of) in arbitration proceedings"); Jennifer J. Johnson, Wall Street Meets the Wild West: Bringing Law and Order to Securities Arbitration, 84 N.C. L. Rev. 123, 175 (2005) ("There is an unspoken bias in [securities] arbitrations that panels should view dispositive motions with much skepticism and proceed as a matter of course to a hearing."); Gary W. Jackson, Prosecuting Class Actions in Arbitration, Assoc. of Trial Lawyers of Am., ATLA Annual Convention Reference Materials, 829 (2006); Harold M. Brody & Anthony J. Oncidi, Careful What You Wish For: Is Arbitration the Employer's Panacea? Perhaps There is a Better Alternative, 9 HR Advisor: Legal & Practical Guidance, Nov./Dec. 2003, at 7.

[249] See, e.g., Am. Arb. Ass'n, Employment Arbitration Rules and Mediation Procedures, Rule 27 ("The arbitrator may allow the filing of a dispositive motion if the arbitrator determines that the moving party has shown substantial cause that the motion is likely to succeed and dispose of or narrow the issues in the case.")

holding that the arbitrators did not exceed their powers by granting a motion for summary judgment.[250] Courts have confirmed arbitration awards based on the documents submitted[251] or grants of summary judgment,[252] over the objections of parties seeking a full hearing.

One study shows that arbitrators frequently grant summary judgment in favor of Kaiser, a large health maintenance organization, to resolve pro se tort claims.[253]

(3) Default or Ex Parte Awards

Much as litigation may result in a default judgment against a party who does not participate,[254] the same can occur in

---

[250] McGee v. Armstrong, 941 F.3d 859, 867 (6th Cir. 2019).

[251] British Ins. Co. of Cayman v. Water Street Ins. Co., Ltd., 93 F. Supp.2d 506 (S.D.N.Y. 2000).

> Oral argument is not a necessary component of due process in all circumstances. While hearings are advisable in most arbitration proceedings, arbitrators are not compelled to conduct oral hearings in every case. The lack of oral hearings does not amount to the "denial of fundamental fairness" required to warrant vacating the award. As long as an arbitrator's choice to render a decision based solely on documentary evidence is reasonable, and does not render the proceeding "fundamentally unfair," the arbitrator is acting within the liberal sphere of permissible discretion.

Id. at 517 (citations omitted). See also FDIC v. Air Florida Sys., 822 F.2d 833 (9th Cir. 1987) (upholding decision of arbitrator to deny one party's request to hold an oral evidentiary hearing and to require all evidence to be submitted in writing where sole issue involved valuation of corporate stock); Intercarbon Bermuda Ltd. v. Caltex Trading & Transport Corp., 146 F.R.D. 64 (S.D.N.Y. 1993) (confirming award after arbitrator refused to conduct oral hearing despite party's repeated requests); Schlessinger v. Rosenfeld, Meyer & Susman, 47 Cal. Rptr. 2d 650 (Ct. App. 1995) (upholding AAA arbitral award based on summary adjudications).

[252] Sheldon v. Vermonty, 269 F.3d 1202, 1206 (10th Cir. 2001) (holding that arbitrators can dispose of legal issues on dispositive motions); Burdette v. FSC Sec. Corp., 1993 WL 593997, at *4 (W.D. Tenn. 1993) (confirming arbitral award in nature of summary judgment); Warren v. Tacher, 114 F. Supp.2d 600, 602 (W.D. Ky. 2000) ("the arbitrators had the authority to decide and grant a pre-hearing motion to dismiss.") See also Unif. Arbitration Act § 15(b) ("An arbitrator may decide a request for summary disposition of a claim or particular issue: (1) if all interested parties agree; or (2) upon request of one party to the arbitration proceeding if that party gives notice to all other parties to the proceeding, and the other parties have a reasonable opportunity to respond."); Am. Arb. Ass'n, Commercial Arbitration Rules, R–34(a) (2022) ("The arbitrator may allow the filing of and make rulings upon a dispositive motion only if the arbitrator determines that the moving party has shown that the motion is likely to succeed and dispose of or narrow the issues in the case.")

[253] Andrea Cann Chandrasekher & David Horton, Arbitration Nation: Data from Four Providers, 107 Cal. L. Rev. 1, 57 (2019) ("we found that summary judgment motions are Kaiser's primary line of defense against pro se patients. A staggering 377 of the 459 self-represented tort plaintiffs (82%) in our dataset lost at the summary judgment stage").

[254] Fed.R.Civ.P. 55(a) ("When a party against whom a judgment for affirmative relief is sought has failed to plead or otherwise defend, and that failure is shown by affidavit or otherwise, the clerk must enter the party's default.").

arbitration,[255] and is sometimes called an "ex parte award."[256] Such default awards are the norm in debt collection arbitrations against consumers, much as default judgments are the norm in debt collection litigations against consumers.[257] In a more complex and higher-stakes case, the Seventh Circuit enforced a default award of over $50 million.[258]

A default award may be enforced against a party that received notice of arbitration, even if the non-defaulting party did not seek a court order compelling arbitration.[259] However, under the AAA Commercial Arbitration Rule 31 "[a]n award shall not be made solely on the default of a party." So, the non-defaulting party must submit "such evidence as the arbitrator may require for the making of an

---

[255] Val-U Construction Co. v. Rosebud Sioux Tribe, 146 F.3d 573, 575 (8th Cir. 1996) ("The AAA held an arbitration hearing and Val-U presented its case. The Tribe was not represented at the hearing."); id. at 579 ("the Tribe never requested that the AAA postpone the hearing until the issue of sovereign immunity was resolved."); AAA Employment Arbitration Rules and Mediation Procedures, Rule 29 ("Unless the law provides to the contrary, the arbitration may proceed in the absence of any party or representative who, after due notice, fails to be present or fails to obtain a postponement. An award shall not be based solely on the default of a party. The arbitrator shall require the party who is in attendance to present such evidence as the arbitrator may require for the making of the award.")

[256] Into the Sunset Revocable Living Tr. v. Design Tech Homes LP, No. 05-18-01272-CV, 2020 WL 1969505, at *1 (Tex. App. Apr. 24, 2020) ("Design Tech instituted arbitration proceedings with the American Arbitration Association and obtained an ex-parte arbitration award against Sunset. When Design Tech attempted to confirm the ex-parte arbitration award, the district court determined Sunset had not received notice concerning the arbitration proceedings and vacated the ex-parte arbitration award.")

[257] Christopher R. Drahozal & Samantha Zyontz, Creditor Claims in Arbitration and in Court, 7 Hastings Bus. L.J. 77, 80 (2011) ("The rate at which consumers responded (i.e., did not default) also did not appear to differ systematically between arbitration and litigation").

[258] Bartlit Beck LLP v. Okada, 25 F.4th 519, 525 (7th Cir. 2022) (respondent "Okada was not denied any right to be heard when the [arbitration] Panel proceeded without evidence that he never offered. As [claimant] Bartlit Beck points out, the Panel proceeded as expressly authorized by the default rule of the parties' chosen arbitral facility: 'The [Panel] may receive [the non-defaulting party's] evidence and argument without the defaulting party's presence or participation.' CPR Rule 16.")

[259] UniFirst Corp. v. Stronger Collision Ctr., LLC, 336 So. 3d 1283, 1286 (Fla. Dist. Ct. App. 2022) (UniFirst was "within its rights under New York law to file a demand for arbitration with the AAA without first exercising its permissive option to seek a court order compelling arbitration. The [AAA] rules agreed to by the parties do not require a court order to compel arbitration and explicitly permit ex parte arbitration where not prohibited by law. Accordingly, UniFirst complied with New York law and the contractual language (incorporating AAA expedited procedures) before seeking and obtaining an arbitral award. The trial court erred in dismissing the petition to enforce the arbitral award on that basis"); Tutti Mangia Italian Grill, Inc. v. Am. Textile Maint. Co., 128 Cal. Rptr. 3d 551, 557 (Ct. App. 2011) ("Because the arbitration proceeded under a self-executing agreement, appellants ignored the arbitration at their peril").

award."[260] Some courts similarly require a non-defaulting party to "prove up" a default judgment.[261]

(e) *Un/Reasoned Awards, and the Role of Precedent*

As the Supreme Court explained in 1956, arbitrators "need not give their reasons for their results."[262] Arbitrator's decisions, called arbitration awards, often lack reasoning, and thus resemble the typical general verdict rendered by a jury, rather than the reasoned opinion of a trial judge. Unreasoned awards can be very brief—perhaps just a couple of sentences finding for the claimant and ordering the respondent to pay a particular dollar amount—or a bit longer.[263] Unreasoned awards are the traditional norm in commercial and related types of arbitration, and thus are often called "standard

---

[260] See also JAMS Rules, R. 22(j) (while the Arbitrator "may proceed" with a Hearing in which a party fails to attend, "[t]he Arbitrator may not render an Award solely on the basis of the default or absence of the Party," and the non-defaulting party must "submit such evidence as the Arbitrator may require for the rendering of an Award.")

[261] The requirements for obtaining a default judgment vary by state. For example, in many cases California requires a "prove-up hearing" at which "The court shall hear the evidence offered by the plaintiff, and shall render judgment in the plaintiff's favor for that relief, not exceeding the amount stated in the complaint * * * , as appears by the evidence to be just." Cal. C. Civ. P. § 585(b).

[262] Bernhardt v. Polygraphic Co. of America, 350 U.S. 198, 203 (1956).

[263] See, e.g., Morgan Keegan & Co., Inc. v. Grant, No. CV0907369SJOFFMX, 2010 WL 11549681, at *3 (C.D. Cal. June 30, 2010), aff'd, 497 F. App'x 715 (9th Cir. 2012) ("the [arbitrators] issued [their] ruling in the form of an unreasoned Award" "in which [they] found for Respondent . . . in the amount of $1,450,000 in compensatory damages, $10,000 in costs, and levied all forum fees against Respondent."); U.S. ex rel. Coastal Roofing Co. v. P. Browne & Assocs., Inc., 771 F. Supp. 2d 576, 580 (D.S.C. 2010) ("In addressing the merits of the parties' dispute, the arbitrator's award stated the following: The Broadband Companies, successor in interest to Broadband Construction Services, LLC, shall recover of Coastal Roofing Company, Inc., the total sum of $719, 203.33, derived as follows: Damages $436,545.13, Pre Award Interest at 8.75% $ 64,465.20, Attorney fees and expenses $218,193.00"); ThyssenKrupp Materials, LLC v. Triumph Grp., Inc., No. 20-CV-11087, 582 F. Supp.3d 449, 452 (E.D. Mich. Jan. 26, 2022) (the parties "agreed that the Arbitrator would issue an unreasoned award. The Arbitrator thereafter held a five-day evidentiary hearing during which the parties presented live testimony from several witnesses and introduced nearly 100 exhibits."); id. ("the Arbitrator ruled in favor of TK. In his unreasoned award, the Arbitrator determined that TGI and TAS were jointly and severally liable to TK for approximately $2.9 million in damages. He also directed TK to deliver to TGI and TAS certain aluminum that TK had acquired on their behalf during the parties' relationship, and he required TGI and TAS to accept delivery of that aluminum from TK.")

awards."[264] Unreasoned awards are unlikely to be published,[265] and thus to serve as precedent for future decisions by arbitrators or courts. An unreasoned award is typically private in the sense of being confidential. And an unreasoned award is in a sense the private property of the parties who paid the arbitrator to produce it.

In contrast, the sort of reasoned decisions commonly issued by judges are sometimes issued by arbitrators ("reasoned awards") in several contexts including: (1) employment,[266] (2) consumer,[267] (3) labor,[268] (4) international commercial and maritime.[269] For example, "arbitral precedent plays a major role [in] labor arbitration, where

---

264 L. Ali Khan, Arbitral Autonomy, 74 La. L. Rev. 1, 48 (2013) ("Litigation is open and accessible to the public; arbitration is frequently confidential, and its records are unavailable to the public. Litigation produces judicial opinions justifying orders and judgments; arbitration renders standard awards without supportive rationale. Published judicial opinions make litigation intellectually transparent; unpublished arbitration awards make arbitration relatively opaque. Judicialization of dispute resolution generates legal precedents that are binding in similar cases; arbitration rarely offers or relies on binding precedents.")

265 See Amy J. Schmitz, Untangling the Privacy Paradox in Arbitration, 54 U. Kan. L. Rev. 1211, 1216 (2006) ("arbitration awards generally are not published"). W. Mark C. Weidemaier, Judging-Lite: How Arbitrators Use and Create Precedent, 90 N.C. L. Rev. 1091, 1104–1111 (2012) ("securities arbitrators may and sometimes do issue reasoned awards. But historically, norms in securities arbitration have disfavored reasoned awards, and the available evidence suggests that securities arbitrators do not often issue them. * * * Most of the securities awards are unreasoned, meaning the arbitrator also provided no narrative explanation whatsoever for his or her decision"); FINRA Customer Code 12904(g), (h).

266 W. Mark C. Weidemaier, Judging-Lite: How Arbitrators Use and Create Precedent, 90 N.C. L. Rev. 1091, 1104–1111 (2012). Id. at 1102–03 ("The AAA's employment arbitration rules provide that arbitrators will provide "written reasons for the award unless the parties agree otherwise." Since 2000, the AAA has published these awards, and current rules require that awards be made available to the public at cost. These awards are also available online through LexisNexis in fully searchable format. Under current practice, however, the names of parties and witnesses are redacted before publication.")

267 Christopher R. Drahozal, Arbitration and Rule Production, 72 Case W. Res. L. Rev. 91, 134 (2021) ("The AAA and JAMS both require arbitrators in consumer and employment arbitrations to issue awards that explain the reasoning behind their decisions. The AAA consumer and employment rules also each authorize the AAA to publish redacted awards. As of June 1, 2021, over 3,500 AAA employment arbitral awards and over 3,000 AAA consumer arbitral awards were available on Westlaw.")

268 W. Mark C. Weidemaier, Judging-Lite: How Arbitrators Use and Create Precedent, 90 N.C. L. Rev. 1091, 1106 (2012) ("most labor arbitration awards are unpublished, and awards that are submitted to the BNA for publication are published only if the BNA decides the award is of sufficiently 'general interest.' ") See also Wolters Kluwer Partners with American Arbitration Association to Enhance Labor and Employment Awards Database, CISION PR NEWSWIRE (June 7, 2018, 01:52), https://www.prnewswire.com/news-releases/wolters-kluwer-partners-with-american-arbitration-association-to-enhance-labor-and-employment-awards-database-300661896.html [https://perma.cc/X79B-WL7L] ("This move is a direct response to our customers, who have requested more awards for their research." (quoting Chris Carr, Labor & Employment Law Portfolio Director for Wolters Kluwer Legal & Regulatory U.S.)).

269 See § 58(c)(4).

arbitrators are engaged primarily in building a 'common law of the workplace.' "[270] Even in domestic commercial arbitration, the practice of reasoned awards is growing.[271]

§ 35 Remedies

(a) Generally Determined by Contract

Remedies, like other aspects of arbitration, are primarily determined by the arbitration agreement. Parties can get creative. For instance, "baseball" arbitration limits the arbitrator to two remedies: each party's final settlement offer. The arbitrator must pick one of those two options (usually a dollar amount) as the award. This approach has been used outside Major League Baseball salaries, such as in determining the rent Saks would pay to operate a department store in San Francisco.[272]

The Supreme Court used a contractual approach to determine whether the arbitrator could award punitive damages in *Mastrobuono v. Shearson Lehman Hutton, Inc.*[273] As the Court said, "the case before us comes down to what the contract has to say about the arbitrability of petitioners' claim for punitive damages."[274] *Mastrobuono* stated that this contractual analysis is mandated by the FAA and that it preempts any state law requiring a non-contractual analysis. New York law at the time prohibited arbitrators from awarding punitive damages regardless of the arbitration

---

[270] W. Mark C. Weidemaier, Judging-Lite: How Arbitrators Use and Create Precedent, 90 N.C. L. Rev. 1091, 1116 (2012). "[L]abor arbitrators often justify their decisions by citing only other arbitration awards." Id. at 1095. See § 48(a)(2).

[271] John Burritt McArthur, Parties Usually Benefit Most from Reasoned Awards, Not Standard Awards, 38 Alts. To Hight Cost Litig. 44, 45 (2020) (JAMS and CPR rules provide for reasoned awards as the default); id. ("in awards issued in 2016, 41% of AAA commercial and construction awards were reasoned, and another 8% were findings of fact and conclusions of law, while 51% were standard awards.").

[272] California Union Square L.P. v. Saks & Co. LLC, 71 Cal. App. 5th 136, 138, 286 Cal. Rptr. 3d 115, 117 (2021).

> [Lease] Section 3.1(c) sets forth the process for settling disputes about the Fair Market Rent. This subsection mandates an arbitration process which is to be conducted under the rules of the American Arbitration Association ("AAA"). It subjects this process to several modifications enumerated in Sections 3.1(c)(i) through 3.1(c)(v). Section 3(c)(i) requires Saks to make a demand for arbitration along with its proposed determination of the Fair Market Rent, and Union Square must respond with its own rent determination. If the parties' positions continue to differ, Section 3.1(c)(ii) specifies the qualifications required for the arbitrator. Section 3.1(c)(iii) provides for what is known as "baseball arbitration," in which each party proposes its own rent determination and the arbitrator "select[s] which of the two determinations proposed . . . most closely approximate[s] [the arbitrator's] determination [of rent]."

Id.

[273] 514 U.S. 52 (1995).

[274] Id. at 58.

agreement's terms.[275] *Mastrobuono* found that the FAA preempted that New York law.[276] The Court pointed out that the contract authorized arbitration in accordance with the rules of the National Association of Securities Dealers ("NASD") and a NASD manual provided to NASD arbitrators contained this provision: "The issue of punitive damages may arise with great frequency in arbitrations. Parties to arbitration are informed that arbitrators can consider punitive damages as a remedy."[277] Thus the Court found that the arbitration clause "contradicts * * * the conclusion that the parties agreed to foreclose claims for punitive damages."[278] The Court then went on to cite two further reasons for interpreting the contract to permit arbitrators to award punitive damages: (1) "the federal policy favoring arbitration,"[279] which means that "ambiguities as to the scope of the arbitration clause itself are resolved in favor of arbitration," and (2) "the common-law rule of contract interpretation that a court should construe ambiguous language against the interest of the party that drafted it."[280] These final two points suggest that the Court favors interpretations of arbitration agreements that preserve the full remedies of the parties, especially parties to adhesive arbitration agreements drafted by the opposing party.

Some courts have gone beyond interpretating arbitration agreements to hold that certain contractual remedy-limitations are unenforceable. These cases tend to arise in the context of consumer and employment arbitration agreements, and rest on contract law's unconscionability doctrine, special concerns regarding the vindication of federal statutory rights, or a combination of the two.[281] However, the 2003 Supreme Court case of *Pacificare Health Systems, Inc. v. Book*,[282] indicates that in at least some cases involving contractual remedy-limitations, courts should send to the arbitrators the question whether to enforce those limitations. In *Book*, physicians brought claims under a statute (RICO) that provides for treble damages. The defendants' motion to compel arbitration was

---

[275] See Garrity v. Lyle Stuart, Inc., 386 N.Y.S.2d 831 (Ct. App. 1976).

[276] The Court said its "decisions in Allied-Bruce, Southland, and Perry make clear that if contracting parties agree to include claims for punitive damages within the issues to be arbitrated, the FAA ensures that their agreement will be enforced according to its terms even if a rule of state law would otherwise exclude such claims from arbitration." 514 U.S. at 58. "[I]n the absence of contractual intent to the contrary, the FAA would pre-empt the Garrity rule." Id. at 59.

[277] Mastrobuono, 514 U.S. at 61 (quoting Mastrobuono v. Shearson Lehman Hutton, Inc., 20 F.3d 713, 717 (7th Cir. 1994)).

[278] Mastrobuono, 514 U.S. at 61.

[279] Id. at 62.

[280] Id.

[281] See § 24; Graham Oil Co. v. Arco Products Co., 43 F.3d 1244 (9th Cir. 1994).

[282] 538 U.S. 401 (2003).

denied by the district court because the arbitration agreement prohibited the arbitrators from awarding "punitive damages."[283] The Supreme Court found the agreement ambiguous on whether it prohibited the arbitrators from awarding treble damages.[284] "[W]e should not, on the basis of 'mere speculation' that an arbitrator might interpret these ambiguous agreements in a manner that casts their enforceability into doubt, take upon ourselves the authority to decide the antecedent question of how the ambiguity is to be resolved."[285] "Since we do not know how the arbitrator will construe the remedial limitations," the Court concluded "the proper course is to compel arbitration."[286]

(b) Typical Contract Terms

Many arbitration agreements provide that the arbitrator may order any remedy that a court could order.[287] And this seems to be the usual default interpretation of arbitration agreements that are silent on remedies. For example, arbitrators order parties to pay

---

[283] Id. at 403.

[284] Id. at 405.

[285] Id. at 406–07.

[286] Id. at 407. Arbitrators may decide the enforceability of remedy-limitations not only when the arbitration agreement is ambiguous (as in *Book*) but also when the arbitration agreement provides that the arbitrator shall decide the enforceability of the arbitration agreement. Id. at 406–07. See Terminix International Co. v. Palmer Ranch Ltd. Partnership, 432 F.3d 1327, 1331–32 (11th Cir. 2005) (by incorporating AAA Rules—including rule that "[t]he arbitrator shall have the power to rule on his or her own jurisdiction, including any objections with respect to the existence, scope or validity of the arbitration agreement"—into their agreement, the parties agreed that the arbitrator should decide the validity of the arbitration clause, including its provisions on remedies.)

[287] See, e.g., Am. Arb. Ass'n, Commercial Arbitration Rules, R–49(a) (2022) ("The arbitrator may grant any remedy or relief that the arbitrator deems just and equitable and within the scope of the agreement of the parties, including, but not limited to, specific performance of a contract."); id. R-38(a) ("[t]he arbitrator may take whatever interim measures he or she deems necessary, including injunctive relief and measures for the protection or conservation of property and disposition of perishable goods."); Providian Bancorp Servs. v. Thomas, 255 S.W.3d 411, 418 (Tex.App.2008) (holding that arbitrator's award of attorneys' fees was proper because "the parties agreed that the arbitrator could award any recovery or remedy that he deemed just and equitable").

punitive damages[288] and issue injunctions[289] even though the arbitration agreement may not expressly authorize those remedies. Injunctions can be far-reaching, so parties may want to limit arbitrators' discretion to order them. For instance, the California Supreme Court upheld from an unconscionability challenge an auto dealers' consumer arbitration agreement providing that "an arbitrator's award 'shall be final and binding on all parties, except that in the event the arbitrator's award for a party is $0 or against a party is in excess of $100,000, or includes an award of injunctive relief against a party, that party may request a new arbitration under the rules of the arbitration organization by a three-arbitrator panel.' "[290] The court acknowledged the auto dealer's "concern that the scope of an injunction can extend well beyond the transaction at issue and can compel a car seller to change its business practices. Because of the broad impact that injunctive relief may have on the car seller's business, the additional arbitral review when such relief is granted furnishes a 'margin of safety' that provides the party with superior bargaining strength a type of extra protection for which it has a legitimate commercial need."[291]

Arbitration can be less suited than litigation as a forum for an emergency, provisional remedy, such as a temporary restraining order (TRO) or preliminary injunction. This is because arbitration cannot award any remedy until an arbitrator has been appointed, and the party against whom a TRO or preliminary injunction is sought likely can delay that appointment until it does whatever the

---

[288] See Bowen v. Amoco Pipeline Co., 254 F.3d 925, 940 (10th Cir. 2001) ("In the case before us, the parties agreed to be governed by rules that authorize any remedy or relief which the Tribunal deems just and equitable and within the scope of the agreement of the parties. Given the broad scope of this rule, the arbitrators did not exceed their powers in awarding punitive damages") (internal citations and quotation marks omitted); Emerald Aero, LLC v. Kaplan, 215 Cal. Rptr. 3d 5, 17 (Ct. App. 4th Dist. 2017), as modified on denial of reh'g (Mar. 21, 2017) ("Although plaintiffs did not specifically identify punitive damages in the Arbitration Claim form, there was nothing in the submission preventing the Arbitrator from awarding those damages"); Bosack v. Soward, 586 F.3d 1096 (9th Cir. 2009); Todd Shipyards Corp. v. Cunard Line, 943 F.2d 1056 (9th Cir. 1991); Raytheon Co. v. Automated Business Sys., Inc., 882 F.2d 6 (1st Cir. 1989); Bonar v. Dean Witter Reynolds, Inc., 835 F.2d 1378 (11th Cir. 1988).

[289] Intl. Petroleum Products and Additives Co., Inc. v. Black Gold, S.A.R.L., 418 F. Supp. 3d 481 (N.D. Cal. 2019); Yahoo! Inc. v. Microsoft Corp., 983 F. Supp. 2d 310, 314 (S.D.N.Y. 2013) (confirming award in which arbitrator "issued an injunction that 'restores the parties to the activities they were ready to proceed with before the pause.' The Arbitrator ordered that Yahoo is 'restrained and enjoined from continuing any pause in transitioning' and is 'commanded to use all efforts' to complete the Taiwan transition by October 28, 2013 and the Hong Kong transition by November 11, 2013.' "); Western Tech. Services Intern., Inc. v. Caucho Industriales S.A., 2010 WL 1848949 (N.D.Tex.2010); Grossman v. Ilowitz, 898 N.Y.S.2d 621, 623 (App.Div.2010)("An arbitration award may grant injunctive relief").

[290] Sanchez v. Valencia Holding Co., LLC, 353 P.3d 741, 751 (Cal. 2015).

[291] Id.

other party sought to restrain or enjoin. For this reason, arbitration organizations "have responded by creating standing tribunals to address issues of emergency relief."[292] For instance, an emergency arbitrator appointed by the AAA issued an award in a dispute between Microsoft and Yahoo.[293]

Many arbitration agreements permit parties to seek preliminary injunctive relief from a court in disputes that are ultimately to be resolved in arbitration. Courts are willing to grant such contractually-authorized relief.[294] In contrast, authorities are split on courts' granting preliminary injunctive relief pending arbitration when not so authorized by the agreement. Some states' statutes authorize such preliminary relief. For instance, a California statute authorizes a court to issue before arbitration "a provisional remedy * * * upon the ground that the award to which the applicant may be entitled may be rendered ineffectual without provisional relief."[295] And a New York statute permits courts to "entertain an application for an order of attachment or for a preliminary injunction in connection with an arbitration that is pending or that is to be commenced inside or outside this state," "but only upon the ground that the award to which the applicant may be entitled may be rendered ineffectual without such provisional relief."[296] And even without contractual or statutory authorization, some cases hold that courts may grant injunctive relief pending arbitration because it is necessary to hold the status quo while arbitration is pending.[297]

---

[292] Christopher R. Drahozal, Why Arbitrate? Substantive Versus Procedural Theories of Private Judging, 22 Am. Rev. Int'l Arb. 163, 178 (2011).

[293] Yahoo! Inc. v. Microsoft Corp., 983 F. Supp. 2d 310, 314 (S.D.N.Y. 2013) (confirming award issued by arbitrator appointed under agreement providing, "Except with respect to claims for interim, injunctive or emergency relief, where an Emergency Arbitrator will be appointed pursuant to Rule O–1 of the AAA Emergency Measures of Protection, the arbitration will be heard and determined before arbitrators selected in accordance with the remainder of this Section 17.5.")

[294] See, e.g., Variable Annuity Life Ins. Co. v. Laferrera, 680 F. App'x 880, 885–86 (11th Cir. 2017) ("the parties agreed to allow a court of competent jurisdiction to grant temporary injunctive relief pending arbitration"; "as Defendants concede, the agreements to arbitrate, which incorporate the FINRA rules, provide that the parties 'may seek a temporary injunctive order from a court of competent jurisdiction.' "); Toyo Tire Holdings of Americas, Inc. v. Continental Tire North America, Inc., 609 F.3d 975, 977–81, 983 (9th Cir. 2010) (agreement incorporated "International Chamber of Commerce Rules allow judicially imposed interim relief, including injunctive relief"; "If Toyo loses its customers before interim relief is possible, any subsequent relief could be useless"; "court may issue interim injunctive relief on arbitrable claims if interim relief is necessary to preserve the status quo and the meaningfulness of the arbitration process").

[295] Cal. Civ. Proc. Code § 1281.8.

[296] N.Y. C.P.L.R. § 7502.

[297] Performance Unlimited, Inc. v. Questar Publishers, Inc., 52 F.3d 1373, 1380 (6th Cir. 1995) (concluding that district court erred as a matter of law when it concluded that it could not enter preliminary injunctive relief because the parties'

Conversely, other cases have held that "courts should not grant injunctive relief unless there is 'qualifying contractual language' " in the arbitration agreement "which permits it."[298]

dispute was the subject of arbitration); Merrill Lynch, Pierce, Fenner & Smith v. Salvano, 999 F.2d 211, 214 (7th Cir. 1993) ("the weight of federal appellate authority recognizes some equitable power on the part of the district court to issue preliminary injunctive relief in disputes that are ultimately to be resolved by an arbitration panel"). In addition, the Fifth Circuit has held that a "court can grant preliminary relief before deciding whether to compel arbitration." Janvey v. Alguire, 647 F.3d 585, 593 (5th Cir. 2011).

298 Manion v. Nagin, 255 F.3d 535, 538–39 (8th Cir. 2001) (quoting Merrill Lynch, Pierce, Fenner & Smith, Inc. v. Hovey, 726 F.2d 1286, 1292 (8th Cir. 1984)). See also Simula, Inc. v. Autoliv, Inc., 175 F.3d 716, 726 (9th Cir. 1999) (affirming denial of preliminary injunction because plaintiff's claims were arbitrable and arbitral panel was authorized to grant provisional remedies).

Chapter 6

ENFORCEMENT AND VACATUR OF ARBITRATION AWARDS

Table of Sections

A. ENFORCEMENT OF ARBITRATION AWARDS

Table of Sections

Sec.

§ 36 Confirmation

As a general rule, arbitration awards are final and binding on the parties with only very limited grounds for judicial review. If the parties comply with the award, that ends the dispute. If the losing party refuses to comply, however, the prevailing party may seek court enforcement of the award. One option is for the prevailing party to seek a court order *confirming* the award.[1] A confirmed award in favor of the claimant is enforced in the same manner as other court judgments[2]: through judicial liens, garnishment, orders to turn over property, etc. In addition, arbitration awards generally have preclusive effect—that is, the arbitrator's ruling precludes re-litigating or re-arbitrating the claims resolved in arbitration.

---

[1] 9 U.S.C. § 9.

[2] FAA § 13 provides:

The party moving for an order confirming, modifying, or correcting an award shall, at the time such order is filed with the clerk for the entry of judgment thereon, also file the following papers with the clerk:

(a) The agreement; the selection or appointment, if any, of an additional arbitrator or umpire; and each written extension of the time, if any, within which to make the award.

(b) The award.

(c) Each notice, affidavit, or other paper used upon an application to confirm, modify, or correct the award, and a copy of each order of the court upon such an application.

The judgment shall be docketed as if it was rendered in an action.

The judgment so entered shall have the same force and effect, in all respects, as, and be subject to all the provisions of law relating to, a judgment in an action; and it may be enforced as if it had been rendered in an action in the court in which it is entered.

9 U.S.C. § 13.

§ 37 Claim Preclusion (Res Judicata)

The doctrine of claim preclusion (or *res judicata*) bars *adjudication*[3] of claims that have already been adjudicated in a prior proceeding. Arbitration awards have claim-preclusive effect in that they preclude later claims covered by the award.[4] Most courts hold that this is true whether or not a court has confirmed the award.[5] As the Restatement points out, "once an award has been confirmed, there is no need to give it preclusive effect as an award; the court judgment confirming the award is itself entitled to preclusive effect."[6]

Suppose Ann asserts a claim in arbitration against Bob and the arbitrator rules for Bob. If Ann then asserts the same claim in litigation, a court will grant Bob's motion to dismiss the case. The court treats the prior arbitration award in Bob's favor just as it would treat a prior court decision in Bob's favor, as precluding further litigation of that claim. Finality is central to binding adjudication, whether that adjudication be litigation or arbitration.

---

[3] See § 1, n.1.

[4] Restatement (Second) of Judgments § 84 (1982); Charles Alan Wright et al., Federal Practice and Procedure § 4475.1 (2005). For cases giving claim-preclusive effect to arbitration awards, see, e.g., Myer v. Americo Life Inc., 469 F.3d 731, 733 (8th Cir. 2006); IDS Life Ins. Co. v. Royal Alliance Assocs., Inc., 266 F.3d 645 (7th Cir. 2001); Century Int'l Arms, Ltd. v. Fed. State Unitary Enter. State Corp., 172 F. Supp.2d 79, 95–96 (D.D.C. 2001); Ruth R. Remmel Revocable Tr. v. Regions Fin. Corp., 369 Ark. 392, 403, 255 S.W.3d 453, 462 (2007) ("we hold that the circuit court correctly ruled that the arbitration award is res judicata to the claims asserted by the Remmels in their third-amended complaint"); Fink v. Golenbock, 680 A.2d 1243, 1252 (Conn. 1996); Sartor v. Superior Court, 187 Cal.Rptr. 247 (Ct. App. 1982) (award in favor of architectural firm is res judicata barring homeowner's identical causes of action against firm's employees).

[5] Val-U Const. Co. v. Rosebud Sioux Tribe, 146 F.3d 573, 581 (8th Cir. 1998) ("[t]he fact that the award in the present case was not confirmed by a court * * * does not vitiate the finality of the award."); Jacobson v. Fireman's Fund Ins. Co., 111 F.3d 261, 267 (2d Cir. 1996) ("[the] contention that only a judicially confirmed arbitration award may form the basis for the defenses of res judicata and collateral estoppel is without merit * * * [These] doctrines are applicable to issues resolved by arbitration where there has been a final determination on the merits, notwithstanding a lack of confirmation of the award."); Freecharm Ltd. v. Atlas Wealth Holdings Corp., 2011 WL 4591929 (S.D. Fla. Sep. 30, 2011) ("an unconfirmed arbitration award has a preclusive effect on subsequent litigation proceedings"); Camp v. Kollen, 567 F. Supp.2d 170 (D.D.C. 2008) (unconfirmed award given claim preclusive effect); Thibodeau v. Crum, 6 Cal.Rptr.2d 27 (Ct. App. 1992) (unconfirmed award in arbitration between homeowner and general contractor is res judicata barring homeowner's identical claim against subcontractor). But see Gruntal & Co., Inc. v. Steinberg, 854 F. Supp. 324, 337–338 (D.N.J. 1994) (requiring award to be confirmed before it can be considered "final"), aff'd, 46 F.3d 1116 (3d Cir. 1994); In re Interdiction of Wright, 2010-1826 (La. 10/25/11), 75 So. 3d 893, 894 ("we find an unconfirmed arbitration award does not have a preclusive effect").

[6] Restatement (Third) U.S. Law of Int'l Comm. Arb. § 4.35, Reporters' Note c (2019).

The claim-preclusive effect of labor arbitration awards can be less clear, as discussed in Section 49.

§ 38 Issue Preclusion (Collateral Estoppel)

The doctrine of issue preclusion bars adjudication of issues that have been decided in a prior case. The doctrine of issue preclusion can apply if that prior case was an arbitration,[7] but issue preclusion from arbitration is a matter of judicial discretion,[8] and thus less reliable than issue preclusion from litigation or claim preclusion from litigation or arbitration. To put it another way, proving that an earlier arbitration resolved an issue tends to be harder than proving that an earlier litigation resolved an issue, and also harder than proving that either an earlier arbitration or litigation resolved a claim.

While issue preclusion can only be asserted *against* one who was a party to the prior case, it can be asserted *by* one who was a stranger to that prior case.[9] When issue preclusion is asserted by a stranger to the prior case, it is called "non-mutual" issue preclusion. Suppose that Ann asserts a claim in arbitration against Bob and the arbitrator rules that certain conduct by Bob was negligent. If Carlos then sues Bob for damages arising out of the same conduct, the court hearing Carlos's case may hold, under the doctrine of non-mutual issue preclusion, that Carlos does not have to re-prove Bob's negligence. The court adopts the arbitrator's ruling regarding Bob's negligence and moves on to the other issues of Carlos's suit, such as whether his damages were caused by Bob's negligence. The court treats the prior

---

[7] Manganella v. Evanston Ins. Co., 700 F.3d 585, 591 (1st Cir. 2012) (affirming issue preclusive effect of arbitration award; "Generally, final arbitral awards are afforded the same preclusive effects as are prior court judgments."); B-S Steel of Kan., Inc. v. Tex. Indus., Inc., 439 F.3d 653, 666 (10th Cir. 2006) (affirming issue preclusive effect of arbitration award); id. ("This circuit has previously applied collateral estoppel to a confirmed arbitration award.") (citing Coffey v. Dean Witter Reynolds Inc., 961 F.2d 922, 927–28 (10th Cir. 1992)); Weizmann Inst. of Sci. v. Neschis, 421 F. Supp.2d 654, 676–77 (S.D.N.Y. 2005) ("The Requirements of Collateral Estoppel Have Been Satisfied With Respect To Mrs. Gelman's Testamentary Capacity" because "this Court finds that the issue of Mrs. Gelman's testamentary capacity was necessarily decided by the Arbitration Award and is 'decisive of the present action.' "); Maidman v. O'Brien, 473 F. Supp. 25, 29 (S.D.N.Y. 1979) (collateral estoppel effect of arbitrators' decision barred federal securities law claim against broker, when controlling issues in suit were identical to those decided by arbitrators and when investor had fair opportunity to present her claims).

[8] Universal American Barge Corp. v. J-Chem, Inc., 946 F.2d 1131, 1137–38 (5th Cir. 1991) (courts must "carefully consider whether procedural differences between arbitration and the district court proceeding might prejudice the party challenging the use of offensive collateral estoppel. The district court specifically must determine whether procedural opportunities available to the party in the subsequent action might be likely to cause a different result.")

[9] Ian R. Macneil, Richard E. Speidel & Thomas J. Stipanowich, Federal Arbitration Law § 39.1.1 (1994); Jack H. Friedenthal, Mary Kay Kane & Arthur R. Miller, Civil Procedure § 14.14 (4th ed. 2005).

arbitration ruling against Bob just as it would treat a prior court ruling against Bob, as precluding further litigation of that issue, even against a new party.[10]

In practice, however, a challenge for Carlos will be proving to the court that the arbitrator really did rule that Bob was negligent. Many arbitration awards are not accompanied by reasoned opinions.[11] As the Second Circuit explained, "Application of [collateral] estoppel following arbitration," "may be problematic because arbitrators are not required to provide an explanation for their decision."[12] If the arbitration award for Ann contained no reasoning, a court may not be able to learn *why* the arbitrator ruled against Bob. Perhaps the arbitrator concluded that Bob was negligent or perhaps the arbitrator concluded that Bob was not negligent but was liable to Ann for some other reason. If the latter, Bob is not precluded from arguing the negligence issue in Carlos's suit. Courts have denied issue-preclusive effect from arbitration awards because the court could not infer the factual basis for the arbitrator's decision.[13] In addition, under the law of some states, arbitration awards have non-mutual issue-preclusive effect only if the arbitration agreement provides that they will have such effect.[14]

B. VACATUR OF ARBITRATION AWARDS

Table of Sections

Sec.

---

[10] See, e.g., Riverdale Dev. Co. v. Ruffin Bldg. Sys. Inc., 146 S.W.3d 852, 854 (Ark. 2004) ("a third party * * * is entitled to rely upon an arbitration award such as [the one] here under the doctrines of collateral estoppel or res judicata").

[11] See § 34(e).

[12] Postlewaite v. McGraw-Hill, 333 F.3d 42, 48 (2d Cir. 2003).

[13] See, e.g., Postlewaite v. McGraw-Hill, Inc., 333 F.3d 42, 49 (2d Cir. 2003) ("[T]he party asserting preclusion bears the burden of showing with clarity and certainty what was determined by the prior judgment."; "issue preclusion will apply only if it is quite clear that this requirement has been met."); Hybert v. Shearson Lehman/American Express, Inc. 688 F. Supp. 320 (N.D.Ill.1988); Sports Factory, Inc. v. Chanoff, 586 F. Supp. 342, 346 (E.D. Pa. 1984); Lee L. Saad Constr. Co. v. DPF Architects, P.C., 851 So.2d 507 (Ala. 2003).

[14] Buckner v. Kennard, 99 P.3d 842, 846 (Utah 2004) ("a private arbitration award does not have nonmutual collateral estoppel effect unless the parties expressly provide for such preclusive effect beforehand"); Vandenberg v. Superior Court, 88 Cal. Rptr. 2d 366, 377–81 (Cal. 1999) ("a private arbitration award, even if judicially confirmed, may not have nonmutual collateral estoppel effect under California law unless there was an agreement to that effect in the particular case.")

---

§ 39 Overview of Vacating Arbitration Awards

(a) Vacatur of Award Contrasted with Appellate Reversal of Trial Court

A party disappointed with an arbitrator's decision may ask a court to vacate the arbitration award. In some ways, a court considering whether to vacate an arbitration award is like an appellate court considering whether to reverse the decision of a trial court. But "the grounds on which courts review arbitration awards are much narrower than the grounds on which appeals courts review decisions of trial courts."[15] While appellate courts usually give some deference to trial courts' factual findings—reversing only those that are "clearly erroneous"—trial courts' conclusions of law receive no

---

[15] Christopher R. Drahozal, Commercial Arbitration: Cases and Problems 564 (3d ed. 2013).

appellate deference,[16] so any error of law by the trial court may be reversed under an appellate court's de novo review of questions of law.

In contrast, arbitrators' conclusions of law rarely receive de novo review by courts considering a motion to vacate an arbitration award.[17] In fact, the FAA may not allow courts to review arbitrators' conclusions of law at all because "error of law" by the arbitrator is not even a ground for vacating an arbitration award. The FAA only permits courts to vacate:

> (1) Where the award was procured by corruption, fraud, or undue means;
>
> (2) Where there was evident partiality or corruption in the arbitrators, or either of them;
>
> (3) Where the arbitrators were guilty of misconduct in refusing to postpone the hearing, upon sufficient cause shown, or in refusing to hear evidence pertinent and material to the controversy; or of any other misbehavior by which the rights of any party have been prejudiced; or
>
> (4) Where the arbitrators exceeded their powers, or so imperfectly executed them that a mutual, final, and definite award upon the subject matter submitted was not made.[18]

Why are the FAA's grounds for vacating arbitration awards so narrow that they do not even include "error of law" by the arbitrator? The following two subsections summarize two common explanations.

(b) Narrow Grounds for Vacatur Save Time and Money

One explanation of why the FAA's grounds for vacating arbitration awards are so narrow that they do not even include "error of law" by the arbitrator is that such a ground would reduce the efficiency of arbitration. As the Supreme Court's 2008 opinion in *Hall Street Associates, L.L.C. v. Mattel, Inc.* ,[19] recognized, arbitration's propensity to save time and money is strengthened by the narrowness of the FAA's grounds for vacatur. *Hall Street* described

---

16 "For purposes of standard of review, decisions by judges are traditionally divided into three categories, denominated questions of law (reviewable de novo), questions of fact (reviewable for clear error), and matters of discretion (reviewable for 'abuse of discretion')." Pierce v. Underwood, 487 U.S. 552 (1988).

17 The FAA's "grounds are narrower than the standards for appellate review in a judicial case where a court reviews a lower court's legal rulings de novo and factual findings for clear error." Maureen A. Weston, The Other Avenues of Hall Street and Prospects for Judicial Review of Arbitral Awards, 14 Lewis & Clark L. Rev. 929, 933–34 (2010).

18 9 U.S.C. § 10(a).

19 552 U.S. 576 (2008).

the FAA's provisions on confirmation and vacatur of arbitration awards

> as substantiating a national policy favoring arbitration with just the limited review needed to maintain arbitration's essential virtue of resolving disputes straightaway. Any other reading opens the door to the full-bore legal and evidentiary appeals that can render informal arbitration merely a prelude to a more cumbersome and time-consuming judicial review process and bring arbitration theory to grief in post-arbitration process.[20]

In other words, the FAA's narrow grounds for vacatur reduce the likelihood that a court will vacate an award and thus reduce the likelihood that a party disappointed with an award will incur the time and expense necessary to challenge it in court.[21] The FAA's narrow grounds for vacatur increase the finality of the arbitrator's decision and thus reduce costs to both parties and to the court system.[22]

In contrast, if the FAA had listed "error of law" among the grounds for vacating an arbitration award, more parties disappointed with their arbitration awards would challenge those awards in court.[23] In addition to the costs of those challenges themselves, attempts to vacate awards on that basis might also make the

---

[20] 552 U.S. 576 (internal quotation omitted).

[21] Courts grant a significant minority of motions to vacate awards. Michael H. Leroy & Peter Feuille, The Revolving Door of Justice: Arbitration Agreements That Expand Court Review of an Award, 19 Ohio St. J. on Disp.Resol. 861, tbl.1 (2004) (at first-level of court review, 139 (92.1%) arbitration awards were confirmed, while 12 (7.9%) were vacated. 118 of initial court decisions were appealed. At higher levels of court review, 102 (86.4%) awards were confirmed, while 16 (13.6%) were vacated); Lawrence R. Mills et al., Vacating Arbitration Awards, Disp. Resol. Mag., Summer 2005, at 23, 24 (20% vacatur rate). However, because of arbitration's usual privacy, no data indicates the number of awards that never become the subject of a motion to vacate.

[22] See also Henry S. Noyes, If You (Re)Build It, They Will Come: Contracts to Remake the Rules of Litigation in Arbitration's Image, 30 Harv. J.L. & Pub. Pol'y 579, 592 (2007) ("limited appellate review encourages finality and discourages parties from pursuing dubious, costly appeals"); Jackson Williams & Morgan Lynn, Public Citizen Releases the Costs of Arbitration, PIABA B.J., Summer 2002, at 52 ("Public Citizen agrees that proponents of arbitration are undoubtedly correct that the limited, narrow grounds upon which an arbitration award can be appealed will reduce litigation costs. Parties will avoid paying court reporters to record or transcribe hearings or appellate attorneys to write briefs.")

[23] Abbott v. Mulligan, 647 F. Supp.2d 1286,1291–92 (D. Utah 2009) ("If a misinterpretation or misapplication of the law was a sufficient basis upon which a district court could overturn an arbitration panel's ruling, district courts would become routine avenues for appeal every time a plausible argument could be made that the arbitration panel got the law wrong. An appeal to the district court would be virtually guaranteed if one of the parties felt they had grounds to argue that the arbitrators got the law *really* wrong. Such review would defeat the rationale and purposes behind the FAA.")

underlying arbitration process more expensive. Currently, arbitrators in many cases do not write reasoned opinions explaining their decisions,[24] and arbitration may not produce a transcript or other record of the arbitration hearing.[25] These cost-saving aspects of arbitration might have to change if courts vacated awards lacking a basis from which the court could determine whether the arbitrator correctly applied the law. The Supreme Court has said that "A prime objective of an agreement to arbitrate is to achieve 'streamlined proceedings and expeditious results.' "[26] These goals of saving time and money are advanced by the FAA's narrow grounds for vacatur and would be hindered if courts reviewed arbitrators' legal rulings as closely as appellate courts review trial courts' legal rulings.

(c) Arbitration Award as Contract Term

Another explanation of why the FAA's grounds for vacating arbitration awards are so narrow that they do not even include "error of law" by the arbitrator is that such a ground would conflict with the contractual core of arbitration law. As the Supreme Court said in 2022, "an arbitral award" "is no more than a contractual resolution of the parties' dispute."[27] So, as Judge Richard Posner explained:

> It is tempting to think that courts are engaged in judicial review of arbitration awards under the Federal Arbitration Act, but they are not. When parties agree to arbitrate their disputes they opt out of the court system, and when one of them challenges the resulting arbitration award he perforce does so not on the ground that the arbitrators made a mistake but that they violated the agreement to arbitrate, * * * conduct to which the parties did not consent when they included an arbitration clause in their contract.[28]

In other words, the FAA does not make "error of law" a ground for vacatur because arbitrators are not necessarily supposed to apply the law. They are supposed to apply the contract.

This understanding of arbitrators bound by contract, rather than by law "external" to the contract, has two main features. First, some courts have long stated that arbitrators are not obligated to apply the law and may, without fear of vacatur, decide the case by

---

24 See § 34(e).

25 See § 34(a).

26 Preston v. Ferrer, 552 U.S. 346, 357 (2008).

27 Badgerow v. Walters, 142 S. Ct. 1310, 1316 (2022).

28 Wise v. Wachovia Sec., LLC, 450 F.3d 265, 269 (7th Cir. 2006).

applying something other than law, such as industry custom or the arbitrator's own sense of equity.[29]

Second, the understanding that arbitrators are bound by contract, rather than by law "external" to the contract, generally leads courts and commentators to see issues of vacatur through a contractual lens. Although arbitrators, like courts, are adjudicators issuing legally binding rulings, an arbitrator's power to issue such a ruling comes from the parties' contract. "In the main, an arbitrator acts as the parties' agent and as their delegate may do anything the parties may do directly."[30] As the Supreme Court said in a labor arbitration case, "we must treat the arbitrator's award as if it represented an agreement between" the parties themselves.[31] In short, a court enforcing an arbitration award is a court enforcing a contract. The parties agreed to comply with the arbitrator's decision and if a party refuses to do so then that party is in breach of contract. Just as courts routinely enforce most other sorts of contracts without assessing the wisdom of the contract's terms, so courts routinely enforce arbitration awards without assessing the wisdom of the award's terms.

However, not all contracts are enforceable and, similarly, not all arbitration awards are enforceable. Just as contract law has long recognized defenses to contract enforcement, arbitration law has long recognized defenses to the enforcement of an arbitration award. Contract law's defenses include misrepresentation, mistake, duress, undue influence, unconscionability, illegality, impracticability, and frustration of purpose. These contract defenses generally resemble the FAA's grounds for vacating an arbitration award. FAA § 10(a) permits courts to vacate:

> (1) Where the award was procured by corruption, fraud, or undue means;
>
> (2) Where there was evident partiality or corruption in the arbitrators, or either of them;
>
> (3) Where the arbitrators were guilty of misconduct in refusing to postpone the hearing, upon sufficient cause

---

29 See § 41(c).

30 George Watts & Son, Inc. v. Tiffany and Co., 248 F.3d 577, 580 (7th Cir. 2001) (Easterbrook, J.).

31 Eastern Associated Coal Corp. v. United Mine Workers, 531 U.S. 57, 62 (2000). See also United Paperworkers Int'l Union v. Misco, Inc., 484 U.S. 29, 42 (1987) ("A court's refusal to enforce an arbitrator's award * * * because it is contrary to public policy is a specific application of the more general doctrine, rooted in the common law, that a court may refuse to enforce contracts that violate law or public policy."); Seymour v. Blue Cross/Blue Shield, 988 F.2d 1020, 1023 (10th Cir. 1993) ("The public policy exception is rooted in the common law doctrine of a court's power to refuse to enforce a contract that violates public policy or law.")

shown, or in refusing to hear evidence pertinent and material to the controversy; or of any other misbehavior by which the rights of any party have been prejudiced; or

(4) Where the arbitrators exceeded their powers, or so imperfectly executed them that a mutual, final, and definite award upon the subject matter submitted was not made.[32]

Subsection 1's "corruption, fraud, or undue means" resembles contract law's defenses of illegality, misrepresentation, undue influence, and duress. Subsection 2's "partiality or corruption" and subsection 3's "misconduct" or "misbehavior" resemble contract law's defenses of unconscionability, illegality, and undue influence. Subsection 4's "exceeded * * * powers" or "imperfectly executed them" resembles contract law's defenses of illegality, mistake, impracticability, and frustration of purpose.

These "statutory" grounds for vacatur—the grounds expressly stated in FAA § 10(a)—are discussed next.

§ 40 Statutory Grounds for Vacatur

(a) Corruption, Fraud or Undue Means

FAA § 10(a)(1) permits courts to vacate an arbitration award where the "award was procured by corruption, fraud, or undue means."[33] To vacate, there must be a close causal connection between the wrongdoing—corruption, fraud (including perjury) or undue means—and the award.[34] The party seeking vacatur must also show that the wrongdoing was "(1) not discoverable upon the exercise of due diligence prior to the arbitration, (2) materially related to an issue in the arbitration, and (3) established by clear and convincing evidence."[35] If the alleged wrongdoing was brought to the attention

---

[32] 9 U.S.C. § 10(a).

[33] 9 U.S.C. § 10(a)(1). "The best reading of the terms 'undue means' * * * is that it describes underhanded or conniving ways of procuring an award that are similar to corruption or fraud, but do not precisely constitute either." Nat'l Casualty Co. v. First State Ins. Group, 430 F.3d 492, 499 (1st Cir. 2005). "Ex parte contact [between the arbitrator and a party] involving disputed issues raises a presumption that the arbitration award was procured by fraud, corruption, or other undue means." Rosenthal-Collins Group, L.P. v. Reiff, 748 N.E.2d 229, 232 (Ill. Ct. App. 2001) (vacating award) (applying state law rather than FAA).

[34] See Ian R. Macneil, Richard E. Speidel & Thomas J. Stipanowich, Federal Arbitration Law § 40.2.2 (1994). See Odeon Capital Group LLC v. Ackerman, 864 F.3d 191 (2d Cir. 2017) (refusing to vacate award based on perjury during the arbitration because it was not material to the award); Envtl. Barrier Co., LLC v. Slurry Sys., Inc., 540 F.3d 598, 608 (7th Cir. 2008) (award enforceable when there was no nexus between purported fraud and arbitrator's final decision).

[35] A.G. Edwards & Sons, Inc. v. McCullough, 967 F.2d 1401, 1404 (9th Cir. 1992). Accord Bauer v. Carty & Co., Inc., 246 Fed.Appx. 375, 377 (6th Cir. 2007).

of the arbitrators then the award will not be vacated on this ground.[36] Vacatur under FAA § 10(a)(1) is not common but does happen occasionally. For example, the Eleventh Circuit vacated an award due to perjury by an expert witness as to his qualifications.[37] The Ninth Circuit affirmed vacatur of an award procured by fraud "not discoverable by due diligence before or during the proceeding" and "materially related to the submitted issue."[38]

(b) Evident Partiality or Corruption

(1) Arbitrator's Disclosure

FAA § 10(a)(2) permits courts to vacate an arbitration award where "there was evident partiality or corruption in the arbitrators."[39] But while arbitrator partiality is a ground for vacating an award, issues of partiality often arise much earlier in the arbitration process—at the arbitrator-selection stage, when possible arbitrators disclose their experiences, connections, and financial interests. For example, the AAA's Commercial Arbitration Rules say,

> Any person appointed or to be appointed as an arbitrator, as well as the parties and their representatives, shall disclose to the AAA any circumstance likely to give rise to justifiable doubt as to the arbitrator's impartiality or independence, including any bias or any financial or personal interest in the result of the arbitration or any past or present relationship with the parties or their representatives.[40]

During the arbitrator-selection process,[41] a party may challenge the appointment of an arbitrator on the ground that the arbitrator is partial to the opposing party. "The primary remedy sought at this early stage is disqualification of the partial arbitrator and the

---

[36] Barahona v. Dillard's, Inc., 2010 WL 1655322, at *2 (5th Cir. 2010). Forsythe Intern., S.A. v. Gibbs Oil Co., 915 F.2d 1017, 1022–1023 (5th Cir. 1990)(award not affected by alleged fraud since arbitrators heard argument on allegations of fraud and rendered decision that rested on parties' intent as measured by their actions, and not allegedly fraudulent witness testimony); Belmont Partners v. Mina Mar Group, Inc., 741 F. Supp. 2d 743, 753–754 (W.D. Va. 2010) (allegedly fraudulent statement was central to the parties' dispute, fully briefed by both sides, and essentially a credibility determination for arbitrator to make).

[37] Bonar v. Dean Witter Reynolds, Inc., 835 F.2d 1378, 1383 (11th Cir. 1988) ("Nix's perjury requires vacation of the punitive damages portion of the arbitration award.")

[38] Williams v. Laimana, 21-55053, 2022 WL 563250, at *1 (9th Cir. Feb. 24, 2022). See also Satcomm v. PayPal, 5:19-MC-10-MTT, 2020 WL 1609503, at *2 (M.D. Ga. Apr. 1, 2020) (vacating award due to fraud).

[39] 9 U.S.C. § 10(a)(2).

[40] Am. Arb. Ass'n, Commercial Arbitration Rules, R–18(a) (2022).

[41] See § 33(a).

appointment of a substitute."[42] While this remedy can be ordered by a court, such pre-award disputes over arbitrator partiality tend to be resolved by the parties themselves, by the arbitrator (perhaps by resigning her appointment), or by the organization administering the arbitration.

Of the court decisions vacating arbitration awards under FAA § 10(a)(2) "evident partiality," many are because of insufficiencies in the arbitrator's disclosures. The leading non-disclosure partiality case is *Commonwealth Coatings Corp. v. Continental Casualty Co.*,[43] decided by the Supreme Court in 1968. In *Commonwealth Coatings*, a subcontractor sued a surety on the prime contractor's bond to recover money due for a painting job.[44] Each party appointed an arbitrator and the two party-appointed arbitrators appointed a third, neutral arbitrator.[45] The arbitrators unanimously ruled for the surety.[46] Then the subcontractor learned for the first time that the neutral arbitrator, an engineering consultant, had a business relationship with the prime contractor.[47] The prime contractor had paid the arbitrator consulting fees of about $12,000 over a period of four or five years.[48] Although there was no evidence of actual bias or prejudice by the neutral arbitrator, the Supreme Court reversed the lower courts and vacated the arbitration award. Justice Black's opinion for the Court's plurality held that non-disclosure of "any dealings that might create an impression of possible bias" or creating "even an appearance of bias" would warrant vacating.[49] In contrast, Justice White's concurring opinion required disclosure of substantial relationships only.[50] Justice White wrote "arbitrators are not automatically disqualified by a business relationship with the parties before them if both parties are informed of the relationship in advance, or if they are unaware of the facts but the relationship is trivial."[51]

What particular dealings or relationships trigger a duty to disclose can only be determined case-by-case in a fact-intensive

[42] Ian R. Macneil, Richard E. Speidel & Thomas J. Stipanowich, Federal Arbitration Law § 28.1.1 (1994).

[43] 393 U.S. 145 (1968).

[44] Id. at 146.

[45] Id.

[46] Id.

[47] Id.

[48] Id.

[49] Id. at 149.

[50] 393 U.S. at 150 (White, J., concurring).

[51] Id.

inquiry.[52] Nevertheless, the Fourth Circuit has identified four factors to be considered:

(1) the extent and character of the personal interest, pecuniary or otherwise, of the arbitrator in the proceeding;

(2) the directness of the relationship between the arbitrator and the party he is alleged to favor;

(3) the connection of that relationship to the arbitration; and

(4) the proximity in time between the relationship and the arbitration proceeding.[53]

The Restatement adds:

(5) any relevant industry practices that may affect the parties' expectations regarding relationships between the arbitrator, and the parties and their dispute; and

---

[52] Compare, e.g., Positive Software Solutions, Inc. v. New Century Mortgage Corp., 436 F.3d 495 (5th Cir. 2006) (vacating award where arbitrator failed to disclose that seven years before the arbitration, he and his former law firm were co-counsel in a lengthy litigation matter with law firm and particular lawyer representing winning party in arbitration); Schmitz v. Zilveti, 20 F.3d 1043, 1044 (9th Cir. 1994), (vacating award where the arbitrator failed to disclose that his law firm had represented the corporate parent of the defendant corporation involved in the arbitration in 19 matters over a 35-year period ending some 21 months before the arbitration.); Neaman v. Kaiser Found. Hosp., 11 Cal. Rptr. 2d 879 (Ct. App. 1992) (failure of neutral arbitrator to reveal that he had served as a party-arbitrator for one of the parties required the award to be set aside); Wages v. Smith Barney Harris Upham Co., 937 P.2d 715 (Ariz. Ct. App. 1997) (vacating award when arbitrator failed to disclose that he had represented investors with similar claims against predecessor-in-interest to respondent), with Lucent Techs. Inc. v. Tatung Co., 379 F.3d 24 (2d Cir. 2004) (arbitrator's prior service as expert witness for one of the parties does not constitute evident partiality when that service involved matter unrelated to dispute at issue and engagement concluded prior to arbitration); Freeman v. Pittsburgh Glass Works, LLC, 709 F.3d 240, 254–55 (3d Cir. 2013) (party's undisclosed campaign contributions to arbitrator's election campaign not evidence of partiality because they are on the public record and because opposing party's lawyers contributed more); Apusento Garden (Guam) Inc. v. Superior Court of Guam, 94 F.3d 1346, 1352 (9th Cir. 1996) (confirming award of arbitrator who failed to disclose that he and Apusento Garden's expert witness were both limited partners in a partnership unrelated to the arbitration); Woods v. Saturn Distribution Corp., 78 F.3d 424 (9th Cir. 1996) (no evident partiality arising from arbitrators' financial dependence on Saturn where arbitrators, like Woods, were Saturn auto dealers); Casden Park La Brea Retail LLC v. Ross Dress For Less, Inc., 75 Cal. Rptr. 3d 763 (Ct. App. 2008) (neutral arbitrator had no duty to disclose employer's prior dealings with a party because the arbitrator did not participate in or have a pecuniary interest in those transactions); Guseinov v. Burns, 51 Cal. Rptr. 3d 903 (Ct. App. 2006) (declining to vacate award despite arbitrator's nondisclosure of prior service as a pro bono mediator in an unrelated case involving a party's attorney).

[53] ANR Coal Co., Inc. v. Cogentrix of North Carolina, Inc., 173 F.3d 493, 500 (4th Cir. 1999). By statute, California requires extensive disclosures by neutral arbitrators of potential conflicts of interest. See § 33(a)(3). Gray v. Chiu, 151 Cal. Rptr. 3d 791, 797 (Ct. App. 2013) (vacating award).

(6) the extent to which the arbitrator undertook a reasonable investigation to discover potential conflicts and actually knew of, or should have known of, the information that was not disclosed.[54]

Arbitrator investigation is significant, as is party investigation. Courts may vacate an award by an arbitrator who did not know of her relationship with a party if she would have discovered the relationship had she engaged in a reasonable investigation.[55] Conversely, courts have refused to vacate where the arbitrator's inadequate disclosure disclosed enough to put a party on notice to investigate further rather than wait to see if the award ruled against that party.[56]

The Ninth Circuit perhaps tightened standards for arbitrator disclosure in the 2019 case of *Monster Energy Co. v. City Beverages*.[57] In *Monster Energy*, two "sophisticated companies," a supplier and a distributor of beverages, arbitrated a dispute before a JAMS arbitrator who had disclosed his "economic interest in the overall financial success of JAMS" and further informed the distributor that JAMS previously had "participated in" a dispute resolution proceeding with the supplier. Neither party objected to the arbitrator's disclosures. After the arbitrator ruled for the supplier, the distributor learned that the arbitrator had a personal "ownership" interest in JAMS beyond his economic interest as a JAMS arbitrator. While the district court rejected the distributor's "evident-partiality" challenge to the award, the Ninth Circuit reversed and vacated the award. The Ninth Circuit found the arbitrator's "ownership interest" in JAMS to be a "crucial fact" not

---

54 Restatement (Third) U.S. Law of Int'l Comm. Arb. § 4.18 (2019).

55 New Regency Productions, Inc. v. Nippon Herald Films, Inc., 501 F.3d 1101, 1107–08 (9th Cir. 2007) ("an arbitrator's lack of actual knowledge of the presence of a conflict does not excuse non-disclosure where the arbitrator had a duty to investigate, and thus had constructive knowledge of, the conflict.") See also Applied Indus. Materials Corp. v. Ovalar Makine Ticaret Ve Sanayi, A.S., 492 F.3d 132, 138 (2d Cir. 2007) ("where an arbitrator has reason to believe that a nontrivial conflict of interest might exist, he must (1) investigate the conflict (which may reveal information that must be disclosed under Commonwealth Coatings) or (2) disclose his reasons for believing there might be a conflict and his intention not to investigate."); id. (if an arbitrator fails to follow this rule by investigating or disclosing a potential nontrivial conflict of interest, such a failure "is indicative of evident partiality.")

56 Cox v. Bonni, 241 Cal. Rptr. 3d 359, 373 (Ct. App. 2018) ("While failure to disclose properly a ground for disqualification generally mandates vacation of the award, this rule only applies if the party moving to vacate had no reason to know of the existence of a nondisclosed matter. If a party is aware that a disclosure is incomplete or otherwise fails to meet the statutory disclosure requirements, the party cannot passively reserve the issue for consideration after the arbitration has concluded.")

57 Monster Energy Co. v. City Beverages, LLC, 940 F.3d 1130 (9th Cir. 2019).

adequately disclosed by the arbitrator's disclosure of his "economic interest in the overall financial success of JAMS."[58]

(2) Arbitrator's Conduct

Courts may vacate arbitration awards under FAA § 10(a)(2) because arbitrators showed "evident partiality" in their conduct of the arbitration. However, courts disagree about whether Justice White's concurring opinion in *Commonwealth Coatings* makes Justice Black's opinion a plurality or a majority opinion, and thus courts "have diverged significantly in attempting to define 'evident impartiality.' "[59] The quickest courts to vacate, "consistent with Black's plurality opinion, require only proof of a reasonable impression or appearance of bias."[60] At the other extreme of most reluctant to vacate are courts requiring proof of actual bias.[61] The intermediate position "adopted by a majority of courts, and by the Restatement, requires an objective, disinterested observer who is fully informed of the facts relevant to the arbitrator's conduct or alleged conflicts to develop a serious doubt regarding the fundamental fairness of the arbitral proceedings."[62]

As the Fourth Circuit explained:

> The party asserting evident partiality has the burden of proof. The alleged partiality must be direct, definite, and capable of demonstration rather than remote, uncertain or speculative. Therefore, the burden on a claimant for vacation of an arbitration award due to "evident partiality"

---

[58] Id. at 1135.

[59] Restatement (Third) U.S. Law of Int'l Comm. Arb. § 4.18 (2019).

[60] Id. (citing New Regency Productions, Inc. v. Nippon Herald Films, Inc., 501 F.3d 1101, 1106 (9th Cir. 2007); Montez v. Prudential Sec., Inc., 260 F.3d 980, 983 (8th Cir. 2001); Olson v. Merrill Lynch, Pierce, Fenner & Smith, Inc., 51 F.3d 157, 160 (8th Cir. 1995); Schmitz v. Zilveti, 20 F.3d 1043, 1045 (9th Cir. 1994)).

[61] Id. (citing Positive Software Solutions v. New Century Mortgage Corp., 476 F.3d 278, 281 (5th Cir. 2007) (en banc); Sphere Drake Ins. Ltd. v. All Am. Life Ins. Co., 307 F.3d 617, 621–623 (7th Cir. 2002); Health Servs. Mgmt. Corp. v. Hughes, 975 F.2d 1253, 1264 (7th Cir. 1992); Ormsbee Dev. Co. v. Grace, 668 F.2d 1140, 1150 (10th Cir. 1982)).

[62] Id. (citing Dauphin Precision Tool v. United Steelworkers of Am., 338 F. App'x 219, 223 (3d Cir. 2009) (unpublished opinion); Applied Indus. Materials Corp. v. Ovalar Makine Ticaret Ve Sanayi, A.S., 492 F.3d 132, 137 (2d Cir. 2007); Nationwide Mut. Ins. Co. v. Home Ins. Co., 429 F.3d 640, 644 (6th Cir. 2005); JCI Commc'ns, Inc. v. Int'l Broth. of Elec. Workers, Local 103, 324 F.3d 42, 51 (1st Cir. 2003); ANR Coal Co., Inc. v. Cogentrix of N.C., Inc., 173 F.3d 493, 500–501 (4th Cir. 1999); Gianelli Money Purchase Plan & Trust v. ADM Investor Servs., Inc., 146 F.3d 1309, 1312–1313 (11th Cir. 1998); Al-Harbi v. Citibank, N.A., 85 F.3d 680, 683 (D.C. Cir. 1996); Morelite Constr. Corp., 748 F.2d at 82–85; Merit Ins. Co. v. Leatherby Ins. Co., 714 F.2d 673, 681 (7th Cir. 1983), cert. denied, 464 U.S. 1009, modified, 728 F.2d 943 (7th Cir. 1984); DeBaker v. Shah, 194 Wis. 2d 104, 118 (Wis. 1995)).

is heavy, and the claimant must establish specific facts that indicate improper motives on the part of an arbitrator.[63]

Parties have alleged that evident partiality was demonstrated by an arbitrator who "appeared disinterested" during one party's presentation,[64] an arbitrator who made "several comments" indicating "empathy" for the opposing party,[65] an arbitrator who called a party's lawyer "bitter and irresponsible,"[66] and an arbitrator who used the term "young lady" in addressing a party's lawyer.[67] But in none of these cases did the court vacate the award. Courts have also rejected the "structural bias" argument that arbitrators of industry associations are biased against claims brought against the industry.[68]

(3) Tripartite Arbitration

The topic of arbitrator partiality gains another layer of complexity when the arbitrator alleged to be partial is a party-appointed arbitrator in tripartite arbitration, (arbitration with three-arbitrators). For example, conduct that would be a troubling indicator of partiality in a single arbitrator—speaking with one party beyond the presence of the other party—is common of party-appointed arbitrators. As the Ninth Circuit said in one case, "before the submission of the parties' pre-hearing briefs * * * , each party had ex parte contact with its party arbitrator. This is customary in tripartite arbitration panels."[69] Accordingly, Judge Easterbrook, writing for the Seventh Circuit, suggested that very different partiality standards be applied to party-appointed arbitrators "because in the main party-appointed arbitrators are *supposed* to be advocates. In labor arbitration a union may name as its arbitrator the business manager of the local union, and the employer its vice-president for labor relations. Yet no one believes that the predictable loyalty of these designees spoils the award."[70]

---

63 Peoples Sec. Life Ins. Co. v. Monumental Life Ins. Co., 991 F.2d 141, 146 (4th Cir. 1993).

64 Austin South I, Ltd. v. Barton-Malow Co., 799 F. Supp. 1135, 1143 (M.D. Fla. 1992).

65 Remmy v. Paine Webber, Inc., 32 F.3d 143, 148 (4th Cir. 1994).

66 InterChem Asia 2000 Pte. Ltd. v. Oceana Petrochemicals AG, 373 F. Supp.2d 340, 348 (S.D.N.Y. 2005).

67 Smith v. Prudential Securities, Inc., 846 F. Supp. 978, 980 (M.D. Fla. 1994).

68 Harter v. Iowa Grain Co., 220 F.3d 544 (7th Cir. 2000) (National Grain & Feed Association arbitration); Scott v. Prudential Sec., Inc., 141 F.3d 1007, 1015–16 (11th Cir. 1998) (National Futures Trading Association arbitration).

69 U.S. Life Ins. Co. v. Superior Nat. Ins. Co., 591 F.3d 1167, 1171 n.1 (9th Cir. 2010).

70 Sphere Drake Ins., Ltd. v. All Am. Life Ins. Co., 307 F.3d 617, 620 (7th Cir. 2002) (emphasis in original).

On the other hand, the Wisconsin Supreme Court "prescrib[ed] presumptive impartiality as the appropriate role for the party-appointed arbitrator, unless the parties contract for non-neutral arbitrators or the arbitration rules otherwise provide for non-neutral arbitrators."[71] Relatedly, the AAA and American Bar Association in 2004 approved a "Code of Ethics for Arbitrators in Commercial Disputes." It "establishes a presumption of neutrality for all arbitrators, including party appointed arbitrators, which applies unless the parties' agreement, the arbitration rules agreed to by the parties or applicable laws provide otherwise."[72] The AAA Commercial Arbitration Rules say: "Any arbitrator shall be * * * subject to disqualification for partiality or lack of independence."[73] "The parties may agree in writing, however, that arbitrators directly appointed by a party pursuant to Section R–13 shall be non-neutral, in which case such arbitrators need not be impartial or independent and shall not be subject to disqualification for partiality or lack of independence."[74]

(c) Arbitrator Misconduct

FAA § 10(a)(3) permits courts to vacate an arbitration award where "the arbitrators were guilty of misconduct in refusing to postpone the hearing, upon sufficient cause shown, or in refusing to hear evidence pertinent and material to the controversy; or of any other misbehavior by which the rights of any party have been prejudiced."[75] This provision has been summarized by courts as requiring arbitrators to provide the parties with a "fundamentally fair hearing," which requires only notice and an opportunity to be

---

[71] Borst v. Allstate Ins. Co., 717 N.W.2d 42, 48 (Wis. 2006). See also Metro. Prop. & Cas. Ins. Co. v. J.C. Penney Cas. Ins. Co., 780 F. Supp. 885, 892 (D. Conn. 1991) (expressing concern about party-appointed arbitrator's ex parte meetings party to discuss the merits of the case prior to his appointment as arbitrator, "The fact that party selected arbitrators are not expected to be 'neutral', however, does not mean that such arbitrators are excused from their ethical duties and the obligation to participate in the arbitration process in a fair, honest and good-faith manner.")

[72] The Code of Ethics for Arbitrators in Commercial Disputes, Mar. 1, 2004.

[73] Am. Arb. Ass'n, Commercial Arbitration Rules, R–19(a) (2022).

[74] Id. at R-19(b).

[75] 9 U.S.C. § 10(a)(3). See, e.g., Tempo Shain Corp. v. Bertek, Inc., 120 F.3d 16 (2d Cir. 1997); Goldfinger v. Lisker, 500 N.E.2d 857 (N.Y. Ct. App. 1986) (vacating award due to arbitrator's ex parte contacts).

heard.[76] An arbitration award may be rendered against a party who does not participate in arbitration after receiving notice.[77]

Courts are cautious about vacating an award due to an arbitrator's ruling on a procedural or evidentiary issue. Most hold that "a challenge to an arbitrator's evidentiary rulings or limitations on discovery should not provide a basis for vacating an award unless the error substantially prejudiced a party's ability to present material evidence in support of its case."[78] An award has been vacated, however, where the arbitrator misled a party about what evidence had been admitted.[79] Also, ex parte evidence received by arbitrators has triggered vacatur.[80]

(d) Exceeded Powers

FAA § 10(a)(4) permits courts to vacate an arbitration award where, among other things, "the arbitrators exceeded their powers."[81] These powers are largely determined by the arbitration agreement.[82] So, courts vacate awards under this provision "in cases where the

---

[76] See, e.g., Legacy Trading Co., Ltd. v. Hoffman, 2010 WL 325893, at *3 (10th Cir. 2010) ("a fundamentally fair arbitration hearing requires only notice, opportunity to be heard and to present relevant and material evidence and argument before the decision makers, and that the decision-makers are not infected with bias") (citation omitted); Nationwide Mut. Ins. Co. v. Home Ins. Co., 278 F.3d 621, 625 (6th Cir. 2002) ("Fundamental fairness requires only notice, an opportunity to present relevant and material evidence and arguments to the arbitrators, and an absence of bias on the part of the arbitrators."); Roche v. Local 32B-32J SEIU, 755 F. Supp. 622, 624 (S.D.N.Y. 1991) (for arbitrator misconduct to be found under this ground, misconduct must amount to denial of fundamental fairness of arbitration proceeding).

[77] See § 34(d)(3).

[78] Schlessinger v. Rosenfeld, Meyer & Susman, 47 Cal. Rptr. 2d 650, 659 (Ct. App. 1995). See also U.S. Life Ins. Co. v. Superior Nat. Ins. Co., 591 F.3d 1167, 1174 (9th Cir. 2010) ("the phrase 'refusing to hear evidence pertinent and material to the controversy' necessarily implies prejudice to the rights of a party"); Nat'l Casualty Co. v. First State Ins. Group, 430 F.3d 492, 499 (1st Cir. 2005) (vacatur only where "the exclusion of relevant evidence so affects the rights of a party that it may be said that he was deprived of a fair hearing.").

[79] Gulf Coast Industrial Workers Union v. Exxon Co., USA, 70 F.3d 847 (5th Cir. 1995).

[80] Pac. Reins. Mgmt. Corp. v. Ohio Reins. Corp., 935 F.2d 1019, 1025 (9th Cir. 1991); Totem Marine Tug & Barge, Inc. v. N. Am. Towing, Inc., 607 F.2d 649, 653 (5th Cir. 1979) ("[a]rbitrators cannot conduct ex parte hearings or receive evidence except in the presence of each other and of the parties, unless otherwise stipulated"); Goldfinger v. Lisker 500 N.E.2d 857 (N.Y. 1986) (private communication between arbitrator and party constitutes misconduct sufficient to vacate award), with U.S. Life Ins. Co. v. Superior Nat. Ins. Co., 591 F.3d 1167, 1176 (9th Cir. 2010) ("Ex parte conduct by an arbitration panel requires vacatur of an award only if the ex parte contact constitutes misbehavior that prejudices the rights of a party.")

[81] 9 U.S.C. § 10(a)(4).

[82] Vaughn v. Leeds, Morelli & Brown, PC, 315 Fed.Appx. 327, 330 (2d Cir. 2009) ("this Court has consistently accorded the narrowest of readings to this statutory ground [§ 10(a)(4)], focusing on whether the arbitrators had the power, based on the parties' submissions or the arbitration agreement, to reach a certain issue, not whether the arbitrators correctly decided that issue").

arbitrators somehow alter the parties' contractual obligations" or "fail to meet their obligations, as specified in a given contract, to the parties."[83] On the other hand, where an agreement provided that a majority of three arbitrators were to "render a brief reasoned decision" that "shall include all claims and defenses of the parties," but failed to do so, the Sixth Circuit refused to vacate the award for exceeding their powers under § 10(a)(4).[84] "The proper remedy for falling short of the level of explanation agreed to by the parties is remanding back to the panel, rather than starting from scratch" with vacatur.[85]

In *Stolt-Nielsen S.A. v. AnimalFeeds International Corp.*,[86] the Supreme Court relied on FAA § 10(a)(4) to vacate an award permitting classwide arbitration where the arbitration agreement did not authorize it. The Court said "an arbitration decision may be vacated under § 10(a)(4) of the FAA on the ground that the arbitrator 'exceeded [his] powers,' for the task of an arbitrator is to interpret and enforce a contract, not to make public policy. In this case, we must conclude that what the arbitration panel did was simply to impose its own view of sound policy regarding class arbitration."[87] By contrast, in *Oxford Health Plans LLC v. Sutter*, "[t]he parties agreed that the arbitrator should decide whether their contract authorized class arbitration," so the Supreme Court affirmed denial of a motion to vacate the award permitting classwide arbitration.[88] The *Oxford* Court said "A party seeking relief under [§ 10(a)(4)] bears a heavy burden. It is not enough to show that the arbitrator committed an error—or even a serious error. Because the parties bargained for the arbitrator's construction of their agreement, an arbitral decision even arguably construing or applying the contract must stand, regardless of a court's view of its (de)merits."[89] Nevertheless, some courts continue to vacate awards "[w]hen an arbitrator disregards the plain text of a contract without legal justification simply to reach a result that he believes is just."[90]

FAA § 10(a)(4)'s "exceeded powers" ground for vacatur relates to the "scope of arbitration agreement" topic discussed in Section 26.[91]

---

83 Western Employers Ins. Co. v. Jefferies & Co., Inc., 958 F.2d 258, 262 (9th Cir. 1992).

84 In re Romanzi, 31 F.4th 367, 375 (6th Cir. 2022).

85 Id.

86 559 U.S. 662 (2010).

87 Id. at 672.

88 569 U.S. 564, 566 (2013).

89 Id. at 569.

90 Aspic Eng'g & Constr. Co. v. ECC Centcom Constructors LLC, 913 F.3d 1162, 1169 (9th Cir. 2019).

91 See § 26.

As explained there, if a party seeks to litigate rather than arbitrate a particular claim, the court will send that claim to arbitration only if the parties agreed to arbitrate that claim. That the parties agreed to arbitrate *some* claim is not enough. They must have agreed to arbitrate *that* claim. This point about the enforcement of executory arbitration agreements has its counterpart with respect to enforcement of arbitration awards. Courts enforce an arbitrator's award on a claim only if the parties agreed to arbitrate *that* claim, and they vacate awards deciding issues beyond the scope of the arbitration agreement.[92]

If the parties used a broad arbitration agreement, such as one covering all disputes "relating to" the parties' relationship, then the arbitrator likely had the power to rule on all claims between the parties. But when parties use narrower arbitration agreements, the possibility arises of an arbitration award that exceeds the arbitrator's power by ruling on claims not properly before the arbitrator. However, even if the arbitrator ruled on a claim not covered by the written arbitration agreement, the arbitrator may have received the power to rule on that claim from the parties' conduct—if they argued the merits of that claim in arbitration without either party objecting that it was beyond the scope of the arbitration. In other words, a party's right to object to the arbitrator's ruling on a claim beyond the scope of the arbitration agreement may be waived by the party arguing the merits of that claim in arbitration without clearly objecting to the arbitrator's power to reach those merits.[93] In

[92] Jock v. Sterling Jewelers Inc., 646 F.3d 113, 122 (2d Cir. 2011) ("an arbitrator may exceed her authority by, first, considering issues beyond those the parties have submitted for her consideration"); Hebbronville Lone Star Rentals, L.L.C. v. Sunbelt Rentals Indus. Servs., L.L.C., 898 F.3d 629, 633 (5th Cir. 2018) (holding that arbitrator exceeded his powers by ordering reformation of contract when arbitration clause authorized arbitrator to "resolve only 'any remaining dispute over Seller's proposed adjustments to a Revenue Calculation' "); Raymond James Fin. Servs., Inc. v. Bishop, 596 F.3d 183, 193 (4th Cir. 2010) ("[B]y rendering an award whose underlying legal basis exceeded the bounds of arbitrable employment-related disputes cognizable under NASD Rule 10101 . . ., the panel 'exceeded [its] powers' under 9 U.S.C. § 10(a)(4).")

[93] Environmental Barrier Co., LLC v. Slurry Systems, Inc., 540 F.3d 598, 606 (7th Cir. 2008) (rejecting SSI's argument that arbitrator exceeded his powers because "SSI never told the arbitrator that it thought this dispute was nonarbitrable. To the contrary, it voluntarily submitted to the arbitrator's authority, filed a counterclaim, and confined its objections to EBC's standing to arbitrate. Only after the arbitrator issued an award unfavorable to SSI and the case wound up in court did SSI raise an objection to the arbitrator's authority to decide the dispute."); Fortune, Alsweet & Eldridge, Inc. v. Daniel, 724 F.2d 1355, 1356–57 (9th Cir. 1983) ("[a]n agreement to arbitrate an issue need not be express; * * * it may be implied from the conduct of the parties"; appellant's "conduct demonstrated he agreed to submit this conflict to arbitration and waived any right to object."); Tristar Pictures, Inc. v. Director's Guild of America, Inc., 160 F.3d 537, 540 (9th Cir. 1998) ("Tristar's challenge to the arbitrator's jurisdiction fails, not only because of the broad language of the arbitration clause, but also because of Tristar's prior actions. Although Tristar did suggest at the arbitration hearing that the arbitrator had no authority to decide certain issues, it chose to argue that the arbitrator lacked authority rather than simply refusing to come

contrast, parties who do object in arbitration to the arbitrator's power to reach the merits presumably do not waive their right to make this "exceeded powers" argument in a motion to vacate under FAA § 10(a)(4) because the Supreme Court has held that "merely arguing the arbitrability issue to an arbitrator does not indicate a clear willingness to arbitrate that issue."[94]

Broader questions about arbitrators exceeding their powers are discussed next.

§ 41 Formerly Non-Statutory Grounds for Vacatur

(a) Un/Restricted Submissions

In addition to the statutory grounds for vacating arbitration awards, which are discussed in Section 40, courts used to—and perhaps still do—recognize additional grounds for vacatur. These *non-statutory* grounds consisted of *contractually-created* grounds for vacatur and *judicially-created* grounds for vacatur. Both categories of non-statutory grounds for vacatur were undermined by the Supreme Court's 2008 opinion in *Hall Street Associates v. Mattel,*[95] which stated that the FAA's four grounds for vacatur are "exclusive."[96] Nevertheless, important questions remain about the extent to which some formerly non-statutory grounds for vacatur can

---

to the table.") (internal quotations omitted); Metzler Contracting Co. LLC v. Stephens, 774 F. Supp.2d 1073 (D. Haw. 2011) ("the Stephenses voluntarily submitted their argument concerning these issues to the arbitrator, and cannot now claim that the arbitrator had no authority to decide them"); Data Mountain Solutions, Inc. v. Giordano, 680 F. Supp.2d 110, 124 (D.D.C. 2010) ("If a party has not consented to arbitration of a given issue, then an arbitrator 'exceed[s][his] powers' by reaching that issue, and any consequent award may be vacated by a court upon judicial review. 9 U.S.C. § 10(a)(4)."); id. at 131 ("Mr. Giordano has failed utterly to demonstrate that he made a "clear and explicit" objection to the presentation of the fee-splitting dispute to the arbitrator. He therefore consented to the arbitration of that issue and may not challenge the arbitrator's authority").

[94] First Options of Chicago v. Kaplan, 514 U.S. 938, 946 (1995). See also Dedon GmbH v. Janus et Cie, 411 Fed. Appx. 361, 364 (2d Cir. 2011); Opals on Ice Lingerie v. Bodylines Inc., 320 F.3d 362, 368–69 (2d Cir. 2003).

[95] 552 U.S. 576 (2008).

[96] Id. at 584. Those four grounds are:

(1) Where the award was procured by corruption, fraud, or undue means;

(2) Where there was evident partiality or corruption in the arbitrators, or either of them;

(3) Where the arbitrators were guilty of misconduct in refusing to postpone the hearing, upon sufficient cause shown, or in refusing to hear evidence pertinent and material to the controversy; or of any other misbehavior by which the rights of any party have been prejudiced; or

(4) Where the arbitrators exceeded their powers, or so imperfectly executed them that a mutual, final, and definite award upon the subject matter submitted was not made.

9 U.S.C. § 10(a).

be re-characterized to fit within the four statutory grounds and thus continue to apply after *Hall Street.*

Context for these issues and the impact of *Hall Street* comes from distinguishing arbitration agreements that require the arbitrator to apply the law correctly to the merits of the parties dispute and arbitration agreements that do not so require. When the FAA was enacted in 1925 (and, to a lesser extent, still today), agreements that required the arbitrator to apply the law correctly were called "restricted submissions" because the agreement submitting the dispute to arbitration[97] imposed an important restriction on the manner in which the arbitrator was authorized to decide the case.[98] In contrast, an "unrestricted submission" allows the arbitrator to decide the case according to law or according to some other source of norms, such as the customs in a particular industry or the arbitrator's own sense of equity. The next two subsections discuss arbitration arising out of restricted and unrestricted submissions, respectively, and the state of the law governing each of them after *Hall Street.*

(b) Restricted Submissions: Agreements Requiring Arbitrators to Apply the Law Correctly

(1) Hall Street and Interpretation of the FAA

An agreement may attempt to require the arbitrator to apply the law correctly by authorizing a court to vacate an arbitration award that does not apply the law correctly. For example, one arbitration agreement said "The Court shall vacate, modify or correct any award: (i) based upon any of the grounds referred to in the Federal Arbitration Act, (ii) where the arbitrators' findings of fact are not supported by substantial evidence, or (iii) where the arbitrators' conclusions of law are erroneous."[99] This language purports to create, by contract, grounds for vacatur—numbers ii and iii—not otherwise found in the law. Prior to *Hall Street,* courts split on whether to

---

[97] Today, the term "submission agreement" is perhaps used more often to describe *post-dispute* arbitration agreements than pre-dispute arbitration agreements, see § 3(a), because a post-dispute agreement clearly submits a particular dispute to arbitration, while the parties to a pre-dispute agreement probably hope at the time of the agreement that they will not have a dispute at all, let alone one requiring arbitration. Prior to the FAA, pre-dispute arbitration agreements were generally not enforceable so presumably a higher percentage of arbitration in that era than today arose out of post-dispute "submission" agreements.

[98] As Professor Drahozal points out, "submissions can be restricted in any number of ways. But in this context, the most relevant restriction is one that requires the arbitrators to follow the law." Christopher R. Drahozal, Contracting Around Hall Street, 14 Lewis & Clark L. Rev. 905, 914 n.50 (2010).

[99] Kyocera Corp. v. Prudential-Bache Trade Services, Inc., 341 F.3d 987, 990–91 (9th Cir. 2003).

enforce such contractually-created grounds for vacatur,[100] but *Hall Street* resolved this split against enforcement. *Hall Street* refused to enforce a clause providing that "[t]he [District] Court shall vacate, modify or correct any award: (i) where the arbitrator's findings of facts are not supported by substantial evidence, or (ii) where the arbitrator's conclusions of law are erroneous."[101] The Supreme Court rejected such contractually-created grounds for vacatur, which it called "expandable judicial review authority."[102] *Hall Street* stated that the FAA's four grounds for vacatur are "exclusive" and cannot be "supplemented by contract."[103]

(2) State Law Departures from Hall Street

Since *Hall Street*, a few state supreme court decisions have enforced agreements requiring arbitrators to apply the law correctly.[104] For example, the 2011 Texas Supreme Court decision in *Nafta Traders, Inc. v. Quinn*,[105] enforced an arbitration agreement that said "The arbitrator does not have authority (i) to render a decision which contains a reversible error of state or federal law, or (ii) to apply a cause of action or remedy not expressly provided for under existing state or federal law."[106] The Texas Supreme Court recognized the similarity between this clause and the arbitration clause in *Hall Street*.

---

[100] Hall Street, 552 U.S. at 583 n.5.

[101] Hall Street Associates v. Mattel, 552 U.S. 576, 579 (2008).

[102] Id. at 584.

[103] Id.

[104] Raymond James Financial Services, Inc. v. Honea, 55 So.3d 1161, 1169 (Ala. 2010) ("Under the Alabama common law, courts must rigorously enforce contracts, including arbitration agreements, according to their terms in order to give effect to the contractual rights and expectations of the parties. Applying that principle in this case requires us to give effect to the provision in the arbitration agreement authorizing a court having jurisdiction to conduct a de novo review of the award entered as a result of arbitration proceedings conducted pursuant to that same agreement."); Cable Connection, Inc. v. DirectTV, Inc., 190 P.3d 586, 589 (Cal. 2008) (discussing *Hall Street* and concluding that FAA does not preempt state law enforcing arbitration agreement providing that "The arbitrators shall not have the power to commit errors of law or legal reasoning, and the award may be vacated or corrected on appeal to a court of competent jurisdiction for any such error."); Nafta Traders, Inc. v. Quinn, 339 S.W.3d 84 (Tex. 2011) (enforcing restricted submission).

In contrast, several states' courts hold that their state law does not enforce contractually-created grounds for vacatur. Brookfield Country Club, Inc. v. St. James-Brookfield, LLC, 696 S.E.2d 663, 667 (Ga. 2010); HL 1, LLC v. Riverwalk, LLC, 2011 WL 816811 (Me. 2011); Brucker v. McKinlay Transp., Inc., 557 N.W.2d 536, 540 (Mich. 1997); John T. Jones Constr. Co. v. City of Grand Forks, 665 N.W.2d 698, 704 (N.D. 2003); Pugh's Lawn Landscape Co., Inc. v. Jaycon Dev. Corp., 320 S.W.3d 252, 260 (Tenn. 2010).

[105] 339 S.W.3d 84 (Tex. 2011).

[106] Id. at 88.

> [W]hile the Supreme Court and the parties in *Hall Street* framed the issue as "expandable judicial review authority", the flip-side is limited arbitral decision-making authority * * * . The parties in *Hall Street* attempted to accomplish indirectly the same end that Quinn and Nafta sought directly—a limit on the arbitrator's authority.[107]

In other words, directing the court to vacate "where the arbitrator's conclusions of law are erroneous" (as the *Hall Street* agreement did) is just an indirect way of doing what the *Nafta Traders* agreement did directly, that is, deprive the arbitrator of "authority * * * to render a decision which contains a reversible error of state or federal law." Further highlighting the similarities between the two cases, the Texas Supreme Court noted that the Texas Arbitration Act (TAA), much like FAA § 10(a)(4), instructs courts to vacate arbitration awards if the arbitrators "exceeded their powers."[108] With such strong similarities between the cases, how did the Texas Supreme Court reach a different result from *Hall Street*?

It did so by interpreting the TAA differently than *Hall Street* interpreted the FAA. "We must, of course, follow *Hall Street* in applying the FAA, but in construing the TAA, we are obliged to examine *Hall Street*'s reasoning and reach our own judgment."[109] The Texas Supreme Court said that *Hall Street* "did not discuss [FAA] section 10(a)(4)" and this

> omission appears to us to undercut the Supreme Court's textual analysis. When parties have agreed that an arbitrator should not have authority to reach a decision based on reversible error—in other words, that an arbitrator should have no more power than a judge—a motion to vacate for such error as exceeding the arbitrator's authority is firmly grounded in the text of section 10. The Supreme Court's reasoning that an arbitrator's merely legal errors are not the kind of "egregious departures from the parties' agreed-upon arbitration" section 10 addresses loses force when such errors directly contradict the parties' express agreement and deprive them of the benefit of their reasonable expectations.[110]

Accordingly, the Texas Supreme Court interpreted the TAA to enforce agreements requiring arbitrators to apply the law correctly

---

[107] Id. at 92.

[108] Id. at n.15 (citing Tex. Civ. Prac. & Rem. Code § 171.088(a)(3)(A)).

[109] Id. at 91–92.

[110] Id. at 92–93.

and thus require courts to vacate awards in which arbitrators exceed their powers by failing to apply the law correctly.

So interpreted, the TAA differs from the FAA as interpreted by the U.S. Supreme Court in *Hall Street*, which raises the question whether the former is preempted by the latter. While the U.S. Supreme Court has long held that FAA § 2 preempts inconsistent state law,[111] the Court has never extended that holding to the FAA's provisions on confirmation and vacatur of awards, FAA §§ 9–11.[112] *Nafta Traders* said its holding is not preempted by the FAA, even though it recognizes a ground for vacatur not found in the FAA.[113] Moreover, *Hall Street* itself said:

> In holding that [FAA] §§ 10 and 11 provide exclusive regimes for the review provided by the statute, we do not purport to say that they exclude more searching review based on authority outside the statute as well. The FAA is not the only way into court for parties wanting review of arbitration awards: they may contemplate enforcement under state statutory or common law, for example, where judicial review of different scope is arguable. But here we speak only to the scope of the expeditious judicial review under §§ 9, 10, and 11, deciding nothing about other possible avenues for judicial enforcement of arbitration awards.[114]

So *Hall Street* may support *Nafta Traders*' holding that the FAA does not preempt the TAA's additional grounds for vacatur.

(c) Unrestricted Submissions: Agreements Not Requiring Arbitrators to Apply the Law Correctly

(1) Uncertainty About When Arbitrators Must Apply the Law

As noted above, arbitration agreements can be divided into two types: those that require the arbitrator to apply the law correctly and those that do not.[115] Agreements that do not ("unrestricted submissions") give the arbitrator discretion whether to decide the case according to law or according to some other source of norms, such

---

[111] See § 7.

[112] See § 42. The Supreme Court of Alabama said "in Hall Street, the Supreme Court of the United States acknowledged that state statutory or common law might permit arbitration awards to be reviewed under standards different from those enumerated in [FAA] § 10, thus effectively stating that § 10 represents procedural as opposed to substantive law." Raymond James Financial Services, Inc. v. Honea, 55 So.3d 1161, 1168 (Ala.2010).

[113] 339 S.W.2d at 100–01.

[114] Hall St. Assocs., L.L.C. v. Mattel, Inc., 552 U.S. 576, 590 (2008).

[115] See § 41(a).

as the customs in a particular industry,[116] religious principles,[117] or the arbitrator's own sense of equity.[118] Some courts have long stated their commitment to enforce such agreements by enforcing arbitration awards arising out of them without considering whether the award rests on a correct application of law. For example, the California Supreme Court said:

> As early as 1852, this court recognized that, 'The arbitrators are not bound to award on principles of dry law, but may decide on principles of equity and good conscience, and make their award ex aequo et bono [according to what is

---

[116] Some industries have developed their own bodies of law applied by their own arbitrators, who are often merchants rather than lawyers. See Lisa Bernstein, Merchant Law in a Merchant Court: Rethinking the Code's Search for Immanent Business Norms, 144 U. Pa. L. Rev. 1765 (1996) (grain); Lisa Bernstein, Opting Out of the Legal System: Extralegal Contractual Relations in the Diamond Industry, 21 J. Legal Stud. 115 (1992) (diamonds); Lisa Bernstein, Private Commercial Law in the Cotton Industry: Creating Cooperation Through Rules, Norms, and Institutions, 99 Mich. L. Rev. 1724 (2001) (cotton); see also Lisa Bernstein, Private Commercial Law, in 3 Palgrave Dictionary of Economics and the Law 108, 108 (Peter Newman ed., 1998) ("Private commercial law exists in over fifty industries including diamonds, grain, feed, independent films, printing, binding, peanuts, rice, cotton, burlap, rubber, hay and tea.").

[117] See, e.g., Lang v. Levi, 16 A.3d 980, 982 (Md.2011) ("The arbitration agreement provided that if the parties no longer lived together as husband and wife, they authorized an arbitration panel, the Beth Din, to decide all issues involving the Jewish divorce and premarital agreements, including monetary disputes. This agreement stated: 'The decision of the Bet Din shall be made in accordance with Jewish Law (Halakhah) and/or the general principles of arbitration and equity (Pesharah) customarily employed by rabbinical tribunals.' "); Itzhakov v. Segal, No. A-2619-17T4, 2019 WL 4050104, at *1 (N.J. Super. Ct. App. Div. Aug. 28, 2019) ("It is hereby agreed between us that any questions of Jewish law that are relevant to this sale and to this document shall be decided by the Lakewood Rabbinical Court, and we are required to do as they decide, and signing this document constitutes an acceptance of everything in the arbitration agreement that the said court regularly uses, and under no circumstances shall any dispute between us come to the civil courts, G-d forbid."); Prescott v. Northlake Christian Sch., 141 F. App'x 263, 265 (5th Cir. 2005) ("After being fired from her job as principal at [Northlake Christian School], Prescott brought suit in the district court, alleging Title VII and various state law claims"; "After NCS moved successfully to compel arbitration, such proceedings were conducted according to the Rules of Procedure for Christian Conciliation of the Institute for Christian Conciliation. In arbitration, Prescott * * * was awarded approximately $ 150,000 in damages"; "In reaching his decision, the arbitrator determined that NCS had wrongfully discharged Prescott by failing to follow Biblical precepts, as required in her employment contract; specifically, the conflict resolution process described in Matthew 18."); Jabri v. Qaddura, 108 S.W.3d 404, 408 (Tex. App. 2003) ("The Parties agree to arbitrate all existing issues among them," "the determination of each party's responsibilities and duties according to the Islamic rules of law by Texas Islamic Court.")

[118] A small number of arbitration agreements call for application of the arbitrator's own sense of equity. Christopher R. Drahozal, Contracting Out of National Law: An Empirical Look at the New Law Merchant, 80 Notre Dame L.Rev. 523, 538–39 (2005); Christopher R. Drahozal, Is Arbitration Lawless?, 40 Loy. L.A. L. Rev. 187, 206–07 (2006).

> just and good].' As a consequence, arbitration awards are generally immune from judicial review.[119]

Similarly, in this century the Connecticut Supreme Court said "[u]nder an unrestricted submission, the arbitrators' decision is considered final and binding; thus the courts will not review the evidence considered by the arbitrators nor will they review the award for errors of law or fact."[120] And the Second Circuit quoted New York's highest court for the proposition that "absent provision in the arbitration clause itself, an arbitrator is not bound by principles of substantive law."[121]

On the other hand, the Supreme Court's change, starting in the 1980s, to enforcing predispute agreements to arbitrate federal statutory claims, rested on the Court's oft-repeated premise that "judicial scrutiny of arbitration awards * * * is sufficient to ensure that arbitrators comply with the requirements of the statute."[122] This

---

[119] Moncharsh v. Heily & Blase, 832 P.2d 899, 904 (Cal. 1992) (citations omitted).

[120] Industrial Risk Insurers v. Hartford Steam Boiler Inspection & Ins. Co., 779 A.2d 737, 744 (Conn. 2001).

[121] State Farm Mut. Automobile Ins. Co. v. Mallela, 372 F.3d 500, 507 n.5 (2d Cir. 2004) (quoting Silverman v. Benmor Coats, Inc., 61 N.Y.2d 299, 308 (N.Y. 1984)). See also Bull NH Infor. Sys., Inc. v. Hutson, 229 F.3d 321, 330 (1st Cir. 2000) ("To determine whether an arbitrator has exceeded his authority under § 10 * * * , courts do not sit to hear claims of factual or legal error by an arbitrator as an appellate court does in reviewing decisions of lower courts * * * and even where such error is painfully clear, courts are not authorized to reconsider the merits of the arbitration awards."); T.Co. Metals, LLC v. Dempsey Pipe & Supply, Inc., 592 F.3d 329, 339 (2d Cir. 2010) (vacating an award requires more than error or misunderstanding of the law); Puerto Rico Tel. Co. v. U.S. Phone Mfg. Corp., 427 F.3d 21, 32 (1st Cir. 2005) ("a mere mistake of law by an arbitrator cannot serve as the basis for judicial review.");Wallace v. Buttar, 378 F.3d 182, 189–90 (2d Cir. 2004) ("A federal court cannot vacate an arbitral award merely because it is convinced that the arbitration panel made the wrong call on the law."); Univ. Commons-Urbana, Ltd. v. Universal Constructors Inc., 304 F.3d 1331, 1337 (11th Cir. 2002) ("Only a manifest disregard for the law, in contrast to a misinterpretation, misstatement, or misapplication of the law, can constitute grounds to vacate an arbitration decision."); Todd Shipyards Corp. v. Cunard Line, 943 F.2d 1056, 1060 (9th Cir. 1991) ("[C]onfirmation is required even in the face of erroneous* * * misinterpretations of law* * * . It is not enough that the Panel may have failed to understand or apply the law * * *. An arbitrator's decision must be upheld unless it is completely irrational, or it constitutes a manifest disregard for the law.") (internal citations omitted); Advest, Inc. v. McCarthy, 914 F.2d 6, 8 (1st Cir. 1990) (courts are not authorized to reconsider the merits of arbitration awards "[e]ven where such error is painfully clear"); Miller v. Prudential Bache Secs., 884 F.2d 128, 130 (4th Cir. 1989) ("mere" error of law is insufficient to set aside arbitrator's award); Miller v. Prudential Bache Secs., 884 F.2d 128, 130 (4th Cir. 1989) ("mere" error of law is insufficient to set aside arbitrator's award); Moseley, Hallgarten, Estabrook & Weeden, Inc. v. Ellis, 849 F.2d 264, 272 (7th Cir. 1988) ("mistake" of law is insufficient to vacate arbitration award); WHD, LP. v. Mayflower Capital, LLC, 673 S.E.2d 168, 2009 WL 368335, at *4 (N.C. App. 2009) (table) ("our Courts have long held that if an arbitrator makes a mistake, either as to law or fact, it is the misfortune of the party, and there is no help for it.") (internal quotations omitted).

[122] Shearson/American Express, Inc. v. McMahon, 482 U.S. 220, 232 (1987). Accord 14 Penn Plaza LLC v. Pyett, 556 U.S. 247, n.10 (2009); Gilmer v. Interstate/Johnson Lane Corp., 500 U.S. 20, 32 n.4 (1991). These statements followed

assurance that courts scrutinize arbitration awards closely enough to ensure that arbitrators correctly apply statutory law conflicts with courts' statements (quoted in the previous paragraph) that they will not consider whether arbitration awards correctly apply the law because arbitrators are not bound to decide cases according to law. This conflict relates to an unresolved tension between arbitration's traditional role of resolving contract disputes—where an arbitrator is merely the parties' agent interpreting the parties' contract—and the post-1980s growth of arbitration resolving statutory claims, many of which are mandatory law in the sense that they override contract terms contrary to the statute.[123]

This distinction was recognized by the 1953 Supreme Court case, *Wilko v. Swan*,[124] overturned by the Court in the 1980s.[125] In holding Securities Act claims non-arbitrable, *Wilko* contrasted claims under this investor "protective" statute with "commercial controversies" where the *Wilko* Court "[r]ecogniz[ed] the advantages that prior agreements for arbitration may provide."[126] In other words, *Wilko* refused to enforce a predispute agreement to arbitrate a statutory claim, thus largely avoiding worries that arbitrators will not apply mandatory/statutory law correctly, while *Wilko* praised enforcement of predispute agreements to arbitrate commercial claims, which tend to turn on contract interpretation and thus not raise concerns about arbitrators' application of mandatory/statutory law. This distinction between statutory claims and commercial claims largely prevailed until the 1980s, so before then, "arbitration * * * functioned almost entirely in either the area of labor disputes or in 'ordinary disputes between merchants as to questions of fact.' "[127] Arbitrators in these two traditional contexts resolved almost exclusively contract claims, as labor arbitration was traditionally limited to alleged breaches of collective bargaining agreements, and merchants allege breach of contracts for the sale of goods that raise "questions of fact—quantity,

---

the Supreme Court's earlier consideration of the issue in an international arbitration context. Mitsubishi Motors Corp. v. Soler Chrysler-Plymouth, Inc., 473 U.S. 614, 637 n.19 (1985).

123 See §§ 5(e)(1), 39(c).

124 346 U.S. 27 (1953).

125 See § 5(e)(1).

126 Wilko v. Swan, 346 U.S. 427, 438 (1953) ("Recognizing the advantages that prior agreements for arbitration may provide for the solution of commercial controversies, we decide that the intention of Congress concerning the sale of securities is better carried out by holding invalid such an agreement for arbitration of issues arising under the Act.")

127 Mitsubishi Motors Corporation v. Soler Chrysler-Plymouth Inc., 473 U.S. 614, 650 (1985) (Stevens, J. dissenting).

quality, time of delivery, compliance with terms of payment, excuses for non-performance, and the like."[128]

When hearing breach-of-contract claims, the arbitrator is not so much applying the law as applying the contract. Put another way, the arbitrator is resolving questions that the parties could have resolved when they formed the contract. The arbitrator is resolving questions that arise because the parties chose to draft a contract in broad, general terms, rather than detailed, specific terms. For example, a collective bargaining agreement might say the employer must have "just cause" before terminating an employee, and the labor arbitrator may be asked to decide whether shouting obscenities at a supervisor is "just cause." The parties could have resolved this question themselves by specifically defining "just cause" in the agreement to include or exclude "using foul language" or "shouting at a supervisor." But the parties' broad language left a gap in the agreement, and it is the arbitrator's job, as the parties' agent, to fill that gap by interpreting or applying the agreement.

The Supreme Court emphasizes that courts should not substitute their own judgment for that of the arbitrators on such questions of contract interpretation. "[A]s long as the arbitrator is even arguably construing or applying the contract and acting within the scope of his authority, that a court is convinced he committed serious error does not suffice to overturn his decision."[129] On this view, contracts are private matters between the parties and the parties have hired the arbitrator as their agent to interpret and apply their contract.[130] Arbitration is private, contractual self-governance by which parties hire their agent, the arbitrator, to resolve their disputes.[131] As the Supreme Court put it, "we must treat the

---

[128] Id. at 646, n.11 (quoting Cohen & Dayton, The New Federal Arbitration Law, 12 Va. L. Rev. 265, 281 (1926)).

[129] United Paperworkers Int'l Union v. Misco, Inc., 484 U.S. 29, 38 (1987). See also Oxford Health Plans LLC v. Sutter, 569 U.S. 564 (2013).

> A party seeking relief under [§ 10(a)(4)] bears a heavy burden. It is not enough to show that the arbitrator committed an error—or even a serious error. Because the parties bargained for the arbitrator's construction of their agreement, an arbitral decision even arguably construing or applying the contract must stand, regardless of a court's view of its (de)merits. Only if the arbitrator acts outside the scope of his contractually delegated authority—issuing an award that simply reflects his own notions of economic justice rather than drawing its essence from the contract—may a court overturn his determination. So the sole question for us is whether the arbitrator (even arguably) interpreted the parties' contract, not whether he got its meaning right or wrong.

Id. at 2068 (quotations and citations omitted).

[130] "In the main, an arbitrator acts as the parties' agent and as their delegate may do anything the parties may do directly." George Watts & Son, Inc. v. Tiffany and Co., 248 F.3d 577, 580 (7th Cir. 2001) (Easterbrook, J.).

[131] See, e.g., United Steelworkers of America v. Warrior & Gulf Nav. Co., 363 U.S. 574 (1960).

arbitrator's award as if it represented an agreement between" the parties themselves.[132] So arbitration of most breach-of-contract claims fits comfortably with courts' statements that they will not consider whether arbitration awards correctly apply the law. For example, if the arbitrator is resolving a contract-interpretation issue, the arbitrator is reaching a result that the parties could have reached themselves (by simply contracting for it expressly) when they agreed to arbitrate, and thus the arbitrator is acting within her powers derived solely from the parties. The same is true when the arbitrator is deciding many other issues of contract and commercial law because these bodies of law consist largely of default rules, that is, rules the parties can alter or avoid by predispute contract.[133]

In contrast, arbitrators are doing more than the parties could have done when they formed their contract when arbitrators are deciding claims under statutes parties cannot alter or avoid by predispute contract. For example, statutes designed to protect consumers and employees often consist of such mandatory rules.[134]

> A collective bargaining agreement is an effort to erect a system of industrial self government. . . . Gaps may be left to be filled in by reference to the practices of the particular industry and of the various shops covered by the agreement. Many of the specific practices which underlie the agreement may be unknown, except in hazy form, even to the negotiators . . . [The arbitration] grievance machinery under a collective bargaining agreement is at the very heart of the system of industrial self government. Arbitration is the means of solving the unforeseeable by molding a system of private law for all the problems which may arise and to provide for their solution in a way which will generally accord with the variant needs and desires of the parties. The processing of disputes through the grievance machinery is actually a vehicle by which meaning and content are given to the collective bargaining agreement.

Id. at 580–1.

132 Eastern Associated Coal Corp. v. United Mine Workers, 531 U.S. 57, 62 (2000).

133 See Alan Scott Rau, The Culture of American Arbitration and the Lessons of ADR, 40 Tex. Int'l L.J. 449 (2005).

> Of course, in thinking about judicial review [of arbitration] on matters of "law" we should distinguish between mere rules of construction, which come into play in the absence of a contrary agreement, and mandatory rules. After all, most "rules" of contract or commercial law are nothing more than "gap-fillers." They supply a term where the parties have not expressly supplied one themselves; modern commercial law looks in particular to industry custom and course of dealing to furnish the "framework of common understanding controlling any general rules of law which hold only when there is no such understanding." But where the parties have bargained for dispute resolution through arbitration, the method they have chosen to fill any gaps in the agreement is the arbitrator's interpretation. His interpretation is their bargain. In contrast, legal "rules" in other areas may reflect stronger and overriding governmental or societal interests. In such cases, obviously, some greater degree of arbitral deference should be expected.

Id. at 521.

134 David S. Schwartz, Understanding Remedy-Stripping Arbitration Clauses: Validity, Arbitrability, and Preclusion Principles, 38 U.S.F. L. Rev. 49 (2003).

> Many regulatory statutes—particularly those protecting consumers or investors—contain "anti-waiver" provisions that expressly guarantee against

Indeed, an important purpose of these statutes is often to protect consumers and employees from contract terms unfavorable to them. When arbitrators resolve such claims (e.g., employment discrimination,) they are not resolving questions the parties could have resolved themselves when the parties formed their contract. And it was in the context of these sorts of statutory claims—which the Supreme Court began sending to arbitration in the 1980's—that the Court said that "judicial scrutiny of arbitration awards" "is sufficient to ensure that arbitrators comply with the requirements of the statute."[135] Perhaps the Court was suggesting that courts tightly review arbitrators' conclusions of law because the Court was trying to make its then-new enforcement of predispute agreements to arbitrate statutory claims less controversial by calming fears that claims in areas such as employment discrimination and investor protection would be sent to "lawless" arbitration.

(2) Manifest Disregard of Law

Following the Supreme Court's 1980s cue, some federal appellate courts in the 1990s began tightening judicial review of arbitrators' legal rulings on statutory claims. While many courts had held out the possibility that they could vacate awards in cases of "manifest disregard of the law" by the arbitrator,[136] the manifest-disregard doctrine was very narrow[137] so it was nearly impossible,

---

> contract terms purporting to waive the statutes' protections. Even without such statutory provisions, prospective waivers of such statutory protections are routinely struck down as unconscionable, void as against public policy, or simply because they would " 'nullify the purposes' of the statute." The principle is sufficiently clear and uncontroversial that the Supreme Court could flatly assert, without further explanation, "To begin, we think it clear that there can be no prospective waiver of an employee's rights under Title VII."

Id. at 54.

135 Shearson/American Express, Inc. v. McMahon, 482 U.S. 220, 232 (1987). Accord 14 Penn Plaza LLC v. Pyett, 556 U.S. 247, n.10 (2009); Gilmer v. Interstate/Johnson Lane Corp., 500 U.S. 20, 32 n.4 (1991). These statements followed the Supreme Court's earlier consideration of the issue in an international arbitration context. Mitsubishi Motors Corp. v. Soler Chrysler-Plymouth, Inc., 473 U.S. 614, 637 n.19 (1985).

136 Every United States Court of Appeals and many state appellate courts adopted some version of the "manifest disregard" doctrine, Birmingham News Co. v. Horn, 901 So.2d 27, 48–50 (Ala. 2004) (citing cases), and the Supreme Court apparently endorsed it in First Options of Chicago, Inc. v. Kaplan, 514 U.S. 938, 942 (1995) (citing Wilko v. Swan, 346 U.S. 427, 436–37 (1953)). See also Ga. Code Ann. § 9–9–13(b)(5) (Supp. 2006) ("The award shall be vacated * * * if the court finds that the rights of that party were prejudiced by: * * * The arbitrator's manifest disregard of the law.")

137 An oft-cited Second Circuit opinion said that an error of law should lead to vacatur for "manifest disregard" only if the error is "obvious and capable of being readily and instantly perceived by the average person qualified to serve as an arbitrator. Moreover, the term 'disregard' implies that the arbitrator appreciates the existence of a clearly governing legal principle but decides to ignore or pay no attention to it." Merrill, Lynch, Pierce, Fenner & Smith, Inc. v. Bobker, 808 F.2d 930, 933 (2d Cir. 1986).

until about 1997, to find a case vacating an arbitration award in reliance on it.[138] But then some courts began expanding the "manifest disregard" doctrine to conform more closely to the Supreme Court's repeated statement that "judicial scrutiny of arbitration awards" "is sufficient to ensure that arbitrators comply with the requirements of the statute" giving rise to the claim. For example, the D.C. Circuit, in *Cole v. Burns International Security Services*,[139] held that agreements to arbitrate statutory employment discrimination claims were enforceable "only if judicial review under the 'manifest disregard of the law' standard is sufficiently rigorous to ensure that arbitrators have properly interpreted and applied statutory law."[140] The *Cole* opinion went on to assert that "the courts are empowered to review an arbitrator's award to ensure that its resolution of public law issues is correct."[141] *Cole*, in essence, called for the "manifest disregard of law" standard to become a *de novo* "error of law" standard, at least with respect to claims under statutory or public law.

Along these lines, the following year the Second Circuit in *Halligan v. Piper Jaffray, Inc.*,[142] reversed a district court's denial of a motion to vacate for manifest disregard of employment discrimination law. *Halligan* said that "when a reviewing court is inclined to hold that an arbitration panel manifestly disregarded the law, the failure of the arbitrators to explain the award can be taken into account."[143] *Halligan* seemed to challenge the longstanding practice (in many sorts of cases) of arbitrators not to write reasoned opinions justifying their decisions.[144] That practice had largely ensured that parties challenging arbitration awards had little to point to and, consequently, little chance of persuading a court to vacate the award.[145] If the law of vacatur had continued moving in the direction exemplified by *Cole* and *Halligan*, arbitrators might have been required to write reasoned opinions, giving parties more

---

138 See Ian R. Macneil, Richard E. Speidel & Thomas J. Stipanowich, Federal Arbitration Law § 40.7.1, at 40:84–40:85 (1994); Cole v. Burns Int'l Security Services, 105 F.3d 1465 (D.C. Cir. 1997).

139 105 F.3d 1465 (D.C. Cir. 1997). This case is also discussed in § 31.

140 105 F.3d at 1487.

141 Id.

142 148 F.3d 197 (2d Cir. 1998).

143 Id. at 204.

144 See § 34(e).

145 Trivisonno v. Metropolitan Life Ins. Co., 39 Fed.Appx. 236, 241 (6th Cir. 2002) ("The Sixth Circuit has continued to hold that arbitrators are not required to explain their decisions. That remains the law in this circuit, however desirable it might be, despite the recognition that should arbitrators choose not to explain their decisions it becomes all but impossible to determine whether they acted with manifest disregard for the law.")

opportunity to identify manifest disregard, or other erroneous conclusions, of law by arbitrators.[146]

However, the law of vacatur in federal courts moved in the opposite direction. Some federal appellate courts weakened the "manifest disregard" ground for vacatur,[147] with the Seventh Circuit even suggesting that it could be eliminated.[148] This eliminationist view received support from the Supreme Court's 2008 opinion in *Hall Street Associates v. Mattel*,[149] which stated that the FAA's four grounds for vacatur are "exclusive."[150] And several courts shortly after *Hall Street* read it as abolishing manifest disregard as a basis for vacatur.[151] However, the Supreme Court left the survival of "manifest disregard" unresolved in the post-*Hall Street* case of *Stolt-Nielsen S.A. v. AnimalFeeds International Corp.*,[152] in which it said "We do not decide whether 'manifest disregard' survives our decision in [*Hall Street*], as an independent ground for review or as a judicial gloss on the enumerated grounds for vacatur set forth at 9 U.S.C. § 10."[153] And since *Stolt-Nielsen*, some courts have said that

---

146 See generally Stephen L. Hayford, A New Paradigm for Commercial Arbitration: Rethinking the Relationship Between Reasoned Awards and the Judicial Standards for Vacatur, 66 Geo. Wash. L. Rev. 443, 445 (1998).

147 See Sarofim v. Trust Company Of The West, 440 F.3d 213, 217 (5th Cir. 2006) (confining manifest disregard doctrine to cases in which enforcement of the award would "result in significant injustice.").

148 Wise v. Wachovia Securities, LLC, 450 F.3d 265, 268–69 (7th Cir. 2006) (Posner, J.) ("we have defined 'manifest disregard of the law' so narrowly that it fits comfortably under the first clause of the fourth statutory ground—'where the arbitrators exceeded their powers.' For we have confined it to cases in which arbitrators 'direct the parties to violate the law.' ")

149 552 U.S. 576 (2008).

150 Id. at 1403.

151 Medicine Shoppe Int'l, Inc. v. Turner Investments, Inc., 614 F.3d 485, 489 (8th Cir. 2010) (citing *Hall Street* for the proposition that a "claim that the arbitrator disregarded the law" is "not included among those specifically enumerated in § 10 and [ ] therefore not cognizable"); Frazier v. CitiFinancial Corp., LLC, 604 F.3d 1313, 1322–24 (11th Cir. 2010) ("Although our prior precedents have recognized these three non-statutory grounds for vacatur [arbitrary and capricious, public policy, and manifest disregard] * * * We hold that our judicially-created bases for vacatur are no longer valid in light of Hall Street"); Citigroup Global Markets, Inc. v. Bacon, 562 F.3d 349, 358 (5th Cir. 2009); Robert Lewis Rosen Assocs., Ltd. v. Webb, 566 F. Supp.2d 228, 233 (S.D.N.Y. 2008) (due to *Hall Street,* "manifest disregard of the law standard is no longer good law."); Carey Rodriguez Greenberg & Paul, LLP v. Arminak, 583 F. Supp.2d 1288, 1290 (S.D. Fla. 2008) (citing *Hall Street* and stating that "An allegation that the Award violates public policy is not one of the four exclusive statutory grounds upon which the Award may be vacated."); Hereford v. D.R. Horton, Inc., No. 1070396, 2008 WL 4097594, at *5 (Ala. 2008) ("we hereby overrule our earlier statement * * * that manifest disregard of the law is a ground for vacating * * * an arbitrator's award"); Ancor Holdings, LLC v. Peterson, Goldman & Villani, Inc., 294 S.W.3d 818, 829 (Tex. Ct. App.2009) ("manifest disregard of the law and gross mistake are not grounds for vacating an arbitration award under the FAA").

152 559 U.S. 662 (2010).

153 Id. at 672 n.3.

"manifest disregard" survives as an example of arbitrators' "exceed[ing] their powers" under FAA § 10(a)(4).[154]

This uncertainty about the survival of manifest disregard is part of broader uncertainty about the extent to which arbitrators are bound to apply the law at all and how, in arbitration of statutory claims, "judicial scrutiny of arbitration awards" "is sufficient to ensure that arbitrators comply with the requirements of the statute."[155] While, as noted above, federal courts did not continue expanding "manifest disregard" to vacate legally-erroneous awards on statutory claims, California courts have held that "an arbitrator exceeds its powers" "by issuing an award that violates a party's statutory rights."[156] And some California courts seem to be using this reasoning to vacate awards that fail to apply correctly mandatory rules of statutory law.[157]

(3) Public Policy

"Although FAA § 10 does not expressly list public policy as a ground for vacating an arbitral award," the Restatement argues that

---

154 In re Romanzi, 31 F.4th 367, 375 (6th Cir. 2022) ("Section 10(a)(4) also allows an arbitration award to be vacated if it was made in 'manifest disregard of the law.' ");

Wachovia Securities, LLC v. Brand, 671 F.3d 472, 483 (4th Cir. 2012) (reading *Stolt* "to mean that manifest disregard continues to exist either 'as an independent ground for review or as a judicial gloss on the enumerated grounds for vacatur set forth at 9 U.S.C. § 10.' Therefore, we decline to adopt the position of the Fifth and Eleventh Circuits that manifest disregard no longer exists."); Johnson v. Wells Fargo Home Mortg., Inc., 635 F.3d 401, 415 (9th Cir. 2011) (while *Stolt* "expressed some doubt as to whether the 'manifest disregard' [standard] survive[d] [its] decision in Hall Street," "in this Circuit the 'manifest disregard' standard has survived Hall Street intact, and so we are bound to apply it") (citing Comedy Club, Inc. v. Improv West Assocs., 553 F.3d 1277, 1290 (9th Cir. 2009). See also Sands v. Menard, Inc., 787 N.W.2d 384, 397 (Wis. 2010) ("a court must overturn an arbitrator's award when the panel exceeds its powers. Wis. Stat. § 788.10(1)(d). An arbitration panel exceeds its powers when it engages in perverse misconstruction or positive misconduct, when the panel manifestly disregards the law, or where the award itself is illegal or violates strong public policy."); Broom v. Morgan Stanley DW Inc., 236 P.3d 182, 184 (Wash. 2010) ("in Boyd v. Davis, * * * we approved of facial legal error as an accepted basis for vacating an arbitral award. In Boyd, we suggested that such error indicates that the arbitrators exceeded their powers.").

155 Shearson/American Express, Inc. v. McMahon, 482 U.S. 220, 232 (1987). Accord 14 Penn Plaza LLC v. Pyett, 556 U.S. 247, n.10 (2009); Gilmer v. Interstate/Johnson Lane Corp., 500 U.S. 20, 32 n.4 (1991). These statements followed the Supreme Court's earlier consideration of the issue in an international arbitration context. Mitsubishi Motors Corp. v. Soler Chrysler-Plymouth, Inc., 473 U.S. 614, 637 n.19 (1985).

156 Brown v. TGS Mgmt. Co., LLC, 271 Cal. Rptr. 3d 303, 313 (Ct. App. 2020), as modified on denial of reh'g (Nov. 12, 2020).

157 Id. at 318 ("Because the arbitration award is inconsistent with the protection of Brown's rights under section 16600, the award exceeded the arbitrator's powers. Consequently, the trial court erred in denying the petition to vacate the arbitration award and in entering judgment on the award").

"such a ground is a necessary part of a national arbitration law."[158] However, "[a]ll or most of the cases in which courts of appeals have vacated awards on public policy grounds are labor arbitration cases,"[159] which are not primarily governed by the FAA.[160] The Supreme Court has not decided whether public policy is a ground for vacatur under the FAA. And a few courts have cited the Supreme Court's 2008 opinion in *Hall Street Associates v. Mattel*,[161] which stated that the FAA's four grounds for vacatur are "exclusive,"[162] for the proposition that public policy is not a ground for vacatur under the FAA.[163]

Even in labor arbitration, the public policy ground for vacatur is narrow. In a 2000 labor case, *Eastern Associated Coal Corp. v. United Mine Workers of America*, the Supreme Court stated that to deny enforcement of an award as contrary to public policy, enforcement must "run contrary to an explicit, well-defined, and dominant public policy, as ascertained by reference to positive law and not from general considerations of supposed public interests."[164] In *Eastern Associated*, a truck driver subject to Department of Transportation regulations requiring random drug testing of workers engaged in "safety-sensitive" tasks twice tested positive for marijuana, so Eastern sought to discharge him. Each time, the union went to arbitration, and the arbitrator concluded that the drug use did not amount to "just cause" and ordered the driver's reinstatement on certain conditions. The Supreme Court held that this arbitration

---

158 Restatement (Third) U.S. Law of Int'l Comm. Arb. § 4.20 (2019).

159 Id. (citing Gary B. Born, International Commercial Arbitration 3403–3404 (2d ed. 2014)).

160 See § 44(a)(1).

161 552 U.S. 576 (2008).

162 Id. at 584.

163 Frazier v. CitiFinancial Corp., LLC, 604 F.3d 1313, 1322–24 (11th Cir. 2010) ("Although our prior precedents have recognized these three non-statutory grounds for vacatur [arbitrary and capricious, public policy, and manifest disregard] * * * We hold that our judicially-created bases for vacatur are no longer valid in light of Hall Street"); Marquis Yachts v. Allied Marine Grp., Inc. (N.), No. CIV 09-1770 JRT/FLN, 2010 WL 1380137, at *10 (D. Minn. Mar. 31, 2010) ("public policy is not one of the exclusive statutory grounds that the FAA provides for vacating arbitration awards"); Carey Rodriguez Greenberg & Paul, LLP v. Arminak, 583 F. Supp.2d 1288, 1290 (S.D. Fla. 2008) (citing *Hall Street* and stating that "An allegation that the Award violates public policy is not one of the four exclusive statutory grounds upon which the Award may be vacated.") See also ESCO Corp. v. Bradken Res. Pty Ltd., No. CIV. 10-788-AC, 2011 WL 1625815, at *9 (D. Or. Jan. 31, 2011), report and recommendation adopted, No. CV 10-788-AC, 2011 WL 1630355 (D. Or. Apr. 27, 2011) ("It is unclear whether a public policy defense is available under Chapter I of the FAA in light of Hall Street Assocs., L.L.C. v. Mattel, Inc., in which the Supreme Court determined that § 10(a) lists the exclusive grounds for vacating an arbitration award.")

164 531 U.S. 57, 63 (2000).

award did not violate public policy.[165] The Supreme Court's other two cases considering the public policy ground for vacatur—also both labor cases—also found that the ground had not been satisfied.[166]

Apart from labor arbitration, another example of public policy as a ground for vacatur may be in child custody arbitration. Section 13(b) notes that some courts refuse to enforce agreements to arbitrate child custody disputes. In contrast, other courts enforce agreements to arbitrate child custody but then review the resulting arbitration awards (awarding custody) with less deference than courts ordinarily give arbitrators rulings on such fact-intensive questions, thereby retaining for the court a significant role in furthering the public policy of protecting children's' interests.[167]

§ 42 Federal Preemption of State Law on Vacatur

(a) State Grounds for Vacatur Broader than Federal Grounds

Some state courts have applied the FAA's grounds for vacating arbitration awards. For example, New York's highest court said in 2011, "[a]s this matter affects interstate commerce, the vacatur of the arbitration award is governed by the Federal Arbitration Act."[168] And where state law grounds for vacatur are, in relevant respects, the same as the FAA's grounds, as they often are, then little turns on

---

[165] Id. at 58 ("The Court cannot find in the Act, the regulations, or any other law or legal precedent an explicit, well defined, dominant public policy to which the arbitrator's decision runs contrary").

[166] W.R. Grace & Co. v. Loc. Union 759, Int'l Union of United Rubber, Cork, Linoleum & Plastic Workers of Am., 461 U.S. 757, 771 (1983); United Paperworkers Int'l Union v. Misco, Inc., 484 U.S. 29, 42 (1987)(reversing Fifth Circuit holding that arbitration award reinstating employee violated public policy).

[167] Compare Schechter v. Schechter, 881 N.Y.S.2d 151, 152 (App. Div. 2009) (reversing confirmation of arbitration award on custody and visitation), with Fawzy v. Fawzy, 973 A.2d 347, 360–61 (N.J. 2009) ("the constitutionally protected right to parental autonomy includes the right to submit any family controversy, including one regarding child custody and parenting time, to a decision maker chosen by the parents. * * * [T]he review of an arbitration award is to take place within the confines of the Arbitration Act, unless there is a claim of adverse impact or harm to the child. Only in that case will further review be required"). See also E. Gary Spitko, Reclaiming the "Creatures of the State": Contracting for Child Custody Decisionmaking in the Best Interests of the Family, 57 Wash. & Lee L. Rev. 1139, 1165–66 n.98 (2000) ("Given that agreements to arbitrate child support issues also strongly and directly implicate the interests of a child who is not a party to the arbitration agreement, * * *[m]ost courts * * * have held that arbitration awards of child support should be subject to a high level of judicial review.")

[168] US Elecs., Inc. v. Sirius Satellite Radio, Inc., 958 N.E.2d 891, 892 (N.Y. 2011). See also, Hereford v. D.R. Horton, Inc., 13 So. 3d 375, 379 (Ala. 2009); A.G. Edwards & Sons, Inc. v. Petrucci, 525 So. 2d 918, 921 (Fla. Dist. Ct. App. 1988) (finding that "the trial court did have jurisdiction to enter an order vacating the arbitrator's award" under FAA § 10); Dowd v. First Omaha Secs. Corp., 495 N.W.2d 36, 41–42 (Neb. 1993); Vold v. Broin & Assocs., Inc., 699 N.W.2d 482, 487 (S.D. 2005).

whether a state court uses the state or federal grounds.[169] But if application of state grounds for vacatur would lead to a different result than application of the FAA's grounds, a party may argue the FAA preempts the state grounds.

Initially, this preemption argument seems weak because FAA § 10 applies only in federal court, as it specifies the grounds on which "the United States court in and for the district wherein the award was made may make an order vacating the award." Nevertheless, the Restatement says, "federal law preempts" "a state law ground" for vacatur "when application of the ground would substantially impair the parties' agreement to arbitrate."[170] This is because "[a]lthough the FAA § 10 grounds for post-award relief do not apply in state court, FAA § 2—which makes arbitration agreements valid, irrevocable, and enforceable—does apply in state court and preempts conflicting state law."[171]

Consequently, the FAA preempts state law grounds for vacatur that "interfere with the command of FAA § 2 that arbitration agreements be valid, irrevocable, and enforceable."[172] An extreme hypothetical example would be a state law permitting vacatur whenever the arbitrator who issued the award is human. This would prevent any arbitration in the state, except perhaps if the arbitrators were monkeys,[173] from producing a legally-binding award because all awards of human arbitrators could be easily vacated. In other words, this ground for vacatur would make unenforceable agreements for binding arbitration by effectively converting them into agreements for non-binding arbitration.

Relatedly and more realistically, the Restatement says federal law preempts a state ground for vacatur "when the ground substantially interferes with fundamental attributes of arbitration. This basis for FAA preemption is derived from the Supreme Court's decision in *AT&T Mobility LLC v. Concepcion*," which held that the

---

169 See Restatement (Third) U.S. Law of Int'l Comm. Arb. § 1.9 (2019) ("In most cases, the available grounds for post-award relief under state law are the same as those provided by the FAA, and so no preemption issue arises.") (citing Conn. Gen. Stat. §§ 50a–134, 50a–136; Fla. Stat. §§ 684.0046, 684.0048; Ga. Code Ann. §§ 9–9–56(b), 9–9–58; Hawaii Rev. Stat. § 658D–9(a); La. Stat. Ann. §§ 9:4274, 9:4276). See also Unif. Arbitration Act (1956) § 12, 7 U.L.A. 497–500 (2005) (grounds for vacating the award); 7 U.L.A. 95 (2005) (table of jurisdictions adopting the act); Unif. Arbitration Act (2000) § 23, 7 U.L.A. 73–74, 81–83 (2005) (grounds for vacating the award); 7 U.L.A. 1 (2005) (table of jurisdictions adopting the act).

170 Restatement (Third) U.S. Law of Int'l Comm. Arb. § 1.9 (2019).

171 Id.

172 Id.

173 Baravati v. Josephthal, Lyon & Ross, Inc., 28 F.3d 704, 709 (7th Cir. 1994) (Posner, J.) ("short of authorizing trial by battle or ordeal or, more doubtfully, by a panel of three monkeys, parties can stipulate to whatever procedures they want to govern the arbitration of their disputes").

FAA preempts state law denying enforcement to many agreements for individual, rather than classwide, arbitration.[174] So, as the Restatement says, "a state court decision that vacates an arbitral award on the ground that the arbitration clause must authorize class arbitration for any resulting award to be enforceable" would, "[b]y analogy to *Concepcion*," "interfere with fundamental attributes of arbitration by conditioning the enforceability of the award on the availability of class arbitration, and thus is preempted by the FAA."[175]

A state ground for vacatur that survived FAA preemption challenge is New Hampshire's statute permitting courts to "correct[ ] or modify[ ]" an arbitration "award for plain mistake."[176] The New Hampshire Supreme Court rejected a FAA preemption challenge to this ground in *Finn v. Ballentine Partners, L.L.C.*[177] In *Finn*, the trial court refused to confirm a portion of an award the trial court held "barred, under settled principles of res judicata, by the award of damages" the claimant received from an earlier arbitration award.[178] *Finn* interpreted the parties' ordinary choice of law clause—"This Agreement shall be governed by and construed in accordance with the internal laws of the State of New Hampshire"—as "[t]heir choice to govern their agreement by New Hampshire law."[179] So, "the parties opted for judicial review through a mechanism other than the FAA, an avenue left undisturbed by the Court in *Hall Street*."[180] This interprets an ordinary choice of law clause as choosing, not just the law of one state over that of other states, but also as choosing state law over federal law. Thus, this interpretation contrasts with the bulk of cases, which hold that ordinary choice of law clauses do not contract out of FAA § 2 preemption.[181]

The Washington Supreme Court also rejected a FAA preemption challenge in the 2010 case of *Broom v. Morgan Stanley DW Inc.*[182] It affirmed a lower court order vacating an award on the ground that the award contained facial legal error.[183] The dissent argued that this

---

174 Restatement (Third) U.S. Law of Int'l Comm. Arb. § 1.9 (2019) (citing AT&T Mobility LLC v. Concepcion, 563 U.S. 333 (2011)). See § 29.

175 Restatement (Third) U.S. Law of Int'l Comm. Arb. § 1.9 (2019).

176 N.H. Rev. Stat. Ann. § 542:8.

177 143 A.3d 859, 869–870 (N.H. 2016).

178 Id. at 864.

179 Id. at 872.

180 Id.

181 See § 16(b).

182 236 P.3d 182 (Wash.2010).

183 "[T]he arbitration panel ruled that all of the Brooms' claims except for the CPA claim were barred by state and federal statutes of limitations." Id. at 183–84. "The Brooms filed a complaint in superior court and moved to vacate the arbitration award. They argued that the award contained facial legal error because state statutes of

is not a ground for vacatur under the FAA and that the FAA preempts Washington law to the extent it has this ground.[184] The majority did not respond to this argument or otherwise mention the FAA.

(b) State Grounds for Vacatur Narrower than Federal Grounds

While the FAA may preempt some state grounds for vacatur not found in federal law,[185] little support can be found for the argument that the FAA preempts state law recognizing *fewer* grounds for vacatur than are found in federal law. For example, federal law used to (and may still) recognize a ground for vacatur, "manifest disregard of law," not found in California law.[186] If a California court confirms an arbitration award notwithstanding the court's finding that the arbitrator manifestly disregarded the law, the party seeking to vacate the arbitration award may argue that FAA preemption of state arbitration law requires an order vacating the award. This argument was rejected by the California Court of Appeals in *Siegel v. Prudential Ins. Co.*[187]

> California's rule precluding on the merits review of an arbitration award does not stand as an obstacle to full effectuation of the purpose of the [FAA]—enforcement of arbitration agreements * * *. California's rule evidences no hostility towards arbitration. In fact, California's rule furthers the use of arbitration by somewhat more strictly limiting judicial review of the merits of an award. California's rule against on the merits review furthers rather than defeats full effectuation of the federal law's objectives.[188]

Similarly, a Kentucky appellate court applied state, rather than federal, law of vacatur to a case involving interstate commerce because Kentucky law recognized narrower grounds for vacatur than

---

limitations do not apply to arbitration. The trial court agreed and vacated the award." Id. at 184.

[184] Broom v. Morgan Stanley DW Inc., 236 P.3d 182, 192 (2010) (Madsen, C.J., dissenting).

[185] See § 42(a).

[186] Moncharsh v. Heily & Blase, 10 Cal. Rptr. 2d 183, 190 (Cal. 1992). This ground is discussed in § 41(c).

[187] 79 Cal. Rptr. 2d 726 (Ct.App.1999).

[188] Id. at 735.

were found in federal law and thus did not "frustrate" Congress' purpose in enacting the FAA.[189]

[189] Strausbaugh v. H & R Block Fin. Advisors, Inc., 2007 WL 3122257, at *4–5 (Ky. Ct. App. 2007) ("Based on our analysis of federal and state law, we hold that Kentucky courts are not compelled by federal preemption to substitute and apply 9 U.S.C. § 10 (2002), and the federal case law interpreting it, in place of the [Kentucky Uniform Arbitration Act], even when reviewing arbitration awards involving interstate commerce.")

Chapter 7

LABOR ARBITRATION

Table of Sections

§ 43 Labor Law, Labor Unions, and Labor Arbitration

Labor arbitration arises out of a collective bargaining agreement between an employer and a labor union, in contrast to employment arbitration, which arises out of a contract between an employer and an individual employee.[1] Labor arbitration grew with the growth of labor unions, and thus collective bargaining, during and after the 1930s.[2] Before then, courts often enjoined strikes as violating tort or antitrust law; and employers usually had the legal powers to fire and replace employees asserting grievances, and to enforce—with injunctions against union organizers—contracts in which workers agreed not to join, form, or help a union.[3] However, the 1932 Norris-LaGuardia Act prohibited such contracts,[4] and greatly reduced the labor injunctions that had been based in tort or antitrust law.

The Wagner Act of 1935, the core of what is now known as the National Labor Relations Act (NLRA),[5] went further in encouraging the formation of labor unions and strengthening their bargaining position with employers. Section 1 of the NLRA begins "[t]he denial by some employers of the right of employees to organize and the refusal by some employers to accept the procedure of collective bargaining lead to strikes and other forms of industrial strife." Section 1 then refers to "[t]he inequality of bargaining power between employees who do not possess full freedom of association or actual liberty of contract and employers," before declaring:

> Experience has proved that protection by law of the right of employees to organize and bargain collectively safeguards commerce from injury * * * by encouraging practices fundamental to the friendly adjustment of industrial disputes * * * and by restoring equality of bargaining power between employers and employees.[6]

---

1 See § 45(b)(1)(C).

2 R. W. Fleming, Reflections on the Nature of Labor Arbitration, 61 Mich. L. Rev. 1245, 1246 (1963) (the timing of "[t]he tremendous growth of grievance arbitration *** is not surprising. Grievance arbitration presupposes the existence of collective bargaining agreements. Collective bargaining agreements, in turn, presuppose union organization. The great growth in the labor movement, especially in the mass production industries, occurred in the years following passage of the Wagner Act in 1935.").

3 See, e.g., Stephen J. Ware, Labor Unions, Cartelization, and Arbitration: Replacing at-Will Employment with Arbitration of Employee Grievances, 12 Penn. St. Arb. L. Rev. 19, 37–58 (2020).

4 29 U.S.C. § 103.

5 National Labor Relations Act, 49 Stat. 449 (1935). The Wagner Act was the first of three pieces of legislation commonly known as that National Labor Relations Act. The Wagner Act was later modified by two major pieces of legislation. The Taft-Hartley amendments of 1947 added regulation of union's unfair labor practices, among other changes. See Taft-Hartley Act, Pub. L. No. 80-101, 61 Stat. 136 (1947) (codified as amended at 29 U.S.C. §§ 141–187 (2006)). The Landrum-Griffin amendments in 1959 were primarily directed at the protection of members of unions vis-à-vis their unions, including a workers Bill of Rights. See Landrum-Griffin Act, Pub. L. No. 86-257, 73 Stat. 519 (1959) (codified as amended at 29 U.S.C. §§ 401–531).

6 29 U.S.C. § 151.

Accordingly, Section 1 of the NLRA declared "the policy of the United States to" be "encouraging the practice and procedure of collective bargaining."

The NLRA created the National Labor Relations Board (NLRB) to enforce employee rights. Key is NLRA Section 7, which protects employees' rights:

> to self-organization, to form, join or assist labor organizations, to bargain collectively through representatives of their own choosing, and to engage in other concerted activities for the purpose of collective bargaining or other mutual aid or protection.[7]

The NLRA prohibits employers from interfering with protected Section 7 rights, discriminating against employees for engaging in Section 7 rights, and refusing to bargain with the employees' union.[8]

Empowered by the NLRA, unions increasingly succeeded in securing from employers collective bargaining agreements (CBAs) replacing the employer's ability to discipline or discharge employees at will with the employer's promise to discipline or discharge employees only "for cause" and to arbitrate disputes about whether such cause exists in a particular case.[9] Such discipline and discharge cases make up many of the *grievances* (labor arbitration's usual word for *claims*) resolved in labor arbitration. In addition, labor arbitrators resolve grievances over other CBA provisions, which often address a wide range of workplace issues, such as wages and benefits, discipline, scheduling, and job security.[10]

---

7 Id.

8 29 U.S.C. § 158(a).

9 Elkouri & Elkouri, How Arbitration Works § 3.3.A & § 15.2.A.ii (BNA Dec. 2020) (most union contracts require cause for dismissal, and discipline is often a subject of arbitration); Nicole B. Porter, The Perfect Compromise: Bridging the Gap Between At-Will Employment and Just Cause, 87 Neb. L. Rev. 62, 69 (2008) ("Most collective bargaining agreements incorporate a 'just cause' standard for termination of employees."); Smith v. Kerrville Bus Co., 709 F.2d 914, 917 (5th Cir. 1983) ("In instances where the language of a collective contract does not explicitly prohibit dismissal except for just cause, arbitrators typically infer such prohibitions from seniority clauses or grievance and arbitration procedures."). But see Elkouri, § 15.2.A.ii. ("However, some arbitrators have held to the contrary, concluding that, where a collective bargaining agreement exists but contains no express limitation on the employer's right to discharge and discipline employees, an employer may discharge for any reason it chooses.").

10 Elkouri, supra note 9, at § 3.3.A & § 15.2.A.ii ("Among the infinite number of matters that may be the subject of rights arbitration are questions with respect to seniority rights, vacations, holidays, discharge and discipline, layoffs, job bidding and classifications, and harassment.").

Although some CBAs allow employers to bring arbitration claims alleging union breach of a no-strike clause,[11] many CBA arbitration clauses do not allow the employer to assert claims in arbitration.[12] So, labor arbitration nearly always involves grievances against employers, which distinguishes labor arbitration from much other arbitration in which either side to a transaction might, depending on the case, assert a claim against the other. This trait of labor arbitration arose, the Supreme Court concluded, from a "history indicat[ing] that the agreement to arbitrate grievance disputes was considered as quid pro quo of a no-strike agreement."[13] This deal is central to the Supreme Court's understanding of what makes labor arbitration different from other arbitration. As the Court said in the landmark labor arbitration case, *United Steelworkers v. Warrior & Gulf Navigation Co.*,

> The present federal policy is to promote industrial stabilization through the collective bargaining agreement. A major factor in achieving industrial peace is the inclusion of a provision for arbitration of grievances in the collective bargaining agreement.
>
> Thus the run of [non-labor] arbitration cases * * * becomes irrelevant to our problem. There the choice is between the adjudication of cases or controversies in courts * * * on the one hand and the settlement of them in the more informal arbitration tribunal on the other. In the commercial case, arbitration is the substitute for litigation. Here arbitration is the substitute for industrial strife.[14]

While non-labor arbitration basically resolves claims (asserted by either party) that would otherwise likely have been resolved in litigation, labor arbitration basically resolves worker grievances that would otherwise likely have been resolved by strikes and other "industrial strife." In addition to defusing potential employee unrest, parties to CBAs use arbitration for the same reasons as parties to

---

11 See e.g., Lincoln Mills, 353 U.S. 448, 449 (1957) ("The agreement provided that there would be no strikes or work stoppages and that grievances would be handled pursuant to a specified procedure. The last step in the grievance procedure—a step that could be taken by either party—was arbitration.").

12 Dennis R. Nolan, Labor and Employment Arbitration in a Nutshell 165 (2d ed. 2007). See, e.g., Std. Concrete Prods. Inc. v. Gen. Truck Drivers, Office, Food & Warehouse Union, Local 952, 353 F.3d 668 (9th Cir. 2003).

13 Lincoln Mills, 353 U.S. 448, 455 (1957). See also Local 174, Teamsters v. Lucas Flour Co., 369 U.S. 95 (1962) (courts should imply a no-strike clause with respect to any dispute which a CBA "provides shall be settled exclusively and finally by compulsory arbitration.").

14 United Steelworkers v. Warrior & Gulf Navigation Co., 363 U.S. 574, 577–78 (1960).

other contracts, which include the desire for speedy, informal, inexpensive, and expert adjudication.[15]

CBAs commonly make labor arbitration the endpoint of a multi-stage grievance process.[16] A grievance arbitration process is generally one section in a lengthy collective bargaining agreement that addresses a wide range of workplace issues. If an employee encounters a problem with terms or conditions of work, such as wages, benefits, scheduling, or job security, or is disciplined, the union files a grievance. The union and employer attempt to resolve the grievance by having different agents negotiate. If negotiation cannot resolve the grievance, the parties ultimately arbitrate to obtain a resolution from the arbitrator.

For instance, the first step of the process may be that the employee informally brings the concern to the attention of a supervisor. If the supervisor is unable to resolve the situation, then the second step may require that the union shop steward file a written grievance with a manager, and that the steward and manager meet within a set short time to discuss the grievance and their interpretations of the CBA. If the manager is unable to remedy the grievance, then the third step may require that the union president and company president or director of labor relations meet. If that third step fails to resolve the grievance, then at the fourth step, the union files for arbitration.

Labor arbitration is "part and parcel" of the CBA and provides "meaning and content" to it.[17] The CBA cannot enumerate all of the practices of a particular industry or workplace and cannot anticipate every dispute that may arise. Arbitration fills in the gaps through interpretation and application of the CBA. The grievance arbitration process provides a form of workplace self-governance that is more responsive to the parties' needs in a particular workplace than decisions of a court of general jurisdiction could be.[18]

Most CBAs provide that the union, rather than an employee with a concern, decides whether to file a grievance with a manager and, if that does not produce a resolution, whether to pursue

---

[15] See Douglas E. Ray, et al., Understanding Labor Law 284 (5th ed. 2019) (identifying reasons arbitration provisions are included as 1) informality of hearing, 2) inexpensive nature of arbitration compared to litigation, 3) neutrality of third-party expert, and 4) "defusing potential employee unrest.").

[16] Ariana R. Levinson, What the Awards Tell Us About Labor Arbitration of Employment-Discrimination Claims (hereinafter Labor Arbitration), 46 Mich. J.L. Reform 789, 794 (2013).

[17] United Steelworkers of Am. v. Warrior & Gulf Nav. Co., 363 U.S. 574, 580–81 (1960).

[18] Id.

arbitration.[19] For examples, see the arbitration provisions in Section 46(a). Union control of grievances aims to assure that employees are aided by a union representative and that the CBA is interpreted in a consistent manner that is fair to all represented employees.[20] A basic precept of labor law is that employees can better achieve improved terms and conditions of work acting collectively through their union than individually. Because of this the union represented worker is constrained to act with other employees through the union rather than bargain over individual grievances.[21]

Some contracts, nevertheless, provide both the union and the employee the right to bring a grievance and/or pursue arbitration of a contract violation. For example, in one case a Connecticut state employee was able to bring a statutory claim through the negotiated union arbitration process with individual, rather than union, representation.[22]

In the usual situation where the union controls the grievance, if the union declines to proceed with a grievance, the employer's action, with which the employee is concerned, stands. The employee's only recourse in such a situation is to sue the union, alleging that not pursuing the grievance breached the union's duty of fair representation.[23] Generally it is only when a court holds that a union breached its duty of fair representation that an affected employee can pursue a claim against the employer for its breach of CBA.[24] However, proving breach of the duty of fair representation involves a high standard, and most courts hold that mere negligence on a union's part does not result in a breach of the duty. Instead, the employee must prove that the union acted arbitrarily, discriminatorily, or in bad faith.[25]

Generally, unions can bring grievances for contract violations that affect all or a sub-group of workers. For instance, a union could file a grievance for a violation of a wage provision on behalf of all servers if tips were being calculated inconsistently with a contract provision. The arbitrator would be able to order back-pay to all affected employees as well as direct the employer to use the correct method of calculation going forward. Similarly, if the union pursues

---

[19] Dennis Nolan, Labor and Employment Arbitration: What's Justice Got to Do with It?, 53 Disp. Resol. J. 40, 44 (1998).

[20] See Nolan, supra note 19, at 44.

[21] Emporium Capwell Co. v. Western Addition Community Organization, 420 U.S. 50 (1975).

[22] Serafin v. Connecticut, 2005 WL 578321 (D. Conn. Mar. 9, 2005).

[23] Vaca v. Sipes, 386 U.S. 171 (1967).

[24] Hines v. Anchor Motor Freight, 424 U.S. 554, 567 (1976).

[25] Id. at 570.

a contract violation on behalf of an individual, the resultant award will inform the employer's actions as to other employees. For example, a union could grieve a suspension because the worker was not on notice that the conduct, perhaps storing alcohol in their locker, was against the rules and could result in suspension. The arbitrator then orders the suspension removed from the worker's personnel file and that the worker be paid for the lost pay. The employer likely will inform all the workers that they can be disciplined for storing alcohol in their lockers so that they will be able to suspend future workers who do so. Because the union grievance and arbitration process effectively represents the interest of many employees, the issue of class actions is not extensively litigated as it is in other arbitration setting as discussed in Section 29.

The grievance arbitration process is sometimes termed "rights arbitration" because it resolves the union and employees' rights under the CBA. Some CBAs also include a different type of arbitration termed "interest arbitration" which is discussed in Section 46(b)(3). Interest arbitration is a process where the arbitrator determines what the provisions of a CBA are, rather than how the provisions of an existing CBA should be interpreted or applied.

§ 44 Law Governing Labor Arbitration

(a) LMRA Rather than FAA

(1) Section 301

The foundational labor arbitration case is *Textile Workers Union v. Lincoln Mills*,[26] decided by the Supreme Court in 1957. *Lincoln Mills* held that courts must enforce arbitration clauses in CBAs.[27] *Lincoln Mills* rested its holding on Section 301 of the Labor Management Relations Act of 1947 ("LMRA").[28] The Labor Management Relations Act was part of the Taft-Hartley Act, a management-friendly bill intended to curb the power of unions that were engaging in strike activity that some viewed as disruptive to industrial peace.[29] Section 301 was intended to enable unions to be sued, and particularly, to compel unions to comply with no-strike

---

[26] Textile Workers v. Lincoln Mills of Alabama, 353 U.S. 448 (1957).

[27] 353 U.S. at 456 ("Congress adopted a policy which placed sanctions behind agreements to arbitrate grievance disputes, by implication rejecting the common-law rule * * * against enforcement of executory agreements to arbitrate.") (citation omitted) (footnote omitted).

[28] 29 U.S.C. §§ 141–44, 171–88.

[29] Theodore J. St. Antoine, Charles B. Craver, & Marion G. Crain, Labor Relations Law: Cases and Materials 16–17 (12th ed. 2011); Diversity Jurisdiction Under 303(B) of the Taft-Hartley Act, 59 Yale L.J. 575, 575, 579–80 (1950); Alan I. Horowitz, The Applicability of Boys Markets Injunctions to Refusals to Cross a Picket Line, 76 Colum. L. Rev. 113, 114 (1976).

clauses in CBAs.[30] Before enactment of Section 301, the legal status of unions was uncertain, and different state courts had ruled differently as to whether unions could sue or be sued.[31] Section 301 authorizes suing for violation of a CBA in federal district court. It also establishes that a union can be sued as an entity and may sue as an entity and on behalf of its members.

(2) Lincoln Mills

In *Lincoln Mills*,[32] the union and employer had entered into a CBA wherein the union agreed not to strike, and the parties agreed to use a grievance-arbitration process to resolve disputes arising under the CBA. When the employer refused to arbitrate a grievance, the union sued to compel arbitration. The Supreme Court compelled arbitration and reasoned that the union had given up the right to strike in return for the employer's promise to arbitrate, so the promise must be enforceable.

While *Lincoln Mills* held that arbitration clauses in CBAs are enforceable under the LMRA, *Lincoln Mills* ignored the FAA. Because *Lincoln Mills* did not mention the FAA, the "most natural reading" of *Lincoln Mills* is that the FAA does not govern labor arbitration.[33] The Supreme Court's subsequent opinions on labor arbitration did not address the FAA until 1987.[34] That year, the Court suggested that, although the FAA does not govern labor

---

[30] Archibald Cox, Grievance Arbitration in the Federal Courts, 67 Harv. L. Rev. 591, 602, 606 (1954); James E. Pfander, Federal Jurisdiction Over Union Constitutions After Wooddell, 37 Vill. L. Rev. 443, 465–66 (1992).

[31] Ray, supra note 15, at 285.

[32] Textile Workers v. Lincoln Mills of Alabama, 353 U.S. 448 (1957).

[33] Ian R. Macneil, Richard E. Speidel & Thomas J. Stipanowich, Federal Arbitration Law: Agreements, Awards, and Remedies under the Federal Arbitration Act § 11.3.1, § 11:9 (1994). See also, Lincoln Mills, 353 U.S. at 466 (Frankfurter, J., dissenting).

> Naturally enough, I find rejection, though not explicit, of the availability of the Federal Arbitration Act to enforce arbitration clauses in collective-bargaining agreements in the silent treatment given that Act by the Court's opinion. If an Act that authorizes the federal courts to enforce arbitration provisions in contracts generally, but specifically denies authority to decree that remedy for 'contracts of employment,' were available, the Court would hardly spin such power out of the empty darkness of § 301. I would make this rejection explicit, recognizing that when Congress passed legislation to enable arbitration agreements to be enforced by the federal courts, it saw fit to exclude this remedy with respect to labor contracts.

Id.

[34] Macneil, Speidel & Stipanowich, supra note 33, at § 11.3.1. See, e.g., United Steelworkers v. American Mfg. Co., 363 U.S. 564 (1960); United Steelworkers v. Warrior & Gulf Navigation Co., 363 U.S. 574 (1960); United Steelworkers v. Enterprise Wheel & Car Corp., 363 U.S. 593 (1960).

arbitration, courts may look to the FAA for guidance in labor cases.[35] Then in *Penn Plaza v. Pyett*, a 2009 case, the Court decided a labor arbitration case seeking to compel arbitration under the FAA without addressing whether the FAA is an additional basis for enforcing labor arbitration agreements or simply remains a source of guidance in labor cases.[36]

Although the LMRA, rather than the FAA, primarily governs labor arbitration, the LMRA says nothing about arbitration. It does not even mention the word "arbitration."[37] Because the LMRA says nothing about arbitration, courts must make common law to govern labor arbitration. *Lincoln Mills* held that this is *federal* common law. LMRA Section 301 grants jurisdiction to federal courts and *Lincoln Mills* held that this provision does not merely give federal courts jurisdiction to apply *state* law, but rather gives them authority to create substantive *federal* law.[38] State courts have concurrent jurisdiction to enforce CBAs,[39] including arbitration clauses, but they must apply the federal common law of collective bargaining and enforcement.[40]

The FAA and labor arbitration law are similar in an important respect. Both require courts to use an especially powerful remedy, specific performance, in enforcing arbitration agreements. While

---

35 See United Paperworkers Int'l Union v. Misco, Inc., 484 U.S. 29 (1987). ("The Arbitration Act does not apply to "contracts of employment of * * * workers engaged in foreign or interstate commerce," 9 U.S.C. § 1, but the federal courts have often looked to the Act for guidance in labor arbitration cases, especially in the wake of [*Lincoln Mills*]."). Id. at 40 n.9.

36 14 Penn Plaza LLC v. Pyett, 556 U.S. 247, 254 (2009).

37 The portion of the LMRA on which *Lincoln Mills* relied (Section 301) provides in pertinent part:

> (a) * * * Suits for violation of contracts between an employer and a labor organization representing employees in an industry affecting commerce as defined in this chapter, or between any such labor organizations, may be brought in any district court of the United States having jurisdiction of the parties, without respect to the amount in controversy or without regard to the citizenship of the parties.
>
> (b) * * * Any labor organization which represents employees in an industry affecting commerce as defined in this chapter and any employer whose activities affect commerce as defined in this chapter shall be bound by the acts of its agents. Any such labor organization may sue or be sued as an entity and in behalf of the employees whom it represents in the courts of the United States. Any money judgment against a labor organization in a district court of the United States shall be enforceable only against the organization as an entity and against its assets, and shall not be enforceable against any individual member or his assets.

29 U.S.C. § 185(a)–(b).

38 Lincoln Mills, 353 U.S. at 456 (the "substantive law to apply in suits under [the LMRA] is federal law, which the courts must fashion from the policy of our national labor laws.").

39 Charles Dowd Box Co. v. Courtney, 368 U.S. 502, 511–14 (1962).

40 Local 174, Teamsters v. Lucas Flour Co., 369 U.S. 95, 102 (1962).

money damages are the ordinary remedy for breach of contract,[41] specific performance, that is, a court order to arbitrate, is the remedy for breach of an arbitration agreement. That is true of non-labor arbitration under the FAA,[42] and it is true of labor arbitration under the LMRA, as interpreted by *Lincoln Mills*.[43] If, for example, Employee sues Employer over a grievance covered by the CBA's arbitration clause, the court will stay or dismiss Employee's case.[44] Alternatively, if Union seeks to arbitrate Employee's grievance but Employer refuses to participate in arbitration, then a court will order Employer to do so.[45]

(b) NLRA

The National Labor Relations Act does not mention arbitration, let alone provide a basis to enforce a labor arbitration agreement or award. Nevertheless, the NLRA, and the NLRB it created, often impact labor arbitration. For example, if an employee or union files with the NLRB a charge that an employer has violated the NLRA by engaging in an unfair labor practice, the NLRB will sometimes "defer" (not hear) an unfair labor practice charge and instead order the parties to resolve it in arbitration. This NLRB deferral to arbitration thus resembles a court staying or dismissing litigation and referring the dispute to arbitration.[46] The NLRB will also sometimes dismiss an unfair practice charge in deference to an arbitration award in a manner similar to how a court might dismiss a suit as barred or estopped by an arbitration award under the FAA.[47] Extensive NLRB decisions address these issues of when to defer a claim to arbitration.

---

[41] Joseph M. Perillo, Calamari and Perillo on Contracts § 14.4 564 (6th ed.2009).

[42] See § 5(b).

[43] Lincoln Mills, 353 U.S. at 451.

[44] Allis-Chalmers Corp. v. Lueck, 471 U.S. 202, 220 (1985) ("A rule that permitted an individual to sidestep available grievance procedures would cause arbitration to lose most of its effectiveness, as well as eviscerate a central tenet of federal labor-contract law under § 301 that it is the arbitrator, not the court, who has the responsibility to interpret the labor contract in the first instance."); Vera v. Saks & Co., 335 F.3d 109 (2d Cir. 2003); National Ass'n of Broadcast Employees & Technicians v. American Broadcasting Co., 140 F.3d 459, 462 (2d Cir. 1998). By contrast, if the employee or union seeks arbitration of a grievance and the employer asserts the grievance arbitration clause is inapplicable and refuses to submit to arbitration then the employee may bring suit. Sidhu v. Flecto Co., 279 F.3d 896, 900 (9th Cir. 2002) ("[i]f the employer repudiates the procedures established in a CBA to govern a particular grievance, the aggrieved employee is relieved of the usual requirement to exhaust administrative remedies as to that grievance.").

[45] See, e.g., Lincoln Mills, 353 U.S. 448; Armco Employees Indep. Fed'n v. AK Steel Corp., 252 F.3d 854 (6th Cir. 2001); Washington Hosp. Center v. Service Employees International Union, 746 F.2d 1503, 1506 (D.C. Cir. 1984).

[46] Collyer Insulated Wire, 192 NLRB 837, 841–42 (1971).

[47] Spielberg Manf. Co., 112 NLRB 1080, 1082 (1955).

(c) RLA

As Section 66(b)(4) explains, the Railway Labor Act ("RLA")[48] requires employers and unions in certain transportation industries, such as railroads and airlines, to submit certain disputes to the Adjustment Board for decision.[49] Thus, the RLA requires arbitration, rather than litigation, of these disputes even when parties have not formed an arbitration agreement, in contrast to other private-sector labor disputes which go to arbitration only when the parties have formed an arbitration agreement. Nevertheless, arbitration under the RLA resembles other private-sector labor arbitration in many respects.

(d) Public Sector Labor Laws

(1) *Labor Arbitration of Federal Employees*

In the public sector, The Civil Service Reform Act ("CSRA") authorizes employees of the federal government to form labor unions and requires employers (the various federal government agencies) to bargain in good faith with these unions.[50] The Federal Service Labor-Management Relations Statute,[51] Title VII of the CSRA, explicitly provides for grievance arbitration and interest arbitration for most federal workplaces.[52] As Section 78(b)(2) explains, Title VII of the Civil Service Reform Act ("CSRA") states that any grievance of a federal employee not excluded from the grievance process by the CBA will be settled through a grievance arbitration process that culminates in "binding arbitration * * * invoked by either the [union] or the agency [employer]." The statute sets the default as grievance arbitration from which the parties may opt out, in contrast to the private sector where parties could negotiate a grievance procedure that does not include arbitration, although that may rarely happen. Thus, the CSRA requires arbitration, rather than litigation, of these disputes even when parties have not formed an explicit arbitration agreement, in contrast to most private-sector labor disputes which go to arbitration only when the parties have formed an arbitration agreement. Either party to a federal employment arbitration may

---

[48] 45 U.S.C. §§ 151–88.

[49] Id. § 153(i).

[50] Civil Service Reform Act of 1978, Pub. L. 95–454, 92 Stat. 111 (codified as amended in scattered sections of 5 U.S.C.).

[51] U.S. Federal Labor Relations Authority, Guide to Arbitration under the Federal Service Labor-Management Relations Statute (Sept. 30, 2016) available at https://www.flra.gov/system/files/webfm/Authority/AR%20Forms,%20Guide,%20Other/Arbitration%20Guide%209.30.16.pdf.

[52] 5 U.S.C. § 7119; 5 U.S.C. § 7121.

appeal to the Federal Labor Relations Authority and may further appeal that Authority's decision to a federal court.[53]

For the Postal Service, the Postal Reorganization Act explicitly provides for interest arbitration, and the courts have interpreted that Act similarly to LMRA Section 301 as to grievance arbitration.[54] The statute, rather than a contract, imposes the duty to arbitrate if the parties have not reached a new agreement within 60 days of the expiration (or date when subject to modification) of the prior CBA.[55] In contrast, grievance arbitration results from a contractual duty.

(2) Labor Arbitration of State and Local Government Employees

Some states provide the right to collectively bargain to their employees, and those statutes generally contain provisions authorizing arbitration.[56] For instance, Illinois permits some employees to strike when "the public employer and the labor organization have not mutually agreed to submit the disputed issues to final and binding arbitration."[57] Similarly, Oregon prohibits striking by any public employee who "is included in an appropriate bargaining unit that provides for resolution of a labor dispute by petition to final and binding arbitration."[58] State and local public sector arbitration is discussed further in Section 66(b)(3).

§ 45 Formation of Enforceable Labor Arbitration Agreements

(a) Labor Arbitration Only Partly Governed by Contract Law

Labor arbitrators and courts often consider contractual canons of interpretation when interpreting CBAs and sometimes apply principles of contract law to labor arbitration issues. But the Supreme Court has explained that "A collective bargaining agreement is not an ordinary contract for the purchase of goods and services, nor is it governed by the same old common-law concepts,

---

[53] 5 U.S.C. §§ 7122(a), 7123(a).

[54] 39 U.S.C. § 1207; 39 U.S.C. § 1208(b); Am. Postal Workers' Union v. U.S. Postal Service, 646 F. Supp. 2d 1 (D.D.C. 2009).

[55] 39 U.S.C. 1207(c).

[56] Elkouri & Elkouri, Chapter 21, 21.1 (citing Alaska Stat. § 23.40.200 (Michie 1997); Haw. Rev. Stat. § 89–12 (1997); Idaho Code § 44–1811 (1997); 5 Ill. Comp. Stat. 315/17 (West 1997); Minn. Stat. § 179A.18 (1996); Mont. Code Ann. §§ 39-32-110, 39-34-105 (1997); Ohio Rev. Code Ann. §§ 4117.15–16 (Anderson 1997); Or. Rev. Stat. § 243.726 (1996); 43 Pa. Cons. Stat. §§ 1101.1001–1003, 1101.2201 (1997); Vt. Stat. Ann. tit. 21 § 1730 (1997); Wis. Stat. § 111.70(4)(cm)(6)(c) (1995–96)).

[57] 5 Ill. Comp. Stat. 315/17 (West 2022).

[58] Or. Rev. Stat. § 243.726 (West 2022).

which control such private contracts."[59] So, the following pages show many examples of labor arbitration law differing from the ordinary contract law that more thoroughly governs non-labor arbitration. Several of these differences can even appear in a single case—for instance, one observing that "collective bargaining agreements are enforced 'without question as to consideration,' " traditional contract notions such as "meeting of the minds" "do not apply to enforcement of collective bargaining agreements," and fraud in the inducement of a CBA "is no defense" to its enforcement.[60] More generally, the NLRB has stated that "In determining whether [a CBA] has been reached, the Board uses general contract principles adapted to the context of collective bargaining, but it is not bound strictly by technical rules of contract law.[61]

(b) Mutual Manifestations of Assent and Consideration

(1) Manifestations of Assent

(A) Manifestations of Assent by Employer and Union

The general requirements to form a contract are: (1) mutual manifestations of assent, and (2) consideration, as discussed in §§ 18 & 19. The parties to a CBA—employer and union—nearly always manifest assent to it by signing it in ink or, more recently, electronically.[62] The NLRA requires "execution of a written contract incorporating any agreement reached if requested by either party."[63] The widespread use of signed writings enables employers, unions, employees, and arbitrators to know and be able to reference the agreed upon terms and conditions of employment.

The widespread use of signed writings enables labor law to avoid many of the assent issues that arise outside the labor context, such

---

[59] Transportation-Commc'n Emp. Union v. Union Pac. R. Co., 385 U.S. 157, 160–61 (1966).

[60] Greater St. Louis Construction Laborer Welfare Fund v. Hancock Demolition & Excavation Co., 2009 WL 2568049, at *8 (E.D. Mo. Aug. 18, 2009) (citations omitted).

[61] Intermountain Rural Elec. Ass'n, 309 NLRB 1189, 1192 (1992) (holding that an employer did not agree through a series of letters with the union to pay the full cost of benefits but leaving a statutory ruling that the employer unlawfully ceased full payment in effect) (citations omitted).

[62] For examples of electronic rather than ink, see, e.g., Centers for New Horizons, Inc., 2015 NLRB Reg. Dir. Dec. LEXIS 18, at *9–13 (Jan. 30, 2015) (recognizing formation of a CBA and thus a "contract bar,"—labor law's time period in which an existing CBA prohibits other unions from trying to represent employees or an employee from attempting to decertify the union—when employer's attorney's typed name and signature block were affixed to the e-mailed CBA offer); Makro Services Inc., 2008 NLRB Reg. Dir. Dec. LEXIS 6 at *6–7 (Jan. 16, 2008) (recognizing contract bar based on series of emails even where most recent does not include signature block).

[63] NLRA Section 8(d); The term "execute" in Section 8(d) means "to sign" the "written contract."

as assent by performance, on a website, or through the battle of the forms.[64] In contrast to the quick or doubtful assent to arbitration agreements prevalent in those non-labor contexts, the negotiation of and assent to CBAs is typically quite thorough.[65] When a union is first recognized by the NLRB as the exclusive bargaining agent for some employees of the employer, it takes an average of 465 day from then and a mean of 374 days for those parties who do reach agreement on a first CBA to do so.[66] Private-sector CBAs typically expire after 3 years, as discussed below in Section 43(b)(3), so the parties to an existing CBA often negotiate subsequent CBAs by proposing changes to or deletion of existing CBA provisions or addition of new provisions. Often when negotiating parties conditionally agree to a provision, such as a grievance arbitration provision, they will initial to indicate they tentatively agree, dependent on reaching agreement on all provisions of the CBA.

In some significant percentage of first-time CBA negotiations, and a smaller percentage of later negotiations, the employer never agrees to a CBA and thus does not agree to arbitration.[67] But in contrast to parties considering most non-labor sorts of contracts—where neither party has any duty to negotiate with the other, let alone negotiate exclusively with the other—the NLRA requires the employer and union to engage in good faith bargaining with each other, "as opposed to dealing with other parties."[68] The purpose of requiring employers to bargain exclusively with the union when employees elect union representation is to protect the employees, who generally have less power than the employer, to democratize economic decision making by operating as a means for employees to

---

64 See § 18(b) & (c); John E. Higgins, Jr., The Developing Labor Law: The Board, the Courts, and the National Labor Relations Act § 13.II.C (John E. Higgins, Jr. et al. eds., 7th ed. 2020) ("[T]he refusal to sign a written memorandum of the agreement made has been uniformly regarded as a per se refusal to bargain.").

65 Exceptions from the norm of thorough negotiation and assent tend to be unusual circumstances such as when an employer signs on to an existing multi-employer CBA or parties enter into a mid-term side agreement to an existing CBA.

66 Robert Combs, Analysis: Now It Takes 465 Days to Sign a Union's First Contract (Bloomberg Law Aug. 2, 2022) available at https://news.bloomberglaw.com/daily-labor-report/analysis-how-long-does-it-take-unions-to-reach-first-contracts.

67 The National Labor Relations Act (NLRA): Union Representation Procedures and Dispute Resolution, at 11–12 (Congressional Research Service Dec. 11, 2013) available at https://crsreports.congress.gov/product/pdf/RL/RL32930/37.

68 United Steelworkers of Am. v. Warrior & Gulf Nav. Co., 363 U.S. 574, 580 (1960)("[w]hen most parties enter into contractual relationship they do so voluntarily, in the sense that there is no real compulsion to deal with one another, as opposed to dealing with other parties. This is not true of the labor agreement."); NLRA Section 8(d) ("but such obligation does not compel either party to agree to a proposal or require the making of a concession").

have a voice in decisions, and to reduce economic strife by providing an orderly process for resolution of disputes.[69]

Labor law's duty to bargain in good faith informs some issues regarding manifestation of assent. For instance, good faith bargaining typically involves a back and forth between the parties. So, if an employer offers a take-it-or-leave it proposal, the NLRB will consider that as a factor potentially indicating bad faith bargaining, which would lead to the NLRB ordering the employer to resume bargaining in good faith.[70] In collective bargaining, employers generally avoid take-it-or leave-it proposals of the sort that are routine in the adhesive arbitration agreements of consumers and employees not represented by a union discussed in Section 18(a)–(e).

Labor law's duty to bargain in good faith also informs decisions when one of the parties—typically the employer—refuses to sign a CBA that the other party—typically the union—claims both parties agreed to with spoken words and a handshake.[71] In these instances, the union may file a charge with the NLRB alleging the employer violated the NLRA by refusing to bargain in good faith. If the Board finds the parties shook on an agreement, stipulated to sign the agreement at a later time, had a meeting of the minds, orally ratified an agreement, or otherwise agreed to a contract, the Board will order the employer to sign and abide by the CBA.[72] Courts treat the Board's factual finding as to whether a CBA was agreed to by the parties with substantial deference.[73] As explained by the Supreme Court, a business person who enters into an agreement with numerous provisions "with the reservation" that they "will not reduce it to writing or sign it" bargains in bad faith.[74] Even more so does the

---

69 NLRA Section 1 (describing inequality of bargaining power between employees and employers who are organized in corporate or other associational form and how protecting the right of employees to bargain collectively encourages friendly adjustment of disputes); Emporium Capwell Co. v. Western Add. Comm. Org., 420 U.S. 50, 62 (1975) (explaining that majority rule is a source of collective employee strength).

70 Ray, supra note 15, at 170.

71 Demolition Workers Union Loc. 95 & Mack Royce Dismantling, Ltd., 330 NLRB 352, 358 (1999) (union ordered to sign agreement that was reached with employer before union's negotiating party changed and refused to honor the original agreement).

72 N.L.R.B. v. New Orleans Stevedoring Co., 997 F.2d 881, 1993 WL 261072, at *4 (5th Cir. 1993); N.L.R.B. v. Coletti Color Prints, Inc., 387 F.2d 298, 304 (2d Cir. 1967); Demolition Workers, 330 NLRB at **28 ("The ultimate question in these cases is, of course, whether there was a meeting of the minds on all material terms of the contract"); Newspaper and Mail Deliverers' Union of New York and Vicinity & NYP Holdings, Inc., 348 N.L.R.B. 312, at **30 (2006).

73 New Orleans Stevedoring Co., 997 F.2d at *7 ("where substantial evidence on the record as a whole supports the Board's finding that an agreement between an employer and a union existed, we will not reverse its finding-even if we justifiably might have made a different finding from the Board.").

74 H.J. Heinz Co. v. NLRB, 311 U.S. 514, 526 (1941).

employer, who by "refusal to honor with [their] signature, the agreement which [they] have made with a labor organization, discredits the organization, impairs the bargaining process and tends to frustrate the aim of the statute to secure industrial peace through collective bargaining," bargain in bad faith.[75]

(B) Conditions Sometimes Required to Form a CBA—Including Ratification by Employees

While the previous subsection explains that the widespread of use of signed writings enables labor law to avoid many of the assent issues that arise outside the labor context, collective bargaining agreements sometimes raise issues similar to those raised in other settings about assent by an agent. Basic agency law allows one party to act through another, for example, to form a contract.[76] Labor law uses a concept similar to that of an agent, representative, in binding individual employees to the CBA their representative, the union, formed on their behalf.[77] So, to form a CBA, a union is not obligated to obtain employees' individual assent to or even ratification by a majority of the employees of any negotiated collective-bargaining agreement.[78]

In contrast, some CBAs make ratification in a specified manner, such as by a majority of unit employees (rather than only union members) or within a certain time frame, a condition of contract formation.[79] Employee ratification is a prerequisite for contract acceptance only when both parties (union and employer) discuss the ratification process and agree that it is a condition precedent to a binding contract.[80] For instance, in *Granite Rock Co. v. Int'l Bhd. of*

---

75 Id.

76 See § 18(g).

77 Mendez v. Starwood Hotels & Resorts Worldwide, Inc., 346 F. App'x 602, 602–03 (2d Cir. 2009) ("Pursuant to the National Labor Relations Act, a designated bargaining representative has exclusive authority to bargain over 'rates of pay, wages, hours of employment, or other conditions of employment.' 29 U.S.C. § 159(a). In NLRB v. Allis-Chalmers Mfg. Co., 388 U.S. 175, 87 S. Ct. 2001, 18 L.Ed.2d 1123 (1967), the Supreme Court confirmed that where a union functions as an exclusive bargaining representative, 'only the union may contract the employee's terms and conditions of employment.' Id. at 180. Represented employees are bound by these negotiated terms and conditions of employment, which are mandatory subjects of bargaining.").

78 North Country Motors, 146 NLRB 671, 674 (1964) ("The Act imposes no obligation upon a bargaining agent to obtain employee ratification of a contract it negotiates in their behalf."); see also Beatrice/Hunt-Wesson, 302 NLRB 224, 225 (1991) (Stephens concurring).

79 Beatrice/Hunt-Wesson, 302 NLRB at 226 (1991) (Stephens concurring).

80 Beatrice/Hunt-Wesson, 302 NLRB at 224 n.1 (1991); Williamhouse-Regency of Delaware, 297 NLRB 199, 199 n.5 (1989) (union negotiators informing the employer in writing at outset of negotiations and orally during negotiations that an agreement would have to be ratified by union members before it becomes binding does not create a condition precedent).

Teamsters, "the parties [rightly] characterize[d] as a formation dispute" a dispute about when ratification occurred, "because a union vote ratifying the CBA's terms was necessary to form the contract."[81] As the *Granite Rock* Court said, "when a contract is formed can be as critical as whether it was formed. That is the case where, as here, the date on which an agreement was ratified determines the date the agreement was formed, and thus determines whether the agreement's provisions were enforceable during the period relevant to the parties' dispute."

In some other instances, parties agree to a condition precedent to formation of the CBA, such as a vote by the employer's board of trustees or a union obtaining dismissal of a pension fund lawsuit against an employer.[82]

(C) CBA Distinguished from Employment Contract

Most workers in the U.S. are employed at will without any written employment contract,[83] and whether an at-will employment relationship is a contract has been a subject of debate.[84] To the extent it is a contract, the agreement is simply that the employee will show up and work and in return the employer will pay an agreed rate for the work. Because each party can terminate the relationship at any time without notice, any further protections or benefits for the employee result not from an employment contract, but from implied contracts, promissory estoppel, or statutory or court-created rights.[85] On the other hand, some employees, primarily high-level executives and managers, have individual employment contracts that are written signed documents that may provide for termination only for cause, certain wages and benefits, a bonus structure, severance, non-competition, or other terms.[86]

---

[81] Granite Rock, 561 U.S. 287, 303–04 (2010).

[82] Kent Engineering, Inc., 180 NLRB 86, 88 (1969); Bronson Methodist Hosp., 223 NLRB 95, 98 (1976); see also Air-Vac Industries, Inc., 259 NLRB 336 (1981) (finding parties did not agree that supplemental bargaining agreement was conditioned on the employer obtaining a higher pay rate from the contracting municipalities).

[83] Rachel Arnow-Richman, Modifying At-Will Employment Contracts, 57 B.C.L. Rev. 427, 428 (2016); Ray, supra note 15, at 39 ("The at will employment rule governs over half of the total civilian non-agricultural workplace" [sic.]).

[84] Harry Hutchison, The Collision of Employment-at-Will, Section 1981 & Gonzalez: Discharge, Consent and Contract Sufficiency, 3 U. Pa. J. Lab. & Emp. L. 207, 207, 214 (2001); see also Arnow-Richman, supra note 83 at 436 ("Currently, both workers and employers operate in a state of perpetual uncertainty as to which promises are contractually binding, which reflect extra-contractual norms, and which are mere aspirations, not rising to the level of a promise at all.").

[85] Ray, supra note 15, at 45–58.

[86] Arnow-Richman, supra note 83, at 435 n.34.

In contrast, a labor contract (CBA) is negotiated by a union, rather than an individual employee, and its terms govern the workplace. When a union negotiates a labor contract, labor law prohibits the employer from entering into any employment contract with an individual worker or group of individual workers that contradicts the CBA.[87] The principal Supreme Court case, *J.I. Case* from 1944, determined that employers cannot enter into individual employment agreements that contradict the CBA. The court explained that a CBA is not "a contract of employment except in rare cases; no one has a job by reason of it and no obligation to any individual ordinarily comes into existence from it alone." Instead, the court analogized a CBA to "tariffs established by a carrier, to standard provisions prescribed by supervising authorities for insurance policies, or to utility schedules of rates and rules for service, which do not of themselves establish any relationship, but which do govern the terms of the shipper or insurer or customer relationship whenever and with whomever it may be established." The *J.I. Case* court recognized that if the CBA does not provide an employer can discipline only for just cause that the employer in most U.S. states remains free to hire and fire at will. Other than that, the employee is entitled to the benefits of the CBA, even if they would waive its benefits and agree to less favorable terms.

Another significant Supreme Court case, *Emporium Capwell* from 1975, extended the prohibition on entering individual employment contracts to entering into contracts with groups of individuals.[88] The case held an employer can terminate employees who seek to bargain with an employer over racially discriminatory conduct because the employees must negotiate only through the union, which was selected by a majority of employees.[89] The Supreme Court explained: "[Labor] policy therefore extinguishes the individual employee's power to order his own relations with his employer and creates a power vested in the chosen representative to act in the interests of all employees."[90]

(2) Consideration

As explained in Section 19, consideration is normally required to form a contract, and in many non-labor contexts the consideration for each party's promise to arbitrate a dispute is the other party's reciprocal promise to arbitrate that dispute. Some courts have refused in non-labor contexts to enforce agreements obligating one

---

87 J.I. Case Co. v. N.L.R.B., 321 U.S. 332 (1944).

88 Emporium Capwell Co. v. Western Addition Community Organization, 420 U.S. 50 (1975).

89 Id. at 52, 72.

90 Id. at 63.

party to pursue its claims in arbitration, while allowing the other party to pursue its claims in litigation.[91] In contrast, unions have not similarly asked courts to refuse to enforce CBAs obligating a union to pursue its claims in arbitration, while allowing the employer to pursue its claims in litigation.[92] Perhaps this is because unions generally want arbitration clauses enforced and an argument that an employer's promise to arbitrate lacks consideration was foreclosed by the Supreme Court's foundational labor arbitration case, *Textile Workers Union v. Lincoln Mills*,[93] which said the quid pro quo for the employer's agreement to arbitrate is the union's no-strike agreement. Even when a CBA does not include an express promise by the union not to strike during the CBA's term, courts imply such a promise when the CBA contains an arbitration clause.[94]

On the other hand, in cases not involving the enforceability of an agreement to arbitrate, courts have explicitly stated that consideration is not required to render a CBA enforceable.[95] Because a CBA as an attempt at self-governance is more than a contract, courts "should not be preoccupied with principles which might apply to an ordinary contract."[96] For instance in one Eighth Circuit case an individual employer signed a stipulation agreeing to be bound by an earlier-formed multi-employer CBA.[97] The employer stopped making

---

[91] § 19.

[92] Monetary judgments against a union are enforceable "only against the organization as an entity and against its assets" and not against "any individual member," similar to money judgments against a business entity that are enforceable only against the entity and not against owners and employees of the entity. Labor Management Relations Act, Section 301(b), 29 U.S.C. § 185(b). Employer damages from a union's CBA breach are likely to be low, unless the breach was of the CBA's no-strike clause, so that is the union breach most likely to be worth an employer suing a union for money. Additionally, the LMRA Section 303 specifically provides employers the ability to go to court and seek damages in litigation for unlawful strikes and boycotts, so it makes economic sense that these are the circumstances in which an employer would most likely also sue for breach of contract. 29 U.S. Code § 187; 2 Guide to Employment Law & Regulations § 17A:21 Breach of contract (July 2022 Update). While the LMRA permits employers to sue unions for CBA breaches, the LMRA did not repeal the Norris LaGuardia Act, which prohibits courts from issuing injunctions in most labor disputes. 29 U.S.C. § 101 et seq. However, the Supreme Court held that the Norris LaGuardia Act does not preclude courts from enjoining a strike in breach of a no-strike clause where the strike is over a grievance covered by the arbitration clause. Boys Mkts. v. Retail Clerks Local 770, 398 U.S. 235 (1970). So, it makes sense for an employer to sue in such a case because immediate relief is available.

[93] Lincoln Mills, 353 U.S. at 448 (1957).

[94] Local 174, Teamsters, Chauffeurs, Warehousemen and Helpers v. Lucas Flour Co., 369 U.S. 95 (1962).

[95] Greater St. Louis Construction Laborer Welfare Fund v. Hancock Demolition & Excavation Co., 2009 WL 2568049 at *8 (E.D. Mo. Aug. 18, 2009); Lumpkin v. International Harvester Co., 1986 WL 1996, at *18 (N.D. Ill. Feb. 10, 1986); Certified Corp. v. Hawaii IBT Local 996, 597 F.2d 1269, 1271 (9th Cir. 1979).

[96] Certified Corp. 597 F.2d at 1271.

[97] Darnel v. East, 573 F.2d 534, 537 (8th Cir. 1978).

payments required by the CBA, and the lower court permitted this, finding the stipulation was invalid for lack of consideration.[98] The appellate court reversed explaining that CBAs are not "ordinary contracts and are not governed by the common law concepts which govern private agreements." Agreements to be bound by a multi-employer contract are enforced "without question as to consideration."[99] In any event, the quid pro quo, which is similar to consideration in other contexts, of giving up the right to strike for labor arbitration agreements is well-established.[100]

(c) Defenses to Enforcement of Labor Arbitration Agreements

(1) Contract Defenses and the Separability Doctrine

The FAA says arbitration agreements shall be enforceable "save upon such grounds as exist at law or in equity for the revocation of any contract."[101] This savings clause permits parties challenging arbitration agreements to invoke any of contract law's defenses to enforcement, such as unconscionability, misrepresentation, duress, undue influence, mistake, impracticability, frustration of purpose, the statute of limitations, the statute of frauds, and illegality. Most of these defenses, however, are brought as to the overall contract including the arbitration agreement and are subject to the separability doctrine, and thus heard by arbitrators rather than courts.[102] In contrast, courts hear arguments that no contract containing an arbitration agreement was formed.[103]

The same distinction between contract formation issues, which are for courts to decide, and contract validity issues (defenses to enforcement), which are for arbitrators to decide, applies in labor arbitration. The courts will decide issues concerning formation of the CBA[104] but will not decide whether the overall CBA is valid. Courts

---

98 Id.

99 Id.

100 Local 174, Teamsters v. Lucas Flour Co., 369 U.S. 95, 102 (1962).

101 9 U.S.C. § 2.

102 See §§ 19–21.

103 § 21(a).

104 Granite Rock Co. v. IBT, 561 U.S. 287 (2010).

It is well settled in both commercial and labor cases that whether parties have agreed to "submi[t] a particular dispute to arbitration" is typically an " 'issue for judicial determination.' " Howsam v. Dean Witter Reynolds, Inc., 537 U.S. 79, 83, 123 S. Ct. 588, 154 L.Ed.2d 491 (2002) (quoting AT & T Technologies, Inc. v. Communications Workers, 475 U.S. 643, 649, 106 S. Ct. 1415, 89 L.Ed.2d 648 (1986)); see John Wiley & Sons, Inc. v. Livingston, 376 U.S. 543, 546–547, 84 S. Ct. 909, 11 L.Ed.2d 898 (1964). It is similarly well settled that where the dispute at issue concerns contract formation, the dispute is generally for courts to decide. See, e.g., First Options of Chicago, Inc. v. Kaplan, 514 U.S. 938, 944, 115 S. Ct. 1920, 131 L.Ed.2d 985 (1995) ("When deciding whether the parties agreed to will, thus, address issues about whether the parties entered into, or formed, an agreement to arbitrate.[105] For example, in *Granite Rock Co. v. IBT*, the Supreme Court held that a dispute that turned on when a CBA was formed—which in that case required by ratification of the CBA by the union members—should be determined by a court rather than an arbitrator. If the CBA was ratified before the strike, then the strike was subject to the arbitration clause, but if the CBA was ratified after the strike, then no agreement to arbitrate the strike was formed.[106]

In labor arbitration as well, the Supreme Court has held challenges to the issue of validity of a CBA are for the arbitrator.[107] An example of a labor case applying the separability doctrine of *Prima Paint* is *Mery Steel Works, Inc. v. Int'l Assoc. of Bridge, Structural, Ornamental & Reinforcing Iron Workers Local 580*.[108] In *Mery* a non-union building trades company, Mery, accepted a bid on project that required using union members.[109] The company signed an agreement with the union to be bound by the union's collective bargaining agreement.[110] Mery refused to make payments required by that CBA, and the union notified the company it was commencing arbitration. Mery sought to stay the arbitration because it entered the CBA due to fraud and mistake.[111] The court refused to grant a preliminary injunction staying the arbitration, citing *Prima Paint* for the proposition that "to avoid an apparent agreement to arbitrate, a petitioner must establish 'fraud in the inducement of the arbitration clause itself-an issue [that] goes to the 'making' of the agreement to arbitrate."[112]

---

arbitrate a certain matter . . . courts generally . . . should apply ordinary . . . principles that govern the formation of contracts"); AT & T Technologies, supra, at 648–649, 106 S. Ct. 1415 (explaining the settled rule in labor cases that " 'arbitration is a matter of contract' " and "arbitrators derive their authority to resolve disputes only because the parties have agreed in advance to submit such grievances to arbitration"); Buckeye Check Cashing, Inc. v. Cardegna, 546 U.S. 440, 444, n. 1, 126 S. Ct. 1204, 163 L.Ed.2d 1038 (2006) (distinguishing treatment of the generally nonarbitral question whether an arbitration agreement was "ever concluded" from the question whether a contract containing an arbitration clause was illegal when formed, which question we held to be arbitrable in certain circumstances).

Id. at 296–97 (2010).

[105] Id.

[106] Granite Rock, 561 U.S. at 303–04.

[107] Granite Rock, 561 U.S. at 301.

[108] 2007 WL 2349916 (S.D.N.Y. Aug. 16, 2007).

[109] Id. at *1.

[110] Id.

[111] Id.

[112] Id. at *3.

Similarly, in another labor case, *United Assoc. Local 26 v. Big Rooter/Nelson Plumbing*, the court held that the attacks on the CBA for fraud in the inducement and mistake must be arbitrated whereas the court addressed the defenses that the arbitration provision itself was substantively and procedurally unconscionable.[113] The court reasoned that fraud in the execution is where the party does not understand what type of agreement it is signing, such as believing a person is signing a will when actually signing a quit claim deed, which is an issue for the court to determine. On the other hand, fraud in the inducement occurs when a party misrepresents a provision of a contract, but not the type of contract. Because the employer knew it was signing a CBA, the issue of fraud in inducement, of whether the union misrepresented the terms of the deal would permit two employees not to join the union, was for the arbitrator to determine.[114] After noting that an attack on the arbitrability clause itself for fraud in the inducement would be for the court, rather than the arbitrator to decide,[115] the court moved on to address the attacks on the arbitration clause for unconscionability, presumably reasoning those were for the court to determine because they did attack the arbitrability clause itself.[116]

At least one court has held that participation in an arbitration and arguing a formation defense to the arbitrator does not waive the right to litigate the issue thereafter.[117]

While the previous paragraphs discuss labor cases applying the separability doctrine to send contract defenses to arbitrators, such cases seem to arise less frequently in the labor context, perhaps because CBAs are negotiated by union and employer representatives who are often experienced negotiators who have negotiated multiple CBAs together over the years and have a standing relationship that does not involve any type of misrepresentation, duress, unconscionability, illegality, or other generally-applicable contract defense. And if such bad behavior is detected during bargaining, the party who believes the other party is bargaining in bad faith will file a charge with the NLRB. Also, conduct that might be considered duress or undue influence—such as threats by employers to lock employees out of work and permanently replace them or by unions to go to the press about an employer's refusal to agree to certain terms—

---

113 2011 WL 130335 (W.D.Wa. Jan. 14, 2011).

114 Id. at *3.

115 Id. at *3.

116 Id. at *4.

117 Houston Refining, 765 F.3d at 396 (5th Cir. 2014) (relying on First Options, 514 U.S. 938 for proposition that "merely arguing the arbitrability issue to an arbitrator does not illustrate a clear willingness" to arbitrate a formation issue).

are expressly condoned by labor law as part of the free play of bargaining.[118]

(2) Non-Contract Defenses to Enforcement

Like contract defenses, statutory defenses will generally be for the arbitrator to determine. In *Prime Healthcare Services v. United Nurses and Allied Professionals, Local 5067*, the employer argued that ERISA preempted the union's arbitration claim.[119] The First Circuit held that "a statutory bar to or preemption of arbitration is not an issue of arbitrability—and ERISA does not bar or preempt the arbitration of this claim."[120] The First Circuit identified two categories of threshold arbitrability issues where the court, rather than the arbitrator, will decide the matter unless the parties have clearly and unmistakably committed the matter to the arbitrator.[121] One, discussed above in Section 45(c)(1), is a dispute about whether the parties are bound by an arbitration clause. The other, discussed below in Section 46, is a dispute about whether an arbitration clause that concededly applies to the parties applies to a particular type of controversy.[122] The First Circuit explained in *Prime Healthcare* that the employer had entered into an agreement to arbitrate disputes about employee retirement benefits and so the parties were bound to arbitrate, and the type of dispute was precisely that covered by the arbitration clause.[123] The court reasoned that statutory defenses, such as ERISA arguments, are suitable for arbitration except in certain cases, which are mentioned in the statute or would give rise to an inherent conflict with the goals of the statute.[124] The court reasoned that the arbitrator could determine whether or not ERISA renders the union's claims unsuitable for arbitration.[125]

§ 46 Terms of Labor Arbitration Agreements

(a) Freedom of Contract

Because the grievance process—which as explained above typically involves several steps culminating in arbitration—is contractual, the parties in good faith can agree to any reasonable

---

118 NLRB v. Mackay Radio & Tel. Co., 304 U.S. 333 (1938); Machinists Lodge 76 v. Wisconsin Employment Relations Commission, 427 U.S. 132 (1976).

119 Prime Healthcare Services v. United Nurses & Allied Professionals, Local 5067, 848 F.3d 41 (1st Cir. 2017).

120 Id. at 47.

121 Id. at 46.

122 Id.

123 Id. at 47.

124 Id. at 48.

125 Id. at 49.

process to address disputes that suits their needs.[126] The agreed-upon procedure may limit grievances to complaints that provisions of the CBA have been violated or may permit employees to raise any type of workplace complaint. Some agreements provide the names of a set number of arbitrators, for which the parties select a single arbitrator for each dispute that goes to arbitration; others provide one arbitrator will be selected through an arbitration organization; some name a permanent panel of arbitrators; sometimes each party selects an arbitrator and those two select a neutral third; and sometimes an arbitration organization selects all three. The number of day or months by which the other party must be notified of arbitration vary. Some arbitrations are simply a decision by a committee made up of people in the industry with three appointed by the union and three by a multi-employer association.[127] Some agreements provide for emergency on the spot arbitration in a situation that is an emergency safety issue where the industry arbitrator reports to the work site and makes an immediate verbal ruling on whether work should stop until the emergency is resolved.[128]

Many grievance processes resemble each other and use a stepped procedure progressively elevating a grievance to higher levels of decision makers.[129] For instance, the first step of the process may be that the employee informally brings the grievance to the attention of a supervisor. If the supervisor is unable to remedy the grievance, then the second step may require that the union shop steward file a written grievance with a manager, and that the steward and manager meet within a set short time to discuss the grievance and their interpretations of the CBA. If the manager is unable to remedy the grievance, then the third step may require that the union president and company president or director of labor relations meet. At each step, there may be an informal exchange of documents between the parties.[130] If that third step fails to resolve the grievance, then at the fourth step, the union files for arbitration. Some CBAs include time limitations at each step whereas others do not but may require prompt movement from step to step. The period in which to file at each step is often short, varying between three to

---

[126] A union is limited by the duty of fair representation it owes to its members. See Ray, supra note 31, at 350 (discussing how union must act with good faith and a legitimate purpose when negotiating a CBA).

[127] See e.g., Hines, 424 U.S. at 557, n.2; Ford Motor Co. v. Huffman, 345 U.S. 330, 337–38 (1953).

[128] See e.g., Article 17.6 Informal hearings and interim rulings, of the Pacific Coast Longshore Contract Document, July 1, 1999–July 1, 2002 between International Longshore and Warehouse Union and Pacific Maritime Association.

[129] Levinson, Labor Arbitration, supra note 16, at 824.

[130] Levinson, Labor Arbitration, supra note 16, at 824.

60 days.[131] In most instances, the union, rather than the grievant, controls the process, so the union decides whether to move the grievance to each successive step and whether to invoke arbitration.[132]

One example of a typical arbitration provision is Article 19—Grievance Procedure in the contract between Walt Disney World Co. and the Service Trades Council Unions, UNITE HERE 737 effective May 2, 2004 through April 28, 2007 at pages 26–27.

> Step 5 If the grievance shall have been submitted but not adjusted under Step 4, either party may within seven (7) calendar days after receipt of the written reply request in writing that the grievance be submitted to an Arbitrator mutually agreed upon by the Company and the Union. If agreement is reached, the arbitration must occur within thirty (30) days after the joint selection of the arbitrator. If the Company and the Union do not mutually agree upon the selection of an Arbitrator, then an Arbitrator shall be selected from a panel of seven (7) Arbitrators furnished by the Federal Mediation and Conciliation Service. Either party, at their discretion may refuse one list, which has been presented by a Federal Mediation and Conciliation Service for a pending arbitration hearing. At this point, the parties have a maximum of fourteen (14) calendar days from the date the list is received, to strike the panel. The Rules for the Federal Mediation and Conciliation Service shall govern the selection of an Arbitrator and the conduct of the arbitration hearing. The Arbitrator shall not have the authority to alter, amend, change, modify, add to or subtract from or reform any provision, Article or language of this Agreement. The Decision of the Arbitrator shall be final and binding on all parties with no further appeal, except for reasons of setting aside an Arbitrator's Award, as set forth in applicable Federal and Florida Statutes. Any joint expense incidental to or arising out of the arbitration shall be borne equally by the Company and the appropriate Union. Only one grievance shall be before a specific Arbitrator at one time.

Another example of a typical arbitration provision is Article XIV, Grievance Procedure in the contract between Riser Foods Company

---

131 See Collective Bargaining Negotiations & Contract Manual, Methods of Settling Disputes, CBNC 9:2106 (Bloomberg BNA) (noting that filing deadlines at the initial step vary from three to 60 days); CBNC 170:1302, 170:1303, 170:2302; 170:2601, 170:2602 (example clauses from CBAs where arbitration must be filed by deadlines ranging from five to 60 days).

132 Levinson, Labor Arbitration, supra note 16, at 818.

d/b/a Giant Eagle (Cleveland Clerks) and United Food and Commercial Workers Union Local No. 880, effective September 14, 2008 through September 11, 2011 at pages 53–54.

Section 2. The Union may refer a dispute or grievance which has not been resolved to arbitration on the forty-fifth (45th) day after the dispute or grievance has been submitted in writing to the Employer in Step 1, or at any time thereafter. The Union must refer a dispute or grievance to arbitration no later than thirty (30) days after the last Step 3 meeting is held.

Section 3. The arbitrator's decision shall be issued within thirty (30) days after the dispute or grievance is submitted to the arbitrator and shall be final and binding upon the Employer, the Union, and the employee or employees involved. The expenses of the arbitrator shall be borne equally by the Employer and the Union.

Section 4. The time limits specified in Section 1 above may be extended by mutual agreement but shall otherwise be enforced in that the dispute or grievance shall be decided against any employee or party failing to observe the time limits.

Section 5. In the event a grievance goes to arbitration, this Agreement, including any Supplements or Addenda, shall be the basis on which the arbitrator's decision is rendered, and in reaching his or her decision the arbitrator shall have no authority to amend, modify, or in any way change its terms.

Section 6. At any step in this grievance procedure, the Executive Board of the Local Union shall have final authority in respect to any aggrieved employees covered by this Agreement to decline to process further a grievance, complaint, disagreement or dispute if in the judgment of the Executive Board such grievance or dispute lacks merit or justification under the terms of this Agreement, or has been adjusted or rectified under the terms of this Agreement to the satisfaction of the Union Executive Board.

Section 7. In the investigation and processing of a dispute or grievance, the Union and the Employer shall upon request provide each other all relevant and pertinent records, papers, and data including the names of any and all witnesses whose testimony would have bearing on the grievance, except where a failure to follow established check-out procedure may be involved or where the security of the Union and/or the Employer would be at issue.

Some parties have longer more detailed arbitration provisions. One example is Article 11, Grievance and Arbitration in the UAW (United Automobile, Aerospace, and Agricultural Implement Workers of American International Union) AFL-CIO Student Association of Graduate Employees and UCLA, effective June 1, 2000–Sept. 30, 2003, at pages 11–13.

F. APPEAL TO ARBITRATION

An appeal to arbitration may be made only by the UAW and only after the timely exhaustion of the Grievance Procedure. The written appeal to arbitration must be received by the campus labor relations office within 45 calendar days of the date of issuance of the final University decision to the UAW. The written appeal must be signed by an authorized representative of the UAW and must include: 1. The name and address of the UAW representative who is responsible for the appeal to arbitration and to whom all correspondence relating to the arbitration is to be sent. 2. A copy of the completed grievance form; and 3. A statement setting forth the unresolved issue(s), the Articles of the Agreement alleged to have been violated, and the remedy requested. If a grievance is not appealed to arbitration, the University's Step 3 response shall be final.

G. The UAW representative shall contact the campus labor relations office within 30 calendar days of the appeal to arbitration in order to select an arbitrator from the panel set forth in Appendix B. The arbitrator shall be selected within 45 calendar days from the date of the appeal. Failure to contact the campus labor relations office within the established time frame will be considered as a withdrawal of the appeal to arbitration. 1. If the parties cannot mutually agree to an arbitrator from the panel, the parties shall alternately strike one name each from the list of panel members. Unless the parties agree otherwise, the party selecting first shall be determined by the flip of a coin. The remaining name shall be designated as the arbitrator. 2. Within 60 calendar days from selection, the parties shall attempt to agree to a hearing date, but if are unable to agree, the authority for scheduling a hearing date shall reside with the arbitrator.

H. BIFURCATION

1. The arbitration process shall be bifurcated where the University asserts that there are procedural (e.g. timeliness, standing) and/or arbitrability issues that preclude the UAW from proceeding to a hearing on the merits of the claim. 2. When practicable, the University shall inform the Union in writing of its intent to assert the issue of arbitrability prior to the selection of the arbitrator or 45 days prior to the scheduled arbitration. The issue(s) of arbitrability shall be resolved in a hearing prior to and separate from the hearing (if any) on the merits of the claim, except as provided in Section 3 below. If possible, after an arbitrator is selected, the dates for the arbitrability hearing and the hearing on the merits shall be scheduled at the same time. Unless the parties agree otherwise, the arbitrator shall issue a bench decision on the issue of arbitrability. 3. Subject to the above, a single hearing on the issue of arbitrability and the merits will be held, unless the parties agree otherwise. If the arbitrator finds the grievance to be not arbitrable, the substantive facts of the case need not be heard and the grievance shall be denied. If the arbitrator finds in favor of arbitrability, the hearing shall proceed to the substantive issues raised.

I. PROCEDURAL/EVIDENTIARY ISSUES AT HEARING

1. At least seven calendar days prior to the arbitration the parties shall exchange lists of known witnesses. 2. During the hearing the parties shall have the opportunity to examine and cross examine witnesses under oath and to submit relevant evidence. Issues and allegations shall not be introduced at the hearing unless they were introduced prior to or during Step 3 of the Grievance Procedure. 3. Upon request by either party but not upon his/her own motion, the arbitrator shall have the authority to subpoena relevant documents and/or witnesses. 4. The arbitration hearing shall be closed to anyone other than the participants in the hearing unless the parties agree otherwise in writing. 5. In all cases appealed to arbitration except for actions taken pursuant to Article 7, Discipline and Dismissal, the UAW shall have the burden of proceeding.

J. SCOPE OF ARBITRATOR'S AUTHORITY

The arbitrator shall consider the evidence presented and render a written decision within thirty (30) calendar days of the close of the record of the hearing. The arbitrator's

> decision will set forth the findings of fact, reasoning, and conclusions on issues submitted by the parties. The arbitrator's authority shall be limited to determining whether the University has violated arbitrable provisions of this contract and to ordering corresponding remedies. The arbitrator shall not have jurisdiction or authority to add to, amend, modify, nullify, or ignore in any way the provisions of this contract nor shall the arbitrator have the authority to review any academic judgment. * * * The arbitrator's fees and the costs of transcripts requested by the arbitrator or both parties shall be equally born by the parties. Costs for transcripts requested by only one party, shall be born by the requesting party. 3. The party that cancels or postpones an arbitration will be liable for any cancellation/postponement fees charged by the arbitrator or court reporter.

Another example is Article V—Adj. of Complaints and Grievances in the contract between Acme Steel Company (Riverdale Plant) and Acme Packaging Corporation (Riverdale Plant) and United Steelworkers of American (USWA), AFL-CIO-CLC, dated September 1, 1993, at pages 44–49.

> Section 10 Arbitration.
>
> There shall be a mutually agreed to permanent arbitrator who shall serve in accordance with the conditions and procedures mutually agreed upon by the parties. In the event a grievance is appealed to arbitration in accordance with the provisions of this Article for filing notice of appeal from a decision in Step 4 when there is no permanent arbitrator, the parties shall meet for the purpose of agreeing upon an arbitrator. If they are unable to reach such an agreement within ten (10) days after the written request for arbitration, the Company and the Union shall jointly request the Chicago office of the Federal Mediation and Conciliation Service to submit a list of five (5) arbitrators. If the parties are unable to agree upon one of these five (5) arbitrators, the party requesting arbitration shall first strike two (2) names, and the other party shall next strike two (2) names, and the remaining person shall be the arbitrator. The parties shall submit the grievance or grievances to be arbitrated in a written stipulation to the arbitrator. The arbitrator may consider and decide only the particular grievance or grievances presented to him in a written stipulation of the Company and the Union, and his

decision shall be based solely upon his interpretation of the provisions of this Agreement.

The arbitrator shall not have the right to amend, take away, modify, add to, or change any of the provisions of this Agreement. * * * The decision of the arbitrator shall be final and binding on the Company, the Union, and the employee or employees involved. The expense and fee of the arbitrator shall be divided equally between the Company and the Union. Settlement of grievances may or may not be retroactive as the equities of particular cases may demand, but the following limitations shall be observed by arbitrators where the arbitrator's award is retroactive. In any case where the arbitrator determines that the award should be retroactive, the retroactive date shall be as follows: * * *

Section 11 Suspension and Discharge Cases. The purpose of this Section is to provide for the disposition of complaints and grievances involving suspensions or discharges and to establish a special procedure for the prompt review of all cases involving discharge or suspension of more than four (4) calendar days. Complaints concerning suspensions of four (4) calendar days or less shall be handled in accordance with the procedures set forth in Sections 4 and 10 of this Article. Grievances concerning suspensions of five (5) calendar days or more and discharges shall be handled in accordance with the procedures set forth below, including the procedures set forth in Sections 4 and 10 of this Article.

* * *

(C) Jurisdiction of the Arbitrator.

Should it be determined by the arbitrator that an employee has been suspended or discharged without proper cause therefor, the Company shall reinstate the employee and make him whole for the period of his suspension or discharge, which shall include providing him such earnings and other benefits as he would have received except for such suspension or discharge, and offsetting such earnings or other amounts as he would not have received except for such suspension or discharge. Should it be determined by the arbitrator that an employee has been suspended or discharged for proper cause therefor, the arbitrator shall not have jurisdiction to modify the degree of discipline imposed by the Company; provided, however, that in a discharge case, the arbitrator shall have discretion, if he finds that the Company has proper cause for discipline, but does not have proper cause for discharge, to modify the penalty; provided, further, that in case the arbitrator modified the discipline, the arbitrator shall have discretion to reduce or not require the Company to pay the compensation provided in Section 10, Subparagraph (A) above, if, in his judgment, the facts warrant such an award. The provisions of Section 11 (C) apply to all suspensions regardless of the number of days involved. In suspension and discharge cases only, the arbitrator may, where circumstances warrant, modify or eliminate the offset of such earnings or other amounts as would not have been received except for such suspension or discharge.

* * *

(b) Scope of Labor Arbitration Agreements

(1) Court Determines Scope Unless Agreement Clearly Says Arbitrator Does

As Section 26(a) explains, "the question whether the parties have submitted a particular dispute to arbitration," is one of two common meanings of "arbitrability." Because labor arbitration is contractual, the issue is focused on whether the dispute is covered by the CBA and falls within the coverage or "scope" of the arbitration provision. Courts, following the premise of the *Steelworkers Trilogy*, presumptively decide questions of arbitrability, while leaving questions about contractual preconditions discussed in § 30—sometimes termed "procedural arbitrability"—to the arbitrator.[133] Thus, the arbitrator, rather than the courts, generally decides whether an arbitration is barred by the failure to comply with grievance time limits or other procedural requirements in the grievance-arbitration process.[134]

As Section 26(b) explains, the Supreme Court holds that the FAA presumptively sends disputes about an arbitration agreement's scope to courts, rather than to arbitrators, and this rule applies to

---

[133] John Wiley & Sons v. Livingston, 376 U.S. 543, 546–47 (1964); Oil, Chem. & Atomic Workers Local 4-447 v. Chevron Chem. Co., 815 F.2d 338, 340 (5th Cir. 1987). Some parties contract for the arbitrator to decide questions of substantive as well as procedural arbitrability. To do so requires a clear and unmistakable waiver of the right to go to a court to determine substantive arbitrability. The Common Law of the Workplace: The Views of Arbitrators, § 2.23, at 94–95 (2d ed. 2005).

[134] Elkouri, supra note 9, § 6.2.B; John Wiley & Sons v. Livingston, 376 U.S. 543, 557 (1964) (whether preliminary steps of grievance process were exhausted); Oil, Chem. & Atomic Workers Local 4-447 v. Chevron Chem. Co., 815 F.2d 338, 340 (5th Cir. 1987) (whether grievance timelines were met).

labor arbitration as well.[135] As Section 26(b) further explains, this rule that courts, rather than arbitrators, resolve disputes about the scope of arbitration agreements is merely a default rule, because parties can contract around this rule if they do so "clearly and unmistakably."[136] One Fifth Circuit case found that parties had not done so clearly and unmistakably.[137] The D.C. Circuit has recognized that disputes over the process to select the arbitrator can be subject to a clear and unmistakable delegation to the arbitrator.[138] Additionally, one court has held that when a party participates in an arbitration, they waive the right to pursue substantive arbitrability issues in litigation.[139]

Because of the strong presumption of arbitrability, discussed in the next section, the courts should not classify disputes over the meaning of the other provisions of the CBA as issues of substantive arbitrability to be decided by the courts. As to an issue that is about substantive arbitrability rather than the merits of the dispute, the parties can contract around this rule by using an arbitration agreement that clearly and unmistakably states such disputes shall be resolved by the arbitrator rather than the court.[140]

---

[135] First Options of Chicago, Inc. v. Kaplan, 514 U.S. 938, 943 (1995) (arbitration is "a matter of contract between the parties; it is a way to resolve those disputes—but only those disputes—that the parties have agreed to submit to arbitration."). See also Howsam v. Dean Witter Reynolds, Inc., 537 U.S. 79, 83 (2002) ("the question whether the parties have submitted a particular dispute to arbitration, i.e., the 'question of arbitrability,' is an issue for judicial determination unless the parties clearly and unmistakably provide otherwise. * * * Similarly, a disagreement about whether an arbitration clause in a concededly binding contract applies to a particular type of controversy is for the court.")

[136] Howsam v. Dean Witter Reynolds, Inc., 537 U.S. 79, 83 (2002) ("the question whether the parties have submitted a particular dispute to arbitration, i.e., the 'question of arbitrability,' is an issue for judicial determination unless the parties clearly and unmistakably provide otherwise.") See also First Options of Chicago, Inc. v. Kaplan, 514 U.S. 938, 946–47 (1995); AT & T Technologies, Inc. v. Communications Workers of Am., 475 U.S. 643 (1986) .

[137] Houston Refining v. Steelworkers, 765 F.3d 396, 408 (5th Cir. 2014) ("[L]ike any other disputed issue, even the gateway question of arbitrability can be given to an arbitrator . . . [b]ut the party contending that an arbitrator has authority to decide arbitrability 'bears the burden of demonstrating clearly and unmistakably that the parties agreed to have the arbitrator decide . . .' ").

[138] Pacific Coast District 1, Marine Engineers' Beneficial Assoc. v. Liberty Maritime Corp., 998 F.3d 449, 460 (D.C. Cir. 2019) ("While we thus decide that the gateway issue of whether the arbitrator was appointed by mutual agreement is a 'question of arbitrability' that means that the issue is only presumptively for a court to resolve. The presumption is overcome if parties clearly and unmistakably assign a question of arbitrability to the arbitrator.")

[139] See Cleveland Elec. Illuminating Co. v. Utility Workers, 440 F.3d 809 (6th Cir. 2006).

[140] AT & T Technologies, Inc. v. Communications Workers of Am., 475 U.S. 643 (1986).

(2) *Courts Generally Interpret Labor Arbitration Agreements Broadly*

The second case in the Steelworkers Trilogy, *United Steelworkers of America v. Warrior & Gulf Nav. Co.,*[141] explicitly established a presumption of arbitrability. The union filed a grievance because the employer subcontracted out unit work. The arbitration clause included disputes about the meaning and application of the CBA and about "local trouble of any kind." It excluded matters which are "strictly a function of management." Citing the exclusion, the employer refused to arbitrate the subcontracting grievance. The Supreme Court held that whether subcontracting was a management function was for the arbitrator, and not the courts, to decide. The language of the CBA excluding management functions from arbitration was unclear and created ambiguity better resolved by the arbitrator. Under the presumption of arbitrability, only in the narrowest of circumstances, when there is "forceful evidence" of excluding the particular type of dispute from the arbitration clause, should a court refrain from enforcing a labor arbitration agreement. Otherwise, courts would become involved in labor cases, creating inefficiency and removing the cases from the expertise provided by the parties' mutually selected arbitrator. Thus, courts must compel arbitration "unless it may be said with positive assurance that the arbitration clause is not susceptible of an interpretation that covers the asserted dispute."

The first case in the trilogy similarly established that courts will not address the merits of a dispute even if an employer believes that arbitration is clearly not warranted based on agreements separate from the collective bargaining agreement or impossible given the physical reality of complying with the union's interpretation of the CBA. In *United Steelworkers of America v. American Mfg. Co.,*[142] a disabled employee attempted to return to work, and the employer refused to permit it. The CBA contained a no-strike clause and an arbitration provision. The union argued that under a seniority provision in the CBA the grievant should be returned to work and sought arbitration. The employer argued that the claim was frivolous because the employer could not return the grievant to work. The employer asserted the grievant was unable to physically perform his job and had entered a workers' compensation settlement agreeing he was permanently partially disabled. The Court determined that even where a grievance is frivolous it must be determined in the first instance by the arbitrator. The Court emphasized that the role of a court is simply to ascertain whether "the party seeking arbitration is

---

141 363 U.S. 574 (1960).

142 363 U.S. 564 (1960).

making a claim which on its face is governed by the contract." Questions of contract interpretation are for the arbitrator, and the court should not usurp the arbitrator's role by "weighing the merits of the grievance, considering whether there is equity in a particular claim, or determining whether there is particular language [in the contract to] support the claim." The Court reasoned that the union had agreed not to strike so the employer's return promise to arbitrate disputes must be honored. The Court recognized that "processing of even frivolous claims may have therapeutic value of which those who are not part of the [work] environment may be quite unaware."[143] Finally, the Court reasoned that the courts should not remove the case from the bargained for decision maker—the arbitrator.

The agreed upon procedure may limit grievances to complaints that provisions of the CBA have been violated or may permit the union, or employees, to raise any type of workplace complaint. CBAs often include provisions setting wage scales, providing benefits, providing just cause for discipline, promoting safety and health, prohibiting discrimination, providing for dues check-off, explaining how seniority is measured, governing lay-offs, and addressing the use of technology, among others.

(3) Temporal Scope of Labor Arbitration Agreements

While non-labor arbitration agreements are often written broadly to cover all disputes arising out of a transaction whenever they arise, labor arbitration agreements often cover only grievances arising during the term of the CBA. After the CBA expires, labor law requires the employer to keep in place all CBA terms and conditions of employment, with few exceptions, until it has reached a good faith agreement with the union or they have reached impasse, upon which the employer can unilaterally implement the terms and conditions contained in its last best CBA offer.[144] Typically, an expired CBA is extended by agreement of the parties or replaced with a new contract that largely mirrors the old with only some added provisions, deleted provisions, or changes to certain provisions, such as increases to the wage scale. Many CBAs in the private sector are for a term of three years because the NLRB provides for a contract bar of three years duration or less during which a union typically cannot be de-certified

[143] 363 U.S. at 568.

[144] NLRB v. Katz, 369 U.S. 736, 743 (1962) ("We hold that an employer's unilateral change in conditions of employment under negotiation is similarly a violation of Section 8(a)(5), for it is a circumvention of the duty to negotiate which frustrates the objectives of Section 8(a)(5) much as does a flat refusal."); Wilkes-Barre Hospital Co. v. NLRB, 857 F.3d 364, 373 (D.C. Cir. 2017) ("This 'unilateral change doctrine' extends to cases " 'where, as here, an existing agreement has expired and negotiations on a new one have yet to be completed.' ")

and another union cannot petition to represent the employees.[145] The purpose of the contract bar is to promote stable employment relationships and predictable terms and conditions of employment.[146]

Sometimes parties disagree over whether the conduct underlying the dispute arose during the term of the CBA. The courts will compel arbitration even when the specific dispute arose after expiration of the agreement if the decision requires interpretation of the CBA.[147] For instance, when a union sought arbitration over an employer's failure to pay severance and argued the severance pay accrued to the workers while working under the CBA, the Supreme Court compelled arbitration.[148] But if a dispute arises after the CBA expired and does not involve conduct arising before the CBA expiration, then the CBA does not arguably govern the dispute, and the dispute is not arbitrable.[149]

In a 2017 unpublished opinion[150] the Eastern District of Virginia court held it had authority to issue a declaratory judgment that the CBA had expired rather than send the dispute to arbitration for a determination.[151] The court explained that it must first decide who decides whether a particular dispute is arbitrable, the arbitrator or the court. Then, when the court should decide, the court should determine whether the particular dispute is arbitrable.[152] The parties agreed, in this instance, the court should determine whether the dispute was arbitrable. The court noted that the parties had not clearly and unmistakably waived the right to have the court determine the arbitrability question.[153] The court held the dispute was not subject to arbitration because the CBA provision was clear as to the date upon which the CBA could expire.[154] The court held

---

145 1 Labor and Employment Law § 12.04 [3][b][iv][D] (Matthew Bender & Co. 2022).

146 See id. [d][c][ii].

147 See District No. 1, Pacific Coast District, 815 F.3d 834 (delegating to arbitrator decision of whether parties reached impasse thereby causing expiration of CBA by its terms); but see AECOM Special Mission Services, Inc. v. Operating Engineers, Local No. 99, 2017 BL 53904 (E.D. V. Feb. 21, 2017) (determination of whether employer withdrew from CBA for the courts).

148 Nolde Bros. v. Bakery & Confectionery Workers Local 358, 430 U.S. 243, 255 (1977).

149 Litton Financial Printing Division, 501 U.S. 190, 206 (1991).

150 AECOM Special Mission Services, Inc. v. Operating Engineers, Local No. 99, 2017 BL 53904, 2017 WL 710055 (E.D.V. Feb. 21, 2017); see also Culinary Workers Joint Exec. Board v. Mirage Casino-Hotel, Inc., 911 F.3d 588 (9th Cir. 2018).

151 AECOM, 2017 WL 7110055 at *1.

152 Id. at *3.

153 Id. at *3 n.1.

154 Id. at *5.

that the employer had not agreed to submit issues regarding the duration and expiration of the CBA to arbitration.[155]

While grievance arbitration describes the bulk of labor arbitration, interest arbitration is also used by unions and employers.[156] Interest arbitration is a process where the arbitrator determines what the provisions of a CBA are, rather than how the provisions should be interpreted or applied. The parties agree that if they reach an impasse when negotiating for a CBA, they will arbitrate rather than striking or locking out, and the arbitrator will settle the terms of the CBA. An interest arbitrator may be required to pick one party's final offer, may have authority to pick any offer that represents a compromise between the two parties' position, or may have authority to craft any sensible resolution for the parties.[157] Interest arbitrators are most often used to settle wage provisions of the CBA, but may settle any term of a CBA, ranging from leave policies, seniority rules, subcontracting restrictions, or discipline policies.[158]

Interest arbitration is often used in the public sector because many public sector employees are forbidden from striking.[159] Statutes may provide for interest arbitration in lieu of a strike or lock-out if the parties reach impasse, or the parties may voluntarily agree to use interest arbitration.[160] Statutes may also provide principles which the arbitrator should use to determine the provisions of the CBA.[161] Many statutes provide that the parties must mediate and engage in a fact-finding process before invoking arbitration.[162] In a minority of states, interest arbitration has been held unconstitutional as a delegation of the legislature's authority to private citizens.[163]

Interest arbitration is used less often in the private sector.[164] A common example of interest arbitration in the private sector is

---

155 Id. at *6.

156 Dennis R. Nolan & Richard A. Bales, Labor and Employment Arbitration, at 70 (Thomson West 2017).

157 Cf. Martin H. Malin, Ann C. Hodges & Joseph E. Slater, & Jeffrey M. Hirsch, Public Sector Employment Cases and Materials, at 804 (3d ed. Thomson West 2016)(mentioning traditional interest arbitration, final offer issue-by-issue arbitration, and final offer package arbitration).

158 Elkouri, supra note 9, at § 22.1.

159 Elkouri, supra note 9, at § 22.4; Nolan, supra note 156, at 76.

160 Elkouri, supra note 9, at § 22.4.

161 Elkouri, supra note 9, at § 22.5.C; Nolan, supra note 156, at 77.

162 Elkouri, supra note 9, at § 22.5.B. Fact-finding is a process where the parties present evidence to a neutral factfinder who issues a report. The government employer and the union can then elect to adopt, or refuse to adopt, the report.

163 Elkouri, supra note 9, § 22.6 Malin, supra note 157, at 805.

164 Nolan, supra note 156, at 71, 75.

baseball arbitration.[165] In baseball, the CBA sets minimum salaries.[166] Particular salaries are negotiated between a team and a player's agent.[167] If the team and player cannot agree on the salary, they invoke arbitration.[168] Baseball arbitration is, thus, a somewhat unique form of interest arbitration because the salaries of each player are set forth in an individual contract that supplements the terms of the CBA.[169] Each party presents the arbitrator with its final offer and material supporting that offer.[170] The arbitrator then selects one party's salary offer as the one the player will receive.[171]

Interest arbitration is sometimes agreed upon by other private sector parties as a method to settle disputes arising in negotiating an initial or subsequent collective bargaining agreement.[172] For example, an agreement between IBEW and San Diego Gas and Electric provided that if the parties were unable to settle on amendments to the CBA after its termination, then the dispute would be submitted to an arbitration board.[173] In another instance, the UAW negotiated a letter agreement, with an employer regarding a plant they were organizing and other unorganized plants, that provided for interest arbitration of unresolved issues if the parties remained in negotiations beyond a certain time period.[174] More often, however, parties agree after reaching impasse to submit certain determinations to an interest arbitrator.[175] Private sector employers governed by the NLRA and the unions representing their employees have an obligation under the NLRA to bargain in good faith.[176] Interest arbitration is enforceable under Section 301, and courts

---

165 Nolan, supra note 156, at 92–93; Barry Winograd, An Introduction to the History of Interest Arbitration in the United States, 61 Lab. Law J. 11230499 (C.C.H.) 164, 165 (2010).

166 Nolan, supra note 156, at 94.

167 Nolan, supra note 156, at 94.

168 Frederick N. Donegan, Examining the Role of Arbitration in Professional Baseball, 1 Sports Law J. 183, 191 (1994).

169 Benjamin A. Tulis, Final-Offer "Baseball" Arbitration: Contexts, Mechanics & Applications, 20 Seton Hall J. Sports & Ent. L. 85, 87 (2010) (describing baseball arbitration as a unique form of interest arbitration because it sets the terms of an individual contract rather than a CBA).

170 Nolan, supra note 156, at 95.

171 Nolan, supra note 156, at 95; Donegan, supra note 168, at 191.

172 Theodore J. St. Antoine, Charles B. Craver, & Marion G. Crain, Labor Relations Law: Cases and Materials, 590 (12th ed. 2011) (discussing Steelworkers CBA in 1970's that required interest arbitration).

173 Elkouri, supra note 9, at § 22.2.A & n.64.

174 Dana Corp., 356 NLRB 256, 257 (2010).

175 Elkouri, supra note 9, at § 22.2.A

176 NLRA Section 8(a)(5) & (b)(3) & (d).

review interest arbitration under the same highly deferential standards used in grievance arbitration award enforcement.[177]

When a statute or the parties do not specify criteria for the interest arbitrator to follow, the arbitrator has wide discretion. Parties should present the arbitrators with the data necessary to explain their position and influence the arbitrator to rule in their favor. Often the parties present evidence in written form via exhibit books that contain pertinent data, with limited or no testimony from witnesses.[178] Arbitrators may consider what, in their opinion, the parties would have agreed to and what would be reasonable and fair to the employees and the employer.[179] They will offer a workable solution that can be effectively implemented by the parties.[180] They may tend to take a more conservative approach and implement less than a party seeks reasoning that incremental change is best when the parties are faced with a new practice or process.[181] Arbitrators, however, do use recognizable standards in making their determinations.[182] In wage disputes, for instance, arbitrators compare the wages to those of other similarly situated employees, consider the employer's ability to pay, and factor in the cost-of-living and inflation.[183]

Reform proposals such as the Employee Free Choice Act have contemplated revising the NLRA to require interest arbitration in all first contract situations. Interest arbitration is more widely used in other countries, such as Canada.[184]

(4) Parallel Contract and Statutory Claims

(A) Narrow Arbitration Agreements Covering Only Contract Claims

While non-labor arbitration agreements typically cover all claims whether arising out of contract, tort, statute, or other area of law, labor arbitration agreements traditionally cover only claims arising out of contract—breach of the CBA.

Where a CBA requires arbitration only of contractual, not statutory, claims an employee may have—arising out of the same conduct—both a contractual grievance in arbitration and a statutory

---

[177] Elkouri, supra note 9, at § 22.2.A.

[178] Malin, supra note 157, at 803.

[179] Elkouri, supra note 9, at § 22.3; Nolan, supra note 156, at 81.

[180] Elkouri, supra note 9, at § 22.3

[181] Malin, supra note 157, at 816.

[182] Elkouri, supra note 9, at § 22.7; Malin, supra note 157, at 816.

[183] Elkouri, supra note 9, at § 22.7.

[184] St. Antoine, Craver, supra note 172, at 591.

claim in litigation.[185] For example, if a CBA contains a no-discrimination clause that prohibits discrimination based on sex, and an employee is denied a promotion because of her sex, then she can file a grievance, and the union can pursue the claim that she was discriminated against in violation of the no-discrimination clause to arbitration if the union and the employer are unable to resolve the grievance at lower levels of the process. The employee can also file a charge with the EEOC and hire counsel to pursue her claim for a violation of Title VII of the Civil Rights Act, which prohibits employment discrimination because of sex, in litigation.

These parallel proceedings perhaps involve some redundancy but follow from the narrow scope of the arbitration agreement and the same substantive prohibition against sex discrimination in both the contract and the statute. Moreover, as the Supreme Court emphasized in a 1974 case denying preclusive effect to an arbitration award, *Alexander v. Gardner-Denver Co.*,[186] labor arbitration processes were not suited to deciding discrimination claims, and unions, which rely on majoritarian decision-making and processes, cannot adequately protect statutory rights of minorities. Additionally, at that time, labor arbitrators were experts in interpreting CBAs but not statutory law. The Court also emphasized that labor arbitration is a substitute for industrial strife, and not for litigation.[187]

In allowing the employee's statutory case to proceed in court despite the arbitrator's ruling against the employee, *Gardner Denver* explained that the trial court could consider a labor-arbitration award for the weight it was worth in the discrimination case.[188] The Court set out relevant factors trial courts could consider including whether the CBA provisions conform to the statutory ones, whether the arbitration forum was procedurally fair, whether the record adequately addressed the statutory claim, and the "special competence of particular arbitrators." The Court permitted lower courts, in their discretion, to accord the labor arbitration award great weight but urged the lower courts to be mindful of Congress's decision to "provide a judicial forum for the ultimate resolution of discriminatory employment claims." Some trial courts will consider the labor award and the opinion's reasoning, and some will give an

[185] See e.g., St Aubin v. Unilever HPC NA, 2009 WL 1871679, at *2–4 (N.D. Ill. June 26, 2009) (permitting plaintiff who lost related claim in arbitration to pursue FMLA claim in court).

[186] 415 U.S. 36 (1974).

[187] Gardner-Denver, 415 U.S. at 54–55.

[188] Gardner-Denver, 415 U.S. at 60 n.21.

award no weight. A minority determine the weight of the prior award is such that it should be given claim preclusive effect.[189]

(B) Broader Labor Arbitration Agreements Covering Statutory Claims

One of the most important labor arbitration developments of recent decades is the expansion of some labor arbitration agreements to cover statutory claims and courts' increasing willingness to enforce those broader agreements.[190] In contrast to the traditional narrow labor arbitration agreement covering only contractual grievances, the CBA in *14 Penn Plaza v. Pyett*,[191] named statutes, such as Title VII and the ADEA, and stated that "[a]ll such claims shall be subject to the grievance and arbitration procedures * * * as the sole and exclusive remedy for violations."[192] The Supreme Court enforced this agreement, and reversed lower court orders denying the employer's motion to compel arbitration of the employees' statutory claims.

The Supreme Court held that a CBA's clear and unmistakable waiver of the right to litigate requires a union-represented employee to arbitrate statutory anti-discrimination claims.[193] The Court explained that arbitration agreements concerning employment claims are within the realm of workplace terms and conditions over which unions have bargaining power.[194] The Court addressed concerns about the majoritarian union processes by noting that anti-discrimination statutes and the duty of fair representation deter

---

189 See Martin H. Malin, Revisiting the Meltzer-Howlett Debate on External Public Law in Labor Arbitration: Is it Time for Courts to Declare Howlett the Winner?, 24 Lab. Law 1, 20 (2008) (suggesting that some courts rely on arbitration awards rather than providing de novo review of statutory claims); Courtney Lamont Phelps, Lifting Gardner-Denver Footnote 21: The Heavy Burden to Give "Appropriate Weight" to Arbitration Decisions on Subsequent Judicial Review (2011) (unpublished student independent study paper) (on file with author) (outlining various ways courts have treated arbitration awards in employment discrimination cases).

190 See e.g. Darrington v. Milton Hershey School, 958 F.3d 188 (3d Cir. 2020) (compelling arbitration under CBA's clear and unmistakable waiver of discrimination claims); Savant v. APM Terminals, 776 F.3d 285, 291 (5th Cir. 2014) (court held that while CBA's arbitration clause did not waive judicial forum a separate memorandum of understanding covering ADEA claims did); Hamzaraj v. ABM Janitorial Northeast Inc., No. 15 Civ. 2030, 2016 WL 3571387, at *5 (S.D.N.Y. June 27, 2016) (compelling arbitration when CBA provided a means for plaintiff to pursue claims in arbitration independent of the union); Bouras v. Good Hope Mgmt. Corp., No. 11 Civ. 8708, 2012 WL 3055864, at *4 (S.D.N.Y. July 24, 2012) (dismissing suit when union refused to represent plaintiff in arbitration); Acevedo v. Tishman Speyer Props. L.P., No. 12 Civ. 1624, 2013 WL 1234953, at *3 (S.D.N.Y. Mar. 26, 2013) (compelling arbitration because CBA waived judicial remedy despite ADEA's "Right of Action" provision.)

191 556 U.S. 247 (2009).

192 Id. at 252.

193 Id. at 251. For a discussion that sets labor arbitration in the context of the jurisprudential change from permitting only arbitration of contract claims to also permitting arbitration of statutory claims see §§ 27 and 28(a).

194 Id. at 255–56.

unions from unfairly treating minorities and that collective strength is the central premise of labor law.[195] The Court interpreted *Gardner-Denver* as addressing only contractual claims[196] and explained that the negative view of arbitration portrayed by *Gardner-Denver* is outmoded.[197] The Court's current view is that many arbitrators address complex statutory issues and have the skills and expertise necessary to decide statutory discrimination issues.[198] The Court also views arbitration as a more efficient alternative for resolving employment disputes than litigation.[199]

(C) Broad Versus Narrow Contract Language

In *Pyett*, the Court stated several times that the CBA included a clear and unmistakable waiver,[200] but did not discuss the requisites for a clear and unmistakable waiver.[201] The Court had previously explained that inclusion of a general arbitration clause wherein the parties agree to arbitrate disputed matters does not preclude an employee from litigating statutory claims, particularly when the CBA contains no explicit incorporation of antidiscrimination standards.[202] Since the *Pyett* decision, courts have reaffirmed that a general provision providing for arbitration of contract disputes and a general no-discrimination clause forbidding discrimination on listed grounds, such as race or gender, does not constitute a clear and unmistakable waiver.[203]

---

[195] Id. at 261, 270–72.

[196] Id. at 262.

[197] Id. at 265.

[198] Id. at 268–69.

[199] Id. at 269.

[200] Id. at 259 (stating that the CBA explicitly stated the agreement to arbitrate statutory claims), at 260 (stating the CBA clearly and unmistakably required arbitration of the age discrimination claims at issue in the case).

[201] Mark S. Mathison & Bryan M. Seiler, What 14 Penn Plaza LLC v. Pyett Means for Employers: Balancing Interests in a Landscape of Uncertainty, 25 ABA J. Lab. & Emp. L. 173, 181 (2010) (noting Pyett provides "no additional guidance" on what constitutes a clear and unmistakable waiver because the Court "refused to consider the arguments . . . that the CBA did not clearly and unmistakably require arbitration . . .").

[202] Wright v. Universal Maritime Serv. Corp., 525 U.S. 70, 80–81 (1998).

[203] Amalgamated Transit Union v. New Orleans Reg'l Transit Auth., No. 21-1790, 2022 WL 1238608, at *5 (E.D. La. Apr. 27, 2022) (provision stating "all claims are subject to mandatory grievance procedures and arbitration" does not constitute clear and unmistakable waiver for statutory claims); Mansaray v. Kraus Sec. Sys., No. 20-CV-1415, 2021 WL 183275, at *3 (S.D.N.Y. Jan. 19, 2021) (clauses requiring use of grievance arbitration for disputes over "interpretation or application" of the CBA and requiring employers to comply with state and federal antidiscrimination statutes too general to constitute a waiver of a judicial forum.); Jordan-Rowell v. Fairway Supermarket, No. 18 cv01938, 2019 WL 570709, at *10 (S.D.N.Y. Jan. 16, 2019) (general arbitration clause in CBA did not constitute a clear and unmistakable waiver); Kovac v. Superior Dairy, Inc., 930 F. Supp. 2d 857 (N.D. Ohio 2013); Harrell v. Kellogg Co., 892 F. Supp. 2d 716 (E.D. Pa. 2012); see Wawock v. CSI Elec.

Courts have enumerated two circumstances in which a clear and unmistakable waiver will be found.[204] First, a CBA clearly and unmistakably waives the right to litigate a statutory claim when the CBA explicitly incorporates the statutory claim into the CBA.[205] For instance, the Fifth Circuit found that a CBA clearly and unmistakably waived an employee's right to go to court with a Rehabilitation Act claim, but not a Family Medical Leave Act (FMLA) claim.[206] The CBA defined a grievance as "a dispute, difference, disagreement or complaint between the parties related to wages, hours, and conditions of employment.[207] The grievance/arbitration provision stated a grievance includes "but is not limited to," one involving "interpretation, application of, or compliance with" the CBA.[208] The CBA incorporated an employee handbook that provided policies for compliance with the FMLA.[209] The Court reasoned those policies did not "purport to make the FMLA a part of the agreement" and were insufficient to create a clear and unmistakable waiver.[210] On the other hand, the Court ruled that the

---

Contractors, Inc., No. 14-56810, 649 Fed.Appx. 556 (9th Cir. April 6, 2016) (requiring arbitration of "all grievances or questions in dispute" does not constitute a clear and unmistakable waiver of a claim for violation of state wage statutes); Manning v. Boston Medical Center, 725 F.3d 34, 53 (1st Cir. 2013) ("broadly-worded arbitration clause" does not constitute clear and unmistakable waiver of FLSA claim); Quintanilla v. Suffolk Paving Corp., No. CV 09-5331, 2011 WL 1323033, at *5 (E.D.N.Y. Feb. 10, 2011) (general arbitration clause concerning "interpretation, application, performance, or alleged breach" of CBA did not clearly and unmistakably waive right to bring wage and hour suit under FLSA and state labor law); Sinley v. Safety Controls Tech., Inc., No. 109065, 2020 WL 4700641, at *5 (Ct. App. Aug. 13, 2020) (language stating 'any employment-related law or statute" is not clear and unmistakable because it does not mention the specific statute at issue); See also Holladay v. Rockwell Collins, Inc., No. 3:17-CV-00078, 2018 WL 7351693, at *4 (S.D. Iowa Apr. 11, 2018) (CBA that waived right to litigate discrimination claims did not require arbitration of FMLA claims); Alfonso v. Maggies Paratransit Corp., 203 F. Supp.3d 244, 249–50 (E.D.N.Y. 2016) (holding that a provision which allowed the union the sole discretion of whether to arbitrate claims does not constitute a substantive waiver exception under *Pyett*.).

204 Lawrence v. Sol G. Atlas Realty Co., 841 F.3d 81, 84 (2d Cir. 2016); Carson v. Giant Food, Inc., 175 F.3d 325, 331 (4th Cir. 1999).

205 Abdullayeva v. Attending Homecare Services LLC, 928 F.3d 218, 224–25 (2d Cir. 2019); Gilbert v. Donahoe, 751 F.3d 303, 310 (5th Cir. 2014); Montgomery v. Compass Airlines, LLC, 98 F. Supp. 3d 1012, 1029 (D. Minn. 2015); Ibarra v. United Parcel Service, 695 F.3d 354, 359–60 (5th Cir. 2012); Quint v. A.E. Staley Mfg. Co., 172 F.3d 1, 9 (1st Cir. 1999). Cf. Cloutier v. GoJet Airlines, LLC, 996 F.3d 426, 439 (7th Cir. 2021) (specific statutory claims must be specified as encompassed by arbitration provision rather than simply mentioned elsewhere in the CBA); Manning v. Boston Medical Center Corp., 725 F.3d 34, 52 (1st Cir. 2013) ("something closer to specific enumeration of the statutory claims to be arbitrated is required" to constitute clear and unmistakable waiver).

206 Gilbert, 751 F.3d at 310.

207 Id.

208 Id.

209 Id.

210 Id.

CBA incorporated the Rehabilitation Act.[211] The CBA stated, "consistent with the other provisions of this Agreement, there shall be no unlawful discrimination against handicapped employees, as prohibited by the Rehabilitation Act."[212]

Second, a CBA clear and unmistakably waives the right to litigate a statutory claim when the CBA includes an arbitration clause that explicitly refers to arbitration as the sole forum for deciding statutory claims.[213] For example, the language "the 'grievance and arbitration provisions of this [CBA] shall be the sole and exclusive remedy for any employee who believes that he or she had been subjected to illegal discrimination in violation of applicable law and/or this [CBA]' constitutes a clear and unmistakable waiver of a court claim under Title VII."[214]

Some questions regarding labor arbitration of discrimination claims remain post-*Pyett*. Generally, when a union and an employer reach an impasse in CBA negotiations, the employer is free to implement its last final offer.[215] If an employer includes a clear and unmistakable waiver in its contract proposal, the employer may

---

211 Id.

212 Id.; but see Restea v. Brown Harris Stevens LLC, No. 17 Civ. 4801, 2018 WL 1449183, at *5 (S.D.N.Y. Mar. 23, 2018) (holding arbitration clause applying to "interpretation, application or performance" of the CBA when clause mentioned Title VII clearly and unmistakably waived the right to a judicial forum").

213 Nelson v. City of Live Oak, 2011 WL 5006472 (M.D.Fla. 2011); but see Coleman v. S. Wine & Spirits of Cal., Inc., 2011 WL 3359743 at *1 (N.D. Cal. Aug. 2, 2011) (holding provision broad enough to require arbitration of discrimination claim when it simply states "disputes and grievances arising hereunder involving interpretation of application of the terms of this Agreement, including any statutory or common law claims of sex, race, age, disability or other prohibited discrimination, shall be settled *** by final and binding arbitration").

214 Nelson, at *1–2. See also, Darrington v. Milton Hershey Sch., 958 F.3d 188, 195 (3d Cir. 2020) ("the Union *** on behalf of the allegedly aggrieved, waive any right to institute or maintain any private lawsuit alleging employment discrimination in any state or federal court ***"); Maldonado v. SecTek, Inc., 2019 WL 3759451, at *7 (E.D. Pa. Aug. 8, 2019) (Any claim *** the Company has breached any federal, state, or local civil rights law, shall be resolved exclusively pursuant to binding arbitration); NBCUniversal Media, LLC v. Pickett, 2017 WL 4708019, at *2 (C.D. Cal. July 19, 2017), affd, 747 F. Appx. 644 (9th Circ. 2019) (The dispute resolution process "set forth in the CBA 'shall provide *the sole and exclusive procedure* for resolution of such claims, and neither the Union nor any aggrieved employee may file an action or complaint in court on any claim that arises under Section 2.1, having expressly waived the right to so file.'"). Cf. Thompson v. Air Transp. Int'l L.L.C., 664 F.3d 723, 726–27 (8th Cir. 2011) (holding that despite arbitration clause including language that employees waive "each and every cause of action *** provided under these statutes," an FMLA claim was not waived because a different clause specified that FMLA governs FMLA claims); Bradley v. Compass Airlines, LLC, No. 12-cv-2471 2013 WL 2443848, at *5 (D. Minn. June 5, 2013) (holding that because CBA mentioned no federal or state laws, it did not clearly an unmistakably waive the employee's right to a judicial forum for a state race discrimination claim).

215 Ray, supra note 15, at 175 ("[U]nilateral changes after impasse that implement proposal consistent with final offers made to the union do not violate Section 8(a)(5))."

argue for implementation of the waiver post-impasse, as part of the last final offer. Because the union did not actually agree to the clause, however, courts are unlikely to find this a true clear and unmistakable waiver and are likely to determine the requisite knowledge and intent to form an agreement are absent.

Another issue that remains is what occurs when a union and employer have entered into a clear and unmistakable waiver, but the union declines to pursue a discrimination or other employment claim to arbitration.[216] Because the union, and not the grievant, normally controls the grievance arbitration process, the union need not take any particular grievance to arbitration. One solution to this problem is for CBAs to include a right for an individual grievant to proceed with statutory claims in arbitration.[217] A similar proposal is to let each grievant choose between arbitration or litigation post-dispute.[218] Permitting individual control of the process, however, weakens the union's ability to ensure an appropriate process is used in labor arbitration and to obtain standard treatment for all employees and opens the process to displaying conflict rather than solidarity among employees to the employer.[219] Another solution that some courts have adopted is to require the employer to litigate the statutory claim when the union declines to pursue it to arbitration.[220]

(c) Multi-Party Agreements and Disputes

As discussed in Section 27, in the non-labor context cases about non-signatories to an arbitration agreement generally involve a non-

---

[216] Stuart M. Boyarsky, Not What They Bargained For: Directing the Arbitration of Statutory Antidiscriminatory Rights, 18 Harv. Negot. L. Rev. 221, 254 (2013).

[217] Levinson, Labor Arbitration, supra note 16, at 806. Gildea v. BLDG Mgmt., 2011 WL 4343464, at *5 (S.D.N.Y. Aug. 16, 2011) (requiring individual to proceed to arbitration without the union); Molina v. Harvard Maint., No 20 Civ. 10993, 2021 WL 5281098, at *4 (Nov. 11, 2021).

[218] Levinson, Labor Arbitration, supra note 16, at 854–55; cf. Maldonado v. SecTek, Inc., 2019 WL 3759451, at *7 (E.D. Pa. Aug. 8, 2019) (staying litigation while plaintiff and union determine whether to arbitrate when arbitration is exclusive means to settle statutory discrimination claim).

[219] Levinson, Labor Arbitration, supra note 16, at 855; David L. Gregory & Edward McNamara, Mandatory Labor Arbitration of Statutory Claims, and the Future of Fair Employment: 14 Penn Plaza v. Pyett, 19 Cornell J.L.& Pub. Pol'y 429, 452 (2010).

[220] See e.g., Espada v. Guardian Serv. Indus., No. 18-CV-5443, 2019 WL 5309963, at *7 (E.D.N.Y. Oct. 18, 2019); Drake v. Hyundai Rotem USA, Corp., 2013 WL 4551228) (E.D. Pa. Aug. 28, 2013); Brown v. Services for the Underserved, 2012 WL 3111903 (E.D.N.Y. 2012); Silva v. Pioneer Janitorial Services, 777 F. Supp. 2d 198, 207 (D. Ma. 2011); Veliz v. Collins Bldg. Serv., Inc., No. 10 Civ. 06615 (RJH), 2011 WL 4444498, at *4 (S.D.N.Y. Sept. 26, 2011); De Souza Silva v. Pioneer Janitorial Servs., 777 F. Supp. 2d 198, 206 (D. Mass. 2011); Morris v. Temco Serv. Indus., Inc., No. 09 Civ. 6194 (WHP), 2010 WL 3291810, at *6 (S.D.N.Y. Aug. 12, 2010); Borrero v. Ruppert Hous. Co., Inc., No. 08 CV 5869 (HB), 2009 WL 1748060, at *2 (S.D.N.Y. June 19, 2009); Kravar v. Triangle Serv., Inc., 186 L.R.R.M. 2565 (S.D.N.Y. May 19, 2009).

signatory compelling arbitration, rather than being compelled to participate. But because the labor grievances arise from allegations of employers attempting to avoid their obligations under a CBA, labor non-signatory cases focus on compelling the non-signatory to arbitrate.[221] For example, non-signatories to labor arbitration agreements will be compelled by the courts to arbitrate disputes with a union in instances involving companies who merge with a signatory or who are owned by a signatory.

In addition, the Sixth Circuit in *Greenhouse* explained an arbitrator can bind a non-signatory to an arbitration award "if there's clear and unmistakable evidence that the non-signatory agreed to arbitrate that question."[222] In *Greenhouse* the union had a CBA with a company in Tennessee owned by the same owners as a company in Kentucky that had not signed the CBA and was permitting non-union employees to perform work covered by the CBA. The union and a representative of both companies proceeded to arbitrate the dispute. The district court ruled that the Kentucky company was not bound by the arbitration because they were not a signatory to the CBA. The Sixth Circuit reversed and ordered the lower court to decide whether the Kentucky company had consented to the arbitrator determining arbitrability—whether the non-signatory was bound by the CBA.[223] The lower court would need to determine whether the representative spoke on behalf of the Kentucky company, and if so, whether the representative consented to the arbitration of the question of whether the Kentucky company was bound by the CBA.[224]

As stated by the Tenth Circuit, because "a party cannot be forced to arbitrate any issue [it] has not agreed to submit to arbitration,"[225] non-signatories resisting arbitration should have their resistance adjudicated by courts rather than arbitrators. The Supreme Court held that a dispute over whether a company resulting from a merger was bound by the collective bargaining agreement of one of the merging corporations should be determined by the court.[226] Lower courts have addressed whether a particular employer who purchased

---

[221] Some of these cases could be categorized as cases about whether a non-party formed a contract with a union but for ease of understanding they are discussed here as issues of scope.

[222] Greenhouse Holdings v. Intern. Union of Painters & Allied Trades, Council 91, 43 F.4th 628 (6th Cir. Aug. 8, 2022).

[223] Id. at 633

[224] Id.

[225] Communications Workers v. Avaya, 693 F.3d 1295, 1300 (10th Cir. 2012).

[226] John Wiley & Sons Inc. v. Livingston, 376 U.S. 543 (1964) ("Thus, just as an employer has no obligation to arbitrate issues which it has not agreed to arbitrate, so a fortiori, it cannot be compelled to arbitrate if an arbitration clause does not bind it at all.").

a company bound by a multi-employer CBA continued to be bound by the CBA,[227] and whether a company opened by the son of a deceased prior owner continued to be bound by the CBA.[228] In another instance, the Tenth Circuit addressed whether managers were covered by a labor agreement.[229] The court reversed the district court's order compelling arbitration to determine whether certain engineers were management, a category of employees not covered by the CBA. The court recognized the presumption in favor of arbitration but prioritized the principle that because arbitration is contractual, "a party cannot be forced to arbitrate any issue [it] has not agreed to submit to arbitration."[230] The court asserted that the court must reach the merits of the dispute over the CBA terms to determine the threshold issue of arbitrability, "whether the parties consented to submit a particular dispute to arbitration."[231] The court reasoned that "compelling evidence" supported the employer's assertion that the CBA, and a related neutrality agreement, used the term management to mean nonoccupational employees not subject to the CBA. The court concluded the employer and union had not consented to submit the dispute to arbitration.[232]

§ 47 Grievance-Arbitration Process

(a) The Grievance Process

Because the grievance process is contractual, the parties can agree to any reasonable process to address disputes that suits their needs.[233] The agreed upon procedure may limit grievances to complaints that provisions of the CBA have been violated or may permit employees to raise any type of workplace complaint. Many grievance processes resemble each other and use a stepped procedure progressively elevating a grievance to higher levels of decision makers.[234] For instance, the first step of the process may be that the employee informally brings the grievance to the attention of a supervisor. If the supervisor is unable to remedy the grievance, then the second step may require that the union shop steward file a

---

227 Peabody Holding Co., LLC v. Mine Workers, 665 F.3d 96 (4th Cir. 2012).

228 Sheet Metal Workers Local 36 v. Whitney, 670 F.3d 865, 868 (8th Cir. 2012). ("As the Supreme Court has made clear, [u]nless the parties clearly and unmistakably provide otherwise, the question of whether the parties agreed to arbitrate is to be decided by the court, not the arbitrator.' ").

229 Communications Workers v. Avaya, 693 F.3d 1295 (10th Cir. 2012).

230 Id. at 1300.

231 Id. at 1300.

232 Id. at 1302.

233 A union is limited by the duty of fair representation it owes to its members. See Ray, supra note 15, at 350 (discussing how union must act with good faith and a legitimate purpose when negotiating a CBA).

234 Levinson, Labor Arbitration, supra note 16, at 824.

written grievance with a manager, and that the steward and manager meet within a set short time to discuss the grievance and their interpretations of the CBA. If the manager is unable to remedy the grievance, then the third step may require that the union president and company president or director of labor relations meet. At each step, there may be an informal exchange of documents between the parties.[235] If that third step fails to resolve the grievance, then at the fourth step, the union files for arbitration. Some CBAs include time limitations at each step whereas others do not but may require prompt movement from step to step. The period in which to file at each step is often short, varying between three to 60 days.[236] In most instances, the union, rather than the grievant, controls the process, so the union decides whether to move the grievance to each successive step and whether to invoke arbitration.[237] Having described the grievance process, this section next explains how to invoke labor arbitration, advises on how to prepare for the hearing, and describes a typical arbitration hearing.

(b) Invoking Arbitration and Arbitrator Selection

Invoking labor arbitration is typically even less formal than the informal demand process used in many types of arbitration.[238] Labor arbitration is usually invoked simply by the union providing to the employer a written statement that states the union is moving to the last step of the grievance arbitration process and filing for arbitration. In some situations, the parties list the names of arbitrators in the collective bargaining agreement and rotate through those arbitrators.[239] The arbitrators listed are sometimes referred to as a permanent panel of arbitrators. In this situation, the parties call the arbitrator next in rotation to schedule the arbitration hearing.

In other situations, the CBA specifies an arbitration organization, and the parties contact the organization to request a list of arbitrators. The use of the AAA and the FCMS are common for labor arbitration.[240] Public sector unions may commonly use a state

---

[235] Levinson, Labor Arbitration, supra note 16, at 824.

[236] See Collective Bargaining Negotiations & Contract Manual, Methods of Settling Disputes, CBNC 9:2106 (Bloomberg BNA) (noting that filing deadlines at the initial step vary from three to 60 days); CBNC 170:1302, 170:1303, 170:2302; 170:2601, 170:2602 (example clauses from CBAs where arbitration must be filed by deadlines ranging from five to 60 days).

[237] Levinson, Labor Arbitration, supra note 16, at 818.

[238] See § 33(b) for discussion of arbitration pleadings.

[239] Levinson, Labor Arbitration, supra note 16, at 815.

[240] Levinson, Labor Arbitration, supra note 16, at 814. In the railway and transportation industry, employers and unions are governed by the Railway Labor Act (RLA) and arbitration is organized through the National Mediation Board. Elkouri, supra note 9, § 1.5.B.

or local arbitration organization.[241] The parties' lawyers or other representatives,[242] should read the applicable service rules on requesting an arbitrator list and follow those rules precisely to ensure receipt of a list. Once the parties receive the list, they research the arbitrators to decide how to rank their choices. Research involves looking at any past published decisions and contacting others in the field who have appeared before the arbitrators. Many labor arbitrators belong to the National Academy of Arbitrators (Academy), a professional organization of distinguished labor arbitrators,[243] and some may have authored a paper available from the Academy.[244] A lawyer must carefully assess how each arbitrator is likely to rule on the kind of case at issue. For instance, if the case involves an argument that a union missed a deadline for moving to the third step of the grievance process then knowing that a particular arbitrator often rules for the union is not enough information. The lawyer must also know how the arbitrator tends to rule about procedural errors and, best case scenario, about missing deadlines. To select an arbitrator, the parties can either send their ranking to the arbitration organization and rely on the organization to select the appropriate arbitrator or can determine the arbitrator themselves. The former may involve a fee so the parties, or their lawyers, often simply meet telephonically to strike names until only one remains. The parties then jointly contact the arbitrator selected to schedule a hearing date. Parties and their representatives should not contact the arbitrator ex parte without permission from the opposing party, which may be given to accomplish an administrative task such as setting a hearing date and location.[245]

In other instances, the parties have not listed arbitrators or a organization in the CBA but instead must mutually agree to an arbitrator.[246] In this instance, each party may propose names until agreement is reached. A lawyer can propose names based on prior experience with a particular arbitrator or based on research, and before deciding on a particular arbitrator must also research those proposed by the opposing party. Because arbitration is contractual, a

---

241 See Elkouri, supra note 9, § 1.5.B (mentioning New York State Board of Mediation maintains a panel of private arbitrators).

242 Parties to labor arbitration are often represented by non-attorneys, such as a union representative or human resources director. This book provides advice for attorneys because law students and attorneys are the target audience, but the advice applies equally to non-attorney representatives. See § 34(b) for a discussion of the role of lawyers in arbitration.

243 Elkouri & Elkouri, supra note 9, § 1.5.A.

244 Proceedings of the Academy are available on the Academy website at http://naarb.org/proceedings/index.asp.

245 St. Antoine, Common Law, supra note 133, § 1.4, at 6.

246 Levinson, Labor Arbitration, supra note 16, at 815.

CBA may specify some other process for invoking arbitration and selecting an arbitrator. Whatever the process, a lawyer must begin by consulting the relevant CBA provisions and complying with them.

The arbitrator can be any neutral person selected by the parties but most often is someone who specializes in labor arbitration and is familiar with collective bargaining and the industry or workplace involved. Often the arbitrator is a lawyer, but many are not lawyers but other types of experts in workplace relations.[247]

(c) Preparing for the Hearing

Typically, the hearing dates and location are arranged by an email to the arbitrator and a pre-hearing conference is not held. Motion practice is generally not involved in labor arbitration.[248] When preparing for an arbitration hearing, the first items that the lawyer should attend to are making a case timeline and outlining the issues, contract language and/or law, and evidence supporting each.[249] Some lawyers find using a case matrix useful for the latter tasks. A review of the pertinent CBA language is crucial. Research will also involve locating relevant prior arbitration decisions between the parties and published outcomes in similar arbitration cases confronting other parties. If the issues involve statutory or other legal issues in addition to CBA issues, the lawyer must also research the relevant law. An effective lawyer refers to the timeline and outline throughout case preparation and updates them as the case preparation progresses.

If the lawyer has not already interviewed all the witnesses during the grievance process, the lawyer must interview them. The initial interview could be by phone or virtual meeting and involves finding out what the witness has to say about the case. A follow-up phone call or interview, in-person or virtual, focused on obtaining additional information identified as necessary after research, may sometimes be necessary. Documents and other evidence should be identified and obtained by the lawyer. The other party may have provided all relevant documents informally during the grievance process so that they are available to the client and lawyer. If documents were not produced during the grievance process, the

---

247 Michel Picher, Ronald L. Sabeer & David Lipsky, Cornell/PERC Institute on Conflict Resolution, The Arbitration Profession in Transition: A Survey of the National Academy of Arbitrators, at 276 (2000) available at http://naarb.org/proceedings/synopses.asp (finding that in 1999 61.4% of NAA arbitrators had a law or JD degree).

248 See Richard A. Bales, Normative Consideration of Employment Arbitration at Gilmer's Quinceanera, 81 Tul. L. Rev. 331, 348 (2006). For discussion of dispositive motions in other types of arbitration, see § 34(d)(2).

249 Ariana R. Levinson, Lawyering Skills, Principles and Methods Offer Insight as to Best Practices for Arbitration (hereinafter Lawyering Skills), 60 Baylor L. Rev. 1, 52 (2008).

lawyers often exchange documents once arbitration is requested. If a party fails to produce relevant documents, the opposing lawyer can ask the arbitrator to subpoena documents to the hearing,[250] but this will likely result in a delay of the hearing to review the documents. As noted in § 36(d), courts are split on whether arbitrators have authority to subpoena documents pre-hearing or only to the hearing.

To obtain documents during the grievance process and before arbitration, parties often file a written request for information with the other party. These requests resemble a request for production of documents in litigation. In the private sector, if the opposing party fails to produce the information, the party seeking information can file a charge with the National Labor Relations Board (NLRB),[251] and, after investigation, the NLRB, through the regional general counsel, will issue a complaint. The National Labor Relations Act (NLRA) requires that parties bargain in good faith, and a refusal of an employer or union to provide information related to conditions of employment and necessary to proceed with or defend against a grievance is a violation of the NLRA. When the NLRB issues a complaint, an agent may help the parties settle and exchange information. If that does not happen, the case will proceed to a hearing in front of an Administrative Law Judge, but due to the length of time that may take, the party requesting the information may then have to rely on the arbitrator's subpoena power and delay the arbitration hearing or proceed without the information.[252] In the public sector, a state law that requires bargaining in good faith may provide a similar right to information,[253] and even if no law so provides, parties may have an established practice of exchanging information during the grievance process. Generally, litigation discovery tools, such as interrogatories and depositions, are not available in labor arbitration, and so a lawyer does not need to spend time preparing discovery beyond an information request.[254] The level of discovery is generally even less than the minimal discovery traditionally involved in other types of arbitration and certainly less

---

250 Levinson, Labor Arbitration, supra note 16, at 824–25; St. Antoine, Common Law, supra note 133, § 1.14, at 12.

251 Levinson, Labor Arbitration, supra note 16, at 824. In the public sector, a similar process may be used involving a state labor agency.

252 Levinson, Labor Arbitration, supra note 16, at 828.

253 See e.g., Liebert Cassidy Whitmore, Labor Relations in and Negotiations in Local Government at 6, 9 (discussing California Public Employee Relations Board requiring employers to supply relevant information to unions) available at http://www.counties.org/sites/main/files/file-attachments/153-labor_relations_course_materials_2013.pdf; 20 No. 11 Mich. Emp. L. Letter 3, 3 (2012) (discussing duty to provide information under Michigan Public Employment Relations Act).

254 Levinson, Labor Arbitration, supra note 16, at 824.

than the expanded discovery being utilized in some arbitrations today.[255]

Once the lawyer has interviewed the relevant witnesses, obtained and reviewed relevant documents and real evidence, and modified the case timeline and outline accordingly, the lawyer prepares witness examinations. The lawyer should practice direct examination with each witness and should practice admitting or referring to exhibits with the witness. These practice sessions should be in-person if the hearing will be in person and virtual if the hearing will be virtual so that the client is familiar with the actual process to be used at the hearing. The lawyer should also prepare the witness for anticipated cross-examination as well. The lawyer should explain what to expect at the arbitration hearing to the witness and should make sure the witness understands that while the process is informal, they should act professionally and respectfully toward everyone present. The lawyer should also draft a statement of the issue or issues to submit to the arbitrator at the start of the hearing and an opening and closing statement. Even when a lawyer anticipates filing a brief in lieu of closing argument, drafting the argument in advance of the hearing will help clarify the important points the lawyer needs to make during the hearing and will provide a basis for the brief.

A lawyer should prepare the exhibits for the hearing. If it is possible to stipulate with the opposing advocate to the exhibits in advance, the exhibits can be marked. Whether or not marked, they can be three-hole punched and placed into a binder to create exhibit books. Make an exhibit book for each arbitrator and each lawyer and a witness copy. Also, place the exhibits on a flash drive to provide to the arbitrator. Providing a Microsoft Word version in addition to a PDF version permits the arbitrator to cut and paste from the exhibits into the opinion.

Lawyers should also consider creating demonstrative exhibits. While in many hearings, no demonstrative exhibits are used, an eye-catching and interesting demonstrative exhibit can help persuade the arbitrator.[256] Effective demonstrative exhibits can be large reproductions of exhibits, a timeline or map, or a Power-Point bulleting the main conclusions of the argument. If a witness will refer to a demonstrative exhibit during testimony, the lawyer should prepare the witness using the demonstrative exhibit. Providing a demonstrative exhibit, such as a timeline, map or Power-Point, in

---

[255] For a discussion of the minimal, yet expanding, discovery in other types of arbitration, see § 33(d).

[256] Cooley, supra note 277, at 104.

electronic form that the arbitrator can take after the hearing will enable the arbitrator to refer to it when writing the opinion.[257]

(d) Conferring with the Opposing Advocate

Although arbitrators do not typically hold pre-conference hearings,[258] sometimes the lawyers informally confer with each other before the hearing. Doing so can reduce cost and increase efficiency by minimizing the amount of time needed for preliminary matters at the hearing. Parties can stipulate to authenticity or admissibility of documents and decide which documents to mark as joint exhibits.[259] They can also stipulate to the issues submitted to arbitration. Because the issue provides an opportunity to frame the case at the start of the hearing, a lawyer should not stipulate to the issue pre-hearing unless the agreed issue persuasively frames the case. The advocates can also discuss the order of witnesses and the amount of time they estimate each witness examination will take, better enabling them to estimate when a particular witness needs to be available.[260] The parties can agree on whether a reporter will be used, and if so, who will pay,[261] or on whether to record and transcribe a hearing. They can also agree on whether closing briefs will be filed, and, if so, the deadline by which the briefs will be submitted.

(e) The Arbitration Hearing

The parties in the arbitration are normally the union, rather than the individual grievant, and the employer.[262] Because the process is contractual, the parties may agree to any reasonable type of hearing that suits their needs. For instance, some parties use a joint board composed of an equal number of representatives from the union and the employer and a decision-making process that resembles negotiation rather than arbitration. Traditional labor arbitration, however, is an adjudicatory process normally in front of a single arbitrator, but sometimes in front of a panel of three.[263] When a panel is used, each party selects one arbitrator, and the arbitrators select a third. As discussed in § 47(c), party appointed arbitrators are normally neutral, but parties to labor disputes do sometimes agree that the party appointed-arbitrators are not

---

257 See Rick Bales, Labor Arbitration: Practical Ways to Cut Costs without Sacrificing Quality, 44 ABA Section of Labor & Employment Law Newsletter 10, 11 (summer 2016).

258 Bales, Labor Arbitration, supra note 257, at 11.

259 Bales, Labor Arbitration supra note 257, at 11.

260 Bales, Labor Arbitration supra note 299, at 11.

261 Bales, Labor Arbitration supra note 299, at 11.

262 Levinson, Labor Arbitration, supra note 16, at 818.

263 For a discussion of the similarities and differences of the adjudicatory process to litigation, see § 34(a).

neutral.[264] The parties may or may not be represented by a lawyer at the arbitration hearing.[265] Parties who are not represented by a lawyer are represented by a human resource representative or a union business agent, who are generally familiar with the process.[266]

Often at the beginning of the hearing, each party provides a statement of the issues in the case to the arbitrator. The arbitrator generally desires the parties to reach agreement on the issue because the jurisdiction of the arbitrator is determined by the issue.[267] In labor cases, like other cases, courts determine some arbitrability issues unless clearly and unmistakably delegated to the arbitrator, and an award can be vacated if the parties had not agreed to arbitrate that particular type of claim.[268] For instance, a CBA may grant the arbitrator authority to determine whether an employee was disciplined for just cause, but not explicitly grant the arbitrator authority to determine the remedy if just cause is found. If the parties did not agree to have the arbitrator determine the latter issue, a court may vacate the award as to the remedy.[269] The parties may also agree to let the arbitrator determine the issues.[270] In routine cases, such as terminations, the parties generally agree to the issues. In more complex cases, however, the parties may not agree. Other preliminary matters will also be addressed before opening statements. For instance, parties may have subpoenaed documents and review those. Or parties may have stipulated to the authenticity or admissibility of certain exhibits and present those joint exhibits to the arbitrator.[271] Preliminary matters may also include simple requests such as to use a slide show or other visual in opening statement. Lawyers sometimes request sequestration of witnesses, and all the witnesses who are not entitled to remain are asked to leave and admonished by the arbitrator not to discuss the case with any other witnesses.[272] Normally, the grievant and one union and one employer representative are permitted to remain throughout the hearing.

---

[264] See Seth H. Liebman, Something's Rotten in the State of Party Appointed Arbitration: Healing ADR's Black Eye That Is "Nonneutral Neutrals," 5 Cardozo J. Conflict Resol. 215, 221–23 (2004).

[265] Levinson, Labor Arbitration, supra note 16, at 817.

[266] Levinson, Labor Arbitration, supra note 16, at 819, 846–47; Dennis R. Nolan, Disputatio: "Creeping Legalism" as a Declension Myth, 2010 J. Disp. Resol. 1, 7 (2010).

[267] Levinson, Lawyering Skills, supra note 249, 57.

[268] St. Antoine, Common Law, supra note 133, § 1.21, at 16. ("But if no agreement is reached, the arbitration proceeds at the risk of a posthearing attack on the grounds that the resulting award exceeded the jurisdiction of the arbitrator.").

[269] See Elkouri, supra note 9, § 15.3.E.i. & ii.

[270] St. Antoine, Common Law, supra note 133, § 1.21, at 16.

[271] St. Antoine, Common Law, supra note 133, § 1.27, at 19.

[272] St. Antoine, Common Law, supra note 133, § 1.32, at 22.

After the issues are determined and other preliminary matters are attended to, the party representatives provide opening statements.[273] In discipline cases, the burden is on the employer, and the employer representative gives the first opening statement.[274] In contract interpretation cases, the burden is on the union, and the union representative gives the first opening statement.[275] An effective opening statement tells a compelling story, summarizes the relevant CBA provisions, and provides an overview of the conclusions that the evidence will prove.[276] Often an opening statement starts by introducing the parties, the lawyers, and the theme of the case, provides a summary of the relevant law and/or CBA provisions and the theory of the case, describes the facts via a chronological story, rebuts the anticipated case theory of the opposing side, and makes a specific request for relief.[277] Sometimes a lawyer will delay providing an opening statement until immediately before presenting the client's case.[278] Effective lawyers seldom do so because the opening statement is the best opportunity to influence the arbitrators' decision before any evidence is presented.[279] If the arbitrator hears only one side of the story, all the initial evidence will be filtered only through that perspective.[280]

After opening statements, the party with the burden of proof presents its case.[281] Normally the employer proceeds first in a discipline case, and the union proceeds first in a contract interpretation case. The witnesses are sworn to tell the truth,[282] and the arbitrator may swear all witnesses as a group before sequestration or may swear in each witness immediately before the witness testifies. The party calls witnesses[283] and directly examines them using open and closed questions that permit the witness to tell the story.[284] The lawyer will introduce relevant documents or real

---

[273] Levinson, Labor Arbitration, supra note 16, at 818.

[274] Elkouri, supra note 9, §§ 7.4.G.iii, 7–29, 8–13.

[275] Id.

[276] Levinson, Lawyering Skills, supra note 249, at 64.

[277] John W. Cooley & Steve Lubet, Arbitration Advocacy, at 111, 115, 117 (2d ed. 2003).

[278] Levinson, Lawyering Skills, supra note 249, at 26.

[279] Levinson, Lawyering Skills, supra note 249, at 29–31.

[280] Levinson, Lawyering Skills, supra note 249, at 33.

[281] See St. Antoine, Common Law, supra note 133, § 1.33, at 22–23.

[282] Levinson, Labor Arbitration, supra note 16, at 817.

[283] Levinson, Labor Arbitration, supra note 16, at 804, 818.

[284] An open question is one that leaves room for the witness to answer as the witness sees fit, such as "What happened next?" A closed question is one that narrows the options but does not suggest the answer, such as "What color was the automobile?" A leading question is one that suggests the answer, such as "that was the red car, wasn't it?" Leading questions are generally used only sparingly on direct exam, such

evidence not contained in joint exhibits through the witnesses. The opposing counsel then cross-examines the witness[285] using leading questions to emphasize significant points to the arbitrator. Sometimes cross-examination is brief or waived altogether,[286] and focusing cross-examination on only one, two, or three key points is particularly effective. Parties are permitted re-direct, and then generally re-cross or re-re-direct with permission of the arbitrator. Once the initial party rests its case, the other party calls and presents its witnesses in the same manner. In some cases, the parties may request that the arbitrator visit the site involved in the incident. For instance, if there is an allegation that a manager smelled marijuana on the grievant before the grievant was discharged, the parties may want to demonstrate where the manager was in relation to the grievant and other odors emanating from the site. As a lawyer, you should definitely consider arranging a site visit if one may be dispositive in the case.

Labor arbitration is less formal than litigation, and the hearing normally takes place around a conference room table. As discussed in § 34(c), rules of evidence are used, but only loosely followed.[287] Most arbitrators tend to admit most evidence "for the weight it is worth."[288] One of the limited grounds upon which a federal district court can reverse an award is when the labor arbitrator failed to admit all relevant evidence, which explains this tilt toward admission of evidence.[289] Some arbitrators do explain how much weight they believe any objected to piece of admitted evidence holds.[290] Objecting to a piece of evidence is intended to alert the arbitrator to flaws in the evidence. For example, a lawyer might make a hearsay objection to alert the arbitrator that the evidence is second-hand and not verified by witnesses or documents.

Once the testimony has been given and other evidence admitted, the parties have the opportunity to make closing arguments. The order of arguments may depend on the arbitrator, who may permit the party with the burden of proof to argue first, last, or both first and last. Closing arguments are an opportunity to outline the applicable contract law, relevant arbitration awards, and any

---

as to establish preliminary background such as education and profession or to establish a time or date.

285 William H. Holley, Kenneth M. Jennings & Roger S. Wolters, The Labor Relations Process 483 (10th ed. 2011).

286 Levinson, Lawyering Skills, supra note 267, at 27.

287 Levinson, Labor Arbitration, supra note 16, at 821.

288 Michael Z. Green, No Strict Evidence Rules in Labor Arbitration, 15 Tex. Wesleyan L. Rev. 533, 536 (2009).

289 Green, supra note 288, at 537.

290 Green, supra note 288, at 537.

relevant statutory or case-law and to explain how the evidence presented proves the party's position. Often a closing argument begins with the theme and theory of the case, provides an overview of the conclusions on each major legal or contractual issue, proceeds to argue the outcome of each conclusion in more detail focusing on significant facts, requests specific relief, and concludes by thanking the arbitrator.[291] The parties often elect to file closing briefs rather than provide an oral closing argument.[292] They may do so because they wish to cite to arbitration opinions and awards, because they believe writing is more precise than oral argument, or because they want to insure the arbitrator has the argument available in writing to refer to while writing the opinion. Filing briefs increases the length of time until a decision, and the arbitrator may have already made a fairly firm decision about the case before the briefs arrive.[293] For these reasons, lawyers should strongly consider coming to the hearing prepared to make a precise closing statement with citation to opinions and awards.[294] Some parties use a modified process where each lawyer individually presents the argument to the reporter, who then provides a written copy to the arbitrator and opposing lawyer after both arguments have been made.[295]

Sometimes transcripts are not taken in labor arbitration hearing[296] because of the added cost of having one prepared.[297] Sometimes the arbitrator records the hearing to refer to when writing the award and opinion.[298] If a reporter is used, a lawyer should make introductions and provide a business card to insure proper spelling of names and identification. At the close of the hearing, the parties should thank the arbitrator and make cordial goodbyes to everyone present, including the opposing party and counsel.

A hearing may last one day or several depending upon the complexity of the issue and the number of witnesses the parties call. When scheduling the hearing, a lawyer must properly estimate the amount of time needed to avoid having to schedule an additional day of hearing at the end of the first hearing date. If the parties end up needing a day they did not anticipate, in many instances, the proceeding will be significantly delayed because of the difficulty of

---

291 Cooley, supra note 277, at 207, 208, 213, 219, 220.

292 See Levinson, Labor Arbitration, supra note 16, at 819.

293 Lawyering Skills, supra note 267, at 44.

294 Levinson, Lawyering Skills, supra note 267, at 44–45.

295 Levinson, Lawyering Skills, supra note 267, at 41.

296 Levinson, Labor Arbitration, supra note 16, at 819. For a discussion of other aspects of confidentiality of arbitration hearings, see § 37(b).

297 St. Antoine, Common Law, supra note 133, § 1.12, at 11.

298 Levinson, Labor Arbitration, supra note 16, at 819.

finding a day that the arbitrator, parties, and lawyers are all available.[299]

Increasingly, labor arbitration hearings are held virtually. Lawyers should be familiar with the platform that will be used and arrange for witnesses to come to their location or to have reliable internet service and access from their location. If possible, lawyers should prepare the exhibits in advance and deliver copies to the arbitrator(s), witnesses they will call, and opposing counsel, including an extra copy or two for the witnesses who will be called by the opposing party. A virtual hearing may enable free recording and transcription of the hearing, and parties should agree before the hearing and discuss with the arbitrator whether they wish to have access to a recording and transcript.

(f) Payment of Fees

The employer and union generally each pay for their own lawyer fees. Because the union provides representation, the grievant generally does not pay to hire a lawyer.[300] As discussed in § 3(c), parties to arbitration must pay the arbitrator a fee for the time spent on the case. Generally, the parties split equally the arbitrator's fee. Sometimes, however, a contract provides that the losing party must pay the arbitrator's fee.[301] Lawyers should be sure to check the CBA for any provision regarding payment of fees and discuss and consider the fees with the client when determining whether to proceed to arbitration.

§ 48 The Private Law of Labor Arbitration

(a) Written Opinions and Awards

As discussed in § 34(e), unlike traditional commercial arbitration where an award is typically only a couple sentences, labor arbitrators normally provide a more extensive written opinion and award to the parties.[302] Many of these awards are published by BNA (Bloomberg) or CCH (Wolters Kluwer),[303] and AAA labor arbitration awards are available on Westlaw and LEXIS Advance. Westlaw also

---

[299] Bales, Labor Arbitration, supra note 257, at 11.

[300] Most union represented employees pay dues or an equivalent fee to enable the union to provide services, such as representation, including by an attorney, at arbitration.

[301] Levinson, Labor Arbitration, supra note 16, at 843.

[302] W. Mark C. Weidemaier, Toward a Theory of Precedent in Arbitration, 51 Wm. & Mary L. Rev. 1895, 1910–11 (2010) (using labor arbitration as one example of an arbitration system that generates precedent); Theodore J. St. Antoine, Gilmer in the Collective Bargaining Context, 16 Ohio St. J. on Disp. Resol. 491, 509 (2001).

[303] Levinson, Labor Arbitration, supra note 16, at 810.

provides access to CCH and Federal Labor Relations Authority awards.[304]

(b) Persuasive Precedent

While an arbitrator is not bound by any previous award between different parties, many arbitrators rely on them as persuasive precedent.[305] As discussed in § 34(e), arbitration precedent plays an important role in labor arbitration. Over the years, labor arbitrators have begun predictably considering certain concepts and factors for some particular types of cases. Most cases involve discharge or some other type of discipline, but some involve other issues of contract interpretation or application. This section discusses concepts involved in discipline cases, other types of CBA interpretation cases, interesting issues addressing the use of technology in the workplace, and finally discrimination and other cases that raise statutory as well as contractual claims.

(c) Substance of Opinions and Awards

(1) Discharge and Discipline

An employee could be discharged or otherwise disciplined for many different reasons, including tardiness, absence, insubordination, inability to perform tasks properly, use of drugs, theft, or possession of a weapon. Most CBAs include what is often termed a just-cause provision.[306] For instance, one CBA states in its Article for Discipline & Adverse Actions, "Discipline and adverse action must be consistent with applicable laws and regulations and will be taken only for just cause."[307] A just-cause provision requires that an employer only discipline an employee for a good reason. Another CBA states the employer may "discipline, suspend or discharge any employee for just cause and shall comply with the principles of progressive discipline" and references Appendix B as explaining "the principles of 'just cause.' "[308] In the appendix, the

---

304 A comprehensive list of available arbitration awards, including labor arbitration awards, is available on Cornell Library's web page at http://guides.library.cornell.edu/c.php?g=31398&p=199822.

305 Nolan, Disputatio, supra note 266, at 5.

306 Elkouri & Elkouri, supra note 9, § 15.2.A.ii; Clyde W. Summers, Individualism, Collectivism and Autonomy in American Labor Law, 5 Employee Rts. & Emp. Pol'y J. 453, 478 (2001); Basic Patterns in Union Contracts, at 7 (BNA 14th ed. 1995).

307 CBA between Department of Interior and Federal Indian Service Employees AFT Local 4524, Article 23 Discipline and Adverse Actions, at 77, available at http://www.bie.edu/cs/groups/xbie/documents/text/idc016461.pdf.

308 Working Agreement between SEIU, Local 925 and Bremerton School District 100-C, Article XII. Termination of Employment, Section A. Discharge for Good and Just Causes, at 12-1, (effective through August 31, 2024) available at https://www.

CBA states that the "concept of 'just cause' . . . requires that there be fundamental fairness in decisions related to the discipline and discharge of employees" and then enumerates seven factors to consider.[309]

In the private sector, the default employment rule is that employees are employed at will. Employers can fire at-will employees for any reason or no reason at all. Many situations create exceptions to this default rule. For instance, a CEO may have an individual employment contract requiring termination only for cause or an employee may be able to show that she was fired because she is a woman, which is a prohibited reason to terminate an employee under the federal statute known as Title VII. A CBA containing a just-cause provision creates another situation where the default at-will rule does not apply.

Many arbitrators agree on the types of principles that determine whether an employer had a good reason to terminate an employee. These principles explore not only the substantive reasons for the discipline but also the process used to determine that the discipline was appropriate. The employer has the burden of proof to demonstrate that the grievant engaged in the alleged infraction.[310] Often arbitrators require the employer to prove by a preponderance of the evidence that the grievant engaged in the infraction. If the alleged infraction is criminal in nature or involves moral turpitude, then many require a higher standard of proof of "clear and convincing evidence" and a minority sometimes require "beyond a reasonable doubt."[311] And recently, arbitrators have used the "clear and convincing evidence" standard in termination cases, whether or not they involve allegations of criminal behavior.[312] Some arbitrators do not specify the quantum of proof necessary to prevail, preferring instead to focus on making factual findings.

Many arbitrators require that notice be given of the types of behavior that warrant discipline and the type of discipline that is appropriate for each type of behavior.[313] For instance, a rule may

---

bremertonschools.org/cms/lib/WA01001541/Centricity/Domain/60/SEIU%2021-24%20CBA%20Final%2012.8.21.pdf.

309 Working Agreement between SEIU, Local 925 and Bremerton School District 100-C, Appendix B, What Does "Just Cause" Mean?, at A-3 (effective through August 31, 2024) available at https://www.bremertonschools.org/cms/lib/WA01001541/Centricity/Domain/60/SEIU%2021-24%20CBA%20Final%2012.8.21.pdf.

310 Elkouri, supra note 9, § 15.3.D.i. St. Antoine, Common Law, supra note 133, § 6.9, at 190.

311 Elkouri, supra note 9, § 15.3.D.ii.a; St. Antoine, Common Law, supra note 133, § 6.10, at 192–93.

312 Elkouri, supra note 9, § 15.3.D.ii.a.

313 Ariana R. Levinson, Industrial Justice: Privacy Protection for the Employed, 18 Cornell J .L.& Pub. Pol'y, 609, 640 (2009) (hereinafter Industrial Justice); See e.g.,

state that an employee who is absent three times receives a written warning while another warns that insubordination will result in immediate termination. Arbitrators are more likely to uphold discipline against an employee who, having previously engaged in a similar infraction, has been warned that a specific disciplinary action will result from further infractions.[314]

Most arbitrators interpret a just-cause provision to require progressive discipline. Progressive discipline means that for each transgression an employee receives a greater penalty.[315] For instance, a first absence for which an employee provides no notice to the employer may warrant an oral reprimand, a second, a written warning, a third a suspension, and a fourth termination. The purpose of progressive discipline is to enable an employee to correct the problematic behavior. Some offenses are so serious, however, that discharge without lesser preceding discipline is appropriate.[316] For instance, arbitrators have found assaulting a co-worker or selling drugs on the employer's premise to warrant discharge without progressive discipline.[317] In each instance, the discipline must "fit the crime," meaning that a less significant penalty is warranted for being tardy than for assaulting a co-worker.[318]

Many arbitrators also require that the employer give notice to the employee of the reason for the discipline and an opportunity for the employee to respond before the discipline is imposed.[319] Providing this opportunity prevents employers from implementing discipline without sufficient evidence to prove the grievant committed the infraction.[320]

Some arbitrators also require that the employer use an adequate process to investigate the incident causing the discipline.[321] For instance, if an anonymous note says that an employee has liquor in a company locker provided for personal use, the company should not rely on the note, but should ask the employee for permission to open

---

Gaylord Container Corp., 107 Lab. Arb. Rep.(BNA) 1138 (1997) (Allen, Jr., Arb.) (overturning demotion for absenteeism when employer failed to mention that demotion could be penalty for additional infractions).

314 Elkouri, supra note 9, § 15.3.F.xi.

315 Levinson, Industrial Justice, supra note 313, at 644–45.

316 Elkouri, supra note 9, § 15.3.F.xi.

317 Elkouri, supra note 9, § 15.3.F.i. See e.g., Burger Iron Co., 92 Lab. Arb. Rep.(BNA) 1100, 1105 (1989) (Dworkin, Arb.) (upholding discharges for selling drugs on the employer's premise).

318 Levinson, Industrial Justice, supra note 313, at 646.

319 Levinson, Industrial Justice, supra note 313, at 656–57; Bud Indus. Inc., 124 Lab. Arb. Rep.(BNA) 908, 914 (2007) (Miles, Arb.); Penn Window Co., 120 Lab. Arb. Rep.(BNA) 298, 303 (2004) (Dissen, Arb.).

320 Elkouri, supra note 9, § 15.3.F.ii.

321 Levinson, Industrial Justice, supra note 313, at 644.

the locker and should investigate whether anyone else had access to the locker.

Generally, the discipline must be for a work-related reason and not because of an employee's actions away from the workplace during personal time.[322] For instance, if an employee is out drinking and dancing and someone posts a photo of the drunk grievant on Facebook so a manager finds out about the behavior, typically that would not warrant discipline.[323] Other examples of off-duty conduct that do not warrant discipline include flying a Nazi flag on a private house porch[324] and selling marijuana.[325] Off-duty actions must significantly and concretely harm the employer to warrant discipline.[326] Examples where a grievant engages in such off-duty conduct include directly competing with the employer's business, a role model engaging in obscene conduct of which the community becomes aware, and financially harming an employer by taking unwarranted leave.[327]

Most arbitrators also consider whether the grievant was treated in the same way that others who committed the same infraction were.[328] For instance, if the grievant was terminated for assault on a co-worker, but in two prior instances employees were suspended for assault, the arbitrator may find no good cause for termination and reduce the penalty to a suspension. Consistent enforcement of rules is necessary if an employer wishes to discipline an employee for running afoul of a rule.[329] When rules are inconsistently enforced or not enforced at all, employees are led to believe that violations will go unsanctioned.[330] Employers must promulgate only reasonable rules necessary for safe and efficient business operations.[331] Rules must be disseminated and known to employees.[332]

---

[322] Summers, supra note 306, at 478–79; Levinson, Industrial Justice, supra note 313, at 677.

[323] Cf. Shawnee County, 123 Lab. Arb. Rep.(BNA) 1659 (2007) (Daly, Arb.) (termination relating to photo of grievant dancing at a bar posted on public web page overturned).

[324] Dept. of Corr. Servs., 114 Lab. Arb. Rep.(BNA) 1533, 1542 (1997) (Simmelkjaer, Arb).

[325] Lockheed Aeronautical Sys. Co., 92 Lab. Arb. Rep.(BNA) 669 (1989) (Jewett, Arb.).

[326] Levinson, Industrial Justice, supra note 313, at 677.

[327] Levinson, Industrial Justice, supra note 313, at 676–79.

[328] Levinson, Industrial Justice, supra note 313, at 644.

[329] Levinson, Industrial Justice, supra note 313, at 640.

[330] Levinson, Industrial Justice, supra note 313, at 669.

[331] Levinson, Industrial Justice, supra note 313, at 643.

[332] Elkouri, supra note 9, § 15.3.F.x.

Arbitrators recognize that employees have a right to privacy when being disciplined.[333] Arbitrators may find an investigation inadequate because the employer failed to interview co-worker witnesses individually in private.[334]

Some CBAs expressly limit an arbitrator's ability to lessen the level of discipline imposed by the employer when the arbitrator finds the grievant committed the alleged infraction.[335] Many CBAs provide no such limit, and arbitrators often consider mitigating factors when determining whether an employer imposed an appropriate level of discipline.[336] For instance, long seniority weighs against imposing the most severe discipline of termination.[337] Other factors that weigh against severe penalties are honesty and acceptance of responsibility for an infraction, a work record devoid of other discipline, and commendations and promotions.[338] Arbitrators will also reduce discipline when management is at least partially at fault for the infraction.[339] For instance, an arbitrator reinstated, without back pay, a severely depressed employee discharged for assaulting a supervisor who had demeaned the employee.[340] Other factors, such as lack of seniority or a poor work record, tend to support a high level of discipline.[341]

Arbitrators also follow the principle that employees should obey their employers' orders and grieve later, except in certain situations involving imminent safety risks, an intrusive invasion of privacy, or direction of unlawful behavior, where it is permissible for an employee to refuse a direct order.[342] Thus, employees who decide to refuse an employer's order risk being disciplined without recourse to a successful grievance.

(2) Contract Interpretation

Unions not only bring discipline cases, but also arbitrate cases involving any alleged breach of a CBA provision. These cases might involve any number of issues such as an allegation that an employer

---

[333] Levinson, Industrial Justice, supra note 313, at 639; Rhodia, Inc., 118 Lab. Arb. Rep.(BNA) 455, 464 (2003) (Neas, Arb.).

[334] ESAB Welding & Cutting Prods., 115 Lab. Arb. Rep.(BNA) 79, 83 (2000) (Wolkinson, Arb.).

[335] Elkouri, supra note 9, § 15.3.E.ii.

[336] Levinson, Industrial Justice, supra note 313, at 645.

[337] Elkouri, supra note 9, § 15.3.F.ix.

[338] Levinson, Industrial Justice, supra note 313, at 645.

[339] Elkouri, supra note 9, § 15.3.F.xv.

[340] Bethlehem Structural Prods. Corp., 106 Lab. Arb. Rep. (BNA) 452, 456 (1995) (Witt, Arb.).

[341] Elkouri, supra note 9, §§ 15.3.F.viii &15.3.F.ix.

[342] Levinson, Industrial Justice, supra note 313, at 649.

has sub-contracted work in violation of a work-preservation provision, a dispute over whether a certain scheduling system is permissible, a request to accommodate a disabled employee, or allegations that pay or break provisions are not being properly followed. Although less frequent, employers too can sometimes seek arbitration in a CBA interpretation dispute.[343]

The arbitrator will examine all relevant contract language, the intent of the parties as expressed when negotiating the provision, and the past practice of the parties.[344] For a simple dispute, the arbitrator may simply have to read the wage and hour provision, identify that it states a person in the grievant's position should be paid a certain amount, and order the employer to pay that amount. Such simple disputes, however, normally settle earlier in the grievance process. Thus, arbitrators generally confront situations where the contract language is not clear. For instance, the CBA may contain a work-preservation clause that states "employees not hired as custodians cannot perform cleaning tasks and whenever the number of custodians present is inadequate another custodian will be called in to work." The CBA also contains a management rights clause that states, "management reserves to itself all rights not explicitly curtailed by this agreement." The arbitrator presented with no specific language about sub-contracting must determine whether the work-preservation clause explicitly curtails the ability to use a sub-contractor not hired by the employer as a custodian. To do so, the arbitrator may turn to the parties' negotiations. The arbitrator may find that the union offered a clause that prohibited sub-contracting but it was rejected by management, which would suggest sub-contracting out all the custodial work is permissible. Or the arbitrator may find that the work-preservation clause was sought by the union in response to sub-contracting out of administrative services which the employer ceased because of the new provision. Such history would suggest that sub-contracting is not permissible. The arbitrator may also look at the past practice of the parties. If other non-custodial work has been sub-contracted out that suggests the work-preservation clause does not prohibit it. On the other hand, if no type of work has been sub-contracted out, that suggests the work-preservation clause prohibits sub-contracting the cleaning work.

---

343 Employers can sometimes grieve because the CBA makes express provision for it at some stage of the grievance procedure. Elkouri, supra note 9, at Chapter 5, Section 5.4.B. & n.77 (stating that of 400 agreements examined in one survey, 26% provided for company grievances) (citing Basic Patterns in Union Contracts 34 (BNA Books 14th ed 1995)). Employers have, for instance, arbitrated against a union to receive damages for violation of a no-strike clause in a CBA. Elkouri, supra note 9 at § 18.3.D.i.

344 Elkouri, supra note 9, at § 9.3.A.ii.

Ambiguity in CBA terms and a conflict over their interpretation can arise for several different reasons. As in any contract case, it is difficult to precisely describe every concept. The parties may use inherently vague terms or create ambiguity due to grammar or typographical errors. Provisions may conflict with each other, such as in the example above with the conflict between the work-preservation clause and the management rights clause. Even within one provision, contradictory language may be used. Application of a provision to a particular situation often is not foreseen.[345] Indeed, one of the reasons parties put arbitration clauses in their CBAs is precisely to deal with that type of unanticipated situation.[346] Sometimes parties intentionally agree to ambiguous language, reasoning that leaving the interpretation to an arbitrator is preferable to failing to reach agreement on the CBA as a whole.

The intent of the parties as expressed when negotiating the agreement is often used to interpret CBA language.[347] If available, bargaining history can point strongly toward the correct interpretation in an ambiguous situation. When a party has attempted and failed to include a certain provision, arbitrators are unlikely to read the CBA as including that provision. If the party, however, offered the provision as a clarification then the arbitrator may read the CBA to include the provision even if it was not ultimately integrated into the express terms of the agreement.[348] Because the clause is presented as clarifying the parties' current interpretation of the CBA, failure to include it does not indicate the parties understanding differed from the offered clause. When assessing the parties' intent, many arbitrators take into consideration the level of sophistication of the negotiating parties and are more likely to hold sophisticated negotiators to the plain meaning of the drafted provision.[349]

Arbitrators also rely on past practice to interpret ambiguous CBA language,[350] and often past practice is the only evidence of intent relied upon by arbitrators.[351] Parties, both employer and union, are assumed to know what is occurring at the workplace,[352] and even practices which are not regularly occurring will be considered by arbitrators to interpret ambiguous language.[353] In

---

345 St. Antoine, Common Law, supra note 133, § 2.2, at 71.

346 Elkouri, supra note 9, § 9.2.C.

347 Elkouri, supra note 9, at 9.3.A.ii.

348 Elkouri, supra note 9, § 9.3.A.ii.a.

349 Elkouri, supra note 9, § 9.3.A.xvi.

350 Elkouri, supra note 9, § 9.3.A.v.

351 Elkouri, supra note 9, § 12.1.

352 Elkouri, supra note 9, § 12.8.

353 Elkouri, supra note 9, § 12.8.

reliance on past practice, arbitrators rely on prior arbitration awards between the same company and union dealing with the same issue. They also honor past grievance settlements between the parties.[354] In most instances, employer handbooks are not considered because they are simply a unilateral statement not binding on the union, but, in some instances, a longstanding handbook rule may evidence a past practice.[355] If the past practice of the parties is unclear, arbitrators may rely on industry practice or practice between the employer and another union when the same CBA language is used between them.[356]

Not all arbitrators rely on the language of the CBA, the expressed intent of the parties, and past-practice. Some rely only on the plain meaning of the terms used,[357] and interpret the terms according to their "usual and ordinary meaning."[358] Others permit extrinsic evidence, such as expressions of intent during negotiations and past practice, only to determine if the terms of the CBA are ambiguous or not, in which case the plain language would prevail.[359] Other arbitrators consider all the evidence,[360] and some will even interpret the CBA contrary to what the terms taken out of context suggest.[361] Generally though, arbitrators agree that a party's subjective intent which was not expressed across the table does not bear on the meaning of the CBA terms.[362]

Even in situations where an agreement is absolutely silent on a subject, an arbitrator may determine that past practices prohibits the employer from making a unilateral change.[363] While the precise test a particular arbitrator may use varies, generally arbitrators consider whether the practice was known to both parties and consistently used over a period of time rather than only sporadically.[364] For instance, if the employees have always had ten paid minutes to change into their uniforms before starting their shift, and the employer cuts it to five minutes, an arbitrator may find that

---

354 Elkouri, supra note 9, § 9.3.A.iii.

355 Elkouri, supra note 9, § 9.3.A.ix.

356 Elkouri, supra note 9, § 9.3.A.vi.

357 Elkouri, supra note 9, § 9.2.A; St. Antoine, Common Law, supra note 133, § 2.21, at 72.

358 St. Antoine, Common Law, supra note 133, at 69.

359 TriMas Corp., 125 Lab. Arb. Rep. (BNA) 911, 921 (2008) (Nolan, Arb.).

360 Considering all the evidence may be based on the "theory that all language is infected with ambiguity." St. Antoine, supra note 133, at 75.

361 Elkouri, supra note 9, § 9.2.A.i.

362 Elkouri, supra note 9, § 12.1.

363 Elkouri, supra note 9, § 12–2–3; St. Antoine, Common Law, supra note 133, § 2.21, at 90–91. See United Steelworkers v. Warrior & Gulf Navigation Co., 363 U.S. 574 (1960).

364 Elkouri, supra note 9, § 12.2.

violates the CBA because the practice is incorporated into the pay provision. The party urging the use of past practice bears the burden of proving the requirements.[365] Many arbitrators will find a binding past practice as to wages and benefits, but permit management to make unilateral changes to "methods of operation and direction of the workforce" reasoning the latter are generally reserved to management through a management rights clause in the CBA.[366] In other situations where a CBA is silent on a subject, arbitrators may rely on common arbitration principles, such as the requirements for just cause discussed in § 48(c), assuming they were known to the parties or may determine what the parties would have agreed had they bargained over the subject.[367] For example, if a CBA contains a description of the bargaining unit, seniority provisions, and a grievance and arbitration procedure, most arbitrators will infer "employees cannot be discharged without just cause."[368] Or if a CBA contains a grievance and arbitration procedure, an arbitrator may infer the union thereby agreed not to strike.[369] An arbitrator may also award damages when a union violates a no-strike clause in the CBA even though the clause does not mention damages.[370]

Many contract interpretation principles used by labor arbitrators will be familiar to anyone involved in any type of contract interpretation.[371]

- Critically, as mentioned above, most arbitrators will determine the meaning of a particular term in light of the contract as a whole, factoring in all relevant provisions.[372]
- Words will be provided their common meanings and industry or technical terms theirs unless otherwise defined or proven that the terms should otherwise be interpreted.[373]

---

365 Id.

366 Elkouri, supra note 9, § 12.5.C.

367 Elkouri, supra note 9, § 9.2.D; St. Antoine, Common Law, supra note 245, § 2.22, at 92–94.

368 St. Antoine, Common Law, supra note 133, § 2.22, at 92–94.

369 Handsaker, Morrison & Marjorie L., Remedies & Penalties for Wildcat Strikes: How Arbitrators & Federal Courts Have Ruled, 22 Cath. U.L. Rev. 279, 292 (1972–73).

370 Elkouri, supra note 9, § 18.3.D.i.

371 St. Antoine, Common Law, supra note 133, § 2.1, at 70.

372 Elkouri, supra note 9, § 9.3.A.viii.

373 Elkouri, supra note 9, § 9.3.A.i & 9.3.A.i.a.

- The use of the same word will indicate the same concept, while the use of different words will indicate a distinction was intended by the parties.[374]
- Terms will be interpreted consisted with the underlying purpose of the relevant provision.[375]
- "The expression of one thing is the exclusion of another."[376]
- When a list of specific items is followed by a more general term, the general term includes only items similar to the specific ones.[377]
- A provision will be interpreted against the party drafting it.[378]
- An interpretation resulting in a just result is preferred to one resulting in a harsh or arbitrary result.[379]
- As with most agreements, arbitrators will prefer an interpretation that renders a CBA provision valid and enforceable over one that renders it unlawful.[380]

(3) Technology

As technology advances, it sometimes raises new workplace issues. For instance, the use of social media by employees has received much attention, both by human resources professionals and in the public media. New techniques to monitor employees, such as GPS or Google watches, that raise privacy concerns have also received attention.[381] Cases involving new technology generally reach labor arbitrators before they reach the courts because of the shorter time period to reach arbitration and because of the greater workplace protection granted to employees by a CBA with a just-cause provision.

---

[374] Elkouri, supra note 9, § 9.3.A.i.c.

[375] Elkouri, supra note 9, § 9.3.A.vii.

[376] Elkouri, supra note 9, § 9.3.A.xi. This doctrine is known by the Latin phrase "*expressio unius est exclusio alterius.*"

[377] Elkouri, supra note 9, § 9.3.A.xii. This doctrine is known by the Latin phrase "*ejusdem generis.*"

[378] Elkouri, supra note 9, § 9.3.B.ii.

[379] Elkouri, supra note 9, § 9.3.B.v.

[380] Elkouri, supra note 9, § 9.3.B.vi.

[381] See Ariana R. Levinson, What Hath the Twenty First Century Wrought? Issues in the Workplace Arising from New Technologies and How Arbitrators Are Dealing with Them, 11 Transactions Tn. J.Bus. L 9, 9 (2010) (hereinafter New Technologies).

Arbitrators have applied principles relating to just cause in cases involving new technologies.[382] For example, in cases involving personal use of employer-issued equipment, such as computers or cell phones, arbitrators generally uphold discipline if the employee knew of the rule prohibiting personal use and the rule was equally enforced.[383] Sometimes, even when the rule has been enforced, arbitrators mitigate the level of damage due to seniority.[384] Additionally, arbitrators require the use of progressive discipline in situations involving personal use of employer-issued equipment.[385]

Similarly, rules prohibiting use of technology to make racially or sexually offensive communications are generally considered reasonable[386] if employees are aware of the rules[387] and the rules are consistently enforced.[388] Some arbitrators have reduced discipline for such inappropriate use of technology because the communication was private,[389] shared only with a few people,[390] or did not result "in loss or other harm."[391]

Generally employees cannot be disciplined for their use of technology while off-duty and away from the workplace.[392] As well stated by one arbitrator, "[a]s a general rule, once an employee is off duty and away from the workplace, there is a presumption that the

---

382 Levinson, New Technologies, supra note 381, at 13.

383 Levinson, New Technologies, supra note 381, at 13; Conneaut Sch. Dist., 104 Lab. Arb. Rep. (BNA) 909, 914 (1995) (Talarico, Arb.); Chevron Prods. Co., 116 Lab. Arb. Rep. (BNA) 271, 2715 (2001) (Goodstein, Arb.); AlliedSignal Engines, 106 Lab. Arb. Rep.(BNA) 614, 624 (1996) (Rivera, Arb.); Co. of Sacramento, 118 Lab. Arb. Rep.(BNA) 699, 701 (2003) (Riker, Arb.).

384 City of El Paso, 123 Lab. Arb. Rep. (BNA) 691–92 (2001) (Greer, Arb.).

385 Levinson, New Technologies, supra note 381, at 15; Clatsop County, 126 Lab. Arb. Rep. (BNA) 620, 635 (2009) (Reeves, Arb.).

386 Levinson, New Technologies, supra note 381, at 19; MT Detroit, 118 Lab. Arb. Rep. (BNA) 1777, 1779, 1782 (2003) (Allen, Arb.); U.S. Dept. of Agric., 118 Lab. Arb. Rep. (BNA) 1212, 1216 (2003) (Cook, Arb.).

387 Levinson, New Technologies, supra note 381, at 22; S. Cal. Edison, 117 Lab. Arb. Rep. (BNA) 1066, 1071–72 (2002) (Prayzich, Arb.).

388 Levinson, New Technologies, supra note 381, at 22; Chevron Prods. Co., 116 Lab. Arb. Rep. (BNA) 271, 272 (Goodstein, Arb.); Snohomish Co. Pub. Util. Dist. No. 1, 115 Lab.Arb.Rep. (BNA) 1, 8 (2000) (Levak, Arb.).

389 Levinson, New Technologies, supra note 381, at 20; City of Fort Worth, Tex., 123 Lab. Arb. Rep. (BNA) 1125, 1130 (2007) (Moore, Arb.); Snohomish Co. Pub. Util. Dist. No. 1, 115 Lab. Arb Rep. (BNA) 1, 8 (2000) (Levak, Arb.); Ga. Power Co., 123 Lab. Arb. Rep. (BNA) 936, 948 (2006) (Nolan, Arb.). Cf. City of Fort Lauderdale, 125 Lab. Arb. Rep. (BNA) 1249, 1254 (2008) (Abrams, Arb.) (reducing length of suspension when employee only accidently made communication available to others because of a printer paper jam).

390 Levinson, Industrial Justice, supra note 313, at 676 n.392 (2009); Chevron Prods. Co., 116 Lab. Arb. Rep. (BNA) 271, 274, 280, 281 (2001) (Goodstein, Arb.).

391 Am. Red Cross, 125 Lab. Arb. Rep. (BNA) 1969, 1715 (2008) (Ruben, Arb.).

392 Levinson, New Technologies, supra note 381, at 24.

employee's private life is beyond the employer's control."[393] In some instances, however, arbitrators have found the necessary significant concrete harm to the employer resulting from the off-duty conduct to justify discipline.[394] Some cases involve an employee who is competing with the employer's business,[395] some involve role models, such as teachers, engaging in publicly observed obscene conduct,[396] and some involve deleterious communications between co-workers.[397]

In discipline cases, arbitrators normally assess the reliability and accuracy of evidence.[398] When modern technology is involved, such as images stored in a computer temporary file, expert testimony may be necessary to help the arbitrator assess the evidence.[399] Additionally, evidence is considered as a whole so consistency with other evidence can boost the reliability of unclear evidence.[400]

In discipline cases, arbitrators also address the issue of whether employer technological monitoring is appropriate. Whether an employee is provided notice of the monitoring of actions, such as by GPS, and also of the type of conduct which constitutes an infraction of the rules is sometimes a determinative factor in monitoring cases.[401] Yet, there is no consensus among arbitrators as to the validity of surreptitious on-duty monitoring by GPS or webcams.[402] As to monitoring electronic communications, many arbitration awards permit employers doing so, even without any notice of monitoring to employees, "provided the employer has a reasonable

---

393 Dep't. of Corr. Servs., 114 Lab. Arb. Rep. (BNA) 1533, 1536 (1997) (Simmelkjaer, Arb.).

394 Levinson, New Technologies, supra note 381, at 24; Levinson, Industrial Justice, supra note 313, at 636.

395 GFC Crane Consultants, Inc., 122 Lab. Arb. Rep. (BNA) 801, 804 (2006) (Abrams, Arb.); Fox Television Station, 118 Lab. Arb. Rep. (BNA) 641, 645 (2003) (Allen, Arb.).

396 Warren City Bd. of Educ., 124 Lab. Arb. Rep. (BNA) 532, 535 (2007) (Skulina, Arb.); Phoenix City Bd. of Educ., 125 Lab. Arb. Rep. (BNA) 1473 (2009) (Baroni, Arb.). Cf. L'Anse Creuse Pub. Schs., 125 Lab. Arb. Rep. (BNA) 527 (2008) (Daniel, Arb.) (reducing termination to paid administrative leave where obscene photo of teacher was posted on a publicly available website).

397 WMATA/Metro, 124 Lab. Arb. Rep. (BNA) 972, 976 (2007) (Evans, Arb.); City of Quincy, 126 Lab. Arb. Rep. (BNA) 534, 539 (2008) (Finkin, Arb.).

398 Levinson, New Technologies, supra note 381, at 28.

399 Levinson, New Technologies, supra note 381, at 29. See e.g., Indep. Sch. Dist. #284, 125 Lab.Arb.Rep.257, 264 (BNA) (2008); AK Steel, 125 Lab. Arb. Rep. (BNA) 903, 904 (2008) (Dean, Arb.).

400 Levinson, Industrial Justice, supra note 313, at 656.

401 Levinson, New Technologies, supra note 381, at 30. Cf. Orange Co., Fla. 123 Lab. Arb. Rep. (BNA) 460, 463 (2007) (Smith, Arb.) (overturning suspension for driving employer-owned vehicle home where no notice that doing so would violate company policy); Embarq, 123 Lab. Arb. Rep. (BNA) 923, 932 (2007) (Armedariz, Arb.) (upholding discipline for time misrepresentation discovered by GPS where employer previously warned employee about falsifying time records).

402 Levinson, New Technologies, supra note 381, at 31.

cause to believe a violation of company policy has taken place and is monitoring for that reason."[403]

Some arbitration opinions address employer monitoring of employees' off-duty conduct. For instance, cases arise where employers hire investigators to examine employees conduct while on FMLA leave. One arbitrator held surreptitious surveillance of an employee and his truck while outside a relative's home, at an ATM, and at two shopping stores was appropriate when the employer had a reasonable suspicion of misconduct.[404] Another arbitrator permitted surreptitious surveillance of an employee using FMLA leave even though the employer had no suspicion of misconduct but was concerned about the large amount of leave taken by the employee.[405] The arbitrator overturned the termination, however, because the surveillance video demonstrated the grievant would only have been able to work a portion of his shift.[406]

Some cases involving new technology arise out of CBA provisions other than the just-cause provision. In some cases, unions protest a failure to increase pay commensurate with additional duties created by new technology.[407] In others, disputes arise because employers attempt to prohibit employees from carrying or using personal devices.[408] In one case an arbitrator denied a grievance for identity theft, when two computers containing the employees' names and social security numbers were stolen from the employer's accounting firm, because the health and safety clause could not be read so broadly.[409]

Some CBAs contain provisions specifically addressing the use of technology. For instance, the UPS/Teamsters contract contains a provision limiting the use of GPS data in disciplinary hearings. The data can only be used when there is also other evidence that the

---

403 Levinson, New Technologies, supra note 381, at 33; Dep't of Veterans Affairs, 122 Lab. Arb. Rep. (BNA) 106, 108 (2006) (Hoffman, Arb.); Dep't of Veterans Affairs, 122 Lab. Arb. Rep. (BNA) 300, 306 (2005) (Peterson, Arb.); Tesoro Ref. & Mktg. Co., 120 Lab. Arb. Rep. (BNA) 1299, 1302–03 (2005) (Suntrup, Arb.); AE Staley Mfg. Co., 119 Lab. Arb. Rep. (BNA) 1371, 1375 (2004) (Nathan, Arb.); City of Ft. Worth, 123 Lab.Arb.Rep. (BNA) 1125, 1127 (2007) (Moore, Arb.); S. Cal. Edison, 117 Lab. Arb. Rep. (BNA) 1066, 1069 (2002) (Prayzich, Arb.).

404 Interstate Brands Crop., 121 Lab. Arb. Rep. (BNA) 1580, 1581 (2005) (Skulina, Arb.).

405 Bud Indus., Inc., 124 Lab. Arb. Rep. (BNA) 908, 910 (Miles, Arb.).

406 Id.

407 Levinson, New Technologies, supra note 381, at 39–40; Stanford Hosp. & Clinics, 123 Lab. Arb. Rep. (BNA) 1697, 1702 (2007) (Staudohar, Arb.); Agric. Research Serv., 122 Lab. Arb. Rep. (BNA) 1469, 1472 (2006) (Feldman, Arb.).

408 See e.g. OZinga Ill. RMC, Inc., 123 Lab. Arb. Rep. (BNA) 198, 200 (Simon, Arb.).

409 Chicago Bd. of Educ., 125 Lab. Arb. Rep. (BNA) 1168 (2008) (Goldstein, Arb.).

employee was not at the correct location at the correct time.[410] Sports CBAs also address the use of technology because "data analytics is used by sports teams to improve recruiting, which is often referred to as the 'Moneyball' approach."[411] The National Basketball Players Association (NBPA) and Major League Baseball Players Association (MLBPA) CBAs provide examples of the types of provisions,[412] which include the right to decline the use of a sensor, notice of data collection, access to the data collected, and limitations on the purposes for which the data can be used.[413]

(4) Discrimination Cases

In some labor arbitrations, arbitrators address statutory claims in addition to claims that the CBA has been violated.[414] This may be because the CBA permits such claims to be raised, because a statute is incorporated into the CBA,[415] or, in some limited number of cases, because the union has agreed that arbitration, rather than litigation, is the only available forum.[416] Sometimes arbitrators will refuse to hear statutory claims because they consider it outside their jurisdiction, which is limited to interpreting the CBA.[417] Many arbitrators, however, are lawyers familiar with statutory interpretation and employment law. Normally the statutes at issue are employment statutes such as Title VII of the Civil Rights Act of 1964, the Americans with Disabilities Act, the Age Discrimination in Employment Act, or the Family Medical Leave Act. In these cases, some arbitrators consider the statute, administrative guidance, and case law just as a judge would in deciding such a case.[418] One study found that while in fact-specific cases arbitrators are less likely to

---

410 National Master United Parcel Service Agreement for the Period August 1, 2018 through July 31, 2023, at 20, https://teamster.org/wp-content/uploads/2018/12/ups18nationalmaster.pdf [https://perma.cc/V2P8-GZHS].

411 Maria Macaluso & Ariana R. Levinson, Collective Action, Legislation, and Creative Litigation at the Intersection of Geospatial Data & Workers' Rights, 36 ABA J. Lab. &Emp. L 299, 311 (2022); see also Matthew T. Bodie, Miriam A. Cherry, Marcia L. McCormick & Jintong Tang, The Law and Policy of People Analytics, 88 U. Colo. L Rev. 961, 968 (2017).

412 2017 NBA-NBPA Collective Bargaining Agreement 359-61 (Jan. 19, 2017) [hereinafter NBA CBA], https://cosmic-s3.imgix.net/3c7a0a50-8e11-11e9-875d-3d44e94ae33f-2017-NBA-NBPA-Collective-Bargaining-Agreement.pdf [https://perma.cc/3L37-F8HP]; Major League Clubs and MLBPA 2017-2021 Basic Agreement 334–36 (Dec. 1, 2016), https://d39ba378-ae47-4003-86d3-147e4fa6e51b.filesusr.com/ugd/b0a4c2_95883690627349e0a5203f61b93715b5.pdf [https://perma.cc/H9VJ-NVKM].

413 Macaluso, supra note 411, at 312.

414 Nolan, Disputatio, supra note 266, at 11.

415 Levinson, Labor Arbitration, supra note 16, 812–13.

416 See § 46(b)(4)(B) for a discussion of cases where the CBA waives the right to go to court.

417 See Levinson, Labor Arbitration, supra note 16, at 811.

418 Elkouri, supra note 9, § 10.2.A.

cite court decisions, in many employment discrimination cases, arbitrators cite multiple decisions and apply appropriate standards of proof and burden shifting.[419] The American Arbitration Association (AAA) instituted a panel of labor arbitrators with employment law experience to select from as arbitrators in such cases.[420]

(5) Remedies

When determining a remedy, arbitrators normally strive to make the parties whole by placing them in the position they would have been had no CBA violation occurred.[421] Typical remedies in discipline cases are reinstatement[422] or elimination of the discipline, back pay, and benefits. The amount of back pay is generally mitigated by the grievant's earnings during the period of unemployment.[423] In addition to these remedies, in other types of cases arbitrators award lost wages, medical costs, promotions, pension fund contributions, and recall rights. Arbitrators may order a grievant to undergo a medical examination, drug testing, or treatment or order parties to cease and desist from certain conduct.[424] Arbitrators have awarded lost overtime and premium pay, pay for travel time,[425] reimbursement for medical and dental expenses, health insurance premiums, and tuition.[426] They have ordered employers to issue parking permits, to cease interfering with issuance of event passes,[427] to revise employee evaluations, to reopen a closed plant,[428] or to provide a grievant special training or equipment.[429] Arbitrators may issue creative remedies, dissimilar to those typically issued by courts, such as posting of an apology, requiring an employee to continue medication, or granting a union representative a meeting with employees on company time.[430] One

---

419 See Levinson, Labor Arbitration, supra note 16, at 830–32.

420 Daily Labor Report: News Archive June 1, 2011, 105–DLR C–3, available to subscribers at https://news.bloomberglaw.com/daily-labor-report/fmcs-aaa-representatives-discuss-past-years-developments?context=search&index=0

421 Elkouri, supra note 9, § 18.3.A.i.

422 Levinson, Labor Arbitration, supra note 16, at 852.

423 Elkouri, supra note 9, § 18.3.I.

424 Levinson, Labor Arbitration, supra note 16, at 839; Elkouri, supra note 9, § 18.4.A.iii.

425 Elkouri, supra note 9, § 18.3.A.ii.

426 Elkouri, supra note 9, § 18.3.A.vi.

427 Elkouri, supra note 9, § 18.3.A.i.

428 Elkouri, supra note 9, § 18.3.A.ii.

429 Elkouri, supra note 9, § 18.3.A.vi.

430 Levinson, Labor Arbitration, supra note 16, at 840–41.

arbitrator ordered reinstatement of a grievant with training "appropriate to polish her interpersonal skills."[431]

In one case, the union grieved a rule requiring employees to wear pagers, respond within 15 minutes, and arrive at work within an hour. The arbitrator ordered that employees disciplined under this unreasonable unilaterally-implemented rule be made whole. The remedy included rectifying "wage loss, back pay, job demotion, blemished work record, promotion denial, seniority, or any other employment related benefit loss directly attributable to any disciplinary action stemming from the violation of the on-call pager policy."[432]

Sometimes after finding a contract violation, an arbitrator will order the parties to negotiate for an appropriate remedy.[433] Generally, arbitrators do not award mental distress damages for non-statutory breach of CBA claims[434] and are reluctant to award punitive damages.[435]

While most awards benefit employee-grievants, some awards go to an employer or a union. For instance, employers have won damages from unions that violate no-strike clauses.[436] And unions and union trust funds have won damages from employers when an employer has violated a CBA provision the benefit of which inures to the union as a whole. For instance, damages have been awarded for violations of union-representational rights and union-security clauses and for plant closures and sub-contracting.[437]

§ 49 Enforcement and Vacatur of Labor Arbitration Awards

(a) Enforcement of Labor Arbitration Awards

(1) Confirmation of Labor Arbitration Awards

In most cases, the parties voluntarily comply with the labor arbitration award, but in some a party seeks enforcement of the award.[438] Unlike in the FAA which sets out detailed provisions,

---

431 Elkouri, supra note 9, § 18.3.A.vi. (quoting Mount Sinai Hospital, 105 Lab. Arb. Rep. (BNA) 1047, 1050 (1995) (Duff, Arb)).

432 Lyondell Citgo Ref., 120 Lab. Arb. Rep. (BNA) 360, 364 (2004) (Moreland, Arb.).

433 Elkouri, supra note 9, § 18.1.A.

434 Elkouri, supra note 9, § 18.3.C.

435 Elkouri, supra note 9, § 18.3.F.

436 Elkouri, supra note 9, § 18.3.D.i.

437 Elkouri, supra note 9, § 18.3.D.ii.f.

438 Elkouri, supra note 9, § 2.1 (citing LeRoy & Feuille, Final and Binding, But Appealable to Courts: Empirical Evidence of Judicial Review of Labor and Employment Arbitration Awards, in Arbitration 2001: Arbitrating in an Evolving

including a statute of limitations and notice requirements, there is no statute or provision other than the civil rules of procedure that govern filing for confirmation of a labor award. Some courts may simply follow the FAA provisions, especially when parties file to confirm the award under the FAA § 9 in addition to under the LMRA Section 301.

If parties are operating under traditional 301 practice, enforcement of the award is generally the equivalent of confirmation of an award in the FAA context, meaning that in labor arbitration parties move or petition to enforce an award in the initial court in order to obtain a judicial order adopting the award.[439] For example, in one case a union filed a complaint to confirm an arbitration award where the employer refused to reinstate an employee to her prior position and make her whole, even though an arbitrator had ordered that remedy after finding she was discharged without cause.[440] The court heard the matter on written cross-motions for summary judgment and classified the dispute as one for specific enforcement. The court granted summary judgment to the union and ordered the employer to pay attorneys' fees.[441] In another case, a union filed an action to enforce an arbitration award finding the employer violated the CBA by subcontracting to a non-union contractor.[442] The court found it had jurisdiction to confirm the award and granted the union's motion for summary judgement on "its action to enforce the arbitration award."[443]

Because Section 301 contains no statute of limitations when enforcing labor arbitration awards, courts usually borrow the most closely analogous state statute of limitations, which often have a statute of limitations significantly less than the year provided for in FAA § 9.[444]

Legal Environment, Proceedings of the 54th Annual Meeting of NAA 49, 62 (Grenig & Briggs eds., BNA Books 2002)).

439 Milk Drivers, Dairy and Ice Cream Employees, Local Union No. 387 v. Roberts Dairy, 294 F. Supp.2d 1050, 1058 (C.D.IA Nov. 26, 2003) (explaining that while titled a complaint to confirm an award, the union's request is "more along the lines of a request for enforcement").

440 Complaint to Confirm Arbitration Award, 2006 WL 2426847, Local 509, SEIU v. Fidelity House (July 17, 2006).

441 Local 509, Service Employees Intern. Union v. Fidelity House, Inc., 518 F. Supp. 2d 317 (D. Ma. Sept. 28, 2007).

442 International Broth. of Elec. Workers, Local Union No. 124 v. Alpha Elec. Co., Inc., 759 F. Supp. 1416, 1418 (W.D.Miss. Jan. 24, 1991).

443 Id. at 1421, 1427.

444 5 National Labor Relations Act: Law & Practice § 41.09 (Matthew Bender 2022); Local 802, Musicians v. Parker Meridien Hotel, 145 F.3d 85 (2d Cir. 1998); Sullivan v. Lemoncello Plumbing Co., 36 F.3d 676 (7th Cir. 1994).

(2) *Claim Preclusive Effect of Labor Arbitration Awards*

(A) *Generally*

Generally if an employee sues for violation of a collective bargaining agreement because they are dissatisfied with an arbitration award, they are precluded from doing so unless they can prove the union breached its duty of fair representation.[445] If an employee sues for a separate claim, not a violation of the collective bargaining agreement, the claim will be preempted if it depends on interpretation of the CBA.[446] These doctrines reduce the number of instances where a party to litigation might argue claim preclusion applies.

At least a couple of state courts have discussed issue preclusion (collateral estoppel) and held it applies to the findings in a labor arbitration award when employees bring a tort common law claim.[447] Generally, however, if an employee sues for a violation distinct from the CBA that relates to the same nexus of facts as a labor award, such as a statutory discrimination claim, then the court will consider the claim de novo,[448] providing appropriate weight to the arbitration award as discussed further below in Section 49(a)(2)(B).

(B) *Statutory Claims*

As discussed in Section 46(b)(4)(A), *Gardner Denver* explained that the trial court could consider a labor-arbitration award for the weight it was worth when deciding a statutory claim, such as a discrimination case, de novo.[449] The Court set out relevant factors trial courts could consider including whether the CBA provisions conform to the statutory ones, whether the arbitration forum was procedurally fair, whether the record adequately addressed the statutory claim, and the "special competence of particular arbitrators." The Court permitted lower courts, in their discretion, to accord the labor arbitration award great weight but urged the lower courts to be mindful of Congress's decision to "provide a judicial forum for the ultimate resolution of discriminatory employment claims." Per *Gardner Denver*, some trial courts will consider the labor

---

[445] Hines v. Anchor Motor Freight, 424 U.S. 554, 571 (1976); Ford Motor Co. v. Huffman, 345 U.S. 330, 338 (1953).

[446] Allis-Chalmers Corp. v. Lueck, 471 U.S. 202, 218–19 (1985).

[447] Kelly v. Vons Companies, Inc., 67 Cal. App. 4th 1329 (1998); Taylor v. People's Gas Light & Coke Co., 275 Ill. App. 3d 655, 661 (Ill. App. 1995); see also Brock v. Lucky Stores, Inc., 2000 WL 288395, at *8 (N.D. CA March 14, 2000) (applying preclusive effect under California state law).

[448] Taylor v. Lockheed Martin Corp., 113 Cal. App. 4th 380, 387 (Nov. 17, 2003) (collateral estoppel does not apply to statutory claim).

[449] Gardner-Denver, 415 U.S. at 60 n.21.

award and the opinion's reasoning, and some will give an award no weight.[450] Despite *Gardner Denver*'s guidance, at least one federal judge gave issue-preclusive effect to a labor arbitration award's factual findings about the cause of a termination in a parallel Title VII suit.[451] Another judge determined that great weight required by *Gardner Denver* did not mean preclusive effect and so would not apply collateral estoppel.[452]

Some courts that may previously have declined to consider arbitration awards are now giving them greater weight in discrimination cases due toward the favorable position toward arbitration taken in *Pyett*.[453] Three circuits have, however, confirmed that *Gardner-Denver* continues to govern statutory claims when a CBA contains no clear and explicit waiver. They have each reversed a lower court that applied issue preclusion or claim preclusion.[454]

Even prior to *Pyett*, some courts were more deferential to arbitration awards than others. For instance, the Second Circuit continues to hold that an arbitration opinion and award resulting from substantial evidence presented during an evidentiary hearing will preclude a plaintiff from litigating a discrimination claim unless "evidence that the decision was wrong as a matter of fact" or "the impartiality of the" evidentiary hearing "was somehow compromised."[455] Even so one court within the Second Circuit decided

---

450 See Martin H. Malin, Revisiting the Meltzer-Howlett Debate on External Public Law in Labor Arbitration: Is it Time for Courts to Declare Howlett the Winner?, 24 Lab. Law 1, 20 (2008) (suggesting that some courts rely on arbitration awards rather than providing de novo review of statutory claims); Courtney Lamont Phelps, Lifting Gardner-Denver Footnote 21: The Heavy Burden to Give "Appropriate Weight" to Arbitration Decisions on Subsequent Judicial Review (2011) (unpublished student independent study paper) (on file with author) (outlining various ways courts have treated arbitration awards in employment discrimination cases).

451 Franklin v. Liberty Lines Transit, Inc., 2016 WL 1078283, at *16 (S.D.N.Y. March 16, 2016).

452 Pender v. Dist. Council 37 AFSCME, 223 F. Supp. 2d 534, 542 (S.D.N.Y. September 30, 2002).

453 See e.g. Hawkins v. Leggett, 955 F. Supp. 2d 474 (D. Md. 2013) (Title VII decision providing great weight to an arbitrator's just cause finding); Tewolde v. Owens & Minor Distribution, Inc., No. 07-CV-4075, 2009 WL 1653533, at *9 (D. Minn. June 10, 2009) ("Therefore, a court affords an arbitrator's decision interpreting and applying the terms of a CBA 'an extraordinary level of deference' in a later Title VII action in federal court and confirms the decision 'so long as the arbitrator is even arguably construing or applying the contract and acting within the scope of his authority.' ")

454 Grimes v. BNSF Ry. Co., 746 F.3d 184 (5th Cir. 2014); Coleman v. Donahoe, 667 F.3d 835, 854 (7th Cir. 2012); Mathews v. Denver Newspaper Agency LLP, 649 F.3d 1199, 1204–05 (10th Cir. 2011). See also Gautier v. Celanese, 143 F. Supp. 3d 429, 437 (W.D. Va. 2015) ("But where a contract is silent about arbitration of statutory claims, courts need not raise the insurmountable hurdles of claim preclusion and issue preclusion.")

455 Attard v. City of New York, No. 10-4224-cv, 2011 WL 6225249 (2nd Cir. Dec. 15, 2011) (quoting Collins v. N.Y.C. Transit Auth., 305 F.3d 113, 119 (2d Cir. 2002));

providing an arbitration award under a state statute great weight in a parallel statutory discrimination claim was inappropriate because the arbitrator did not permit testimony of comparators necessary to determine the claim.[456]

In cases where the union has unmistakably waived an employee's right to litigate a statutory claim, courts are likely to find the award precludes litigation of the same claim. For example, one pre-*Pyett* case found (albeit likely erroneously) that the CBA clearly and unmistakably waived an employees' right to litigate a sexual harassment claim. The union had proceeded to arbitration on the employee's claim and had lost. The court applied collateral estoppel precluding the employee from relitigating the factual determinations made by the arbitrator in the labor award and granted summary judgment to the employer.[457] Additionally, some atypical CBAs permit an individual employee to arbitrate a statutory claim, without the union's participation. In one case involving a public sector employee in Connecticut, an employee arbitrated her FMLA claim without her union's participation. The arbitrator decided against the employee and for the employer on the statutory claim. The court decided that under Connecticut law, the doctrine of res judicata barred her re-litigation of the FMLA claim in a federal suit and granted the employer summary judgment on her claim.[458]

(b) Vacatur of Labor Arbitration Awards

(1) Generally

While FAA § 10 specifies grounds for vacatur, the LMRA "is much less specific. It simply provides federal jurisdiction to enforce collective bargaining agreements, including arbitration clauses in these contracts. Addressing this statutory void, the U.S. Supreme Court has [in labor cases] provided standards for enforcing arbitration agreements and arbitrator awards."[459] The Supreme Court case *Enterprise Wheel* established that a court must confirm any arbitration award that "draws its essence from the" CBA, even if the award is in error.[460] Only under narrow circumstances should an award be vacated. These circumstances are:

---

see also D'Agosta v. Geren, 2011 U.S. Dist. LEXIS 86902, at *25 (E.D.N.Y. July 13, 2011).

456 Colon v. Fashion Inst. of Tech. (State Univ. of N.Y.), 983 F. Supp. 2d 277, 285 (S.D.N.Y. October 18, 2013).

457 Clarke v. UFI, Inc., 98 F. Supp.2d 320, 336 (E.D.N.Y. 2000).

458 Serafin v. Connecticut, 2005 WL 578321 (D. Conn. Mar. 9, 2005).

459 Michael H. LeRoy, Irreconcilable Deferences? The Troubled Marriage of Judicial Review Standards under the Steelworkers Trilogy and Federal Arbitration Act, 30 J. Disp. Resol. 89, 91 (2010).

460 United Steelworkers v. Enterprise Wheel & Car Corp., 363 U.S. 593 (1960).

1) The award results from procedural unfairness, such as fraud, corruption, or bias.

2) The arbitrator "clearly exceeded" the authority granted "by contravening a clear provision of the" CBA.

3) The award violates a fundamental and well-defined public policy.[461]

The Railway Labor Act sets out a similar standard for vacatur, and RLA cases cite to LMRA cases when determining whether the award fails to "confine itself to matters within the scope" of the arbitrators' jurisdiction.[462] The RLA specifies that "judicial review is limited to (1) whether the Board failed to comply with the RLA; (2) whether the Board failed to conform or confine itself to matters within the scope of its jurisdiction; and (3) whether the Board's decision was the result of fraud or corruption."[463]

Since the *Steelworkers Trilogy*, different courts have interpreted the standards for confirmation and enforcement and vacatur of labor arbitration awards differently.[464] This section discusses each of the three most recognized grounds for vacatur of a labor arbitration award as well as other possible grounds. It then discusses vacating an award due to the union's breach of fair representation and modification of awards.

(2) Procedural Unfairness

As to ground one, procedural unfairness (fraud, corruption, or bias), an arbitration award will be vacated because of bias if the arbitrator had a "personal stake" in the arbitration.[465] In one case, where the arbitrator was the son of an officer of an international union to which the local union bringing the grievance belonged, a court determined that bias sufficient to vacate the award was shown simply because of the particular family relationship.[466] One court found, however, that when an employer sued an arbitrator post-award and the arbitrator filed for Rule 11 sanctions against the

---

[461] Ray, supra note 15, at 290.

[462] Continental Airlines, Inc. v. Teamsters, 391 F.3d 613, 620 (5th Cir. 2004); Union Pac. R.R. Co. v. Am. Ry. & Airway Supervisors' Ass'n, 838 F. App'x 846, 849 (5th Cir. 2020). ("This court has also held that we may vacate an arbitrator's decision pursuant to an exceedingly narrow, judicially created exception for public policy concerns.").

[463] 45 U.S.C. § 153(1)(q)(2004); Continental, 391 F.3d at 620.

[464] While in other context confirmation and enforcement are two separate parts of the process, in labor arbitration parties tend to move for enforcement, intending to include confirmation of the award and orders to comply with it.

[465] Pitta v. Hotel Ass'n of New York City, 806 F.2d 419, 423 (2d Cir. 1986).

[466] Morelite Constr. Corp. v. New York City Dist. Council Carpenters Benefit Funds, 748 F.2d 79, 84 (2d Cir. 1984).

employer's lawyer, that action did not demonstrate bias undermining the award.[467] Even situations that raise an appearance of impropriety, which would require recusal of a federal judge, do not amount to sufficient bias to vacate a labor arbitration award.[468] In one case, for instance, the court permitted an employer-appointed co-arbitrator to determine a case involving his former law partners' actions during the partnership.[469]

Similar to cases of bias resulting in vacatur, where an employer and union purposefully select an arbitrator they believe will be biased against a grievant, the award will be vacated.[470] The procedural unfairness in the process justifies vacating the award regardless of whether the arbitrator was actually biased. Likewise, labor awards will be vacated for corruption. In a RLA case, the Ninth Circuit described corruption sufficient to merit vacatur of an award as including violence, threats of violence, bribery, extortion, and other acts that threaten the integrity of an arbitration proceeding, including threats of economic injury, such as an employer-appointed representative threatening to blacklist a neutral member.[471]

At least one party has sought vacatur of a labor arbitration award on FAA § 10 grounds of evident partiality. The First Circuit held that participation on an arbitration committee (board) of representatives from companies in the same industry as one of the parties is not evident partiality, even when they may be from competitor companies.[472]

(3) Exceeding Authority

As to ground two, clearly exceeding authority by contravening a clear provision of the CBA, the Supreme Court has reaffirmed the narrow circumstances where an arbitrator clearly exceeds the authority granted by the CBA. A court should not vacate an award even if convinced the arbitrator "committed serious errors" when the arbitrator is "arguably construing or applying the contract and acting within the scope of his authority."[473] Most courts vacate a labor arbitration award only where the award violates the clear language

---

[467] Toyota of Berkeley v. Automobile Salesmen's Union Local 1095, 834 F.2d 751, 756 (9th Cir. 1987).

[468] Pitta, 806 F.2d at 423; Apperson v. Fleet Carrier Corp., 879 F.2d 1344, 1350, 1360 (6th Cir. 1989).

[469] Apperson, 879 F.2d at 1360–61.

[470] Elkouri, supra note 9, § 2.2.A.ii.c.(9); Allen v. Allied Plant Maint. Co., 881 F.2d 291 (6th Cir. 1989).

[471] United Transp. Union v. BNSF Ry. Co., 710 F.3d 915, 932 (9th Cir. 2013).

[472] JCI Communs., Inc. v. IBEW, Local 103, 324 F.3d 42, 52 (1st Cir. 2003).

[473] Major League Baseball Players Ass'n v. Garvey, 532 U.S. 504 (2001); Michigan Family Res. v. SEIU, 475 F.3d 746 (6th Cir. 2007).

of the agreement.[474] For instance, in one case an arbitrator awarded no remedy where the plain language of the CBA required awarding a remedy if a violation was found.[475]

The Eleventh Circuit has explained that in circumstances where the arbitrator may have interpreted the CBA, or may not have, the award should not be vacated. "The rule of *Enterprise Wheel* is that, when it is 'not apparent' from the arbitrator's stated reasoning (or lack thereof) whether she permissibly interpreted a collective bargaining agreement or impermissibly modified it, and one can plausibly read the award either way, the court must resolve the ambiguity by finding that the award is an interpretation of the contract and enforcing it. The rule reflects a strong, albeit not irrebuttable, presumption that the arbitrator has interpreted the agreement instead of modifying it."[476]

(4) Public Policy

In limited circumstances, a court may vacate an arbitration award because it conflicts with public policy.[477] The public policy must be an explicit, fundamental, and well-defined one ascertainable from a specific statute or law.[478] For instance, an award reinstating a truck-driver who tested positive twice for marijuana use, during random drug tests, did not violate public policy.[479] The Court recognized truck drivers, like the grievant, are extensively regulated by federal law and that random testing of truck drivers is required.[480] The Court, however, reasoned that the applicable federal law's "remedial aims are complex," promote rehabilitation, and do not

---

[474] Elkouri, supra note 9, § 2.2.A.ii.c.(4); Michigan Family Res. v. SEIU, 475 F.3d 746, 753 (6th Cir. 2007); CenterPoint Energy Res. Corp. v. Gas Workers Union, Local No. 340, 920 F.3d 1163, 1168 (8th Cir. 2019) ("Here, the arbitrator explained at length why he interpreted the contract to allow for review of the discipline. Even if there was serious error in the analysis, the arbitrator was arguably construing the contract."); Monongahela Valley Hosp., Inc. v. United Steel Paper & Forestry Rubber Mfg. Allied Indus. & Serv. Workers Int'l Union AFL-CIO CLC, 946 F.3d 199, 201 (3d Cir. 2019) ("An arbitration award does not "draw[ ] its essence" from a CBA where, as here, an arbitrator not only fails to heed the plain language of the agreement but also exceeds his authority by injecting language into it that was already rejected in prior bargaining.") cf. Delek Ref., Ltd. v. Local 202, United Steel, Paper & Forestry, Rubber, Mfg., Energy, Allied Indus. & Serv. Workers Int'l Union, 891 F.3d 566, 570 (5th Cir. 2018) (noting one rare circumstance when court will vacate a labor award is when the arbitrator ignores the plain language of the CBA).

[475] Operating Eng'rs Local 9 v. Shank-Artukovich, 751 F.2d 364 (10th Cir. 1985).

[476] Wiregrass Metal Trades Council AFL-CIO v. Shaw Envtl. & Infrastructure, Inc., 837 F.3d 1083, 1091–92 (11th Cir. 2016).

[477] Paperworkers v. Misco, Inc., 484 U.S. 29, 43 (1987).

[478] Id.

[479] Eastern Associated Coal Corp. v. Mine Workers District 17, 531 U.S. 57, 65–66 (2000).

[480] Id. at 63–4.

prohibit reinstatement of an employee who fails a random drug test twice.[481] The Court noted that the federal law encouraged collective bargaining rather than requiring a certain outcome for employees who test positive.[482] The Court determined that in light of these "several policies, taken together," the award did not condone drug use or ignore the risk to public safety, but rather punished the grievant with a suspension, required substance-abuse treatment, and provided only one further last chance if the grievant again tests positive.[483] Moreover, the award did not violate any "specific provision of any law or regulation."[484]

(5) Manifest Disregard of Law

Sometimes parties urge vacatur of a labor arbitration award on grounds of manifest disregard of the law. Courts reviewing arbitration under the FAA have occasionally vacated an award because of an arbitrator's manifest disregard of the law.[485] The Supreme Court has left open the issue about whether manifest disregard is a valid basis for vacatur under the FAA, either as an independent ground for review or as a "judicial gloss on the enumerated grounds."[486] The Supreme Court has not yet addressed the issue under Section 301.[487] Some courts have, however, applied the standard of "manifest disregard of the law" to review a labor arbitration award,[488] and some courts have traditionally used the term "manifest disregard of the CBA" to describe one circumstance when an arbitrator exceeded authority.[489] If a case implicates "manifest disregard" as a standard for review, detailed research of the governing law in that jurisdiction is required.

(6) Breach of DFR

In some instances, a court will vacate an arbitration award due to the union's breach of the duty of fair representation during the

---

[481] Id. at 64–65.

[482] Id. at 66.

[483] Id. at 66.

[484] Id. at 66.

[485] Elkouri, supra note 9, § 2.2.A.ii.b.(2); see § 44 for discussion of the relationship between Section 301 and the FAA.

[486] Stolt-Nielsen S.A. v. AnimalFeeds Int'l Corp., 559 U.S. 662, 671 n.3 (2010).

[487] National Football League Players Ass'n v. National Football League Management Council, 2011 WL 31068 (S.D.Ca. 2011) (noting that the Ninth Circuit has not yet decided whether the FAA applies to suits brought under Section 301 and assuming, without deciding, that the manifest disregard of the law standard applies to review a labor arbitration award).

[488] Regional Local Union No. 846 v. Gulf Coast Rebar, Inc., 83 F. Supp. 3d 997, 1010, 1012, 1014 (2015).

[489] Major League Umpires Ass'n v. American League of Professional Baseball Clubs, 357 F.3d 272, 280 (3d Cir. 2004).

arbitration process and permit an employee to litigate de novo the breach of CBA claim against the employer under Section 301.[490] This type of claim is termed a "hybrid 301-DFR" claim because it must be brought against both the union and the employer.[491]

(c) Modification of Awards

If a party seeks enforcement of an award that is incomplete, courts will send the case back to arbitration to complete the award.[492] For instance, the arbitrator may not have calculated the specific amount of damages, and the parties cannot agree on how to calculate them. The Court will send the issue back to the parties to resolve through arbitration.[493]

---

[490] UPS v. Mitchell, 451 U.S. 56, 61–62 (characterizing hybrid DFR suit as one to vacate award); Hines v. Anchor Motor Freight, 424 U.S. 554, 567 (1976); Hypes v. Cyprus Kanawha Corp., 1994 WL 660695, at *4 (4th Cir. November 23, 1994); Goodman v. Potter, 2003 WL 21359535, at *4 (D.D.C. Jan. 29, 2003).

[491] Elkouri, supra note 9, § 2.2.A.ii.d.(2).

[492] Courier-Citizen Co. v. Boston Electrotypers Union No. 11, 702 F.2d 273, 279 (1983).

[493] Elkouri, supra note 9, § 2.2.A.ii.b.(3).

Chapter 8

INTERNATIONAL ARBITRATION

Table of Sections

A. OVERVIEW

Table of Sections

Sec.

§ 50 Introduction: Commercial Arbitration and Public Law Arbitration

International disputes are often arbitrated. That generalization includes disputes between national governments ("States"), disputes between private parties who are citizens of different States, and disputes between States and private parties who are citizens of other States. The "citizens" involved in international arbitration are often giant corporations, and the disputes routinely involve large amounts of money. Rarely is an individual consumer or employee a party in international arbitration, although it does happen.[1] And athletes participating in the Olympic Games are required to sign entry forms in which they agree to settle all Games-related disputes through arbitration before the Court of Arbitration for Sport (CAS).[2]

International arbitration is commonly divided into commercial arbitration and public law arbitration. Of the two, international commercial arbitration is more similar to the domestic arbitration discussed above so international commercial arbitration is discussed next, before turning to international public law arbitration. The first section on international public law arbitration distinguishes it from international commercial arbitration.[3]

§ 51 International Commercial Arbitration: Sources of Law

(a) Treaties, Primarily the New York Convention

(1) Basic Provisions

The most important body of law governing international commercial arbitration is the United Nations Convention on the

[1] For instance, people who work on ships may be involved in international employment arbitration. See, e.g., Lim v. Offshore Specialty Fabricators, 404 F.3d 898 (5th Cir. 2005). See generally Catherine A. Rogers, The Arrival of the "Have-Nots" in International Arbitration, 8 Nev. L.J. 341, 361–63 (2007).

[2] History of the Court of Arbitration for Sports, https://www.tas-cas.org/en/general-information/history-of-the-cas.html (last visited Aug. 8, 2022).

[3] See § 61.

Recognition and Enforcement of Foreign Arbitral Awards.[4] (See Appendix C). This treaty is called the "New York Convention" after its birthplace. It has been ratified by 175 States, including those with the most significant presence in international business, such as the United States, China, Japan, India, Germany, Russia, Brazil, the United Kingdom, France, Italy, Canada, and the Netherlands.[5] States that have ratified (or "acceded to") the New York Convention are known as "Contracting States."

The New York Convention's primary purpose is to make arbitration awards rendered in one State enforceable in the courts of other States.[6] Accordingly, it begins "[t]his Convention shall apply to the recognition and enforcement of arbitral awards made in the territory of a State other than the State where the recognition and enforcement of such awards are sought."[7] The Convention provides that "[e]ach Contracting State shall recognize arbitral awards as binding and enforce them."[8] It contains a narrow list of grounds upon which "[r]ecognition and enforcement of the award may be refused."[9]

The New York Convention succeeded in making enforcement of foreign arbitration awards more routine. So it has long been said that it is generally easier to enforce foreign arbitral awards than foreign court judgments.[10] While enforcing foreign judgments may become as easy as enforcing foreign arbitral awards as more States adopt the 2019 Hague Judgments Convention on the Recognition and Enforcement of Foreign Judgments,[11] that has not yet occurred, so

---

4 Convention on the Recognition and Enforcement of Foreign Arbitral Awards, June 10, 1958, 21 U.S.T. 2517, 330 U.N.T.S. 3, available at https://uncitral.un.org/sites/uncitral.un.org/files/media-documents/uncitral/en/new-york-convention-e.pdf (last visited Nov. 27, 2022).

5 See New York Convention, Contracting states—list of Contracting States New York Arbitration Convention, https://www.newyorkconvention.org/list+of+contracting+states (last visited Aug 9, 2022).

6 Alan Scott Rau, Edward F. Sherman & Scott R. Peppet, Processes of Dispute Resolution: The Role of Lawyers 960 (4th ed. 2006).

7 New York Convention, art. I(1).

8 Id. art. III.

9 Id. art. V.

10 Alan Scott Rau, Edward F. Sherman & Scott R. Peppet, Processes of Dispute Resolution: The Role of Lawyers 961 (4th ed. 2006) ("Under the Convention, enforcement in other jurisdictions of a foreign arbitral award has become considerably more simple and certain than would be the enforcement of the judgment of a foreign court."); Ronald A. Brand, The Continuing Evolution of U.S. Judgments Recognition Law, 55 Colum. J. Transnat'l L. 277, 334–35 (2017) ("the New York Convention provides benefits of arbitration agreement and award recognition and enforcement that are not available on an equal basis to choice of court agreements," so "the ability to choose a court instead of arbitration, and to have that choice supported by the legal system, remains significantly impaired without the Hague Convention in effect.")

11 "At present, there is no federal law that governs the recognition of foreign judgments in the United States, nor is there an international treaty in force." Gibson Dunn, The United States Becomes the Sixth Signatory to the 2019 Hague Judgments

ease of enforcement remains a major reason why parties to international contracts agree to arbitrate.[12] For example, it is generally easier to persuade a United States court to enforce a foreign arbitration award than it is to persuade a United States court to enforce a foreign court's judgment. Similarly, it is generally easier to persuade a foreign court to enforce an arbitration award made in the United States than it is to persuade a foreign court to enforce a United States court's judgment.

In addition to requiring enforcement of arbitration awards rendered in another State, the New York Convention also requires enforcement of executory arbitration agreements.[13] The New York Convention's remedy for breach of such agreements, like the remedy under FAA §§ 3 and 4, is specific performance, that is, a court order to arbitrate.[14] While the New York Convention requires enforcement of executory arbitration agreements, its provisions on that topic reflect less "drafting attention" than was given to its provisions on enforcing arbitration awards.[15] In other words, the gist of the New York Convention is less about getting parties to arbitration than about getting arbitrators' decisions enforced.

In contrast, the FAA's more important impact was on getting parties to arbitration because, prior to its enactment, courts around

---

Convention on the Recognition and Enforcement of Foreign Judgments, March 18, 2022, https://www.gibsondunn.com/the-united-states-becomes-the-sixth-signatory-to-the-2019-hague-judgments-convention-on-the-recognition-and-enforcement-of-foreign-judgments/. However, in 2022 the United States signed the Convention of 2 July 2019 on the Recognition and Enforcement of Foreign Judgments in Civil or Commercial Matters, which "seeks to enhance" "the free flow of judgments across national borders" "by providing a set of clear, predictable rules under which civil and commercial judgments rendered by the courts of one Contracting State are recognized and enforced in other Contracting States." Id. This Convention is "not yet in force," in the U.S. as it "must first undergo a ratification process in U.S. Congress, a procedure that can in some cases take several years." Id.

[12] Christian Bühring-Uhle, Arbitration and Mediation in International Business 135–43 (1996).

[13] New York Convention, art. II(1):

> Each Contracting State shall recognize an agreement in writing under which the parties undertake to submit to arbitration all or any differences which have arisen or which may arise between them in respect of a defined legal relationship, whether contractual or not, concerning a subject matter capable of settlement by arbitration.

[14] Id. art. II(3).

> The court of a Contracting State, when seized of an action in a matter in respect of which the parties have made an agreement within the meaning of this article, shall, at the request of one of the parties, refer the parties to arbitration, unless it finds that the said agreement is null and void, inoperative or incapable of being performed.

Id. See § 52(a).

[15] Gary B. Born, International Commercial Arbitration 839 (2d ed. 2014) ("Article II was added to the Convention in the closing days of negotiations. Little drafting attention was given to the Article.")

the United States generally refused to enforce executory arbitration agreements, but did enforce arbitration awards.[16] So the main arbitration law reform needed in the early 1900s United States was holding parties to their promises to arbitrate rather than litigate, while the main arbitration law reform needed globally in the late 1900s was holding States' to their promises to enforce arbitration awards against their own citizens.

(2) U.S. Ratification and Implementation of the New York and Panama Conventions

In 1970, the United States ratified the New York Convention and Congress enacted Chapter 2 of the FAA (§§ 201–208) to make the New York Convention enforceable in United States courts.[17] The ratification came with the reservation that it would be applied "on the basis of reciprocity, to the recognition and enforcement of only those awards made in the territory of another Contracting State."[18] As a result, an arbitration award rendered in another Contracting State (or an agreement to arbitrate in another Contracting State) is generally enforceable in United States courts.[19]

Additionally, the United States and most States in the Western Hemisphere have ratified the Inter-American Convention on International Commercial Arbitration, also known as the Panama

---

[16] Ian R. Macneil, Richard E. Speidel & Thomas J. Stipanowich, Federal Arbitration Law: Agreements, Awards, and Remedies under the Federal Arbitration Act ch.4 (1994). See also Ian R. Macneil, American Arbitration Law: Reformation, Nationalization, Internationalization 19 (1992).

[17] 9 U.S.C. § 201.

[18] See New York Convention, Contracting states—list of Contracting States New York Arbitration Convention, https://www.newyorkconvention.org/list+of+contracting+states (last visited Aug 09, 2022) (listing ratifying states and their reservations). See also New York Convention, art. I(3) ("When signing, ratifying or acceding to this Convention, or notifying extension under article X hereof, any State may on the basis of reciprocity declare that it will apply the Convention to the recognition and enforcement of awards made only in the territory of another Contracting State.")

[19] Whether the New York Convention applies turns on where the arbitration award is made (or is to be made), not the citizenship of the parties. See, e.g., E.A.S.T., Inc. v. M/V Alaia, 876 F.2d 1168 (5th Cir. 1989); Ministry of Defense of the Islamic Republic of Iran v. Gould, Inc., 887 F.2d 1357 (9th Cir. 1989); Continental Transfert Technique Ltd. v. Federal Government of Nigeria, 697 F. Supp.2d 46, 56 (D.D.C. 2010) ("the critical element is the place of the award: if that place is in the territory of a party to the Convention, all other Convention states are required to recognize and enforce the award, regardless of the citizenship or domicile of the parties to the arbitration") (quoting TermoRio S.A. E.S.P. v. Electranta S.P., 487 F.3d 928, 934 (D.C. Cir. 2007)).

However, the New York Convention does not govern arbitration "entirely between citizens of the United States" unless their "relationship involves property located abroad, envisages performance or enforcement abroad, or has some other reasonable relation with one or more foreign states." 9 U.S.C. § 202.

Convention.[20] The New York Convention does not govern "[i]f a majority of the parties to the arbitration agreement are citizens of a State or States" that have signed the Inter-American Convention,[21] which also enforces arbitration awards.[22] The Inter-American Convention "was obviously modeled"[23] on the New York Convention and the Second Circuit has stated that "Congress intended the Inter-American Convention to reach the same results as those reached under the New York Convention."[24] According to the Eleventh Circuit, "it is well-settled that where the New York and Panama Conventions are substantively the same," "decisions under the New York Convention apply with equal force to cases under the Panama Convention."[25]

However, while Article 1 of the Inter-American Convention provides that arbitration agreements are "valid," one of the Convention's "major deficiencies" is that it lacks a provision obligating courts to enforce arbitration agreements by ordering parties to arbitration.[26] Nevertheless, some U.S. courts have ordered such parties to arbitration in reliance on FAA § 307, which provides that FAA "Chapter 1 [9 U.S.C. §§ 1–16] applies to actions and proceedings brought under this chapter to the extent chapter 1 is not in conflict with this chapter or the Inter-American Convention as ratified by the United States."[27] In this indirect fashion, courts have applied FAA § 2 and § 4 to order arbitration in Inter-American Convention cases.[28]

---

[20] 9 U.S.C. § 305(1). See Inter-American Convention on International Commercial Arbitration, Jan. 30, 1975, 1975 O.A.S.T.S. No.42, 14 I.L.M. 336, available at http://www.oas.org/DIL/CIDIPI_convention_arbitration.htm (last visited Aug.1, 2011). See generally John P. Bowman, The Panama Convention and Its Implementation under the Federal Arbitration Act (2002).

[21] 9 U.S.C. § 305(1). For a list of signatories, see Department of International Law, https://www.oas.org/juridico/english/sigs/b-35.html (last visited Aug.09, 2022).

[22] Inter-American Convention on International Commercial Arbitration, OAS, http://www.oas.org/en/sla/dil/inter_american_treaties_B-35_international_commercial_arbitration.asp (last visited Nov. 29, 2022).

[23] Alan Scott Rau, Edward F. Sherman & Scott R. Peppet, Processes of Dispute Resolution: The Role of Lawyers 968–69 (4th ed. 2006).

[24] Productos Mercantiles E Industriales, S.A. v. Faberge USA, Inc., 23 F.3d 41, 45 (2d Cir. 1994). The Organization of American States promulgated the Inter-American Convention at a time when only three Latin American states had ratified the New York Convention. See Jonathan C. Hamilton, Three Decades of Latin American Commercial Arbitration, 30 U. Pa. J. Int'l L. 1099, 1100 (2009).

[25] Tecnicas Reunidas de Talara S.A.C. v. SSK Ingenieria y Construccion S.A.C., 40 F. 4th 1339, 1344 (11th Cir. 2022).

[26] Claus von Wobeser, The Influence of the New York Convention in Latin America and on the Inter-American Convention on International Commercial Arbitration, 2 No. 1 Disp. Resol. Int'l 43, 51 (May 2008).

[27] 9 U.S.C. § 307.

[28] Paramedics Electromedicia Comercial Ltda. v. Medical Sys. Info. Techs., Inc., 2003 WL 23641529 (S.D.N.Y. June 4, 2003) (FAA § 4), remanded on other grounds,

(3) U.S. Exceptions from New York Convention

The general enforceability in United States courts of foreign arbitration agreements and awards is subject to two important exceptions found in FAA § 202.

First, the New York Convention does not govern an arbitration agreement or award "entirely between citizens of the United States," unless their "relationship involves property located abroad, envisages performance or enforcement abroad, or has some other reasonable relation with one or more foreign states."[29] Courts have held that agreeing to arbitrate in another State is not, without more, enough of a relation with a foreign state to bring the arbitration within the coverage of the Convention.[30] In contrast, "location of property, or designation of performance or enforcement, in a foreign jurisdiction are examples of non-U.S. elements whose presence is sufficient," "even if the arbitration agreement is exclusively between U.S. parties."[31]

Second, the United States ratified the New York Convention with the reservation that it does not govern an arbitration agreement

369 F.3d 645, 658 (2d Cir. 2004); Siderurgica del Orinoco (SIDOR), CA v. Linea Naviera de Cabotaje, C.A., 1999 WL 632870 (S.D.N.Y. Aug. 19, 1999) (FAA § 2).

29 9 U.S.C. § 202.

30 Jones v. Sea Tow Services Freeport NY Inc., 30 F.3d 360 (2d Cir. 1994); Reinholtz v. Retriever Marine Towing & Salvage, 1993 WL 414719 (S.D. Fla.1993); Brier v. Northstar Marine, Inc., 1992 WL 350292 (D.N.J. 1992). See also Ensco Offshore Co. v. Titan Marine L.L.C., 370 F. Supp. 2d 594, 601 (S.D. Tex. 2005)(granting Texas rig owner's motion for a declaration that the arbitration clause compelling arbitration in London with Florida salvor was invalid because there was "not a reasonable link between the legal relationship and England or any other foreign state"; court did not order arbitration anywhere); Nomanbhoy v. Vahanvaty, No. 11 C 2456, 2011 WL 6736052, at *5 (N.D. Ill. Dec. 21, 2011) (denying Illinois CEO of Illinois company's motion to confirm an arbitration award under the New York Convention from an arbitration in Sri Lanka, between CEO and CEO's siblings and niece who were also shareholders of the company, holding the parties' agreement did not meet the reasonable relationship requirement of 9 U.S.C. 202 because the legal relationship at issue, the parties' ownership and operation of the company which had no property or operations in a foreign state, was completely domestic; court did not order arbitration anywhere); Armstrong v. NCL (Bahamas) Ltd., 998 F. Supp. 2d 1335 (S.D. Fla. 2013) (denying Bahamian employer's motion to compel arbitration in the U.S. under Bahamian law, as a Seaman who fell from stage on which he was performing while aboard a ship brought action in state court against his employer. The court held a provision in the employee's employment agreement stating arbitration must occur under Bahamian Law in the county of citizenship of the employee (the United States) was unenforceable because the parties' relationship did not have sufficient foreign nexus for removal jurisdiction under the Convention on Recognition and Enforcement of Foreign Arbitral Award because the plaintiff worked only aboard the ship and was never requested to perform work or services on foreign soil; court did not order arbitration anywhere.).

31 Restatement (Third) U.S. Law of Int'l Comm. Arb. § 1.4 (2019).

or award not "considered as commercial."[32] However, FAA § 202's definition of "commercial" incorporates FAA § 2's "involving commerce," which has been broadly interpreted by the Supreme Court.[33] As a result, the definition of "commercial" in United States law may be "the broadest of any signatory to the Convention."[34] For example, employment relationships are generally considered "commercial" by United States courts,[35] but courts of other States might disagree. What sorts of disputes might not be "considered as commercial"? Perhaps examples would include "family law disputes, state boundary disputes, and disputes presenting political issues."[36]

(4) Awards Made in the U.S. but "Not Considered as Domestic"

In addition to generally making enforceable in United States courts arbitration awards rendered in another Contracting State, the New York Convention also applies to awards made in the United States if those awards are "not considered as domestic."[37] An oft-cited Second Circuit case, *Bergesen v. Joseph Muller Corp.*,[38] says awards "not considered as domestic" are "made within the legal framework of another country, e.g., pronounced in accordance with foreign law or involving parties domiciled or having their principal place of business outside the enforcing jurisdiction."[39] An award rendered in

---

[32] 9 U.S.C. § 202 ("An arbitration agreement or arbitral award arising out of a legal relationship, whether contractual or not, *which is considered as commercial*, including a transaction, contract, or agreement described in section 2 of this title, falls under the Convention.") (emphasis added); New York Convention, Art. I(3) ("When signing, ratifying or acceding to this Convention, or notifying extension under article X hereof, any State * * * may also declare that it will apply the Convention only to differences arising out of legal relationships, whether contractual or not, *which are considered as commercial* under the national law of the State making such declaration.") (emphasis added).

[33] See § 5(c).

[34] Ian R. Macneil, Richard E. Speidel & Thomas J. Stipanowich, Federal Arbitration Law § 44.9.3.3 (1994).

[35] Rogers v. Royal Caribbean Cruise Line, 547 F.3d 1148, 1155 (9th Cir. 2008) ("The employment contracts of seafarers 'aris[e] out of legal relationship[s] . . . which [are] considered as commercial,' and therefore those contracts 'fall[ ] under the [C]onvention.' "); Bautista v. Star Cruises, 396 F.3d 1289, 1297–1300 (11th Cir. 2005).

[36] Christopher R. Drahozal, Commercial Arbitration: Cases and Problems 306 (2d ed.2006). See also Island Territory of Curacao v. Solitron Devices, Inc., 356 F. Supp. 1, 13 (S.D.N.Y. 1973) ("Research has developed nothing to show what the purpose of the 'commercial' limitation was. We may logically speculate that it was to exclude matrimonial and other domestic relations awards, political awards, and the like.") See also Gary B. Born, International Commercial Arbitration 299–302 (2d ed.2014).

[37] New York Convention, art. I(1) ("This Convention * * * shall also apply to arbitral awards not considered as domestic awards in the State where their recognition and enforcement are sought.")

[38] 710 F.2d 928, 932 (2d Cir. 1983).

[39] Id. at 932. See also Ledee v. Ceramiche Ragno, 684 F.2d 184, 187 (1st Cir. 1982) (relevant question is "Is a party to the agreement not an American citizen, or does the commercial relationship have some reasonable relation with one or more foreign states?"); Kaliroy Produce Co., Inc. v. Pacific Tomato Growers, Inc., 730 F.

the United States may be "not considered as domestic" (and thus governed by the New York Convention) even if the arbitration was between United States citizens, so long as it involved performance abroad.[40]

(b) National Law

(1) Implementing Legislation

In addition to the New York Convention and other treaties, international arbitration is also governed by national arbitration law. "In virtually all Contracting States, the New York Convention has been implemented through national legislation."[41] While many States have implemented the New York Convention by adopting the United Nations Commission for International Trade Law (UNCITRAL) Model Law on International Arbitration,[42] the United States has not.[43] Instead, the United States legislation implementing the New York Convention is Chapter 2 of the FAA.[44] The United States legislation implementing the Panama Convention is Chapter 3 of the FAA.[45] These chapters of the FAA are the core of the United States' national law on international commercial arbitration. In addition, U.S. law on international commercial arbitration includes

---

Supp.2d 1036, 1039 (D. Ariz. 2010) (award rendered in Arizona "is non-domestic and within the scope of the Convention" because the case "involves one foreign party (ALP) and two domestic parties (PTG and Kaliroy), and principally involved conduct and contract performance in the United States and Mexico. Moreover, the Tribunal applied Arizona law in issuing the Award."); Matter of Arbitration Between Trans Chemical Ltd. and China Nat. Machinery Import and China National Machinery Import and Export Corp., 978 F. Supp. 266, 297 (S.D. Tex. 1997) ("adopt[ing] the Bergesen definition of 'nondomestic' as encompassing actions to confirm arbitration awards rendered in the United States between two foreign parties.")

[40] See Lander Co., Inc. v. MMP Investments, Inc., 107 F.3d 476, 482 (7th Cir. 1997). In Lander Co., the Seventh Circuit held that such cases are governed by both the Convention and the FAA. Id. at 481. Accord Freudensprung v. Offshore Technical Services, Inc., 379 F.3d 327, 341 (5th Cir. 2004); Bergesen v. Joseph Muller Corp., 710 F.2d 928, 934 (2d Cir. 1983) ("no reason to assume that Congress did not intend to provide overlapping coverage between the Convention and the Federal Arbitration Act.").

[41] Gary B. Born, International Commercial Arbitration 113 (2d ed.2014).

[42] See UNCITRAL Arbitration Rules—United Nations, https://uncitral.un.org/sites/uncitral.un.org/files/media-documents/uncitral/en/uncitral-arbitration-rules-2013-e.pdf (last visited Aug 9, 2022).

[43] However, California, Texas and a few other U.S. states have enacted the UNCITRAL Model Law. Id.

[44] 9 U.S.C. §§ 201–08. And one might say Chapter 1 of the FAA also implements the New York Convention because FAA § 208 provides that "Chapter 1 applies to actions and proceedings brought under this chapter to the extent that chapter is not in conflict with this chapter or the Convention as ratified by the United States."

[45] 9 U.S.C. §§ 301–07. And one might say Chapter 1 of the FAA also implements the Panama Convention because FAA § 307 provides that "Chapter 1 applies to actions and proceedings brought under this chapter to the extent chapter 1 is not in conflict with this chapter or the Inter-American Convention as ratified by the United States."

case law, which is helpfully summarized in the Restatement on The United States Law of International Commercial Arbitration.

If an arbitration agreement or award is covered by (within the scope of) the New York Convention or other treaty, then the treaty might be expected to supersede any conflicting national law. But national courts have not always readily subordinated their national laws to the treaties.[46] For instance, in the United States "acts of Congress remain on a par with treaties,"[47] "the Constitution trumps treaties,"[48] and at least one court has refused to enforce an international commercial arbitration award on constitutional grounds.[49] In sum, "the practical effect" of the New York Convention depends on national law—including case law interpreting the Convention and statutes implementing it—and therefore varies from State to State.[50]

With national law on arbitration continuing to vary from State to State, cases can turn on the question of which State's arbitration law governs, a question generally determined by the seat of arbitration.

(2) The Choice of National Arbitration Law: The "Seat" of Arbitration

The place (or "seat") in which an international commercial arbitration occurs is significant because, under widely recognized choice-of-law principles, it is the seat State's *arbitration* law that governs the dispute, even if some other State's *substantive* law governs that dispute.[51] For instance, a contract might contain a New

---

[46] Margaret L. Moses, The Principles and Practice of International Commercial Arbitration 17 (2008) (the New York Convention "should supercede domestic law regarding the proper form of an arbitration agreement. However, State courts have not always viewed the Convention as superceding their domestic law.") For example, the United States Supreme Court has held "that an Act of Congress * * * is on a full parity with a treaty, and that when a statute which is subsequent in time is inconsistent with a treaty, the statute to the extent of conflict renders the treaty null." Breard v. Greene, 523 U.S. 371, 376 (1998) (quotations omitted).

[47] William W. Park & Alexander A. Yanos, Treaty Obligations and National Law: Emerging Conflicts in International Arbitration, 58 Hastings L.J. 251, 252 (2006).

[48] Id.

[49] Base Metal Trading, Ltd. v. OJSC "Novokuznetsky Aluminium Factory," 283 F.3d 208 (4th Cir. 2002) (due process requirements for personal jurisdiction). For contrary authority on that personal jurisdiction issue, see Christopher R. Drahozal, Commercial Arbitration: Cases and Problems 620–22 (3d ed.2013).

[50] Gary B. Born, International Commercial Arbitration 113 (2d ed. 2014).

[51] Restatement (Third) U.S. Law of Int'l Comm. Arb. § 1.3 (2019) ("an arbitral proceeding is ordinarily governed by the arbitration law of the jurisdiction in which it is seated. It would, for example, be subject to any mandatory rules in the arbitration law of the seat. Similarly, the grounds for vacating or setting aside the award would be those in the arbitration law of the seat."). See, e.g., Balkan Energy Ltd. v. Republic of Ghana, 302 F. Supp. 3d 144, 152–153 (D.D.C. 2018) ('In this case, because the parties designated in the arbitral clause that The Hague, Netherlands was to serve as

York choice-of-law clause but provide for arbitration in Mexico. While the arbitrators would likely apply New York substantive law to the merits of the underlying dispute, any judicial involvement in the arbitration would likely be by a Mexican court applying Mexican arbitration law.[52] Possible topics for such judicial involvement (all likely governed by the seat's arbitration law) include arbitrator selection, the arbitration process, and the enforcement or setting aside of the arbitration award.[53]

With the seat's arbitration law governing all this, a lot can turn on the choice of seat, so that choice may be a topic of negotiation at the time a contract is formed. "Parties frequently choose a seat of arbitration in a country where neither party's business interests are located. In addition, the seat may be chosen simply because it is convenient to both parties."[54] The seat can, many authorities suggest, be different from where the arbitration hearing actually occurs.[55] If, for example, the parties want English arbitration law to apply, they can contractually designate England as the seat of arbitration and then hold the arbitration hearings in some other country.[56]

---

the seat of arbitration, Dutch law supplied the law applicable to the arbitration agreement."), appeal dismissed, 2018 WL 5115572 (D.C. Cir. Oct. 12, 2018).

[52] See International Standard Elec. Corp. v. Bridas Sociedad Anonima Petrolera, Indus. Y Comercial, 745 F. Supp. 172 (S.D.N.Y. 1990). In *Bridas*, the arbitration occurred in Mexico City under a contract with a New York choice of law clause. The federal court in New York held that it lacked jurisdiction to set aside award because New York Convention art. V's reference to the country "under the laws of which [the] award was made" refers

> exclusively to procedural and not substantive law, and more precisely, to the regimen or scheme of arbitral procedural law under which the arbitration was conducted, and not the substantive law of contract which was applied in the case.
>
> In this case, the parties subjected themselves to the procedural law of Mexico. Hence, since the situs, or forum of the arbitration is Mexico, and the governing procedural law is that of Mexico, only the courts of Mexico have jurisdiction under the Convention to vacate the award. ISEC's petition to vacate the award is therefore dismissed.

Id. at 178.

[53] Alan Scott Rau, Edward F. Sherman & Scott R. Peppet, Processes of Dispute Resolution: The Role of Lawyers 962 (4th ed. 2006).

[54] Margaret L. Moses, The Principles and Practice of International Commercial Arbitration 56 (2008).

[55] Restatement (Third) U.S. Law of Int'l Comm. Arb. § 1.3 (2019) ("The seat is not necessarily the location at which any arbitral hearings are held. Although the two often are the same, they need not be: the parties or arbitrators can agree to hold the hearings at a location other than the seat."); English Arbitration Act of 1996 § 100(2) ("an award shall be treated as made at the seat of the arbitration, regardless of where it was signed, dispatched or delivered to any of the parties.")

[56] "England is one of the leading jurisdictions in the world for international commercial arbitration (the other two top contenders are France and Switzerland)." S.I. Strong, Border Skirmishes: The Intersection Between Litigation and International Commercial Arbitration, 2012 J. Disp. Resol. 1, 5 (2012).

The parties' contract can select the seat of arbitration directly by naming it, or indirectly by delegating the choice of seat to the arbitration organization the contract names to administer the arbitration, such as the International Chamber of Commerce. Another such organization is the American Arbitration Association ("AAA"). When the AAA decides the seat (or "locale") of arbitration, it will consider:

1. Location of parties and attorneys.
2. Location of witnesses and documents.
3. Location of records.
4. Where the evidence is located (i.e., location of a construction site).
5. Consideration of the relative difficulty in traveling and cost to parties.
6. Place of performance of the contract.
7. Place of previous court actions.
8. Location of most appropriate panel.
9. Any other reasonable arguments that might affect the locale determination.[57]

What happens if the parties neither select the seat of arbitration directly nor delegate seat-choice to an arbitration organization? If such parties cannot resolve their dispute about where to seat the arbitration, they may litigate the question in national courts. However, most States' arbitration laws deny courts the power to select an arbitral seat. Instead, most States' arbitration laws give arbitrators and arbitration organizations the power to select an arbitral seat, but these laws only apply to arbitrations already seated within that State.[58] Accordingly, some States' arbitration laws hold that arbitration clauses that do not specify an arbitral seat or a means of selecting the arbitral seat are invalid.[59] And when national courts do decide the arbitral seat, there is a risk that different States' courts will select different arbitral seats for the same case.[60]

---

57 Am. Arb. Ass'n, Locale Determinations: ICDR, available at https://www.icdr.org/sites/default/files/document_repository/AAA360_ICDR_Council_Standards.pdf.

58 Gary B. Born, International Commercial Arbitration 2105 (2d ed. 2014) ("[T]he absence of agreement on the arbitral seat arguably prevents application of [national arbitration law] statutory mechanisms that empower the arbitrators to select an arbitral seat."). So a court may refuse to select a seat and refuse to grant anyone else the power to select a seat. In sum, circularity or bootstrapping problem arises.

59 Id.

60 See Tonicstar Ltd v. Am. Home Assur. Co. [2004] EWHC 1234 (Q.B.). This case involved parallel judicial proceedings in New York and England, and later requests for

(c) *Contracting for the Procedural Rules and Substantive Law to Be Applied to a Particular Case*

While international commercial arbitration is typically slower and more costly than domestic arbitration,[61] that is not much of a criticism because the alternative to international arbitration is not domestic arbitration but international litigation. And parties often fear home-party bias in foreign courts along with the unfamiliarity of foreign law.[62]

International arbitration avoids the unfamiliarity and possible bias of foreign courts by substituting the procedures and arbitrators chosen by the parties.[63] International commercial arbitration agreements often incorporate the procedural rules of an arbitration organization such as the International Chamber of Commerce[64] or the London Court of International Arbitration.[65] These organizations provide procedural rules and administer arbitrations according to them. In contrast, another organization—the United Nations Commission for International Trade Law (UNCITRAL)—promulgates a popular set of procedural rules but does not administer arbitration.[66]

---

arbitration in both England and New York. The English courts issued an antisuit injunction to prevent the respondents from getting a U.S. court to compel arbitration in New York. The English court reasoned that the dispute was more closely connected to England, and that English courts should therefore decide the arbitral seat. Although there was no conflicting US court decision, such a scenario is conceivable.

61 Alan Scott Rau, Edward F. Sherman & Scott R. Peppet, Processes of Dispute Resolution: The Role of Lawyers 631 (4th ed. 2006) ("It is inevitable that international arbitration will often turn out to be considerably more protracted and expensive than its domestic counterpart.")

62 Edward Brunet, Charles B. Craver & Ellen E. Deason, Alternative Dispute Resolution: The Advocate's Perspective 442–44 (4th ed. 2011). "Parties choose international arbitration primarily because they fear being subject to the potentially biased decisions of the national courts of their business-partner-turned-adversary." George A. Bermann, Jack J. Coe, Jr., Christopher R. Drahozal & Catherine A. Rogers, Restating the U.S. Law of International Commercial Arbitration, 113 Penn St. L. Rev. 1342 (2009).

63 International commercial arbitration offers a "time-tested blend of common law and civil law procedures (as opposed to international litigation, which typically gives one party a home-court advantage in terms of procedure)." S.I. Strong, Navigating the Borders Between International Commercial Arbitration and U.S. Federal Courts: A Jurisprudential GPS, 2012 J. Disp. Resol. 119, 124.

64 Alan Scott Rau, Edward F. Sherman & Scott R. Peppet, Processes of Dispute Resolution: The Role of Lawyers 628 (4th ed. 2006). ("A large number of other organizations besides the AAA compete in the administration of international commercial arbitrations; by far the most important of these is the International Chamber of Commerce (ICC) in Paris.")

65 See London Court of International Arbitration (LCIA), http://www.lcia.org (last visited Aug. 10, 2022).

66 See UNCITRAL Arbitration Rules (as revised in 2021), https://uncitral.un.org/sites/uncitral.un.org/files/media-documents/uncitral/en/21-07996_expedited-

Parties in international arbitration can avoid application of foreign law through *amiable composition*, the arbitrator's power to ignore any State's law and apply instead the customs of international commerce,[67] but parties rarely choose this sort of arbitration.[68] More often, they include a choice of law clause agreeing that a particular State's substantive law will govern any dispute they have.

B. FORMATION OF ENFORCEABLE INTERNATIONAL COMMERCIAL ARBITRATION AGREEMENTS

Table of Sections

---

§ 52 Formation

(a) Enforcement of Executory Arbitration Agreements

The New York Convention makes executory arbitration agreements enforceable. Article II(1) says:

> Each Contracting State shall recognize an agreement in writing under which the parties undertake to submit to arbitration all or any differences which have arisen or which may arise between them in respect of a defined legal relationship, whether contractual or not, concerning a subject matter capable of settlement by arbitration.[69]

Just as the remedy for breach of a domestic executory arbitration agreement is specific performance, rather than money damages,[70] the

---

arbitration-e-ebook.pdf; Margaret L. Moses, The Principles and Practice of International Commercial Arbitration 9 (2008).

[67] See generally Lex Mercatoria and Arbitration (Thomas Carbonneau ed., Rev.ed.1998).

[68] Christopher R. Drahozal, Contracting Out of National Law: An Empirical Look at the New Law Merchant, 80 Notre Dame L. Rev. 523 (2005).

[69] New York Convention, art. II(1).

[70] See § 5(b).

New York Convention also does not direct courts to award money damages for breach of international executory arbitration agreements. Rather it directs courts to "refer the parties to arbitration," that is, specifically enforce the agreement to arbitrate:

> The court of a Contracting State, when seized of an action in a matter in respect of which the parties have made an agreement within the meaning of this article, shall, at the request of one of the parties, refer the parties to arbitration, unless it finds that the said agreement is null and void, inoperative or incapable of being performed.[71]

For example, if Buyer sues Seller despite an international commercial arbitration agreement between them, Seller can get a court to stay or dismiss Buyer's lawsuit.[72]

(b) National Law Governs Formation

Suppose though that Buyer denies that its contract with Seller contains an arbitration clause. That is, suppose Buyer denies that "the parties have made an agreement within the meaning of" Article II of the New York Convention. "It is axiomatic," the Restatement says, "that 'arbitration is a matter of contract' and that arbitrators enjoy authority to resolve disputes only because the parties have agreed to submit their grievances to arbitration. Thus, a court may not compel arbitration until it has resolved the question of the very existence of an arbitration agreement. An abundant case law so holds."[73]

---

[71] New York Convention, art. II(3). See also Domenico Di Pietro & Martin Platte, Enforcement of International Arbitration Awards 66 (2001) ("refer the parties to arbitration" "means that the Court becomes incompetent to entertain the case and must stay proceedings"); 9 U.S.C. § 206 ("A court having jurisdiction under this chapter may direct that arbitration be held in accordance with the agreement at any place therein provided for, whether that place is within or without the United States. Such court may also appoint arbitrators in accordance with the provisions of the agreement."). FAA § 208 provides that "Chapter 1 applies to actions and proceedings brought under this chapter to the extent that chapter is not in conflict with this chapter or the Convention as ratified by the United States." As Chapter 1 includes FAA § 3 staying litigation, this provision presumably applies to actions under FAA Chapter 2.

[72] Restatement (Third) U.S. Law of Int'l Comm. Arb. § 2.1(b) (2019) ("A court enforces an international arbitration agreement by either or both of the following: (1) staying or dismissing judicial proceedings regarding a dispute that is subject to the agreement; and (2) compelling arbitration of a dispute that is subject to the agreement.") See, e.g., Rhone Mediterranee Compagnia Francese Di Assicurazioni E Riassicurazioni v. Lauro, 555 F. Supp. 481 (D.V.I. 1982), aff'd, 712 F.2d 50 (3d Cir. 1983) (stay): Filanto, S.p.A. v. Chilewich Intern. Corp., 789 F. Supp. 1229 (S.D.N.Y.1992) (dismiss).

[73] Restatement (Third) U.S. Law of Int'l Comm. Arb. § 2.13 Note a (2019).

As in the domestic context, challenges to the existence of international arbitration agreements can take a wide variety of forms, so the Restatement lists arguments:

(a) that there was no assent;

(b) that there was no offer or acceptance;

(c) that the offer was revoked prior to acceptance;

(d) that the arbitration term constituted a proposal to materially alter the contract not accepted by the resisting party thus preventing a contract from being formed;

(e) that there was a counteroffer rather than an acceptance;

(f) that there was merely an agreement to agree;

(g) that there was a lack of consideration;

(h) that the contract was not yet formed;

(i) that there was a lack of authority to bind the party sought to be bound;

(j) that essential terms of the contract, upon which assent depends, had not been agreed upon;

(k) that the contract was superseded; and

(*l*) that the alleged agreement or contract was a forgery or sham.[74]

What body of law resolves these issues? An example is *Matter of Ferrara S.p.A.*,[75] in which the arbitration clause apparently appeared, not right above the signature line, but rather on the back of the page containing signatures of the parties' agents.[76] This location of the arbitration clause made it unenforceable under Italian law, according to the buyer.[77] The buyer argued that Italian law governed the question whether the parties formed an arbitration agreement.[78] In contrast, according to the United States district court, the arbitration clause *would* be enforceable under United States law. So, the *Ferrara* court confronted a choice-of-law question, that is, whether Italian or United States law governed the question whether the parties formed an arbitration agreement.

Upon analysis, the *Ferrara* court chose to apply United States law. Other United States cases similarly apply U.S. law to determine

---

74 Id.

75 441 F. Supp. 778 (S.D.N.Y. 1977), aff'd mem., 580 F.2d 1044 (2d Cir. 1978).

76 Id. at 779.

77 Id. at 780.

78 Id.

whether the parties have formed an international arbitration agreement.[79] This is understandable, as Article II of the New York Convention provides courts with little guidance about how to determine whether the parties have formed an arbitration agreement. The little Article II provides is its requirement that the agreement be "in writing."[80] But Article II provides no legal rules on mutual assent, offer and acceptance, consideration, or any other topics that might factor into determining whether the parties have formed an arbitration agreement. Nor does Article II tell courts where to look to find such legal rules. In other words, Article II lacks a choice-of-law rule.[81] It does not say, for example, to apply the law of the State in which the agreement was allegedly formed. Or to apply the law of the State in which the alleged agreement would be performed (the "seat" of arbitration). "Neither the New York Convention nor the FAA prescribes the law applicable to the existence of an arbitral agreement on the occasion of the agreement's enforcement," so "the Restatement takes the view that the issue should be subject to the law indicated by the choice-of-law rules of the forum."[82]

(c) The Requirement of a Writing

Under domestic United States law, an oral arbitration agreement is likely unenforceable[83] and many other States' national laws also enforce only written arbitration agreements.[84] Similarly, the New York Convention suggests that only written arbitration agreements are enforceable, as it provides that "Each Contracting State shall recognize an *agreement in writing* under which the parties undertake to submit to arbitration."[85] It then defines "agreement in writing" to "include an arbitral clause in a contract or

---

79 Aggarao v. MOL Ship Mgmt. Co., 675 F.3d 355, 367 (4th Cir. 2012) (in a Convention case, applying Maryland law).

80 See § 52 (c).

81 As Gary Born explains:

> Article II's terms reflect the fact that the New York Convention was, until late in its drafting process, directly solely at the recognition of arbitral awards, and not arbitration agreements. When Article II of the Convention was expanded, to require recognition of arbitration agreements, relatively little thought was directed towards choice-of-law or other issues relating to the new provisions.

Gary B. Born, International Commercial Arbitration 462 (2009).

82 Restatement (Third) U.S. Law of Int'l Comm. Arb. § 2.13 Note d(i) (2019).

83 See § 17(a).

84 See, e.g., UNCITRAL Model Law, art. 7 (Option I, as amended); Swiss PILA, art. 178(I); English Arbitration Act, § 5; French Code of Civil Procedure, art. 1443.

85 New York Convention, art. II(1).

an arbitration agreement, signed by the parties or contained in an exchange of letters or telegrams."[86]

The reference to "letters or telegrams" evokes the technology of the era in which the Convention was written. In contrast, international commercial arbitration agreements formed through more-modern electronic communication, such as email, may be enforceable but few reported cases have addressed the question.[87]

Even if the communications technology used by the parties fits within the Convention's definition of "agreement in writing," the arbitration agreement may not be enforceable because it fails the signature requirement. As noted above, Article II(2) defines "agreement in writing" to "include an arbitral clause in a contract or an arbitration agreement, *signed by the parties* or contained in an exchange of letters or telegrams."[88] To what does this signature requirement apply? Most United States courts hold that the signature requirement applies to both the typical predispute arbitration agreement (the "arbitral clause in a contract") and a standalone "arbitration agreement," which is more often formed post-dispute and called a "submission agreement,"[89] but does not apply to

---

[86] New York Convention, art. II(2). Whether an "agreement in writing" in fact occurred can be a fact-intensive inquiry. See, e.g., Filanto, S.p.A. v. Chilewich Intern. Corp., 789 F. Supp. 1229, 1236–37 (S.D.N.Y. 1992).

[87] See § 17(a). There is a United Nations Convention on the Use of Electronic Communications in International Contracts (ECC). G.A. Res. 60/21, U.N. Doc. A/Res/60/21, U.N. Sales No E.07.V.2 (Dec. 9, 2005), available at https://www.parliament.gov.fj/wp-content/uploads/2017/02/ECC-Convention-2005.pdf. It provides that "[w]here the law requires that a communication or a contract should be in writing, or provides consequences for the absence of a writing, that requirement is met by an electronic communication if the information contained therein is accessible so as to be usable for subsequent reference." Id. art.9(2). The ECC applies to the New York Convention. Id. art. 20(1). See also Chloe Z Fishing Co., Inc. v. Odyssey Re (London) Ltd., 109 F. Supp. 2d 1236, 1250 (S.D. Cal. 2000) ("Under plaintiffs' unduly restrictive definition, only a written message sent in an envelope with a signature or a message transmitted by telegraph would satisfy the letter and telegram requirements respectively. However, the Court finds that Article II section 2 of the Convention could not have intended to exclude all other forms of written communications regularly utilized to conduct commerce in the various signatory nations by failing to provide an exhaustive list of 'letters' or 'telegrams.' ") But see Decision of the Hologaland Court of Appeal, 16 August 1999, Yearbook on Commercial Arbitration XXVII, at 519 (2002) (exchange of emails did not satisfy writing requirement).

[88] New York Convention, art. II(2) (emphasis added).

[89] See Czarina, LLC v. W.F. Poe Syndicate, 358 F.3d 1286, 1290–91 (11th Cir. 2004) (affirming refusal to enforce an arbitration award based on an unsigned arbitration clause); Kahn Lucas Lancaster, Inc. v. Lark International Ltd., 186 F.3d 210, 217 (2d Cir. 1999), abrogated in part on other grounds by Sarhank Group v. Oracle Corp., 404 F.3d 657, 660 n. 2 (2d Cir. 2005), ("Grammatically, the comma immediately following 'an arbitration agreement' serves to separate the series ('an arbitral clause in a contract or an arbitration agreement') from the modifying phrase ('signed by the parties or contained in an exchange of letters or telegrams'), and suggests that the modifying phrase is meant to apply to both elements in the series. Indeed, this comma can serve no other grammatical purpose.") But see Sphere Drake Insurance PLC v.

an arbitration agreement formed by "an exchange of letters or telegrams."[90]

§ 53 Separability

In the domestic United States context, the Supreme Court has repeatedly held that "a challenge to the validity of the contract as a whole, and not specifically to the arbitration clause, must go to the arbitrator."[91] These cases occurred before arbitration—when one party sought in court to compel arbitration and the other party resisted on the ground that the contract containing the arbitration agreement was voidable.[92] This pre-arbitration separability is not widely adopted outside the United States.[93]

By contrast, in the international commercial context post-arbitration separability is a firmly established legal concept. If the arbitrators hold invalid the contract containing the arbitration agreement, the losing party may argue the arbitration award is a nullity because the arbitrators' jurisdiction to render the award rests entirely on a now-invalidated contract. This argument is precluded by treating the arbitration agreement as separate from the invalidated contract containing it. "As a consequence," flowing from this post-arbitration separability, the Restatement says, "an arbitral tribunal is able to find on the merits that the underlying agreement is invalid or unenforceable, without retroactively undermining the tribunal's authority to make that determination in the first place."[94] Many States' national laws adopt this post-arbitration separability.[95]

In addition, international commercial arbitration agreements governed by U.S. law are also subject to the pre-arbitration separability doctrine discussed in Sections 21–23. Consequently,

---

Marine Towing, Inc., 16 F.3d 666, 667–69 (5th Cir. 1994) (signature not required to enforce "arbitral clause in a contract").

90 See Standard Bent Glass Corp. v. Glassrobots Oy, 333 F.3d 440, 449–50 (3d Cir. 2003).

91 Buckeye Check Cashing, Inc. v. Cardegna, 546 U.S. 440, 449 (2006). See §§ 21–23.

92 See §§ 21–23.

93 George A. Bermann, The "Gateway" Problem in International Commercial Arbitration, 37 Yale J. Int'l L. 1, 22–23 (2012)("Unlike elsewhere, separability in American law essentially serves two distinct purposes."); id. (separability's "less universally acknowledged" "function in U.S. law," from "the seminal Prima Paint case," "permits courts to entertain challenges specifically applicable to the arbitration agreement, and not to the contract as a whole.")

94 Restatement (Third) U.S. Law of Int'l Comm. Arb. § 2.7 cmt. a (2019).

95 Gary B. Born, International Commercial Arbitration 349–50 (2d ed. 2014) ("An international arbitration agreement is almost invariably treated as presumptively 'separable' or 'autonomous' from the underlying contract within which it is found.") See, e.g., UNCITRAL Model Law, art. 16; English Arbitration Act § 30; UNCITRAL rules, art. 21(I); LCIA Rules, art. 23.

defenses to enforcement of contracts containing international arbitration clauses are heard by arbitrators, not courts, unless those challenges are "directed to the arbitration clause itself" rather than to the whole contract containing that clause.[96] As the Restatement puts it,

> whether a court determines the nullity or voidness of an agreement to arbitrate at the outset depends on whether the challenge is directed specifically to the arbitration agreement or is equally applicable to the contract as a whole. A court entertains a challenge directed specifically to the arbitration agreement but refers to the arbitral tribunal a challenge that applies equally to the arbitration agreement and the main contract.[97]

"The separability of the arbitration agreement" "allows a court to refer issues concerning the validity of the underlying contract to an arbitral tribunal even when there may be reason to doubt that the underlying contract is valid or enforceable."[98]

§ 54 Contract Law Defenses

While defenses to enforcement of contracts containing international arbitration agreements are subject to the separability doctrine discussed in the previous section, courts nevertheless hear contract law defenses directed to the arbitration agreement itself. The New York Convention requires courts to enforce arbitration agreements unless a court finds that a particular agreement "is null and void, inoperative or incapable of being performed."[99] This phrase may sound foreign to United States lawyers but most domestic contract defenses seem to fall into one of the Convention's three categories: "null and void," "inoperative," or "incapable of being performed."[100] As the Restatement says, "[t]he terms 'null and void, inoperative or incapable of being performed' in Article 2 of the New York Convention are sufficiently capacious to encompass the full range of circumstances that would justify nonenforcement."[101] According to Gary Born:

---

96 See § 21.

97 Restatement (Third) U.S. Law of Int'l Comm. Arb. § 2.14 cmt. b (2019).

98 Restatement (Third) U.S. Law of Int'l Comm. Arb. § 2.7 cmt. a (2019).

99 New York Convention, art. II(3).

100 Lindo v. NCL (Bahamas), Ltd., 652 F.3d 1257, 1272 (11th Cir. 2011) (reiterating court's earlier holding "that Article II's 'null and void' clause was confined to standard breach-of-contract defenses and that the limited scope of the Convention's null and void clause must be interpreted to encompass only those situations—such as fraud, mistake, duress, and waiver—that can be applied neutrally on an international scale.") (internal quotes omitted).

101 Restatement (Third) U.S. Law of Int'l Comm. Arb. § 2.9 cmt. b (2019).

- "null and void" refers to "cases in which an arbitration agreement was defective or invalid from the outset," such as "fraud * * * , unconscionability, illegality and mistake."[102]
- "inoperative" "refers to agreements that were at one time valid, but which thereafter ceased to have effect (or to be 'operative'), * * * includ[ing] cases of waiver, revocation, repudiation, or termination of the arbitration agreement, or failure to comply with jurisdictional time limits prescribed by the arbitration agreement."[103]
- " 'incapable of being performed' includes cases where the parties have agreed upon a procedure that is physically or legally impossible to follow."[104]

What law determines whether an agreement "is null and void, inoperative or incapable of being performed"? In addressing this question as it relates to international arbitration agreements under the New York Convention, in an oft-cited case, the Third Circuit said:

> an agreement to arbitrate is "null and void" only (1) when it is subject to an internationally recognized defense such as duress, mistake, fraud, or waiver, or (2) when it contravenes fundamental policies of the forum state. The "null and void" language must be read narrowly, for the signatory nations have jointly declared a general policy of enforceability of agreements to arbitrate.[105]

In other words, the New York Convention, like FAA § 2, allows courts to decline to enforce arbitration agreements only on such grounds as exist at law or in equity for the revocation of any contract. As with domestic arbitration agreements, parties who deny the enforceability of an international commercial arbitration agreement generally must find their arguments in contract law, not in some other body of law.[106]

---

[102] Gary B. Born, International Commercial Arbitration 841 (2d ed.2014).

[103] Id. at 842–43.

[104] Id. at 844.

[105] Rhone Mediterranee Compagnia Francese Di Assicurazioni E Riassicurazoni v. Lauro, 712 F.2d 50, 53 (3d Cir. 1983) (citations omitted). See also Ledee v. Ceramiche Ragno, 684 F.2d 184, 187 (1st Cir. 1982) ("must be interpreted to encompass only those situations—such as fraud, mistake, duress, and waiver—that can be applied neutrally on an international scale."); DiMercurio v. Sphere Drake Ins., PLC, 202 F.3d 71, 80 (1st Cir. 2000); Chloe Z Fishing Co., Inc. v. Odyssey Re (London) Ltd., 109 F. Supp.2d 1236, 1259 (S.D.Cal. 2000); Prograph Intern. Inc. v. Barhydt, 928 F. Supp. 983, 989 (N.D. Cal. 1996).

[106] Gary B. Born, International Commercial Arbitration 834 (2d ed. 2014) ("The categories of substantive invalidity of international arbitration agreements contained in the Convention and most developed national arbitration legislation are limited to cases where such agreements are invalid on generally-applicable contract law grounds

§ 55 Non-Contract Law Defenses: Non-Arbitrable Claims

The New York Convention only requires enforcement of agreements to arbitrate disputes "concerning a subject matter capable of settlement by arbitration."[107] Article II(1) provides:

> Each Contracting State shall recognize an agreement in writing under which the parties undertake to submit to arbitration all or any differences which have arisen or which may arise between them in respect of a defined legal relationship, whether contractual or not, concerning a subject matter capable of settlement by arbitration.[108]

In other words, the Convention does not require enforcement of agreements to arbitrate "non-arbitrable" claims.

This topic of non-arbitrable claims in the domestic United States context is discussed in Section 5(e), which summarizes the United States Supreme Court's 1980's expansion of arbitrable claims. Prior to the 1980's, nearly all domestic arbitration occurred in two contexts: (1) labor disputes, and (2) disputes among businesses. With domestic arbitration limited to these contexts, it seemed largely confined to contract claims and little attention was given to the arbitration of non-contract claims. Beginning in the 1980's, (and spurred by an international arbitration case from 1975,[109]) the Supreme Court enforced agreements to arbitrate other claims such as antitrust, securities, and employment discrimination.[110] Domestically, only a few claims are now non-arbitrable.[111]

(e.g., mistake, fraud, unconscionability, impossibility, waiver.)"). See, e.g., Ledee, 684 F.2d at 187 (rejecting provision in Puerto Rico Dealers Act that invalidated, on public policy grounds, arbitration clauses in dealers' contracts, and stating, "[A]n expansive interpretation of the [null and void] clause would be antithetical to the goals of the Convention.")

[107] New York Convention, art. II(1). See also id., art. V(2).

2. Recognition and enforcement of an arbitral award may also be refused if the competent authority in the country where recognition and enforcement is sought finds that:

(a) The subject matter of the difference is not capable of settlement by arbitration under the law of that country; or

(b) The recognition or enforcement of the award would be contrary to the public policy of that country.

Id. (emphasis added).

[108] New York Convention, art. II(1).

[109] Scherk v. Alberto-Culver Co., 417 U.S. 506, 515–520 (1974) (enforcing international agreement to arbitrate a claim arising under the Securities Exchange Act of 1934 notwithstanding Court's assumption, arguendo, that its precedents would bar such enforcement in a domestic context.)

[110] See § 5(e)(1).

[111] See § 5(e).

Similarly, in the international commercial context, most claims are arbitrable. But in many States, including the U.S., "criminal matters, child custody, family matters, and bankruptcy are not arbitrable. It would be against the law or the public policy of the local jurisdiction to try to arbitrate disputes in these areas."[112] Also, the validity of a patent is generally not arbitrable.[113]

Suppose a particular claim is arbitrable under the national law of one party but non-arbitrable under the national law of the other party? Most courts, including United States courts, have applied the non-arbitrability rules of the forum where litigation over the arbitration agreement's enforceability is pending.[114]

C. TERMS OF INTERNATIONAL COMMERCIAL ARBITRATION AGREEMENTS

Table of Sections

---

[112] Margaret L. Moses, The Principles and Practice of International Commercial Arbitration 31 (2008). See also Jean-Francois Poudret & Sebastien Besson, Comparative Law of International Arbitration 295–314 (2007) (under the law of some States, nonarbitrable claims may include those relating to property rights and laws that regulate markets or protect consumers and employees).

[113] Margaret L. Moses, The Principles and Practice of International Commercial Arbitration 31 (2008). William Grantham, The Arbitrability of International Intellectual Property Disputes, 14 Berkeley J. Int'l L. 173 (1996); Deming Liu, Think Twice Before Arbitrating a Patent Dispute?, 23 Am. Rev. Int'l Arb. 313 (2012).

[114] Gary B. Born, International Commercial Arbitration 521 & n.520 (2009).

---

§ 56 Scope of Arbitration Agreements

In domestic arbitration under the FAA, if a party seeks to litigate rather than arbitrate a particular claim, the court will send that claim to arbitration only if the parties agreed to arbitrate that claim.[115] That the parties agreed to arbitrate *some* claim is not enough. They must have agreed to arbitrate *that* claim. Whether they did is a question of interpreting the scope of the arbitration agreement.

The threshold issue regarding scope is who—court or arbitrator—decides whether a claim is arbitrable. The FAA presumptively sends scope disputes to courts, rather than to arbitrators,[116] although many parties contract around this default rule with arbitration agreements delegating scope issues to the arbitrator.[117]

In the international commercial context, parties do this frequently, such as by agreeing to arbitrate under the International Chamber of Commerce's Rules of Arbitration. Article 6(3) of the ICC Rules provides that

> if any party raises one or more pleas concerning the existence, validity or scope of the arbitration agreement or concerning whether all of the claims made in the arbitration may be determined together in a single arbitration, the arbitration shall proceed and any question of jurisdiction or of whether the claims may be determined together in that arbitration shall be decided directly by the arbitral tribunal * * *[118]

"Virtually all other leading institutional arbitration rules are to the same effect."[119] The New York Convention arguably "require[s] Contracting States to 'recognize' such agreements (like other agreements to arbitrate) and to 'refer' the parties to such agreements to arbitration."[120]

Suppose, however, that the parties have not agreed to arbitrate disputes about the scope of the arbitration agreement. Consider, for

---

[115] See § 26.

[116] Id.

[117] Id.

[118] 2021 Arbitration Rules, International Chamber of Commerce, https://iccwbo.org/dispute-resolution-services/arbitration/rules-of-arbitration/#article_6.

[119] Gary B. Born, International Commercial Arbitration 932–33 (2009).

[120] Id. at 860.

example, a contract between Buyer and Seller obligating each party to arbitrate any "controversy or claim arising out of this contract, or the breach thereof." Suppose that Buyer sues Seller, alleging antitrust (or, internationally, "competition law") violations, and Seller moves to stay the litigation and to compel arbitration. Buyer may argue that, while the parties agreed to arbitrate breach-of-contract claims, they did not agree to arbitrate antitrust claims because such claims did not "arise out of" the contract.

If Buyer sues in some nations outside the United States, the foreign court is likely to grant Seller's motion. Some nations' laws generally prohibit courts from ruling on the agreement's scope until after the arbitrator has so ruled.[121] Under such laws, Buyer must go to arbitration to persuade the arbitrator that the parties did not agree to arbitrate antitrust claims. In other words, Buyer must go to arbitration to persuade the arbitrator that the arbitration agreement should be interpreted not to cover Buyer's claim. Only after getting a ruling from the arbitrator to that effect, or successfully challenging in court a contrary ruling,[122] can Buyer proceed to litigate the antitrust claim.

Arguably, this reasoning is required by New York Convention Article II(3) which provides

> The court of a Contracting State, when seized of an action in a matter in respect of which the parties have made an agreement within the meaning of this article, shall, at the request of one of the parties, refer the parties to arbitration, unless it finds that the said agreement is null and void, inoperative or incapable of being performed.[123]

According to Gary Born, "[t]his language is most naturally read as establishing an exception to the general obligation to refer parties to arbitration only in cases where the parties' arbitration agreement is null and void, inoperative or incapable of being performed—and *not* in cases where the scope of the arbitration agreement allegedly does not encompass the parties' dispute."[124] This reading of the

[121] Gary B. Born, International Commercial Arbitration 1049 (2d ed.2014) (France and India "provide that an arbitral tribunal generally has competence-competence to initially decide virtually all jurisdictional disputes * * * subject to eventual judicial review"). However, "a French court is permitted to question arbitral jurisdiction [when] no arbitral tribunal has yet been constituted and the agreement to arbitrate is, for one reason or another, manifestly ineffective or unenforceable." George A. Bermann, The "Gateway" Problem in International Commercial Arbitration, 37 Yale J. Int'l L. 1, 17 (2012).

[122] See id. See also William W. Park, Determining an Arbitrator's Jurisdiction: Timing and Finality American Law, 8 Nev. L.J. 135, 139 (2007) (same).

[123] New York Convention, art. II(3).

[124] Gary B. Born, International Commercial Arbitration 1056 (2d ed. 2014).

Convention would, in the above example, require a court to refer Buyer's claim to arbitration because Buyer concedes that it formed an enforceable arbitration agreement with Seller and is merely arguing about the best interpretation of that agreement. While this reading of the Convention is plausible, many courts do not follow it. "Most national courts have routinely considered disputes concerning the scope of the arbitration agreement in interlocutory judicial proceedings."[125] That is, most national courts have not required Buyer go to arbitration to persuade the arbitrator that the arbitration clause should be interpreted not to cover Buyer's claim.

§ 57 Multi-Party Disputes

(a) Claims by or Against Those Not Party to the Arbitration Agreement

The previous section discusses interpreting international arbitration agreements to decide if they cover a particular claim. A specific application of that "scope" question is whether a particular arbitration agreement covers particular claims by or against a non-party to the arbitration agreement. This "non-party" issue arises with some frequency in international commercial arbitration.[126]

As in domestic arbitration, the non-party issue can arise in various procedural contexts. Three examples include:

(1) a party to the arbitration agreement seeks to litigate its claims against a non-party to the agreement but that non-party seeks to compel arbitration of those claims;

(2) a party to the arbitration agreement seeks to arbitrate its claims against a non-party to the agreement and that non-party refuses to participate in arbitration of those claims; and

(3) a non-party to the agreement seeks to arbitrate its claims against a party to the agreement and that party refuses to participate in arbitration of those claims.

Depending on the procedural context, the relevant legal doctrines may include those noted in this book's discussion of them in the domestic context[127]—third-party beneficiaries, estoppel, agency, assumption of contractual duties, corporate veil piercing.[128] With

---

[125] Id. at 1056, n.47.

[126] See generally W. Laurence Craig, Introduction, in Multiple Party Actions and International Arbitration (The Permanent Court of Arbitration, eds. 2009).

[127] See § 27.

[128] Gary B. Born, International Commercial Arbitration § 10.02 (2d ed. 2014).

respect to all of these doctrines, the relevant law is national,[129] or international principles found outside the New York Convention,[130] as the Convention itself has no provisions on point.

(b) Consolidation of, and Stays Pending, Related Proceedings

As explained in Section 28, rules of civil procedure encourage courts to consolidate related cases and to join multiple parties in a single action if their disputes arise out of the same transaction or occurrence. This consolidation and joinder avoids multiple litigation over the same facts, thus saving time and money and helping to avoid inconsistent results. These same goals also argue for arbitrators to consolidate cases and to join parties. The obstacle to doing so, however, is the contractual nature of arbitration. Parties who have not agreed to arbitrate have a right to litigate rather than arbitrate. And parties who have agreed to arbitrate have a right to arbitrate rather than litigate.

> [P]arties agree to arbitrate with particular other parties, according to specified procedures—not to arbitrate with anybody, in any set of proceedings. Accordingly, most national legislatures, courts and arbitral tribunals have resolved questions of consolidation, joinder and intervention by reference to the parties' arbitration agreement(s), providing for consolidation, joinder and/or intervention where contemplated—and only where contemplated—by the parties' agreement.[131]

This result is consistent with the New York Convention, which has no provisions specifically addressing the consolidation of multiple arbitrations. The Convention's general provisions requiring Contracting States to enforce executory arbitration agreements support national law deferring to party autonomy.[132]

§ 58 Arbitration Procedure

(a) Overview

Section 31 explains that while the presentation of evidence and argument in litigation is governed by rules of procedure and evidence enacted by government, the rules of procedure and evidence in arbitration are, with few exceptions, whatever the parties'

---

[129] Id. § 10.05[B].

[130] Id. § 10.05[A].

[131] Gary B. Born, International Commercial Arbitration 2569 (2d ed. 2014).

[132] Id. ("virtually all authorities have resolved these issues by reference to principles of party autonomy").

arbitration agreement says they are. This point also applies to international commercial arbitration, as the New York Convention and Panama Convention do not regulate the procedures of arbitration. In their international commercial arbitration agreement, the parties can select rules of procedure and evidence, along with the arbitration's location, language, governing law, and other matters. "In essence, the parties create their own private system of justice."[133]

Of course, few parties start from scratch in their agreement in creating their own, completely customized, system of justice. Just as many domestic arbitration agreements incorporate the rules of an arbitration organization, such as the American Arbitration Association's Commercial Rules, many international commercial arbitration agreements incorporate the rules of an arbitration organization, such as the International Chamber of Commerce or the London Court of International Arbitration.[134]

International commercial arbitration procedures often consist of compromises between procedures familiar in legal systems (such as the United States) based on the English common law and procedures used in the civil law systems prevalent in continental Europe, South America, and East Asia. One major difference between the common law and civil law traditions is "that what common lawyers think of as a trial in civil proceedings does not exist in the civil law world."[135]

While a trial in the United States brings together the parties, lawyers, judge, and jury in a single, concentrated event, civil law systems use "an entirely different approach" with "no such thing as a trial in our [common law] sense; there is no single, concentrated event. The typical civil proceeding in a civil law country is actually a series of isolated meetings of and written communications between counsel and the judge, in which evidence is introduced, testimony is given, procedural motions and rulings are made, and so on."[136]

Why this major difference between common law and civil law systems? "The reason is that the right to a jury in civil actions, traditional in the common law world, has never taken hold in the civil law world."[137] Following the civil law approach of a series of isolated meetings at which some, but not all, evidence is introduced would not be practical with a jury because the "lay jury cannot easily be

---

[133] Margaret L. Moses, The Principles and Practice of International Commercial Arbitration 17 (2008). See also Gary B. Born, International Commercial Arbitration 2130–32 (2d ed. 2014).

[134] Gary B. Born, International Commercial Arbitration 2138–40 (2d ed. 2014).

[135] John Henry Merryman & Rogelio Perez-Perdomo, The Civil Law Tradition 113 (3d ed. 2007).

[136] Id.

[137] Id.

convened, adjourned, and reconvened several times in the course of a single action without causing a great deal of inconvenience."[138] So in common law systems a trial must be a single, concentrated event. In contrast, civil law systems can spread out the case over several appearances with each involving the examination of only one witness or the introduction of "only one or two pieces of material evidence."[139]

International commercial arbitration procedures generally look somewhat "civilian" to a lawyer trained in the United States, which is not only a common law jurisdiction, but the common law jurisdiction with the strongest and most broadly applicable civil jury right.

(b) Pre-Hearing

(1) Selection of Arbitrators

While international commercial arbitration sometimes has one arbitrator, three is especially common. For this reason, discussions of international commercial arbitration often refer, not to "the arbitrator," but to "the tribunal."[140] "[W]hen there are substantial amounts of money at stake, most parties feel more comfortable with three arbitrators. * * * In addition when the parties are from different cultural or legal backgrounds, a party may want at least one arbitrator to have some knowledge and understanding of its own culture and legal system."[141] For these reasons, many international commercial arbitration agreements provide for *tripartite* arbitration, in which each party picks one arbitrator and those two agree on the third. This method of arbitrator selection is also the usual method under the rules of important international arbitration organizations, such as the International Chamber of Commerce and London Court of International Arbitration. Many international commercial arbitration agreements provide that arbitration will be conducted according to the rules of these organizations. "According to all of the leading international commercial arbitration rules, party-appointed arbitrators on [a] tripartite panel are expected to be 'independent and impartial' or the substantial equivalent."[142]

---

[138] Id.

[139] Id. at 114.

[140] Restatement (Third) U.S. Law of Int'l Comm. Arb. § 1.1 (2019) ("An 'arbitral tribunal' is a body consisting of one or more persons designated directly or indirectly by the parties to an arbitration agreement and empowered by them to adjudicate a dispute that has arisen between or among them.")

[141] Margaret L. Moses, The Principles and Practice of International Commercial Arbitration 42 (2008).

[142] Thomas J. Stipanowich, Reflections on the State and Future of Commercial Arbitration: Challenges, Opportunities, Proposals, 25 Am. Rev. Int'l Arb. 297, 369–70 (2014).

(2) Pleadings

An expert on international commercial arbitration says parties seek "fair and neutral procedures that are flexible, efficient and capable of being tailored to the needs of their particular dispute, without reference to the formalities and technicalities of procedural rules applicable in national courts."[143] While litigation generally begins with a complaint filed and served by the plaintiff, and domestic arbitration typically begins with a *demand* for arbitration filed and served by the *claimant*, the corresponding document in international arbitration is often called (more politely) a *request* for arbitration or *notice* of arbitration.[144] This document typically states the basic substantive claims, the relief sought, and the jurisdiction of the arbitrators conferred by the agreement to arbitrate. The request for arbitration may also include the claimant's views about the appropriate number or manner of selecting arbitrators and, if that is tripartite arbitration, the request for arbitration may also include claimant's nomination of an arbitrator. One challenge in drafting this—or any—pleading in international arbitration is making it "understandable and persuasive to readers from other legal and linguistic backgrounds."[145]

After a request for arbitration is served, the respondent may reply in several ways. It might answer the claimant's allegations or assert counterclaims. It might nominate an arbitrator, or it might object to the arbitrators' jurisdiction to hear the dispute, perhaps arguing that there is no enforceable arbitration agreement or that any such agreement does not cover this dispute.

(3) Discovery

Like other aspects of international commercial arbitration procedure, discovery is governed primarily by the arbitration agreement, so the parties have great freedom to choose the amount and types of discovery that will be required in their arbitration.[146] Often parties exercise this freedom by agreeing to arbitrate under the rules of an arbitration organization, so the parties indirectly choose the amount and types of discovery provided by those rules. The

[143] Gary B. Born, International Commercial Arbitration 2123 (2d ed. 2014).

[144] Id. at 2213.

[145] Id. at 2217.

[146] "[M]ost national arbitration legislation contains few provisions regarding the disclosure authority of international arbitral tribunals, instead leaving the subject to either the parties' agreements or the arbitrators' inherent or implied authority." Gary B. Born, International Commercial Arbitration 2324 (2d ed. 2014). Gary Born suggests that this is required by the New York Convention. Id. at 2324 ("A Contracting State's prohibition of agreements granting (or denying) the arbitrators disclosure powers would amount to a failure to recognize a material term of the agreement to arbitrate, contrary to Articles II(1) and II(3)."

selected rules, in turn, generally give arbitrators broad discretion over the amount and types of discovery they will require.[147]

While domestic arbitration tends to have less discovery than litigation in the United States,[148] this is even more true of international commercial arbitration—where discovery "is usually materially less extensive and intrusive than in common law litigation."[149] Comfort with extensive and intrusive discovery may be widespread among arbitrators from the United States, and perhaps arbitrators from other systems based on the English common law, but that sort of discovery is generally foreign to arbitrators from the civil law systems prevalent in continental Europe, South America, and East Asia. In most civil law jurisdictions, "[e]vidence-taking is largely controlled by the court and the parties have no (or virtually no) right to demand relevant materials from one another or from witnesses."[150] In much of the world, "United States-style" discovery is as alien and suspect as that other anomalous feature of United States litigation, the civil jury.[151] International commercial arbitration procedures often consist of compromises between the common law and civil law traditions. This is reflected in international commercial arbitration typically having less discovery than litigation or arbitration of comparable cases in the United States and in that lesser discovery consisting primarily in the disclosure of documents, rather than interrogatories or depositions.[152] For these reasons, the word "discovery" might even be ill-suited to international commercial

---

[147] "The prevailing view is, and is increasingly firmly-held, * * * that, even absent express authorization, the power to order discovery or disclosure is inherent in an international arbitral tribunal's mandate." Id. at 2342.

[148] See § 33(d).

[149] Gary B. Born, International Commercial Arbitration 2249 (2d ed. 2014).

[150] Gary B. Born, International Commercial Arbitration 2344–45 (2d ed. 2014).

[151] See § 58(a) (contrasting civil procedure in common law and civil law systems). On the connections between the civil jury and broad discovery, see John Henry Merryman & Rogelio Perez-Perdomo, The Civil Law Tradition 114 (3d ed. 2007); Stephen J. Ware, Consumer and Employment Arbitration Law in Comparative Perspective: The Importance of the Civil Jury, 56 U. Miami L. Rev. 865, 868–69 (2002) (quoting John H. Langbein, The German Advantage in Civil Procedure, 52 U. Chi. L. Rev. 823, 831 (1985), and Paul D. Carrington, The Seventh Amendment: Some Bicentennial Reflections, 1990 U. Chi. Legal F. 33, 40 (1990)).

[152] Gary B. Born, International Commercial Arbitration 2347 (2d ed.2014) ("The most common and significant mode of disclosure in international arbitration is the production of documents."); id. at 2352 ("interrogatories are infrequently used outside of common law settings."); id. at 2354 ("Depositions are not infrequently used in domestic United States arbitrations, but are much less common in international arbitration."); Carolyn B. Lamm et al., International Arbitration in a Globalized World, Disp. Resol. Mag., Winter 2014, at 4, 6 (trend "toward broader document disclosure" but "depositions and interrogatories[ ] are not commonly used in international arbitration").

arbitration,[153] but this book uses the word because it is familiar to lawyers in the United States.

What happens if a party disobeys an arbitrator's discovery order? International commercial arbitrators are "likely to draw adverse inferences from a party's refusal to produce requested documents or witnesses."[154] In addition, it is "possible, but unusual," for arbitrators to seek court enforcement of their discovery orders.[155] Similarly, parties denied discovery may seek to involve courts, who are authorized by some national laws to help parties in arbitration obtain discovery from recalcitrant opponents and non-parties. However, a United States statute giving federal courts the power to order discovery from specified persons "for use in a proceeding in a foreign or international tribunal,"[156] was interpreted by the Supreme Court to "reach[ ] only governmental or intergovernmental adjudicative bodies," rather than arbitral panels.[157]

(c) Hearing

(1) General Comparison with Trial

International commercial arbitration hearings resemble trials and domestic arbitration hearings in the United States, insofar as all three types of proceedings involve adversaries trying to persuade a neutral adjudicator by presenting evidence and making arguments. All three typically proceed with opening statements, presentation of witnesses by the claimant for examination and cross-examination, followed by similar presentation of the respondent's witnesses, and ending with closing statements.

However, international commercial arbitration hearings often differ from United States trials and domestic arbitration hearings in ways that seem to follow from international commercial arbitration's frequent blending of common law and civil law traditions.[158] While trials and hearings in the United States and other common law States generally allow parties (through their lawyers) great latitude

---

153 Peter Ashford, Document Production in International Arbitration: A Critique from 'Across the Pond', 10 Loy. U. Chi. Int'l L. Rev. 1, 1–2 (2012).

154 Gary B. Born, International Commercial Arbitration 2391 (2d ed. 2014).

155 Id.

156 28 U.S.C. § 1782.

157 ZF Auto. US, Inc. v. Luxshare, Ltd., 142 S. Ct. 2078 (2022). The Court held that 28 U.S.C. § 1782 did not apply to an arbitration tribunal selected in accord with "Arbitration Rules of the German Institution of Arbitration e.V. (DIS)," "a private dispute-resolution organization based in Berlin," or investment arbitration [see § 62] by " 'an ad hoc arbitration in accordance with Arbitration Rules of the United Nations Commission on International Trade Law (UNCITRAL),' with each party selecting one arbitrator and those two choosing a third."

158 See § 58(a).

in presenting their cases—including the direct and cross-examination of witnesses—"arbitrators with civil law backgrounds (principally in Continental Europe, Japan, Korea and China) can often be expected to adopt somewhat more 'inquisitorial' procedures, with the tribunal being primarily responsible for identifying issues, seeking evidence and probing the record."[159] Also, civil law systems "favor proof through documents, rather than witness testimony,"[160] and where witnesses are heard, it is generally the judge who examines them.[161] Cross-examination "continues to play virtually no role" in civil law litigation,[162] and in some civil law jurisdictions the parties, their relatives, and other interested persons are disqualified from appearing as witnesses.[163]

With international commercial arbitration generally blending the common and civil law traditions, it is no surprise that international commercial arbitration "tends to rely more heavily on documentary evidence and written witness statements than oral testimony."[164]

(2) Rules of Evidence

The New York Convention does not create rules of evidence for arbitration. The same is true of the FAA, so in the domestic United States context arbitration's evidentiary rules (like other aspects of arbitration) are primarily determined by the arbitration agreement.[165] In a slight contrast, other national arbitration laws, particularly those based on the UNCITRAL Model Law, provide that "[t]he power conferred upon the arbitral tribunal includes the power to determine the admissibility, relevance, materiality and weight of any evidence."[166] This contrast is slight because allowing parties to determine evidentiary rules in their arbitration agreement reaches the same result as a statute giving arbitrators the power to decide evidentiary issues if, as is often true, parties agree to arbitrate pursuant to arbitration organization rules that gives arbitrators the

---

159 Gary B. Born, International Commercial Arbitration 2204 (2d ed. 2014).

160 Id. at 2205.

161 In the civil law, "even the questions asked a witness during civil proceedings are often asked by the judge on the basis of questions submitted in writing by counsel for the parties." John Henry Merryman & Rogelio Perez-Perdomo, The Civil Law Tradition 115 (3d ed. 2007).

162 Gary B. Born, International Commercial Arbitration 2283 (2d ed.2014). Accord John Henry Merryman & Rogelio Perez-Perdomo, The Civil Law Tradition 116 (3d ed. 2007).

163 John Henry Merryman & Rogelio Perez-Perdomo, The Civil Law Tradition 116 (3d ed. 2007).

164 Gary B. Born, International Commercial Arbitration 2255 (2d ed. 2014).

165 See § 34(c).

166 UNCITRAL Model Law, Art. 19(2).

power to decide evidentiary issues. However, parties may not wish to give arbitrators complete discretion over evidentiary issues, so some international arbitration clauses include an agreement that the arbitration be conducted according to the International Bar Association (IBA) Rules on the Taking of Evidence in International Commercial Arbitration.[167] "These rules provide a good harmonization of civil and common law approaches to taking evidence, and provide parties with a fair amount of certainty about the tribunal will deal with documents, witnesses, and experts."[168]

As in domestic United States arbitration, "technical rules of evidence are usually not observed" in international commercial arbitration and arbitrators tend to "err substantially on the side of permitting presentation of the facts that a party desires."[169] Rather than holding defective evidence inadmissible, arbitrators can just give it little or no weight. However, the IBA Rules noted in the previous paragraph give arbitrators the power to exclude evidence on several grounds including irrelevance, privilege, and unreasonable burden.[170]

(3) No Hearing; Dispositive Motions

While much litigation in the United States ends on a grant of a motion to dismiss or for summary judgment, such motions are generally less likely to succeed in arbitration,[171] including international commercial arbitration. However, that does not mean a live hearing is required for an international commercial arbitration award to be enforceable in court. Just as domestic arbitration may result in a default award against a party who does not participate in arbitration, the same is true internationally. A more difficult situation arises when arbitrators decide to forgo live testimony and decide the case on the documentary evidence submitted, despite a party's request for a live hearing. While there is some domestic United States authority in favor of confirming such awards,[172] a leading scholar of international commercial arbitration writes that "[o]ral hearings are mandatory in virtually all international arbitrations (save where the parties agree otherwise)."[173] "Failure to

---

167 Int'l Bar Ass'n, The Rules, IBA Rules on the Taking of Evidence in International Arbitration, at 7, (Dec. 17, 2020), https://www.ibanet.org/MediaHandler?id=def0807b-9fec-43ef-b624-f2cb2af7cf7b.

168 Margaret L. Moses, The Principles and Practice of International Commercial Arbitration 44–45 (2008).

169 Gary B. Born, International Commercial Arbitration 2310 (2d ed. 2014).

170 IBA Rules on the Taking of Evidence, Art. 9(2).

171 See § 34(d).

172 See § 34(d).

173 Gary B. Born, International Commercial Arbitration 2264 (2d ed. 2014). See id. at 3513 ("In some contexts, 'documents only' arbitrations are customary (conducted

hear oral evidence, when requested by a party to do so, would invite a challenge to the resulting award for failure to afford the protesting party the opportunity to present its case."[174]

(4) Written Awards; Reasoned Opinions

While in some types of domestic arbitration the arbitrators' awards tend to be very brief and conclusory,[175] international commercial awards tend to resemble the opinions issued by many courts—lengthy, "careful discussions of the parties' positions and the tribunal's factual and legal analysis."[176] The rules of several leading international arbitration organizations require that arbitration awards be supported by reasoned opinions.[177] In some international fields, arbitrators often cite earlier arbitration awards as precedent.[178]

(d) Remedies

Section 35's discussion of remedies in domestic arbitration notes that remedies, like other aspects of arbitration, are primarily determined by the arbitration agreement. The same is true in international commercial arbitration.[179] While most international commercial arbitration awards are of money damages, "courts have routinely upheld [arbitrators'] grants of injunctive relief, including specific performance of contractual obligations."[180] In addition, "international arbitration tribunals generally possess (and exercise) the authority to award the prevailing party in an arbitration the costs of arbitration, including its legal costs."[181] In contrast, awards of

without oral hearings or testimony). Most national courts have rejected arguments that such procedures are necessarily procedurally improper or inadequate.")

[174] Id. at 2265.

[175] See § 34(e) (explaining that unreasoned awards can be very brief—perhaps just a couple of sentences finding for the claimant and ordering the respondent to pay a particular dollar amount—or a bit longer).

[176] Id. at 2304.

[177] Gary B. Born, International Commercial Arbitration § 23.03 (2d ed. 2014).

[178] Christopher S. Gibson & Christopher R. Drahozal, Iran-United States Claims Tribunal Precedent in Investor-State Arbitration, 23 J. Int'l Arb. 521, 537–44 (2006)("extensive reliance on [Iran-United States Claims] Tribunal precedents" in investor-state arbitration); Gabrielle Kaufmann-Kohler, Arbitral Precedent: Dream, Necessity, or Excuse?, 23 Arb. Int'l 357 (2007).

[179] Gary B. Born, International Commercial Arbitration 3068–69 (2d ed. 2014) ("The remedial powers of an international arbitral tribunal are defined in the first instance by the parties arbitration agreement. * * * Under most developed national arbitration regimes, arbitrators have broad discretion in fashioning relief.")

[180] Id. at 3073.

[181] Id. at 3086.

punitive damages "are arguably contrary to public policy in some civil law jurisdictions."[182]

Section 35 on remedies in domestic arbitration notes that arbitration is generally less suited than litigation as a forum for an emergency remedy, such as a temporary restraining order. This is because arbitration cannot award any remedy until an arbitrator has been appointed. The party against whom a restraining order is sought likely can delay that appointment until it does whatever the other party sought to restrain.[183] This problem applies as well in international commercial arbitration,[184] so "parties to international arbitration agreements who require urgent provisional relief at the outset of a dispute must often seek the assistance of national courts."[185] Some (but probably a minority) of courts in the United States have been reluctant to provide such assistance on the ground that the purpose of the New York Convention is best carried out by restricting pre-arbitration judicial action to enforcement of executory arbitration agreements, that is, sending parties to arbitration.[186] "The Restatement rejects that position, concluding that neither the New York or Panama Convention, nor the FAA, precludes courts from ordering provisional relief in support of an international arbitral proceeding."[187]

D. ENFORCEMENT AND VACATUR OF INTERNATIONAL COMMERCIAL ARBITRATION AWARDS

Table of Sections

---

182 Id. at 3081.

183 See § 35(b). For attempts to remedy this problem, see Erin Collins, Pre-Tribunal Emergency Relief in International Commercial Arbitration, 10 Loy. U. Chi. Int'l L. Rev. 105 (2012).

184 Gary B. Born, International Commercial Arbitration 2450–51 (2d ed. 2014).

185 Id. at 2523.

186 Id. at 2524–32.

187 Restatement (Third) U.S. Law of Int'l Comm. Arb. § 3.3 cmt. b (2019).

(4) Improper Arbitral Procedure or Composition of Arbitral Authority
(5) Set Aside by Court at Seat of Arbitration
(6) Non-Arbitrability
(7) Public Policy

§ 59 Enforcement of International Arbitration Awards

The primary purpose of the New York Convention is to make arbitration awards rendered in one State enforceable in the courts of other States. Accordingly, the Convention begins "[t]his Convention shall apply to the recognition and enforcement of arbitral awards made in the territory of a State other than the State where the recognition and enforcement of such awards are sought."[188] The Convention states that "[e]ach Contracting State shall recognize arbitral awards as binding and enforce them,"[189] and the Convention permits only a narrow list of grounds upon which "[r]ecognition and enforcement of the award may be refused."[190]

To recognize and enforce an award, the Convention prescribes a fairly quick and easy process:

> 1. To obtain the recognition and enforcement mentioned in the preceding article, the party applying for recognition and enforcement shall, at the time of the application, supply:
>
> (a) The duly authenticated original award or a duly certified copy thereof;
>
> (b) The original agreement referred to in article II or a duly certified copy thereof.
>
> 2. If the said award or agreement is not made in an official language of the country in which the award is relied upon, the party applying for recognition and enforcement of the award shall produce a translation of these documents into such language. The translation shall be certified by an official or sworn translator or by a diplomatic or consular agent.[191]

---

188 New York Convention, art. I(1).

189 Id. art. III.

190 Id. art. V. See § 60(b).

191 Id. art. IV.

The speed and ease of this process is facilitated by national courts' "taking a practical and relatively flexible approach" to it,[192] for example by excusing non-compliance with the translation requirement where the award could nonetheless be comprehended by the court.[193]

The Convention's distinction between award recognition and enforcement generally relates to which party—claimant or respondent—prevailed in arbitration. Prevailing claimants typically seek award enforcement to receive the money or other remedy awarded in arbitration, while prevailing respondents typically seek award recognition to increase the award's finality and preclude further arbitration or litigation of the claim respondent defeated in arbitration.[194]

In implementing the New York Convention, Chapter 2 of the FAA provides:

> Within three years after an arbitral award falling under the Convention is made, any party to the arbitration may apply to any court having jurisdiction under this chapter for an order confirming the award as against any other party to the arbitration. The court shall confirm the award unless it finds one of the grounds for refusal or deferral of recognition or enforcement of the award specified in the said Convention.[195]

This provision enables federal[196] courts to confirm awards "falling under" the Convention.[197] For example, if an arbitration tribunal seated outside the United States awards the claimant money damages from the respondent and the respondent has property in the United States then the claimant does not need to involve a court at the seat of the arbitration. The claimant can get a federal court in the U.S. to confirm the award, which converts the award into a judgment of the court.[198] A confirmed award is enforced in the same manner as

---

[192] Gary B. Born, International Commercial Arbitration 3397 (2d ed. 2014).

[193] Id. at 3399.

[194] William W. Park & Alexander A. Yanos, Treaty Obligations and National Law: Emerging Conflicts in International Arbitration, 58 Hastings L.J. 251, 260 (2006).

[195] 9 U.S.C. § 207.

[196] An action to confirm an award falling under the Convention triggers the original, but not exclusive, jurisdiction of the federal courts. 9 U.S.C. § 203. Such an action may be brought in state court but the defendant may then remove it to federal court. 9 U.S.C. § 205. See also Christopher R. Drahozal, The New York Convention and the American Federal System, 2012 J. Disp. Resol. 101, 109–111 (discussing application of FAA Chapter 2 in state court).

[197] For a summary of the scope of the Convention, see § 51(a)(1).

[198] See § 36.

other court judgments: through judicial liens, orders to turn over property, etc.

Conversely, if an arbitration tribunal seated in the United States awards the claimant money damages from the respondent and the respondent has property abroad, say in England, then the claimant does not need to involve a U.S. court before seeking enforcement of the award by an English court.[199]

§ 60 Vacatur and Non-Enforcement of International Arbitration Awards

(a) Introduction: National Law of Vacatur

While the primary purpose of the New York Convention is to make arbitration awards rendered in one State enforceable in the courts of other States, Article V says that "[r]ecognition and enforcement of the award may be refused [if the award] has been set aside or suspended by a competent authority of the country in which, or under the law of which, that award was made."[200] As a result, a party displeased with an international commercial arbitration award can get a national court (of the State that is the seat of the arbitration) to vacate ("set aside" or annul) the award and then use that vacatur as a defense to enforcement of the award in other States.[201] Crucially, the standards for vacatur are found, not in the New York Convention, but in the national law of the arbitration's seat.[202] For example, vacatur of an arbitration award rendered in

---

199 Oriental Commercial & Shipping Co. v. Rosseel, N.V., 769 F. Supp. 514, 516 (S.D.N.Y. 1991) ("Under the Convention, it is no longer necessary to seek leave to enforce in the rendering jurisdiction: the party seeking to enforce an award may proceed directly to the jurisdiction in which it wishes to enforce the award and may apply directly to that jurisdiction's court for an order of enforcement.")

200 New York Convention, art. V(1)(e).

201 Gary B. Born, International Commercial Arbitration 2988 (2d ed.2014) ("the Convention limits actions to annul to (a) the place where the arbitral award was made; and (b) if different, and only exceptionally, the state 'under the law of which' the award was made.") See, e.g., Thai-Lao Lignite (Thailand) Co. v. Gov't of Lao People's Democratic Republic, 864 F.3d 172, 176 (2d Cir. 2017) (explaining that New York Convention "uniquely empower[s] courts in the primary jurisdiction to set aside or annul an arbitral award").

202 "The choice of the seat of arbitration is effectively a choice of law with respect to judicial review of the award." William Laurence Craig, Uses and Abuses of Appeal from Awards, 4 Arb. Int'l 174, 178 (1988). Karaha Bodas Co., L.L.C. v. Perusahaan Pertambangan Minyak Dan Gas Bumi, 364 F.3d 274, 287–88 (5th Cir. 2004) ("the courts of the country of the arbitral situs * * * may apply their own domestic law in evaluating a request to annul or set aside an arbitral award"). Compare Born, International Commercial Arbitration, at 2554 (citing Yusuf Ahmed Alghanim & Sons v. Toys "R" Us, Inc., 126 F.3d 15, 22–23 (2d Cir. 1997) ("Most national courts and commentators have * * * concluded that the New York Convention imposes no limits on the grounds with may be relied upon to annul an award in the arbitral seat."), with id. at 2556–60 (contending that "while this position is very widely repeated, it produces

Mexico City is governed by Mexican law and should only be done by a Mexican court.[203] Vacatur of an arbitration award rendered in New York is governed by FAA § 10 and should only be done by a United States court.[204]

While vacatur of an award by a court of the State that is the seat of arbitration nearly always prevents the award from being enforced by the courts of other States,[205] a rare and well-known exception involved an arbitration award in favor of a United States company against the Government of Egypt. The award was vacated by an Egyptian court but nevertheless enforced by a United States district court in *Chromalloy Aeroservices v. Arab Republic of Egypt*.[206] That court said that, while Article V of the New York Convention says the United States court "*may*, at its discretion, decline to enforce the award," Article VII:

> *requires* that, "The provisions of the present Convention *shall not* * * * deprive any interested party of any right he may have to avail himself of an arbitral award in the manner and to the extent allowed by the law * * * of the count[r]y where such award is sought to be relied upon." 9 U.S.C. § 201 note (emphasis added). In other words, under the Convention, CAS [the United States company] maintains all rights to the enforcement of this Arbitral Award that it would have in the absence of the Convention. Accordingly, the Court finds that, if the Convention did not exist, the Federal Arbitration Act ("FAA") would provide CAS with a legitimate claim to enforcement of this arbitral award.[207]

Here, the *Chromalloy* court reasoned that the quoted language from Article VII of the Convention makes arbitration awards enforceable to the extent permitted by the domestic arbitration law of the State in which enforcement is sought, even if the award has been set aside by a court at the seat of arbitration. Perhaps it was relevant that, at

---

anomalous results which are very difficult to justify in light of the Conventions' overall structure and purposes.")

[203] International Standard Elec. Corp. v. Bridas Sociedad Anonima Petrolera, Indus. Y Comercial, 745 F. Supp. 172 (S.D.N.Y. 1990).

[204] Yusuf Ahmed Alghanim & Sons v. Toys "R" Us, Inc., 126 F.3d 15, 21 (2d Cir. 1997) ("We read Article V(1)(e) of the Convention to allow a court in the country under whose law the arbitration was conducted to apply domestic arbitral law, in this case the FAA, to a motion to set aside or vacate that arbitral award.")

[205] See § 60(b)(5). "An arbitration award does not exist to be enforced in other Contracting States if it has been lawfully 'set aside' by a competent authority in the State in which the award was made." TermoRio S.A., E.S.P v. Electranta S.P, 487 F.3d 928, 936 (D.C. Cir. 2007).

[206] 939 F. Supp. 907 (D.D.C. 1996).

[207] Id. at 909–10.

least according to its lawyer, CAS "was able to show that Egyptian courts had a disturbing propensity to nullify awards in favor of foreign parties against Egyptians or its government for seemingly arbitrary reasons."[208] *Chromalloy* is not unique,[209] but courts generally decline to enforce under their own domestic arbitration law awards that have been vacated by a court of the State that is the seat of arbitration.[210]

In contrast, purported vacatur of an award by a court of a State *not* the seat of arbitration should *not* prevent enforcement of the award by the courts of any State.[211] In fact, the Convention does not even authorize a court to vacate or modify an award made in another State.[212] "The reason for this is evident from the limited purpose of the Convention[ ]: to effectuate the enforceability of awards in foreign nations outside the nation primarily legally responsible for the awards."[213]

To summarize, a party displeased with an international arbitration award has two ways to prevent or limit its enforcement.[214]

---

[208] Gary H. Sampliner, Enforcement of Foreign Arbitral Awards After Annulment in Their Country of Origin, 11 (9) Mealey's Int'l Arb. Rep., Sept.1996, at 22, 28.

[209] W. Laurence Craig, Some Trends and Developments in the Laws and Practice of International Commercial Arbitration, 30 Tex. Int'l L.J. 1, 32 (1995) ("the French statute does not permit nonenforcement on the ground that the award has been set aside by the courts of the country where the arbitration took place. Instead of automatic nonenforcement, the French court will independently examine any reasons for nonrecognition, including the reasons which led to its annulment abroad, in the exercise of its control function.")

[210] See, e.g., Baker Marine (Nig.) Ltd. v. Chevron (Nig.) Ltd., 191 F.3d 194 (2d Cir. 1999) (distinguishing *Chromalloy* and affirming district court holding that "it would not be proper to enforce a foreign arbitral award [rendered in Nigeria] under the Convention when such an award has been set aside by the Nigerian courts."); Spier v. Calzaturificio Tecnica, S.p.A., 77 F. Supp.2d 405 (S.D.N.Y. 1999).

[211] See Karaha Bodas Co., L.L.C. v. Perusahaan Pertambangan Minyak Dan Gas Bumi Negara, 364 F.3d 274 (5th Cir. 2004) (Swiss court refused to set aside arbitration award made in Switzerland but then Indonesian court purported to set it aside; Fifth Circuit held that Indonesian court's ruling could not a be a defense to enforcement under the New York Convention: "there is only one national court system that has jurisdiction to consider an application for annulment of an award."). Accord W. Michael Reisman, Systems of Control in International Adjudication and Arbitration: Breakdown and Repair 114 (1992).

[212] Tesoro Petroleum Corp. v. Asamera (South Sumatra) Ltd., 798 F. Supp. 400, 405 (W.D. Tex. 1992) (the Convention "not appear to this Court to authorize a suit to be initiated for the purpose of vacating an arbitral award, but instead sets forth the specific, limited circumstances in which, in a suit to enforce an award, a court may decline to do so.")

[213] Ian R. Macneil, Richard E. Speidel & Thomas J. Stipanowich, Federal Arbitration Law § 44.40.1.3, at 44:273 (1994).

[214] W. Michael Reisman & Heide Iravani, The Changing Relation of National Courts and International Commercial Arbitration, 21 Am. Rev. Int'l Arb. 5, 12 (2010) ("the Convention establishes two tiers of review competence, making a sharp distinction between so-called 'primary' or 'venue' jurisdictions and 'secondary' or 'enforcement' jurisdictions.")

First, that party can try to persuade a court at the seat of arbitration to "set aside" (vacate), rather than confirm, the award. Vacatur by a court at the seat nearly always prevents enforcement of the award by the courts of any State. Second, even if the court at the seat of arbitration confirms the award, that confirmation only makes the award enforceable in that State, so the party displeased with the award can seek to prevent other States' courts from recognizing and enforcing it.[215] This second topic of enforcement (but not the first topic of vacatur) is governed by the New York Convention, which provides:

> 1. Recognition and enforcement of the award may be refused, at the request of the party against whom it is invoked, only if that party furnishes to the competent authority where the recognition and enforcement is sought, proof that:
>
> (a) The parties to the agreement referred to in article II were, under the law applicable to them, under some incapacity, or the said agreement is not valid under the law to which the parties have subjected it or, failing any indication thereon, under the law of the country where the award was made; or
>
> (b) The party against whom the award is invoked was not given proper notice of the appointment of the arbitrator or of the arbitration proceedings or was otherwise unable to present his case; or
>
> (c) The award deals with a difference not contemplated by or not falling within the terms of the submission to arbitration, or it contains decisions on matters beyond the scope of the submission to arbitration, provided that, if the decisions on matters submitted to arbitration can be separated from those not so submitted, that part of the award which contains decisions on matters submitted to arbitration may be recognized and enforced; or
>
> (d) The composition of the arbitral authority or the arbitral procedure was not in accordance with the agreement of the parties, or, failing such agreement, was not in accordance with the law of the country where the arbitration took place; or
>
> (e) The award has not yet become binding on the parties, or has been set aside or suspended by a competent

[215] As noted above, confirmation by the seat is not required before a court outside the seat can enforce an award. See § 59.

authority of the country in which, or under the law of which, that award was made.

2. Recognition and enforcement of an arbitral award may also be refused if the competent authority in the country where recognition and enforcement is sought finds that:

(a) The subject matter of the difference is not capable of settlement by arbitration under the law of that country; or

(b) The recognition or enforcement of the award would be contrary to the public policy of that country.

These grounds for denying recognition and enforcement to awards are permissive. That is, the Convention authorizes but does not require States to deny recognition and enforcement if one party proves any of the grounds in Article V.[216]

The Convention's grounds for denying recognition and enforcement are discussed in the following subsections.

(b) The Convention's Grounds for Non-Enforcement of Award

(1) Arbitration Agreement Invalid

Article V(1)(a) of the New York Convention says recognition and enforcement of an arbitration award may be refused if "The parties to the agreement referred to in article II were, under the law applicable to them, under some incapacity, or the said agreement is not valid under the law to which the parties have subjected it or, failing any indication thereon, under the law of the country where the award was made."[217] This provision refers to and relates to Article II, which requires enforcement of executory arbitration agreements.[218] So generally, "the same substantive analysis that applies in the context of the enforcement of [executory] arbitration agreements is equally applicable in resolving an application to recognize [or deny enforcement to] an arbitral award."[219] That

---

216 Gary B. Born, International Commercial Arbitration 3428 (2d ed. 2014) ("The English language text of Article V is unmistakably permissive, providing that Contracting States "*may*" refuse recognition of an award").

217 New York Convention, art. V(1)(a).

218 Restatement (Third) U.S. Law of Int'l Comm. Arb. § 4.10 cmt. a (2019) ("Just as parties cannot be required to arbitrate if they have not entered into an arbitration agreement, so too an arbitral award is not enforceable if it is based upon an arbitration agreement that never existed or is invalid.")

219 Gary B. Born, International Commercial Arbitration 3449 (2d ed. 2014). But see China Minmetals Materials Import and Export Co., Ltd. v. Chi Mei Corp., 334 F.3d 274 (3d Cir. 2003) ("there is indeed some distinction between Article II and Article V.

analysis is summarized above in the context of the enforcement of executory arbitration agreements.[220] However, one difference between the earlier stage of enforcing an executory agreement to arbitrate and the later state of vacating an arbitration award is that at the later stage an arbitrator may already have ruled that the parties formed a valid (enforceable) arbitration agreement. Nevertheless, "[a] court reviews de novo an arbitral tribunal's determination of whether an arbitration agreement exists," and "whether a contract that includes an arbitration clause exists."[221] In addition, "[a] court also reviews de novo an arbitral tribunal's determination of the validity of an arbitration agreement," "unless the parties clearly and unmistakably agree that validity is an issue for the arbitral tribunal to decide in a final and binding manner."[222]

An example at the award-enforcement stage is *Sarhank Group v. Oracle Corp.*,[223] in which the Second Circuit held that a district court could find that a parent corporation was not bound by its subsidiary's agreement to arbitrate.[224] Another case denied recognition and enforcement of an arbitration award on the ground that there was no "exchange of letters" or other agreement to arbitrate as required by Article II of the New York Convention.[225]

(2) Inadequate Opportunity to Present Case

Article V(1)(b) of the New York Convention says recognition and enforcement of an arbitration award may be refused if "[t]he party against whom the award is invoked was not given proper notice of the appointment of the arbitrator or of the arbitration proceedings or was otherwise unable to present his case."[226] Some courts have read this provision to "essentially sanction[ ] the application of the forum state's standards of due process."[227] In contrast, the Restatement

---

The former explicitly requires an 'agreement in writing' while the latter requires only that the parties have reached an agreement as to arbitrability under ordinary contract principles.")

[220] See §§ 52–54.

[221] Restatement (Third) U.S. Law of Int'l Comm. Arb. § 4.10 cmt. d, e (2019).

[222] Id.

[223] 404 F.3d 657 (2d Cir. 2005).

[224] Id. at 662–63 (remand[ing] to the district court to find as a fact whether Oracle agreed to arbitrate, by its actions or inaction, or by reason of any action of Systems [Oracle's subsidiary] as to which Oracle clothed Systems with apparent or actual authority to consent on its behalf to arbitration, or on any other basis recognized by American contract law or the law of agency").

[225] Dynamo v. Ovechkin, 412 F. Supp.2d 24 (D.D.C. 2006).

[226] New York Convention, art. V(1)(b).

[227] Parsons & Whittemore Overseas Co., Inc. v. Societe Generale De L'Industrie du Papier (RAKTA), 508 F.2d 969, 975 (2d Cir. 1974). Accord Karaha Bodas Co., L.L.C. v. Perusahaan Pertambangan Minyak Dan Gas Bumi, 364 F.3d 274, 298 (5th Cir. 2004).

says, Article V(1)(b) "is interpreted against the background of the general presumption in favor of giving effect to arbitral awards and the broad discretion that arbitrators enjoy in managing arbitral proceedings," so it "is interpreted narrowly and protects only against serious procedural defects that have a material effect on arbitral proceedings, rendering them fundamentally unfair."[228]

Nevertheless, some cases rely on Article V(1)(b) in denying enforcement to an arbitration award. These cases include facts like lack of an oral hearing,[229] inadequate notice of the hearing,[230] and denial of an opportunity to present evidence. In an example of the latter, the Second Circuit held that arbitrators (the Iran-United States Claims Tribunal[231]) denied a party (Avco) the opportunity to present its claim by first "approving the method of proof proposed by Avco, namely the submission of Avco's audited accounts receivable ledgers," and then ruling against Avco because it did not submit actual invoices.[232] Apart from such cases, showing that a party lacked an opportunity to present its case may require a fact-intensive inquiry about the extent to which arbitrators can reasonably be expected to accommodate the schedule of a party or its witnesses, and

---

[228] Restatement (Third) U.S. Law of Int'l Comm. Arb. § 4.11 cmt. a (2019).

[229] See § 58(c)(3). Restatement (Third) U.S. Law of Int'l Comm. Arb. § 4.11 Note e (2019) ("Generally, denial of a party's request to have even a single oral hearing may be grounds for denying post-award relief. There are, however, exceptions. For example, if the parties have agreed in their arbitral agreement to a 'documents only' or an online arbitration, denial of a subsequently requested oral hearing is not adequate grounds for challenge. Relatedly, if a party requests an additional hearing or hearings, or other procedural opportunities, an arbitral tribunal's ruling on the request is afforded deference and denial of such a request will not generally be sufficient ground for refusing recognition or enforcement of an arbitral award.")

[230] Gary B. Born, International Commercial Arbitration 3507 (2d ed. 2014). On the other hand, "failure to serve legal documents in a manner consistent with national procedural rules is not a ground for challenge" as the "arbitration agreement displaces national rules for service." Restatement (Third) U.S. Law of Int'l Comm. Arb. § 4.11 Note d (2019). See Choice Hotels Int'l, Inc. v. SM Prop. Mgmt., LLC, 519 F.3d 200, 208–209 (4th Cir. 2008) (deferring to arbitrator's decision that service at last-known address was sufficient under AAA rules and that agreement did not require service on representative designated in agreement for notice of other contractual events). See also Bernstein Seawell & Kove v. Bosarge, 813 F.2d 726, 732 (5th Cir. 1987) (holding that even in the absence of actual notice, information provided to party's attorney about arbitration was sufficient to constitute constructive notice); First State Ins. Co. v. Banco de Seguros Del Estado, 254 F.3d 354, 357–358 (1st Cir. 2001) (lack of notice attributed to negligence of party's designated agent).

[231] The Iran-United States Claims Tribunal is discussed further in § 64.

[232] Iran Aircraft Industries v. Avco Corp., 980 F.2d 141 (2d Cir. 1992) ("Having thus led Avco to believe it had used a proper method to substantiate its claim, the Tribunal then rejected Avco's claim for lack of proof. * * *We believe that by so misleading Avco, however unwittingly, the Tribunal denied Avco the opportunity to present its claim in a meaningful manner.")

courts generally defer to arbitrators' judgment about the timing and conduct of the arbitration proceedings.[233]

(3) Arbitrators Exceeded Their Jurisdiction

Article V(1)(c) of the New York Convention says recognition and enforcement of an arbitration award may be refused if

> The award deals with a difference not contemplated by or not falling within the terms of the submission to arbitration, or it contains decisions on matters beyond the scope of the submission to arbitration, provided that, if the decisions on matters submitted to arbitration can be separated from those not so submitted, that part of the award which contains decisions on matters submitted to arbitration may be recognized and enforced.[234]

This ground for non-enforcement resembles FAA § 10(a)(4), which permits courts to vacate an arbitration award where, among other things, "the arbitrators exceeded their powers."[235] Courts and commentators generally speak interchangeably of arbitrators exceeding their powers, exceeding their authority, or exceeding their jurisdiction because whether one calls it "power," or "authority," or "jurisdiction," it comes from the parties.[236] It is conferred by contract, not by statute or other law, so arbitrators exceed it when they decide matters beyond the scope of the arbitration agreement. This is clear in Article V(1)(c) of the New York Convention which refers to "matters beyond the scope of the submission to arbitration."

Courts will enforce an arbitration award on a claim only if the parties agreed to arbitrate that claim. That the parties agreed to arbitrate *some* claim is not enough. They must have agreed to arbitrate *that* claim. However, courts generally presume that the arbitrators acted within their powers,[237] and rarely decline to enforce

---

[233] Parsons & Whittemore Overseas Co., Inc. v. Societe Generale De L'Industrie du Papier (RAKTA), 508 F.2d 969, 973–74 (2d Cir. 1974) (rejecting Article V(1)(b) argument).

[234] New York Convention, art. V(1)(c).

[235] 9 U.S.C. § 10(a)(4). *Parsons*, 508 F.2d at 976 (Article V(1)(c) "tracks in more detailed form" FAA § 10(a)(4). "Both provisions basically allow a party to attack an award predicated upon arbitration of a subject matter not within the agreement to submit to arbitration.")

[236] Restatement (Third) U.S. Law of Int'l Comm. Arb. § 4.12 Note d (2019) ("As a practical matter, the disputes within the tribunal's jurisdiction are defined by the arbitration agreement and by any terms of reference agreed to by the parties. They may also be determined by a joint submission by the parties to the arbitral tribunal.")

[237] Management & Technical Consultants S.A. v. Parsons-Jurden Intern. Corp., 820 F.2d 1531, 1534 (9th Cir. 1987) (stating, in a case to enforce a foreign arbitral award, "Federal arbitration law has established a presumption that an arbitral body has acted within its powers"); *Parsons*, 508 F.2d at 976 (referring to the "powerful presumption that the arbitral body acted within its powers."); Whirlpool Corp. v.

awards as beyond the submission to arbitration.[238] In part, this is because parties often agree to arbitrate pursuant to an arbitration organization's rules, which give to the arbitrators the power to decide whether particular claims are within the scope of the arbitration agreement.[239] However, "although those rules give the arbitrators the authority to determine their own jurisdiction, they do not expressly provide that the arbitrators have the final and unreviewable authority to determine either the claims or issues encompassed by the arbitration agreement."[240] So "if a case proceeds to arbitration and a party raises a jurisdictional objection, the tribunal has the authority to entertain and resolve the jurisdictional question," but courts may review the arbitrators' resolution de novo unless the parties "clearly agreed to have the arbitrators decide (i.e., to arbitrate) the question of arbitrability,' by "indicat[ing] that the tribunal's determination is final and entitled to deference by the courts."[241]

(4) Improper Arbitral Procedure or Composition of Arbitral Authority

Article V(1)(d) of the New York Convention says recognition and enforcement of an arbitration award may be refused if "[t]he composition of the arbitral authority or the arbitral procedure was not in accordance with the agreement of the parties, or, failing such agreement, was not in accordance with the law of the country where the arbitration took place."[242] Several courts have vacated awards where the composition of the arbitration panel departed from the agreement.[243] Other cases relying on Article V(1)(d) in denying

---

Philips Electronics, N.V., 848 F. Supp. 474, 480 (S.D.N.Y. 1994) (arbitrator's "decision as to the scope of its arbitral authority is entitled to deference").

[238] Albert Jan van den Berg, New York Convention of 1958: Refusals of Enforcement, 18(2) ICC Int'l Ct. Arb. Bull. 15, 24 (2007) (finding only two reported cases, neither of which was from the United States).

[239] See, e.g., International Chamber of Commerce Rules of Arbitration, Art. 6, https://iccwbo.org/dispute-resolution-services/arbitration/rules-of-arbitration/#article_6.

[240] Restatement (Third) U.S. Law of Int'l Comm. Arb. § 4.12 Note d (2019).

[241] Id.

[242] New York Convention, art. V(1)(d).

[243] See Encyclopaedia Universalis SA v. Encyclopaedia Britannica, Inc., 403 F.3d 85, 90–92 (2d Cir. 2005) (refusing to recognize award, under Article V(1)(d) of New York Convention, on grounds that chairman was appointed without co-arbitrators attempting to agree on chairman, as provided for by parties' agreement). Courts have reached similar results in the context of vacatur. Cargill Rice, Inc. v. Empresa Nicaraguense de Alimentos Basicos, 25 F.3d 223, 226 (4th Cir. 1994) ("Arbitration awards made by arbitrators not appointed under the method provided in the parties' contract must be vacated."); Szuts v. Dean Witter Reynolds, Inc., 931 F.2d 830, 831 (11th Cir. 1991) (award vacated for failure to maintain three-person tribunal as required by parties' agreement); W. Can. SS Co. v. Cia de Nav. San Leonardo, 105 F.

enforcement to an arbitration award include facts such as the arbitrators' failure to:

- render an award or conduct the proceedings within prescribed time limits,
- conduct the arbitration in the agreed arbitral seat,
- make a reasoned award,
- apply agreed rules of procedure, or
- apply provisions regarding consolidation of arbitrations.[244]

That said, courts are generally reluctant (even in cases with facts like those just listed) to overturn awards for arbitrators' minor violations of agreed procedures.

A leading commentator states that "the most difficult issues that arise under Article V(1)(d) involve cases where the parties' agreed arbitral procedures violate the mandatory laws of the arbitral seat."[245] "The Restatement adheres to a literal reading of the text of the New York Convention, which requires that the parties' agreement be given effect even if that entails violating the mandatory law of the seat."[246] "Accordingly, a court should recognize or enforce (or decline to vacate) an award that complies with the parties' agreement but violates the mandatory law of the seat."[247]

(5) Set Aside by Court at Seat of Arbitration

Article V(1)(e) of the New York Convention says recognition and enforcement of an arbitration award may be refused if "The award has not yet become binding on the parties, or has been set aside or suspended by a competent authority of the country in which, or under the law of which, that award was made."[248] The setting aside of an arbitration award by a court at the seat of arbitration is discussed above.[249] As the Restatement states, "[o]rdinarily, a court will not confirm, recognize, or enforce an award that has been set aside by a competent authority."[250]

Supp. 452, 453 (S.D.N.Y. 1952) (vacating award made by two arbitrators because arbitration agreement required three-person tribunal).

[244] Gary B. Born, International Commercial Arbitration 3565–71 (2d ed. 2014).

[245] Id. at 3573.

[246] Restatement (Third) U.S. Law of Int'l Comm. Arb. § 4.13 Note c (2019).

[247] Id.

[248] New York Convention, art. V(1)(e).

[249] See § 60(a).

[250] Restatement (Third) U.S. Law of Int'l Comm. Arb. § 4.14 cmt. c (2019).

More often debatable is whether a particular award has "become binding on the parties," but courts generally hold awards to be binding even when a party displeased with the award might still seek to have it set aside by a court in the arbitral seat, so confirmation of an award by a court in the arbitral seat is not necessary to make an award binding.[251]

A related provision is Article VI of the Convention which provides:

> If an application for the setting aside or suspension of the award has been made to a competent authority referred to in article V(1)(e), the authority before which the award is sought to be relied upon may, if it considers it proper, adjourn the decision on the enforcement of the award and may also, on the application of the party claiming enforcement of the award, order the other party to give suitable security.[252]

At least one United States court has adjourned its enforcement pending a decision by a court at the seat of arbitration, India, on whether to set aside the award.[253]

(6) Non-Arbitrability

Article V(2)(a) of the New York Convention says recognition and enforcement of an arbitration award may be refused if "the competent authority in the country where recognition and enforcement is sought finds that: The subject matter of the difference is not capable of settlement by arbitration under the law of that country."[254] This provision relates to Article II(1), discussed above, which requires enforcement of agreements to arbitrate only disputes "concerning a subject matter capable of settlement by arbitration."[255] Generally, "if arbitration of a dispute or claim cannot be required under Article II(1), because it is non-arbitrable, then an award dealing with that dispute is generally subject to non-recognition under Article

---

[251] Gary B. Born, International Commercial Arbitration 3613 (2d ed. 2014).

[252] New York Convention, art. VI.

[253] Fertilizer Corp. of India v. IDI Management, Inc., 517 F. Supp. 948, 956–59 (S.D. Ohio 1981) ("The award is presently before the Indian courts for a ruling."); id. at 962 ("this Court has determined to adjourn its decision on enforcement of the Nitrophosphate Award until the Indian courts decide with finality whether the award is correct under Indian law. FCI, of course, may apply to this Court for suitable security, as provided by Article VI.") See also Europcar Italia, S.p.A. v. Maiellano Tours, Inc., 156 F.3d 310, 317–18 (2d Cir. 1998) (listing factors courts should consider when deciding whether to adjourn enforcement proceedings to await the outcome of parallel foreign proceedings).

[254] New York Convention, art. V(2)(a).

[255] See § 55.

V(2)(a)."[256] Non-arbitrability has not often been relied on by courts in declining enforcement of awards.[257]

(7) Public Policy

Article V(2)(b) of the New York Convention says recognition and enforcement of an arbitration award may be refused if "the competent authority in the country where recognition and enforcement is sought finds that * * * [t]he recognition or enforcement of the award would be contrary to the public policy of that country."[258] This provision has been interpreted narrowly by United States courts so, as the Restatement drily notes, "[t]he public policy ground is often invoked, but rarely with success."[259] As the Second Circuit recognized long ago,

> [a]n expansive construction of this defense would vitiate the Convention's basic effort to remove preexisting obstacles to enforcement. Additionally, considerations of reciprocity—considerations given express recognition in the Convention itself—counsel courts to invoke the public policy defense with caution lest foreign courts frequently accept it as a defense to enforcement of arbitral awards rendered in the United States.[260]

Therefore, the court held "enforcement of foreign arbitral awards may be denied on this basis only where enforcement would violate the forum state's most basic notions of morality and justice."[261] Similarly, one commentator observes that courts, especially in developed countries, exercise "a substantial degree of restraint and moderation in the application of public policies under Article V(2)(b)."[262]

---

256 Gary B. Born, International Commercial Arbitration 3696 (2d ed. 2014) However, if non-enforcement of an award (Art. V) is sought in a different State than non-enforcement of an executory agreement (Art. II) than different standards may apply.

257 Restatement (Third) U.S. Law of Int'l Comm. Arb. § 4.15 cmt. a (2019).

258 New York Convention, Art. V(2)(b).

259 Restatement (Third) U.S. Law of Int'l Comm. Arb. § 4.16 cmt. d (2019).

260 Parsons & Whittemore Overseas Co., Inc. v. Societe Generale De L'Industrie du Papier (RAKTA), 508 F.2d 969, 973–74 (2d Cir. 1974). Accord Fertilizer Corp. of India v. IDI Management, Inc., 517 F. Supp. 948 (S.D. Ohio 1981).

261 Parsons, 508 F2d at 974. For an example, see Karen Mar. Ltd. v. Omar Int'l, Inc., 322 F. Supp. 2d 224, 229 (E.D.N.Y. 2004) (contract undertaking to boycott Israel violated U.S. anti-boycott law; "if [e]nforcement of the award * * * legitimized or perpetuated the Arab boycott of Israel, [enforcement] would violate basic American notions of morality and justice.")

262 Gary B. Born, International Commercial Arbitration 3655 (2d ed. 2014).

E. INTERNATIONAL PUBLIC LAW ARBITRATION

Table of Sections

§ 61 Overview of International Public Law Arbitration

International arbitration is commonly divided into commercial arbitration and public law arbitration. Of the two, international commercial arbitration is more like domestic arbitration. Most basically, domestic arbitration is private (non-government) adjudication,[263] and so is international commercial arbitration.[264] In the international commercial context, "[w]hen parties agree to arbitrate their disputes, they give up the right to have those disputes decided by a national court. Instead, they agree that their disputes will be resolved privately, outside any court system."[265]

By contrast, in the international public law context the word "arbitration" is not typically used to describe a private-sector alternative to government courts. International public law disputes often involve claims by and against States. These are generally claims for which no national court has jurisdiction to enter judgment against the defending State because the doctrine of sovereign immunity prevents such jurisdiction.[266] So when States "arbitrate"

---

[263] See § 1.

[264] Gary B. Born, International Commercial Arbitration 257 (2d ed. 2014) ("The non-governmental identity of the decision-maker is a fundamental, distinguishing feature of 'arbitration' agreements.")

[265] Margaret L. Moses, The Principles and Practice of International Commercial Arbitration 17 (2008).

[266] See, e.g., Andreas F. Lowenfeld, International Litigation and Arbitration ch.7 (3d ed. 2006). Sovereign immunity is less of a force in commercial arbitration than in public law arbitration because sovereign immunity often does not protect a State insofar as it is engaged in "commercial," rather than governmental, activity. See, e.g., 28 U.S.C. § 1605.

> A foreign state shall not be immune from the jurisdiction of courts of the United States or of the States in any case—
>
> * * *

their *public law* disputes with each other, they are not giving up the right to have those disputes decided by a national court because they never had any such right. International public law arbitration is not an alternative to international litigation, but rather an alternative to the other ways States interact, such as diplomacy and war. The same is also generally true of public international law arbitration involving claims against States by private parties who are citizens of different States; for example, investment arbitration generally involves claims that would otherwise be barred by sovereign immunity.

Because the claims in public international law arbitration are generally against States, enforcement of an award arising out of such arbitration may face an obstacle not likely present in international commercial arbitration, let alone domestic arbitration: how does a party enforce an arbitration award against a State whose national courts are part of the State and thus share the State's opposition to enforcement of the award?

Public international arbitration agreements can be divided into three types.[267] The first consists of an arbitration clause that is included in a treaty with the purpose of resolving disputes regarding the application of that treaty. A prominent example of this first type

---

(1) in which the foreign state has waived its immunity either explicitly or by implication, notwithstanding any withdrawal of the waiver which the foreign state may purport to effect except in accordance with the terms of the waiver;

(2) in which the action is based upon a commercial activity carried on in the United States by the foreign state; or upon an act performed in the United States in connection with a commercial activity of the foreign state elsewhere; or upon an act outside the territory of the United States in connection with a commercial activity of the foreign state elsewhere and that act causes a direct effect in the United States;

* * *

(6) in which the action is brought, either to enforce an agreement made by the foreign state with or for the benefit of a private party to submit to arbitration all or any differences which have arisen or which may arise between the parties with respect to a defined legal relationship, whether contractual or not, concerning a subject matter capable of settlement by arbitration under the laws of the United States, or to confirm an award made pursuant to such an agreement to arbitrate, if (A) the arbitration takes place or is intended to take place in the United States, (B) the agreement or award is or may be governed by a treaty or other international agreement in force for the United States calling for the recognition and enforcement of arbitral awards, (C) the underlying claim, save for the agreement to arbitrate, could have been brought in a United States court under this section or section 1607, or (D) paragraph (1) of this subsection is otherwise applicable.

Id. § 1605(a) (emphasis added). See also Cargill Intern. S.A. v. M/T Pavel Dybenko, 991 F.2d 1012, 1018 (2d Cir. 1993) ("the [New York] Convention is exactly the sort of treaty Congress intended to include in the arbitration exception" of 28 U.S.C.§ 1605(a)(6).); 9 U.S.C. § 15 ("Enforcement of arbitral agreements, confirmation of arbitral awards, and execution upon judgments based on orders confirming such awards shall not be refused on the basis of the Act of State doctrine.")

[267] Thomas Buergenthal & Sean D. Murphy, Public International Law in a Nutshell 87 (6th ed. 2019).

is investment arbitration. The second type of public international arbitration agreement "consists of treaties whose sole function is to establish a method for the resolution and arbitration of whatever disputes might arise between the parties in the future."[268] And the third type consists of post-dispute arbitration agreements, such as the one establishing the Iran-U.S. Claims Tribunal.[269] These three types of public international law arbitration are discussed in the following three sections.

§ 62 Investment Arbitration

The parties to major transnational business transactions often consist entirely of private-sector businesses based in the most economically developed parts of the world. The contracts facilitating such transactions often have a clause providing for international *commercial* arbitration of any disputes, which subjects them to the law discussed in Sections 51–60. In contrast, other transnational business transactions involve a country's government (a State) as a party. This is especially likely when the transaction will exploit natural resources or require a large investment (e.g., mining) in a less-developed country.[270] With at least one State as a party, arbitration arising out of such transactions is international *public law* arbitration, and commonly falls under the heading of "investment arbitration,"[271] for reasons discussed in the following paragraphs.

---

[268] Id. at 87–88

[269] Id. at 88.

[270] Alan Scott Rau, Edward F. Sherman & Scott R. Peppet, Processes of Dispute Resolution: The Role of Lawyers 628–29 (4th ed. 2006) ("In many countries the government assumes a far more active role in economic transactions—particularly those involving capital investment and the exploitation and development of national resources—than it does in the United States."); Julian D. Lew, Loukas A. Mistelis & Stefan M. Kroll, Comparative International Commercial Arbitration 764 (2003) ("The investment may be considerable which may need years for the investor to recover. In developing countries foreign investment often relates to core components of the national economy. These factors make foreign investment particularly vulnerable to possible interference by the host state.").

[271] S.I. Strong, Navigating the Borders Between International Commercial Arbitration and U.S. Federal Courts: A Jurisprudential GPS, 2012 J. Disp. Resol. 119, 124 ("international commercial arbitration is a private dispute resolution mechanism that relies heavily on the agreement of the parties, both as a means of demonstrating consent to arbitration and as a way of describing the shape of the proceedings. * * * International investment arbitration, on the other hand, is a treaty-based procedure that is rooted in public international law."); Irene M. Ten Cate, International Arbitration and the Ends of Appellate Review 44 N.Y.U. J. Int'l L. & Pol. 1109, 1113 (2012) ("The paradigmatic commercial arbitration case involves contract claims arising out of business transactions between private parties. Investment disputes, on the other hand, always involve claims against state party respondents concerning their interference with investments made by foreign investors (often, but not always, in state-sponsored projects). The private-public distinction also holds true for the sources that govern the disputes.")

While international *commercial* arbitration arises out of an ordinary contract between the parties, (either a predispute arbitration agreement or a post-dispute submission agreement,) the "contract" underlying investment arbitration is typically quite different. Generally, the State in which the investment occurred (the "host" State) previously consented to arbitration by acceding (agreeing) to a treaty providing for the arbitration of investment disputes or by enacting similar legislation. Such a treaty or legislation "constitute[s] a unilateral standing offer" to arbitrate disputes with any investor fulfilling the requirements of the treaty or legislation.[272]

> In what amounts to a sophisticated choice of forum clause, some treaties require investors to choose between litigating their treaty claims in national courts and arbitrating their investment claims before an arbitral panel * * * . Other treaties require investors to arbitrate their claims, but let the investors choose the arbitral body that will administer the dispute.
>
> Investors have overwhelmingly accepted Sovereigns' standing offers to arbitrate.[273]

States typically agree to investment arbitration to attract foreign investment.[274] Historically, investors have been vulnerable to host State seizure of assets (expropriation) or regulation tantamount to expropriation.[275] The doctrine of sovereign immunity might prevent investors from bringing a claim against the host State in the investor's home courts,[276] or in the courts of the host State.[277] The only remedy available to the investor would be diplomatic or military support from its home State against the host State. With investors' home states generally reluctant to do this,[278] investors continue to fear expropriation and similar actions by host states. Reducing these fears is a goal of international investment treaties and their arbitration provisions. Relatedly, collecting on an international investment arbitration award against a State "may be difficult, but

---

272 Julian D. Lew, Loukas A. Mistelis & Stefan M. Kroll, Comparative International Commercial Arbitration 764 (2003).

273 Susan D. Franck, The Nature and Enforcement of Investor Rights Under Investment Treaties: Do Investment Treaties Have a Bright Future, 12 U.C. Davis J.Int'l L. & Pol'y 47, 54–55 (2005). "The offer is accepted by the investor when it initiates arbitration proceedings against the state." Julian D. Lew, Loukas A. Mistelis & Stefan M. Kroll, Comparative International Commercial Arbitration 764 (2003).

274 Christopher F. Dugan et al., Investor-State Arbitration 6 (2008).

275 Jeswald W. Salacuse, The Law of Investment Treaties 285 (2010).

276 Christopher F. Dugan et al., Investor-State Arbitration 20–21 (2008).

277 Id. at 14.

278 See id. at 29.

political repercussions of treaty-based arbitration claims have compelled countries to honor awards—obviating the investor's need to pursue collection through the courts."[279]

The terms of international investment treaties vary. In most, host states do not forego a right of expropriation altogether.[280] Rather, host states limit the circumstances where expropriation can take place and provide for compensating the foreign investor.[281] Host states agree to provide foreign investors with the better of treatment provided to investments of nationals of the host State or of investments of nationals of any other country.[282] Investment treaties usually prohibit the host country from requiring the investment project to export a percentage of its production, use local content, or hire local workers.[283] Investment treaties ensure that the investor can transfer money freely between the host State and the investor's home State.[284]

The number of parties to international investment treaties varies. Some involve only two countries, that is, they are bilateral investment treaties (BITs). A typical BIT obligates the host State to provide foreign investors protection against various forms of expropriation and discrimination by the State.[285] For example, in the Supreme Court's 2014 case of *BG Grp., PLC v. Republic of Argentina*, a British investor in Argentina argued "that Argentina's new laws and regulatory practices violated provisions in the [BIT] forbidding

---

[279] Michael S. Greco & Ian Meredith, Getting to Yes Abroad: Arbitration as a Tool in Effective Commercial and Political Risk Management, Bus.L.Today, March/April 2007, at 23, 25. For a different view, see Joseph M. Cardosi, Precluding the Treasure Hunt: How the World Bank Group Can Help Investors Circumnavigate Sovereign Immunity Obstacles to ICSID Award Execution, 41 Pepp. L. Rev. 125, 126–27 (2013) (although a State agreeing to arbitration "acts as a waiver of sovereign immunity as to jurisdiction, prevailing investors may encounter the obstacle of sovereign immunity following the arbitration when attempting to execute an award against a noncompliant state. If a state refuses to comply with an award, investors must set off on a worldwide search for assets held by that state; if and when investors find state assets, they must overcome the obstacle of sovereign immunity laws governing access to those assets.")

[280] Jeswald W. Salacuse, The Law of Investment Treaties 288 (2010).

[281] Id.

[282] Id. at 245.

[283] Id. at 329.

[284] Id. at 256–57.

[285] Michael S. Greco & Ian Meredith, Getting to Yes Abroad: Arbitration as a Tool in Effective Commercial and Political Risk Management, Bus. L. Today, March/April 2007, at 26. "To facilitate the flow of capital to lesser-developed countries, the United States and other Western nations have entered into more than 2,800 BITs with capital-importing countries. A critical feature of these treaties is that they protect the foreign investor against expropriation or other conduct." Peter B. Rutledge, Arbitration and the Constitution 51–52 (2013).

the 'expropriation' of investments and requiring that each nation give 'fair and equitable treatment' to investors from the other."[286]

Some BITs commit the host State to arbitrate a broad array of claims by foreign investors, while others are narrower. Some treaties allow investors to choose[287] whether the arbitration will be unadministered (ad hoc) arbitration under the UNCITRAL rules or administered by an organization such as the International Chamber of Commerce (ICC) or the International Centre for Settlement of Investment Disputes (ICSID). ICSID was created in 1965 by an international convention (treaty) under the aegis of the World Bank to resolve investment disputes.[288] Including the United States, there are "162 ICSID Convention signatories States. Today, a majority of investor-State disputes are administered by ICSID."[289]

> The ICSID Convention, which sought to establish what has come to be called a "self-contained" system, provides for an [award] annulment procedure within ICSID itself, and bars challenges to awards in national courts. U.S. courts may therefore not entertain actions to vacate awards rendered pursuant to the Convention. The Convention requires States to treat ICSID Convention awards as binding and enforceable. Under Article 54, contracting States must enforce an ICSID Convention award "as if it were a final judgment of a court in that State."[290]

ICSID awards are not subject to the FAA or New York or Panama Conventions.[291]

§ 63 Treaties Focused on Arbitration of Future Public Law Disputes

The Permanent Court of Arbitration (PCA) was established by the 1899 Hague Convention on the Pacific Settlement of International Disputes.[292] "It is not really a court since it is not composed of a fixed body of judges."[293] Rather, it is a panel of persons

---

286 BG Grp., PLC v. Republic of Argentina, 134 S. Ct. 1198, 1204 (2014).

287 Susan D. Franck, The Nature and Enforcement of Investor Rights Under Investment Treaties: Do Investment Treaties Have a Bright Future, 12 U.C. Davis J.Int'l L. & Pol'y 47, 54–55 (2005).

288 Gary B. Born, International Commercial Arbitration 120, n.819 (2d ed. 2014).

289 Restatement (Third) U.S. Law of Int'l Comm. Arb. Introduction, Historical Introduction to International Commercial and Investor-State Arbitration (2019).

290 Id.

291 Id.

292 For the text of the Convention of July 29, 1989, see Treaties and Other International Agreements of the United States of America 1776–1949, Vol. I, 230–46 (Charles I. Bevans ed., 1968).

293 Malcom N. Shaw, International Law 953 (5th ed. 2003).

nominated by the (hundred or so) contracting States. "Where contracting states wish to go to arbitration, they are entitled to choose the members of the tribunal from the panel. Thus, [the PCA] is in essence machinery facilitating the establishment of arbitral tribunals."[294] The PCA says its caseload includes "territorial, treaty, and human rights disputes between states, as well as commercial and investment disputes."[295] The PCA's website contains a partial list of its cases; that list shows no cases between 1935 and 1995, but dozens of cases more recently.[296]

The International Court of Justice (ICJ), also known as World Court, was created as part of the United Nations in 1945. Judges are elected to it when they receive a majority vote in each of the U.N. Security Council and General Assembly.[297] Only States may be parties to contentious (as opposed to advisory) cases before the ICJ[298] and "the most common, and uncontroversial, way for the Court to receive a case" is through the parties' agreement to submit their existing dispute to the ICJ.[299] This post-dispute arbitration agreement is often used for matters, such as boundary disputes, in which "[b]oth sides are prepared to lose [the dispute], in effect, so submitting it to the adjudication of the Court provides a valuable, 'face-saving' device for an embattled government."[300] An increasing number of predispute agreements to resolve disputes before the ICJ are found in various treaties.[301] Examples include the 1948 Genocide Convention, the 1965 Convention on Investment Disputes, the 1965 Convention on the Elimination of All Forms of Racial Discrimination, and the 1970 Hague Convention on Hijacking.[302]

Compliance with ICJ decisions has been characterized in a variety of ways. While some see "the record of compliance" as "only marginally satisfactory,"[303] others say that States have generally,

---

294 Id.

295 Permanent Ct. of Arb., Introduction to the PCA, (Aug. 11, 2022), https://pca-cpa.org/en/about/introduction/

296 Permanent Ct. of Arb., *Cases*, (Aug. 11, 2022), https://pca-cpa.org/en/cases/

297 "The ICJ adjudicates two types of cases: contentious and advisory. In contentious cases, only states may be parties. Statute of the International Court of Justice, Stat 1055, 33 UN Treaty Ser 993, Art 34 (June 26, 1945) (ICJ Statute). In contrast, an advisory opinion may be given in response to 'any legal question at the request of whatever body may be authorized by or in accordance with the Charter of the United Nations to make such a request.' Id at Art 65." Michael P. Scharf & Margaux Day, The International Court of Justice's Treatment of Circumstantial Evidence and Adverse Inferences, 13 Chi. J. Int'l L. 123 (2012).

298 Malcom N. Shaw, International Law 972 (5th ed.2003).

299 Id. at 254.

300 Id.

301 Id.

302 Malcom N. Shaw, International Law 977 (5th ed. 2003).

303 Malcom N. Shaw, International Law 996 (5th ed. 2003).

but not always, complied with ICJ decisions.[304] Perhaps all can agree that ICJ decisions have an impact "on a political level," and thus "should not necessarily be exclusively evaluated on the legal plane" of enforcement.[305] Failure to comply violates the U.N. Charter and would ultimately be enforceable by the Security Council, but each of its five permanent members (China, France, Russia, the United Kingdom, and the United States) maintains a veto power.[306]

The two institutions discussed in this section—the Permanent Court of Arbitration and the International Court of Justice (or World Court)—both have the word "court" in their names. This may suggest a higher level of "governmental-ness," than is found in international investment arbitration or the Iran-United States Claims Tribunal discussed in the next section. Relatedly, some scholars distinguish international "adjudication" before the PCA or ICJ from international "arbitration" before other bodies[307]—perhaps because "arbitration" tends to connote "non-governmental-ness."

§ 64 Public International Arbitration Tribunals Arising out of Post-Dispute Arbitration Agreements

The leading example of a public international arbitration tribunal established by post-dispute agreement is the Iran-United States Claims Tribunal. It was established in 1981 through the Algiers Declarations as part of the resolution of the Iran Hostage Crisis.[308] The Tribunal hears two categories of claims: private claims, which are claims brought by a national of one State against the other State, and inter-governmental claims, which are claims brought by one State against the other, alleging either a violation of the Algiers Declarations or breach of contract.[309] The Tribunal has decided nearly 4,000 cases and awarded more than $2.5 billion approximately $1 billion to Iran and Iranian nationals and a substantially higher

304 Thomas Buergenthal & Sean D. Murphy, Public International Law in a Nutshell 109 (6th ed. 2019).

305 Malcom N. Shaw, International Law 997 (5th ed. 2003).

306 Id.

307 See e.g., Stephen E. Gent, The Politics of International Arbitration and Adjudication, 2 Penn St. J. L. & Int'l Aff. 66, 67 (2013) ("The two methods primarily differ with respect to the identity of the third party. In arbitration, an individual, state, NGO, or panel of states hands down a decision. On the other hand, adjudication is conducted by an international court, such as the International Court of Justice.")

308 Declaration of the Government of the Democratic and Popular Republic of Algeria, Jan. 19, 1981, 1 Iran-U.S.C.T.R. 3; Declaration of the Government of the Democratic and Popular Republic of Algeria Concerning the Settlement of Claims by the Government of the United States of America and the Government of the Islamic Republic of Iran, Jan. 19, 1981, 1 Iran-U.S.C.T.R. 9.

309 Yulia Andreeva, et al., International Courts, 43 Int'l Law. 425, 439 (2009).

amount to the United States and United States nationals.[310] "While successful U.S. nationals were paid out of a security account in the Netherlands, in cases where Iran prevailed but the U.S. national refused to pay, Iran successfully enforced its awards in U.S. Courts through resort to the New York Convention."[311] The Iran-United States Claims Tribunal still exists.[312]

---

[310] Id.

[311] Thomas Buergenthal & Sean D. Murphy, Public International Law in a Nutshell 94 (6th ed. 2019).

[312] Iran-U.S. Claims Tribunal, https://iusct.com/about/ (last visited Aug. 11, 2022).

Chapter 9

PROCESSES SIMILAR TO ARBITRATION

Table of Sections

---

§ 65 Private Judging and Business Courts

(a) Private Judging

So-called "private judging" is much less private (much more governmental) than arbitration. Arbitration is a creature of contract. Not only does the parties' contract determine *whether* a dispute goes to arbitration, the contract also largely determines *what occurs* during arbitration. Parties to arbitration agreements generally have the freedom of contract to determine the identity of the arbitrator(s), the rules of procedure and evidence, and the confidentiality of the proceedings.[1] Judicial enforcement of arbitration awards is contractual in its rationale. Because the parties agreed to comply with the arbitrator's decision, if the losing party refuses to do so then that party is in breach of contract—even if the arbitrator's decision

---

1 See §§ 31–35.

is wrong—so grounds for vacating arbitration awards are narrow and do not include error of law by the arbitrator.[2]

In contrast, private judging is a less contractual, less privatized, process. Party agreement, usually formed post-dispute, does send a case to a private (or "temporary") judge, and parties generally can determine the time and place of trial. However, unlike arbitration, privately judging may limit contractual freedom insofar as state[3] law requires parties to:

(1) use the same rules of procedure and evidence used in ordinary litigation;[4]

(2) open their case to public view;[5]

(3) use only a former judge,[6] or experienced lawyer as their private judge;[7] and

(4) use the same appellate process used in ordinary litigation.[8]

Along these lines, the California Supreme Court contrasted private (or "temporary") judging with arbitration by noting that, unlike private judging, an "arbitrator need not be sworn or take an oath of office," "arbitration proceedings are not governed by the rules of evidence or judicial procedures applicable to superior court trials,"

---

2 See §§ 39–41.

3 Unlike the Federal Arbitration Act, which makes arbitration law nearly uniform around the country, the law on private judging varies from state to state. California is the leader in private judging. See Cal. Const. art. VI, § 21; Cal. Civ. Proc. Code §§ 638–645. Compare, e.g., N.H.Rev.Stat.Ann. § 519:9 ("The superior court with the consent of the parties shall, and without the consent of the parties may, commit to one or more referees any cause at law or in equity, or the determination of any question of fact pending in court wherein the parties are not, as matter of right, entitled to a trial by jury; and with the consent of the parties shall so commit any other cause or the determination of any other question of fact"); N.Y. Civ. Prac. L. & R. § 4301 ("A referee to determine an issue or to perform an act shall have all the powers of a court in performing a like function"); id. § 4317 ("The parties may stipulate that any issue shall be determined by a referee. Upon the filing of the stipulation with the clerk, the clerk shall forthwith enter an order referring the issue for trial to the referee named therein. Where the stipulation does not name a referee, the court shall designate a referee."); Tex.Civ.Prac. & Rem. Code §§ 151.001("On agreement of the parties, in civil or family law matters pending in a district court, statutory probate court, or statutory county court, the judge in whose court the case is pending may order referral of the case as provided by this chapter and shall stay proceedings in the judge's court pending the outcome of the trial. Any or all of the issues in the cases, whether an issue of fact or law, may be referred."); Wash. Rev. Code. Ann § 4.48.010 ("The court shall order all or any of the issues in a civil action, whether of fact or law, or both, referred to a referee upon the written consent of the parties which is filed with the clerk.").

4 Tex. Civ. Prac. & Rem. Code § 151.005.

5 Cal. Ct. R. 2.400(d); 2.833.

6 Tex. Civ. Prac. & Rem. Code § 151.003.

7 Cal. Ct. R. 2.812(a).

8 Tex. Civ. Prac. & Rem. Code § 151.013.

"the arbitrator issues an award, rather than a final appealable judgment," and "the arbitrator's decision generally is not reviewable for errors of fact or law."[9]

In sum, private judging typically resembles ordinary civil litigation except that the parties select and pay for the judge and hearing room, and thus get to jump the queue of parties awaiting action by regular judges in congested court systems.[10] This queue-jumping has led private judging to be labeled "Rent-A-Judge" and criticized as, "an unconstitutional, elitist institution that unfairly grants privileges to the wealthy."[11] California Supreme Court Chief Justice Ronald George was quoted as saying, the state had a "two-track system of justice—one for people who can decide which trial service they want and which judge they will pick" while "others stand at the end of the line."[12] At least one California judge has written that it is time for California "to reconsider" its decision to permit privately compensated temporary judges.[13] "Judges have a conflict of interest in considering how the judiciary should approach private judging. . . . [V]irtually all sitting judges are in favor of private judging . . . because they see that it will personally benefit them when they retire."[14]

Roughly fifty years ago, private judging was perhaps "used primarily in technical and complex business litigation involving substantial amounts of money."[15] Since then, it seems to have grown in family law matters,[16] including Angelina Jolie's divorce from Brad

---

[9] In re Marriage of Assemi, 7 Cal. 4th 896, 908, 872 P.2d 1190, 1197 (1994).

[10] Eileen L. Harris, Private Judging: A Means for Expediting Justice for Litigants, 82 Ala. Law. 266, 268 (2021) ("A case may be heard at any time and at any place. The private judge and the parties have greater flexibility with scheduling the hearing. Private judges typically do not have a full docket to contend with which provides greater latitude for scheduling. The private judge will provide the clerk of the court the dates, times, and places of any proceeding that could result in a judgment.")

[11] Anne S. Kim, Note, Rent-A-Judges and the Cost of Selling Justice, 44 Duke L.J. 166, 199 (1994). See also Note, The California Rent-A-Judge Experiment: Constitutional and Policy Considerations of Pay-As-You-Go Courts, 94 Harv. L. Rev. 1592 (1981).

[12] Eric Berkowitz, Is Justice Served?, L.A. Times (Oct. 22, 2006), https://www.latimes.com/archives/la-xpm-2006-oct-22-tm-arbitrate43-story.html [https://perma.cc/6EUN-L5EU].

[13] Jolie v. Superior Ct. of Los Angeles Cnty., 281 Cal. Rptr. 3d 610, 633 (Ct. App. 2021) (Segal, J., concurring).

[14] Id. (quoting 1992 Judicial Council Report, pp. 30–31, letter from Judge Robert H. O'Brien, July 17, 1992.)

[15] Barlow F. Christensen, Private Justice: California's General Reference Procedure, 1982 Am. Bar Found. Research J. 79, 82.

[16] J. Scott Vowell, Update on Private Judging in Alabama, 79 Ala. Law. 400, 402 (2018) (Alabama's Private Judge Act "has been used primarily in domestic relations cases"); Jacqueline St. Joan, Privatizing Family Law Adjudications: Issues and Procedures, 34 Colo. Law. 95 (2005); Ned I. Price, Binding Arbitration, Voluntary Trial Resolution, and Med-Arb Proceedings in Family Law, Fla. B.J., Nov. 2012, at 48, 50

Pitt.[17] Perhaps less commonly, it has also been used in medical malpractice, with a jury.[18]

(b) Business Courts

Like so-called private judging, business courts are much less private (much more governmental) than arbitration, but often have some features commonly associated with arbitration, such as specialized, expert adjudicators, and expedited case management procedures emphasizing ADR.[19] As with arbitration and private judging, speed may be the main appeal of business courts to many parties "because business-related decisions do not face a delay * * * caused by other matters that often take precedence in state courts of general jurisdiction, such as criminal and domestic disputes."[20] Compared to arbitration and private judging, however, business courts give parties less choice of adjudicator, as parties generally must take whichever judge the business court assigns to their case.

Variations occur among the many states with business courts.[21] For instance, some business courts automatically receive business cases, while others receive cases on party request or a judge's recommendation.[22] Also, business courts tend to:

(explaining that parties in family law disputes in Florida may agree to private judging called "voluntary trial resolution" in which the parties choose a member of the Florida Bar who is in good standing for more than 5 years to act as a private trial resolution judge).

[17] Jolie v. Superior Ct. of Los Angeles Cnty., 66 Cal. App. 5th 1025, 281 Cal. Rptr. 3d 610 (2021), review denied (Oct. 27, 2021).

[18] Barnes v. Univ. Hosps. of Cleveland, 893 N.E.2d 142, 146 (Ohio 2008) (in medical malpractice action, "[a]fter proceeding with discovery, the parties chose to submit the dispute to a private judge for a jury trial pursuant to R.C. 2701.10, the statute allowing for 'private judging.' The parties signed a written agreement to that effect, which was approved by the judge originally assigned to the case.")

[19] Christopher R. Drahozal, Business Courts and the Future of Arbitration, 10 Cardozo J. Conflict Resol. 491, 492 (2009); Ralph Peeples & Hanne Nyheim, Beyond the Border: An International Perspective on Business Courts, Bus. L. Today, Mar.–Apr. 2008.

[20] Roya Naghepour, Boom or Bust: Ensuring the Georgia State-Wide Business Court Fulfills Its Constitutional Promise, 56 Ga. L. Rev. 423, 433–34 (2021).

[21] Lee Applebaum, Mitchell Bach, Eric Milby, Richard L. Renck, Through the Decades: The Development of Business Courts in the United States of America, 75 Bus. Law. 2053, 2071 (2020) (cataloguing business courts); Joseph R. Slights III & Elizabeth A. Powers, Delaware Courts Continue to Excel in Business Litigation with the Success of the Complex Commercial Litigation Division of the Superior Court, 70 Bus. Law. 1039, 1044 (2015) ("Some form of problem-solving business courts has now been established in twenty-four (24) states").

[22] Christopher R. Drahozal, Business Courts and the Future of Arbitration, 10 Cardozo J. Conflict Resol. 491, 498 (2009); Anne Tucker Nees, Making a Case for Business Courts: A Survey of and Proposed Framework to Evaluate Business Courts, 24 Ga. St. L. Rev. 477, 515 (2007).

- have lower filing fees than arbitration, as government subsidizes the cost of business courts;
- generally lack the confidentiality of arbitration; and
- generally have full rights to appeal, as opposed to the narrower grounds for vacating an arbitration award.[23]

In contrast however, a Delaware statute tried to create a business court similar to arbitration on all three of these factors, and even described this court's process as "arbitration" in granting its Court of Chancery "the power to arbitrate business disputes."[24] This forum had high filing fees ($12,000), appeal only under the deferential standards of FAA § 10, and confidential proceedings barring public access.[25] This confidentiality—"[a]ttendance at the proceeding is limited to 'parties and their representatives,' and all 'materials and communications' produced during the arbitration are protected from disclosure in judicial or administrative proceedings"—led the Third Circuit to hold in *Delaware Coalition for Open Government, Inc. v. Strine* that Delaware's business court violated the First Amendment's right of public access to trials.[26]

The Third Circuit pointed out that arbitration's "[c]onfidentiality is a natural outgrowth of the status of arbitrations as private alternatives to government-sponsored proceedings."[27] By contrast, "Delaware's government-sponsored arbitrations * * * differ fundamentally from other arbitrations because they are conducted before active judges in a courthouse."[28] In sum, while arbitration can be highly confidential because it is non-governmental adjudication,[29] a government court—even if it calls itself "arbitration"—is subject to a constitutional right of public access.

Consistent with the Third Circuit decision in *Strine*, the West Virginia Supreme Court upheld a process providing public access to a so-called "arbitration" by a judge in the state court's Business Division.[30] In contrast to the Delaware business court procedure

---

[23] Christopher R. Drahozal, Business Courts and the Future of Arbitration, 10 Cardozo J. Conflict Resol. 491, 498–500 (2009).

[24] H.B. 49, 145th Gen. Assemb. (Del. 2009), cited in Delaware Coal. for Open Gov't, Inc. v. Strine, 733 F.3d 510, 512 (3d Cir. 2013), cert. denied, 134 S. Ct. 1551 (2014).

[25] 733 F.3d at 512–13. Arbitration petitions are "considered confidential" and are not included "as part of the public docketing system." Tit. 10, § 349(b); Del. Ch. R. 97(4). Del. Ch. R. 98(b).

[26] Delaware Coal. for Open Gov't, Inc. v. Strine, 733 F.3d 510, 521 (3d Cir. 2013).

[27] Id. at 518.

[28] Id.

[29] See § 32.

[30] W. Virginia Inv. Mgmt. Bd. v. Variable Annuity Life Ins. Co., 820 S.E.2d 416, 425–26 (W.Va. 2018).

struck down in *Strine*, in West Virginia, "the date, time and location of the parties' arbitration proceedings below were publicly docketed by the court as they would be in any other civil case," "transcripts of the arbitration were available to the public," and the judge/arbitrator "aptly noted prior to the arbitration, 'you cannot preclude the public or anyone from * * * observing [the arbitration].' "[31] So, the West Virginia Supreme Court "view[ed] the parties' agreement to keep matters confidential to the extent allowable by law as little more than an agreed protective order, ultimately rendered moot when this Court unsealed the record. For those reasons, we do not find that the proceedings violated the constitutional right to access the courts."[32]

§ 66 Non-Contractual, Yet Binding, Arbitration

(a) Jury-Trial Right Constrains Non-Contractual Arbitration

Arbitration can be contractual or non-contractual.[33] That is, the duty to arbitrate a dispute can be created by contract or by other law. If the duty to arbitrate is created by contract, then enforcement of that duty is unlikely to violate the constitutional right to a jury trial. Courts typically hold that, by forming a contract to arbitrate, a party waives its right to a trial by jury.[34] In contrast, the parties to non-contractual arbitration have rarely waived the right to a jury trial, so non-contractual arbitration generally must be non-binding to avoid violating this right.[35] Non-binding arbitration has less in common

---

[31] Id.

[32] Id.

[33] Many examples of "non-contractual" arbitration do involve a contract, such as an employment contract or a contract for the sale of an automobile. So, in these contexts the duty to arbitrate is, in a sense, assumed by contract. The difference between "contractual" and "non-contractual" arbitration is whether it is possible to form a contract of the relevant sort without assuming the duty to arbitrate. For example, in transportation industries governed by the Railway Labor Act, it is not possible to form an employment contract without assuming the duty to arbitrate. See § 66(b)(4). In contrast, it is possible to form such an employment contract elsewhere in the private sector. Accordingly, transportation employment arbitration is "non-contractual," while other labor and employment arbitration is "contractual."

[34] See § 2.

[35] Kimbrough v. Holiday Inn, 478 F. Supp. 566, 570–71 (E.D. Pa. 1979) (non-binding arbitration did not violate jury trial right); Hamm v. Arrowcreek Homeowners' Ass'n, 183 P.3d 895, 903 (Nev. 2008) (same); Lisanti v. Alamo Title Ins. of Tex., 55 P.3d 962 (N.M. 2002) (state statute requiring arbitration of all title disputes under one million dollars violated state constitutional right to jury trial); Cooper v. Poston, 483 S.E.2d 750, 751 (S.C. 1997) (state statute allowing one party unilaterally to divert an action for monetary damages arising out a motor vehicle accident to binding arbitration would "abrogate another party's constitutional right to a jury trial"); Grace v. Howlett, 283 N.E.2d 474 (Ill. 1972) (state statute requiring arbitration of certain automobile injury cases violated right to jury trial under Illinois Constitution); Jersey Cent. Power & Light Co. v. Melcar Utility Co., 59 A.3d 561, 575 (N.J. 2013) (statute requiring binding arbitration for disputes involving low-dollar damages to

with arbitration than it does with mediation and other processes in aid of negotiation. However, the difference between binding and non-binding arbitration can be a matter of degree relating to the degree of deference courts show the arbitrators' awards.[36]

The United States Constitution's Seventh Amendment, preserving the right to jury trial, and most state constitutional provisions recognizing this right,[37] were enacted prior to the merger of law and equity. Courts generally interpret these constitutional provisions to confer a jury trial right only in cases arising at law, as opposed to cases in equity.[38] That basically means there is a right to a jury trial of claims for money damages, but not for equitable remedies like injunctions and specific performance.

Legislatures and administrative agencies have created new claims that did not exist at the time the constitutional provisions regarding the right to a jury trial were enacted. Whether there is a right to a jury trial of these claims is determined by the language of the statute creating the claim and by whether these claims bear more resemblance to legal or to equitable claims.[39] For example, the Supreme Court of New Jersey held that a statute requiring binding arbitration for disputes involving low-dollar damages to underground

---

underground facilities violated the constitutionally guaranteed right to a trial by jury for a common-law cause of action in negligence).

[36] See § 66(b)(6) (no-fault insurance).

[37] While the Seventh Amendment is one of the few amendments in the Bill of Rights that constrains only federal, not state, government, see Curtis v. Loether, 415 U.S. 189, 192 n.6 (1974), nearly all state constitutions contain a provision that similarly protects the right to trial by jury. See Martin H. Redish, Legislative Response to Medical Malpractice Insurance Crisis: Constitutional Implications, 55 Tex. L. Rev. 759, 797 (1977); Eric J. Hamilton, Federalism and the State Civil Jury Rights, 65 Stan. L. Rev. 851, 855 (2013)("Today, forty-seven state constitutions provide for the right to a jury trial in civil cases, and most do so in the "Declaration of Rights" article, the state constitution counterpart to the U.S. Constitution's Bill of Rights.")

[38] See, e.g., Feltner v. Columbia Pictures Television, Inc., 523 U.S. 340, 347–48 (1998); Pichler v. UNITE, 542 F.3d 380, 388 (3d Cir. 2008); Marseilles Hydro Power, LLC v. Marseilles Land & Water Co., 299 F.3d 643 (7th Cir. 2002); State v. O'Malley, 95 S.W.3d 82 (Mo.2003); Motor Vehicle Mfrs. Ass'n v. State, 551 N.Y.S.2d 470 (N.Y. 1990).

[39] The Seventh Amendment's jury trial right

> applies not only to common-law causes of action, but also to actions brought to enforce statutory rights that are analogous to common-law causes of action ordinarily decided in English law courts in the late 18th century, as opposed to those customarily heard by courts of equity or admiralty. To determine whether a statutory action is more analogous to cases tried in courts of law than to suits tried in courts of equity or admiralty, we examine both the nature of the statutory action and the remedy sought.

Feltner, 523 U.S. at 348 (internal citations omitted). See, e.g., Braunstein v. McCabe, 571 F.3d 108, 123 (1st Cir. 2009) ("Courts have held that [bankruptcy code] § 549 actions are equitable rather than legal and do not include a jury trial right.")

facilities violated the constitutionally guaranteed right to a trial by jury for a common-law cause of action in negligence.[40]

(b) Examples of Non-Contractual, Yet Binding, Arbitration

(1) Federal Programs

Federal law requires arbitration of certain disputes under particular federal programs.[41] These disputes may involve claims by private parties against the federal government or claims between private parties relating to the rights and duties specified by the particular federal program. Examples of such federal laws include the Comprehensive Environmental Response, Compensation and Liability Act,[42] the Federal Insecticide, Fungicide, and Rodenticide Act,[43] and the Multiemployer Pension Plan Amendments Act.[44] In all these examples, the duty to arbitrate is created by statute in the absence of any contract providing for arbitration. This form of non-contractual arbitration does not, however, violate the constitutional right to a jury trial because that right does not attach to claims under these programs.[45]

(2) Government Employees—Federal

The Civil Service Reform Act ("CSRA") authorizes employees of the federal government to form labor unions and requires employers (the various federal government agencies) to bargain in good faith with these unions.[46] The CSRA states that the collective bargaining agreement "shall provide procedures for the settlement of grievances."[47] "[A]ny grievance not satisfactorily settled under the negotiated grievance procedure shall be subject to binding arbitration."[48] Herein lies the non-contractual source of the duty to arbitrate. A statute, rather than a contract, imposes the duty to arbitrate.[49]

---

40 Jersey Cent. Power & Light Co. v. Melcar Util. Co., 59 A.3d at 561 (N.J. 2013).

41 See Ian R. Macneil, Richard E. Speidel & Thomas J. Stipanowich, Federal Arbitration Law ch. 12 (1994).

42 42 U.S.C. §§ 9601–9675.

43 7 U.S.C. §§ 136–136y.

44 29 U.S.C. §§ 1381–1461.

45 See, e.g., Thomas v. Union Carbide Agricultural Products Co., 473 U.S. 568 (1985); Connors v. Ryan's Coal Co., 923 F.2d 1461 (11th Cir. 1991).

46 Civil Service Reform Act of 1978, Pub. L. 95–454, 92 Stat. 111 (codified as amended in scattered sections of 5 U.S.C.).

47 Id. § 7121(a)(1).

48 Id. § 7121(b)(1)(C)(iii).

49 Dennis R. Nolan & Richard A. Bales, Labor and Employment Arbitration in a Nutshell 102–03 (4th ed. 2020) ("Unless the parties agree otherwise, all collective bargaining agreements must establish a system of binding arbitration to resolve

Either party to a federal employment arbitration may appeal to the Federal Labor Relations Authority and may further appeal that Authority's decision to a federal court.[50]

(3) Government Employees—State and Local

Some state and local government employees are covered by grievance arbitration systems similar to those often created by collective bargaining agreements in the private sector.[51] What stands out about arbitration in the context of state and local employees, however, is the prevalence of interest arbitration.[52] As Chapter 7 explains, interest arbitration is where the arbitrator determines what the provisions of a collective bargaining agreement will be, rather than how the provisions of an existing CBA will be interpreted or applied. Interest arbitration is often used to determine the terms of employment for public school teachers, police, firefighters, etc. Such government employees:

> are usually forbidden to engage in strikes; economic pressure, and the usual tests of economic strength used in the private sector to determine contract terms after a bargaining impasse, are therefore limited in the public interest. "Interest" arbitration to determine the terms of a new contract when bargaining fails provides a common alternative mechanism. In many cases, in fact, state statutes impose this as a *mandatory* means of settlement. * * * Such legislation in effect gives to public employee

grievances. There are a few statutory exceptions (e.g., disputes over examination, certification, or appointment, or involving retirement or insurance plans), but the goal is to make arbitration the normal method of resolving disputes.")

[50] 5 U.S.C. § 7122(a), 7123(a).

[51] Dennis R. Nolan & Richard A. Bales, Labor and Employment Arbitration in a Nutshell 108 (4th ed. 2020) ("State and local governments vary widely in their use of labor arbitration. Some states still prohibit public sector collective bargaining. Others allow only certain categories of state and local government to bargain, most commonly teachers, police, and firefighters. A few permit bargaining but do not regard negotiated agreements as binding; either party can refuse to proceed with an arbitration or to abide by an award. In still other states, courts have held contractual arbitration agreements, even when authorized by statute, unconstitutional as a prohibited delegation of governmental power to a private individual. Notwithstanding these exceptions, in most states public sector labor arbitration is both legal and common.")

[52] See § 44(d)(2); Dennis R. Nolan & Richard A. Bales, Labor and Employment Arbitration in a Nutshell 109 (4th ed. 2020) ("interest arbitration is far more common in state and local government labor relations than elsewhere in the economy. It is almost unknown in the private sector"); Ronald Hoh, Interest Arbitration, 32 Mont. Law. 8 (2007) ("By 1990, 35 states and the District of Columbia had adopted some form of interest arbitration as a means of resolving disputes over new contract terms for some or all of their public employees.")

unions the "right" to resort to the arbitration mechanism to determine the future terms of employment.[53]

Such arbitration is not so much the application of law to resolve a dispute as it is quasi-legislative policymaking, requiring consideration of government spending and taxation priorities.[54]

(4) Railway Labor Act

Employers and employees in certain transportation industries, such as railroads and airlines, are governed by the Railway Labor Act ("RLA").[55] The RLA creates a National Railroad Adjustment Board consisting of representatives selected by the employers and representatives selected by the employees' labor unions.[56] The RLA requires employers and unions to submit certain disputes to the Adjustment Board for decision.[57] So, if the Adjustment Board is considered arbitration, the RLA requires arbitration, rather than litigation, of these disputes, and thus is non-contractual arbitration. Appeals of Adjustment Board decisions may be taken to federal court. Judicial review of these Boards' determinations has been characterized as "among the narrowest known to the law."[58]

(5) State "Lemon" Laws

Many states have enacted "lemon" laws with the goal of ensuring that auto manufacturers satisfy their warranty obligations to consumers. New York State requires manufacturers to arbitrate lemon law disputes with their customers if the customer chooses arbitration over litigation.[59] New York's highest court rejected the manufacturers' contention that this mandatory, binding arbitration violates their constitutional right to a jury trial.[60] However, because

---

[53] Alan Scott Rau, Edward F. Sherman & Scott R. Peppet, Processes of Dispute Resolution: The Role of Lawyers 615 (4th ed. 2006). See, e.g., R.I. Gen. Laws §§ 28–9.1–1 to .2–1

[54] Clyde W. Summers, Public Sector Bargaining: Problems of Governmental Decisionmaking, 44 U. Cin. L. Rev. 669, 672 (1975).

[55] 45 U.S.C. §§ 151–188.

[56] Id. § 153(a).

[57] Id. § 153(i).

[58] Union Pacific R. Co. v. Sheehan, 439 U.S. 89, 91 (1978) (citation omitted); Martino v. Metro North Commuter R. Co., 582 Fed. Appx. 27, 29 (2d Cir. 2014) ("the scope of judicial review of a labor board's arbitral decision is 'among the narrowest known to law' ").

[59] N.Y. Gen. Bus.L. § 198–a(k), (m); Lyeth v. Chrysler Corp., 929 F.2d 891 (2d Cir. 1991); Star Boxing, Inc. v. Daimlerchrysler Motors Corp., 840 N.Y.S.2d 357, 357–58 (App. Div. 2007)("Once the petitioner selected alternative arbitration, the appellant manufacturer was required to 'submit to such alternative arbitration' " (General Business Law § 198–a[k])).

[60] Motor Vehicle Mfrs. Ass'n v. State, 551 N.Y.S.2d 470 (N.Y. 1990).

Lemon Law arbitration is "imposed on" manufacturers, judicial review of its arbitration awards is fairly rigorous.[61]

(6) State Auto Insurance Laws

Many states have enacted "no-fault" auto insurance. For example, New York State requires every vehicle owner to provide herself and certain others with compensation for economic loss resulting from injuries occasioned by the use or operation of that vehicle, regardless of fault.[62] The insurer is statutorily-required to arbitrate disputes over benefits if the claimant chooses arbitration over litigation.[63] When insurers challenged this requirement on a number of federal and state constitutional grounds, a federal court abstained from ruling on whether the requirement conflicts with the state constitutional right to a jury trial.[64] While New York's no-fault-insurance arbitration is binding, the statute "permits an insurer or a claimant to institute a court action to adjudicate the dispute de novo where the master arbitrator's award is $5,000 or greater."[65]

The Minnesota Court of Appeals held that a statute requiring arbitration of no-fault claims under $5,000 does not violate the insurer's state constitutional right to jury trial because a no-fault arbitrator under this statute only decides the amount of loss (a fact issue) and does not determine the insurance company's liability (a legal issue left to the courts).[66]

In another example of non-contractual, yet binding, arbitration in the auto insurance context, some states require arbitration of uninsured motorist claims.[67] The Illinois Supreme Court held that

---

[61] Star Boxing, Inc. v. Daimlerchrysler Motors Corp., 840 N.Y.S.2d 357, 357–58 (App. Div. 2007) ("Once the petitioner selected alternative arbitration, the appellant manufacturer was required to 'submit to such alternative arbitration' " (General Business Law § 198–a[k]). Since arbitration was imposed upon the appellant, the appellant is entitled to the 'expanded judicial review available in compulsory arbitration'. In order to be upheld, an arbitration award must have evidentiary support and cannot be arbitrary and capricious.")

[62] N.Y. Ins. L. § 5103.

[63] Id. § 5106(b).

[64] Country-Wide Ins. Co. v. Harnett, 426 F. Supp. 1030, 1033–34 (S.D.N.Y. 1977) ("Since this is a novel and important issue as to which the state law is evolving, it would appear that this Court should exercise its discretion to refuse to decide this pendent issue of state law.") Other constitutional challenges to New York's "no fault" regime have also been rejected. Green v. Liberty Mutual Insurance Co., 791 N.Y.S.2d 630 (App. Div .2005); 563 Grand Med. P.C. v. New York State Insurance Dept., 787 N.Y.S.2d 613 (Sup. Ct. 2004).

[65] Ave. C Med., P.C. v. Encompass Ins. of MA, 12 N.Y.S.3d 578, 579 (App. Div. 2015).

[66] Neal v. State Farm Ins. Co., 509 N.W.2d 173, 178 (Minn. App. 1993), rev'd on other grounds, 529 N.W.2d 330 (Minn. 1995).

[67] 215 Ill. Comp. Stat. Ann. § 5/143a (West 2015); Cal. Ins. Code § 11580.2(f); and Mass. Gen. Laws ch. 175, § 111D.

such a requirement did not violate the state constitutional jury trial right.[68] Illinois' uninsured motorist arbitration awards are largely binding, but not completely so because the Illinois statute provides: "Any decision made by the arbitrators shall be binding for the amount of damages not exceeding $75,000 for bodily injury to or death of any one person, $150,000 for bodily injury to or death of 2 or more persons in any one motor vehicle accident, or the corresponding policy limits for bodily injury or death, whichever is less."[69]

(7) Attorney Fee Disputes

Some states require lawyers to arbitrate fee disputes with their clients if the client chooses arbitration over litigation.[70] Courts have rejected the contention that this mandatory, yet binding, arbitration violates the lawyer's constitutional right to a jury trial.[71] The courts hold that by accepting a license to practice law the lawyer waived his or her jury trial right for these sorts of disputes.

---

68 Reed v. Farmers Ins. Group, 720 N.E.2d 1052, 1060 (Ill. 1999).

69 215 Ill. Comp. Stat. Ann. 5/143a. See Phoenix Ins. Co. v. Rosen, 242 Ill. 2d 48, 58–59, 949 N.E.2d 639, 646–47 (2011) (upholding this provision against challenge that it "unfairly favors the insurer over the insured.")

70 Anderson v. Elliott, 555 A.2d 1042 (Me. 1989); BiotechPharma, LLC v. Ludwig & Robinson, PLLC 98 A.3d 986, 992 (D.C. 2014) (D.C. Bar rules "give clients the power to require arbitration of fee disputes"); In re LiVolsi, 428 A.2d 1268 (N.J. 1981).

71 BiotechPharma, LLC v. Ludwig & Robinson, PLLC, 98 A.3d 986, 995–96 (D.C. 2014) ("Although other jurisdictions impose rules similar to D.C. Bar Rule XIII, no such rule has ever been struck down for denying an attorney's right to a jury trial. Rather, it has been held that attorneys give up that right by practicing law in a jurisdiction subject to the challenged rule"); Guralnick v. Supreme Court of New Jersey, 747 F. Supp. 1109, 1116 (1990); Kelley Drye & Warren v. Murray Indus., 623 F. Supp. 522, 525, 527 (D. N.J. 1985); Shimko v. Lobe, 790 N.E.2d 335 (Ohio App. 2003); Anderson v. Elliott, 555 A.2d 1042 (Me. 1989); In re LiVolsi, 428 A.2d 1268 (N.J. 1981).

Appendix A

FEDERAL ARBITRATION ACT

9 U.S.C. §§ 1–402

CHAPTER 1. GENERAL PROVISIONS

§ 1. "Maritime Transactions," and "Commerce" Defined; Exceptions to Operation of Title

"Maritime transactions", as herein defined, means charter parties, bills of lading of water carriers, agreements relating to wharfage, supplies furnished vessels or repairs to vessels, collisions, or any other matters in foreign commerce which, if the subject of controversy, would be embraced within admiralty jurisdiction; "commerce", as herein defined, means commerce among the several States or with foreign nations, or in any Territory of the United States or in the District of Columbia, or between any such Territory and another, or between any such Territory and any State or foreign nation, or between the District of Columbia and any State or Territory or foreign nation, but nothing herein contained shall apply to contracts of employment of seamen, railroad employees, or any other class of workers engaged in foreign or interstate commerce.

§ 2. Validity, Irrevocability and Enforcement of Agreements to Arbitrate

A written provision in any maritime transaction or a contract evidencing a transaction involving commerce to settle by arbitration a controversy thereafter arising out of such contract or transaction, or the refusal to perform the whole or any part thereof, or an agreement in writing to submit to arbitration an existing controversy arising out of such a contract, transaction, or refusal, shall be valid, irrevocable, and enforceable, save upon such grounds as exist at law or in equity for the revocation of any contract.

§ 3. Stay of Proceedings Where Issue Therein Referable to Arbitration

If any suit or proceeding be brought in any of the courts of the United States upon any issue referable to arbitration under an agreement in writing for such arbitration, the court in which such suit is pending, upon being satisfied that the issue involved in such suit or proceeding is referable to arbitration under such an agreement, shall on application of one of the parties stay the trial of the action until such arbitration has been had in accordance with the terms of the agreement, providing the applicant for the stay is not in default in proceeding with such arbitration.

§ 4. Failure to Arbitrate Under Agreement; Petition to United States Court Having Jurisdiction for Order to Compel Arbitration; Notice and Service Thereof; Hearing and Determination

A party aggrieved by the alleged failure, neglect, or refusal of another to arbitrate under a written agreement for arbitration may petition any United States district court which, save for such agreement, would have jurisdiction under Title 28, in a civil action or in admiralty of the subject matter of a suit arising out of the controversy between the parties, for an order directing that such arbitration proceed in the manner provided for in such agreement. Five days' notice in writing of such application shall be served upon the party in default. Service thereof shall be made in the manner provided by the Federal Rules of Civil Procedure. The court shall hear the parties, and upon being satisfied that the making of the agreement for arbitration or the failure to comply therewith is not in issue, the court shall make an order directing the parties to proceed to arbitration in accordance with the terms of the agreement. The hearing and proceedings, under such agreement, shall be within the district in which the petition for an order directing such arbitration is filed. If the making of the arbitration agreement or the failure, neglect, or refusal to perform the same be in issue, the court shall proceed summarily to the trial thereof. If no jury trial be demanded by the party alleged to be in default, or if the matter in dispute is within admiralty jurisdiction, the court shall hear and determine such issue. Where such an issue is raised, the party alleged to be in default may, except in cases of admiralty, on or before the return day of the notice of application, demand a jury trial of such issue, and upon such demand the court shall make an order referring the issue or issues to a jury in the manner provided by the Federal Rules of Civil Procedure, or may specially call a jury for that purpose. If the jury find that no agreement in writing for arbitration was made or that there is no default in proceeding thereunder, the proceeding shall be dismissed. If the jury find that an agreement for arbitration was made in writing and that there is a default in proceeding thereunder, the court shall make an order summarily directing the parties to proceed with the arbitration in accordance with the terms thereof.

§ 5. Appointment of Arbitrators or Umpire

If in the agreement provision be made for a method of naming or appointing an arbitrator or arbitrators or an umpire, such method shall be followed; but if no method be provided therein, or if a method be provided and any party thereto shall fail to avail himself of such method, or if for any other reason there shall be a lapse in the naming of an arbitrator or arbitrators or umpire, or in filling a vacancy, then upon the application of either party to the controversy the court shall designate and appoint an arbitrator or arbitrators or umpire, as the case may require, who shall act under the said agreement with the same force and effect as if he or they had been specifically named therein; and unless otherwise provided in the agreement the arbitration shall be by a single arbitrator.

§ 6. Application Heard as Motion

Any application to the court hereunder shall be made and heard in the manner provided by law for the making and hearing of motions, except as otherwise herein expressly provided.

§ 7. Witnesses Before Arbitrators; Fees; Compelling Attendance

The arbitrators selected either as prescribed in this title or otherwise, or a majority of them, may summon in writing any person to attend before them or any of them as a witness and in a proper case to bring with him or them any book, record, document, or paper which may be deemed material as evidence in the case. The fees for such attendance shall be the same as the fees of witnesses before masters of the United States courts. Said summons shall issue in the name of the arbitrator or arbitrators, or a majority of them, and shall be signed by the arbitrators, or a majority of them, and shall be directed to the said person and shall be served in the same manner as subpoenas to appear and testify before the court; if any person or persons so summoned to testify shall refuse or neglect to obey said summons, upon petition the United States district court for the district in which such arbitrators, or a majority of them, are sitting may compel the attendance of such person or persons before said arbitrator or arbitrators, or punish said person or persons for contempt in the same manner provided by law for securing the attendance of witnesses or their punishment for neglect or refusal to attend in the courts of the United States.

§ 8. Proceedings begun by libel in admiralty and seizure of vessel or property

If the basis of jurisdiction be a cause of action otherwise justiciable in admiralty, then, notwithstanding anything herein to the contrary, the party claiming to be aggrieved may begin his proceeding hereunder by libel and seizure of the vessel or other property of the other party according to the usual course of admiralty proceedings, and the court shall then have jurisdiction to direct the parties to proceed with the arbitration and shall retain jurisdiction to enter its decree upon the award.

§ 9. Award of Arbitrators; Confirmation; Jurisdiction; Procedure

If the parties in their agreement have agreed that a judgment of the court shall be entered upon the award made pursuant to the arbitration, and shall specify the court, then at any time within one year after the award is made any party to the arbitration may apply to the court so specified for an order confirming the award, and thereupon the court must grant such an order unless the award is vacated, modified, or corrected as prescribed in sections 10 and 11 of this title. If no court is specified in the agreement of the parties, then such application may be made to the United States court in and for the district within which such award was made. Notice of the application shall be served upon the adverse party, and thereupon the court shall have jurisdiction of such party as though he had appeared generally in the proceeding. If the adverse party is a resident of the district within which the award was made, such service shall be made upon the adverse party or his attorney as prescribed by law for service of notice of motion in an action in the same court. If the adverse party shall be a nonresident, then the notice of the application shall be served by the marshal of any district within which the adverse party may be found in like manner as other process of the court.

§ 10. Same; Vacation; Grounds; Rehearing

(a) In any of the following cases the United States court in and for the district wherein the award was made may make an order vacating the award upon the application of any party to the arbitration—

(1) Where the award was procured by corruption, fraud, or undue means.

(2) Where there was evident partiality or corruption in the arbitrators, or either of them.

(3) Where the arbitrators were guilty of misconduct in refusing to postpone the hearing, upon sufficient cause shown, or in refusing to hear evidence pertinent and material to the controversy; or of any other misbehavior by which the rights of any party have been prejudiced.

(4) Where the arbitrators exceeded their powers, or so imperfectly executed them that a mutual, final, and definite award upon the subject matter submitted was not made.

(b) Where an award is vacated and the time within which the agreement required the award to be made has not expired the court may, in its discretion, direct a rehearing by the arbitrators.

(c) The United States district court for the district wherein an award was made that was issued pursuant to section 580 of title 5 may make an order vacating the award upon the application of a person, other than a party to the arbitration, who is adversely affected or aggrieved by the award, if the use of arbitration or the award is clearly inconsistent with the factors set forth in section 572 of title 5.

§ 11. Same; Modification or Correction; Grounds; Order

In either of the following cases the United States court in and for the district wherein the award was made may make an order modifying or correcting the award upon the application of any party to the arbitration—

(a) Where there was an evident material miscalculation of figures or an evident material mistake in the description of any person, thing, or property referred to in the award.

(b) Where the arbitrators have awarded upon a matter not submitted to them, unless it is a matter not affecting the merits of the decision upon the matter submitted.

(c) Where the award is imperfect in matter of form not affecting the merits of the controversy.

The order may modify and correct the award, so as to effect the intent thereof and promote justice between the parties.

§ 12. Notice of Motions to Vacate or Modify; Service; Stay of Proceedings

Notice of a motion to vacate, modify, or correct an award must be served upon the adverse party or his attorney within three months after the award is filed or delivered. If the adverse party is a resident of the district within which the award was made, such service shall be made upon the adverse party or his attorney as prescribed by law for service of notice of motion in an action in the same court. If the adverse party shall be a nonresident then the notice of the application shall be served by the marshal of any district within which the adverse party may be found in like manner as other process of the court. For the purposes of the motion any judge who might make an order to stay the proceedings in an action brought in the same court may make an order, to be served with the notice of motion, staying the proceedings of the adverse party to enforce the award.

§ 13. Papers Filed with Order on Motions; Judgment; Docketing; Force and Effect; Enforcement

The party moving for an order confirming, modifying, or correcting an award shall, at the time such order is filed with the clerk for the entry of judgment thereon, also file the following papers with the clerk:

(a) The agreement; the selection or appointment, if any, of an additional arbitrator or umpire; and each written extension of the time, if any, within which to make the award.

(b) The award.

(c) Each notice, affidavit, or other paper used upon an application to confirm, modify, or correct the award, and a copy of each order of the court upon such an application.

The judgment shall be docketed as if it was rendered in an action.

The judgment so entered shall have the same force and effect, in all respects, as, and be subject to all the provisions of law relating to, a judgment in an action; and it may be enforced as if it had been rendered in an action in the court in which it is entered.

§ 14. Contracts Not Affected

This title shall not apply to contracts made prior to January 1, 1926.

§ 15. Inapplicability of the Act of State Doctrine

Enforcement of arbitral agreements, confirmation of arbitral awards, and execution upon judgments based on orders confirming such awards shall not be refused on the basis of the Act of State doctrine.

§ 16. Appeals

(a) An appeal may be taken from—

(1) an order—

(A) refusing a stay of any action under section 3 of this title,

(B) denying a petition under section 4 of this title to order arbitration to proceed,

(C) denying an application under section 206 of this title to compel arbitration,

(D) confirming or denying confirmation of an award or partial award, or

(E) modifying, correcting, or vacating an award;

(2) an interlocutory order granting, continuing, or modifying an injunction against an arbitration that is subject to this title; or

(3) a final decision with respect to an arbitration that is subject to this title.

(b) Except as otherwise provided in section 1292(b) of title 28, an appeal may not be taken from an interlocutory order—

(1) granting a stay of any action under section 3 of this title;

(2) directing arbitration to proceed under section 4 of this title;

(3) compelling arbitration under section 206 of this title; or

(4) refusing to enjoin an arbitration that is subject to this title.

CHAPTER 2. CONVENTION ON THE RECOGNITION AND ENFORCEMENT OF FOREIGN ARBITRAL AWARDS

§ 201. Enforcement of Convention

The Convention on the Recognition and Enforcement of Foreign Arbitral Awards of June 10, 1958, shall be enforced in United States courts in accordance with this chapter.

§ 202. Agreement or award falling under the Convention

An arbitration agreement or arbitral award arising out of a legal relationship, whether contractual or not, which is considered as commercial, including a transaction, contract, or agreement described in section 2 of this title, falls under the Convention. An agreement or award arising out of such a relationship which is entirely between citizens of the United States shall be deemed not to fall under the Convention unless that relationship involves property located abroad, envisages performance or enforcement abroad, or has some other reasonable relation with one or more foreign states. For the purpose of this section a corporation is a citizen of the United States if it is incorporated or has its principal place of business in the United States.

§ 203. Jurisdiction; amount in controversy

An action or proceeding falling under the Convention shall be deemed to arise under the laws and treaties of the United States. The district courts of the United States (including the courts enumerated in section 460 of title 28) shall have original jurisdiction over such an action or proceeding, regardless of the amount in controversy.

§ 204. Venue

An action or proceeding over which the district courts have jurisdiction pursuant to section 203 of this title may be brought in any such court in which save for the arbitration agreement an action or proceeding with respect to the controversy between the parties could be brought, or in such court for the district and division which embraces the place designated in the agreement as the place of arbitration if such place is within the United States.

§ 205. Removal of cases from State courts

Where the subject matter of an action or proceeding pending in a State court relates to an arbitration agreement or award falling under the Convention, the defendant or the defendants may, at any time before the trial thereof, remove such action or proceeding to the district court of the United States for the district and division embracing the place where the action or proceeding is pending. The procedure for removal of causes otherwise provided by law shall apply, except that the ground for removal provided in this section need not appear on the face of the complaint but may be shown in the petition for removal. For the purposes of Chapter 1 of this title any action or proceeding removed under this section shall be deemed to have been brought in the district court to which it is removed.

§ 206. Order to compel arbitration; appointment of arbitrators

A court having jurisdiction under this chapter may direct that arbitration be held in accordance with the agreement at any place therein provided for, whether that place is within or without the United States. Such court may also appoint arbitrators in accordance with the provisions of the agreement.

§ 207. Award of arbitrators; confirmation; jurisdiction; proceeding

Within three years after an arbitral award falling under the Convention is made, any party to the arbitration may apply to any court having jurisdiction under this chapter for an order confirming the award as against any other party to the arbitration. The court shall confirm the award unless it finds one of the grounds for refusal or deferral of recognition or enforcement of the award specified in the said Convention.

§ 208. Chapter 1; residual application

Chapter 1 applies to actions and proceedings brought under this chapter to the extent that chapter is not in conflict with this chapter or the Convention as ratified by the United States.

CHAPTER 3. INTER-AMERICAN CONVENTION ON INTERNATIONAL COMMERCIAL ARBITRATION

§ 301. Enforcement of Convention

The Inter-American Convention on International Commercial Arbitration of January 30, 1975, shall be enforced in United States courts in accordance with this chapter.

§ 302. Incorporation by reference

Sections 202, 203, 204, 205, and 207 of this title shall apply to this chapter as if specifically set forth herein, except that for the purposes of this chapter "the Convention" shall mean the Inter-American Convention.

§ 303. Order to compel arbitration; appointment of arbitrators; locale

(a) A court having jurisdiction under this chapter may direct that arbitration be held in accordance with the agreement at any place therein provided for, whether that place is within or without the United States. The court may also appoint arbitrators in accordance with the provisions of the agreement.

(b) In the event the agreement does not make provision for the place of arbitration or the appointment of arbitrators, the court shall direct that the arbitration shall be held and the arbitrators be appointed in accordance with Article 3 of the Inter-American Convention.

§ 304. Recognition and enforcement of foreign arbitral decisions and awards; reciprocity

Arbitral decisions or awards made in the territory of a foreign State shall, on the basis of reciprocity, be recognized and enforced under this chapter only if that State has ratified or acceded to the Inter-American Convention.

§ 305. Relationship between the Inter-American Convention and the Convention on the Recognition and Enforcement of Foreign Arbitral Awards of June 10, 1958

When the requirements for application of both the Inter-American Convention and the Convention on the Recognition and Enforcement of Foreign Arbitral Awards of June 10, 1958, are met, determination as to which Convention applies shall, unless otherwise expressly agreed, be made as follows:

(1) If a majority of the parties to the arbitration agreement are citizens of a State or States that have ratified or acceded to the Inter-American Convention and are member States of the Organization of American States, the Inter-American Convention shall apply.

(2) In all other cases the Convention on the Recognition and Enforcement of Foreign Arbitral Awards of June 10, 1958, shall apply.

§ 306. Applicable rules of Inter-American Commercial Arbitration Commission

(a) For the purposes of this chapter the rules of procedure of the Inter-American Commercial Arbitration Commission referred to in Article 3 of the Inter-American Convention shall, subject to subsection (b) of this section, be those rules as promulgated by the Commission on July 1, 1988.

(b) In the event the rules of procedure of the Inter-American Commercial Arbitration Commission are modified or amended in accordance with the procedures for amendment of the rules of that Commission, the Secretary of State, by regulation in accordance with section 553 of title 5, consistent with the aims and purposes of this Convention, may prescribe that such modifications or amendments shall be effective for purposes of this chapter.

§ 307. Chapter 1; residual application

Chapter 1 applies to actions and proceedings brought under this chapter to the extent chapter 1 is not in conflict with this chapter or the Inter-American Convention as ratified by the United States.

CHAPTER 4. ARBITRATION OF DISPUTES INVOLVING SEXUAL ASSAULT AND SEXUAL HARASSMENT

§ 401. Definitions

(1) Predispute arbitration agreement.—The term "predispute arbitration agreement" means any agreement to arbitrate a dispute that had not yet arisen at the time of the making of the agreement.

(2) Predispute joint-action waiver.—The term "predispute joint-action waiver" means an agreement, whether or not part of a predispute arbitration agreement, that would prohibit, or waive the right of, one of the parties to the agreement to participate in a joint, class, or collective action in a judicial, arbitral, administrative, or other forum, concerning a dispute that has not yet arisen at the time of the making of the agreement.

(3) Sexual assault dispute.—The term "sexual assault dispute" means a dispute involving a nonconsensual sexual act or sexual

contact, as such terms are defined in section 2246 of title 18 or similar applicable Tribal or State law, including when the victim lacks capacity to consent.

(4) Sexual harassment dispute.—The term "sexual harassment dispute" means a dispute relating to conduct that is alleged to constitute sexual harassment under applicable Federal, Tribal, or State law.

§ 402. No validity or enforceability

(a) In general.—Notwithstanding any other provision of this title, at the election of the person alleging conduct constituting a sexual harassment dispute or sexual assault dispute, or the named representative of a class or in a collective action alleging such conduct, no predispute arbitration agreement or predispute joint-action waiver shall be valid or enforceable with respect to a case which is filed under Federal, Tribal, or State law and relates to the sexual assault dispute or the sexual harassment dispute.

(b) Determination of applicability.—An issue as to whether this chapter applies with respect to a dispute shall be determined under Federal law. The applicability of this chapter to an agreement to arbitrate and the validity and enforceability of an agreement to which this chapter applies shall be determined by a court, rather than an arbitrator, irrespective of whether the party resisting arbitration challenges the arbitration agreement specifically or in conjunction with other terms of the contract containing such agreement, and irrespective of whether the agreement purports to delegate such determinations to an arbitrator.

Appendix B

NEW YORK CONVENTION

Convention on the Recognition and Enforcement of Foreign Arbitral Awards Done at New York, 10 June 1958; entered into force, 7 June 1959 United Nations, Treaty Series, vol. 330, p. 38, No. 4739 (1959).

Article I

1. This Convention shall apply to the recognition and enforcement of arbitral awards made in the territory of a State other than the State where the recognition and enforcement of such awards are sought, and arising out of differences between persons, whether physical or legal. It shall also apply to arbitral awards not considered as domestic awards in the State where their recognition and enforcement are sought.

2. The term "arbitral awards" shall include not only awards made by arbitrators appointed for each case but also those made by permanent arbitral bodies to which the parties have submitted.

3. When signing, ratifying or acceding to this Convention, or notifying extension under article X hereof, any State may on the basis of reciprocity declare that it will apply the Convention to the recognition and enforcement of awards made only in the territory of another Contracting State. It may also declare that it will apply the Convention only to differences arising out of legal relationships, whether contractual or not, which are considered as commercial under the national law of the State making such declaration.

Article II

1. Each Contracting State shall recognize an agreement in writing under which the parties undertake to submit to arbitration all or any differences which have arisen or which may arise between them in respect of a defined legal relationship, whether contractual or not, concerning a subject matter capable of settlement by arbitration.

2. The term "agreement in writing" shall include an arbitral clause in a contract or an arbitration agreement, signed by the parties or contained in an exchange of letters or telegrams.

3. The court of a Contracting State, when seized of an action in a matter in respect of which the parties have made an agreement

within the meaning of this article, shall, at the request of one of the parties, refer the parties to arbitration, unless it finds that the said agreement is null and void, inoperative or incapable of being performed.

Article III

Each Contracting State shall recognize arbitral awards as binding and enforce them in accordance with the rules of procedure of the territory where the award is relied upon, under the conditions laid down in the following articles. There shall not be imposed substantially more onerous conditions or higher fees or charges on the recognition or enforcement of arbitral awards to which this Convention applies than are imposed on the recognition or enforcement of domestic arbitral awards.

Article IV

1. To obtain the recognition and enforcement mentioned in the preceding article, the party applying for recognition and enforcement shall, at the time of the application, supply:

(a) The duly authenticated original award or a duly certified copy thereof;

(b) The original agreement referred to in article II or a duly certified copy thereof.

2. If the said award or agreement is not made in an official language of the country in which the award is relied upon, the party applying for recognition and enforcement of the award shall produce a translation of these documents into such language. The translation shall be certified by an official or sworn translator or by a diplomatic or consular agent.

Article V

1. Recognition and enforcement of the award may be refused, at the request of the party against whom it is invoked, only if that party furnishes to the competent authority where the recognition and enforcement is sought, proof that:

(a) The parties to the agreement referred to in article II were, under the law applicable to them, under some incapacity, or the said agreement is not valid under the law to which the parties have subjected it or, failing any indication thereon, under the law of the country where the award was made; or

(b) The party against whom the award is invoked was not given proper notice of the appointment of the arbitrator or of the arbitration proceedings or was otherwise unable to present his case; or

(c) The award deals with a difference not contemplated by or not falling within the terms of the submission to arbitration, or it contains decisions on matters beyond the scope of the submission to arbitration, provided that, if the decisions on matters submitted to arbitration can be separated from those not so submitted, that part of the award which contains decisions on matters submitted to arbitration may be recognized and enforced; or

(d) The composition of the arbitral authority or the arbitral procedure was not in accordance with the agreement of the parties, or, failing such agreement, was not in accordance with the law of the country where the arbitration took place; or

(e) The award has not yet become binding on the parties, or has been set aside or suspended by a competent authority of the country in which, or under the law of which, that award was made.

2. Recognition and enforcement of an arbitral award may also be refused if the competent authority in the country where recognition and enforcement is sought finds that:

(a) The subject matter of the difference is not capable of settlement by arbitration under the law of that country; or

(b) The recognition or enforcement of the award would be contrary to the public policy of that country.

Article VI

If an application for the setting aside or suspension of the award has been made to a competent authority referred to in article V(1)(e), the authority before which the award is sought to be relied upon may, if it considers it proper, adjourn the decision on the enforcement of the award and may also, on the application of the party claiming enforcement of the award, order the other party to give suitable security.

Article VII

1. The provisions of the present Convention shall not affect the validity of multilateral or bilateral agreements concerning the recognition and enforcement of arbitral awards entered into by the Contracting States nor deprive any interested party of any right he may have to avail himself of an arbitral award in the manner and to the extent allowed by the law or the treaties of the country where such award is sought to be relied upon.

2. The Geneva Protocol on Arbitration Clauses of 1923 and the Geneva Convention on the Execution of Foreign Arbitral Awards of 1927 shall cease to have effect between Contracting States on their

becoming bound and to the extent that they become bound, by this Convention.

Article VIII

1. This Convention shall be open until 31 December 1958 for signature on behalf of any Member of the United Nations and also on behalf of any other State which is or hereafter becomes a member of any specialized agency of the United Nations, or which is or hereafter becomes a party to the Statute of the International Court of Justice, or any other State to which an invitation has been addressed by the General Assembly of the United Nations.

2. This Convention shall be ratified and the instruments of ratification shall be deposited with the Secretary-General of the United Nations.

Article IX

1. This Convention shall be open for accession to all States referred to in article VIII.

2. Accession shall be effected by the deposit of an instrument of accession with the Secretary-General of the United Nations.

Article X

1. Any State may, at the time of signature, ratification or accession, declare that this Convention shall extend to all or any of the territories for the international relations of which it is responsible. Such a declaration shall take effect when the Convention enters into force for the State concerned

2. At any time thereafter any such extension shall be made by notification addressed to the Secretary-General of the United Nations and shall take effect as from the ninetieth day after the day of receipt by the Secretary-General of the United Nations of this notification, or as from the date of entry into force of the Convention for the State concerned, whichever is the later

3. With respect to those territories to which this Convention is not extended at the time of signature, ratification or accession, each State concerned shall consider the possibility of taking the necessary steps in order to extend the application of this Convention to such territories, subject, where necessary for constitutional reasons, to the consent of the Governments of such territories.

Article XI

In the case of a federal or non-unitary State, the following provisions shall apply:

(a) With respect to those articles of this Convention that come within the legislative jurisdiction of the federal authority, the obligations of the federal Government shall to this extent be the same as those of Contracting States which are not federal States;

(b) With respect to those articles of this Convention that come within the legislative jurisdiction of constituent states or provinces which are not, under the constitutional system of the federation, bound to take legislative action, the federal Government shall bring such articles with a favourable recommendation to the notice of the appropriate authorities of constituent states or provinces at the earliest possible moment;

(c) A federal State Party to this Convention shall, at the request of any other Contracting State transmitted through the Secretary-General of the United Nations, supply a statement of the law and practice of the federation and its constituent units in regard to any particular provision of this Convention, showing the extent to which effect has been given to that provision by legislative or other action

Article XII

1. This Convention shall come into force on the ninetieth day following the date of deposit of the third instrument of ratification or accession.

2. For each State ratifying or acceding to this Convention after the deposit of the third instrument of ratification or accession, this Convention shall enter into force on the ninetieth day after deposit by such State of its instrument of ratification or accession.

Article XIII

1. Any Contracting State may denounce this Convention by a written notification to the Secretary-General of the United Nations. Denunciation shall take effect one year after the date of receipt of the notification by the Secretary-General.

2. Any State which has made a declaration or notification under article X may, at any time thereafter, by notification to the Secretary-General of the United Nations, declare that this Convention shall cease to extend to the territory concerned one year after the date of the receipt of the notification by the Secretary-General.

3. This Convention shall continue to be applicable to arbitral awards in respect of which recognition or enforcement proceedings have been instituted before the denunciation takes effect.

Article XIV

A Contracting State shall not be entitled to avail itself of the present Convention against other Contracting States except to the extent that it is itself bound to apply the Convention.

Article XV

The Secretary-General of the United Nations shall notify the States contemplated in article VIII of the following:

(a) Signatures and ratifications in accordance with article VIII;

(b) Accessions in accordance with article IX;

(c) Declarations and notifications under articles I, X and XI;

(d) The date upon which this Convention enters into force in accordance with article XII;

(e) Denunciations and notifications in accordance with article XIII.

Article XVI

1. This Convention, of which the Chinese, English, French, Russian and Spanish texts shall be equally authentic, shall be deposited in the archives of the United Nations

2. The Secretary-General of the United Nations shall transmit a certified copy of this Convention to the States contemplated in article VIII.

Appendix C

EXCERPTS FROM LABOR MANAGEMENT RELATIONS ACT

29 U.S.C. §§ 173, 185

Section 203 (29 U.S.C. § 173)

* * *

(d) Final adjustment by a method agreed upon by the parties is hereby declared to be the desirable method for settlement of grievance disputes arising over the application or interpretation of an existing collective-bargaining agreement. The [Federal Mediation and Conciliation] Service is directed to make its conciliation and mediation services available in the settlement of such grievance disputes only as a last resort and in exceptional cases.

Section 301 (29 U.S.C. § 185)

(a) Suits for violation of contracts between an employer and a labor organization representing employees in an industry affecting commerce as defined in this Act, or between any such labor organizations, may be brought in any district court of the United States having jurisdiction of the parties, without regard to the citizenship of the parties.

(b) Any labor organization which represents employees in an industry affecting commerce as defined in this Act and any employer whose activities affect commerce as defined in this Act shall be bound by the acts of its agents. Any such labor organization may sue or be sued as an entity and in behalf of the employees whom it represents in the courts of the United States. Any money judgment against a labor organization in a district court of the United States shall be enforceable only against the organization as an entity and against its assets, and shall not be enforceable against any individual member or his assets.

* * *

Table of Cases

Index

References are to Section Number